Eighth Edition

Stage Makeup

RICHARD CORSON

PRENTICE HALL   Englewood Cliffs, New Jersey 07632

Library of Congress Cataloging-in-Publication Data

Corson, Richard.
    Stage makeup / Richard Corson.—8th ed.
      p. cm.
    Includes index.
    ISBN 0-13-840539-5
    1. Make-up, Theatrical. I. Title.
PN2068.C65 1990
    792′ .027—dc19
                                    89-3447
                                       CIP

To
MARGE BIERSACH
A. REID WINSEY
EVELYN KENT HALE
and
MITCHELL ERICKSON
for their help, encouragement,
and friendship

Also by Richard Corson:
FASHIONS IN HAIR
FASHIONS IN MAKEUP
FASHIONS IN EYEGLASSES

Editorial/production supervision by Mary Kathryn Leclercq
Interior design by Jayne Conte
Cover design by Bruce Kenselaar
Art director: Florence Dara Silverman
Manufacturing buyer: Carol Bystrom

© 1990, 1986, 1981, 1975, 1967, 1960, 1942 by Prentice-Hall, Inc.
A Division of Simon & Schuster
Englewood Cliffs, New Jersey 07632
Copyright renewed 1970 by Richard Corson

Printed in the United States of America

20 19 18 17 16 15 14 13

ISBN   0-13-840539-5

Prentice-Hall International (UK) Limited, *London*
Prentice-Hall of Australia Pty. Limited, *Sydney*
Prentice-Hall of Canada Inc., *Toronto*
Prentice-Hall Hispanoamericana, S.A., *Mexico*
Prentice-Hall of India Private Limited, *New Delhi*
Prentice-Hall of Japan, Inc., *Tokyo*
Prentice-Hall of Southeast Asia Pte. Ltd., *Singapore*
Editora Prentice-Hall do Brasil, Ltda., *Rio de Janeiro*

Contents

Part 1   BASIC PRINCIPLES

Part 2   PLANNING THE MAKEUP

Illustrations

The numbers of the illustrations indicate the number of the chapter or appendix in which the particular illustration appears, followed by the number of the illustration in that chapter or appendix. The titles of the figures are followed by the pages on which they appear.

APPENDICES

Foreword

I recall once needing a pair of ears for Abraham Lincoln. I didn't know if such a thing could be done, but I figured Dick Corson would, so I called.

"You want what?"

"Ears," I said. "For Lincoln. I'm doing Abe for the Phoenix Theatre—you know, Sherwood's play, and I'm working out the makeup."

"And you need ears."

"Yes, they were very big. Enormous, when you think about it," I said. "I figure without the ears it won't come out right."

"But with them . . .?"

"Yeah."

"Why don't you come on over?"

Dick has always had a sense of humor about me. He's also been a friend ever since he helped carry a table to the theatre in Lakeside, Ohio, when I needed help and couldn't get it. That was many years ago. So I went over.

"Now, let me explain, Hal, that I've never done ears like this before. It can be done, of course, but I'm not sure that it has been. There's not a lot of call for big ears, you know. There's a little casting problem, you see—undercuts and all that. How did you want to attach them?"

"I figured I'd just slip them over mine. Like mittens."

"Had you planned to glue them on?"

"Yeah. Once I slip them on, I'll glue them so they can't fall off. Actually, you shouldn't notice them much because his hair came out over them a lot. They shouldn't be grotesque."

"Just large."

"In case someone notices."

"I see."

Patiently he toiled over those ears. Then one night he called me. "Would you like to come down and slip them on?" I did, and they worked beautifully. It was the touch that made the makeup work, although I doubt very many people were aware of them. But Dick and I were enormously proud of them, and they made the makeup work so well in close-up that on the night we closed, the other actors in the cast waited in a local bar for me to take off the makeup so they could remember what I looked like.

Makeup requires patience. Corson is a patient man, a meticulous man, who goes about his work with the care and thought of a scientist. He is multitalented and has used many of them in creating his books—*Stage Makeup, Fashions in Hair, Fashions in Eyeglasses,* and *Fashions in Makeup.* He's taken most of the photographs, done the intricate drawings, experimented on himself and his friends to get the many character effects, and he is a performer himself and understands the nature of the problems actors face on the stage. He's one of those totally dedicated people you sometimes meet or know in your life who make you feel that it's worthwhile to keep trying to do better.

It's been a great pleasure to see his book on makeup become established as the standard one in use wherever I go, knowing something of the toil that went to make it. In the early days when I was creating Mark Twain makeup he would come to see the show and we would discuss its effectiveness and how it could be improved. His eye I could depend on.

He's written the best book around on the subject. To all you actors who don't feel right unless you have the ears on, trust in Dick.

Hal Holbrook

Preface

This book is intended to be used as a text and as a reference by actors and prospective actors who are or expect to be responsible for their own makeup—and by anyone who might in some way be involved with the makeup, whether as a designer, a director, a makeup artist, or a teacher.

As a textbook, it can be used by individuals learning either on their own or in a workshop. Both methods have their advantages. In learning by yourself, it's possible to work at your own convenience and at your own speed and to experiment with your own ideas and develop your own techniques. In a workshop that is not always possible. But a workshop does provide the advantage of not only having the guidance of a teacher but of seeing other students' work and learning from their successes and their failures. If you are or intend to be an actor, it is important that you work on your own face rather than on someone else's. Only if you are planning to be a makeup artist or a teacher is it really useful to work on faces other than your own. But a workshop is only the beginning. You should then continue to practice and experiment, applying what you have learned and developing your skill.

Whether you are working alone or in a group, taking photographs of your makeups will enable you to look at your work objectively. The photographs of student makeups in this book were taken as routine workshop procedure, using costumes and props from the costume shop and improvising when necessary. As most of the photographs were taken with an instant-picture camera, the students could make any improvements they wanted in the makeup before removing it and then have it photographed again for comparison.

Students seriously interested in makeup as a profession would do well to take courses in freehand drawing and to spend some time in art museums, studying paintings and observing how different artists have achieved their effects. They should also train themselves to observe people wherever they go—not just casually, but analyti-cally, noting color and texture of the skin and hair, conformation of wrinkles, and size, shape, color, texture, and location of any blemishes. Students should also make note of any indications of possible profession or type of work and general lifestyle.

Students would also do well, if they have any talent for it at all, to take a course in acting to help them understand the actor's problems. And unless the student has the patience of a saint, the compassion of a doting mother, and the meticulous fingers of a jeweler, he or she might do well to consider choosing another profession.

ACKNOWLEDGMENTS

In this edition of the book, as in previous editions, a number of people have been helpful in various ways. I am grateful to all of them—to John Handy, Gene Bicknell, Jeffrey Hillock, and Tom Lindberg for serving as models in demonstrating makeup techniques; to Bert Roth for his special contributions to the book; to makeup artist Paul Batson for permitting me to use some of his photographs and for sharing with me some of his creative ideas; to Bill Smith, Robert Maverick, and Randall duc Kim for the photographs they have contributed; to Kristoffer Tabori, Tom Tammi, and Alan Sues for their kindness in permitting numerous photographs to be taken as they worked on their makeups for productions that were in rehearsal; to the various makeup companies for their cooperation; to Hal Holbrook and Uta Hagen for providing the Foreword and the Introduction; to Dick Smith, one of the most imaginative and dedicated makeup artists in the country, for allowing me to use a number of photographs of his makeups and for sharing with me the results of his own experimentation; and to my students for working so hard and teaching me so much.

R.C.

Introduction

The actor's dream is to play a wide range of characters, to explore many facets of life in roles that encompass all humanity. To fulfill this dream he requires not only talent and training but an unstinting devotion to his art.

In many areas of this endeavor the actor is assisted by the artistry and technical skills of brilliant craftsmen. From the original script to the set, lighting, and costumes, every effort is made to achieve perfection. Curiously, in the field of makeup the actor is left quite to his own devices. Except for the rare production so exotic or stylized that a specialist is necessary, the actor must design and execute his own makeup.

It is therefore of considerable concern that many young professionals in the theater are unfamiliar with even so elementary a problem as projection of the actor's features, essential to the fullest communication of the character's inner life. Even on the rare occasions when a professional makeup artist is available, it is still the actor who is more aware than anyone else of the special problems posed by his own features and by the character he is playing. Thus, it is the responsibility of each actor to learn the craft of makeup, that final dressing of the character which will enable him to perform his role as fully and as effectively as possible.

In addition to such fundamentals as the assimilation and projection of the character in terms of age, environment, and health, there is an area of psychological support that makeup can give the actor comparable only to the assistance of a perfect costume. Just as robes or rags can give the actor the "feel" of a character, so also can makeup. The visual image reflected in his dressing room mirror can be as important to the actor as it will later become to the audience.

The authority of the arch of a brow or the sweep of a profile can be as compelling as Lear's crown and scepter. The psychological effect of shadows and pallor or glowing health can be as conducive to mood and manner on stage as in life, while an impudent tilt to a nose or the simple graying of the hair will inevitably make more specific the delineation of character. The most detailed and subtle characterization can be performed only with full freedom and authority when the actor knows that the visual image supports and defines his work.

The actor untrained in makeup is deprived of an invaluable aid to his art—and little is done to remedy the situation. Large universities may give courses in makeup intermittently or not at all. Drama schools often merely glance at the problem or train in outmoded techniques. And the actor must shift for himself or hope for the casual assistance and hand-me-down techniques of fellow artists.

It is therefore most exciting and encouraging to all actors when a book such as this comes to our rescue. Richard Corson's approach to makeup is meticulous and eminently practical. Perhaps even more important is his stress on the creative aspects of makeup and the avoidance of stereotypes and formulae. The insistence on supporting technical skill with imagination and individuality reflects a positive and rewarding approach. With fullest exploitation of the mind and the senses, an unsuspected range of roles exists for each of us. It is through the assistance of the art and craft of makeup presented in this book that we can hope for a more complete realization of our goals in acting.

Uta Hagen

1

Facial Anatomy

The first step in preparing to study makeup is to examine the structure of bone, muscle, and cartilage that lies beneath the skin. In remodeling a face to fit a particular character, you should know how the face is constructed. Even when you are merely trying to make your own face look its best, you need to be aware of its strong and its weak points so that you can emphasize the one and minimize the other. Thus, actors or makeup artists, before they ever open their kit, should familiarize themselves not only with the basic structure of a human face but also with the particular structure of any face they make up, whether it be their own or someone else's.

BONES OF THE FACE

A thorough and highly technical knowledge of anatomy is not really essential to the actor or to the makeup artist. It is not even necessary to remember the technical names of bones and muscles as long as you know where they are. There is, for example, no particular virtue in referring to the *zygomatic arch* when the term *cheekbone* is simpler and more generally understood. In a few instances, however, when the precise location of shadows and highlights is to be discussed, it is certainly advantageous to be able to refer to the exact area. The term *forehead* is useful only if we really mean the entire forehead. And in makeup we seldom do. There are two separate and distinct eminences, the *frontal* and the *superciliary*, which must ordinarily be considered separately in highlighting. In this case, then, the technical terms are useful.

Familiarity with the bones of the face becomes increasingly important with the advancing of the character's apparent age since muscles may lose their tonus and begin to sag, flesh may no longer be firm, and the face, in extreme old age, may sometimes take on the effect of a skull draped with skin. This is an effect impossible to achieve unless you know exactly where the bones of the skull are located.

Figure 1–1 illustrates a skull stripped of all cartilage, muscle, and skin. This is the basic structure of all faces, though there are, naturally, variations in exact shapes of bones.

Figure 1–2 is a diagrammatic representation of a skull indicating the names of the various bones and hollows (or fossae). The *maxilla* and the *mandible* are the upper and lower jaws, and the *nasal bone* is simply the bony part of the nose. But observe that only the upper section of the nose is part of the bony structure of the skull. The lower, more movable part is constructed of cartilage attached to the nasal bone.

The importance of distinguishing between the two eminences of the forehead has already been mentioned. In some individuals these are very clearly defined, especially when the source of light is directly overhead, forming a slight shadow between the two. In other individuals the whole forehead may be smoothly rounded with no hint of a depression.

The *cheekbone* or *zygomatic arch* is one of the most important bones of the face for the makeup artist, and familiarity with its location and conformation is essential for accurate modeling. Some people have prominent cheekbones, easily observed, but others may need to prod the flesh with the fingers in order to find them. In studying the bones of your own face, you should locate them by feel as well as by sight. To feel the cheekbone, prod the flesh along the entire length, beginning in front of the ear, until you know its exact shape. Start with the top of the bone, then feel how it curves around underneath. Keep prodding along the bottom until you reach the enlargement of the bone under the eye. Familiarize yourself with the general shape and exact location

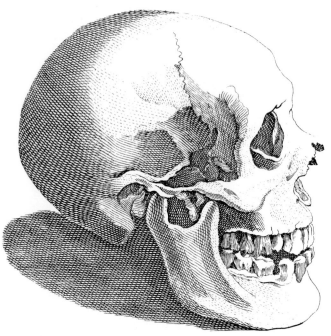

FIGURE 1–1 *A HUMAN SKULL.* From Lavater's Essays on Physiognomy.

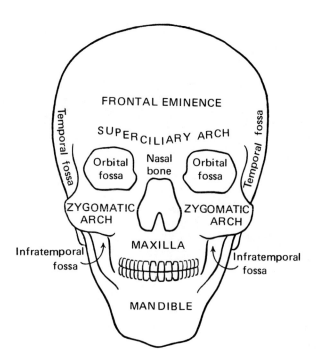

FIGURE 1–2 *DIAGRAM OF PROMINENCES AND DEPRESSIONS IN THE HUMAN SKULL.*

of the bone. Observe, also, the angle of the cheekbone as it slopes gently down from the ear toward the center of the face.

Then there are the hollows in the skull. The *orbital* hollows (or eye sockets) are clear-cut (see Figure 1–3) and easy to feel with your finger. The *temporal* hollows are what are normally referred to as the *temples*. These

FIGURE 1–3 *HEAD OF A MAN IN LATE MIDDLE AGE.*

are not deep, but there is a slight depression that tends to show up increasingly with age. The *infra-temporal* hollows you will have already found in the process of prodding the cheekbone. The lack of bony support here allows the flesh to sink in underneath the cheekbone, resulting in the familiar hollow-cheeked effect. In extreme old age or starvation this sinking-in can be considerable.

Study the bone structure of your own face thoroughly. Then, if possible, study several different types both visually and tactually.

The skull is, as you know, covered with various muscles, which operate the mandible (the only movable part of the skull) and the mouth, eyelids, and eyebrows. In order that the study of these may be made more immediately applicable, they will be noted in Chapter 12 in connection with the individual features that they affect.

CONSTRUCTION OF A HEAD

The best way to arrive at a practical understanding of the structure of the head is actually to construct one. This should be done with artists' modeling clay (such as Plastolene) on a thin but sturdy board. A piece of Masonite about 12 × 16 inches will do very well. Only the front half of the head (from the ears forward) need be done. Figure 1–4 shows such a head being modeled.

In addition to familiarizing yourself with the construction of a human head, there are two additional advantages in working with clay. One is the actual practice in modeling

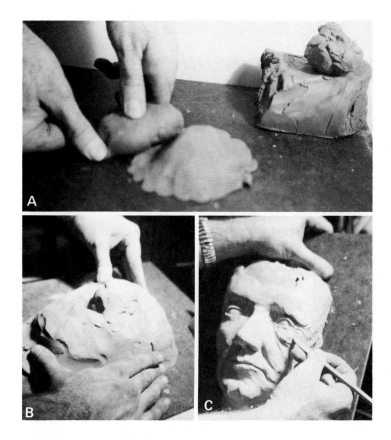

FIGURE 1—4 MODELING A HEAD IN CLAY. A. Clay being pressed against the board to make certain that it sticks. B. Head shaped and nose begun. C. Completed head being aged with a modeling tool.

features—an essential step in making most three-dimensional additions to the face. The other is having available a head that can be remodeled indefinitely. This makes it possible to study the three-dimensional form of sagging flesh, such as wrinkles or pouches, that you are trying to reproduce with paint, as well as to experiment with various shapes of noses, eyebrows, or chins in planning a makeup for a specific character.

MODELING A HEAD IN CLAY

To model a face of approximately life size, you will need about nine pounds of an oil-base clay (see Appendix A), preferably light in color. The area to be developed can be bounded by the hairline, the chin, and a point immediately in front of the ears. (See Figure 1–4.) The clay can be purchased in either five- or one-pound blocks. For easy working, it can be cut into half- or quarter-pound cubes. These cubes should be kneaded and worked with the hands until the mass is soft and pliable. As each piece is softened, it should be pressed to the board with the thumbs, as shown in Figure 1–4A, and additional pieces mashed onto it in the same way. If this is done properly, the completed face can be carried about or hung on the wall with no danger that the clay will pull away from the board. (Figure 1–5A shows a whole head being modeled in clay.)

As each piece of clay is added, the general facial area to be developed should be kept in mind. A face about 7 to 9 inches long and about 5 or 6 inches wide works very well. The softened clay (except for about half a pound, which will be used later) should be molded into a mound resembling half an egg sliced lengthwise. It is by cutting away and building up the various areas in this mound that the face is developed.

Figure 1–6A shows a stylized head construction, emphasizing its three-dimensional quality. In 1–6B you can see how this is related to a real head. In many ways the head, especially the front half, is closer to a cube than to an egg. Although you will probably prefer to use the basic egg shape for your clay model, it is frequently helpful to visualize the cube in order to be sure that your head is really three-dimensional. It is important to be aware that the forehead, for example, has a front plane and two side planes (the temples). The depression for the eyes actually forms a sort of bottom to the forehead box, and the top of the head makes a rounded top.

The nose forms a smaller, elongated box with definite front, sides, and bottom. The front, sides, and bottom of the jaw should be clear-cut, with the lips following the rounded arch of the teeth.

The classic face is divided into three equal parts horizontally, and that division should be your first step. The forehead occupies the top third, the eyes and nose the middle third, and the upper and lower jaws (including

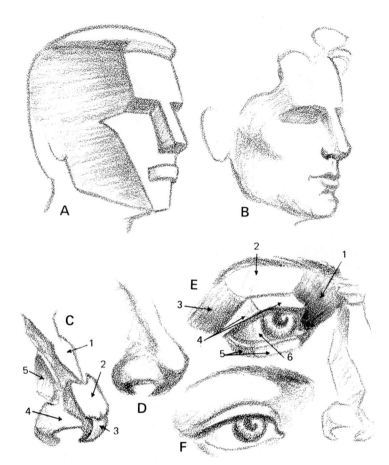

FIGURE 1—6 PLANES OF THE FACE. A, C, and E show planes of the head, nose, and eye flattened to clarify the construction.

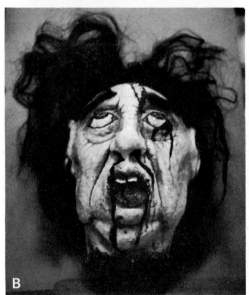

FIGURE 1—5 MAKING A SEVERED HEAD. A. Makeup instructor Bill Smith modeling a clay head on which the B. papier-mâché head was later constructed.

the mouth, of course) the lower third. It is a good idea to model the larger areas and develop the general shape of the head, defining the forehead, the jaw, and the eye sockets before starting on any detailed modeling.

Nose This is usually the simplest single feature to model because its size and location can easily be changed without seriously disturbing the rest of the modeling. This is where you will use the extra bit of clay that was left over. In adding the clay here or elsewhere, it is best to add more

than seems necessary, for it tends to be easier to cut away excess clay than to add on to a feature that has been carefully modeled and then found to be too small.

Figure 1–6C shows a breakdown of the nose into its component parts. Plane 1 represents the slender nasal bone, and 2 and 3 show the two planes of the cartilage that forms the tip. In 4 we see the roughly cylindrical flesh of the nostrils, with 5 representing the side planes. D shows the nose as it actually looks to the observer. But notice in both C and D the subtleties of shape.

The front plane of the nose (1 and 2) is not of even width all the way down. It is narrow at the bridge, then widens and narrows again slightly as it fits into the still wider cartilage of the tip (2). Examine a number of noses carefully to observe this construction. In some noses (Figure 1–3, for example) it will be quite obvious. In others the change will be so subtle that it will be difficult to distinguish it. On your clay head, model these planes carefully to give the feeling of bone and cartilage beneath the skin. Since you will use this particular bit of modeling frequently in your makeup work, it is especially important to become proficient at it now.

Mouth Modeling the mouth is a process of shaping and carving, working for the rounded fleshiness of the lips as opposed to a straight, thin gash in the clay. Start with a cylindrical shape, and model the mouth on that. (Refer to Figure 1–6A.) It is usually helpful in laying out the mouth to establish its exact center by means of the small indentation or cleft that extends from the nose down to the cupid's bow of the upper lip.

Eyes Before beginning on the eyes, be sure the superciliary arch and the cheekbones are carefully modeled since these, along with the nose, will form the eye socket. It is usually wise to model an eye socket before building up an eye. This can be done quite simply by pressing firmly with both thumbs where the eyes are to be. Bear in mind that eyes are normally the width of an eye apart.

As with the nose, the eyes are modeled with extra clay. A piece about the size of a walnut, set into each socket, should prove more than sufficient. This should give you a good start in laying out the correct planes.

Figure 1–6E shows schematically the planes of the eye, and 1–6F shows the normal eye for comparison. Planes 1, 2, and 3 represent the slope from the upper edge of the orbital fossa downward and inward to the eyeball—a slope that lies in three planes blending gently and imperceptibly into each other. Plane 1 is the deepest part of the eye socket, formed by the meeting of the nasal bone and the superciliary arch. Plane 2 is the most prominent part of the upper socket, pushed forward by the bone of the superciliary arch. This is in essentially the same horizontal plane as the forehead. Plane 3 curves backward into the plane of the temple.

Plane 4 represents the upper lid, which comes forward over the eyeball and follows it around so that it is actually in three planes, only two of which are visible in this three-quarter view. Plane 5 represents the lower lid, which, though much less extensive than the upper, follows the same general pattern. Plane 6 represents the eyeball itself.

On your clay head it would probably be well to model the eye as if it were closed, as it is in Figure 1–3. If, however, you prefer the eyes to be open, you can carefully cut away a section of the lid in order to reveal the eyeball itself and give the lid thickness, or you can lay on thin pieces of clay to create the lids. The important thing is to have a three-dimensional eye, correctly placed in the face, well shaped, and set properly into the eye sockets. As with all other features, avoid flatness.

Next, smooth out rough edges and carefully check all planes of the face and of each feature. If the result lacks conviction, analyze it to find your missteps, and redo any problem areas.

But the best way to avoid major problems is first to lay out the proportions with great care, following the measurements of your own features, if you like. Then make sure that the basic head is three-dimensional. Avoid the tendency of some beginners to make heads that are either excessively egg-shaped or very flat. Develop a feeling for both roundness and squareness in the head. Be sure that your individual features are carefully constructed with all of their component parts. Relate the size and placement of features to the head and to each other. A careful modeling of each feature will then result in a three-dimensional head.

The important thing is to follow through each step logically and carefully, progressing from large areas to small ones, taking whatever time is necessary to do the work correctly.

Problems

1. Locate on your own face the various prominences and depressions shown in the diagram in Figure 1–2.
2. Collect photographs and works of art that can be used to illustrate the structure of the face.
3. Model a head in clay. (In most makeup classes there will probably not be sufficient time to do this. It should be done, however, by any student who is considering makeup as a profession.)

2

Light and Shade

Although some three-dimensional changes can be made in creating makeup for the stage, more often than not we create the illusion of three-dimensional changes, using the principles of light and shade.

When we look at an object—any object—what our eye observes depends on the light that is reflected from specific areas of that object to the eye. Thus, because of its structure, your own face will reflect light in a certain pattern, and this pattern of light reflection is what reveals the structure and causes you to look like you instead of like someone else.

But suppose you *want* to look like someone else. You can, if you wish, actually change the shape of your face with three-dimensional makeup. If you do that, the new face will reflect different patterns of light from your normal one, and you will no longer look like you. Instead of actually reshaping your face or parts of it, however, you could simply paint on patterns of light to match those your face would reflect if you were actually to change its shape, thus creating the illusion of the face you want the audience to see.

This is essentially what the painter does. (See Figure 2–1.) But instead of a painter's flat, white canvas, the makeup artist—or the actor—begins with a three-dimensional face—a face that will reflect, as the actor moves his head onstage, a continually changing relationship between the face and the source of light.

In spite of these differences between the painter and the makeup artist, the principles of their art remain the same. Both observe in life what happens when light falls on an object. Both see the patterns of light and shade that reveal to the eye the real shape of an object. Then, with colored paints of varying degrees of lightness and darkness, of brightness and grayness, both re-create those patterns. And if they are sufficiently skillful, observers will be led by those painted patterns of light and shade into believing that they are seeing the real thing. In the case of painted portraits, of course, that is not strictly true, for one is always aware that one is seeing a picture. In fact, only in *trompe l'oeil* paintings is it the aim of the painter to imitate reality so closely that viewers are fooled into believing they are actually seeing the real thing rather than a painted representation of it. But in creating a realistic makeup, the makeup artist *must* aim to convince the audience that they are seeing the real thing.

FIGURE *2–1* LIGHT AND SHADE USED TO CREATE THE ILLUSION OF A *3*-DIMENSIONAL HEAD. *Oil painting.*

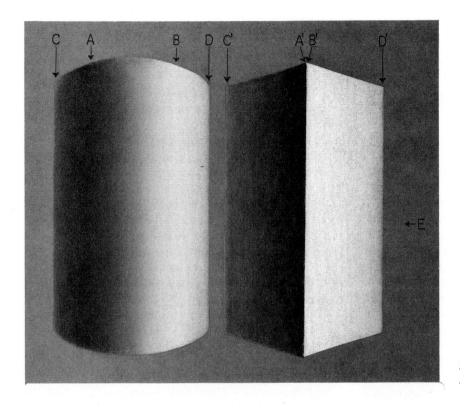

FIGURE **2–2** *MODELING CURVED AND ANGULAR SURFACES.*

Since the basis of actual makeup technique lies, then, in understanding and applying the principles of *chiaroscuro* (or *light and shade*) that have been used by artists for centuries, our next step is to study these principles in theory, to observe them in life, and then to apply them in monochromatic drawing.

FLAT AND CURVED SURFACES

How are we able to tell by sight alone whether a surface is flat or curved? The general outline of the object may provide a fairly reliable clue. But suppose we are trying to distinguish between a cylinder and a box of approximately the same size. If we cover up the ends, the outline will be exactly the same. But we shall still have no difficulty in determining which is which simply because the patterns of light and shade will be completely different, as illustrated in Figure 2–2. What, then, is chiaroscuro?

Perhaps the simplest way to approach it is to imagine the two forms in Figure 2–2 in total darkness. This would result, of course, in their appearing completely black. In other words, there is a total absence of light; and light, after all, provides the only means of our seeing these or any other objects. But if we turn on a light in the position of the arrow E, on the right, the light hits the objects and is reflected from them to our eyes, enabling us to see them. Observe, however, that the light does not illuminate the entire object in either case. Only those surfaces upon which the rays of light fall directly are fully visible because only they receive light rays to reflect to the eye. Surfaces that are situated away from the light source remain in darkness. That enables us to determine the direction in which the surface planes of an object lie and whether they are flat, curved, or irregular. In other words, it tells us the shape of the object.

HARD AND SOFT EDGES

In both of the forms in Figure 2–2 part of the form is lighted, and part remains in darkness. But the shift from the lighted plane to the nonlighted or shadowed plane is entirely different in the two. In one there is a gradual shift from light through semilight (or gray) to dark. In the other the shift is sudden and sharp. Thus, we know that one object has a rounded surface and that the other has flat, angular ones. The sharp division between the two flat surfaces is known as a *hard edge*, and the gradual change between planes on the curved surface, though technically not an edge at all, is known as a *soft edge*. That is a principle basic to all character makeup.

Look, for example, at the two largest wrinkles in the face—the nasolabial folds, which extend from the nose to the lips. In a nasolabial fold, especially if it is well developed, as is the one in Figure 2–3, there is a definite crease in the flesh—and in drawing or painting, the effect of a crease is created by means of a hard

FIGURE 2–3 NASOLABIAL FOLD. *Note the combination of hard and soft edges.*

edge, with the darkest dark next to the lightest light. The puffy part of the fold is somewhat like a half cylinder, with a gradual transition from the dark at the crease to a soft-edged highlight along the most prominent part of the fold and fading away into a soft-edged shadow.

This effect occurs—and can be reproduced with makeup—in various areas of the face, neck, and hands. Forehead wrinkles, eye pouches, sagging jowls, prominent veins in the hands—the illusion of all of these can be created with highlights and shadows—provided one understands the principles of hard and soft edges and learns to apply those principles meticulously in doing character makeups.

DRAWING WITH HIGHLIGHTS AND SHADOWS

In order to make sure that you understand the principle and can apply it, draw some simple, three-dimensional objects, such as a cylinder and a box, with charcoal and chalk on gray charcoal paper. These will serve to demonstrate the principles of light and shade you will use in makeup.

Perhaps the simplest way to begin is to do a drawing similar to the one in Figure 2–2. Before beginning your drawing, pay particular attention to the areas indicated by the arrows. Arrow A designates the darkest area on the cylinder and B, the lightest. You will observe that neither of these areas is precisely at the edge of the cylinder. The edge of the dark side (C) is slightly less dark than the darkest part, whereas the light edge (D) is not quite so light as the highlight (B). The reason for this is simply that on the dark side a small amount of reflected light is always seen at the extreme edge, and on the light side the surface of the edge is curving away from us so abruptly that it seems to be less brightly lighted. If you were to draw a cylinder with maximum light and dark areas at the extreme edges, the cylinder would seem to stop abruptly at the edges instead of continuing around to complete itself.

The source of light in the drawing in Figure 2–2 has been arbitrarily placed in the position of the arrow E. Thus, the right side of the cylinder is in direct light, resulting in a strong highlight and a gradual diminution of light from this highlight to the darkest part of the lowlight, or shadow, on the opposite side of the cylinder. No matter from which direction the light is coming, it will create a highlight on the part of the object on which it falls and leave a lowlight on the opposite side—a natural phenomenon that must be carefully observed in doing makeup.

This phenomenon occurs no matter what the shape of an object may be. In the rectangular object in Figure 2–2, for example, there is a sudden change in the plane of the surface rather than a gradual one, and therefore, a correspondingly sharp contrast in areas of light and shade. This results, of course, in a hard edge and an apparent strengthening of both the highlight and the shadow at the edge. This optical illusion always occurs when strong lights and darks are placed next to each other. It can also be observed at the crease of the nasolabial fold in Figure 2–3. In the drawing (Figure 2–2) the hard edge is intensified by deliberately placing the lightest light next to the darkest dark. In other words, both the strongest highlight and the deepest shadow are at the edge of the object nearest the eye.

In drawing such an object, there is an additional principle—that of aerial perspective—to be taken into consideration. According to that principle, first observed—or at least first applied—by the painter Ucello in the fourteenth century, the centralization of value (the relative brightness or darkness of a color) and of intensity (the relative brightness or dullness of a color) is inversely proportional to the nearness of the color to the eye. In relation to chiaroscuro, this means simply that, with distance, both black and white become more gray—in other words, less strongly differentiated. You have undoubtedly observed this effect in distant mountains or tall buildings or even in cars or houses at a considerable distance. Thus, the near edge of the rectangle is made to appear closer by increasing the intensity, no matter what the value may be. The far edges are made to recede by means of a decrease in intensity and a centralization of value. In makeup, this principle can be applied in highlighting the chin, for example, or the superciliary bone of the forehead in order to make them seem more prominent—in other words, closer to the viewer. Conversely, either one could be made to seem less prominent—farther from the viewer—by decreasing the strength of the highlight or perhaps even using a lowlight instead.

The term *lowlight* is sometimes used to refer to shadows used in makeup and to differentiate them from *cast* shadows. When undirectional light falls upon an object, it not only leaves part of the object itself in shadow, but it also casts a shadow of the object on any area around it from which the light is cut off. In other words, when an object intercepts the light, it casts a shadow. This shadow is known as a *cast* shadow. A cast shadow always has a hard edge, it follows the shape of an object upon which it falls, and it is darkest at the outer edge. Cast shadows are not normally used in makeup because of the continual movement of the actor and the resultant directional changes in light. Probably the only makeup for which they might be used would be one in which both actor and light source were immobile, as in a tableau or for a photograph. In Figure 13–7, for example, the makeup is copied from a painting, using the artist's lighting, which is primarily from one side, instead of imagining the light to be coming from above and center and adjusting the patterns of light and shade accordingly, as would normally be done in makeup.

In doing your own drawings, you might do well to begin with the flat-sided box. Start with your lightest light at what is to be the hard edge, and blend it gradually out toward the outer edge, allowing it to become slightly less light as you go. This can be done by applying the chalk directly, as carefully as you can, then blending with the fingers or with a paper stump to achieve smooth transitions. The precise technique you use is of little impor-

tance as long as you achieve the results you want. When the light side is completed, do the dark side in the same way, starting with a heavy application of charcoal at the hard edge next to the white.

In the cylinder there is a gradual transition from light to dark. Both the light and the dark can be applied in either horizontal or vertical strokes, then blended, leaving the gray paper to serve as the middle tone between the light and the dark.

Figure 12–76 illustrates the principle of modeling a third basic shape—the sphere—and the application of that principle to makeup. Notice how the same principle is used in painting the apple cheeks in Figures 12–51 and 12–75B. In the sphere all shadows and highlights fall in a circular pattern.

Remember that whenever a single light falls on a three-dimensional object, those parts of the object not in the direct line of light will remain in shadow. Conversely, whenever there is a lowlight, or shadow, there is a corresponding highlight. When the surface changes direction abruptly, the shadow and the highlight are immediately adjacent. But when the surface changes direction gradually, shadow and highlight are separated by a gradation of intermediate shades.

Problems

1. With charcoal and chalk on gray paper (obtainable from your local art dealer or stationery store), draw a cylinder, doing the highlights first and completing them before beginning the shadows. Keep the chalk on one side and the charcoal on the other, letting the gray paper serve as a middle tone between them. (See Figure 2–2.) The gray paper can also be allowed to show through at the outer edges. This will decrease the apparent intensity of illumination on the light side and will represent reflected light on the dark side. Then draw a tall, narrow box like the one in Figure 2–2, carefully modeling it with charcoal and chalk, making the hard edge very clean and sharp.
2. Model a sphere in charcoal and chalk, keeping all edges soft. (See Figure 12–76.)

3

Color in Pigment

In addition to understanding the principles of light and shade, you should also be thoroughly familiar with the principles of color, which can then be applied specifically to makeup paints.

All color comes originally from the source of light. White light is a mixture of light rays of all colors. Technically, pigment has no color of its own but has, rather, the ability to absorb certain rays and reflect others. The rays it reflects are the ones that are responsible for the pigment's characteristic color. "Red" lips, for example, absorb all light rays except the red ones, which they reflect, making the lips appear red. A clown's white face reflects all of the component rays of "white" light and therefore appears white. Black eyelashes, on the other hand, absorb all the component rays in white light and therefore appear black.

But since we are concerned here primarily with the artist's point of view, suppose we merely accept for the moment the existence of color in pigment and begin by examining the relationships characteristic of the various colors we see.

CHARACTERISTICS OF COLOR

In order to be able to talk intelligently about color and to approach the problem in an organized way, it is convenient to know three terms usually used to designate the essential characteristics of color—*hue*, *intensity*, and *value*.

Hue The hue of a color is simply the name by which we know it—red or green or blue or yellow. Pink and maroon are both variations of the basic *red* hue; brown is a deep, grayed *orange*; orchid is a tint of *violet*.

If we take samples of all of the major hues with which we are familiar and drop them at random on a table, the result, of course, is chaos. But as we place next to each other hues that are somewhat similar, we begin to see a progression that by its very nature becomes circular—in other words, a color wheel. That is the traditional form of hue arrangement and for our purposes the most practical one.

Since, however, the progression from one hue to another is a steady one, the circle could contain an unlimited number of hues, depending only on one's threshold of perception—the point at which two hues become so nearly alike as to be indistinguishable to the naked eye and, for all practical purposes, identical. But since a wheel containing hundreds of colors would be impractical, certain hues are selected at regular intervals around the circumference. The simplified color wheel illustrated in Figure 3–1A has been chosen because it is the one that is most familiar.

Intensity Thus far we have been speaking only of bright colors. But more often than not we shall be using colors of less than maximum brightness. A gray-blue is still blue, but it is far different from the blue on the color wheel. Although of the same hue, it is lower in intensity. This color would be shown as being nearer the center of the wheel—more gray, in other words. Colors on the periphery are of maximum brilliance. Colors nearer the center are less brilliant (of lower intensity) and are commonly referred to as *tones*.

Value In addition to being blue and low in intensity, a specific color may also be light or dark—light gray-blue, medium gray-blue, dark gray-blue. This darkness or lightness of a color is called its *value*. A light value is high; a dark value is low. Pink is a high value of red; orchid is a high value of violet; midnight blue is a low value of blue. Since the color wheel is only two-dimensional, it obviously cannot be used to demonstrate values,

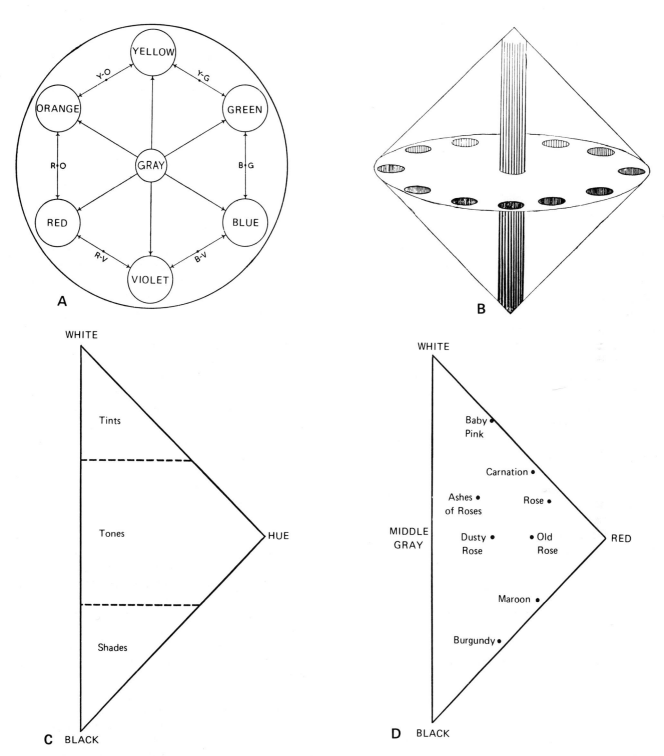

FIGURE 3–1 COLOR DIAGRAMS.   A. Color wheel. B. Double color cone. C. Color triangle. D. Location of values of red on the color triangle.

the third color dimension. But this third dimension can be added simply by placing two solid cones base to base with the flat round color wheel between them, as in Figure 3–1B.

From the color wheel we can go up or down within the cone. As we go up, we approach white, and as we go down, we approach black. Colors in the upper part of the cone are called *tints*; those in the lower part are called *shades*. (See Figure 3–1C.) Straight up the center from tip to tip there is an even progression from black to white; around the periphery, an even progression from one brilliant hue to another; and from any point on the outside to the center, a similar progression from a brilliant hue to gray.

Since any given point within the color cone represents a specific color, a vast number of colors is obviously possible. But *every* one can be located with reasonable accuracy in terms of *hue*, *intensity*, and *value*.

COLOR MIXING

If you don't have the exact color you need, you can, provided you have three primary colors to work with, mix virtually any color you want. These three primary hues are *red*, *yellow*, and *blue*, which can be mixed to achieve three secondary hues—*orange*, *green*, and *violet*, as well as an infinite number of intermediate hues. These hues will not, however, be so brilliant when obtained by mixing as when compounded directly from their sources in nature. Mixed colors always lose some intensity.

A glance at the color wheel (Figure 3–1A) will show why. Blue-green, for example, lies midway on a straight line between blue and green since it is obtained by mixing those two colors. Obviously, that brings it nearer to the gray in the center of the wheel than if it were placed on the periphery, where the primary and secondary colors are located. If the orange on the color wheel were obtained by mixing red and yellow, it too would fall nearer the center.

Colors falling opposite each other on the color wheel are called *complements* and when mixed will produce a neutral gray, as indicated on the color wheel. Blue and orange, for example, can be mixed to produce gray. However, if only a little blue is added to the orange, the result is a burnt orange. Still more blue will give varying intensities of brown.

The same result can be obtained by mixing black and white with the brilliant hue. Any color can be obtained by mixing three pigments—a brilliant hue, black, and white. The color triangle in Figure 3–1C illustrates the principle. This triangle should be imagined as a paper-thin slice cut vertically from the outside of the cone to the center. Since the triangle bounds the complete range of any one hue, a mixture of hue, black, and white at the three points can provide a color at any point within the triangle.

Pink, for example, can be obtained by mixing white with red. Mixing black with red will produce maroon. In order to achieve a dusty rose, both black and white must be added. Figure 3–1D shows where various tints, tones, and shades of red fall on the color triangle.

Problems

1. Translate the following color descriptions as well as you can into terms of hue, value, and intensity: vivid pink, bright orange, pale blue, deep violet, dusty rose, peacock blue, lavender, lemon yellow, brick red, salmon, orchid, turquoise, midnight blue, magenta, coral.
2. Following the principle of complements, what hue would you use to gray each of the following: red-orange, blue-violet, bluish green, greenish yellow, green? Assume that all colors are of maximum intensity.
3. Using red, yellow, blue, white, and black creme makeup or greasepaint, mix the following colors: orchid, turquoise, peach, coral, rust, olive green, cerise, dark brown, ivory.

4

A System for Designating Makeup Colors

Every actor or makeup artist, before beginning a makeup, is faced with choosing from hundreds of available colors those that can best help create his or her character. Unfortunately, one's choice is complicated by the fact that not only does each company have its own method of numbering its colors, but the numbers it assigns to its various colors do not always convey useful information about the colors they designate. The system described in this chapter was designed to alleviate this problem by coordinating the colors of the various makeup companies in a single system which, in essence, describes the color being designated in terms of its hue, value, and intensity.

ORGANIZING THE COLORS

In this system every makeup color is identified by a number that indicates the hue, value, and intensity of the color. In the number S-9-d, for example, S indicates the hue (scarlet); 9, the value (medium); and d, the intensity (medium).

Hue Because of the large number of hues needed to cover the entire range of makeup colors, a few color names, such as *flame* and *chrome*, have been added to the more conventional designations, such as *red*, *yellow*, and *blue*, resulting in the following list of 39 hues (see below):

For those who may not be familiar with all of the added colors, perhaps it should be pointed out that *scarlet* is a bright, orangy red; *flame*, a hot orange; *chrome*, a warm yellow; *lime*, a yellowish green; *turquoise*, a blue-green; and *indigo*, a deep violet-blue. Note that in composite color names, such as *turquoise-blue* and *blue-turquoise*, the second word represents the stronger hue and is modified by the first word. That means that *turquoise-*

39 HUES

Purple-Red	Yellow-Chrome	Blue-Turquoise
Red	Chrome-Yellow	Turquoise-Blue
Scarlet-Red	Yellow	Blue
Red-Scarlet	Lime-Yellow	Indigo-Blue
Scarlet	Yellow-Lime	Blue-Indigo
Flame-Scarlet	Lime	Indigo
Scarlet-Flame	Green-Lime	Violet-Indigo
Flame	Lime-Green	Indigo-Violet
Orange-Flame	Green	Violet
Flame-Orange	Turquoise-	Purple-Violet
Orange	Green	Violet-Purple
Chrome-Orange	Green-	Purple
Orange-Chrome	Turquoise	Red-Purple
Chrome	Turquoise	

blue is a blue that is slightly turquoise, whereas *blue-turquoise* is a turquoise that is slightly blue.

In any particular makeup-color designation in this system of color classification, the hue is indicated by the first letter of the name of the hue or the first two letters for the composite names—for example, R (red), S (scarlet), F (flame), or RS (red-scarlet), SR (scarlet-red), FS (flame-scarlet).

Value The color values range from 1 to 20, 1 being very pale, and 20, very deep. Numbers 8 to 11 indicate a color of medium value. Thus, SF-1 is a pale Scarlet-Flame (or, in more familiar terms, a pale coral pink); SF-20, a deep Scarlet-Flame (a rusty brown); and SF-9, a warm flesh tone of medium value.

Intensity The intensity of the color is indicated by lowercase letters from *a* to *j*, *a* representing a high intensity and *j*, a low intensity approaching gray. SF-9-a, for example, would be a Scarlet-Flame of medium value and high intensity. SF-9-g would be a Scarlet-Flame of the same value but of low intensity.

Gray is technically a neutral (N), having no hue and no intensity. But it does have value, which is indicated as for the hues—N1, N2, etc.

THE MAKEUP-COLOR TABLES

The specific number/letter designation for each of the various makeup colors described above can be found in Tables 1 and 2 in Appendix J. In Table 1 available makeup colors are listed according to the names or numbers assigned to them by the various makeup companies. The most efficient way to make use of these tables of colors is to label all of your own makeup colors in accordance with the lists in Table 2. If you need a color you don't have, you can find out, by consulting Table 1, which company makes it. That will save time and will enable you to make a more accurate color selection than would be possible from the descriptive labels of the makeup companies.

But suppose you have been using one brand of makeup and have recently changed to another, and you now want to know what number in the new brand corresponds to a certain number in the old. First consult Table 2, where the various brands of makeup are listed according to their own numbers, along with the corresponding standardized numbers. Then turn to Table 1 for available colors listed under the standardized numbers. If the color you want is not available in the brand you are using,

look for the nearest number with a listing for that brand.

COLOR MIXING

Sometimes you will need to mix colors in order to produce the exact color of makeup you want. Suppose, for example, that you decide you want an F-9-c foundation color. You have no F-9-c, but you do have lighter and darker F colors of the desired intensity. A mixture of the two should produce the correct color. (If your other F colors are *not* of the right intensity, additional mixing may be required.) If you have nothing at all in the F group, you might use an SF-9-c and an OF-9-c since both are of the same value, the same intensity, and of adjacent hues. They can therefore be mixed to produce the desired color. You can also mix two intensities of the same hue and the same value in order to produce an intensity somewhere between the two—as, for example, mixing F-8-a and F-8-c to get F-8-b.

To simplify your makeup kit, you can rely on mixing a few flesh colors with the more intense shading colors in order to create whatever flesh tones you want. For example, if you have an F-8-c foundation paint but find it isn't quite red enough, you can add a little red. If it is too dark, add some white. If the red makes it too brilliant, add some gray (black and white, if you have no gray). For a fairly grayed color, such as F-11-d, you might begin with F-11-c and simply add a little medium gray. Or if you had an F-11-e, you could mix it with F-11-c to obtain F-11-d.

If, on the other hand, you have F-11-c and want F-8-c, you can add white to lighten it. Or you can get what you want by adding an F color that is lighter and of the same intensity. Different hues can be mixed in the same way. An OF-9-c mixed with SF-9-c will give F-9-c since F falls midway between SF and OF.

Although at first reading this system of color designation may appear complex, once the method of classification is thoroughly understood, the grouping will seem simple and logical, and the advantages of having the makeup colors of the various companies organized into a single system of designation are considerable. The best colors and materials from the different companies can be used together without confusion, you can change from one brand of makeup to another without having to memorize a completely new set of numbers, and you can see at a glance what colors are available in various brands of makeup without having to rely on vague descriptive terms.

Problems

1. Indicate an approximate hue and value (such as light red, dark brown, medium yellow) for each of the following numbers in the color classification: R-2-a, V-1-b, SR-4-c, B-2-a, TB-6-a, SF-9-c, SF-8-g, T-12-b, P-8-b, N-8, B-13-a, C-7-a, O-9-b, R-13-a, F-13-g, VI-7-a, GL-5-a.
2. Select five or six foundation paints from your kit. Then, using only red, yellow, blue, white, and black*, duplicate—as closely as possible—each of the colors.
3. If you are working in a class, mix several samples of paint; then trade samples with another student, and match his samples without knowing what colors he used to mix them. If you are working alone rather than with a group, mix several colors at random without paying any particular attention to the ones selected. Then go back and try to duplicate them.

* If your black paint is not a true black (not completely neutral, that is), it will throw off the color of the mixture. Most black paints in makeup tend slightly toward the blue. To find out whether or not you have a true black, mix a little with some white to make a medium gray. If the gray appears to be neutral, you have a true black, but if it seems to have a cast of any specific color (such as blue), it needs to be adjusted. That can be done by adding a tiny bit of the complementary color to the black. For example, if the gray appears bluish, add a very small amount of the darkest orange you have to the black and test again by mixing with white. If that is not done, and if the black is not true, you will not get the results you want in any mixing in which black is involved.

5

Lighting and Makeup

Since a makeup seen on a stage under colored lights never looks the same as it did in the dressing room mirror, it is to the actor's advantage to know what effect various colors of stage light are likely to have on his makeup so that he can make appropriate adjustments. The purpose of this chapter, therefore, is to consider what happens when colored light falls on colored pigment.

COLOR IN LIGHT

It was mentioned briefly in Chapter 3 that pigment depends for its color on the light that illuminates it. In other words, trees are not green at night—unless, of course, they are artificially illuminated. Nothing has color until light is reflected from it. If all the light is absorbed, the object looks black; if all the light is reflected, it looks white. If certain rays are absorbed and certain others are reflected, the reflected rays determine the color.

The various colors of rays that make up what we call white light can be observed when they are refracted by globules of moisture in the air, forming a rainbow. The same effect can be obtained with a prism. The colored rays are refracted at different angles because of their different lengths, red being the longest and violet the shortest. All matter has the ability to reflect certain lengths of light waves but not others, resulting in color sensations in the eye.

Just as white light can be broken up into its component hues, those hues can be synthesized to produce white light, as well as various other colors. As with pigments, three of the colors can be used as primaries and combined to produce any other color of light, as well as the neutral white. However, the three primaries are not the same in light as in pigment. In light they are *red*, *green*, and *ultramarine* (a deep violet-blue). In mixing lights, *red* and *green* produce *yellow* or *orange*; *green* and *ultramarine* produce *turquoise* or *blue-green*, and

ultramarine and *red* produce *purple*. A mixture of all three primaries produces white light. On the stage these various colored rays are produced by placing a color medium in front of some source of nearly white light, such as a spot or a flood.

LIGHT ON PIGMENT

If the colored rays fall on pigment that is able to reflect them, then we see the color of the light. But if they fall on a pigment that absorbs some of them, the color is distorted. Suppose, for example, that red rays fall on a "red" hat. The rays are reflected, and the hat looks red. But suppose green rays are thrown on the "red" hat. Since the hat is able to reflect only red rays, the green rays are absorbed, nothing is reflected, and the hat looks black.

Imagine a "green" background behind the "red" hat. Add green light and you have a black hat against a green background. Change the light to red, and you have a red hat against a black background. Only white light (or both red and green lights at the same time) will give you a red hat against a green background.

The principle of light absorption and reflection can be used to advantage in certain trick effects, such as apparently changing a white man into a black one before the eyes of the audience. But ordinarily your problem will be to avoid such effects rather than to create them. Usually—unless the makeup is to be seen in simulated moonlight or spotlighted with strong blues or greens—major adjustments will not be necessary.

The problem of becoming familiar with the specific effects of the vast number of possible combinations of light and makeup is a far from simple one. It is impossible to offer a practical panacea for all of the problems you may encounter. A chart could be made, but it would be inaccurate, for not only do exact shades of makeup vary among manufacturers and from stick to stick or cake to cake, but light sources can also vary. Thus, the only practical solution seems to be to generalize and to leave details to the artist himself. Here are a few practical suggestions:

In the first place, try to do your makeup under lighting similar to that under which it will be viewed by the audience. Ideally, dressing-room or makeup-room lights should be arranged to take color media that can be matched with those used on the stage. Since dressing rooms are almost never so equipped, some special arrangement should be made if possible. A pair of small spots in a large dressing room, for example, can be very helpful.

Secondly, whenever possible, look at the makeup from the house. This can usually be done during a full dress rehearsal. If you are doing your own makeup, have someone whose judgment you can trust look at you from the house and offer criticisms. Since final approval of the makeup lies with the director, he is the logical one to do this, but may not be the person best qualified to give the actor constructive suggestions. If a makeup artist is in charge of all the makeup, he will check the makeup under lights and get final approval from the director.

In the third place, you ought to have some familiarity with the general effects of certain colors of light upon certain colors of makeup. Generally speaking, the following principles will hold:

1. Colors of low value will have a maximum effect upon makeup; colors of high value, a minimum.
2. A given color of light will cause a similar color of pigment to become higher in intensity, whereas a complementary color of pigment will be lower in both value and intensity.
3. Any color of pigment will appear gray or black if it does not contain any of the colors composing a given ray of light that falls upon it.

For a better understanding of the effects of colored light on makeup colors, you might examine the color illustrations (Appendix H) under various colors of light. If a spotlight and appropriate color media are not accessible, the following list of colors of light, with their effects upon various colors of makeup, can be used as a guide. You should remember, however, that the effects listed are only approximations, and that the actual effects may upon occasion vary from those indicated here. The names of the colors, rather than their numbers, have been used in this listing since they are more generally understood.

Pink tends to gray the cool colors and intensify the warm ones. Yellow becomes more orange.

Flesh pink affects makeup less strongly than the deeper shades and has a flattering effect on most makeups.

Fire red will ruin nearly any makeup. All but the darker flesh tones will virtually disappear. Light and medium rouge become a pale orange and fade imperceptibly into the foundation, whereas the dark reds turn a reddish brown. Yellow becomes orange, and the cool shading colors become shades of gray and black.

Bastard amber is one of the most flattering colors to makeup. It may gray the cool shading colors somewhat but picks up the warm pinks and flesh tones and adds life to the makeup.

Amber and *orange* have an effect similar to that of red, though less severe. Most flesh colors, except the dark browns, become more intense and more yellow. Rouges tend to turn more orange. Cool colors are grayed. Dark amber has, of course, a stronger effect than light amber.

Light straw has very little effect upon makeup, except to make the colors somewhat warmer. Cool colors may be grayed a little.

Lemon and *yellow* make warm colors more yellow, blues more green, and violets somewhat gray. The darker the color medium, of course, the stronger the effect upon the makeup.

Green grays all flesh tones and rouges in proportion to its intensity. Violet is also grayed. Yellow and blue will become more green, and green will be intensified.

Light blue-green tends to lower the intensity of the foundation colors. Light red becomes darker, and dark red becomes brown. Use very little rouge under blue-green light.

Green-blue will gray medium and deep flesh tones, as well as all reds, and will wash out pale flesh tones.

Blues will gray most flesh tones and cause them to appear more red or purple. Blues and greens become higher in value, violets become more blue, and purples become more violet. The darker the blue, the stronger the effect.

Violet (*light* and *surprise*) will cause orange, flame, and scarlet to become more red. Rouge may seem more intense. Greens are likely to be a little lower in value and intensity. Be careful not to use too intense a red in either foundation or rouge.

Purple will have an effect similar to that of violet, except that the reds and oranges will be intensified to a much greater degree, and most blues will tend to look violet.

DIRECTION OF LIGHT

If, as may occasionally happen, the primary source of light is to be from below rather than from above (see Figure 18–19), the makeup should be done—or, at least, looked at—with light coming from below so that any necessary adjustments can be made.

One problem remains. Since stage lights are likely to change from time to time during a performance, be aware of any radical changes, especially in color, and have your makeup checked under the various lighting conditions that prevail. If such changes do affect your makeup adversely and there is no opportunity for you to adjust the makeup to the lights, try to modify your basic makeup to minimize the problem under all lighting conditions. If this is not successful, consult the director about the possibility of some adjustment of the lighting.

Problems

1. What makeup color and what colors of light would you use to make a white man apparently change suddenly into a black man?
2. What color would each of the following appear to be under the colors of light indicated: A yellow hat under red and green lights? A green hat under red and yellow lights? A red hat under blue and green lights? A red and green hat under yellow lights? A red and yellow hat under green lights? A green and yellow hat under red lights? A red and blue hat under blue lights? A red, yellow, and blue hat under red, green, and ultramarine lights? A purple and white hat under red, green, and ultramarine lights?
3. It has been stated in the chapter that a given color of light raises the intensity of a similar color of pigment. Yet on a stage flooded with red light, all of the clear, bright reds seem to be "washed out." Why is this so?

6

Relating the Makeup to the Character

The foundation on which any character makeup is based is, of course, the character, and the primary purpose of character makeup is to help the actor reveal that character. There are three basic steps that can be followed in arriving at a suitable conception of the makeup for a realistic character:

1. Find out as much as you can (or as much as may be useful) about the character.
2. Visualize the character, considering ways in which what you have learned about him can be reflected in his physical appearance.
3. Adapt, as well as you can, your ideas about the physical appearance of the character to the face of the actor who is playing the part, whether it be yourself or someone else.

FINDING OUT ABOUT THE CHARACTER

The source of information about a fictional character is, of course, the play. For a historical character, there are additional sources, such as biographies, photographs, and works of art. In the play there may or may not be a description of the character by the playwright. In contemporary plays, there usually is. The dialogue contains additional information—from what the character reveals about himself (intentionally or unintentionally) and what other characters say about him. If you are an actor, you will, of course, already have studied the play. If you are designing a makeup for the actor, you *should* do it. And you will, presumably, get from the actor and the director ideas *they* have about the character.

VISUALIZING THE CHARACTER

In arriving at an appropriate visual image of the character, you may find it useful to examine the various factors that might be influential in determining the character's appearance. For convenience, these factors can be divided into seven groups—*genetics, environment, health, disfigurements, fashion, age,* and *personality*. These divisions are obviously not mutually exclusive, nor are they necessarily of equal importance in finding out what you should know about a character.

GENETICS

This category includes those characteristics, physical and mental, with which a person is born. Cyrano's large nose, for example, and the red hair of all the boys in *Life with Father* are clearly genetic in origin. Since they are required by the play, there is no choice to be made. They can simply be noted as required characteristics, as can the character's sex.

In a realistic play, race is always a factor to be considered, whether it is mentioned in the play or not. Members of the same family should, of course, appear to be of the same race—unless there are adopted children of other races, a fact that would surely be brought out in the dialogue. Historical characters should, naturally, appear to be of whatever race or combination of races they actually were—unless the playwright or the director has decided, for whatever reason, to disregard the historical facts. Within a given race, especially the Caucasian, the skin can also be noticeably affected by age, health, and environment and will be discussed under those headings. For two characters created on the same face and illustrating different influences, see Figure 6–1. For an Oriental actor in his makeup as two Caucasian characters, see Figure 12–74. (For information about physical characteristics of the various races, see Appendix E.) For makeups in which sex was a dominant factor, see Figure 20–1 (A–F), which illustrates female characteristics assumed by male characters. (For suggestions on how to change the apparent sex of an actor, see Chapter 20.)

FIGURE **6–1** *CHARACTER MAKEUPS SHOWING DIFFERENCES IN FASHION, PERSONALITY, AND GENETICS.* Makeups by student Elaine Herman. (For another makeup by the same student, see Figure 18–5.)

ENVIRONMENT

In addition to race and other genetic factors, environment is of considerable importance in determining the color and texture of the skin. A Caucasian farmer and a Caucasian bookkeeper are likely to have different colors of skin, and a color that is right for one would probably be inappropriate for the other. A Caucasian man who has lived all of his life in a Scottish village is not likely to have the same sort of complexion as his twin brother who has lived most of his life on the Equator. The color and texture of the skin may be influenced not only by the general climatic conditions of the part of the world in which the character lives but also by the physical conditions under which he works and spends his leisure time. Offices, mines, fields, foundaries, boats, and country estates all have different effects upon the people who work or live there. These environmental effects will, of course, be noticeable primarily on Caucasians.

HEALTH

Unless there are indications in the play to the contrary, a character is assumed to be in good health. If he is not, that fact is usually made evident in either the performance or the makeup or both. Sometimes, as with Camille or with Mimi in *La Boheme*, there are changes in the state of health that should be made apparent to the audience. Physical indications of the general state of health can usually be confined to the skin color, the area around the eyes, and, perhaps, the hair. In general, it is better to do too little than too much. Above all, avoid attributing to specific illnesses physical symptoms that are inaccurate and that will immediately be spotted by doctors and nurses in the audience. In certain areas of makeup it is best to curb the imagination and rely strictly on factual information.

DISFIGUREMENTS

The character may have major or minor disfigurements having genetic causes or resulting from various diseases or from accidents, surgery, fights, attacks, or self-inflicted wounds. If any such disfigurement is essential to the character, it will be specified by the playwright. Sometimes, however, an actor may want to have in the makeup a specific disfigurement—such as a scar or a wart—which, though not indicated in the play, he considers useful and appropriate for the character. Broken noses for prize fighters and scars for underworld characters are familiar choices. For makeups illustrating disfigurements, see Figures 13–33, H–17B, H–19B, and H–20.

FASHION

In the designing of the makeup for most realistic characters, fashion is an essential element to consider since it affects hair and beard styles (see Appendix G) and the use of cosmetics (see Appendix F). Having the wrong look for the period can have a very jarring effect on the audience, whether or not they are conscious of what it is that's jarring. Those who are conscious of it may criticize the actor for not being better informed about the period; those who are not may simply think that he is giving a bad performance. The wise actor avoids the problem by doing his homework, which includes not only being informed about the fashions of the period, but deciding what specific choices—whether fashionable or unfashionable—the character would be likely to make. For illustrations of the effect of fashion on specific makeups, see Figures 6–1, 12–27, 12–30, 12–64, 13–6, 16–1, and 16–5.

AGE

Apparent age (Figures 6–2 and 6–3) is a consideration in every realistic makeup, though it may or may not be important. But whether the exact age is important or not, some decision must be made as to approximately how old the character should look, and that decision will rest with the actor and the director.

Youth The physical attributes of youthfulness—ideally, at least—are a smooth skin, good color in the face, a delicately curved mouth (Figure 6–9O), smooth brows, and an abundance of hair. But genetics, environment, fashion, personality, and health may modify any or all of these.

It is perhaps worth mentioning here the unfortunate custom in the theater of referring to any youthful makeup as a *straight* makeup—a term which implies that you need do nothing but heighten the color and project the features. Designating any makeup as "straight" is a trap that leads to neglect of important work. The term may have a certain validity in the event that a specific role is so cast that the actor's features are precisely right, with not a hair to be changed. But if there is anything at all about the actor's face that is not right for the character, then the actor requires a makeup that will change him to fit the character, and that is called a *character* makeup, no matter what age the character may be.

At times, of course, the actor may not be playing a clearly defined character at all (as may happen in choruses) and can, therefore look exactly like himself. But if the actor wants to look his best—and presumably he does—that, more often than not, will require a *corrective* makeup—in other words, a makeup designed to make the actor look more attractive without relating the changes to a specific character. (See Chapter 10.)

Middle and Old Age The passage of time can bring with it sagging muscles, graying and thinning hair, changes in skin color, and increasing angularity in the lips (Figure 6–9H), the eyebrows, and the cheeks. But the exact nature and extent of these changes and the age at which they become apparent will depend on a

FIGURE 6–2 AND 6–3 ADOLPHE APPIA. Photographs at age 20 and in later years.

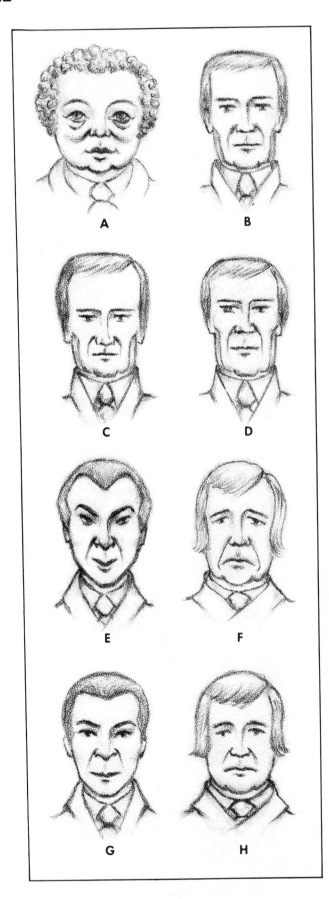

variety of factors, such as genetics, environment, and health. For an illustration of changes in the same face over a period of time, see Figures 6–2 and 6–3.

PERSONALITY

As an example of how physical appearance can help to reveal the personality of the character, look at faces A and B in Figure 6–4, one drawn with curved lines and one with straight. It is quite obvious which face appears more flexible and which more rigid, which one seems more open and which one more reserved. If these were sketches for characters, it is equally obvious which one you might expect to find at a party, and which one working late at the office.

This cartoonist's method of relating straight and curved lines to personality traits can easily be applied to makeup. If, for example, you want a character to look firm and decisive, a straight mouth (Figure 6–4B) will help to give that impression. If, on the other hand, you want to suggest more warmth, cheerfulness, and sociability, you might make the lips fuller and give the corners a slight upward curve (Figure 6–4A). Giving the character a downward curve to the mouth (Figure 6–4F) will, of course, have the reverse effect.

Now look at faces C and D in Figure 6–4. Both are similar to B except that the proportions of the face have been changed to place the emphasis in C on the upper part of the face and in D, on the lower. How does this affect your immediate reaction to each face? Which one, for example, would you expect to belong to a character more inclined to work with his mind than with his muscles, and which to a character more interested in football than in chess? This is not to suggest that emphasis on the upper part of the face will invariably create an impression of a mind-oriented character or that emphasis on the lower part of the face will always suggest a physical orientation. Nonetheless, drawing attention to one section of the face may tend to do just that and can, therefore, be helpful in communicating to the audience what you want them to believe about the character. (Note, for example, the effect of the facial proportions in Figure 7–1C and L.)

In the third set of faces in Figure 6–4, the face is equally divided, but the straight lines have been slanted—up from the center in E and down from the center in F. Note what totally different impressions they create from each other and from the straight lines in B. Note also

FIGURE 6–4 LINE AND PROPORTION IN THE FACE. *These drawings demonstrate the effects of: A. and B. curved and straight lines; C. and D. proportions; and E., F., G., and H. slanted lines.*

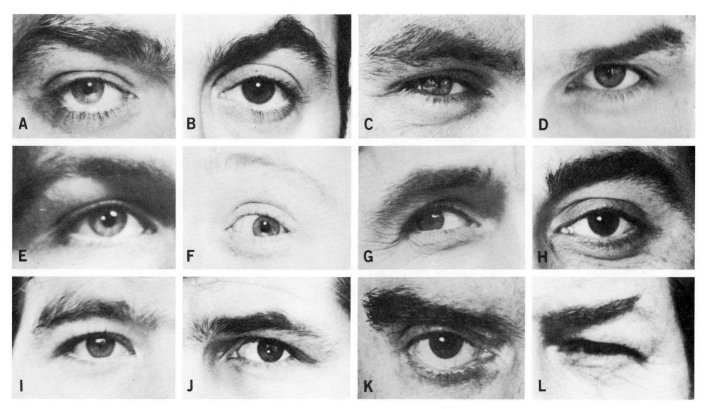

FIGURE 6–5 CHARACTER IN EYES AND EYEBROWS.

how the strong impression created by E is modified by reducing the slant in G. Now look at the various eyebrows in Figure 6–5 and observe the impressions they create.

Other kinds of changes—sometimes involving a single feature—can be equally effective. For example, the eyes of the actor in Figure 6–6A have been made to seem farther apart in B and closer together in C. Observe the difference in the two personalities projected by B and C as a result of this one simple change.

But in making such changes, remember that the impression created by a single feature will be modified to some degree by other elements combined with it in the total picture. Note, for example, how the effect of makeup for eyes close together has been modified in Figure 6–7 by being combined with straight lines for the eyebrows instead of slanted ones. And, in addition, it is modified indirectly by being part of a different face. This indirect modification cannot, of course, be completely controlled unless the actor wears a mask. But direct modification can be controlled, at least to some degree, by deciding what form the modification will take. In other words, the eyebrows in Figure 6–6C could have been straight, or the ones in Figure 6–7B could have been slanted, depending on which seemed more appropriate for the character. The slanted ones could also have been slanted less, slanted more, slanted in the opposite direc-

tion, curved, shortened, lengthened, lightened, thinned, thickened, or made bushy. Any one of these would have modified the impression created by eyes close together.

The apparent length and width of the nose, as viewed from the front, can also be changed with highlights and shadows, as can the length, shape, and prominence of the chin. And the mouth can be made larger or smaller and the lips reshaped.

When considering any of these changes, you may find it helpful to ask yourself what effect the change will have on the audience's perception of the character. (An analytical actor may do this automatically. An intuitive actor will probably not do it at all and may not need to. An actor who is both analytical and intuitive will probably make an intuitive choice, then analyze it to test its validity.)

Changes in the profile may also be helpful in creating an appropriate physical image for the character. (See Figure 6–8.) Sometimes—as with Cyrano, for example—they may be essential. From a practical point of view, changes involving the nose are the easiest to make, though one must keep in mind, obviously, that the actor's nose can only be added to, never subtracted from—except, of course, by surgery.

Similar limitations apply to the forehead and to the chin. However, if a beard is appropriate for the character,

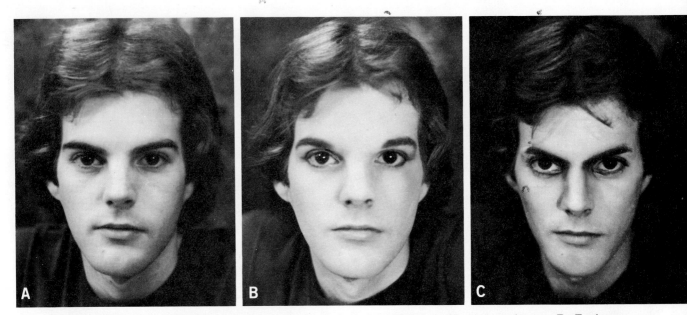

FIGURE 6–6 PLACEMENT OF EYEBROWS. (Actor Jeffrey Hillock.) A. Natural eyebrows. B. Eyebrows farther apart. Inner ends of the brows have been blocked out and the outer ends extended with a pencil. C. Eyebrows closer together. Inner ends of the brows have been extended with a pencil and outer ends blocked out.

FIGURE 6–7 EYES CLOSE TOGETHER. Makeup by student J. C. Stahl. A. Without makeup. B. Eyebrows in a straight line and close together.

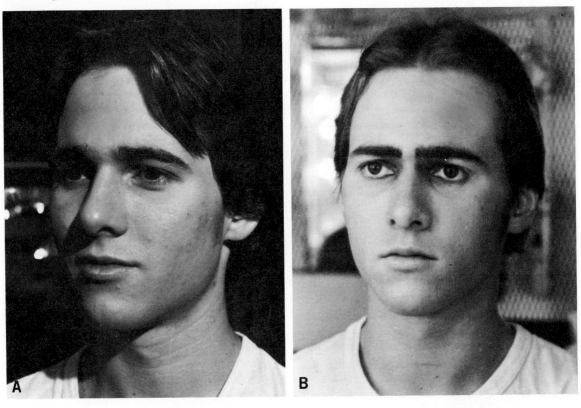

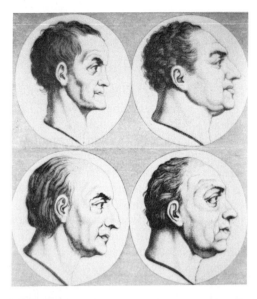

FIGURE **6—8** PROFILES.

FIGURE **6—9** MOUTHS.

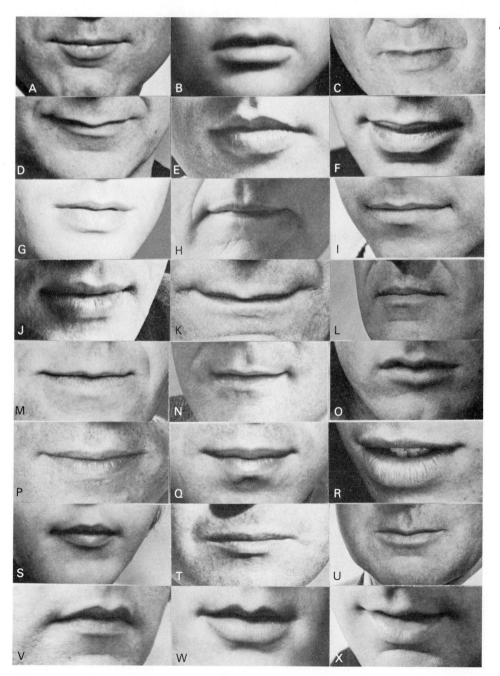

it can be used to conceal the actor's chin, avoiding any three-dimensional remodeling. As for the forehead, making three-dimensional extensions may create practical problems that will cause far more trouble than they're worth. The *height* of the forehead, however, can be easily increased or decreased by wearing a wig or a toupee.

When you have determined what part or parts of the profile you think should be changed and have decided whether or not such changes are practical, the next step is to visualize a specific profile appropriate for the character. Suppose, for example, that you have decided to change the shape or size of the nose. You might begin by asking yourself some questions about the nose. Would it be thin and sharp, long and drooping, short and turned up, thick and rounded? What qualities do roundness or sharpness convey to you? Thickness or thinness? Straight-

ness or crookedness? Which of those qualities are appropriate for the character? Or you might, instead, simply look at a number of profiles and choose a nose that you think would be appropriate. Then, of course, you would have to determine whether or not it would be possible to create that particular nose by adding to the actor's own nose and, if so, whether or not it would look right on the actor's face. If it didn't, additional experimentation would be necessary.

The foregoing approach to creating an appropriate physical image for a character can be profitably applied, at least in part, to most characters who are to be made up realistically. The next step will be to adapt that image to your own face (if you are doing your own makeup) or to the face of the actor who is playing the part. That will be discussed in the next chapter.

7

Designing the Makeup

Once you have decided what you want the character to look like, the next step is to put your ideas into concrete form—either an experimental makeup or a sketch showing what you have in mind. Which you do will probably depend to some extent on whether you are an actor or a makeup designer. In either case, making a sketch or a drawing of the makeup can be extremely helpful. For a makeup designer, professional or nonprofessional, it is almost essential.

THE MAKEUP DESIGNER

If all of the makeups are being designed by one person, he or she will first study the play, then consult with the director, perhaps with the costume designer, and, ideally, with the actors before designing the makeups and will also obtain photographs of the actors before making the sketches. Then, after the sketches have been approved by the director, the designer should make certain that the actor can do the makeup. If not, it is the responsibility of the makeup designer to teach the actor to do it. If, as sometimes happens in the nonprofessional theater, the makeups for all performances are to be done by someone other than the actors, the designer should make sure that the person doing the makeups understands the instructions on the makeup charts. And if the time for actually making up is going to be limited (as with quick changes or with the actor playing more than one part), it is the makeup designer's responsibility to make certain that the makeup, as designed, can be done by the actor (or the makeup artist) in the time available. Unless the makeups are unusually simple, all of this should ordinarily be taken care of before the first dress rehearsal. The makeup designer should be present at the first dress rehearsal with lighting in order to see the makeup in action on the stage. He or she can then consult with the director if necessary and suggest to the actor any

changes that need to be made. Only when the designer is completely satisfied that the makeups are being executed satisfactorily, should the actors be left on their own. In the case of a long run, the designer should check the makeups regularly.

In the professional theater the makeup designer is a professional makeup artist or a costume designer, who may or may not be trained in makeup. In the academic theater the designer may be the makeup teacher, the costumer, or, ideally, one of the more advanced makeup students, who should, when competent to do so, be given the opportunity to design the makeups for public productions. Professional or nonprofessional, the designer should start work well in advance and have it essentially completed before dress rehearsals, which should be used for adjusting the makeup to the lighting and making any other changes that may be needed.

Although in most professional productions (and in some nonprofessional ones) the actors are expected to create their own makeups, there are productions that need the services of a makeup designer. And occasionally, in both professional and nonprofessional productions, a makeup artist may be called in to help an actor who is not prepared, by training or experience, to do the makeup required. In that kind of situation the makeup artist does not usually submit designs to the director, but deals directly with the actor. Thus, instead of determining what the makeup is to be like, the makeup artist works with the actor in creating it.

When the makeup is finished, photographing it with an instant-picture camera can be very helpful and may, in fact, lead to further work on the makeup. When the actor is satisfied with the makeup, he then learns—with the help of the makeup artist, if necessary—to do the makeup himself, using the final photograph or photographs as a guide. He should also keep the photographs on his dressing table until he is secure in doing the makeup without them.

The makeup designer should always allow sufficient time—including additional sessions—for the actor to learn the makeup. If time for doing the makeup in performance is going to be limited, he should make sure that the actor can do the makeup in the time available. And he should, of course, look at the makeup onstage and then make suggestions for any changes he considers desirable.

THE ACTOR AS DESIGNER

If there is no makeup designer for the production and no makeup artist is called in to help individual actors, the actor then becomes his own makeup designer. As such, he has the advantage of knowing, better than anyone else, the character as he wants to portray him. He also has the opportunity to experiment with the makeup over a period of time until he achieves the results he wants. An instant-picture camera with which he can take pictures of himself (or have a friend do it for him) can, if it is available, provide the means of his looking at the

makeup objectively. He can then make any changes or corrections that seem desirable.

In designing his own makeup, the actor can begin either by sketching his ideas on paper, as a makeup designer does, or by experimenting directly with makeup on his own face. He should, of course, choose whichever method works better for him.

If he does do sketches, he may wish to show them to the director for his approval or suggestions. Or he may prefer to show the director photographs of makeup ideas he has been working on. Although neither of these will be expected, either can be useful in avoiding basic disagreements about the makeup the first time the director sees it at a dress rehearsal.

SKETCHES AND DRAWINGS

Two kinds of sketches or drawings can be used in designing makeups—*character* (those which present a visual conception of the character, as in Figure 7–1) and *makeup*

FIGURE **7–1** CHAR-
ACTER SKETCHES.
Pen and Ink.

A   B   C   D

E   F   G   H

I   J   K   L

(those which show the character conception adapted to the actor's face, as in Figures 7–2 and 7–6). Whether they are called *sketches* or *drawings* depends largely on the relative degree of spontaneity with which they are executed. A sketch (Figure 7–1, for example) is the more spontaneous and is usually done more quickly than a drawing (Figures 7–3 and 7–4). It is the makeup drawings, rather than the character sketches, that show what the actor can really be expected to look like when the makeup is finished.

FIGURE 7–3 PORTRAIT OF GEORGE CANNING. *Pencil drawing.*

FIGURE 7–2 PENCIL DRAWING ON COQUILLE BOARD. *One of the wicked stepsisters in Cinderella. In ballet and opera, the stepsisters are usually danced or sung by men. The 1833 hairstyle is based on a drawing in* Fashions in Hair, *Plate 116.*

FIGURE 7–4 PORTRAIT OF ALBERT EINSTEIN. *Pen and ink drawing.*

PRELIMINARY SKETCHES

Preliminary sketches of the character can be done in any medium you choose—pencil (Figure 7–3), charcoal (or charcoal pencil) and chalk, pen and ink (Figures 7–1 and 7–4), pastel, or conté crayon. (Some of the materials used for the various mediums are illustrated in Figure 7–5). They will usually be in black and white or sepia but can, of course, be in color if you wish. If you are inexperienced at sketching, it may be easier for you to use outlines of heads with features indicated, such as those shown on the worksheet in Figure 7–9. Student sketches, using similar worksheets can be seen in Figures 7–10 and 7–11. You may wish to do a number of sketches and then choose the one that seems best to express the character.

ADAPTING THE MAKEUP TO THE ACTOR

If you have chosen to do preliminary sketches and have conceived them strictly in terms of the ideal—that is, if you have created an image intended to fulfill both the playwright's conception and the actor's interpretation—but you have not yet taken into consideration the practical necessity of adapting this ideal conception to the face of the individual actor, the adaptation should be done before the final drawings are made. There is no use presenting to the director or the actor a visual concept of

the character that simply cannot be realized.

One of the simplest—and certainly most reliable—methods of adapting the ideal concept of the character to the face of the actor who is to play the part is to work from photographs—front and profile—of the actor, making sure, of course, that the photographs are recent enough so that the face will not have significantly aged. Place a sheet of tracing paper over the photograph (Figure 7–6A) and sketch the character in pencil (Figure 7–6B–H), being very careful not to change the actor's face in any way in which it cannot actually be changed with makeup. The drawings in Figure 7–7 were done over the photographs in Figure 7–8A and B. Figure 7–8C and D shows the final makeup. Note the close resemblance between the drawing and the makeup—a result of working directly from a photograph of the actor. The drawing in Figure 17–7 was done in the same way.

If you have not previously worked from photographs in this way, you may prefer to begin by making a drawing of the actor as he is. This drawing can then be used with the character drawing (as in Figure 17–7) for a before-and-after comparison. This is the procedure:

1. Place a large glossy photograph of the actor under a sheet of tracing paper. You can tape both the photograph and the tracing paper to a drawing board, or if you prefer to use a pad of tracing paper, you can simply insert the photograph under the top sheet.
2. Using a sharp pencil with a medium (B) lead, trace the outline of the face and the features and fill in lips, eyebrows, eyes, and shadows. Paper stumps can

FIGURE **7–5** DRAWING AND SKETCHING MATERIALS. A. White chalk. B. Cotton swab. C. Paper stump. D. Charcoal pencil. E. Drawing pencil. F. White pencil. G. Drawing pen. H. Conte crayons. I. India ink.

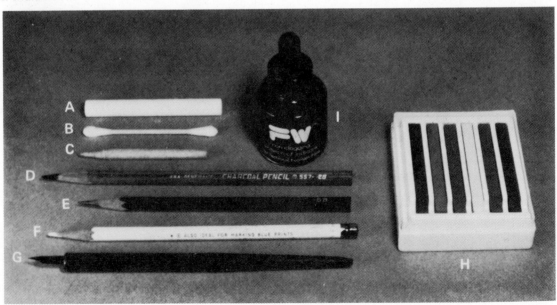

FIGURE 7–6** **MAKING A CHARACTER DRAWING FROM A PHOTOGRAPH. *A. Placing photograph of the actor under a sheet of tracing paper. B. Outlining the face with a drawing pencil. C. Shadows in the eye area being laid in with a pencil. D. Shadows being blended with a paper stump. E. Nose being reshaped. F. Jawline being aged. G. The character's hair being sketched in after the photograph has been removed. H. Finished drawing.*

 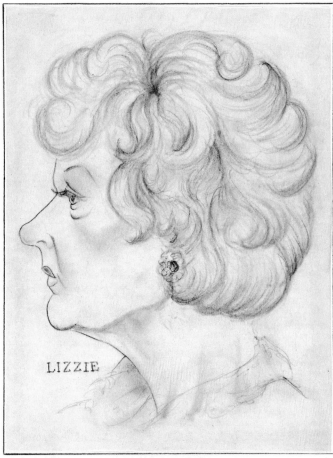

FIGURE 7–7 PENCIL DRAWINGS FOR LIZZIE IN PHILADELPHIA, HERE I COME. *The drawings were made on tracing paper placed over the photographs of the actress in Figure 7–8.*

be used for blending small areas, and the fingers for larger ones.
3. The hair should be sketched in but need not be done in great detail.
4. Remove the photograph and add finishing details to the drawing.

In making a drawing of the character from the photograph, follow the same procedure, but instead of copying the actor's features exactly, change those you wish to alter for the character, as illustrated in Figure 7–6.

QUICK CHANGES

If there are quick changes to be made or if your facilities or your time for making complicated prosthetic pieces are limited, then you should make sure that the requirements for the makeup are reasonable. If they are not, you will need to modify your design to meet practical considerations. In Peter Falk's makeup for Stalin, for example, there was a fairly fast change to be made during intermission—from the first character drawing in Figure

17–7 to the second. Fortunately, the change could be made with cake makeup and the addition of a wig. Therefore, the requirements of the makeup were reasonable. (For suggestions on facilitating quick-change makeups, see Chapter 19).

WORKING DRAWINGS

Working drawings should be provided for the actor or the makeup artist to follow in doing the makeup. They can be in the form either of drawings (such as the *makeup drawings* previously described or the ones used on the worksheets in Figures 7–10 and 7–11) or of diagrams of the face, with indications of changes to be made. The outlines of a face, front and profile, shown on the worksheet in Figure 7–9, could be used for the diagrams. Instructions for the makeup could then be connected to various parts of the diagram with arrows. However, since the drawings show approximately what the makeup will actually look like, whereas the diagrams do not, the drawings are much to be preferred. If you particularly want to relate your written instructions for the makeup to very

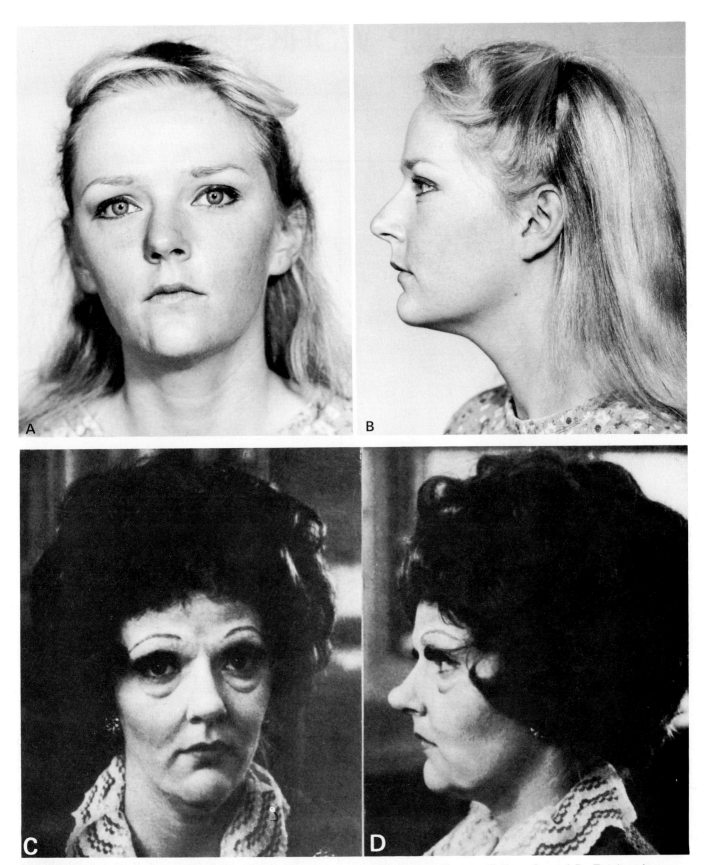

FIGURE 7–8 LIZZIE IN PHILADELPHIA, HERE I COME.   *A. and B. Actress Bonnie Gallup. C. and D. Final makeup based on sketches in Figure 7–7.*

MAKEUP WORKSHEET

PRODUCTION: _____ ACTOR: _____
CHARACTER: _____

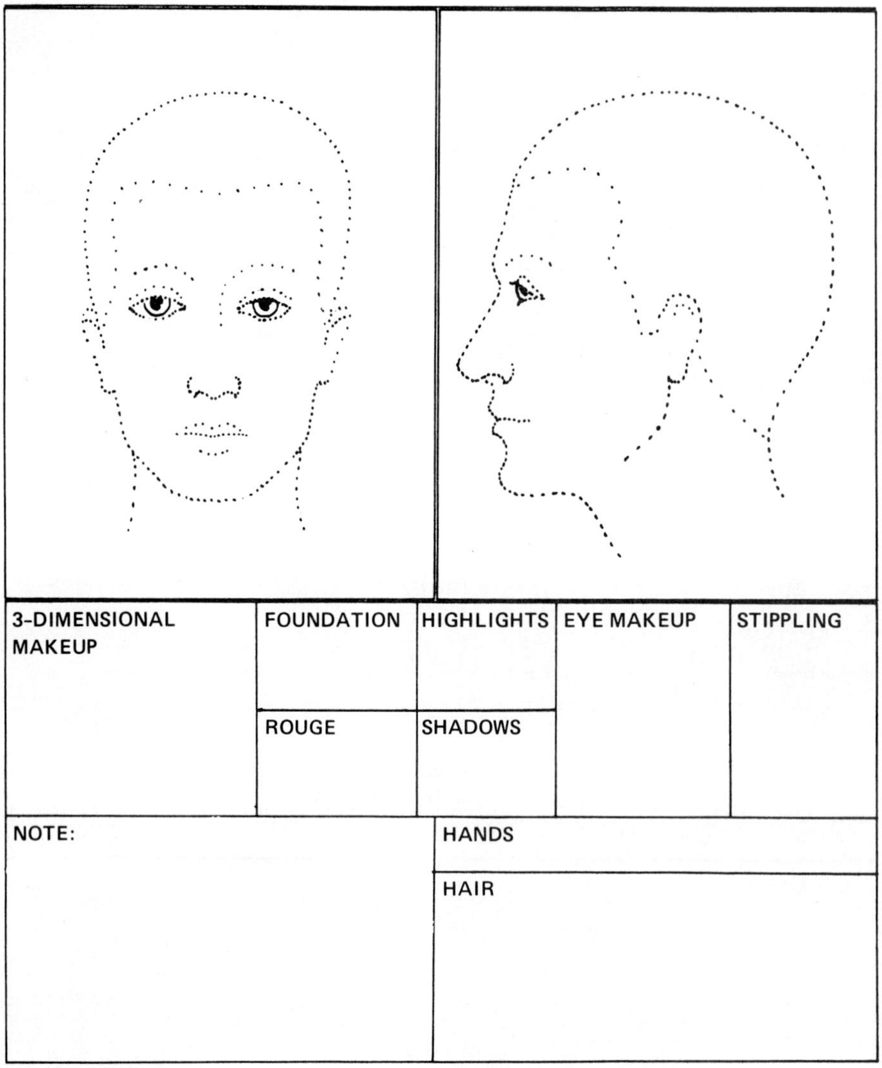

3-DIMENSIONAL MAKEUP	FOUNDATION	HIGHLIGHTS	EYE MAKEUP	STIPPLING
	ROUGE	SHADOWS		

NOTE:	HANDS
	HAIR

FIGURE 7–9 MAKEUP WORKSHEET.

specific areas of the face by means of arrows, that can be done as well with drawings as with diagrams.

The drawings, which can be in either black and white or color and which should include both a front view and a profile, must be carefully rendered to give an accurate impression of what the makeup will look like when it is finished. They can be done on an artist's drawing board, if you have one, or on a clipboard. The drawings (or photocopies of them) should be made available to the actor to mount on or near his makeup mirror (see Figure 17–8C).

For black-and-white drawings, pencil is relatively easy to work with, especially when making revisions. The tracing-paper-over-photograph technique described under "Adapting the Makeup to the Actor" is likely to be the most accurate. If photographs of the actor are not available, pen or pencil drawings can be made directly on the makeup worksheets, as in Figures 7–10 and 7–11, or on separate sheets of paper.

For renderings in color (and color may be advisable for some makeups, especially nonrealistic ones), there are several possibilities. Water colors require the most

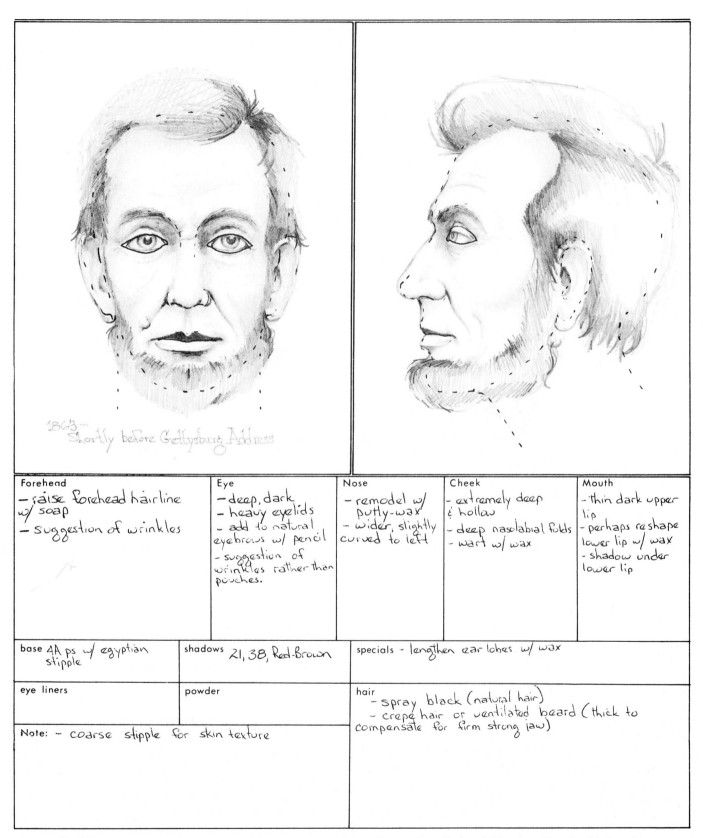

1863 –
Shortly before Gettysburg Address

Forehead	Eye	Nose	Cheek	Mouth
– raise forehead hairline w/ soap – suggestion of wrinkles	– deep, dark – heavy eyelids – add to natural eyebrows w/ pencil – suggestion of wrinkles rather than pouches.	– remodel w/ putty-wax – wider, slightly curved to left	– extremely deep & hollow – deep nasolabial folds – wart w/ wax	– thin dark upper lip – perhaps reshape lower lip w/ wax – shadow under lower lip

base 4A ps w/ egyptian stipple	shadows 21, 38, Red-Brown	specials – lengthen ear lobes w/ wax
eye liners	powder	hair – spray black (natural hair) – crepe hair or ventilated beard (thick to compensate for firm strong jaw)
Note: – coarse stipple for skin texture		

FIGURE 7–10 MAKEUP WORKSHEET FOR ABRAHAM LINCOLN. *By student Richard Brunner. For finished makeup, see Figure 7–12.*

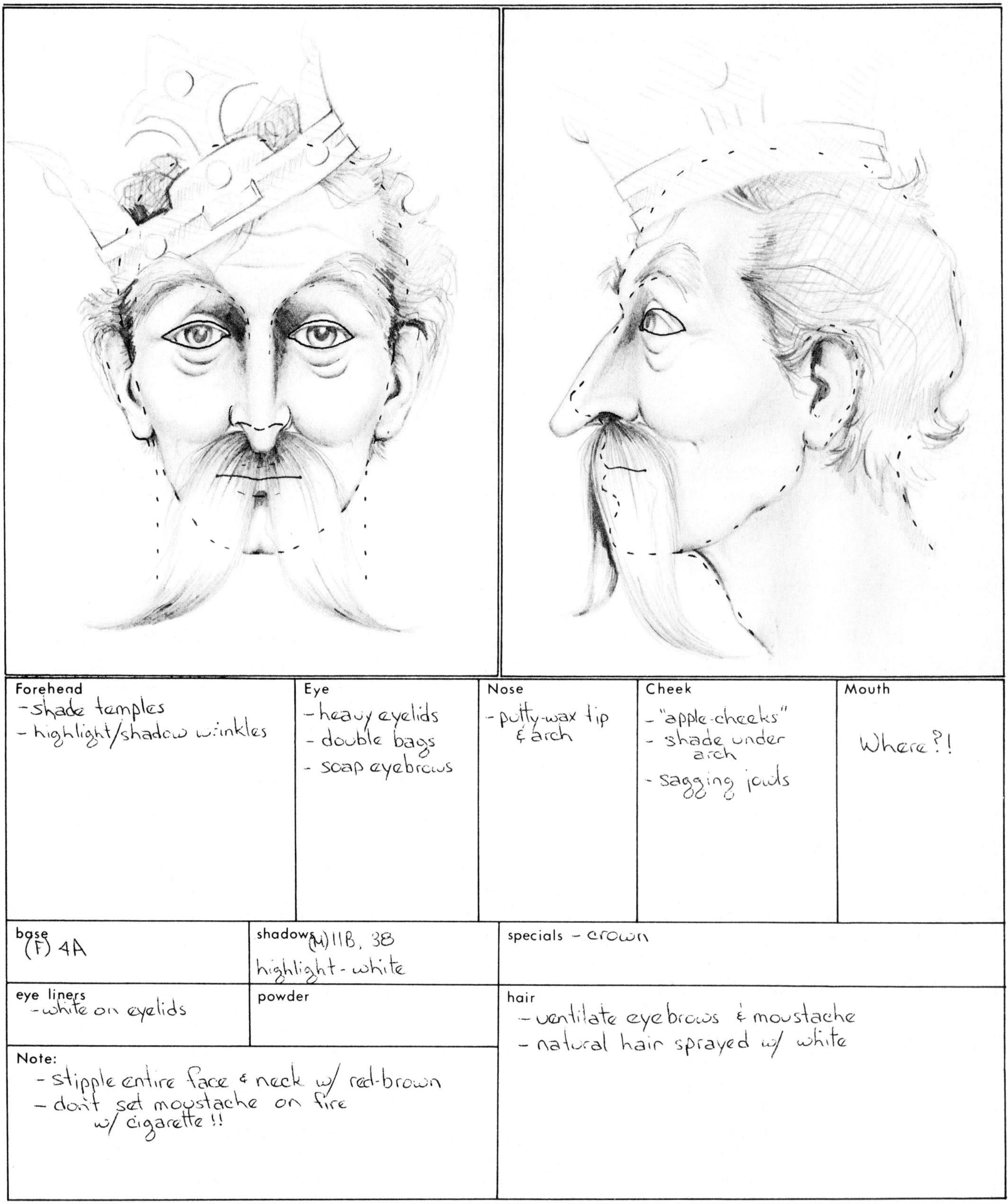

Forehead	Eye	Nose	Cheek	Mouth
-shade temples - highlight/shadow wrinkles	- heavy eyelids - double bags - soap eyebrows	- putty-wax tip & arch	- "apple-cheeks" - shade under arch - sagging jowls	Where?!

base (F) 4A	shadows (M) 11B, 3B highlight - white		specials - crown	
eye liners - white on eyelids	powder		hair - ventilate eyebrows & moustache - natural hair sprayed w/ white	
Note: - stipple entire face & neck w/ red-brown - don't set moustache on fire w/ cigarette !!				

FIGURE **7–11** MAKEUP WORKSHEET FOR KING PELLINORE.   By student Richard Brunner. For finished makeup, see Figure 7–12.

experience for skillful handling and are not easily re-vised—an important consideration in doing makeup drawings. *Colored pencils*—including water-color pen-cils—are easier for the inexperienced to work with but not much easier to revise. *Pastels* and *colored chalk* are relatively easy to work with and have some similarity to makeup paints in color and technique of blending—also in their susceptibility to smudging. The smudging, fortu-nately, can be virtually eliminated, when the drawing is finished, by spraying it with fixative. It's a good idea to protect all such drawings with acetate or transparent plastic sheets.

In general, the advantages of black-and-white pencil drawings outweigh the advantages of drawings in color. If color is important, it can be indicated by referring to specific makeup numbers—either on the worksheet or in the margins of the drawing, possibly with arrows leading to parts of the makeup for which various colors are to be used.

WORKSHEETS

When the final sketch for a makeup has been approved (if approval is required), you should then prepare a makeup worksheet to be followed in doing the makeup. The one in Figure 7–9 is both simple and practical. If you have not already done a finished drawing of the makeup, it can be drawn front view and profile on the worksheet, following the dotted lines or departing from them, using drawing pens or pencils (black or colored), water colors, water-color pencils, or conté crayon (black or sepia). When using pencils or conté crayon, the wrinkles and shadows can be blended with a paper stump or, for larger areas, with the fingers. When using a black lead pencil, it's possible to run the fingers lightly over the entire drawing to gray all the white areas, then to pick out the highlights carefully with an eraser. Since the edges of the erased area will be hard, those edges that should be soft in the makeup should be blended with a stump or with your finger into the adjoining gray area.

Precise information on makeup colors to be used, special techniques of application, hair styles, and any three-dimensional additions to the face, including beards and mustaches, can be entered in the appropriate spaces on the chart. Additional detailed sketches or diagrams can be included when necessary.

Figures 7–10 and 7–11 show completed worksheets for a student makeup. After the final makeup has been approved, you should revise the worksheets, if necessary, to provide all the information required to reproduce the makeup. If possible, a photograph of the final makeup (Figure 7–12) should be attached to the chart. Having an instant-picture camera and high-speed film available will make this a relatively simple matter.

Problems

1. Design realistic makeups for two or more fictional (as opposed to historical) characters. Use any medium you choose for the sketches.
2. Using tracing paper over an 8 × 10 photograph, make a character drawing for a makeup that an actor might reasonably be expected to be able to do himself. (The makeup may be for a specific character if you wish, but it need not be.)
3. Using the tracing-paper-and-pencil technique and an 8 × 10 photograph, adapt one of the character sketches you did for Problem 1 to the face of a specific actor.

8

Makeup Equipment

Before beginning even to experiment with the application of makeup, it is necessary to have suitable equipment with which to work. And until you have learned the tricks of doing good work with whatever equipment happens to be available, you would do well to obtain the best you can afford. That does not mean that you need a *lot* of makeup. In the beginning, a small kit will serve quite well as long as it contains what you really need. From time to time, additional supplies can be added. Materials used in makeup are described in Appendix A.

THE MAKEUP KIT

The term "makeup kit" refers to either a portable container of makeup or just the makeup itself.

Individual Kits These are nearly always portable. (Group kits may or may not be, depending on where and how they are to be used.) They should be large enough to accommodate all of the makeup you usually carry, with room for additional items you may want to add later.

The kits should have compartments or divided trays to keep your materials organized and easily available. Whether they are made of metal, plastic, or wood is a matter of personal preference. What kind of makeup container you have—whether a case with trays or drawers designed specifically for makeup (Figure 8–1B, C, D) or a simple box with a few compartments (Figure 19–2)—doesn't really matter as long as it holds the amount of makeup you need, keeps the makeup in order, is convenient to use, and is generally practical for you.

Group Kits For a small group kit (or a well-stocked individual one) a large fishing-tackle box with cantilever trays (Figure 8–1A) can be used and is likely to be reasonable in price. These boxes come in various sizes. Similar boxes designed to be used as sample cases (Figure 8–1C, for example) may also be suitable for makeup.

If there is no reason to carry the makeup materials from place to place, then wood, metal, or plastic cabinets with small drawers or with shelves and pigeonholes are more easily accessible. The drawers or shelves can be labeled and the paints and powders arranged according to color. Dentists' cases with their many shallow trays and drawers (see Figure 8–2) are ideal for storing makeup.

Makeup Palettes A makeup palette box, though it is not actually a makeup kit, does to some extent function as one since it contains a number of colors. Palette boxes with various selections of colors are available. (See *Makeup palette* in Appendix A.)

Or you can create your own palette by filling an artist's palette box (Figure 8–3A) with your own choice of makeup paints (Figure 8–3B). The paints can be removed from their original containers with a spatula, melted in a metal spoon, and poured into the various compartments of the palette.

You can also buy inexpensive disposable mixing palettes at art supply stores. For use with makeup, the palette can be fitted into a suitable box. If the box you want to use is too small for the palette, take a pair of scissors and simply cut off as many rows of the palette as is necessary to make it fit the box.

Makeup Materials for the Kit After you have determined what kind of makeup container will best fill your requirements, you will need to decide what you want in it—unless, of course, you prefer to buy a complete kit put out by one of the makeup companies—often at a considerable saving over the cost of the makeup materials purchased individually. There are several of these available—some with cake, some with grease, and some with creme makeup. (*See Makeup kits*, Appendix A.)

The main advantage in making up your own kit is

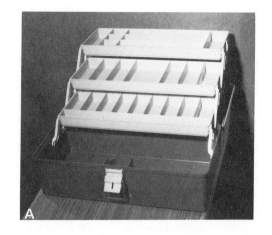

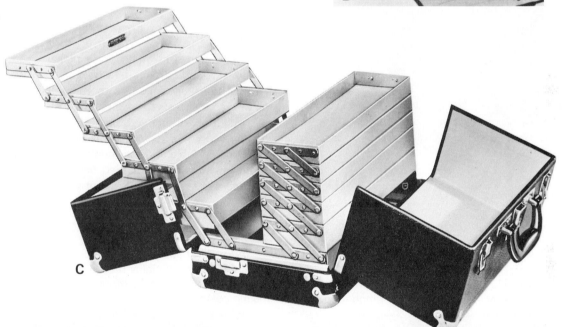

*FIGURE **8—1** MAKEUP KITS.* A. Cantilever fishing-tackle box, which can be filled with suitable items of makeup. An especially practical box of this type is the Fenwick 1080, with 3 trays and adjustable compartments in the top tray. B. Makeup case by Kryolan. Wooden construction, with drawers and compartments. (Kryolan distributors.) C. Ten-tray case suitable for the professional makeup artist or for use as a group kit. (Fibre Products Mfg. Co.) D. Indidivual makeup kit with removable tray.

FIGURE 8–2 ANTIQUE DENTAL CABINET. *Ideal for makeup storage for the professional makeup artist. Made of wood with marble base. There are shelves for bottles and jars behind the glass doors. This type of cabinet is occasionally available in antique shops. Modern dental cabinets can be obtained new from dental supply houses.*

that you can combine items you particularly like from various companies and can select only those items you think you will find useful. If you decide to do this, you may wish to refer to Appendix D (A Basic Makeup Kit) and select those materials best suited to your needs. The kit has been designed to keep the price relatively low. That means fewer colors to work with and more mixing to be done, but that is not necessarily a disadvantage for a student who is learning to mix colors.

THE MAKEUP ROOM

Given the necessary materials, a makeup can be done in any surroundings, but the work can usually be accomplished more efficiently in a room specially designed to fill the requirements for makeup.

The focus of such a room, whether it is an individual dressing room or a large room for group makeup, is the makeup table and the mirror. The average dressing room has mirrors surrounded by rows of naked bulbs. A more satisfactory arrangement would be to have the

FIGURE 8–3 PALETTE BOX. *A. Grumbacher water-color palette box. (Available from artists' supply stores.) B. Palette box filled with creme or grease makeup. The makeup paints are melted in a spoon over a gas or electric burner or a candle flame and poured into the various compartments. The larger of the two center compartments of the box shown here contains a blemish-cover stick for use in highlighting. The compartment might also be used to hold black stipple sponges, filled with an additional color, or left empty and used for mixing colors.*

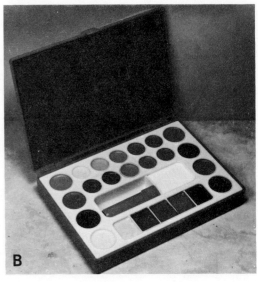

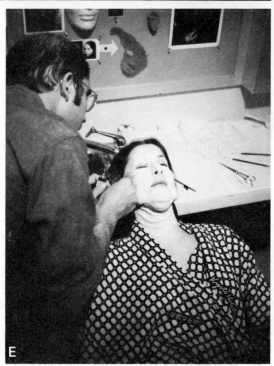

FIGURE *8—4* MAKEUP LABORATORY AT THE CALIFORNIA STATE UNIVERSITY AT LONG BEACH. *Lab is furnished with padded chairs with casters, individual drawers between the chairs, mirrors with non-heating light bulbs, spotlighting in ceiling, 2 adjustable reclining makeup chairs, cork bulletin boards, colored chalkboard, 4 steel sinks, Corning-top electric range for prosthetic work, and built-in storage cabinets. A. Laboratory in new theatre, just after completion. B. and C. Room after the makeup department moved in. D. Ante-laboratory storage area with oven and sink. E. Advanced student, working under the supervision of instructor Bill Smith, applying prosthetic makeup for* The Chairs.

41

FIGURE 8—5 PORTABLE MAKEUP MIRROR WITH ADJUSTABLE LIGHTING AND REVERSIBLE MIRROR.

light source recessed and a slot provided for slipping in color mediums to approximate the stage lighting. This will never give the same effect as the stage lights, but it will come closer to it than the usual dressing room lights. If such an arrangement is not possible, at least be sure that the amount of illumination is adequate. If fluorescent lights are used, install warm-tinted tubes, or else arrange for a color medium to be used over the lights. Even when the lighting around the mirrors is adequate, individual lighted mirrors (Figure 8–5) are very helpful for close-up work.

No matter what type of illumination is used at the dressing tables, it is always desirable to have two spotlights in the general makeup room with colored mediums to approximate the lighting used for the play. The actor can then check his makeup as often as he wishes, at a distance, under appropriately colored lights. The spots should be mounted one on each side of a full-length mirror at a sufficient height for providing a reasonable angle of illumination.

The dressing table should be about 29 inches high and should contain a drawer with a lock for storing the makeup between performances and for keeping the actor's valuables during performances. A dispenser for cleansing tissues either above or to one side of the mirror is a great convenience. Either a wastebasket or a special section built into the table should be provided for disposing of used tissues. If there is an additional space above or at the sides of the mirror, a row of small shelves or pigeonholes for makeup will help to avoid some of the usual clutter on the table. A row of cabinets above the

mirrors can be very useful for getting personal belongings out of the way during performances or for storing wigs on blocks. It's a good idea to equip such cabinets with locks.

A stool is more practical than a chair for use at the makeup table—unless, of course, the chair is padded and has casters, as do those in Figure 8–4—since it enables the actor to get up and back away from the mirror quickly and easily without having to move the chair out and then maneuver it back into position when sitting down. A piano stool is especially practical since the height is adjustable. Padding and upholstering the stool, though not necessary, adds considerably to one's comfort when sitting for several hours at the makeup table.

Still more comfortable (and better for the back) is a Scandinavian padded rocker (Figure 8–8), which is available in various colors.

In the professional theater, actors customarily do their own makeup, but in the nonprofessional theater there may be a makeup person or even a makeup crew. This places an additional burden on dressing rooms, which are often overcrowded anyway. When that situation exists, there should be a special makeup room large enough to accommodate several actors in addition to the makeup people.

There should be running water in every dressing room. A makeup room should contain not only running water but also convenient facilities for storing makeup and wigs. Cases with small drawers are particularly useful. A reclining barber's or dentist's chair (see Figure 8–4B) is enormously helpful to the makeup artist and should be standard equipment in any makeup room.

A general makeup room, when there is one, should be as near to the dressing rooms and to the stage as possible. Since makeup may need to be hurriedly touched up between acts or during an act, having the makeup room near the stage is particularly important. Good ventilation is essential, and air conditioning is usually desirable.

THE MAKEUP WORKSHOP

The makeup workshop differs from the makeup room in that it is used primarily for laboratory work by the makeup artist. It may or may not be used for actual makeup. It should contain equipment and material for modeling and casting (including an oven for foam latex), for the construction and dressing of wigs, and for any experimental or preparatory work done by the makeup artist before actually applying the makeup. It should also contain ample storage facilities, allowing frequently-used items to be within easy reach. The workshop may or may not be equipped with a dentist's or barber's chair

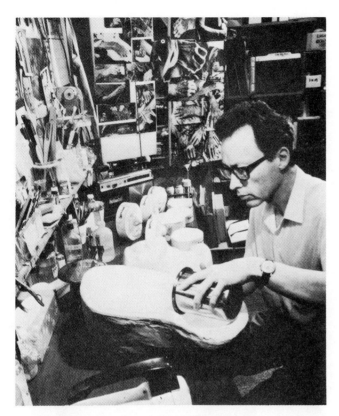

FIGURE 8—6 MAKEUP ARTIST DICK SMITH IN HIS WORK-SHOP. *Shown pouring foamed latex into one of the molds for Dustin Hoffman's makeup in* Little Big Man, *Figure 14–34. (Photo by Dick Smith.)*

for casting or with a mirror and a makeup table. In other words, it should contain whatever is useful to the makeup artist in his work.

The university makeup laboratory shown in Figure 8–4 was designed to function as a makeup room, a workshop, and a classroom. Figure 8–6 shows a corner of a professional makeup artist's workshop.

THE MAKEUP MORGUE

One of the first requisites of a good makeup artist is a keen sense of observation and the ability to apply what he observes to the creation of his makeups. To help him remember what he observes, a makeup morgue (a term used to designate a file of clippings) is indispensable. The morgue should contain, first of all, unretouched photographs of people. Illustrated magazines are a good source for these. Reproductions of works of art are useful for historical characters. Much of this can be found in second-hand bookstores. In addition, your morgue should contain makeup catalogs, price lists, and any information

you collect on makeup techniques. Anything, in fact, that relates to makeup should be included. Clear acetate sheets (see Figure 8–7A) are very helpful in keeping smudges off your pictures.

Below are suggested classifications for your morgue. As your collection grows, you may want to make certain changes or add subdivisions.

AGE, Male	LATEX
AGE, Female	LIGHTING
ANATOMY	MAKEUP MATERIALS*
BALD HEADS	MAKEUP SKETCHES and
BEARDS and MUS-	DRAWINGS
TACHES	MAKEUP TECHNIQUES*
CHEEKS	MOUTHS and CHINS
CHINS	NASOLABIAL FOLDS
COLOR	NECKS and JAWLINES
CORRECTIVE MAKEUP	NONREALISTIC
DISFIGUREMENTS	NOSES
EARS	PAINTINGS, DRAWINGS
EQUIPMENT	PROSTHESIS*
EYES and EYEBROWS	RACES and NATIONALI-
FASHIONS	TIES*
FICTIONAL, Male	SCULPTURE
FICTIONAL, Female	SKIN TEXTURE
FOREHEADS	SUPPLIES
HAIR, Male	TEETH
HAIR, Female	WIGS, Male
HANDS	WIGS, Female
HISTORICAL, Male	WORKSHEETS
HISTORICAL, Female	

A very practical type of morgue is a set of loose-leaf binders with 8½ × 11-inch pages for pasting up your pictures. (See Figure 8–7A.) These pages can be rearranged or temporarily removed at any time. You will probably want to start with a single binder, then expand as your morgue increases in size.

If you want a convenient way to store your pictures until you have time to paste them onto the binder pages, an expanding file (Figure 8–7B) can be very useful. If you have a large collection of pictures, you may find a metal filing cabinet with removable manila folders (Figure 8–7C) more practical. If you also have or expect to have a number of books related to makeup, you should, of course, have bookshelves in your studio or workshop. You may or may not want to combine these with your drawing table and drawing materials, as in Figure 8–8. In any case, keep your pictures organized and ready for instant reference. Keep adding to your morgue continually. It is your private library and an important part of your makeup equipment.

* Can be subdivided.

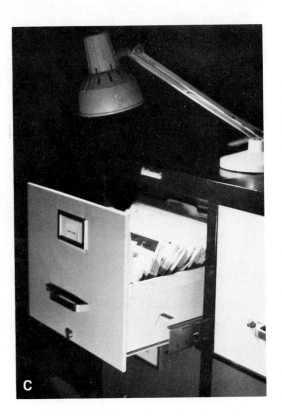

FIGURE **8–7** MAKEUP MORGUES. A. Loose-leaf notebook with acetate protective sheets. B. Expanding file. C. Filing cabinet.

FIGURE **8–8** CORNER OF A MAKEUP ARTIST'S STUDIO WITH REFERENCE BOOKS AND DRAWING TABLE.

Problem

1. Start your own makeup morgue with any photographs you may have already collected. Work out whatever filing system you find most convenient, but be sure there is adequate room for expansion. Label all material you find according to the category in which you file it. This will simplify putting it back each time you have used it.

9

Applying Various Types of Makeup

Since the problems and procedures involved in the application of the various types of makeup are quite different, they will be considered separately. Which type of makeup you choose is a matter of personal preference. (Illustrations of most of the makeup items discussed can be found in the alphabetical listing in Appendix A.)

CAKE MAKEUP

Foundation Cake makeup—dry or moist type—is applied with a sponge (Figure 9–1) for large areas and

FIGURE 9–1 *APPLYING CAKE MAKEUP WITH A NATURAL SILK SPONGE.* (Actor Eugene Bicknell.)

with a brush for small ones. A natural silk sponge is best for the foundation color. The sponge should be damp but not wet. If the makeup does not come off on the sponge easily, you are not using enough water; if it seems thin and runs on the face, you are using too much water. If the paint seems to be thick and heavy, too much water may have soaked into the cake, or the sponge may have been rubbed too hard on the cake. In some brands of *dry* cake makeup the color comes off the cake much more readily than in others. If you use more than one brand of makeup, this difference may require some adjustment. If you have difficulty in getting color off the cake at all, use another brand of makeup.

After the makeup has been taken up on the sponge, stroke the sponge lightly across the face until the whole area is covered smoothly with a thin film of color. Cake makeup requires no powder.

Highlights and Shadows These are normally applied over the foundation. (See Figure 9–2.) It is possible, however, to apply them *under* the foundation for subtle modeling effects or for lightening a heavy beard. A combination of both methods can also be used. When the base is applied *over* shadows and highlights, it should be pressed on lightly with the sponge to avoid smearing the paint underneath and to allow the highlights and shadows to show through.

Highlights and shadows are applied with flat, sable brushes, using appropriate light and dark cake colors. Although a sponge can be used for larger areas, it is easier to control the paint with brushes. For larger areas, a 3/8-inch, 1/2-inch, or 5/8-inch flat sable brush works very well. For smaller areas, including most wrinkles, 3/16-inch, 1/4-inch, and 1/8-inch brushes can be used. Pointed Chinese brushes and eyeliner brushes are useful for small details. In general, it is best to use the largest size brush suitable for the particular job you're doing. Small brushes used for large areas are inefficient and may produce ineffective results.

46

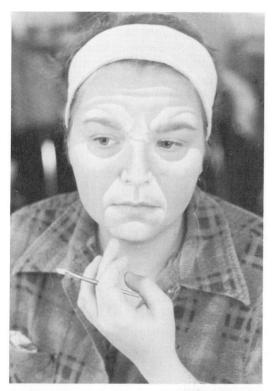

FIGURE 9—2 APPLYING CREME-MAKEUP HIGHLIGHTS OVER A CAKE-MAKEUP FOUNDATION. (Student Susan Lambeth.)

If you are using a sponge to apply highlights and shadows, hold it so that only a small section of it touches the face. Apply the color directly to the face only in the area that is to be most strongly highlighted or shadowed. Then with a clean section of the dampened sponge, using a very light touch, blend the color out over the entire area to be covered, letting it fade out as you go until it blends into the foundation color. It may be helpful to run a clean section of the sponge very lightly over the edge of the shadow or the highlight where it meets the foundation in order to help merge the two.

In working with brushes, the general technique is to lay on color in the darkest area of the shadow or the lightest area of the highlight, then clean the brush and blend the edges of the shadow or the highlight with the damp brush until they blend imperceptibly into the foundation. To save time, use separate brushes for highlights and shadows.

Whether you are using a sponge or a brush, it is always best to build up a highlight or a shadow with several applications rather than trying to get just the right amount the first time. It is much easier to add color than it is to subtract it. If a shadow does become too dark, it should be lightened by lifting the color with a clean damp sponge. Never try to lighten a shadow by brushing a highlight over it! Shadows and highlights can, however,

be toned down or softened by stippling with a sponge, using lighter colors for shadows, darker colors for highlights, or colors in between for toning down both at the same time. (For more detailed instructions in stippling, see Chapter 11.)

DRY MAKEUP

This includes all makeup that is applied dry to the skin—cake rouge, brush-on rouge, brush-on eyeshadow, and face powder. All are, of course, used only as adjuncts to the various types of non-dry makeup.

Dry Rouge Dry (or pressed powder) rouge is best applied with a brush (a rouge brush for larger areas and an eyeshadow brush for small ones), though a rouge puff, a powder puff, a ball of cotton, or, for small areas, a cotton swab can be used if a suitable brush is not available. Dry rouge can be applied over cake makeup, liquid makeup, or any creme or grease makeup that has been powdered.

It is possible to do a certain amount of shadowing with dry rouges and brushes, especially with those dry rouges that are available in brown and gray as well as various shades of red.

Brush-on Rouge This is a form of dry rouge specifically designed to be applied with a soft brush. Such a brush is, in fact, usually included in the box of rouge, though you may prefer the larger rouge brushes that can be purchased separately.

Brush-on Eyeshadow This is similar to brush-on rouge except that it comes in smaller cakes and in different colors and is applied with a small brush or a tiny sponge on a stick. It can also be applied with a cotton swab. Any eyeshadow colors suitable for general shadowing (brown, gray, lake) can, of course, be used for that purpose. White and light flesh tints for highlighting are also available—more often in street makeup, however, than in theatrical.

Face Powder Although deep shades of face powder may occasionally be used for quick makeups to serve as a foundation color, the powder is used primarily to set makeup (to keep it from smearing, that is) and to remove any undesirable shine. It is itself a form of dry makeup, but it is never used over dry makeups since they do not require setting and have no shine to be dulled. Powder is applied with a puff, which is usually loaded with the powder and then pressed firmly onto the makeup (Figure 13—8J). Excess powder is removed with a very soft powder brush or sometimes—especially for small areas—with a clean rouge brush.

CREME MAKEUP

When this type of makeup is applied to the face, it is usually transferred from the stick or the flat container of makeup with the fingers, with a brush, or with a foam-rubber sponge, any of which can also be used for blending. When used for the foundation color, the stick form of creme makeup can also be applied directly with the stick, then blended out with the fingers. If you need to mix colors in order to obtain the shade you want, that can be done on the back of the hand (Figure H–19A) or in a palette box. In applying the makeup, use only a thin film, just enough to color the skin and conceal minor blemishes. Then powder the makeup and go over it lightly with a damp sponge. This removes excess powder and sets the makeup. If a slight sheen is appropriate, the makeup need not be powdered.

Highlights and shadows can be applied either before or after the makeup has been powdered. They can be applied *under* the base for subtle modeling effects or for covering heavy beards. Or you may wish to apply shadows under the base and highlights over. That helps to emphasize the highlights and minimize the shadows. When creme (or greasepaint) highlights are applied *over* the base, they must, of course, be powdered.

Creme rouge is usually applied with a foam-rubber sponge or with the fingers; contour colors, with a wide, flat brush, a foam-rubber sponge, or the fingers. (In general, makeup artists tend to use foam-rubber sponges for applying creme makeup, whereas actors are more likely to use their fingers.)

Creme Makeup Crayons As with any creme makeup, crayons should be applied to skin that is free of grease. For the foundation color, streaks of paint can be applied with the crayons, then blended with the fingers or with a foam-rubber sponge. More than one shade can be used if you want to mix colors. Highlights, shadows, and rouge can be added in the appropriate areas with the crayons, with your fingers, with a foam-rubber sponge, or—especially for smaller areas—with a brush.

When crayons are to be used for highlighting and shadowing, they should first be sharpened into a tentlike shape (*see* Figure 9–3), thus creating a sharp edge, which

*FIGURE **9–3** HIGHLIGHTING WITH A MAKEUP CRAYON. (Actor Eugene Bicknell.) A. Highlighting the crease of the nasolabial fold with a sharpened (flat-cut) makeup crayon. B. Blending the soft edge of the highlight with a wide brush. C. Highlighting to create a sagging jaw line. D. The upper edge of the highlight can then be blended into the foundation color with a brush.*

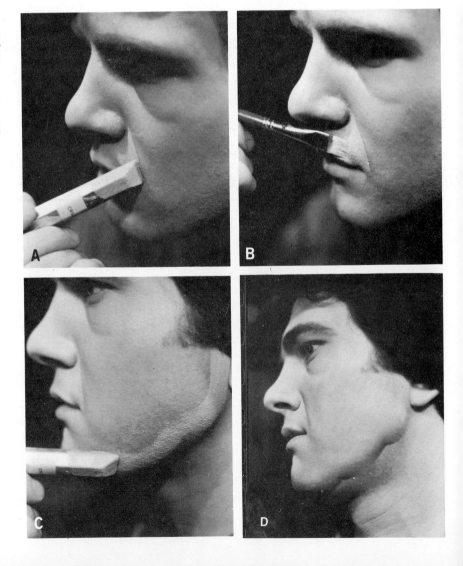

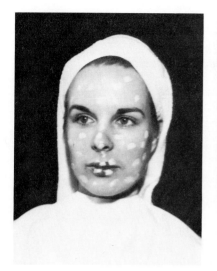 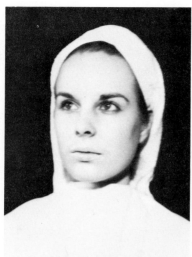

FIGURE 9—4 APPLICATION OF SOFT GREASEPAINT. *Paint is applied in dots, then blended with the fingertips.*

is extremely efficient in making hard-edged highlights (Figure 9–3A). The soft edges can then be blended with a brush (Figure 9–3B).

When crayons are used for stippling, they can be stroked across the face of the stipple sponge, which is then pressed onto the skin.

Crayons, like other creme makeup, can be used in combination with cake makeup, as suggested under Mixed Techniques, Method 1, later in this chapter.

GREASEPAINT

When soft greasepaint in tubes or jars is being used, it is important that the skin be relatively free of grease before the paint is applied. If other makeup has been removed with cleansing cream or any kind of oil, either wash the face with soap and water or use witch hazel or a skin freshener to remove any greasy film before applying the greasepaint.

The paint can be taken directly from the tube or the jar onto your finger and applied in small dots evenly over the face, neck, and ears (Figure 9–4). If you are mixing paints, you may prefer to mix them on the back of your hand or on a palette first to obtain the correct color, then apply the mixed paint in dots. Or you can apply dots of the various colors directly to the skin. When you have dotted the face with paint, dip your fingertips into cold water and blend the base thoroughly, making sure that every exposed part of the flesh is covered, including the neck. Blend it into the hairline so that no line of demarcation is visible, but be careful not to get makeup into the hair. Use very little paint. The purpose of the foundation is to color the face, not to create a mask. However, if there are blemishes to be covered, it may be desirable to use a somewhat heavier foundation.

When you have finished, rub a clean finger lightly across your face. If it leaves a mark or if a noticeable amount of paint comes off on the finger, you have probably used too much paint and should wipe some off. The skin should feel moist and soft to the touch but not slippery.

If you are using stick greasepaint, which is now less frequently used than soft greasepaint, you should first apply cleansing or liquefying cream over the entire face and neck, then wipe it off, leaving only a very thin film. Rub the stick in streaks across the face and neck—about two streaks on each cheek, two on the forehead, one down the nose, one under the nose, one across the chin, and several on the neck. Then blend the paint with your finger tips to make a completely smooth foundation—unless, of course, you want some irregularity in the color for a particular character.

Probably the most common fault in the application of greasepaint is the tendency to use too much, the result of which is a greasy makeup that does not take highlights and shadows well, rubs off easily, induces excessive perspiration, requires an abnormally heavy coating of powder, and creates a masklike effect. For most makeups the foundation color should be used sparingly.

Moist rouge and shading colors (highlights, shadows, eyeshadow) are blended into the foundation, then powdered in order to set the makeup and remove the shine. Creme rouge and shading colors can be used over a greasepaint base in the same way. Dry rouge and eyeshadow, if used, cannot be applied until the makeup has been powdered.

Rubber-mask Greasepaint This is a castor-oil-base greasepaint used primarily over latex, though it can be used over other three-dimensional makeup as well.

FIGURE *9–5* APPLYING RUB-BER-MASK-GREASE PAINT WITH A RED-RUBBER SPONGE. *(Tom Lindberg.)*

Unlike regular greasepaint, it is usually stippled on with a red-rubber sponge (see Figure 9–5). It is never powdered by rubbing or brushing the puff across the surface of the paint but always by pressing a heavily powdered puff firmly into it. Excess powder is removed by brushing lightly with a soft powder brush. If the makeup is to be stippled with various colors, that should be done after the rubber-mask greasepaint has been powdered.

MIXED TECHNIQUES

If you wish to use cake makeup and either creme makeup or greasepaint together, here are a few suggestions for ways in which that can be done.

Method 1 Use creme highlights and shadows over a cake makeup foundation. Then powder and add dry rouge. (If moist rouge is used, it can be applied after highlighting and shadowing but before powdering.) The use of dry rouge, applied last, is especially advantageous because all of the rouging—cheeks, nose, wrinkles, etc.—can be done at once. Then add whatever stippling you wish. If you are stippling with creme makeup (see Chapter

11), powder after each color of stipple, and keep checking from time to time during the performance to see if additional powder is needed.

Method 2 With this method, creme (or grease) highlights, shadows, and rouge are applied first—much stronger than usual but still well blended. Then cake makeup is patted on with a sponge until the makeup underneath shows through only as much as you want it to, after which rouge for cheeks and shadows can be brushed on. If highlights or shadows require touching up, that can be done over the base, preferably with cake makeup. This method can be used for very subtle aging. It would not be a good choice, however, if you want a strong three-dimensional effect. Nor is it suitable if the makeup is to be stippled (see Chapter 11)—unless, of course, you wish to use a light stipple in highlight areas and a dark stipple in shadow areas.

Method 3 Use creme highlights and cake shadows over a powdered creme foundation. This combines the advantage of highlights, which are easily blended, and shadows, which are not likely to develop a shine as the powder wears off. (With highlights, shine doesn't destroy the desired illusion; with shadows, it does.)

10

Corrective Makeup

Corrective makeup (Figure 10–1, for example) is one that is designed to help an actor to look his best. This may involve only minor adjustments, such as changing the curve of the eyebrows, or it may involve making the actor look younger. And, for the stage, it nearly always involves changing the color of the skin.

THE FOUNDATION

In corrective makeup the purpose of the foundation is to provide a skin color that will enhance the actor's appearance under the stage lighting that is used for a particular performance. Since a skin coloring that looks normal and healthy off stage may look pale and washed out under stage lights, some additional color is usually needed. If the skin does not need to be changed in color—this

happens more often with dark-skinned actors than with light—the actor may not need to use a foundation. In this chapter, however, we shall assume that a foundation is needed.

Perhaps the easiest way to choose a suitable foundation (or base) color is to decide, first of all, what hue you want (R, SR, S, FS, etc.), then how light or dark the skin should be, choosing a number between 0 and 21 to indicate the value. A number 8, 9, or 10 is average for Caucasian men (English, northern European), and a 5, 6, or 7 is average for Caucasian women. This average value is the one most frequently employed in corrective makeup, though it will vary with the actor's own coloring. For dark-skinned races the averages will be lower in intensity and usually in value and can vary widely with individuals of a particular race. The fashionable makeup colors of the day may also affect one's choice. If pale skin is

 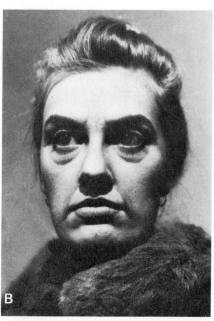

*FIGURE **10–1** A. FEMALE CORRECTIVE AND B. CHARACTER MAKEUPS. By student Laura Love.*

51

in fashion, women may wish to lighten their foundation color. If summer tans are being worn, both men and women may wish to darken it. The actor's natural skin coloring will also have some effect on the color selected. Furthermore, a given color of makeup, unless it is rather heavily applied, will not look the same on a light skin as on a dark one.

As for the hue, you will normally choose, for corrective makeup, one that will help the actor look as attractive as possible under the lights being used on stage. Which color that is will depend, of course, on race. A Caucasian may look for a color in the S group, whereas an Oriental will presumably avoid the redder hues and look for something with more yellow in it. The black and brown races will usually require hues that are neither very red nor very yellow. The F and OF groups contain a number of suitable shades. There are no hard-and-fast rules about what color an actor of any race may or may not use. He should choose one that looks attractive on him in the lighting in which he will be seen.

FACIAL ANALYSIS

Before corrective makeup is applied, the actor's face should be analyzed to determine how it can be made more attractive. If the two sides of the face are sufficiently different to appear obviously asymmetrical, the less pleasing side can be made up to match, as nearly as possible, the more pleasing one. Which side is to be corrected can usually be judged by covering first one half of the face with a sheet of paper, then the other. An even more effective technique is to take a full-face photograph, then to make a reverse print. Both the normal print and the reverse one can be cut vertically in half and the halves switched and pasted together. You will then have two photographs of the face with both sides matching, but one will be based on the right side, the other on the left. The less appealing face will indicate the side that is to be corrected. It is essential, of course, that the photograph be taken straight on if the technique is to work properly.

Decisions as to what is to be corrected will be based on personal taste, which may, in turn, be affected by current fashions. More often than not, however, fashions have to do with individual features—such as eyebrows and lips—rather than with overall proportions. But there are certain classic features and classic proportions that seem to transcend fashion and personal taste and that are, among most Caucasians, considered beautiful.

As noted in the chapter on facial anatomy, the classically proportioned face can be divided horizontally into three equal parts: (1) from the hairline to the eyebrows,

(2) from the eyebrows to the bottom of the nose, and (3) from the bottom of the nose to the tip of the chin. If these three sections are not equal, they can be made to appear equal—or more nearly so—in various ways. But since a face not having classical proportions may sometimes be more interesting on stage than a classically proportioned one, making such a change is not necessarily advantageous.

If you decide that you do want to change the proportions of the face, the following suggestions can be used as a guide.

FOREHEAD

If you want to create the illusion of a lower forehead, darken the area next to the hairline with a foundation color about three shades darker than the rest of the face. This color can be blended downward very gradually so that it disappears imperceptibly into the foundation. That makes the forehead appear lower because light colors reflect light and attract the eye, whereas dark colors absorb light and attract less attention. Following the same principle, a low forehead can be made to look higher by using a color about three shades lighter than the base and applying it at the hairline as before. That will attract the eye upward, emphasizing the height of the forehead.

The forehead can be made to seem narrower by shadowing the temples and blending the shadow onto the front plane of the forehead, thus apparently decreasing the actual width of the front plane by making it appear to turn sooner. Or it can seemingly be widened by highlighting the temples, carrying the highlight to the hairline. This will counteract the natural shadow that results from the receding of the temple areas and will appear to bring them forward. It will also seem to extend the front plane of the forehead horizontally. As always, there should be a difference of only two or three shades between the shadows and the base since deeper shadows at the temples tend to age the face. If the front lobes are too prominent, tone them down with a darker foundation color, and bring forward the depression between the frontal lobes and the superciliary arch with a highlight. If the temples are normally sunken, they can be brought out with a highlight.

NOSE

If you want the nose shorter, apply a deeper color under the tip and blend it up over the tip. That will tone down the natural highlight and take the attention away from the tip. If a short highlight is placed on the upper part

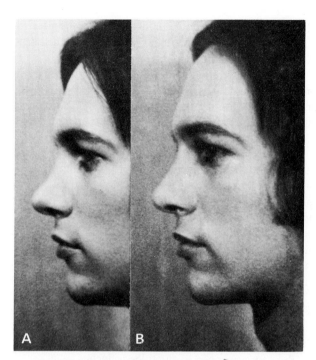

FIGURE 10–2 NOSE RESHAPED WITH PUTTY WAX. A. *Student Lee Austin without makeup. B. Nose reshaped with putty-wax for corrective makeup.*

of the nose, that will attract the eye to that area and help still further to give the illusion of a shorter nose. If you want the nose longer, you can carry a highlight down over and under the tip, pulling the viewer's eye downward and apparently lengthening the nose.

If you want to widen the nose, run a broad highlight down the center and blend carefully. That will appear to widen the front plane of the nose—not the entire nose. You might also highlight the nares to attract the eye outward in both directions, thus giving an illusion of still greater width.

If you want to narrow the nose, reverse the procedure by shadowing the nares and the sides of the nose and running a very narrow highlight down the center. Then blend the edges. That will give the illusion of a sharp and narrow bone and cartilage.

To flatten the nose, reverse the usual modeling by shadowing the front and highlighting the sides. Blend all edges carefully.

If the tip of the nose is fuller than you want it to be, shadow it slightly on either side of the painted highlight to tone down part of the natural highlight.

If the nose is crooked, run a fairly narrow highlight down the nose, then shadow it on either side wherever there is a natural highlight that reveals the crookedness. Blend the highlight and the shadows. The highlight may be straight, or it may bend slightly in the opposite direction

from the real bend. Use whichever method proves the more effective.

In general, then, decide where you want to attract the eye of the viewer, and place the highlights in that area, shadowing areas that you want to recede or to seem smaller or less conspicuous.

Normally, in corrective makeup, highlights and shadows are about three shades darker than the base. But in making up the nose it is often possible and sometimes necessary to use stronger contrasts to achieve the desired effect. This applies particularly when you are using shadows to counteract strong natural highlights.

The corrective techniques just described, though effective from the front, have practically no effect on the nose in profile. That requires a three-dimesional addition. (See Chapter 13.) Obviously, the nose can't be cut down by that method, but it can be built up, as illustrated in Figure 10–2.

JAW LINE AND CHIN

If the jaw line is too square or too prominent, shadow the part that needs to be rounded off or toned down, carrying the shadow both under and over the jawbone, and blend carefully into the foundation. Wearing a fuller hairdo can also be helpful. If you want to make the jaw line more firm and youthful, run a stripe of highlight all along the jawbone, softening the lower edge and blending the top edge imperceptibly into the foundation. A stripe of shadow can be run along under the bone and both edges blended.

If the chin is too prominent—that is, if it juts forward too much—darken the whole chin with a light shadow. If it is too long in proportion to the rest of the face, it can be shortened by shadowing the lower part. Make sure that the edge of the shadow is thoroughly blended. If you want the chin longer, highlight the lower part, and if you want it more prominent, highlight the whole chin. If it's too square, round off the corners with shadows. If it's too pointed, flatten the point with a square shadow. A double chin can be minimized by shadowing it to make it less noticeable.

WRINKLES

Wrinkles can seldom be blotted out completely, but they can be minimized by carefully brushing in highlights where you find the natural shadows and subtly shadowing the prominent part of each wrinkle where you find a natural highlight. This applies also to circles or bags under the eyes.

EYES

In making up the *eyes*, keep in mind that ideally eyes are the width of an eye apart. If they are less than that, you can make them appear to be farther apart than they actually are. For corrective makeup it is seldom that eyes need to be brought closer together, though that may be done for certain character makeups. Either of these changes can easily be brought about by making use of an optical illusion.

If the eyes and the eyebrows are made up as in Figure 10–3A, they will *seem* closer together. If they are made up as in 10–3B, they will *seem* farther apart. For women, false eyelashes can be used instead of—or along with—eye lining and eyeshadow to make the eyes look farther apart. The lashes should be trimmed so that they are fuller at the outer corners, and they can be shortened and placed away from the inner corners of the eye so that they actually extend over only the outer two thirds of the upper lids.

Eyeshadow For corrective makeup for both men and women, appropriate colors for eyeshadow are gray and gray-brown and occasionally, for women, grayed shades of green, blue, or mauve, which can, to increase the subtlety of the color, be applied *over* the gray or gray-

brown. Bright eyeshadow colors should not be used for corrective makeup. For certain *character* makeups, however, they may sometimes be appropriate.

Normally the shadow is placed on the upper eyelid only. The shadow is usually heaviest next to the eye and is more or less confined to the lid itself. The occasionally fashionable practice of carrying the shadow up to the eyebrow is not appropriate for corrective makeup. The upper edge of the shadow should be carefully blended into the foundation. In Figure 10–5A the shadow has *not* been blended. Shadow on the lower lid is also fashionable from time to time but would not normally be used for corrective makeup.

Occasionally the eyelid is highlighted instead of shadowed (see Figure 10–5S) in order to make the eyes more prominent. The method usually used is described in detail in Chapter 12.

A touch of rouge on the bone just below the outer end of the eyebrow will add a youthful sparkle to the eye. This can be done with either creme or dry rouge. The red dot that is sometimes placed at the tear duct for the same purpose is much less effective.

Accents The eyes can be accented by lining them, using a brush or an eyebrow pencil (Figure 10–4A). The brush can be used with cake or liquid eyeliner. If you

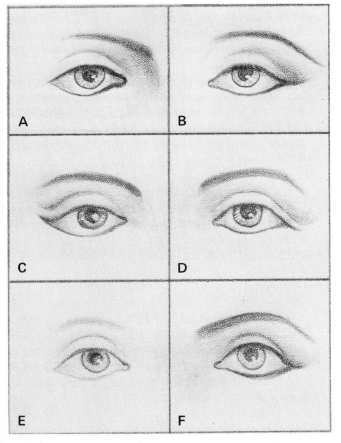

FIGURE 10–3 EYE ILLUSIONS. *A. Shading the eye area and penciling the eyebrow to make the eye appear closer to the nose. Used on both eyes, it will give the illusion of the eyes being closer together. (See Figure 6–6C.) B. Shading the eye area and penciling the eyebrow to make the eye appear farther from the nose. Used on both eyes, it will give the illusion of the eyes being farther apart. (See Figure 6–6B.) C. Shading to turn the eye up at the corner. D. Shading to droop the eye at the outer corner. E. Highlighting (or absence of shading) around the eye to make it smaller. F. Shading the eye and darkening it and extending the brow to make the eye appear larger.*

A

B

C

FIGURE 10—4 MAKING UP THE EYES. *(Actor Kristoffer Tabori.) A. Accenting the eyes with a makeup pencil. B. Softening the pencil with a brush. C. Penciling the eyebrows. Note that both the pencil and the brush are held at some distance from the tip in order to maintain a light touch.*

find that the eyebrow pencil tends to smear, use cake liner instead. With either the brush or the pencil, draw a line along the upper lid close to the lashes. This line should usually start about two-thirds of the way in toward the nose or may even begin close to the tear duct. The line follows the lashes and extends about a quarter inch beyond the outer corner of the eye. It should end in a slight curve (Figure 10–3F), not a straight line, and when a natural effect is desired, it should fade out, not end abruptly.

Then draw a similar line on the lower lid, starting about a third of the way in from the outer corner or a third of the way out from the tear duct, as in Figure 10–5A, and moving outward along the eye, toward the top line. (A line starting in the middle of the eye, as in Figure 10–5B, should be avoided since it tends to divide the eye in half.) This lower line should usually fade out just before it meets the top line. Then both lines may be softened (for men they *should* be) by going over them with a narrow flat shading brush (Figure 10–4B) so that they really become narrow shadows instead of lines. Their purpose is to enlarge the eye slightly as well as to emphasize it. For a natural corrective makeup, they should not completely surround the eye, though for high-fashion makeup in certain periods they occasionally do. Sometimes a small amount of white is brushed or penciled in below the outer quarter inch of the top line in order to help enlarge the eye.

If the eyes are to be made to appear farther apart, the accents should be strongest at the outer ends and carried farther beyond the corner of the eye than usual (Figure 6–6B). If the eyes are to be closer together, the accents are shifted to the inner corners and should not extend to the outer corners at all.

Eyelashes Women's eyelashes are nearly always darkened with mascara or cosmetique (see Appendix A)—usually black or brown, though other colors have occasionally been used for high-fashion makeup. In applying the mascara, hold the wand parallel to the eye and stroke from the roots to the tips of the lashes—upward on the lower side of the upper lashes and downward on the upper side of the lower lashes. Avoid clumps and keep the lashes separated for a natural effect. C and P in Figure 10–5 illustrate a failure to avoid clumps, though the effect in P is obviously intentional. If men's eyelashes are very light or very sparse, brown or black mascara will be helpful in defining the eye. Be extremely careful to avoid getting mascara into the eyes, as it can be painful. If you get smudges of mascara on the skin around the eye, they should be carefully removed with

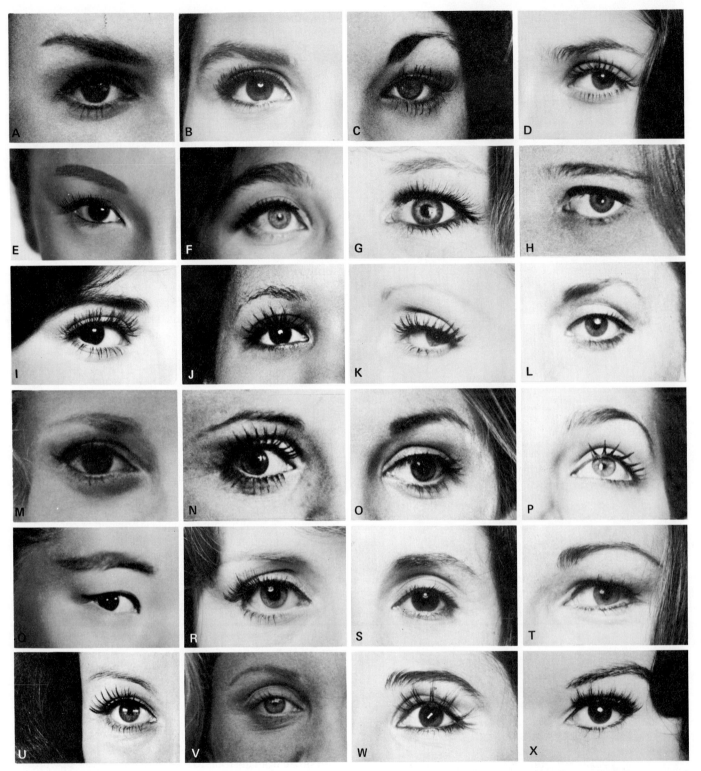

FIGURE 10–5 WOMEN'S EYES. *Illustrates both becoming and unbecoming treatment of eyebrows and the use and misuse of false eyelashes.*

a cotton swab dampened with water or, for waterproof mascara, with mascara remover. *Caution:* Never share your mascara or your mascara brush with anyone else!

In removing mascara, apply the remover to a sheet of cleansing tissue folded into a small square, close one eye, and wipe off the mascara from the lashes on that

eye. (Cotton balls should not be used, for they may leave a residue of fibers.)

Women often wear false eyelashes on the upper lid, less often on the lower. Normally, one false eyelash is cut in two and the hairs cut on the bias so that when the eyelashes are applied, they are long at the outer end and relatively short at the inner end. Be sure to cut the two halves of the lash in reverse so that you will have one left and one right lash. If the lashes are too full, snip out some of the hairs with small pointed scissors—*before* applying the lashes to the eyelid. You can also snip off the ends of some of the lashes to make them less even and more natural looking. Figure 10–5R shows lashes trimmed on the bias, and Figure 10–5K shows lashes that have evidently not been trimmed at all. Using excessively long or heavy lashes may at times be fashionable but does not necessarily make the eyes more attractive.

The eyelashes are attached (see Figure 10–6) with a special eyelash adhesive or with surgical adhesive (see Appendix A). The adhesive is applied to the eyelash strip, which is set in place along the bottom of the eyelid, then secured by pressing carefully and gently with a blunt ended orangewood stick or a paper stump. *Never use any sharp-pointed instrument near the eye!* If the eyes are to be made to seem farther apart, the lashes can be extended beyond the corner of the eye (Figure 10–5G). Mascara should be applied or false eyelashes put on after the makeup has been powdered.

EYEBROWS

For corrective makeup, men's eyebrows should always look natural, whereas women's may or may not. That does not mean that changes should *never* be made in an actor's eyebrows, but it does mean that they should not look made up. Unkempt, scraggly, or excessively heavy brows can be improved by judicious plucking, but that should be done only if you are sure that plucking will improve them. If you're planning to pluck more than a few hairs, it would be wise to experiment with blocking out the portions of the brow to be plucked (see Chapter 12) in order to make sure you're improving the brows, not mutilating them.

In filling out or reshaping men's eyebrows with pencil, be sure to use short, light strokes following the direction of the hairs. Holding the pencil as shown in Figure 10–4C, rather than near the tip, will help to give you a lighter touch in applying the color. If you want to soften the penciling, stroke it lightly with a finger.

Pressed eyeshadow can also be used for both men and women to fill out (though not to reshape) the eyebrows. It is applied with a small, soft eyeshadow brush, which not only fills in the natural eyebrow if it needs filling in, but also produces the effect of a shadow under the brow, making it seem both wider and thicker than it actually is. Whether it can be used alone or should be used in combination with eyebrow pencil will usually depend on how much filling out is required.

If the eyebrows are lighter than the hair, they should

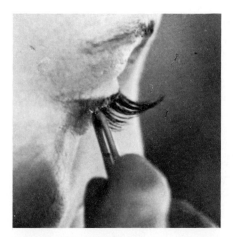

FIGURE 10–6 APPLYING FALSE EYE-LASHES. *Eyelash adhesive has been applied to the lashes, and they are being attached to the skin with tweezers. (Student Janet Lawler.)*

usually be darkened. In darkening men's eyebrows, use either eyebrow pencil or mascara, being careful to maintain a natural look.

Changes in the men's eyebrows illustrated in Figure 10–7 would depend on the hair and on the entire face—and even to some extent on the actor's personality or the aspects of his personality he wished to emphasize. For purposes of projection, however, B and D and possibly A (in Figure 10–7) should usually be darkened. If there is not much space between the eyebrow and the eye (as in Figure 10–7A and D), it may be advantageous to open up the eye area by lifting the outer end of the eyebrow to more nearly approximate the eyebrow in G. That could be done in D, for example, by brushing the hair upward and reshaping the outer end of the brow slightly with a pencil, giving more of a lift to the brow and thus to the entire face. If it proved practicable, a few hairs might be plucked from the bottom of the brow in E. If one wanted a more masculine look, the brow in J might be filled out slightly with a pencil. You can judge for yourself the effect of the various brows illustrated—to what extent they enhance the eye, what quality of personality they suggest, and how they might be improved.

For women's corrective makeup, as for men's, it is not necessary to make the eyebrows fit one single pattern—rather, they should be as flattering as possible to the individual eye and to the face in general. Eyebrows that are too straight, too arched (Figure 10–5C), too slanted (Figure 10–5A), too thick (Figure 10–5F), too thin (Figure 10–5K), too close together, or too far apart might well be corrected. Raising the eyebrow over the outer corner of the eye, as in Figure 10–5B and as suggested for men in the preceding paragraph, can be very helpful in opening up the eye area. Compare, for example, eyebrows B and H in Figure 10–5. Exaggerating the upward curve too much, however, can become grotesque.

A very simple method of determining what shape of brow will look best on a particular face is to manipulate

FIGURE *10–7 YOUNG MEN'S EYES.* *Natural eyebrows without makeup. Some of them could be improved by darkening or reshaping for corrective makeup. Others could be left as they are.*

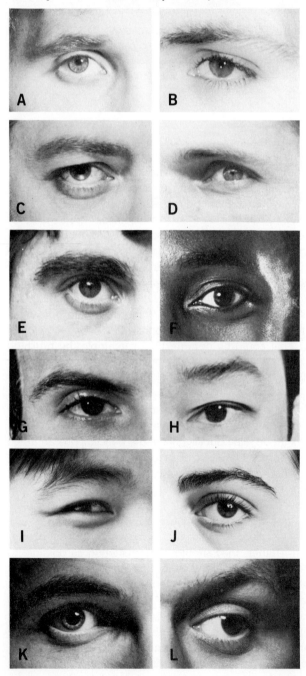

the natural brow with your fingers, as illustrated in Figure 12–26. That can save you a great deal of time in trial and error.

If the brow is well formed and well placed, it can simply be darkened with black or brown mascara or eyebrow pencil. After using mascara, you may wish to touch up the brows with petroleum jelly or cold cream to counteract the flat color of the mascara and restore a natural-looking sheen. With pencils, use short, quick, light strokes, following the direction of the hair. Remember that the intention is to darken the hairs, not the skin underneath—except when the natural brow needs filling out.

If you want to change the line of the brow, that can be done by plucking, penciling, or both. As pointed out above, however, blocking out the parts of the brow to be plucked before actually plucking them would be a wise precaution.

CHEEKS

If the cheeks are too round, the part of the cheek to be made less prominent should be shaded with a base two or three shades darker than that used on the rest of the face. It is important, as always, to blend this lowlight imperceptibly into the lighter base. If the cheeks are too sunken, the procedure can be reversed by using a base a few shades lighter than the rest of the face to counteract the natural shadows that reveal the sunken cheeks.

Color of Rouge Rouge is usually applied after the modeling is done, though it is sometimes used as a shadow in modeling the cheeks. For men, a soft, natural color (such as SR-9½-d, RS-10-b, RS-10-d, or RS-11-b) should usually be used. In selecting a suitable brush-on rouge (as opposed to dry rouge, which can be used in the same way but does not come with its own brush), look for a shade that is not too pink.

For women, the shade of rouge chosen will depend on skin color, fashion, costume, and personal preference. With so many possible variations there can be no hard-and-fast rules. It is usually best to experiment with shades that you think *ought* to be suitable in order to find out which ones actually are the most effective.

Fashions in rouge colors change, but for corrective makeup a flattering conservative shade should always be chosen in preference to an unflattering fashionable one. Costume colors—especially reds, oranges, and purples—may determine to some extent which color should be used. A magenta rouge, for example, is not likely to be the best choice for a woman wearing an orange dress, though magenta accessories might make such a combination possible. Personal preference may also be a factor, provided it does not lead one to choose an unbecoming or unsuitable color.

Placement of Rouge Rouge should usually be placed on the cheekbone rather than low on the cheek, though in glamorizing the face, a soft, medium shade of brush-on rouge can be effectively used as a shadow below the cheekbone in order to sink in the cheeks. (Figure 10–8.) Rouge is usually applied after any modeling with highlights and shadows has been completed. Rouge should not be placed too near the eye or the nose. If the face is narrow, it should be kept even farther from the nose and placed nearer the ears in order to increase the apparent width of the face. If the face is wide, keep the rouge away from the ears and apply it in a pattern more nearly vertical than horizontal. For corrective makeup it should never be applied in a round spot, and it should always be carefully blended.

Rouge is not always used for men, but if color in the cheeks will help to make an actor look healthier or more attractive, it should be used. And it should usually extend over a wider area than it normally does for women—including the temples, if the face is not too wide. Above all, it ought to look as natural as possible. In case of doubt, use none.

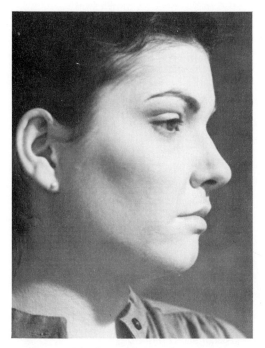

FIGURE **10–8** *CHEEKBONE MODELING.* *Creme makeup highlights and shadows. Makeup by student Nancy Eubanks.*

LIPS

Figures 10–9 and 10–10 illustrate lips of young men and women. In Figure 10–9, E represents the classical ideal—a graceful bow in the upper lip with a dip in the center and a full lower lip not quite so wide as the upper. But the lips need not match this model of classical perfection. Among the other lips in the group, some (A, for example) are well shaped and would not require correction. Although the upper lip in F is thin and out of proportion to the lower lip, the mouth is still attractive, and if it fits the face, it might better be left as it is. The lips in Figure 10–9I do not follow classical proportions, but they are interesting and attractive and should probably not

FIGURE **10–9** *YOUTHFUL LIPS, MALE.* *E. is closest to the classical lip formation.*

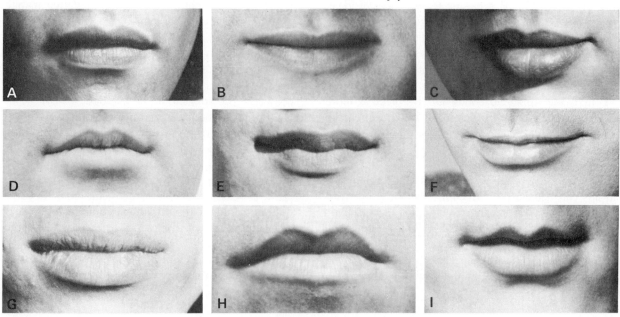

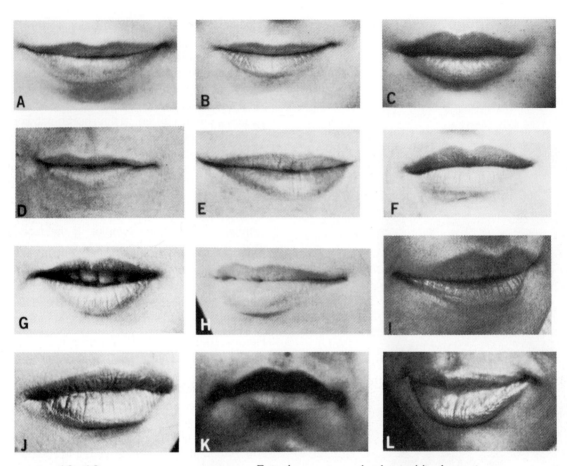

FIGURE 10–10 YOUTHFUL LIPS, FEMALE.   *F. is the most nearly classical lip formation.*

be tampered with. The lower lip should certainly not be darkened. Its fullness works only because it remains light and does not contrast strongly with the skin. Note what happens in C when the lower lip is darkened.

In Figure 10–10, F is closest to the classical ideal. Most of the others might be improved with corrective makeup. In B, for example, the slightly crooked upper lip could easily be reshaped, perhaps giving it a more graceful curve and also widening it a bit in order to make it extend beyond the lower lip. Much the same is true of G. In E the upper lip could also be given a more graceful curve. It might be helpful in I if the upper lip were to be thinned; filling out the lower lip would also help the proportion.

Reshaping   There are various ways of reshaping lips. Thin lips can usually be corrected for women by over-painting—that is, by drawing on new lips of the shape and size wanted. (See Figure 12–59.) This overpainting should be done for men only if the results will seem completely natural. It's usually best to make the lower lip lighter than the upper. A thin highlight over the upper

lip may help to define it. Note the natural highlights over most of the upper lips in Figure 10–9. A similar highlight can be painted in over the corrected lip.

If a man's lips are too full, it is usually best to leave them the natural color (Figure 10–9G). If they are already too red, the lower one can be lightened. If the upper one is very full, it too should be lightened. For women the fullness can be minimized by covering the lips with the foundation, then using the lip color only toward the inside of the lips and fading it outward into the foundation color. Deep colors should be avoided.

For too-wide lips, keep the lip color toward the center of the lips and cover the outer corners with the foundation color. The upper lip may be left slightly wider than the lower. If the mouth is too narrow, carry the lip color out to the extreme corners, particularly on the upper lip. It is seldom possible to carry the color beyond the natural corners of the mouth with any degree of success. The artifice becomes apparent as soon as the mouth is opened.

In the case of a turned-down mouth with a heavy upper lip and a thin lower one, the solution is to overpaint the lower lip to match the upper one and, if possible, to turn up the corners with paint. Or, if the outline of the upper lip is not too definite, it can be partially blocked out with foundation color and the lower one filled in to match. That much correction may not be possible for men.

For a mouth with a thin upper lip, the upper lip can—for women, at least, and sometimes for men—be overpainted to match the lower.

Lip coloring can best be applied with a narrow flat brush and blotted with tissue. The color should usually not be carried to the extreme corners of the mouth unless you wish to widen it. It is frequently helpful, especially when overpainting, to define the lips by outlining them with a brush, using a darker shade of red. The outline should then be blended inward with your brush.

For men, especially when no lip rouge is used at all, the outline of the lips can be defined very subtly with a brown makeup pencil, then blended. Further definition may be possible by deepening the natural shadow immediately below the center of the lower lip. If there is a natural shadow there, this will, of course, not be necessary; but if the natural shadow is slight, it may be helpful. It should, however, be done with great care so as to look completely natural. Observe the shadows under the lips in Figure 10–9.

Color Lip coloring should be compatible with the rouge. And like rouge, it will depend—for women—on color of the skin, hair, costume, and perhaps on colors fashionable at the time. Bizarre fashions (such as white lipstick) should obviously be avoided in corrective makeup. For men a natural color (such as PR-9-d, SR-10-d, or RS-10-b) is safest. Often it is best not to color the lower lip at all.

NECK

If the neck shows signs of age, they can be camouflaged somewhat by shadowing the prominent muscles and highlighting the depressions. Even a sagging neckline can be minimized, at least for the front view, by shadowing. The shadow should be strongest just under the jaw line and should blend gradually into the foundation, which can be darker on the neck than on the face. The neck shadow must never be allowed to come up over the jaw line. The jaw line itself can be defined with a shadow. That will tend to strengthen it and take the attention away from the neck.

When the neck is seen in profile, however, no amount of paint will be really effective. The best solution is actually to tighten the skin under the jaw by pulling the skin in front of the ears upward, backward, or both. That can be done with *facial lifts*, constructed and applied as follows:

1. Cut two rectangles about 3 or 4 inches by ½ inch of mousseline de soie or other very thin, tough fabric. The edges may be pinked or not, as you choose. (See Figure 10–11. Figure 10–12 illustrates the use of three lifts.)
2. Fold over about ½ inch of the fabric at one end to strengthen it, and sew it to a length (about 8 inches) of ½-inch-wide cotton elastic. That should be done for both pieces of the mousseline. After the mousseline is attached to the face, the elastic will go over the top of the head. A dressmaker's hook should be sewn to the free end of one elastic tape (Figure 10–12B) and two or three eyes to the other so that the two ends can be hooked together at just the right tension. If you prefer, you can make the elastic slightly shorter,

FIGURE 10–11 FACIAL LIFT. *The lift (A), made of mousseline de soie, is attached with spirit gum to the skin in front of the ear (B), then pulled tight over the top of the head (C). The tape over the head can be concealed with a wig or sometimes with the natural hair, carefully combed. In the latter case, the tape should more or less match the color of the hair.*

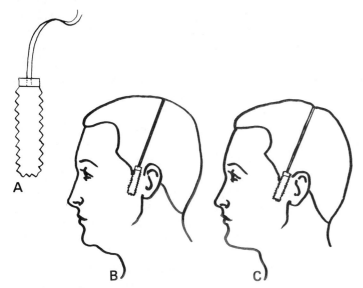

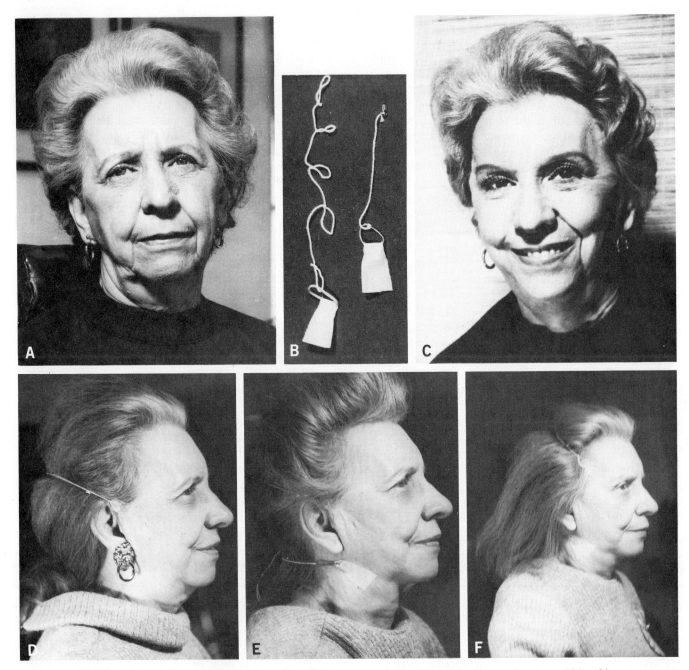

FIGURE 10–12 LIFTS FOR FACE AND NECK. *A and C show model before and after application of lifts. She is wearing her usual street makeup in both pictures. Since the purpose of these pictures is to show how much lifts alone can change the face, no additional corrective makeup has been used. One set of lifts is shown in B and, in D and E, the use of lifts on the cheeks, neck, and temples. Lifts made and applied by Bert Roth, S.M.A.*

fold over the ends to make loops, and tie ordinary string to each loop. Then the string can be tied on top of the head to create the desired tension. Whatever method is used, the construction should be completed in advance so that in making up the actor for the performance, it will be necessary only to attach the pieces.

3. For vertical lifts, the two pieces of mousseline should

be attached to the skin with spirit gum—vertically in front of the ears and below the sideburns. (See Figure 10–11B.) Be sure that the top of the lift, where the elastic is attached to the mousseline, is high enough so that it can be concealed by the hair. It must never, of course, fall below the natural side hair, which should be combed over it.

4. In order to conceal the edges of the fabric, stipple

with Duo adhesive, and allow it to dry along with the spirit gum.

5. Attach the elastic over the head and adjust the tension. (See Figure 10–11C.) Too great tension will result in obvious wrinkles or creases in the skin and must, of course, be avoided.

6. Cover the lifts with plastic sealer and allow it to dry.

7. The foundation color (rubber-mask grease will give the best coverage) can now be stippled over the lifts, blended into the skin around the lifts, then powdered. The makeup can be completed as usual.

8. If the natural hair is to be used, it can be combed over the elastic to conceal it. This, however, may be impossible for men with short hair. If the top hair is long enough to comb over the elastic, false sideburns can sometimes be used to conceal the elastic on the sides. If a wig is to be worn by either men or women, the elastic will very likely be covered.

The lifts can be removed by dabbing the mousseline with spirit gum remover until it comes off easily. If the lifts are to be reused, the mousseline can be cleaned in acetone.

A somewhat simpler method for constructing lifts is to substitute clear plastic adhesive tape (a ½-inch strip about 3 inches long) for the mousseline, and heavy string (two lengths, each about 13 or 14 inches) for the elastic. A matchstick, cut in half, will also be needed. This is the procedure:

1. Fold about an inch of the tape around the matchstick so that the two ends of the stick are protruding beyond either side of the tape. Then press the sticky sides of the tape together firmly.

2. Tie a loop in one end of each length of string, then hook the loop around the folded end of the tape so that the two protruding ends of the matchstick are caught in the loop (Figure 10–13).

In using the lifts, simply stick the tape to the skin (which must be free of grease or makeup), then tie the strings over the head, adjusting them to the correct ten-

FIGURE 10–13 FACIAL LIFT. *Lift made with clear plastic adhesive tape, string, and a matchstick.*

sion. The rest of the procedure is the same as when using the mousseline. The adhesive tape, however, is not reusable, but that scarcely matters since the lifts can be made so quickly.

String can also be used instead of elastic with the mousseline if you prefer. (See Figure 10–12.) When it is, a hook on the end of one string (Figure 10–12B) and a loop on one end of the other string is more practical than tying a knot since the lifts and the strings can be reused. The hook can be attached ahead of time, but the loop should, of course, not be made until the lifts are attached and the tension is being adjusted.

These are not the only methods of constructing facial lifts, but they will serve to illustrate the principle. Each makeup artist has his or her own preference as to materials and exact technique of construction.

TEETH

Dark or discolored teeth can be lightened with tooth enamel. There are several shades of white and cream available. Certain irregularities (such as very long front teeth) can be corrected by shortening the teeth with black tooth enamel or black wax. More serious deficiencies, such as broken, missing, or extremely irregular teeth, require the services of a dentist. This can be expensive, but for the professional actor—unless he is doing only certain types of character roles—it is important to have attractive teeth.

HAIR

The actor's usual hair style should be considered carefully in relation to the shape of the face. If it can be made more becoming, it should be restyled. That can often be done merely by recombing in various ways and checking in the mirror, though it is sometimes better to consult a hairdresser whose work you know and can depend on. Medium long hair usually offers greater potential for change than does short.

If you want to make the face seem shorter and broader, avoid placing the bulk of the hairdo high on the head. Try, instead, to keep it flat on top and wider at the sides. If you want the face longer and narrower, the reverse will apply. If the face is too round, avoid a round hairdo that follows the shape of the face, since that would only emphasize the roundness. But a round hairdo could be helpful for a face that is too square or too angular. If the features are sharp, the hairdo should be soft around the face, not sleek—unless, of course, you have chosen deliberately to emphasize the sharpness.

If a man's hairline is receding slightly, it may be possible to restyle hair to conceal the fact. Or the hairline can sometimes be corrected by using eyebrow pencil of the appropriate color on the scalp. In doing this, never draw a hard, horizontal line; instead, use short strokes of the pencil following the direction of the hair. These strokes should be softened and blurred with the finger so that there is no definite line, and they should also be powdered to avoid shine. Darkening the base color at the hairline will also help. Makeup to match the hair color can be applied to small bald spots and can also be used with some success on the hairline. If the hair has receded beyond the point at which it can be corrected with paint, the actor should procure a toupee or a wig. The best ones are handmade and are expensive, but good inexpensive ones made with synthetic hair are also available. No matter what you pay for a wig or a hairpiece, be sure to have it skillfully styled.

Problems

1. Make your forehead (a) wider, (b) narrower, (c) higher, (d) lower.
2. Using only paint, change the shape of your nose, making it (a) longer and narrower, (b) shorter, (c) broader, (d) flatter.
3. Make your forehead more prominent and your chin less prominent, then your chin more prominent and your forehead less prominent.
4. Make your eyes (a) farther apart, (b) closer together.
5. Make one eye smaller and one eye larger.
6. Change the shape of your eyebrows without blocking them out.
7. Make your mouth (a) wider, (b) narrower.
8. Study your own face, noting prominent bones; size of eyes, nose, mouth, and chin; height of forehead; shape and thickness of eyebrows; shape, width, and fullness of lips; etc. Decide which features you'd like to change for your corrective makeup.
9. Do a complete corrective makeup on yourself.

11
Stippling

Stippling—a method of applying makeup by pressing the color onto the skin rather than stroking it on—is used for giving the effect of skin texture with paint, for toning down shadows or highlights that are too strong, for adding color to or changing the basic color of a makeup, for giving the effect of such skin blemishes as freckles and brown spots, and for helping to conceal the edges of three-dimensional additions to the face. It is usually done with a sponge, occasionally with a brush.

STIPPLING WITH SPONGES

Black plastic stipple sponges (Figure 11–1), red-rubber sponges (Figure 13–8I), natural sponges (Figure 9–1), and some household sponges can be used for stippling. (See *Sponges* in Appendix A.) Red-rubber sponges are used primarily with rubber-mask grease, though they can also be used with creme makeup and with regular grease-paint. Natural sponges are used only with cake makeup; and black stipple sponges and household sponges, with creme makeup, greasepaint, cake makeup, or soft makeup in a tube.

The first step in stippling with sponges is, of course, to apply the stipple color to the sponge. That can be done in four ways:

1. If you are stippling with regular creme makeup (not creme-makeup crayons), with soft grease contour or accent color, or with rubber-mask grease (if it is sufficiently solid and not too sticky or oily), press a flat surface of the sponge into the paint with just enough pressure to transfer paint to the surface of the sponge without clogging the holes. The sponge is then ready to use. In using creme sticks or large sticks of grease-paint, you may prefer to stroke the stick across the surface of the sponge, especially if you are using a fairly large sponge. If you are using a small stipple

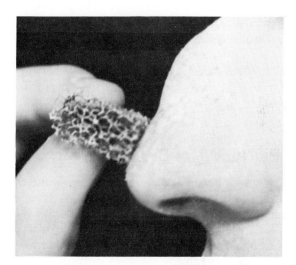

FIGURE *11–1* STIPPLING WITH A BLACK STIPPLE SPONGE.

sponge, you can simply press it into the top of the stick.
2. If you are using creme-makeup crayons or small sticks of greasepaint, stroke the crayon or the stick across a flat surface of the sponge.
3. With makeup in a tube or oily makeup in a jar, apply some paint to the back of the hand, smooth it out, then press the sponge onto the paint on the hand. Or you can, if you prefer, spread the paint onto any convenient flat surface, such as a piece of glass, the top of a container of cake makeup, or the cover of your palette box if you happen to be using one.
4. In using cake makeup (moist or dry type), stroke the dampened (but not wet) sponge across the cake.

When the surface of the sponge is covered with paint, press the sponge gently onto the skin. If the stipple is too faint, keep pressing more firmly until you get the

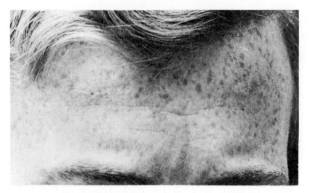

FIGURE 11–2 FRECKLES

effect you want. *Always experiment first on your hand or on your arm before applying the stipple over makeup on the face.*

It is usually best to powder the makeup before stippling over it and also to powder over the stipple. If you are stippling with more than one color, powder after each color. When stippling with cake or other water-soluble makeup, it is, of course, not necessary to powder the stipple.

STIPPLING WITH BRUSHES

For stippling with brushes, small round sables, including eyeliner brushes, can be used. For freckles (Figure 11–2) or other spots of brownish pigmentation in the skin or for spots used for texture (see closeup of Hal Holbrook's Mark Twain makeup in Figure 11–3), narrow, flat brushes are preferable.

In stippling with brushes, the stipple paint is mixed on the back of the hand, in the cover of a makeup palette box, or on any appropriate flat surface, then taken from there with the brush and applied over the makeup. If you are using more than one color of stipple, it is not necessary to powder after applying each color, but only when all of the stippling has been completed.

STIPPLING FOR TEXTURE

In stippling primarily for texture, one or more colors of stipple may be applied over the makeup, using greasepaint, rubber-mask grease, creme makeup, moist cake makeup, or Vitacolor wet makeup. Dry cake makeup is somewhat less effective for stippling but can be used.

If only one color of stipple is used, as in Figure 11–4C, choose a shade between the highlight and the shadow but not, of course, the same as the foundation color—either a bit lighter or darker, a bit higher or lower in intensity, or of a different hue.

If you are not satisfied with the results from using

FIGURE 11–3 STIPPLING DONE WITH A BRUSH. *Detail from Hal Holbrook's makeup for Mark Twain. Three colors were used for the stippling and were applied with a small, flat brush. (For additional illustrations of Mr. Holbrook's makeup, see Chapter 17.)*

just the one color of stipple, you can add additional colors. Three colors are usually more effective than one. Which ones you choose will depend on the effect you want—such as healthy, sickly, tanned, sunburned, or sallow. Keep in mind that colors used for men are usually darker than those used for women. And, of course, dark-skinned actors will require darker stipple colors than those with lighter complexions. The same holds true for light-skinned actors playing dark-complexioned characters.

The first stipple might be about four shades darker than the base. For characters who would normally have red or pink in the complexion, the second might be a shade of red—rose or coral, perhaps, or a bronze rouge. For characters without red tones in the complexion, the second stipple might be used to make adjustments in the color. If the color needs no adjusting, you can simply proceed to the third stipple, which should be lighter than the base but not so light as the highlight. If, after the stippling, the color of the makeup appears to need adjusting—more red, for example, or more pink or more yellow—stipple of the appropriate color can be added.

When you have chosen your stipple colors, apply the first one over the powdered makeup, being careful not to use too much. Avoid smearing the stipple or leaving dark blotches of paint. You should set this first stipple by patting translucent powder over it very carefully so as not to smear it. Slight smears can be retouched by stippling with a small brush.

Follow the same procedure with your second stipple color. If this is a red stipple, you can make it heavier

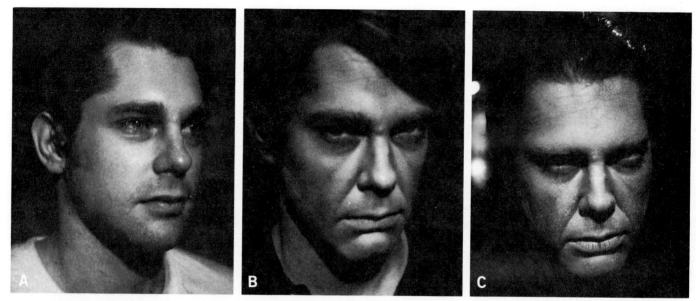

FIGURE 11—4 STIPPLING FOR TEXTURE. *(Actor Graham Beckel.) A. Without makeup. B. Sallow foundation with ivory highlights and rose shadows. Dry rouge (Bob Kelly Bronze) brushed on after powdering. C. Light stipple added for texture, then powdered. Hair combed back and slightly grayed.*

on areas that you wish to appear more red in the final makeup. Powder again.

Then apply your third stipple. Its lightness or darkness will control to some extent the overall lightness or darkness of the final effect. Set this stipple with translucent powder.

Now stipple on the rouge. Even if you included it in the original makeup, you will probably need to add more. Then powder.

Finally, check the makeup and make any adjustments you wish to by additional stippling with a sponge or a brush.

It is also possible to do practically the entire makeup with stippling, including foundation, highlights, shadows, and rouge. This is one possible procedure:

1. Stipple the foundation directly on the skin, using three colors (or more, if you like) that, when juxtaposed in the stippling, will give you the color you want. This will, of course, be somewhat experimental. However, if the three you have chosen do *not* give you what you want, it's very simple to adjust the color by further stippling with whatever color seems needed. Powder after each application of stipple.
2. When the foundation color is satisfactory, carefully stipple on highlights, then shadows. As in working with a brush, always begin at the point of greatest intensity and work away from it toward the edge, stippling more and more lightly to create a soft edge. The density of the stipple can be increased in any particular spot or area by increasing the number of applications of the sponge. This is much safer than increasing pressure on the sponge, which can result

in unsightly blotches. In shadowing, it is also possible to stipple the darkest part of the shadow with a deeper color. Hard edges or areas too small to stipple successfully with a sponge can be stippled with an eyeliner brush. Errors in stippling, if they are not too serious, can usually be corrected by stippling over them with the foundation color. Powder after each stippling.
3. Stipple on the rouge wherever you normally would use it for the particular makeup you're doing—cheeks, nose, jowls, etc. Then powder.

An alternative method—and one which you might prefer for a more subtle effect—is partially to reverse the procedure and stipple on the highlights and the shadows first, making them fairly strong, then stipple on the foundation colors, and, finally, the rouge. Naturally, in stippling with the foundation colors you should proceed cautiously in order not to tone down the highlights and shadows more than you had intended to. However, if you find, when you have finished, that they *have* been toned down too much, it's a very simple matter to make corrections by additional stippling with your original highlight and shadow colors.

STIPPLING TO REDUCE CONTRASTS

Stippling can also be used to reduce contrasts in parts of the makeup that are too dark, too light, or too intense in color. Shadows that are too strong can be toned down with a lighter stipple, and highlights that are too strong, with a darker one. If both the shadows and the highlights are too strong, stippling with the base color will tone down both of them and reduce the overall contrast. If more texture is desirable, stipple the shadows with a color lighter than the base, and the highlights with a color darker than the base. For small areas, use small sponges or brushes, and be careful to confine the stippling to the area for which it is intended. If you inadvertently tone down an area too much, it can be corrected by further stippling with the original color.

Highlights and shadows in youthful makeups should not normally be stippled to reduce contrasts since stippling creates an illusion of texture. That, of course, would work against the smoothness of skin appropriate for most youthful makeups.

If the rouge in age makeups is too strong, it can be stippled with the base color to get the right intensity. Rouge in youthful makeups would not normally be stippled.

STIPPLING TO ADD COLOR

If you are not satisfied with the overall color of a makeup (too red, too yellow, etc.), it is possible to modify the color by stippling over the makeup with another color. This, of course, will also add a certain amount of texture. Or you can use stippling instead of a foundation color by applying highlights and shadows directly onto the skin, then stippling to add an overall color.

If, when you have finished the stippling, you find that the color is still not quite right, you can add additional colors of stipple to correct it. Remember, however, that the more stipple you put over the makeup, the more you are toning down the highlights and shadows underneath. If you inadvertently tone them down too much, you can, of course, restore them by further stippling with the highlight and shadow colors. You may also want to use stippling for adding red to the cheeks, nose, jowls, and other areas of the face.

Unless you are using dry cake or Vitacolor wet makeup, you should usually powder the makeup before stippling and after each color of stipple.

STIPPLING TO CONCEAL EDGES

In using latex pieces, eyebrow covers, bald caps, and various constructions with cotton and tissue, there are sometimes visible edges to be concealed. For the stage, this can often be done with stippling over a rubber-mask grease foundation.

The rubber-mask grease is applied with a red-rubber sponge, which is pressed firmly onto the skin repeatedly, resulting in a thicker-than-usual foundation. Powder is then pressed firmly onto the rubber-mask grease, and the excess is dusted off with a powder brush, as usual. (Since the rubber-mask grease is pressed on without being smoothed out afterward, the technique is referred to as "stippling," even though the skin is completely covered with the paint.) Various colors of stipple can be applied over this with a black stipple sponge (Figure 11–1) or with brushes. The purpose in this case is not primarily to give texture to the skin, but to use the stippled patterns of light and dark colors to break up the tiny line of shadow created by the thickness of the edge being concealed.

12

Modeling with Highlights and Shadows

You have already studied the general structure of the face. The next step is to learn to modify the appearance of this structure through the use of highlights and shadows. Although the illusion created may involve making cheeks rounder, chins more pointed, or noses crooked, more often than not, it will include some aging.

In youth, firm muscles and elastic skin fill out the hollows and smooth over the bumps in the bony structure of the skull. But with age and the accompanying sagging of muscles, this bony structure becomes increasingly evident. Therefore, the first thing to do in learning to age the face is to visualize the bones of the skull and to locate them by prodding with the fingers.

Unquestionably, the single most important factor in learning to create the illusion of three-dimensional changes in bones and flesh through the use of two-dimensional painting techniques is a thorough understanding of what happens when directional light falls on a three-dimensional object (see Chapter 2). Once this is understood, the solution to most problems concerning realistic modeling in makeup can be found simply by asking three questions:

1. What is the exact shape of the structure (a cheekbone, for example, or a wrinkle) that is to be represented?
2. Where is the light coming from? (On the stage it will normally be from above rather than from below.)
3. What happens, in terms of light and shadow, when a light from that direction falls on a structure of that shape?

The answers to these questions will make it clear where the structure (wrinkle or cheekbone) would be light and where an absence of light would make it appear dark. These light and dark areas can then be painted onto the face, creating for the observer the illusion of prominent bones and wrinkles where they do not actually exist.

Before beginning to do this, it's a good idea to take time to practice the technique of modeling hard and soft edges.

MODELING HARD AND SOFT EDGES

It would be best to do the following practice on the back of your hand or the inside of your wrist or your arm if any of those areas is sufficiently free of hair. If you're working on someone else, the back (if not hairy) is a good place to practice. Choose a medium flesh tone for the foundation, a medium dark color (such as S-13-f, FS-13-g, or PR-12-g) for the shadows, and a very light color (such as OF-1-b, OF-1-c, F-1-a, FS-1-a, FS-1-c, or FS-3-a) for the highlights. Use a wide or an extra-wide flat brush. With your brush, take up a small amount of paint and transfer it to the back of your hand—*not* in a spot you plan to use for your practice. Then work from the paint on your hand, using your hand as a palette. This enables you to control the amount of paint on your brush much more effectively than when you work directly from the stick or the container of makeup. (This applies, of course, only to creme makeup or to greasepaint, not to cake makeup. Makeup can be taken directly from cakes without using a palette.) If you are using paint from a palette box (see Appendix A), you can use the inside cover of the box as your palette. Both the hand and the palette box cover can also be used for mixing colors.

The following procedures for modeling hard and soft edges, though they are quite specific as to how to do what and in what order, are not intended to deter you from experimenting with other techniques for achieving the same results.

Soft Edges In making a soft-edged highlight (or a soft-edged shadow), begin with the area of greatest intensity.

1. Using your brush, take up some highlight color from your hand or your palette.
2. With a single, firm stroke of your brush, make a stripe of highlight color. (If you have used a brush of the correct width, taken up the right amount of paint, and used the right amount of pressure in applying it, you will need to make only the one stroke before blending the edges.)
3. Either wipe your brush clean or use a clean brush, then draw the brush lightly along one edge of the highlight, overlapping the edge. Repeat this until the edge blends imperceptibly into the foundation. If you are using cake makeup, the brush should be slightly damp, and you should wipe the makeup off the brush after each stroke, redampening it when necessary.
4. Repeat step 3 with the opposite edge. This should give you a strong highlight with two soft edges. If it is not strong enough, repeat the entire procedure on top of what you have already done.
5. Repeat step 2 with a medium shadow color, applying the stripe of paint a short distance away from the highlight.
6. Repeat step 3 on the side of the shadow away from the highlight.
7. Do the same on the other side of the shadow. In the blending of the shadow color toward the highlight, avoid any overlapping of the highlight color with the shadow. When you have finished, there should be a gradual transition in value between the lightest area of the highlight and the darkest area of the shadow. In other words, you should now have modeled, in essence, a cylinder.

Hard Edges   Hard edges are used in realistic makeup only to create the effect of a crease in the flesh. For a hard edge to be fully effective, the lightest light must meet the darkest dark without any overlapping, smearing, or fuzziness. Hard edges should be clean and sharp. The following steps can be used to practice making a hard edge:

1. Cover a section of skin with a medium foundation color.
2. With your brush, take up some highlight color from your hand or your palette.
3. Holding the brush so that the bristles are perpendicular to the edge you intend to paint, draw it carefully along the skin where you want the hard edge to be. If the hard edge is to fade out at one end (as it usually should), gradually lift the brush so that it touches the skin more and more lightly as you move along. If there are irregularities in the edge, go over the entire edge again in the same way in order to make corrections.
4. Wipe your brush clean. If you are using cake makeup, the brush should be damp.

5. If you want the highlight to be considerably wider than it now is (as on the upper lip when highlighting the nasolabial fold), place your brush in the same position as in step 3 and, barely touching the skin, draw the brush away from the hard edge, pulling some of the paint outward. How far you pull the paint out depends, of course, on the width you want the highlight to be. Moving down along the highlight, keep repeating this stroke for the entire length of the highlight. If you do *not* want to widen the highlight but only to blend the edge, skip this step entirely.
6. In order to soften the outer edge of the highlight, wipe your brush clean, then holding it parallel to the hard edge, stroke it very lightly over the outer edge of the highlight, overlapping the edge with the brush. Keep doing this until you have a soft edge that blends into the foundation color.
7. Examine the highlight. If it needs strengthening, repeat the entire procedure on top of what you have just done. Keep doing this until it is as strong as you want it to be. It would be well at this point to powder what you have already done.
8. Using your shadow color and working in the opposite direction, follow the same procedure as for the highlight, being extremely careful to maintain the clear, sharp edge, and never to let the shadow overlap the highlight.

When you have learned to model hard and soft edges convincingly, you can then apply the technique in creating the illusion of three-dimensional changes on the face.

MODELING THE FACE AND THE NECK WITH HIGHLIGHTS AND SHADOWS

In order to make sure that the final makeup will fit the actor's face, you should always be aware of how *every* highlight and *every* shadow relates to the structure of the face, including bone, cartilage, muscle, fatty tissue, and skin. To demonstrate this, model your entire face and neck by using highlights and shadows to bring out the bone structure and to create the effect of sagging muscles and flesh.

Begin by covering your entire face with a medium deep (8, 9, or 10) cake, creme, or greasepaint foundation color in a shade suitable for aging. This should be a grayed color (d, e, or f) in a warm hue (R, S, FS, or SF). Then, using a pale cream or ivory color, highlight areas of the face as they might look in middle or old age, with bones becoming more prominent and flesh sagging. (See Figure 12–1, which can be used as a guide but should be adapted to your own face rather than copied exactly.) Make the highlights *very strong*, but soften the edges except when creating the effect of creases.

1. Using a wide (Figure 12–2H)or extra-wide (Figure 12–2I) flat shading brush, highlight the area marked H1 in Figure 12–1.
2. Still using your wide brush, apply similar highlights to the superciliary arch, emphasizing the area just above the eyebrows, marked H2 in Figure 12–1. If you look at your forehead in profile, you may find a horizontal break or a change in direction of the planes about halfway up. If you do, this break will represent the top limit of the highlight area.
3. Since the top of the orbital bone above the outer corner of the eye (H3) nearly always catches the light, highlight it, softening the edges. A medium

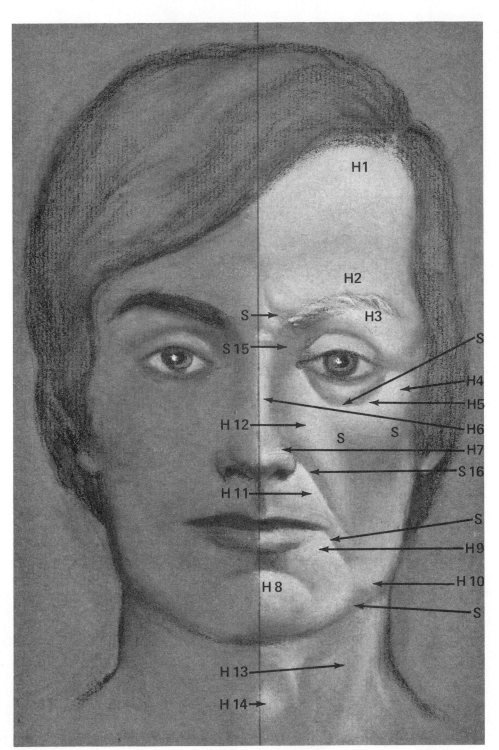

FIGURE 12–1 *HIGHLIGHTING FOR AGE.*

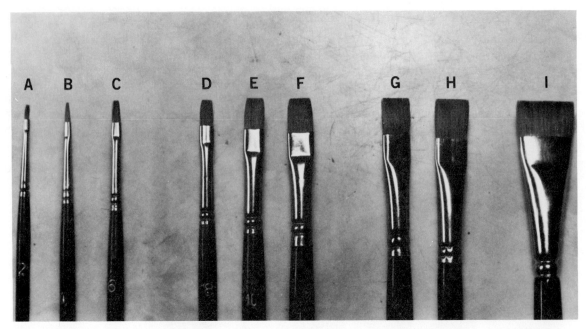

FIGURE 12–2 *FLAT SABLE BRUSHES.*   *A, B, and C, Narrow. D, E, and F, Medium. G and H, Wide. I, Extra wide. All brushes by Kryolan, illustrated in actual size. (Kryolan numbers are 2, 4, and 6 for narrow; 8, 10, and 12 for medium; 14 and 16 for wide; and ⅝-inch for extra wide.)*

brush (Figure 12–2E or F) can be used for this. You may also wish to highlight the lid itself, though if you were creating a very deepset eye, it would be shadowed instead.

4. Using a medium-wide (Figure 12–2G) brush, highlight along the *top* of the cheekbone (H4), softening both edges of the highlight. (See Figure 12–45.) To locate the top, lay one finger horizontally across your temple, press firmly, and move it down until you find it being pulled outward by the cheekbone. Then press *downward* against the bone. Where your finger rests will be the top of the bone. It is the top plane of the bone, not the outside or the underside, that normally receives the most light.

5. If you want a pouch under the eye, continue the cheekbone highlight to the pouch, letting it stop with a hard edge along the lower boundary of the pouch and making it strongest at the very edge of the pouch (H5).

6. Using a medium brush (Figure 12–2E or F), highlight the bone and the cartilage that form the top or front of the nose (H6) since these invariably catch the light strongly (See Figure 12–36A,B.) Keep the highlight off the sides.

7. With the same brush, add a small highlight to the tops of the nares. (See Figure 12–36C,D.)

8. Highlight the chin rather strongly with a wide or a medium-wide brush. Be sure to keep the highlight below the break between the lip and the chin, making it strongest right at the break (H8), where there will

be a fairly hard edge in the very center. (See Figure 12–63A,B.) This edge softens as it moves away to the right and to the left.

9. Now you can begin to use sagging muscles and flesh along with the bone structure in placing your highlights. The flesh at the corners of the mouth may puff out or sag with age, catching the light. Highlight this area (H9) with a medium or a wide brush. (See Figure 12–63C,D.)

10. The jaw line (H10) normally catches a highlight; but since, in age, it is the sagging flesh rather than the bone that is most strongly lighted, highlight this area with a wide or an extra-wide brush, keeping your edges soft and emphasizing the irregularity caused by the sagging flesh. (See Figure 12–55A,B,C.) If your own jawbone is firm and youthful, you can use photographs, paintings, or drawings to determine what might happen to it and how it might catch the light if there actually were sagging flesh.

11. The upper lip, all the way from the nose to the mouth, catches light, especially at the crease of the nasolabial fold (H11 in Figure 12–1). With a wide or an extra-wide brush, held as shown in Figure 12–50C,D, start your highlight at the nose, making a very sharp, clean edge along the crease, then fade it out (Figure 12–50E) as it moves toward the center of the lip.

12. Now observe the area marked H12 in Figure 12–1. This is the top of the nasolabial fold. It may not always be this pronounced, but the area is nearly always prominent in age. It catches a strong highlight

FIGURE 12–3 MODELING THE FACE WITH HIGHLIGHTS AND SHADOWS. *A. Highlighting completed. Makeup by student Milton Blankenship. B. Applying shadows. Makeup by student Joe Allen Brown. C. Highlights and shadows completed. Makeup by student Gigi Coker. (For the same student without makeup, see Figure 16–4.)*

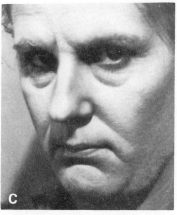

with soft edges. Be sure not to carry the highlight all the way to the crease. A medium brush can be used. To the outside of the crease is an area (S16) that folds under and away from the light and therefore should not be highlighted.

13. Since, with age, the sterno-cleido-mastoid muscles of the neck (H13) usually become more prominent and catch the light, highlight them as you would a cylinder. If your own are not obvious, you can usually find them by turning your head as far as possible to the side and feeling the opposite side of your neck with your fingers.

14. There is likely to be a little light picked up by the larynx and the tracheal column (H14). Make the edges of the highlight soft.

Now, if you have done your highlighting skillfully, your skull structure should be more apparent, and your flesh, in some areas, should have begun to seem more puffy and perhaps to sag. Observe yourself in a spotlight at some distance from the mirror to determine to what extent this has happened. Although the highlights ought to be stronger than you want them to be in the finished makeup (see Figure 12–3A), they should, nonetheless, have begun to give an effect of age.

You will notice, provided you have used a sufficiently dark foundation color, that, as a result of the contrast between it and the very light highlights, the foundation color appears darker than it actually is. As a result of this optical illusion, you will need to add less shadow color than would be required if you had used a lighter foundation color. You may, in fact, need only to deepen the shadow slightly in certain areas—the eye sockets, for example, the deepest part of the wrinkles, or the underside of the jowls. Use your shadow color sparingly. Avoid adding any more than is necessary in order to create the three-dimensional effect that you want.

15. Brush a little deep shadow into the part of the eye socket next to the nose (S15 in Figure 12–1), keeping the edges soft. A medium-wide brush is a good choice for this area.

16. Using the same color and a narrow or a medium-narrow brush, merely suggest a shadow beginning at the root of the nasolabial fold just above S15. The edge of the shadow along the crease should be hard; the other edge should be soft. It is not necessary to draw in a complete fold.

17. Deepen any other areas (such as those marked S in Figure 12–1) that obviously need deepening.
18. If you have been using creme or grease makeup, it should now be powdered. Press translucent powder into the makeup, and remove the excess with a powder brush. (Be sure to choose a translucent powder that does not darken the highlights too much.)

You may find that, although you have achieved a three-dimensional effect, the results are quite stark and unlifelike. The next step, therefore, is to add a touch of rouge—not only on the cheeks, but also on the nose, on the jowls, and in some of the shadow areas. Use a natural shade of dry rouge and apply it with a rouge brush. You may even wish to add rouge around the eyes to make them look weaker. *Always be very careful not to get the rouge into the eye.* Look again in the mirror to see how the rouge creates the effect of blood under the skin and begins to bring your makeup to life. With every realistic makeup you do, always consider the possibility of touching shadow areas with rouge for a more lifelike effect.

If the makeup is still too white or too contrasting, the solution—not only here but in most makeups that need toning down or pulling together—is to use stippling.

Stippling Colors darker than the highlight and lighter than the deep shadow are usually best for stippling. Use your base color, if you like, or for a pinker effect, either use a pinker color or add a stipple of rouge. If you want the foundation color more yellow, stipple with something yellowish. This is a good opportunity to experiment with different colors of stipple. In any case, stipple gently, barely touching the sponge to the face, so as to give added texture to the skin. Keep examining the results in the mirror as you go, and observe that, as you tone down the highlights, the makeup begins to lose its three-dimensional quality. It is important, therefore, to avoid over-stippling. (For more detailed instructions in stippling, see Chapter 11.)

The preceding instructions are for an exercise in modeling technique not necessarily related to a particular character. To check the effectiveness of your modeling before you stipple, it's a good idea to take a closeup black-and-white photograph of your makeup with an instant-picture camera, making sure that the light is coming from the direction you imagined it to be coming from when you did the makeup.

After you have studied the photograph carefully to see if the makeup looks the way you meant it to, turn it upside down and look at it again. That will help you determine how convincingly three-dimensional the modeling really looks. Then, after making any improvements you would like to, it would be a good idea, for purposes of comparison, to photograph the makeup again, both before and after it has been stippled.

The next step is to refine the approach to a makeup by making choices related to a particular character, beginning with colors for foundation, highlights, and shadows.

FOUNDATION COLORS

In selecting the foundation color (unless you already know approximately what color you want), you would do well to analyze the character as suggested in Chapter 6. On the basis of your analysis, decide first on the appropriate hue (such as red or orange), then on the value (the relative lightness or darkness of the skin color you want), and finally on the intensity (the brightness or grayness of the color). That should automatically lead you to the correct section of the color tables, and from the listings there you can select one that seems appropriate. If you do not have the color you select, choose the nearest one you do have, and mix the color you want, using the colors you have available. You may, of course, wish to choose a darker foundation color than the character would normally require in order to decrease the amount of shadow needed, as was done for the preceding exercise.

If your own skin—whether it is dark or light—is the right color for the character, then you may not need a foundation. If you choose to use one for other reasons (to cover skin blemishes, for example), it can be the color of your own skin.

HIGHLIGHT COLORS

Since highlights, in a realistic makeup, represent the character's skin color seen in strong light, they will usually be of a higher value of the foundation hue. For corrective makeup they will normally be about three shades lighter and for a very subtle aging effect, a bit more. For a greater aging effect, increase the contrast between the foundation color and the highlight.

Some useful highlight colors for Caucasian characters are Mehron's Shado-Liner #17, Ben Nye's Extra-Lite and Medium, Joe Blasco's TV White, Bob Kelly's Pale Light (HL-1), Medium Light (HL-2), and Ivory (S-21), Kryolan's O1s, P1, FS4, G16, and 522, and in cake makeup, Mehron's 1B and 4B and Kryolan's TV-White. Kryolan's and Bob Kelly's sticks for covering blemishes can be used when you prefer makeup in stick form for highlighting.

Dark-skinned actors can choose a color six to eight shades lighter than their own skin. Ben Nye's Medium and Dark highlights and his Olive Beard Cover, Kryolan's O5 and FC, and Bob Kelly's Medium Olive, Medium

Brunette, Dark Brunette, and Tantone foundation colors are good possibilities. Joe Blasco has highlighting and shading colors specifically for dark-skinned actors for use on the stage.

Highlights used in age makeups will nearly always be toned down somewhat by being stippled and should, therefore, usually be lighter—sometimes considerably lighter—than you want them to appear in the final makeup. How much they are toned down can be controlled by stippling.

SHADOW COLORS

Whereas shadow colors for modeling in corrective makeup are usually about three shades darker than the base, they can be many shades darker for stronger contrasts in age. They may be of the same intensity as the foundation or grayer, but they should rarely be brighter. For character makeups it is advisable to use two shadow colors—a medium one (which is applied first) and a deep one, which adds depth to the shadows. The medium shadow can be either a grayed version of the foundation color or, more often than not for Caucasians, a shade with more red in it than the base. In realistic makeup, shadows that are too cool for the base color tend to look dirty. If the actor is going to be wearing a red costume, more red than usual can be used in the shadows. The deep shadow should be several shades deeper in value than the medium one. Low values and intensities of Red, Scarlet-Red, Red-Scarlet, and Scarlet are the ones most commonly used for Caucasian makeup and for some American Indians. For Oriental makeups, the shadow colors will, of course, be less red than for most Caucasians but never less red than the foundation color. For makeups for daker skinned races, the shadow colors—both the medium and the deep—will, of course, be darker. How dark will depend on the darkness of the foundation color. And the hue will, as always, depend on the hue of the foundation. As with Caucasians, American Indians, and Orientals, the shadow colors should rarely be less red than the foundation. The one exception would be the use of black in the shadows for dark-skinned Blacks.

There is no universal shadow color suitable for all base colors, but there are currently available ones that can be used with a number of different foundation colors. For medium shadows, Bob Kelly's Medium Rose Shadow (SL-16), Ben Nye's Character Shadow, Joe Blasco's Shading #2, Kryolan's EC4, and Mehron's Mocha Rose (RC11) are especially effective. For deep shadows, Joe Blasco's Character Gray, Mehron's Greyed Mocha (RC14), Bob Kelly's Grey Violet (SL-17), Ben Nye's Dark Brown Shadow #43, and Kryolan's 050 are all useful.

Both medium and deep gray shadow colors are also available. Any of these can, of course, be mixed with

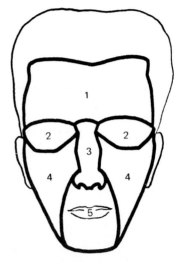

FIGURE 12–4 DIVISION OF THE FACE INTO AREAS.

other colors to lighten them, darken them, gray them, or change the basic hue. Or you can mix your own shadow color for each makeup to go with the foundation color you're using. If there is a shadow color of your own mixing that you find useful with various foundation colors, you might mix up a batch in a small flame-proof container and heat it over a gas flame, a candle, or an electric burner, then pour it into small containers or a palette (see Chapter 8) for future use.

If you are using cake makeup (dry or moist type) and have a shadow color that is not red enough, instead of mixing colors, as you would with creme or grease makeup, you can apply the shadow, then add red to it afterward by brushing on dry rouge as you are completing the makeup.

Now that you have experimented with highlights and shadows in restructuring the face as a whole and considered the problem of choosing colors for specific characters, the face will be divided into areas so that you can examine in detail the modeling of these areas. The five area divisions—forehead, eyes, nose, cheeks, and jaws—are diagrammed in Figure 12–4. Each area will then be subdivided into planes for more detailed analysis. The discussion of each area will indicate the various possible treatments of that area.

AREA 1: FOREHEAD

Planes The forehead is divided into five planes, as shown in Figure 12–5. Planes A and C are the frontal and the superciliary bones; D, the temporal hollows; and B, the slight depression between the two prominences.

A simple method of aging the forehead is to highlight and shadow these planes. The two prominences, A and

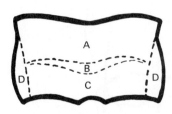

FIGURE 12—5 AREA 1: FOREHEAD.

C, catch the light (Figure 12–6A and C) and should, therefore, be highlighted. The depression, B, falling between them, may be slightly shadowed. Be careful, however, in doing a realistic makeup, not to emphasize the transverse shadow too strongly. If you are using a fairly dark foundation color, you will probably not need to add any shadow at all since the foundation color, if dark enough, will itself serve as a shadow.

The highlighting can be done with a brush, a sponge, or the fingers. Figure 12–7 illustrates the technique that can be used with a brush. A wide or an extra-wide brush should be used. If you have only narrow brushes, then use your fingers for creme or grease makeup or a sponge for cake.

For a prominent overhanging brow, carry a strong highlight all across the front plane of the superciliary arch, rather than just over the eyebrows, and shadow deeply across the bridge of the nose to sink it in.

The temples (Figure 12–6D) are nearly always shadowed for age. These shadows may be barely perceptible in middle age but are usually quite pronounced in later years. The shadows tend to be more intense at the inner edge and to lighten as they approach the hair.

In placing the highlights, keep in mind the light source on the stage. With light coming from above, a strong light will fall on the upper part of the frontal bone. If there is a horizontal division approximately in the middle of your forehead (most clearly observable in profile), the area coming forward below this division will catch another strong highlight, and the area immediately above the division will be less strongly lighted. This is the area where you may or may not wish to use a very slight shadow. When there are no wrinkles to crease the skin, all edges of highlights and shadows will be soft. If you want to make the forehead more rounded or bulging, apply the highlights and shadows in a curved pattern.

Wrinkles If you want to give the effect of a wrinkled forehead, make sure that you model the wrinkles meticulously and that you follow the natural wrinkles—otherwise, you will have a double set of wrinkles when the forehead is raised. Young people who have not yet developed any natural creases and cannot form any by raising the forehead may wish to use photographs of wrinkled foreheads as a guide.

FIGURE 12—6 FOREHEADS. *A. and C. indicate prominences that are normally highlighted for age; B., a slight depression that may or may not be lightly shadowed; and D., a depression that is usually shadowed for age.*

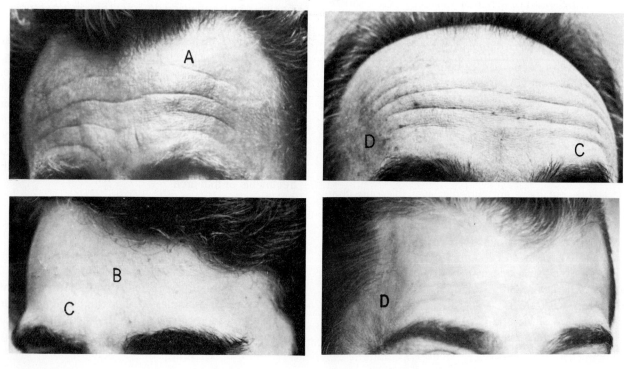

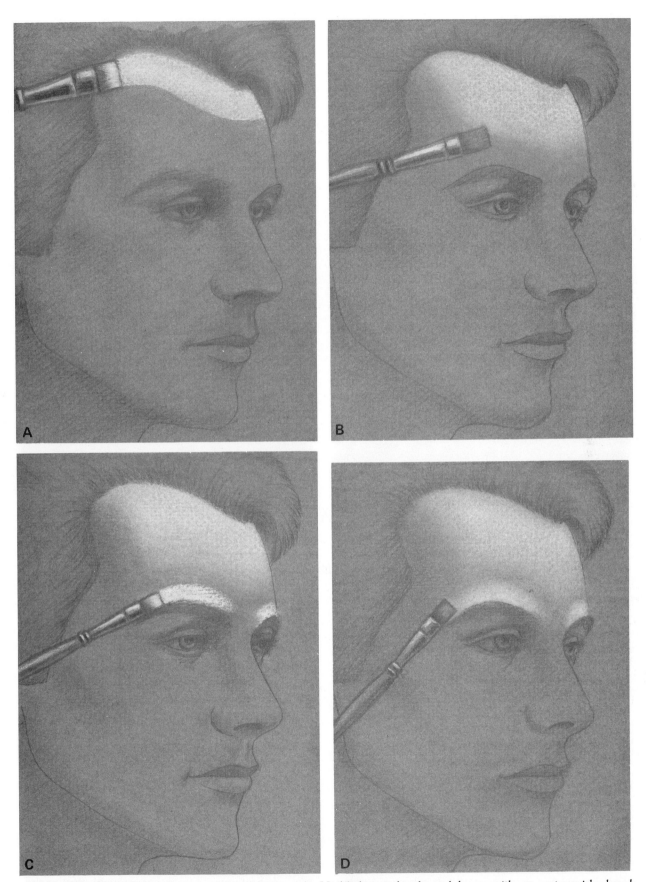

FIGURE 12-7 HIGHLIGHTING THE FOREHEAD. *A. Highlighting the frontal bone with an extra-wide brush. B. Blending the lower edge of the highlight. C. Highlighting the superciliary bone with a medium-wide brush. D. Blending the superciliary bone highlight with a clean brush. E. Highlighting the vertical edge of the frontal bone with a wide brush. F. Blending the edge of the highlight with a clean brush.*

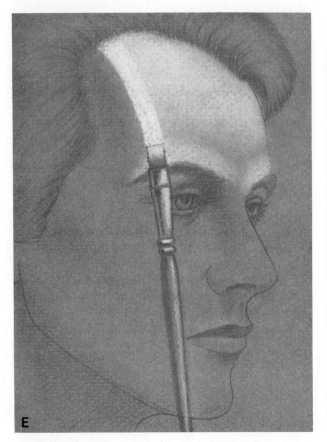

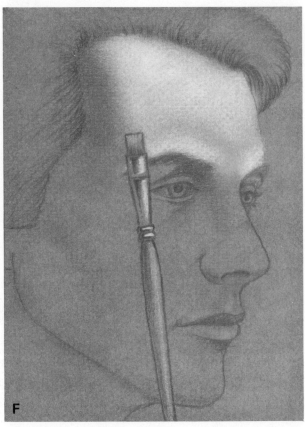

FIG. 12-7   *Cont.*

Before beginning to model forehead wrinkles, observe your own or someone else's natural wrinkles, and with your light source from above, note where the wrinkles catch the light. Is it above or below the crease? Carefully examine photographs in your morgue and those in this chapter (especially Figure 12–8) to see exactly how the light pattern falls, giving the effect of a series of half cylinders. (The lower photograph shows what happens when the light source is from below.) Once you understand the principle involved, you will never make the mistake of painting wrinkles upside down, and you will always keep your hard edges crisp and clean in order to form sharp creases. Following the steps given below may be of help:

1. Using a medium flat brush with your highlight color and holding it so that the flat end of the brush lies parallel to, and barely touches, one of the natural creases in the forehead (Figure 12–9A), draw the brush along the crease, fading the color out at each end. Make sure the paint touches the natural crease at all times but never crosses it. It is best not to try to model wrinkles with the forehead raised, since

the paint is very likely to smudge in the creases, resulting in messy edges.

2. Holding the brush in the same position (Figure 12–9B) and starting near but not *at* one end of the highlight you have just applied, move the brush along the length of the wrinkle again, almost to the end, this time pulling it downward in a series of short, vertical strokes in order to increase the width of the highlight. Be sure, however, not to make these strokes the full width you want the finished highlight to be since space must be left for blending.

3. Using a clean brush, soften the lower edge of the highlight until it blends imperceptibly into the foundation. This should be done by drawing the flat of the brush along the highlight, overlapping the edge. (See Figure 12–9C.) Repeat this until you have a good blend. If you blend downward, the highlight will tend to become too wide. However, highlights for forehead wrinkles are usually wider than the shadows because of the angle of the light source. If the light were coming from directly above, highlights and shadows would be the same width. But as the light source moves forward, the light area is naturally in-

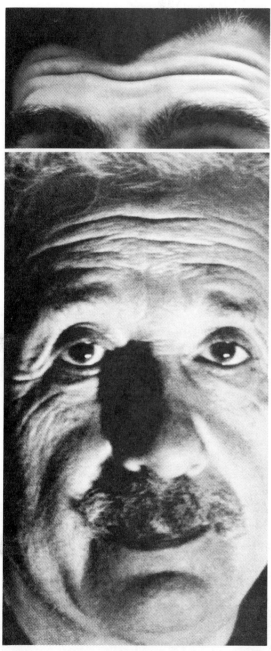

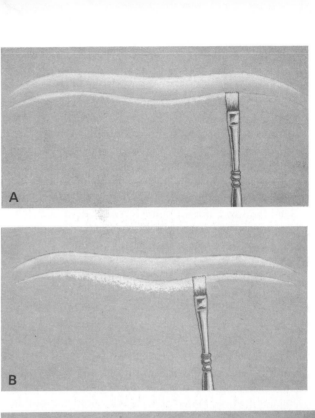

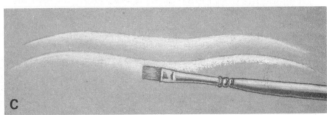

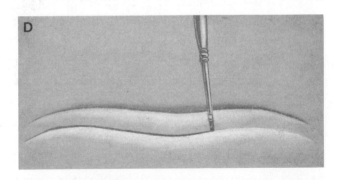

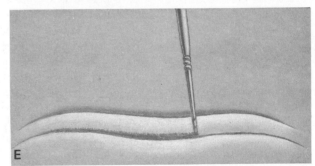

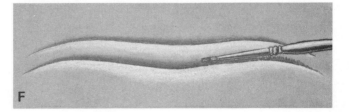

FIGURE **12–8** *FOREHEAD WRINKLES—LIGHT COMING FROM ABOVE AND FROM BELOW.* Note *the reversal of highlights and shadows as a result of the reversal of normal lighting.*

FIGURE **12–9** *MODELING FOREHEAD WRINKLES WITH PAINT.* A, B. Highlighting the wrinkle. C. Blending the highlight. D, E. Shadowing wrinkle. F. Blending shadow.

creased and the dark diminished. Observe the relative widths of highlights and shadows in Figure 12–8. Make sure that the ends of wrinkles, instead of being thick and blunt, are fine and delicate, disappearing imperceptibly into the foundation.

4. Since you must treat not only the wrinkles in a wrinkled forehead, but the entire forehead area, highlight the superciliary arch and the frontal bone, making all edges soft.

5. Using a very narrow brush, paint a line of shadow immediately adjacent to the hard edge of the highlight. (Figure 12–9D.)

6. Following the technique described for blending the highlight in step 2, pull the shadow upward, away from the crease, keeping it narrower than the highlight. (See Figure 12–9E.)

7. With a clean brush, and using the technique described for softening the edge of the highlight in step 3, blend the upper edge of the shadow into the foundation color. (See Figure 12–9F.)

8. Check your wrinkles for roundness and depth, making sure that hard edges are strong and crisp and that soft ones fade away subtly. Check also for projection—in a spotlight, if possible—and make any necessary adjustments. Then powder—unless you are using cake makeup, in which case powdering will not be necessary.

9. Unless there are reasons for its not being done (wanting a pale and bloodless look, for example), a touch of rouge should be added to the shadows and should extend into the highlights. A small, soft brush can be used to apply the rouge. If you prefer to use moist rouge, it should be applied with a narrow shading brush before the makeup is powdered.

10. If the wrinkles look too strong and obvious, stipple the entire forehead, as illustrated in Figure 12–10B, with the base color or any other color or colors you consider appropriate. Using more than one color tends to give a more natural effect. Stipple carefully, watching the effect as you go so that you don't wipe out everthing you've done. If the stippling grays the shadows too much, you can add more rouge. If you use a red stipple, extra rouge will probably not be necessary.

In making wrinkles, you may prefer to use flat-cut pencils (see Figure 12–11) for *applying* the color. For *blending* the color, however, brushes should be used, though cotton swabs (Figure 12–12) can be substituted if a proper brush is not available.

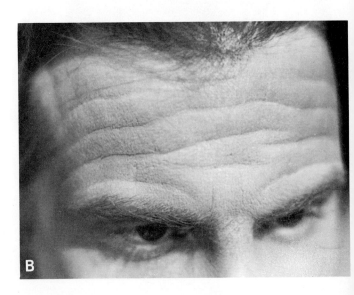

FIGURE *12–10* MODELING WRINKLES. *Makeup by student Douglas Parker. A. Applying creme-makeup highlights and shadows for forehead wrinkles. B. Forehead wrinkles powdered and stippled.*

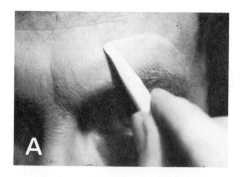

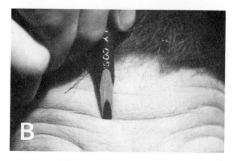

FIGURE 12–11 A. HIGHLIGHTING AND B. SHADOWING FOREHEAD WRINKLES WITH FLAT-CUT MAKEUP PENCILS.

FIGURE 12–12 BLENDING FORE-HEAD-WRINKLE HIGHLIGHTS WITH A COTTON SWAB. (Student J. C. Stahl).

AREA 2: EYES

No feature is more important in suggesting character than the eyes, and none can be changed in a greater variety of ways. Figure 12–13 illustrates a few of the changes that can be made in a single eye. For photographs of youthful eyes and eyebrows, see Figures 10–5 and 10–7; and for aged ones, Figures 12–16, 12–17, 12–18, and 12–19. In studying these photographs, always determine the light source in the photograph and make the necessary adjustments for stage lighting.

PLANE A (Figure 12–14) extends forward from the eye to the bridge of the nose and is nearly always shadowed for age. It is seldom highlighted except for Oriental makeups or for counteracting heavy shadows in deepset eyes. The center of this plane is usually one of the darkest parts of the whole orbital area. (See Figure 12–13F.) The lower edge fades into the shadow on the side of the nose. The outer edge is soft and turns into a highlight on the bridge of the nose. The inner edge is always soft, fading into plane B. In general, the greater the age, the deeper this shadow. A medium or a wide brush can be used for this area.

PLANE B is a transition area that is either left the base color or included with A. In the latter case, the shadow of A is usually lightened as it crosses B and approaches C.

PLANE C is often rouged for youthful makeups and is usually highlighted for age makeups (Figures 12–13F, 12–15A and H–6A). In old age, the skin in plane C may sag and actually cover a part of the open eye. (See Figures 12–16A and 12–18C and G.) Although we cannot do that with paint, we can approach the effect by strongly highlighting C_1 and shadowing the lower edge of C_2 (Figure 12–25A). A medium or a wide brush can be used for C_1 and a narrow one for C_2. If the light is coming from above, the lightest part of the highlight will be nearest the eyebrow—in other words, on the superciliary bone where it forms the outer edge of the eye socket. It will gradually recede into a soft shadow as it approaches the B–C division, whether or not a fold is to be made. (See Figure 12–13F.)

The deepest part of the shadow is at the bottom of the area, and it turns very gradually into a highlight as it approaches C_1. The dotted line indicates only a general division of the whole plane, not a specific one. The inner edge of plane C is a definite division, however, and should be heavily shadowed if sagging flesh is to be represented. If not, then the transition to B is a gradual one.

It is usually best to use two colors for the narrow shadow that creates the impression of a fold of flesh. With the basic shading color, a medium shadow can be applied along the division between B and C and blended carefully to form two soft edges. Then the simulated crease

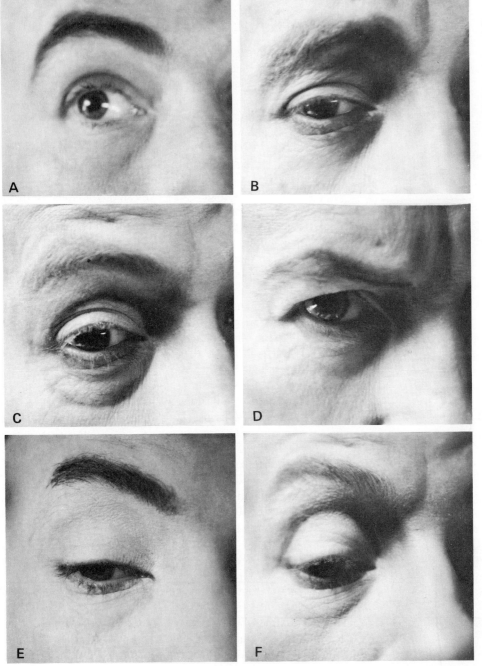

FIGURE **12–13** CHANGING THE EYE WITH MAKEUP. *All makeups are on the same eye. Cake makeup used throughout, except for darkening the brows and lining the eye in E. Outer end of the brow in E. was blocked out with spirit gum.*

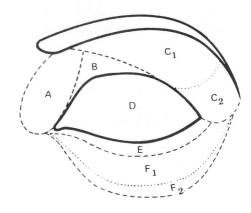

FIGURE **12–14** DIVISION OF THE ORBITAL AREA INTO PLANES FOR HIGHLIGHTING AND SHADOWING.

 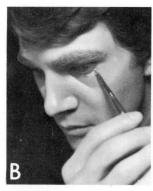 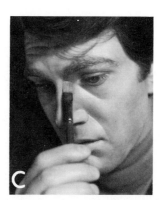 

FIGURE 12–15 MODELING FOR THE ORBITAL AREA. *(Actor Eugene Bicknell.) A. Highlighting plane C with a medium brush. B. Highlighting plane F with a narrow brush. The top edge should be hard. (The highlight under plane F_2 is actually part of the nasolabial fold and will be illustrated in that section.) C. Shadowing plane A of the eye with a medium-wide brush. D. Shadowing plane F of the eye with a medium brush.*

can be deepened with a darker shadow. This deep shadow should also be lightly blended. If the whole orbital area is to appear sunken, then plane C may be shadowed rather than highlighted.

Frequently, wrinkles (commonly known as crow's feet) cut across the outer edge of plane C_2, as in Figure 12–18F. If you use these wrinkles, be sure to make them true wrinkles, not lines (see discussion of forehead wrinkles). Model the wrinkles first with highlights, using a ⅛-inch brush or an eyeliner brush, then add the shadows with an eyeliner or a pointed Chinese brush, keeping the creases very sharp and clear.

PLANE D is the eyelid itself and may be either highlighted (Figure H–3D) or shadowed. If the whole eye is to appear sunken, plane D may be shadowed; but if the eyeball itself protrudes, catching the light, D should be highlighted and the upper division between it and the other areas deeply shadowed. (See Figure 12–13F.) When D catches a highlight, C_1 normally does too (Figure 12–16B), though there may be a deep shadow between the areas.

PLANE D is sometimes highlighted in the same way for glamor makeups, with the eyeshadow used only on the lower part, close to the eye. For either age or glamor, the actor may, at times, want to create the effect of a more prominent lid than he has naturally. This can often be faked quite successfully with paint. (See Figure 17–11.) With a medium brush and your highlight color, draw the enlarged lid on the natural eyelid in approximately the pattern shown in Figure 12–13F. Then, with a deep shadow, outline the new lid and, with a medium brush, shadow upward toward the eyebrow, just as you would if there were a natural crease. The secret of modeling this false eyelid convincingly is to make the shadow edge very dark so that it gives the effect of a deep crease. (See Figure 17–10H.) The effect is more convincing if the eye is not opened too wide.

If the character would be wearing eyeshadow, it will usually be concentrated largely on plane D, though fashion has sometimes decreed that the color be extended over the whole orbital area. In any case, for realistic plays, if the eyeshadow is supposed to be apparent, the placement and the color should be determined on the basis of what choice the character would make. Would she follow the latest fashion or would she not? (If she would, what *was* the latest fashion at the time?) Would she choose a conspicuous color or a conservative one? (A color that might seem conservative in one period might be conspicuous in another.) Would she take care to avoid colors that clashed with her costume or wouldn't she? (Eyeshadow colors that do clash with the costume can be somewhat jarring and should be used only when that effect is intended.) Would she wear false eyelashes or wouldn't she? (If she wouldn't, don't let the eyelashes be obviously false.)

To give the effect of weak eyes, which may accompany extreme old age, the lower part of D and all of Plane E can be rouged with a narrow brush. Using red around the eye opening tends to give an effect of age or weakness of the eyes (Figure H–7I) or may indicate that the character has been crying. In using red around the eyes, apply and remove it with great care so as not to get any into the eyes. And never under any circumstances use *any* makeup inside the lashes, next to the eye itself. If there is a warning on any particular red makeup not to use it around the eye, use another shade of red or another form of red makeup that is not considered unsuitable for use in that area.

PLANE E is usually shadowed for age (see Figure 12–22F), the division between E and F usually having a fairly hard edge. Since a strong shadow under the eye (plane E) tends to add strength, it should usually not be very pronounced for extreme old age. Rouging helps give an appearance of weakness and age. As noted earlier, any red makeup this close to the eye should be applied and removed very carefully.

PLANE F is seldom shadowed in its entirety. Usually the shadow starts at the inner corner of the eye (Figure 12–21I), then fades out along the lower edge, never reaching the outer corner. This can be done with a single shadow color (Figure 12–13B, D, and F) or with two. A deep shadow color (dark brown, gray violet, or dark gray) can be added—also beginning under the inner corner of the eye but fading out sooner than the medium shadow. A medium or a medium-narrow brush can be used. (See Figure 12–15D.) Be careful not to shadow plane F too heavily unless you mean to suggest dissipation, illness, or lack of sleep.

The whole F plane sometimes becomes rather wrinkled (Figure 12–18F), and diagonal wrinkles may cut across the lower edge of F_2 on the side away from the nose (Figure 12–18A). These should be carefully modeled like tiny cylinders. An eyeliner brush or the narrowest available flat brush can be used. If you want plane F slightly puffy, it can be highlighted as shown in Figure 12–15B, using a narrow brush. This same kind of highlight is used when making a full pouch (see the following section).

The secret of shading the various planes of the eye effectively lies in a constant variation of intensity of shadow and highlight and in some variation in color. Not one of these areas should ever be flatly shadowed or flatly highlighted. You should start your shading at the point of maximum intensity, then decrease it gradually in other parts of the area. The use of two colors in the shadow and the addition of rouge can be very helpful in achieving a convincing effect.

EYE POUCHES

In order to make a pouch (Figures 12–16, 12–17, 12–18, 12–19 and 12–20), highlight F_1 and shadow F_2 as if you were modeling a half cylinder that ended abruptly along the bottom edge of F_2. The entire lower edge of F_2 should be hard, with a deep shadow that blends up across F_2 and turns into a highlight on F_1. The division between F_1 and F_2 should always be a soft edge. The cheek area below the pouch will catch light coming from above and will therefore be strongly highlighted.

One of the secrets of making a convincing pouch is to keep the shadow heaviest at the bottom, where the fold of skin naturally falls, creating a deep shadow, and to let it become thinner and thinner, usually fading out almost completely before it reaches the corner of the eye (Figure 12–22K). The fact that these subtle variations must be made in a very small area means that pouches, in order to be convincing, should be modeled with care and precision, keeping the hard edge clean and sharp.

Always use both a medium and a deep shadow, and make sure the pouches look rounded at the bottom, where the sagging skin turns under. A flatly painted shadow will look exactly like paint, not like a pouch.

If you have the beginning of a natural pouch of your own, it will be easy to determine the correct size and shape. If you do not, then you should decide on the basis of what seems to fit in best with your eye.

Following is a step-by-step procedure for modeling a relatively simple eye pouch with paint, as illustrated in Figure 12–22. Other pouches will require a similar technique, with some variations, depending on the particular effect desired.

1. Very carefully highlight the area around the pouch (Figure 12–22A), keeping the edge of the highlight next to the pouch very strong and sharp and clean. Pull the highlight away from the edge, as illustrated in Figure 12–22B. Then, with a clean brush, soften the lower edge of the highlight so that it disappears into the foundation color. (See Figure 12–22C.) This highlight should be modeled with a medium or a medium-wide flat brush. Holding the brush as shown in Figure 12–22A will give you a clean, sharp edge.

2. Highlight the inside of the pouch with a narrow brush, as shown in Figure 12–22D. If the lower lid (plane E) is going to be shadowed, the highlight can begin at the division between E and F, with a definite edge. If the lower lid is puffy and becomes part of the pouch (Figure 12–17H), the upper edge will be immediately below the eyelashes. In either case, soften the lower edge of the highlight in order to make a gradual transition—as if you were modeling a tiny half cylinder. This can be done either by stroking it gently with a clean narrow brush or by patting it lightly with a cotton swab.

3. With a medium shadow, model the fullness at the bottom of the pouch, keeping the lower edge very clean and sharp and letting the upper edge fade out toward the highlight (Figure 12–22E). This fading out can be done, as with the highlight, by using either a clean narrow brush or a cotton swab. (For an alternative procedure for steps 3 and 4, see the paragraphs following step 10.)

4. With your deepest shadow color and your smallest brush, deepen just the bottom edge (not the side edges) of the pouch (Figure 12–22G), then pull the paint upward slightly to soften the upper edge of the shadow. Have the courage to make this shadow extremely dark. (Note the darkness of this lower edge in Figure 12–17B and F.)

5. At this point you may wish to add a touch of rouge to the area between the shadow and the upper highlight, using a small brush. Or you can add the rouge later. (See step 10.)

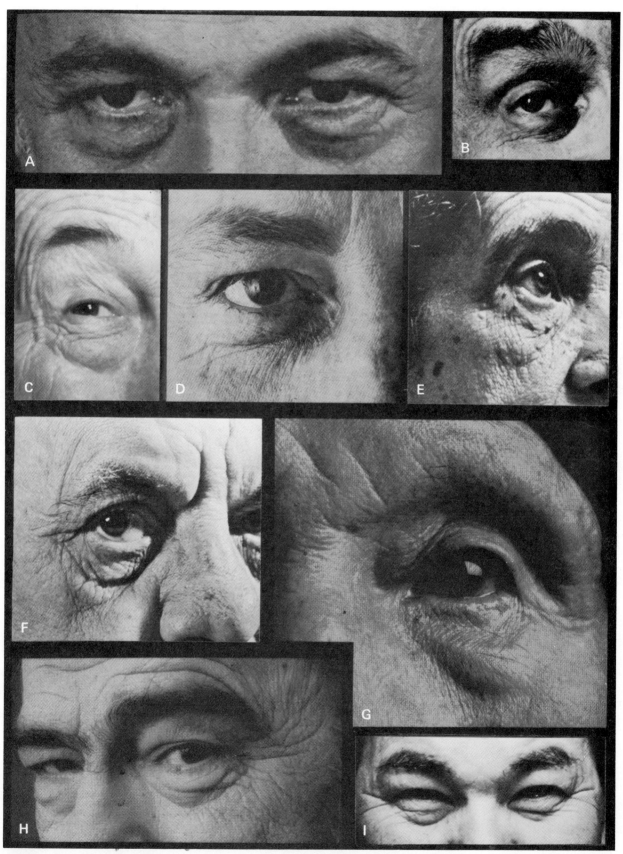

FIGURE **12–16** *EYES AND EYE-BROWS.*

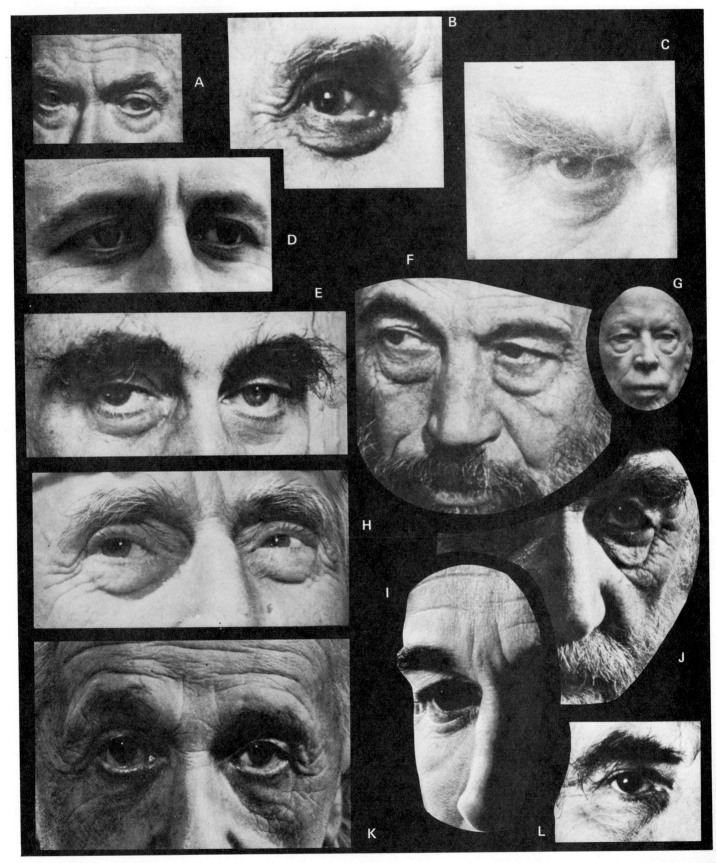

FIGURE **12—17** EYES AND EYE-
BROWS.

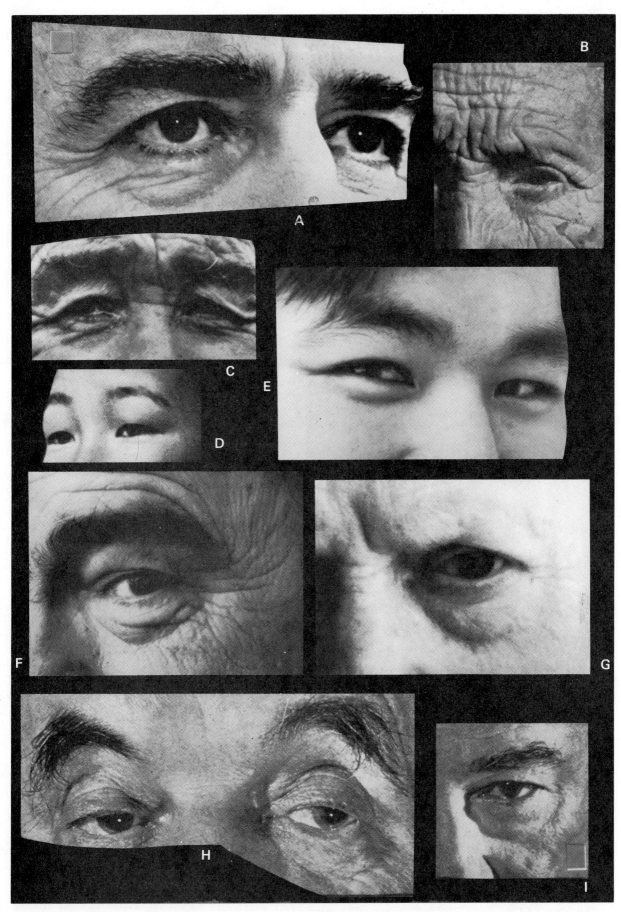

FIGURE **12–18** EYES AND EYE-
BROWS.

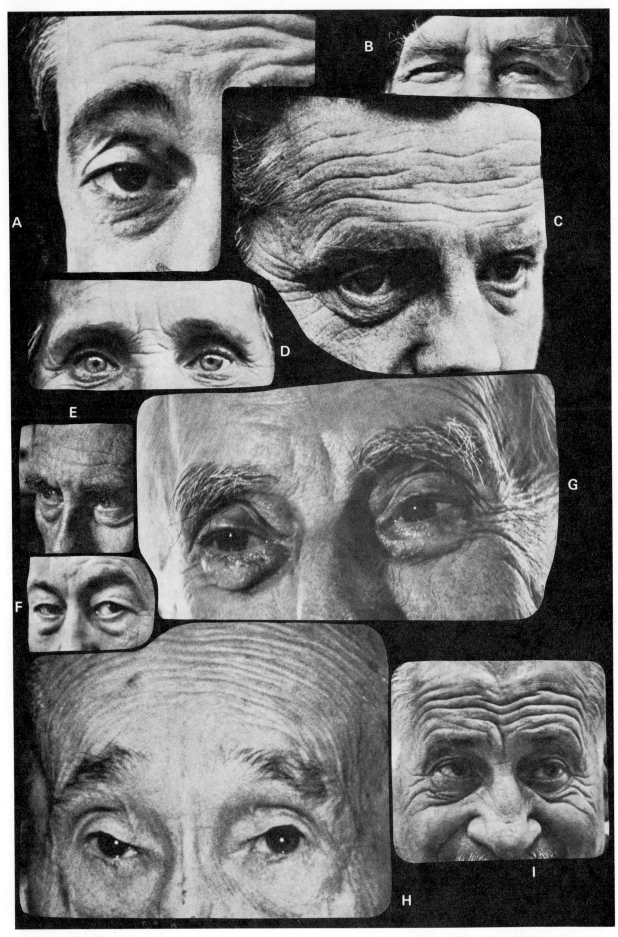

FIGURE **12–19** EYES AND EYE-
BROWS.

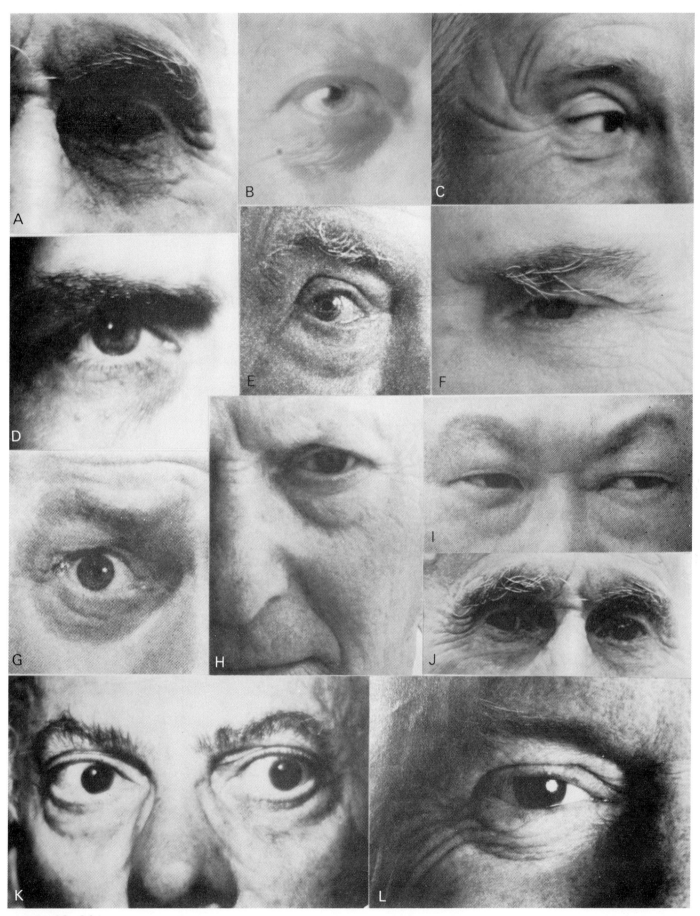

FIGURE **12–20** *MALE EYES AND EYE-BROWS*

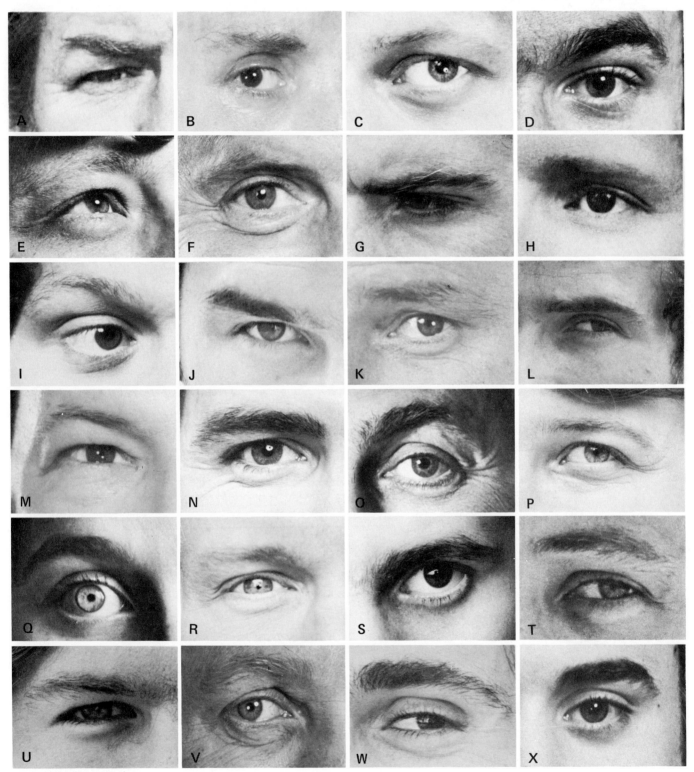

FIGURE **12–21** *MALE EYES AND EYE-BROWS.*

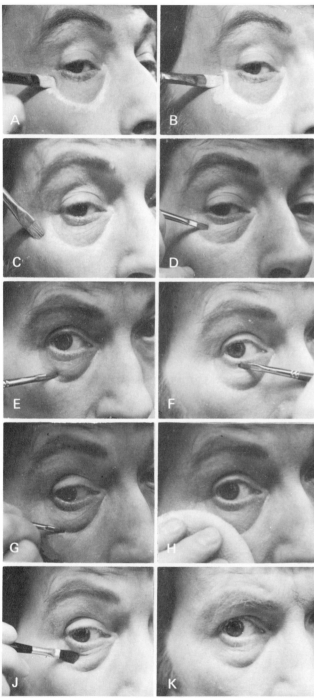

FIGURE 12–22 MODELING A DEEP EYE POUCH. *A. Outlining pouch with highlighting, using medium brush. B. Widening highlight by pulling paint away from hard edge. C. Softening outer edge of highlight with clean brush. D. Highlighting top of pouch with small brush. E. Shadowing bottom of pouch with medium shadow. F. Shadowing lower lid with medium shadow. G. Deepening bottom edge of pouch with very dark shadow. H. Powdering pouch. J. Adding dry rouge with soft eyeshadow brush. K. Finished pouch, after stippling. Stippling is used here primarily to add texture.*

6. If the lower lid (Figure 12–14E) is not actually part of the pouch itself, as in Figure 12–17A, it is usually shadowed. This can be done with a flat brush approximately the same width as the lower lid. It's usually best to begin at the outer corner of the eye and brush across the lid, allowing the shadow to fade out a bit as it approaches the inner corner of the eye. (See Figure 12–22F.) If, however, it is to be puffy (Figure 12–20I), it can be modeled like a wrinkle or a miniature pouch.

7. Powder the pouch with a puff, and remove excess powder with a powder brush. (If you are using cake makeup, this step will, of course, not be necessary.)

8. If the pouch looks too smooth for wrinkled skin in the rest of the face, or if the contrasts are too strong for the rest of the makeup, stipple it very carefully with your sponge.

9. The stippling should now be powdered.

10. If you have not added creme rouge in step 5, or if you have and it is not strong enough, brush the lower part of the pouch with dry rouge, using a small eyeshadow brush. (See Figure H–5A.)

It is possible to vary this technique for modeling pouches by substituting red for the medium shadow. Highlights are applied as usual (steps 1 and 2). The variation comes in step 3. Instead of applying a medium shadow, model the area with red, bringing the color up a bit higher than you normally would for the shadow. This color can then serve as the red between the shadow and the highlight, thus eliminating step 5.

For step 4, instead of using a brush, you can, if you prefer, use a dark pencil that will be compatible in color with your deep shadow. In working with a conventionally sharpened pencil, draw your hard edge with the point, then shade with the side of the lead. With a flat-cut pencil (Figure 12–11B), run the sharp edge along the crease to form a hard edge, then pull the pencil upward, away from the crease, to complete the shadow in the same manner that you would use a flat brush. In shading with your pencil, decrease the pressure of the pencil as you move away from the hard edge, then blend the edge with a clean brush to soften it.

Check your morgue and the various illustrations in this book for other types of eye pouches and for ideas on aging the eyes without the use of pouches.

ORIENTAL EYES

Because Oriental eyes require very special treatment, it will be more practical to consider them separately. An examination of photographs of Oriental eyes will show that they are occasionally quite slanted (Figure 10–5Q), more often slightly slanted (Figure 12–18E), and sometimes not slanted at all (Figure 12–18D).

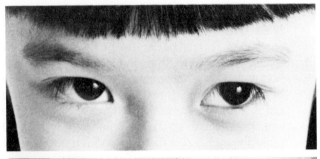

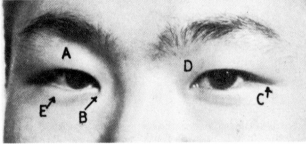

FIGURE 12—23 ORIENTAL EYES. *B. is the epicanthic fold.*

The lid itself ordinarily disappears completely under a fold of flesh that is really an extension of planes A, B, and C in Figure 12–14. (See Figure 12–23A.) This fold overlaps the lower lid slightly at the tear duct (Figure 12–23B). It is this *epicanthic fold* that is particularly characteristic of Orientals. Sometimes there is also an overlap at the outer corner of the eye (Figure 12–23C).

One of the most striking characteristics of the Oriental eyes is the flatness of the orbital area. Because the eye itself is prominent and the bridge of the nose is not built

up, the dip between the two (plane A) is likely to be relatively slight (Figure 12–23D).

If the Oriental eye is to be achieved with paint alone, it is usually necessary to highlight the entire orbital area, and especially plane A, in order to bring the eye forward and counteract the natural shadows. Sometimes there is a slightly puffy effect in plane E (Figure 12–23E). If you wish to create this effect you can model it as a pouch or as a transverse wrinkle with the usual shadow and highlight.

In addition to the highlighting, two small shadows are necessary. One is a crescent-shaped shadow at the tear duct, which gives the illusion of the epicanthic fold. This shadow must be precisely placed, as shown in Figure 12–13E. The second shadow is placed on the outer third of the upper lid and may extend very little beyond the eye. For women who would be using makeup, a slight upward curve to this shadow is often effective.

The eyebrows normally are slanted slightly upward or are rather short and relatively straight. Instead of following the eye downward in a curve, as is usual for youthful brows in Caucasians (Figure 12–13A), Oriental brows may taper off quite abruptly at the ends (Figure 12–13E). There are, however, variations. (See Figures 10–5Q, and 12–23.) For aged Oriental eyes, see Figure 12–24.

For Caucasian eyes that do not adapt easily to this painting technique, three-dimensional makeup (Chapter 13) may be required.

Orientals who wish to play Caucasians can shadow plane A, simulate a tear duct with makeup, using a touch of red for the mucous membrane, and extend their eyebrows downward (Figure 12–74B). They may or may not find it necessary to highlight planes B and C and

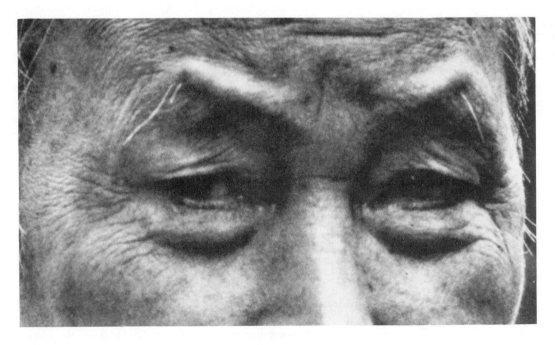

FIGURE 12—24 EYES OF AN ELDERLY CHINESE.

shadow the division between them. Slanting eyes, unless they are very pronounced, are not always a problem, for Caucasian eyes are sometimes slanted. But if they *are* a problem, the slant can be counteracted to some extent by bringing the shadow at the outer corner of the eye downward instead of upward.

EYEBROWS

Changing the eyebrows for corrective makeup has been dealt with in Chapter 10. But besides having the potential for making the face more attractive, eyebrows provide a particularly useful means of characterization. Figure 12–13 illustrates a few such changes that can be made with an eyebrow pencil, paint, and an eyebrow brush in order to age the eye as well as to suggest character. (See also Figure 12–25.)

But using the eyebrows to suggest character can be just as important in makeups for youth as for age. Figure 6–6A, for example, shows a straight (not a corrective) makeup with no changes for character. In B and C the eyebrows and the eyeshadowing have been changed—not to improve the face or to age it but to create a look more appropriate for a specific character. In this case, the principles of optical illusions for making eyes appear farther apart and closer together (see Figure 10–3) have been used. Note how the general look of the face has been altered as a result of this relatively simple change. And note also what character impressions each change creates.

In determining what you want to do with the eyebrows for characters of any age, it's a good idea to manipulate the natural eyebrows with your fingers, as previously suggested in Chapter 10 and illustrated in Figure 12–26, in order to help determine the effect on the face of different eyebrow shapes and positions. Unless your eyebrows (or those of your subject) are unusually adaptable, you might do well to add hair to them, cover them completely with additional hair, or block them out (Figure 12–27) by one of the methods suggested below or others you may devise. If part of the natural brow can be used, you may prefer to block out only the part that needs to be eliminated, as was done in Figure 12–13E, for example.

In blocking out the brows, the problem is twofold—to flatten the hairs against the skin so that they will stay down for the duration of the performance and to cover the flattened hairs by some method that will conceal their color, using a flesh tone to match the rest of the skin.

Blocking Out with Soap In soaping, rub a moistened bar of soap repeatedly over the brows, which must be free of grease, until they are flattened down. In flattening the brows, spread the hairs with a fine-tooth comb, as shown in Figure 12–32B. When they are dry, cover them with a heavy coat of greasepaint or creme stick or, preferably, with rubber-mask grease. Make very sure that you blend the paint carefully into the skin at the edge to prevent the outline of the brows from becoming obvious when the makeup is finished. Then press powder into the paint and remove the excess with a powder brush. If the brows still show through, add alternate layers of paint and powder until they are effectively blocked out. If the brows are heavy, one or more coats of plastic sealer can be applied over the dried soap. For firm adhesion, be sure to spread the sealer beyond the soaped area. Apply the makeup over the dried sealer. Unless the brows are very light, soaping is probably the least satisfactory method of covering them, since with this method the hairs are more likely to loosen during a performance, allowing the brows to become visible. The brows in Figure 18–2 have been soaped out.

Blocking Out with Spirit Gum A more effective method than soaping is to flatten the hairs with spirit gum. Brush the gum well into the brows, comb the hairs upward at an angle onto the forehead, then when the gum is very tacky, press the brows down with a damp cloth so that they will lie flat and give as smooth a surface as possible. When the spirit gum is dry, it should be covered with sealer in order to keep the paint from loosening the gum. Rubber-mask grease, greasepaint, or creme stick can then be stippled over the brow, using more than one coat if necessary. Cake makeup should not be used; it will not adhere properly to sealer.

The spirit gum can be removed with alcohol or spirit-gum remover or, if necessary, with acetone. Be very careful, however, not to let the liquid run down into the eyes. The safest procedure is to dampen cotton or a cloth with the remover, then bend over so that the eyebrow is lower than the eye *before* removing the spirit gum. Or you can use a makeup remover that will remove both makeup and spirit gum. (See *Makeup removers* in Appendix A.)

Blocking Out with Wax You can also mat the brows down with derma wax or, preferably, with Kryolan's stick of Eyebrow Plastic (Figure 12–28), blending the wax carefully into the skin at the edges, then covering it with one or two coats of sealer. If the brows are very heavy, it may help if you flatten them with spirit gum and let it dry before applying the wax, in order to help keep the wax from loosening. In flattening them, spread the hairs with a comb (Figure 12–32B). After the sealer over the wax is dry, makeup can be applied. Rubber-mask greasepaint gives the best coverage.

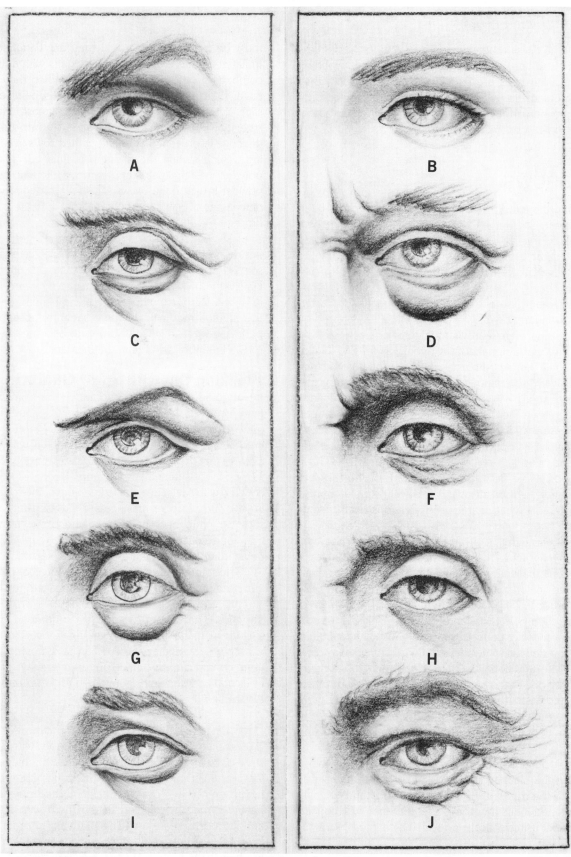

FIGURE 12–25 **CHANGING THE EYE.** *Ten sketches of possible makeups for the same eye. All of the changes can be made by blocking out all or part of the eyebrow in A and creating a new brow and by remodeling the eye area with highlights and shadows.*

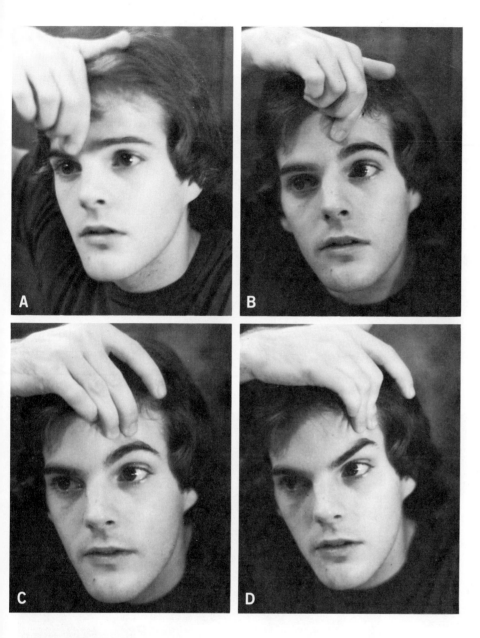

FIGURE **12–26** MANIPULATING THE NATURAL EYEBROW BEFORE BEGINNING THE MAKEUP. *A simple method of selecting the most appropriate shape and position of the eyebrows for the character. (Demonstrated by actor Jeffrey Hillock.)*

FIGURE **12–27** SIXTEENTH-CENTURY LADY. *Eyebrows blocked out. Putty-wax nose. Makeup by student Carolyn Bain.*

FIGURE **12–28** BLOCKING OUT EYEBROWS WITH KRYOLAN'S EYEBROW PLASTIC. *(Student Kitty Reilly.)*

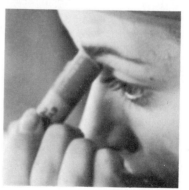

95

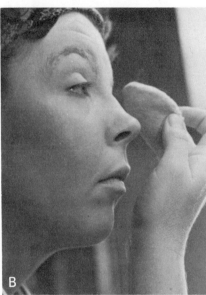
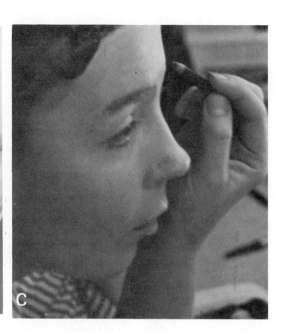

FIGURE 12–29 PARTIALLY BLOCKING OUT EYEBROWS. *Makeup by student Margaret Spicer. A. Both ends of the brows have been flattened with Kryolan's Eyebrow Plastic, then covered with sealer. Flattened sections are being covered with rubbermask grease and will then be powdered, covered with the creme makeup foundation and another application of powder. B. New eyebrows being sketched on with a brown eyebrow pencil. C. Eyes being lined with a brush. The lines will then be softened for a more natural look. D. Finished makeup, based on a photograph of the Duchess of Marlborough, 1905.*

FIGURE **12–30** *BLOCKED OUT EYEBROWS.* *Makeup by student Debbie Hobbs. A. Eyebrows have been blocked out with Kryolan's Eyebrow Plastic, then covered with sealer and creme stick and powdered. (Hair at temples was blocked out later.) New eyebrows are being sketched on very lightly with a small brush. A brush is being used instead of a pencil in order not to damage the eyebrow cover. B. Finished makeup. White highlights used over a pink creme-stick foundation (mixture of SR-2-b and S-9-d). A mixture of PR-12-g, O-18-e, and RS-10-d was used for shadows. For the cheek color, RS-10-d was mixed with PR-12-g. Red was added to the mixture for the lip color.*

Blocking Out with Plastic Film Eyebrows can also be blocked out by covering them with plastic film (see Appendix A). These are the steps involved:

1. Prepare the plastic film by painting liquid plastic (see Appendix A) on glass (Figure 12–31A) or any smooth surface, such as formica, that will not be affected by the plastic, or on the outside of a grapefruit (Figure 12–31C), an orange, or even a large lemon. For eyebrow covers, the fruit is preferable since it gives a simulated skin texture. The plastic can be applied with a brush (Figure 12–31A), an orangewood stick (Figure 12–31C), or a glass rod. Using a rod or an orangewood stick saves cleaning the brush. Three coats of the plastic should be sufficient. Each coat should be thoroughly dry before another coat is applied. In order to avoid trimming, paint the plastic on the glass or the fruit in the shape and size required to cover the eyebrow, overlapping it all around.

2. When the plastic is dry, powder it, then lift one end with tweezers or a fingernail. Powder the underside as you pull it up (Figure 12–31B and D).

3. Cover the eyebrow with eyebrow paste, derma wax, or spirit gum (Figure 12–32A). Then comb the brow upward (Figure 12–32B), spread the hairs, and press them flat against the skin.

4. Press powder into the flattened brows (Figure 12–32C). If the brows are dark, it may be helpful to stipple the brows with a little makeup. Confine the makeup to the brows, and keep it off the surrounding skin. If grease or creme makeup has been used for this stippling, powder again.

5. Apply spirit gum to the skin around the brow (Figure 12–32D) or to the plastic piece, then very carefully lay the plastic piece over the brow (Figure 12–32E), making sure there are no wrinkles or rippling of the edges. Press the plastic down firmly with a damp sponge.

6. Using a small brush dipped in acetone, go over the edges of the plastic (Figure 12–32F) in order to dissolve them and blend the plastic into the skin. (If you are going to apply three-dimensional eyebrows—crepe hair or real hair ventilated on lace—it should be done at this point.)

7. Stipple your makeup (rubber-mask greasepaint gives

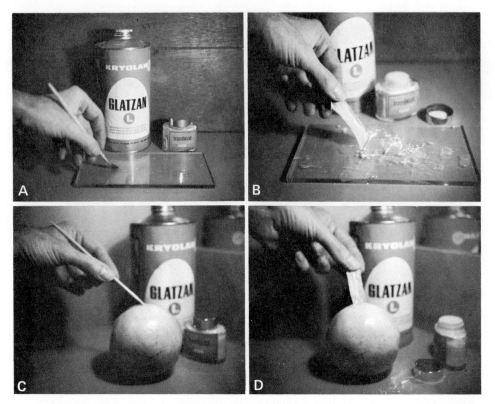

FIGURE 12–31 MAKING PLASTIC FILM FOR COVERING EYEBROWS. *A. Painting liquid plastic on glass. B. Removing dry and powdered film. C. Spreading liquid plastic on grapefruit. D. Removing dry and powdered film.*

the best coverage) over the plastic and onto the skin area around it (Figure 12–32G),then powder, pressing the powder into the makeup with a puff. Remove the excess powder with a powder brush (Figure 12–32H). If the makeup is not covering adequately, stipple on more makeup, then powder again.

Blocking Out with Fabric   Instead of using plastic film, you can follow the same procedure using peach, pink, or beige chiffon, organza de soie, or sheer nylon stocking material obtained by cutting up old nylons. The technique is very similar to that for blocking out with plastic film:

1. Cut your chiffon (or other fabric) large enough to cover the eyebrow, allowing at least 3/16- or 1/4-inch of material around the eyebrow for attaching the fabric to the skin. This can be done by holding the fabric over the brow and marking with an eyebrow pencil or a soft-lead pencil the outline of the area to be covered. Or a paper pattern can be made in the same way, then cut, tested (on both eyebrows), and adjusted before using it to cut the fabric. Then hold the fabric over the eyebrow (Figure 12–33A) to make sure it fits properly.
2. Comb the eyebrows upward, then flatten them against the skin with Kryolan's Eyebrow Plastic (Fig-

ure 12–32A), derma wax, or spirit gum. Recomb (Figure 12–32B), making sure the hairs are pressed flat against the skin.
3. Press powder into the flattened brows (Figure 12–32C).
4. Apply spirit gum to the brows and the area of skin around them to be covered by the fabric (Figure 12–33B).
5. Place the fabric carefully over the gummed area, and press it firmly into the gum with a damp sponge.
6. When the spirit gum is dry, brush liquid sealer over the fabric (Figure 12–33C). (If you are going to apply three-dimensional eyebrows—crepe hair or real hair ventilated on lace—it should be done at this point.)
7. Stipple the eyebrow covers and a bit of the area around them with makeup—preferably rubber-mask grease (Figure 12–33D). Then be sure to blend the edges of the stipple makeup smoothly into the surrounding skin. You may wish to apply the entire foundation color at this point.
8. Press powder into the makeup (Figure 12–33E). Remove excess powder with a powder brush.
9. If the edges of the fabric or any irregularities in the surface of the fabric are obvious, stipple the area with two or three colors, using a black stipple sponge. If you are going to stipple the entire makeup, you can wait and do all the stippling at once. Powder each color of stipple before adding another.

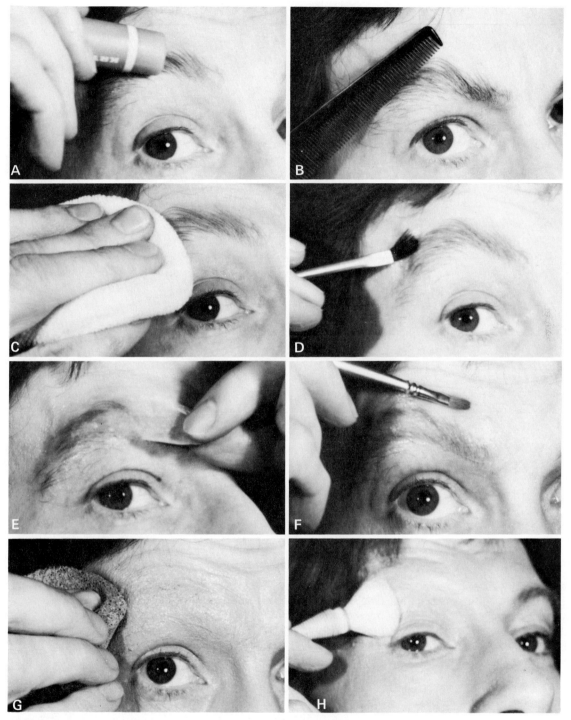

FIGURE 12–32 BLOCKING OUT EYEBROW WITH PLASTIC FILM. *A. Covering brow with Kryolan's Eyebrow Plastic. B. Combing hair upward to flatten it. C. Pressing powder into the flattened brow. D. Painting spirit gum around eyebrow. E. Covering eyebrow with plastic film. F. Dissolving edges of plastic film with acetone for blending. G. Stippling rubber-mask grease over brow area. H. Dusting powder off blocked-out brow.*

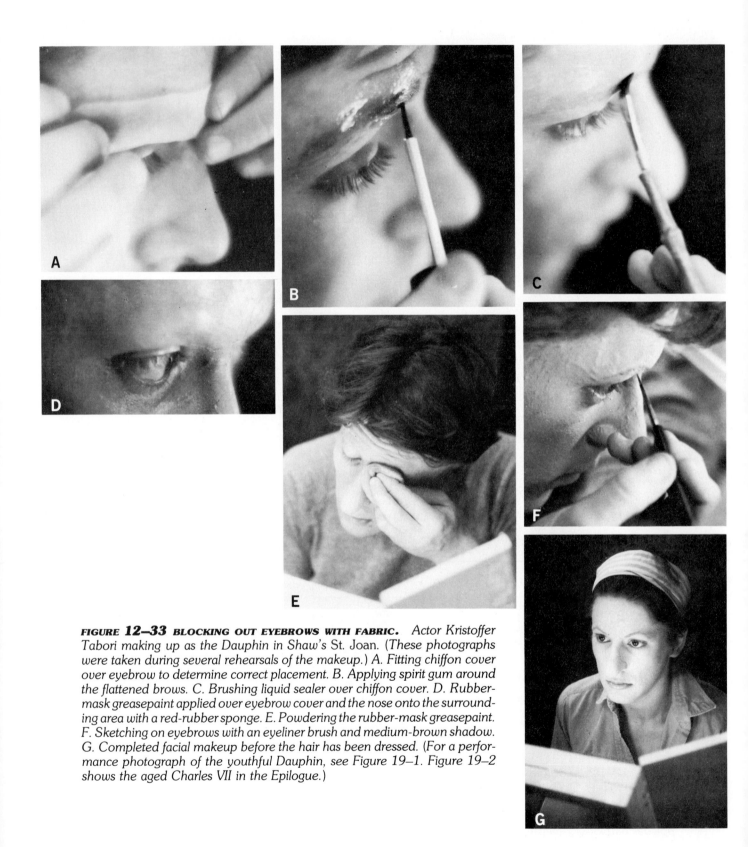

FIGURE **12–33** *BLOCKING OUT EYEBROWS WITH FABRIC.* Actor Kristoffer Tabori making up as the Dauphin in Shaw's St. Joan. (These photographs were taken during several rehearsals of the makeup.) A. Fitting chiffon cover over eyebrow to determine correct placement. B. Applying spirit gum around the flattened brows. C. Brushing liquid sealer over chiffon cover. D. Rubber-mask greasepaint applied over eyebrow cover and the nose onto the surrounding area with a red-rubber sponge. E. Powdering the rubber-mask greasepaint. F. Sketching on eyebrows with an eyeliner brush and medium-brown shadow. G. Completed facial makeup before the hair has been dressed. (For a performance photograph of the youthful Dauphin, see Figure 19–1. Figure 19–2 shows the aged Charles VII in the Epilogue.)

FIGURE 12–34 PAINTING EYES FOR NEFERTITI. *Eyebrows have been flattened with Kryolan's Eyebrow Plastic and covered with sealer and creme makeup foundation. Eyebrows have been painted on, and the eyes are being outlined with a brush. Makeup by student Kitty Reilly.*

If you are going to paint or pencil on eyebrows (Figure 12–33F), that can be done now.

Painted Eyebrows In addition to coloring the natural brows and filling out and reshaping them with pencil, it is possible to pencil or paint certain types of eyebrows over natural brows that have been blocked out. (See Figures 12–27, 12–29, 12–30, and 12–34). If the penciling is to give the illusion of natural hairs, it should be carefully done with short, light, sketchy strokes in order to avoid a flat, painted look.

Crepe-Hair Eyebrows Crepe hair can be added to the natural brows or applied over brows that have already been blocked out. When using hair to fill out the natural brows, add a few hairs at a time, touching the ends with spirit gum and putting them in place with a pair of tweezers. The added hairs can be trimmed after the spirit gum has dried.

When the brows are to be blocked out with spirit gum, crepe hair can be attached to the whole spirit-gummed brow or to any part of it while the gum is still tacky. In fact, if any part of the natural brow is to be covered by a false brow of at least equal thickness, it is usually best to attach the crepe hair, a few hairs at a time, directly to the gummed area rather than to apply the whole false brow over a blocked-out one. The makeup to cover any exposed part of the natural brow can be applied after the false brow is securely in place.

For natural-looking crepe-hair eyebrows, it is usually best to mix at least two colors. If you want the hair to have a natural sheen, you can apply a small amount of brilliantine, hair dressing, petroleum jelly, or even cold cream to the surface of the brows. If you want smooth, neat-looking brows, comb very carefully, pull out loose hairs, and trim away scraggly ones. Further instructions for using crepe hair can be found in Chapter 15.

Ventilated Eyebrows When false eyebrows are to be used for a number of performances, real or synthetic hair ventilated on lace is more satisfactory than crepe hair. Instructions for ventilating are given in Chapter 16.

Aging the Eyebrows In aging the eyebrows, first decide exactly what effect you want, then determine how that can best be achieved. The brows may take a variety of forms. They may be sparse (Figure 12–19H), irregular (Figure 12–16B), bushy (Figure 12–17E), or overhanging (Figure 12–19G). They may be wide (Figure 12–18A), narrow (Figure 12–18D), thick (Figure 12–18A), or thin (Figure 12–18B). But in suggesting age they should never look plucked unless that is really appropriate for the character.

Eyebrows can be aged quickly, when that is necessary, by running a white stick liner, white creme stick, or stick hair whitener through them against the direction of hair growth (Figure 12–13B). This can also be done with clown white, cake makeup, or white mascara.

AREA 3: NOSE

If the nose tends to flatten out under lights or if it is to be altered in appearance for either corrective or character requirements, it will need a certain amount of remodeling. The nose area has seven planes (Figure 12–35).

PLANE A is the very small depression usually found, except in the classic nose, between the superciliary arch and the nose. It is shadowed for age and usually contains one to three vertical wrinkles (Figures 12–16F, 12–17A,D, and 12–53H). The two appearing at the inner ends of the eyebrows have their inception in plane A of the eye socket (area 2) and usually become narrower as they continue upward (Figure 12–49). The center wrinkle may be narrow at both ends and wider in the middle. These are the frowning wrinkles and if made rather deep, they will lend severity to the facial expression. Like all facial wrinkles, they should follow the actor's natural ones if he has any. Painted wrinkles must never conflict with an actor's natural wrinkles—including those that appear when he smiles or frowns.

FIGURE 12–35 PLANES OF THE NOSE.

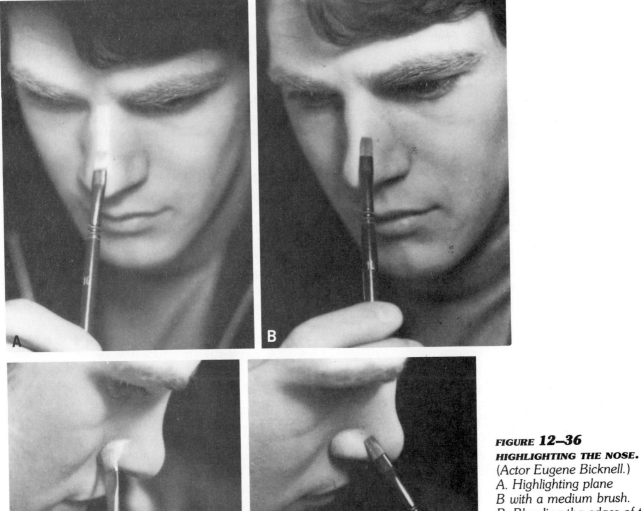

FIGURE 12–36
HIGHLIGHTING THE NOSE.
(Actor Eugene Bicknell.)
A. Highlighting plane
B with a medium brush.
B. Blending the edges of the
highlight with a clean brush.
C. Highlighting the nostrils
with a medium brush. D.
Blending the highlight with
a clean brush.

FIGURE 12–37 SHADOWING THE SIDES OF THE
NOSE. (Actor Kristoffer Tabori.)

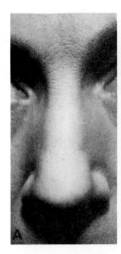
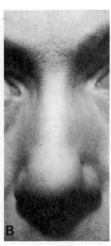
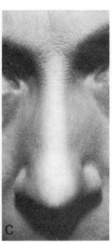

FIGURE *12–38* REMODELING *THE NOSE WITH PAINT.* *A. Wide. B. Shortened. C. Long and thin. D. Crooked.*

PLANE B is the prominent part of the nose and is highlighted both in indicating age and in sharpening and narrowing the nose. If the nose is too long, the lower end of the plane can be left the base color or lightly shadowed (Figure 12–38B) as indicated for corrective makeup. The width of the highlight will largely determine the apparent width of the nose. (See Figure 12–38.) If the nose is too sharp and needs to be broadened or flattened, plane B can be left the base color or lightly shadowed. If the tip is to be broadened or rounded slightly without the use of prosthesis, it can be done by rounding and broadening the highlight (Figure 12–38A). Applying and blending the highlight on plane B is illustrated in Figure 12–36A and B.

The effect of a broken nose can be achieved by giving the illusion of a crook or a curve in plane B. (See Figures 12–38D, 12–39, 12–40, and 12–41.) This is done by using not only a crooked or a curved highlight to reshape plane B but also shadows to counteract the natural highlights on those parts of plane B which should not be prominent on the crooked or broken nose. In Figure 12–39, for example, A represents a normal nose, and B, C, and D show three possible shapes which could

be created by the application of highlights and shadows to the nose in A.

Once you have decided on the shape you want, this is the procedure:

1. Using a flat shading brush of the width the highlighted area is to be, paint a strong highlight on plane B to create the shape you want for the new nose. (See Figure 12–41.) Drawings B, C, and D in Figure 12–39 are diagrammatic representations of two possible broken or crooked noses which could be created with highlights and shadows on the nose in drawing A. Note that in neither case does the highlight extend beyond plane B into plane C. Any extension of the

FIGURE *12–40* MODELING A *CROOKED NOSE.* *Curved highlight has been applied, then shadows added to counteract the natural highlights that would destroy the illusion being created. Makeup by student Susan Lambeth. (For another makeup by Miss Lambeth, see Figure 12–5.)*

FIGURE *12–39* PLACEMENT OF HIGHLIGHTS AND SHADOWS FOR CROOKED NOSES. *A. Normal nose. B., C., and D. Crooked noses. The shaded areas show the placement of shadows; the unshaded areas would be highlighted.*

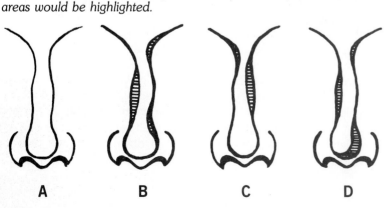

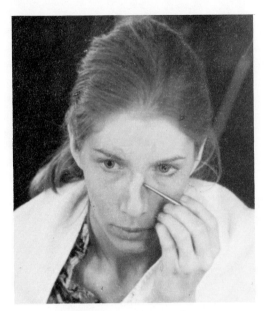

FIGURE *12–41* *MODELING A BROKEN NOSE.* *Crooked highlight has been painted on, and shadows are being added with a medium narrow brush. Makeup by student Laura deBuys.*

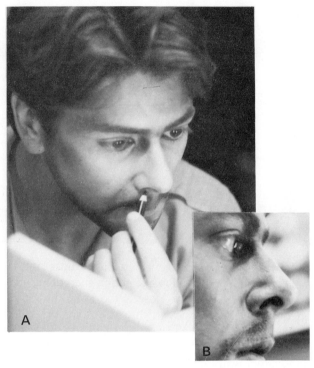

FIGURE *12–42* *ENLARGING THE NOSTRILS.* *A. Enlarging nostrils with a black eyebrow pencil. B. Closeup of enlarged nostril. (Actor Kristoffer Tabori.)*

highlight onto the sides of the nose (plane C) would result in part of the highlight's disappearing whenever the head was turned at more than a very slight angle. The edges of the highlight should, of course, be slightly softened.

2. The three shaded areas in Figure 12–39B and D and the two in C show the correct placement of the shadows for the noses illustrated. The purpose of the shadows is to counteract those natural highlights which would destroy the illusion of the crooked nose. In other words, the shadowed areas are supposed to look as though they are part of the side of the nose. To work effectively they must be fairly dark and be confined to plane B. They must not extend into plane C. Since any part that did extend into plane C would not be receiving as much light as the part on plane B, the part that extended would seem darker than the rest of the shadow and would tend to destroy the illusion. All edges of the shadow should be softened and blended into the highlight on one side and into the foundation on the other. To check the effectiveness of the illusion, look at the nose in a mirror with a spotlight on the face from at least several feet away. This particular illusion should always be checked at a distance—in a spotlight, if possible—to determine how effective it really is.

3. Unless you are using a water-base makeup, powder the nose, making certain that the shadows do not

shine. If they do, the illusion will be destroyed. And keep checking from time to time throughout the performance. A real broken nose can be straightened by reversing this procedure, as explained in Chapter 10.

PLANE C is nearly always shadowed for age. For realistic makeups, the edges between planes B and C, as well as the outer edges of plane C, must always be soft. If the nose tends to flatten out under light, as it sometimes does in youthful makeups, plane C can be subtly shadowed to give the nose greater depth.

PLANE D may be shadowed with plane C, especially if the nares are too wide, but usually a highlight on the upper part of the nare, as in Figure 12–36D, will give the nose more form. To widen the nares, highlight plane D. Applying and blending the highlight in plane D are illustrated in Figure 12–36C and D. To make the nostrils appear larger, outline them with a black eyebrow pencil. (See Figure 12–42.)

PLANE E is usually shadowed for age, but the fact that it receives only reflected light from the floor and sometimes a little from the footlights, if there are any, means that it is automatically in natural shadow. Carrying the highlight from plane B down into E will give the nose a droopy effect.

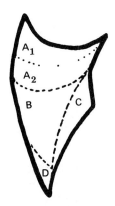

FIGURE *12–43 PLANES OF THE CHEEK.*

AREA 4: CHEEKS

The use of rouge for cheeks and lips will depend on the natural skin pigmentation and on whether natural or artificial coloring is being represented. For creating natural coloring in the cheeks for youth, avoid rouges that are either too purple or too orange. The lighter values are easier to control than the deeper ones. The SR, RS, S, and FS shades from 6 to 12 (*a*, *b*, and sometimes *c* or *d* intensity) are useful for Caucasian women, and RS-10-d, RS-11-b, FS-9-b, or similar shades are effective for Caucasian men. Whether dark-skinned races will use any rouge at all will depend on what is natural for the particular race or ethnic group. Study people to determine the natural placement. There is a great deal of variation. Rouge may be high or low, near the ear or near the nose, confined to a small area, or spread over most of the cheek. Note also other areas of the face—such as nose, forehead, and chin—that may show some color. In makeups for Caucasians, a touch of rouge in these areas can increase the realism of the makeup.

In representing street makeup, ask yourself what color the character might choose, how much she would use, and where she would place it. Would she follow the fashions or be ultraconservative? Might she use too much or none at all? Would she apply it carefully or carelessly? Might she notice whether it clashed with her dress, or wouldn't she care?

In other words, the problem of the addition of artificial coloring to the natural should be considered from the point of view of the character, since it is, after all, a choice over which she (or sometimes he) presumably has control. But remember one thing above all—if a character would not be wearing makeup, don't let her look as if she is.

Modeling As you have already discovered in the study of facial anatomy, the cheekbone (Figure 12–44) is rounded, so that when light is coming from above (the

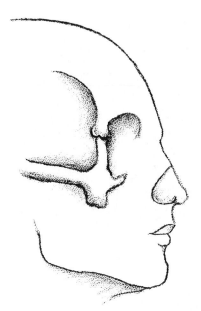

FIGURE *12–44 CHEEKBONE.*

usual assumption in makeup for the stage), the upper part of the bone receives strong light, whereas the lower part, which curves downward and inward, does not receive direct light and therefore appears considerably darker. This means that in modeling the cheeks for age or to achieve the effect of prominent cheekbones in youth, the cheekbone should be highlighted and the hollow below it shadowed. (See Figure 12–46.) The following is a step-by-step procedure for modeling the cheekbone:

1. First, prod the bone (as you have done before in the study of anatomy) in order to find the underside of the bone that curves back in and does not receive direct light. Then, with a medium or a medium-wide brush, lay on a strip of highlight along the top of the bone (Figure 12–45A), making sure that it is actually on top of the bone, where light from above would hit most strongly, and not on the side of the bone, which would be strongly highlighted only if light were coming from the side. With a clean brush, blend the upper edge out so that it disappears into the foundation, and very carefully soften the lower edge as if you were modeling a cylinder.

2. With a medium or a medium-wide brush, lay on the shadow color along the lower half of the cheekbone, (Figure 12–43), taking care to leave a space between the shadow and the highlight above.

3. With a clean brush, soften the lower edge of the shadow, which should now blend into plane B of the diagram in Figure 12–43. Then very carefully soften the upper edge of the shadow so that there is a gradual transition from the light (A_1) to the dark (A_2). Avoid a definite line between the two.

FIGURE 12—45 HIGHLIGHTING THE CHEEKBONE. (*Actor Eugene Bicknell.*) *A. Applying the highlight to the top of the cheekbone with a wide brush. B. Blending the edges of the highlight with a clean brush.*

How much the cheek sinks in and how prominent the bone is will depend on the intensity of the highlight and the shadow. For youthful makeups the contrast may be fairly subtle. For age makeups it may be relatively strong.

The treatment of plane B varies considerably with individuals. The area just below the cheekbone usually catches a little light (Figure 12–46C), and the bottom of that area will, of course, be in shadow as it curves around the jawbone. But in between, various things may happen. Study some of the faces in Figure 12–46 and in your own morgue. Then analyze your own face, or the one you're working on, in order to determine what treatment is likely to work best, making sure it is suitable for the character. If it isn't, you may have to compromise between the ideal cheek you have in mind and the specific potential of the face you're making up.

NASOLABIAL FOLDS

Plane C includes the nasolabial folds—the wrinkles running from either side of the nose downward to the mouth. These folds vary considerably in form and development. (See Figures 12–46, 12–47, and 12–48.) Each one has one hard edge and one soft edge. Wherever there is a crease in the flesh, as there is in the nasolabial fold, a hard edge is automatically formed (Figure 12–49E). Outward from this crease, the shadow lightens (Figure 12–49B) and turns gradually into a highlight as the crest of the fold is reached (Figure 12–49A,A'). Here is one possible technique of application:

1. With a medium or a medium-wide flat brush, starting near the inner corner of the eye, bring a stripe of highlight down along the fleshy area between the nose and the cheekbone (see Figure 12–50A). The upper edge of the highlight, falling along part of plane F_2 of the orbital area, should be kept fairly hard. The width and the conformation of this highlight will depend, of course, on the type of nasolabial fold you have in mind, which must, in turn, be related to the face of which it is a part. If the fold is to be full at the nostril and taper off into nothing near the mouth, the highlight will follow a similar pattern. It will become not only narrower and closer to the crease as it moves downward but also less strong so that at its lower end it may simply disappear into the foundation. This can be done in a single stroke by twisting your brush as you go down in order to narrow the stripe and also by using less and less pressure. Other types of nasolabial folds will, of course, require different conformations of the highlight. These you can work out through observation and experimentation.

2. With a clean brush, blend the lower inside edge of the highlight (see Figure 12–50B) and the part of the upper outside edge which does not fall alongside plane F_2 of the orbital area.

   NOTE: You may prefer to begin your nasolabial fold with step 3 instead of step 1, in which case steps 1 and 2 should be done following step 5.

3. With a wide or an extra-wide brush held at right angles to the natural crease in the skin and the ends of the bristles butting up against the crease, as in Figure 12–50C, move the brush downward along the crease, leaving a narrow stripe of strong highlight. Make sure that the outer edge of the stripe coincides exactly with the crease and does not overlap it. This is your hard edge, and it must be kept sharp and crisp.

4. Starting again at the top of the crease, pull the brush away from the crease, this time letting the highlight fade out as it leaves the crease (Figure 12–50D). Repeat this movement until you have gone the entire length of the crease.

5. Repeat the same horizontal strokes once more (Figure 12–50E), this time fading the highlight imperceptibly before it reaches the center of the lip. Additional strokes can be made for proper blending.

   NOTE: If you chose to begin your fold with step

FIGURE 12–46 CHEEKS.

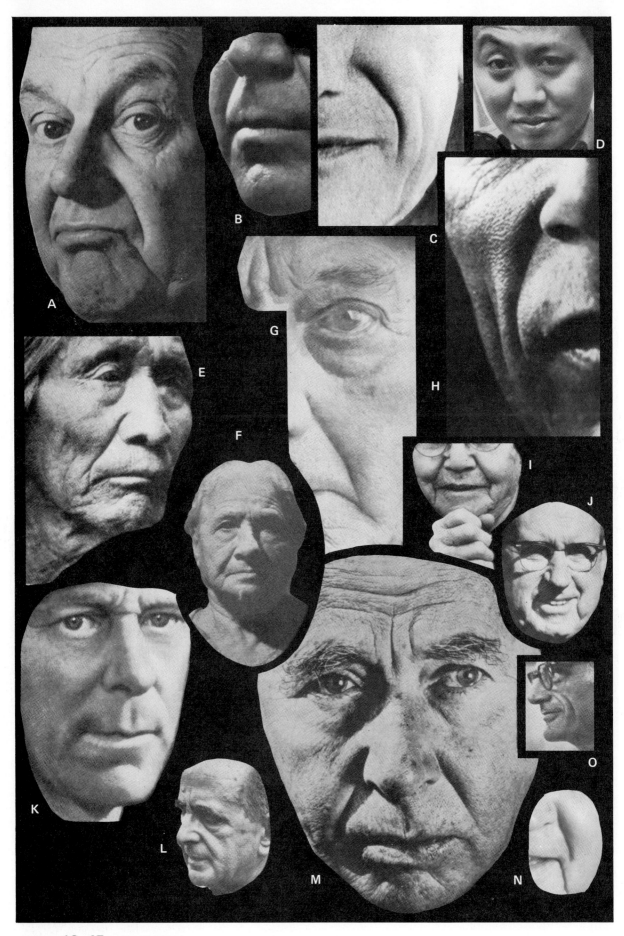

FIGURE **12—47** *NASOLABIAL FOLDS.*

108

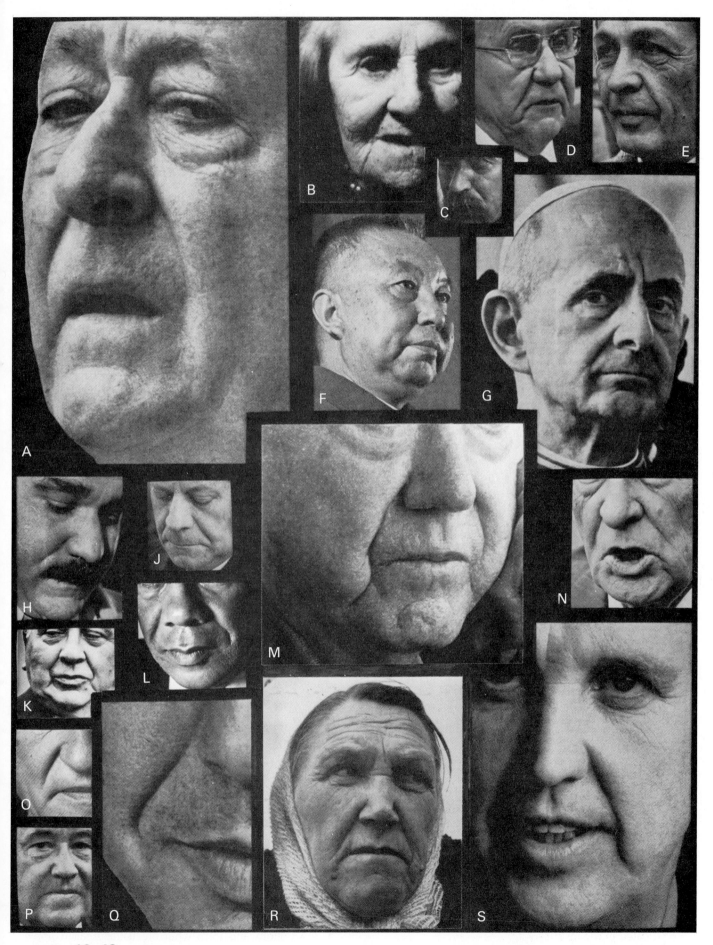

FIGURE **12—48** NASOLABIAL
FOLDS.

109

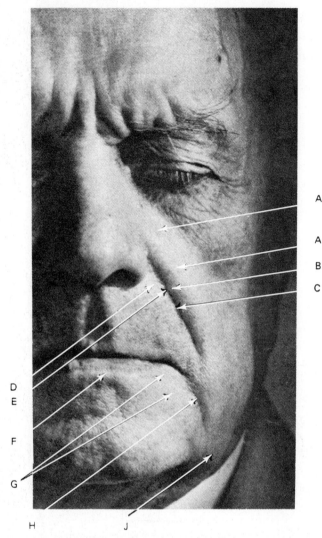

A

A

B

C

D
E

F

G

H   J

FIGURE 12—49 *PLACEMENT OF HIGHLIGHTS AND SHAD-OWS FOR AGE.* (*See text.*)

of the stripe by pulling it away from the crease (Figure 12–50G) so that it blends imperceptibly into the foundation. There should be just a little of the foundation color showing as a middle tone between the highlight and the shadow. Wipe your brush and soften the outside edge of the shadow by overlapping it with the brush, held parallel to the crease (see Figure 12–50H), and moving the brush downward the entire length of the shadow.

8. With your narrowest flat brush and a deep shadow color, go over the hard inside edge of the medium shadow, fading it out at the bottom. (This is a repetition of step 6, using a deeper shadow color and a narrower brush.)

9. Wipe your brush and, barely touching the outer edge of the deep shadow, soften it along its entire length. (This is a repetition of the technique in step 7 but without carrying the shadow so far from the crease.) (If you have used red instead of a medium shadow for step 4, you will need to make this deep shadow wider.) You should now have a sharp, clean edge with a strong contrast between light and dark.

10. In order to give the fold an even more three-dimensional effect, extend a touch of light or medium shadow downward from the eye pouch along the highlight. Observe this shadow in Figure 12–47A, for example.

11. If the fold seems well modeled but too strong, stipple it with your foundation color or with any other color or colors you think would be helpful. (See Chapter 11.) Be very careful to avoid overstippling and, as a result, losing the three-dimensional quality of your fold.

12. For most Caucasian characters—unless they are to be very sickly—some red should be added to the fold. There may be only a little, or there may be a great deal. Observe people for amount and placement. The red can be applied after powdering by brushing on dry rouge or by stippling on creme rouge with a black stipple sponge. If you are also stippling with other colors, you can add the red at the same time. However, after the stipple is powdered, you can still add additional red, if you want to, by brushing with dry rouge.

The preceding instructions are intended for one specific form of nasolabial fold but can easily be adapted to other forms—narrow at the top and wider at the bottom (Figure 12–47F), narrow at the top and bottom and wider in the middle (Figure 12–46G), short (Figure 12–47K), full and puffy (Figures 12–47A and 12–48F), or long and sharply defined and sometimes joined to other wrinkles (Figure 12–47G). For folds which curve outward at the bottom and form what are usually called apple cheeks, see the discussion following.

3 instead of step 1, steps 1 and 2 should be done now.

6. Using a medium or a wide flat brush held at right angles to the crease, with the ends of the bristles butting against it (the same way as in step 1, but from the opposite direction), paint in a narrow stripe of medium shadow color (Figure 12–50F), tapering it as you go down. The lower end should fade away into nothing. The inside edge of this stripe must follow exactly the hard edge of the highlight, barely touching it but never overlapping it. (Instead of a shadow color here, you may wish to substitute red, carrying it out farther beyond the crease than you would the shadow, as was suggested in the instructions for modeling eye pouches. If you do this, the deep shadow—step 7—will be somewhat wider than indicated in the instructions.)

7. With a clean, narrow brush, soften the outside edge

FIGURE 12–50 MODELING A NASOLABIAL FOLD. (Actor Eugene Bicknell.) A. Highlighting the top of the fold with a medium brush. B. Blending the lower edge of the highlight. C. Making a hard edge along the crease with an extra-wide brush. D. Pulling the highlight away from the crease. E. Blending the highlight into the foundation. F. Applying a medium shadow along the crease. G. Pulling the shadow away from the crease. H. Blending the outer edge of the shadow. Steps F, G, and H have been repeated with a deep shadow, which has been kept narrower than the medium shadow.

FIGURE 12–51 *APPLE CHEEKS. A. Student Joe Allen Brown. (For other makeups by the same student, see Figures 12–3B, 12–71, and 20–2.) B. Student Clista Towne-Strother. (Compare with Figure 12–75.)*

Apple Cheeks The term as used here refers not to enormous fat cheeks, no matter how apple-like they may be, but to a nasolabial fold that spreads out and turns into a ball of flesh centered around the knob of the cheekbone. (See Figure 12–46F and 12–47D.) The nasolabial fold begins as usual, sharp and clear, but very narrow at the top and widening as it goes down. As the fold turns outward, the crease disappears and the shadow becomes quite wide, so that in essence you are painting a small sphere. In fact, one of the best ways of beginning the apple cheek is to smile as broadly as possible, then place a spot of highlight on the most prominent part of the round fleshy area that is formed. This highlight will usually be centered on the ball of the cheekbone under the eye. Then, using a wide brush and a medium shadow, paint in the shadow area as if you were modeling a sphere. Starting with the brush in the crease of the nasolabial fold, sweep down from the nostril, following the natural crease until it turns toward the chin. Then move away from the nose, around the ball of the cheek, and into the shadow under the cheekbone. This will give you a very narrow shadow at the beginning and a wide one on the lower part of the "apple." The top edge of this shadow should be very soft and fade imperceptibly into the foundation. The bottom edge gradually softens as it moves away from the nose. (See Figures 12–51 and 12–75B.)

Apple cheeks will look more apple-like with a gener-
ous touch of rouge. They are not invariably red, but more often than not there is some color. The red can either be substituted for the medium shadow or be brushed on with dry rouge after the modeling has been completed and powdered. Stippling can also be used to redden the cheeks, provided you also want to add texture. In applying dry rouge, start at the nostril and brush downward and outward, following the form of the sphere but usually keeping the stronger color near the nose. You may want a little rouge on the nose as well.

JAWLINE

Plane D of area 4 is the mandible, or jawbone. One of the most effective ways of adding age to the youthful face is to create the illusion of sagging jowls. The correct placement of the jowls can usually be determined by gently squeezing the flesh of the jaw between the fingers to see where it creases naturally or by pulling back the chin and turning the head in various ways until creases or bulges appear. (See Figure 17–5B.) It is also possible to estimate the usual position from photographs in Figures 12–46F and H, 12–48F, 12–53B,D,E,J,N,Q, and 12–54.

The point at which the front and back areas of sagging flesh meet can nearly always be located by pressing the

FIGURE 12–52 *HIGHLIGHTING CREASE IN CHEEK.* *The highlight is being applied along a natural crease created when the actor smiles. (Actor Eugene Bicknell.)*

thumb or a finger upward somewhat beyond the middle of the jaw until you locate an indentation in the bone. This will be the correct point for ending the front sag and beginning the back one.

There are too many possible variations in jaws and sagging muscles at the jaw line to make it possible to give precise instructions for modeling that will fit every case, but general principles can be adapted and applied to individual faces. In any case, this is the procedure for modeling one particular kind of jowl:

1. Using a wide brush, sweep the highlight color down from the ear, around the curve in the jawbone, then up (see Figure 12–55A). This upward curve will take place at the indentation in the jawbone described above. Then sweep the brush in another wide arc along the lower part of the jawbone, leaving a small triangle of the foundation color showing at the point where the second arc begins. (See Figure 12–55B.) The second arc should end at the point you have already determined. A third and smaller arc starts at this point and then becomes part of the chin highlight. (See Figure 12–55B.)

2. Using a wide brush, fade the top edge of the highlight upward into the cheek area (Figure 12–55C).
3. Using a clean brush, soften the lower edge of the highlight. (See Figure 12–55D.)
4. Using a medium highlight, make two small triangles just below the two points at which the arcs of the jaw line highlights meet. These triangles should have fairly hard edges along the two diagonal sides and a very soft edge along the bottom. Figure 12–55E and F shows the first triangle. Be sure to leave enough space to add a shadow between the main jaw line highlights and the little triangles.
5. Using a medium-narrow brush (Figure 12–55G), paint a medium shadow beneath the large highlight and above the small triangular ones, touching the lower highlight but not the upper one. Because this represents the underside of the sagging flesh, which would normally be in shadow, it should be modeled like a cylinder with the upper edge fading into the highlight. The lower edge can be softened slightly with a clean narrow brush, or it can be left hard (see Figure 12–55H).
6. In order to increase the three-dimensional quality of the fold of flesh above the two triangles, darken the lower edge of the fold with a deep shadow color (Figure 12–55I), then soften the upper edges of this shadow with a clean brush. The lower edge can also be softened slightly but need not be. The jowls should now appear to be three-dimensional.
7. A more realistic effect can usually be achieved by adding a touch of rouge. (See Figure 12–55K.) This can be done after powdering by stippling with creme rouge or brushing on dry rouge.
8. Stipple with one or more colors, then powder. (See Figure 12–55L and M.)

With some faces, there may be a deep vertical crease cutting up from the jaw line across the cheek. This varies with the individual, but this is the basic technique:

1. With a medium-wide brush, sweep a highlight down from the upper plane of the chin to the bottom of the jaw line, then back up in a small curve. (Figure 12–56A.) Blend both edges.
2. Locate any natural or potential crease in the flesh. This can usually be done either by squeezing the flesh together or by twisting the head around until a crease forms. Note that with light coming from the front, the roll of flesh behind the crease will catch the light; highlight this area, as shown in Figure 12–56B. The lower part of the highlight should be rounded to give a sagging effect. The crease edge will, of course, be hard and the other edges soft.
3. With your highlight, make another sag (C) at the turn of the jawbone. Soften all edges.

FIGURE 12–53 NECK AND JAW LINES.

114

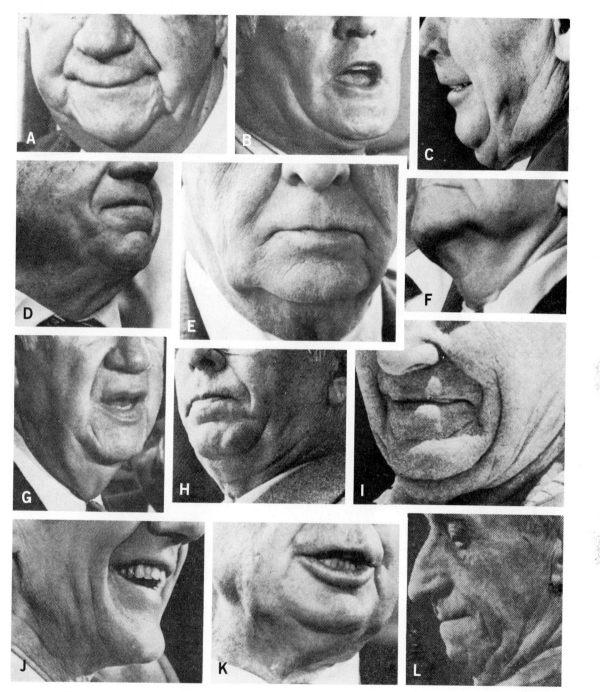

FIGURE 12–54 JAW LINES.

4. Using a medium shadow, make an arc (D) under the first highlight, carrying it up along the crease (E). This crease edge will be hard, the others soft. Both shadow and highlight should fade out before reaching the cheekbone.
5. Add two more areas of shadow (F and G) under the two remaining highlight areas, softening the top edge. The bottom edge may be semi-hard or slightly softened. In the illustration (Figure 12–56) the area toward the chin is semi-hard, whereas farther back

it is slightly softer. Note the very dark triangle of shadow just below the crease in area F.

Sagging muscles in the neck (Figure 12–55H) can contribute to the effectiveness of the sagging jaw line.

In aging the jaw line, it is often helpful, especially with youthful actors, to work from within as well as without. A small bit of sponge (either foam rubber or natural silk) can be placed between the lower jaw and the cheek

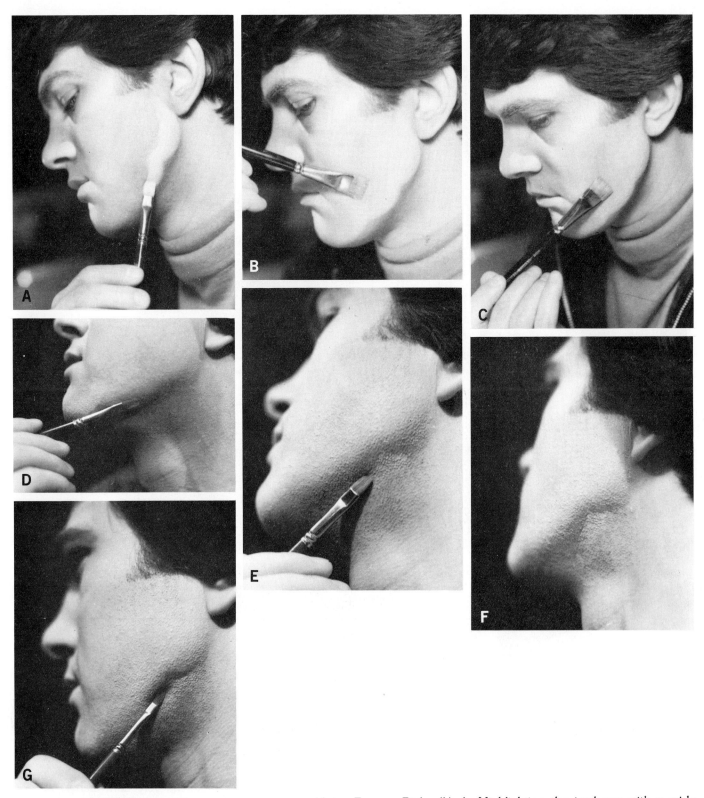

FIGURE 12–55 MODELING SAGGING JOWLS. (Actor Eugene Bicknell.) A. Highlighting the jawbone with a wide brush. B. Blending the upper edge of the highlight. C. Using a clean, extra-wide brush for additional blending of the edges. D. Softening the lower edge of the highlight with a clean brush. E. Adding triangles of highlight with a medium brush. F. First of two triangles of highlight completed, with the bottom edge blended into the foundation. G. Adding a medium shadow, with a hard edge on the bottom where it meets the triangle of highlight, and a soft edge on the top, blending into the soft edge of the upper highlight. H. Medium shadow completed. I. Deepening the bottom edge of the shadow next to the lower highlights. J. Modeling completed. K. Adding dry rouge with a soft eyeshadow brush. L. Stippling the highlights and shadows. M. Completed jaw line.

116

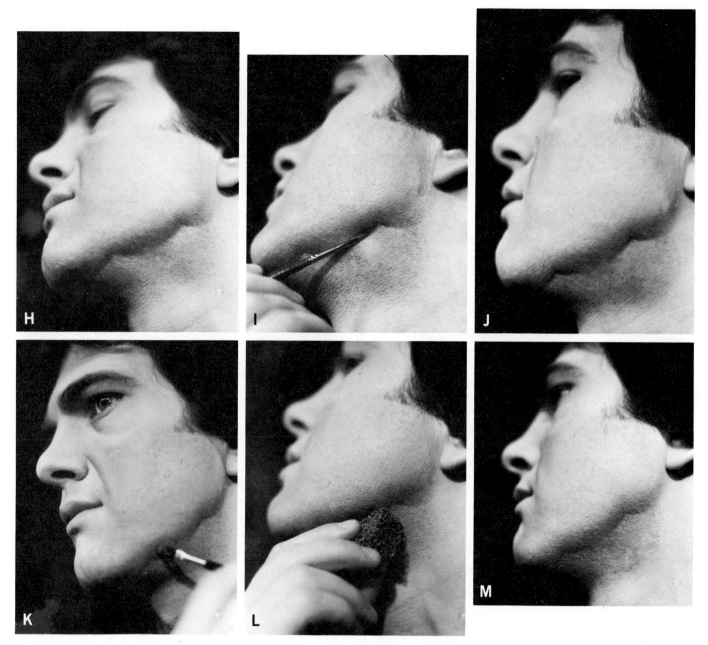

FIG. **12–55** Cont.

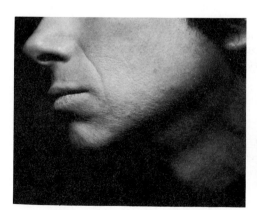

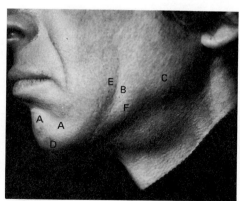

FIGURE **12–56** JAW LINE SAGGED WITH GREASE IN CHEEK.

117

to make the cheek protrude. Absorbent cotton or cleansing tissues can also be used. Naturally, the sponge must be sanitary. A new sponge or a sponge that is reserved for this purpose, and for the one individual, should be used, and whether new or not, it should be sterilized before use. The exact size and shape can be determined by experimentation, starting with a slightly oversize piece and cutting it down. Once the pieces are cut to the right size, they can be preserved for future use. They should be thoroughly washed and dried after each wearing and kept in a tightly covered box or jar.

The actor may object at first to sponges in his mouth, but is not difficult to adjust to them. They do not interfere with articulation or projection, though they may change the quality of the voice slightly.

For a greater effect of puffiness in the cheeks, as well as in the jowls (as for the aged Victoria, for example), a large piece of sponge or cotton can be used. It would be well to start with an entire small or medium-size sponge and then cut it down as much as necessary. The larger the sponge, of course, the more uncomfortable it is likely to be and the more difficulty it is likely to cause for the actor. If sponges are to be used at all, they must be used for a number of rehearsals to enable the actor to become accustomed to them. No actor can be expected to go through a dress rehearsal, let alone a performance, with a mouth unexpectedly full of sponges.

Studying people and photographs of people and modeling sagging jaw lines in clay before modeling them in paint can be very helpful.

AREA 5: MOUTH AND CHIN

This area includes seven planes (Figure 12–57). When there are well-developed nasolabial folds, the outer edge of plane A is always hard (Figure 12–49E). The highlight (Figure 12–49D) decreases in intensity as it approaches plane B, which may or may not be shadowed.

Depending on the natural formation of the actor's upper lip, it is sometimes possible to model the areas A, B, and C in such a way that areas A and B appear to curve outward, with area C sinking in, as if the character had no upper teeth. This can be done by modeling the areas like a horizontal cylinder—strongly highlighting the upper part of areas A and B, then letting the highlight fade into a medium shadow on the lower part of A and B and into a deep shadow on area C. (See Figure 12–58B.)

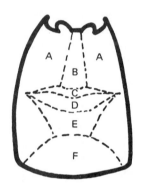

FIGURE 12–57 PLANES OF THE UPPER AND LOWER JAWS.

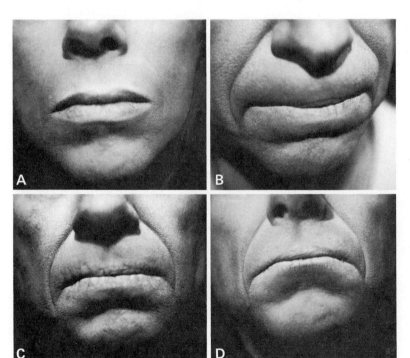

FIGURE 12–58 CHANGING THE MOUTH. All makeups on the same actor. A. Youthful mouth—upper lip reshaped. B. Convex upper lip. Area from nose to mouth shaded from a very light highlight to a deep shadow. Although the actor's lips are pressed together, the rounded effect is achieved largely with paint—with no inside padding. C. Aged mouth. Upper lip slightly convex; lips wrinkled with highlights and shadows. D. Lower lip thinned by painting in a false shadow over the bottom part of the lower lip and highlighting the upper part as if it were a naturally thin lip.

Conversely, the upper lip can be made to seem to protrude by highlighting the lower part of plane A and fading the highlight upward into the foundation color as it approaches the nose.

The treatment given the lips for a specific character can be analyzed on the basis of color, size, shape, and texture.

Lip Color

In deciding on the color for the lips, determine first whether you are representing natural lips or painted ones. If natural, then choose a color that will look natural on stage. What that color is to be will probably depend on the character's age, race, sex, and state of health. In any case, it should relate to the color you have already chosen for the rouge, if any.

If the character's lips would be painted, the decision will be made in terms of what lip coloring she would choose to wear and how heavily she would apply it. Fashion may or may not be a factor; personal taste or lack of it certainly would be. Normally the lip coloring will match the rouge unless the character would be likely to mismatch them or unless the lips would be painted and the cheeks natural (in which case, the color might or might not match.) Lip makeup is usually applied with a flat sable brush.

Size of Lips

The size of the lips (both width and thickness) will depend to some extent on the actor's own lips and how much they can be changed. For a realistic makeup, a very narrow mouth, for example, cannot successfully be made into a very wide one, but a wide one can sometimes be narrowed. The techniques for changing the apparent size of the lips have already been discussed as part of corrective makeup in Chapter 10.

Reshaping the Lips

Reshaping the lips may or may not involve a change of size. It will involve either changing the apparent natural shape to fit the character (Figure 12–59) or painting on a new shape as the charac-

ter might. The reshaping by the character would presumably be intended either to produce what she considered a more becoming shape or to follow a particular fashion, such as the bee-stung lips of the twenties or the Joan Crawford mouth of the thirties.

Lip Texture

Observe in Figure 12–60 the variations in lip texture, which have to do largely with age, environment, and health. In youth the texture is usually smooth, but later in life, depending on the condition of the skin generally, the lips may be rough, cracked, or wrinkled. It is, therefore, important in aging youthful faces that the lips be aged as well. (See Figure 12–58C.) This caution is based on observation of too many makeups in which youthful lips in a wrinkled face have destroyed the believability of an otherwise effective makeup. Suggestions for aging the lips are given below.

Aging the Lips

In addition to causing changes in texture, aging and changes inside the mouth (loss of teeth or wearing of false ones) can bring about changes in shape, size, and general conformation of the mouth. Lips are likely to become thinner (Figure 12–61A,D,E,F,I), and they may be cut by numerous vertical wrinkles, as in Figure 12–61E and I.

The most effective changes in texture can best be accomplished with three-dimensional makeup (see Chapter 13). But in using paint, you can stipple the lips or break the smoothness of the outline with wrinkles. The stippling is done along with that of the rest of the face, using the same colors. The lips should already have been reshaped, and if there are wrinkles cutting into the lip area, they should also have been done before the stippling.

If the mouth is to be wrinkled, it is helpful to make it smaller and, if possible, thinner—unless, of course, it is already small and thin. With a narrow brush, model the wrinkles carefully, using strong highlights with very narrow, deep shadows to form deep creases. Be sure

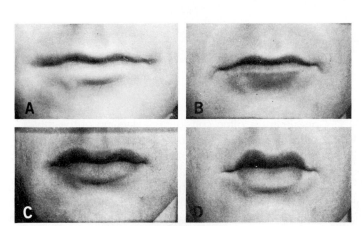

FIGURE 12–59 RESHAPING THE LIPS. *A. Natural lips. B. Lips thinned. C. Lips made fuller. D. Lips made very full and mouth narrowed. Makeup by student David Moffat.*

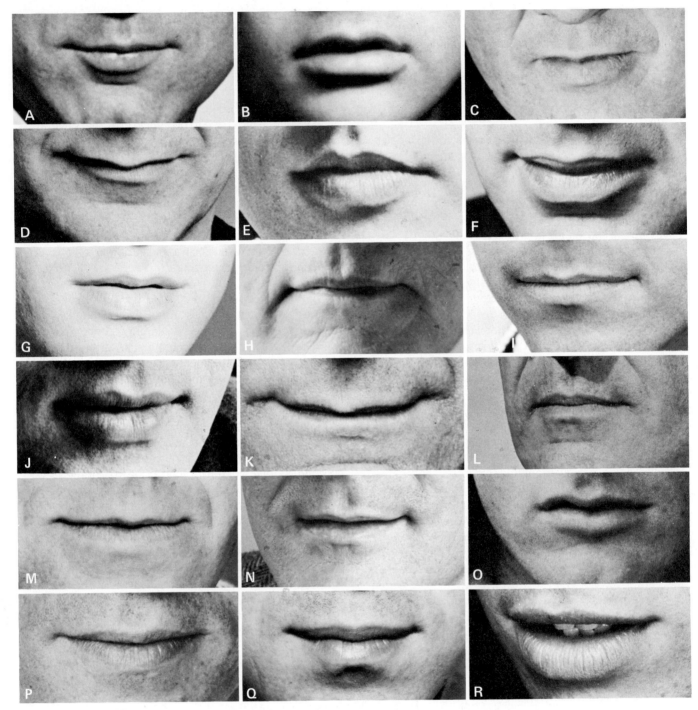

FIGURE 12–60 MOUTHS, MALE.

that each highlight has one hard edge and that the hard edge is very sharp and clean. (See Figure 12–62.) If the wrinkles are too strong, they can be toned down by stippling. The important thing is to make them convincingly three-dimensional.

In addition to the lips, the area around the mouth should also be aged. In old age, and sometimes in middle age, there is often considerable sagging of the muscles, particularly at the corners of the mouth. This frequently results in a crease angling downward from the corners of the mouth, with a roll of flesh above it (Figure 12–60H). Light falling on this roll of flesh from above will create a soft-edged highlight on top and a shadow with one hard and one soft edge below, just as it does with

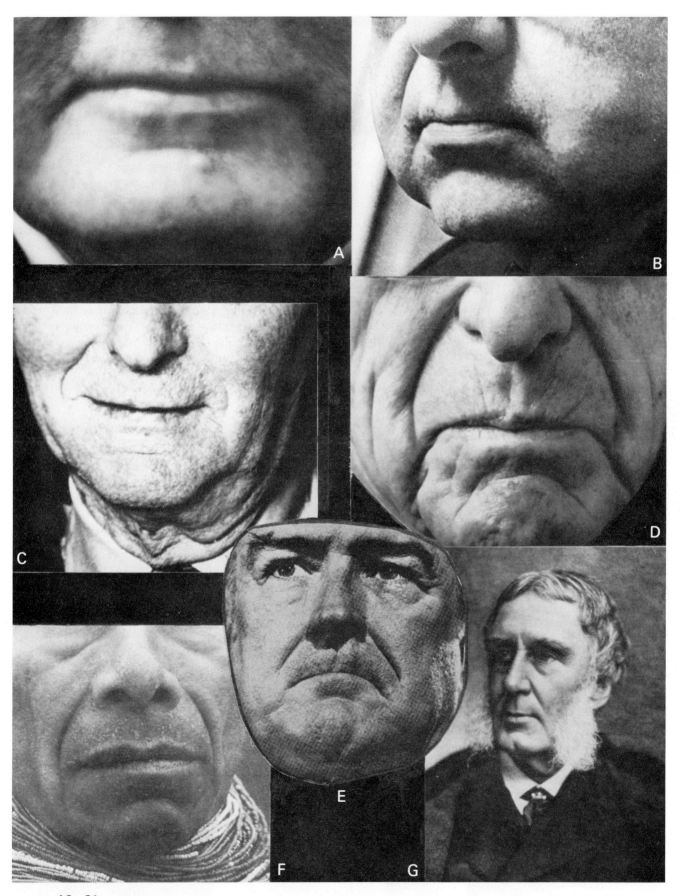

FIGURE **12–61** *MOUTHS AND CHINS.*

121

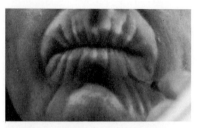

FIGURE 12–62 AGING THE MOUTH. *Painting on wrinkles with highlights and shadows, which will later be stippled. Makeup by student Barbara Murray.*

a nasolabial fold or a forehead wrinkle. The area immediately below the fold will be highlighted with one hard and one soft edge (Figure 12–63C and D).

This highlight may very well become part of a larger sagging area (Figure 12–58D) that does not usually have a sharp crease below it but often ends—in part, at least—where the chin begins. The exact conformation of this area and of the fold above varies considerably—not only with age, but with the individual. It's best to study faces and photographs, then adapt the information you have accumulated in your mind to the requirements of the specific character, relating it, as always, to the individual actor's face.

Study also the variations in plane A immediately below the lips, noticing particularly that this area can be either concave (Figure 12–61G) or convex (Figure 12–61A). Concave is normal in youth, but it may sometimes become convex in old age.

Chin Suggestions for changing the chin to make it more attractive have already been given in the chapter on corrective makeup. These same techniques can be used for character makeup.

The chin itself changes relatively little with age, except for the changes in the texture of the skin, which can be achieved with stippling. What is usually called a double chin (Figure 12–64) is actually a sagging neckline, resulting from a relaxing of the muscles of the jaw and neck area. It begins just behind the chin and cannot be effectively simulated with paint unless the actor already has the beginnings of one that can be highlighted. Lowering the head slightly and pulling it back will help to emphasize whatever fullness is already there. (See Figure 12–64.)

A crease may develop, with age, between areas E and F (see Figure 12–54D). Or there may be a rather abrupt change of plane without an actual crease. In either case, the top of the chin should be more strongly highlighted than it would be in youth in order to emphasize the increased angularity. (See Figure 12–63A and B.)

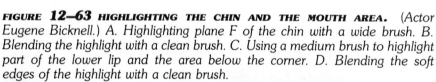

FIGURE 12–63 HIGHLIGHTING THE CHIN AND THE MOUTH AREA. *(Actor Eugene Bicknell.) A. Highlighting plane F of the chin with a wide brush. B. Blending the highlight with a clean brush. C. Using a medium brush to highlight part of the lower lip and the area below the corner. D. Blending the soft edges of the highlight with a clean brush.*

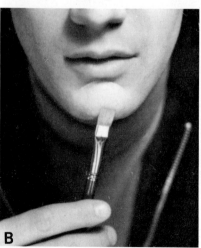

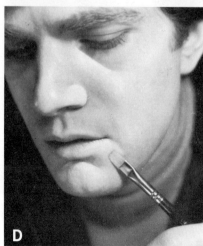

FIGURE *12—64* SIXTEENTH-
CENTURY LADY. *Makeup by
student Carol Doscher.*

NECK

The neck, of course, ages (see Figures 12–53 and 12–54) along with the face and sometimes even more rapidly. A youthful neck, like youthful lips, can destroy the believability of an otherwise effective age makeup. It has already been mentioned that both the front and the back of the neck should be made up. For juveniles, nothing else is likely to be necessary. But for age, the neck requires modeling.

There are four prominences in the neck that are important in makeup. They are labeled A, B, C, and D in Figure 12–65. Because the muscles, along with the top of the larynx and parts of the tracheal column, catch the light, they should be highlighted. All of these, being roughly cylindrical in shape, should be modeled like cylin-

FIGURE *12—65* MUSCLES OF THE NECK AND JAW.

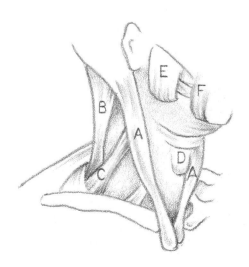

FIGURE *12—66* MODELING THE JAWLINE AND THE NECK FOR AGE. *Makeup by student Clista Towne-Strother. (For other makeups by the same student, see Figures 12–51B and 12–75.*

ders, with the highlight fading around to a shadow. The hollow at the breastbone, where the sterno-cleido-mastoid muscles almost meet, is usually in shadow. In old age there may be two folds of flesh starting above the larynx and hanging down like wattles (Figure 12–53C, H, and M). Small ones can be effectively painted on for a front view (Figure 12–67) but are, of course, ineffective in profile.

FIGURE *12—67* NECK AGED WITH CAKE MAKEUP.

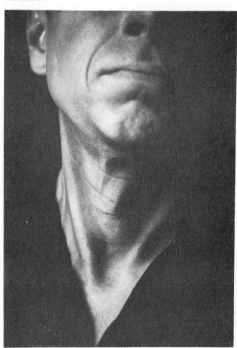

It is also possible to model the wrinkles that form around the neck and diagonally upward toward the ears. To determine the correct placement of the wrinkles, it is usually necessary to twist and turn the head until natural wrinkles are formed. These can be carefully modeled with highlights and shadows. For aging plumper characters, these transverse wrinkles should nearly always be used, but they should be wider and fewer in number.

HANDS

In representing youth, the hands should always be made up to go with the color of the face. The extent of modeling needed for bone, knuckles, and veins of the hands will depend on both age and the care that the hands have been given. Usually, unless the character tends to be quite pudgy, the bones of the hands, in age, tend to become more prominent and the veins begin to stand out (Figures 12–68 and 12–69). The bones, both in the back of the hand and in the fingers (Figure 12–69) should be modeled like cylinders, with highlights along the top and shadows along the sides. The joints may sometimes swell and often, with light skins, redden. A little rouge will give the color. The swelling can be suggested by rounded highlights on top of the joint and narrow, crescent-shaped shadows around them.

A dark-skinned actor who wants to create the effect with makeup can make his hand into a fist and cover the joints with very dark brown makeup. The hand can then be straightened out and the dark brown makeup wiped off the surface of the joint, which can be shadowed, slightly highlighted, and powdered. This technique will leave natural-looking dark ridges in the deepest part of the wrinkles on the joints.

The veins, if at all prominent, should appear three-dimensional, not flat, which means that there should be a highlight along one side of every vein and a shadow along the other. (See Figure 12–70.) Decide arbitrarily which way the light is coming from. Veins should be

treated as elongated cylinders. Their roundness will be particularly pronounced as they cross over bones. They are nearly always irregular, often forking out and meandering across the hand. If the actor's natural veins are visible, they can be followed; and if his veins are prominent, they *should* be followed. (See Figure 12–71). Otherwise, it is possible to place the veins wherever they appear to be most effective. Be careful, however, not to use too many. A few veins carefully placed and convincingly painted will be far more effective than a complicated network.

The color of veins will depend on the type and color of the hand. A pale, delicate, fine-skinned hand will naturally reveal much more blue in the veins than a deeply tanned or a black or a brown one, on which the veins may not appear blue at all and can be modeled with the normal highlight and shadow colors. Often veins that are not extremely prominent are a light greenish blue, in which case a very pale tint of blue-green can be used for highlighting. Very prominent veins under a delicate white skin are likely to be a much deeper blue, with no green cast, and would be expected to have blue-gray shadows. Observe the coloration in elderly hands—of the skin as well as the veins.

The brown spots so often found on older hands (see Figure 12–68) can be painted on with a yellowish brown—about the same color as freckles (FO-13-c/d). They should be of various sizes and unevenly distributed. If the hand is to be rough textured, it should be stippled or given a three-dimensional skin texture (see Chapter 13).

Fingernails In aging the hands, always make sure that the nails are aged in harmony with the rest of the hand. The aging may involve filing or cutting the nails (either real or artificial) to a length and shape appropriate for the character, and it may also require changing the color and the apparent texture of the nails, both of which can be done with creme makeup and makeup pencils, used with latex, sealer, flexible collodion, or spirit gum.

The color can be brushed on (see Figure 12–72C)

FIGURE *12–68* FEMALE HANDS WITH BROWN SPOTS.

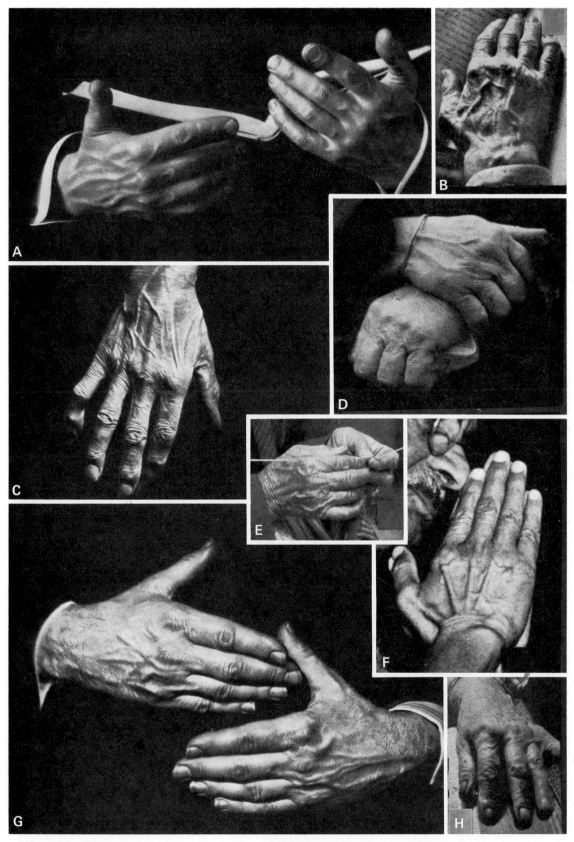

FIGURE **12–69** *HANDS.*

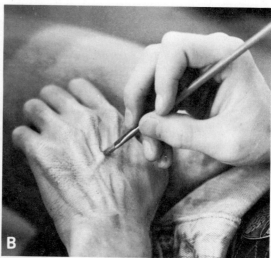

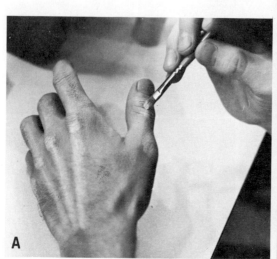

FIGURE 12–70 *AGING A MALE HAND.*
Makeup by student Milton Blankenship. A.
Highlighting the bones of the hand. B.
Shadowing between the bones. C. Powdering
the highlights and shadows. D. Adding final
touches. E. Finished makeup after powdering.
(For the same makeup in color, see Figure
H–8D.)

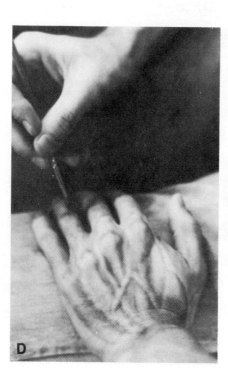

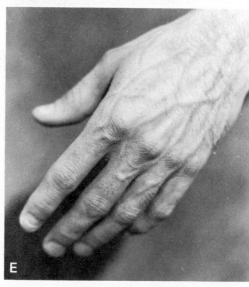

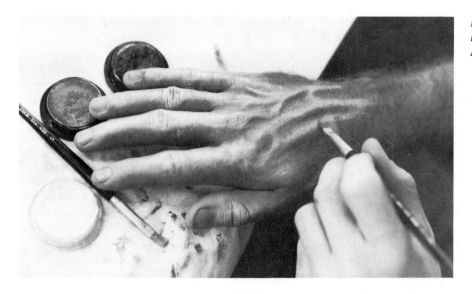

FIGURE 12–71 *AGING A MALE HAND.* Makeup by student Joe Allen Brown.

FIGURE 12–72 *AGING A FEMALE HAND.* Makeup by Gigi Coker. A. Highlighting the bones. B. Blending the shadows. C. Aging the fingernails.

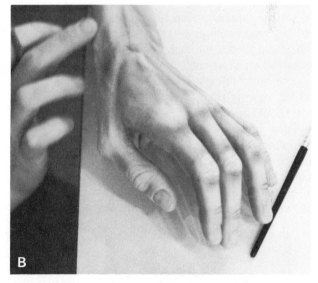

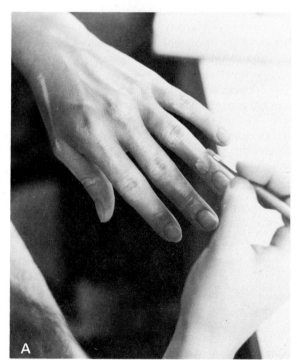

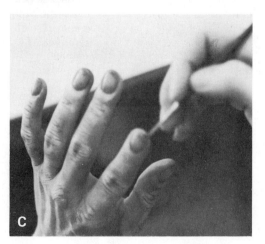

when using creme makeup or stroked on when using creme-makeup crayons or makeup pencils. In general, creme-makeup crayons are preferable to regular creme makeup. Makeup pencils, if you happen to have the right color or colors, are especially useful for creating the effect of ridges in the nails. Vertical strokes can be applied with a white pencil, leaving slight spaces between the strokes to allow the natural color of the nail to show through. Or, instead of leaving spaces between the strokes, you can make alternating strokes of two colors, such as white and ochre, to give a yellowish cast to the nails. You can also achieve the same effect by applying creme makeup or makeup crayon with a very narrow brush.

Pencils can also be used for coloring the nails without giving the effect of ridges. After the color has been penciled on, you can blend it with a fingertip so as to color the entire nail—evenly or unevenly, whichever is appropriate. You may wish to apply the color heavily to conceal the natural color of the nails or sparingly to allow some of the natural color to show through. Any color applied to the nails should be powdered before proceeding with the next step.

When the nails have been appropriately colored, they should be coated with clear latex, sealer, or nonflexible collodion. No matter which one you use, it should be powdered when it has dried in order to remove the shine and give a duller finish to the nail—unless the character would be wearing clear nail polish, in which case the powder should be omitted or clear nail polish used instead of the latex, sealer, or collodion.

An alternative method of aging the nails is to coat them with spirit gum, then, with one finger, to tap the gum until it becomes tacky, at which point you can press white or neutral face powder into the gum. That gives a dull, whitish effect suitable for some aged characters.

If dirt under the nails is appropriate, gray or gray-brown creme makeup can be applied with a small brush.

To create the effect of colored nail polish on aged nails, you can use red makeup pencil or apply lipstick, creme makeup, or makeup crayons with a narrow brush to make vertical stripes of color, as previously suggested. The red should then be powdered and coated with latex. If you want the effect of frosted nail polish, powder the latex; otherwise, leave it unpowdered. Red pencils can be used on the nails without a protective coating of spirit gum; but since some reds stain the nails (or the skin), direct application of the pencils to the nails is *not* advisable—unless, of course, you have already experimented with the red you plan to use and have determined that it does not stain.

For removing makeup from the nails, latex can be peeled off, sealer and collodion removed with acetone, and spirit gum, with spirit-gum remover or acetone.

TEETH

Teeth, if too white and even for the character, can be darkened with an appropriate shade of tooth enamel. The effect of chipped or missing teeth can be created with black tooth enamel or black wax. Black eyebrow pencil can also be used, but it may require touching up during the performance. The teeth should always be dried with a tissue before being blocked out.

Black tooth enamel can also be used to make the edges of the teeth uneven. If they are already uneven and the character should have even teeth, the process can be reversed.

For stained or discolored teeth (Figure 12–73), you can rub brown mustache wax on the teeth with the fingers

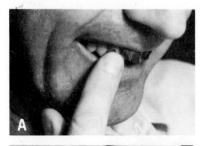

FIGURE 12–73 DISCOLORING THE TEETH. *Makeup by Bert Roth, S.M.A. A. Rubbing brown mustache wax over the teeth. B. Removing some of the mustache wax with a cotton swab. C. Some of the wax removed. D. Most of the wax removed.*

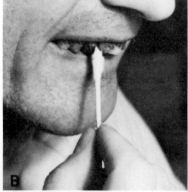
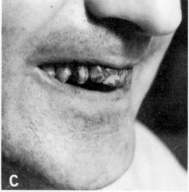
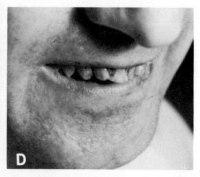

(Figure 12–73A), then partially remove it with a cotton swab (Figure 12–73B). If you want additional color along the sides of the teeth, you can add more wax with another cotton swab. The teeth must, of course, be dried before any wax is applied. The wax can be removed with a cleansing tissue.

If you do not have brown mustache wax, you can color clear mustache wax or derma wax with brown cake makeup by scraping the top of the cake with a knife to obtain a small amount of brown powder, then mixing the powder with the wax, using a palette knife or a modeling tool. When the powder is thoroughly embedded in the wax, it will, of course, be impervious to saliva in the mouth. For nicotine stains, you can use an appropriate shade of cake makeup or mix colors if you don't have the right shade.

RESHAPING THE FACE

There are times when, in addition to working with individual features, you may wish to think in terms of reshaping the face—making it more square, long, wide, round, or oval—in order to make it more appropriate for a particular character. (See Figure 12–74.) This can be done—at

FIGURE **12–74** *ORIENTAL ACTOR AS TWO CAUCASIAN CHARAC-TERS.* *A. Actor Randall duc Kim in his own makeups for B. Titus Andronicus and C. Falstaff.*

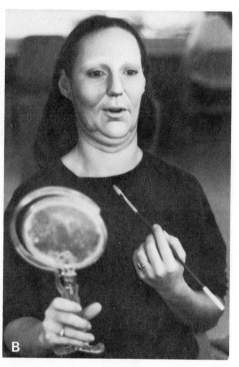

FIGURE **12–75** LENGTH AND ROUND-
NESS IN THE FACE.   *A. Increasing the illusion of length in the nose. B. The same
face with the illusion of roundness created
in the cheeks, the jowls, and the neck.
The horizontal effect in the modeling of
the rounded areas also creates an illusion
of greater width in the face as a whole.
Makeup   by   student   Clista   Towne-
Strother.*

least to some degree—by means of highlights and shadows and beards, mustaches, hair, and eyebrows.

The Long Face A face can be made to look longer
by increasing the apparent height of the forehead and
the apparent length of the nose (Figure 12–75A) and
the chin by highlighting. (See Chapter 10.) Narrowing
the face by subtly shading the sides of the forehead and
the cheeks will also make it seem longer, as will a high,
narrow hair style or one which covers the sides of the
face. A pointed goatee (Figure G–9S) or a long, narrow
beard will have the same effect. A long nose and long
nasolabial folds (Figure 12–74B) will also contribute to
the illusion.

To make a long face look less long, follow the suggestions below for the wide face.

The Wide Face To make a face look wider, you
can do just the reverse of lengthening—lower the forehead
(which can be done with the hair style, as well as with
the makeup) and shorten the chin (if doing so would
not be inappropriate for the character), highlight rather
than shadow the sides of the forehead and the cheeks,

shorten the nose, flatten and widen the hair style, and
dress any facial hair horizontally (Figure 12–74C) rather
than vertically. Making the eyebrows farther apart will
also help, as will avoiding long nasolabial folds and making
apple cheeks instead. In order to decrease the apparent
width of a wide face, follow any of the suggestions for
the long face that seem appropriate.

The Square Face To make a face more square,
the forehead should be vertical at the temples, giving a
squared-off effect, and should usually be made to look
as broad as possible. This can be done by highlighting
the temples and even blocking out the hairline, if necessary, in order to take it farther back at the sides. The
top hairline should be fairly straight across. If much hair
needs to be blocked out, it would usually be better to
wear a wig that will cover the natural hairline and provide
a hairline more suitable for the character.

The jaw can be highlighted at the sides, if necessary,
to make it look wider, and the chin can sometimes be
squared off a bit. A square-cut beard (Figure G–18Y)
can be very helpful. Straight eyebrows will also contribute
to the illusion.

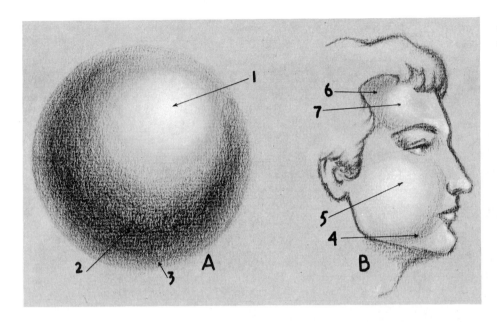

FIGURE *12–76* MODELING A ROUND CHEEK.

If the face is noticeably longer than it is wide, follow the instructions for the wide face in order to give a squarer look.

A square face can be made to look less square by rounding off the forehead, the jaw, and the chin, wearing a longer and more rounded beard, and giving the face an illusion of greater length (see *The Long Face*).

The Oval Face A face—unless it is already too round—can be made to look more oval by rounding off the upper corners of the forehead either by shadowing or by changing the hairline and doing the same to the jaw with shading or with a beard, creating a sweeping curve down to a rounded chin. A round face can be made to look less round by shadowing the sides of the cheeks, curving the shadow gently downward at an angle toward the chin.

The Round Face To round a youthful face and keep it youthful, follow the principles used in modeling a sphere, as illustrated in Figure 12–76, in which drawing A illustrates the shading and highlighting for a sphere, and drawing B, the outline of a youthful face. The effect of roundness is achieved with a highlight (B_5) made in a round pattern in about the center of the cheek, and a thin, crescent-shaped shadow drawn in an arc from close to the eye, past the nostrils and the mouth, and around to the back of the jaw, as shown in B_4. All edges should be soft, and the shadow very subtle. Although some faces cannot be made to look round without the use of three-dimensional makeup, an *effect* of roundness can usually be achieved by rounding various features or areas of the face, as illustrated in Figure 12–75B. Compare with the same face in Figure 12–75A. Rouging the face in a round pattern can also be helpful. An effect of round-

ness can also be achieved by rounding individual features rather than the face as a whole.

In addition, whatever effect of roundness you have achieved with makeup can often be enhanced with the hairstyle (see Figure 12–77). A rounded collar in the costume may also help.

A naturally round face cannot be made thin, but it can be thinned somewhat by highlighting the cheekbones

FIGURE *12–77* EMPHASIZING ROUNDNESS IN THE FACE. *Makeup by student Victoria Thys. The natural roundness of the face is exaggerated, expressing the personality of the character with a makeup based on curves and a wig that makes the face look even more round.*

and shading the whole cheek with a color two or three shades darker than the base. In *aging* a round face, this same technique can be used, as illustrated in Figure 12–78. Or you may wish to age the face with sagging apple cheeks (see Figure 12–61F and I), which give the impression of a happier disposition than would long, drooping nasolabial folds.

Sponges or absorbent cotton can be used in the

FIGURE 12–78 ***CHANGING THE SHAPE OF THE FACE.*** *(For other makeups on the same face, see Figures 12–80 and 17–10.) A. The illusion of width is achieved by carrying the light foundation color from ear to ear and pulling the hair and beard out horizontally. B. The face and the nose have been narrowed by shadowing. The nasolabial folds and the long narrow nose help to lengthen the face.*

FIGURE 12–79 ***AGING A ROUND FACE.*** *Makeup by student Susan Lambeth. A. Very light highlights are being applied over a powdered creme-makeup foundation. B. Finished makeup, after creme shadows have been added and the entire makeup has been stippled with the foundation color, the two shadow colors, and creme rouge (RS-10-b).*

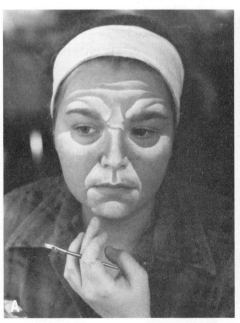

cheeks to fill them out, as suggested earlier under the discussion of modeling jowls for age. The technique is the same, but the modeling with paint will be used to suggest fullness or roundness rather than age. This modeling will, of course, be the same as if sponges were not being used since they merely help the illusion. This technique is suggested only as a possibility and is not recommended as an ideal solution to every problem of making an actor's face rounded.

In this chapter we have concentrated on makeup for the face, the neck, and the hands, but other exposed parts of the body may require makeup as well. Cake makeup can be used for relatively small areas; but to cover large areas, body makeup is usually more practical. For details, *see Body makeup* in Appendix A.

BRINGING THE MAKEUP TO LIFE

Bear in mind, as you work on any realistic character makeup, such as those in Figure 12–80, for example, that the actor you are making up (whether it be yourself or someone else) is the only one who can bring the makeup to life and that until he gets into character, the makeup will be incomplete. Assuming the character before the makeup begins and as needed thereafter is an essential part of the creative process. Note that in Figure 12–75B, for example, the actress is assuming the character while checking the progress of the makeup. Bear in mind also that whenever the makeup is being photographed or checked, either in the mirror or onstage, the actor should *always* be in character.

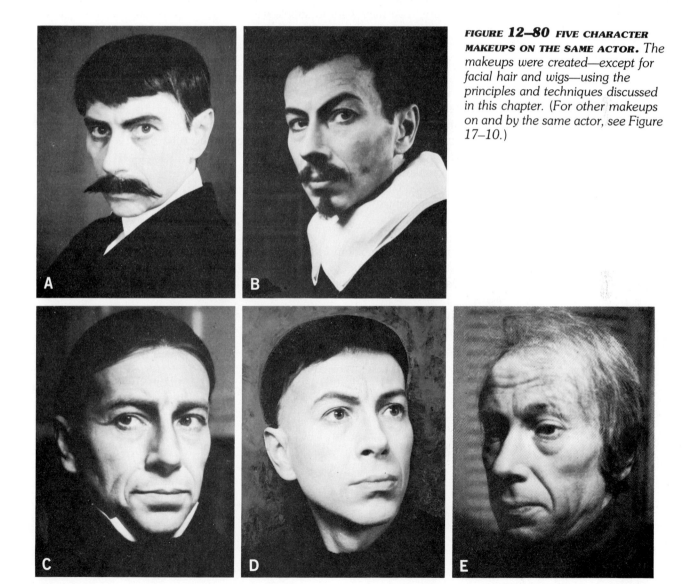

FIGURE 12–80 FIVE CHARACTER MAKEUPS ON THE SAME ACTOR. The makeups were created—except for facial hair and wigs—using the principles and techniques discussed in this chapter. (For other makeups on and by the same actor, see Figure 17–10.)

Problems

1. Design and execute makeups for a pair of characters, both youthful, but sufficiently different that the difference will be apparent in the makeup—as, for example: Katharina and Bianca (*Taming of the Shrew*); Barbara and Sarah (*Major Barbara*); Ophelia (*Hamlet*) and Audrey (*As You Like It*); Canina and Columba (*Volpone*); Joan of Arc (*St. Joan*) and Laura (*The Glass Menagerie*); Romeo and Hamlet; Stanley Kowalski and A Young Collector (*A Streetcar Named Desire*); Marchbanks (*Candida*) and Leo (*The Little Foxes*); Charles Lomax and Bill Walker (*Major Barbara*); Antonio and Launcelot Gobbo (*Merchant of Venice*); Mosca (*Volpone*) and Orlando (*As You Like It*).

2. Follow the step-by-step instructions under *Modeling Hard and Soft Edges* early in the chapter.

3. Following the instructions under *Modeling the Face and the Neck with Highlights and Shadows*, model your face—first with highlights only, then adding shadows, rouge, and stipple.

4. Model your cheekbones with highlights and shadows, taking care to follow your bone structure. You may want to stipple with one or more colors after you have finished.

5. Model a broken or a crooked nose.

6. Practice doing nasolabial folds until you can do them convincingly. If you think it will be helpful, you might model them on your clay head first before modeling them with paint.

7. Do at least three different aged eyes. Make sure that one of the eyes has a full pouch, and keep working on the pouch until it is convincingly three-dimensional. With at least one of the eyes, begin by blocking out the eyebrow.

8. Age your mouth.

9. Age your forehead, using only highlights and shadows.

10. Age your forehead, using wrinkles.

11. Age your neck and jaw line.

12. Age your hands.

13. Age your teeth.

14. Design and execute a makeup for a middle-aged character from a play.

15. Choose from your morgue or from photographs or works of art in this book, three elderly people. Determine what makes them look old rather than middle-aged.

16. Design and create a makeup for an elderly character from a play.

17. Do worksheets for the makeups you designed for problem 1, Chapter 7.

13

Three-Dimensional Makeup

In modeling with paint, there was no attempt to make actual changes in the natural shape of the actor's features but merely to give the impression that such changes had been made. Three-dimensional makeup involves actually building up parts of the body—usually the face, neck, or hand—with various materials, such as nose putty, derma wax, cotton, cleansing tissues, latex, gelatine, and liquid plastic. *Molded* latex processes will be discussed in the next chapter.

NOSE PUTTY

Nose putty is used primarily for changing the shape of the nose (see Figures 13–1 and 13–2), though it does have other uses as well. An actor who settles for his own nose instead of the nose of the character is failing to take advantage of a particularly useful and relatively simple means of physical characterization.

The use of nose putty need not be restricted to fantastic noses or even to large ones. There are minor changes that can easily be made in order to give the actor a nose more suited to the character. But whether the changes are major or minor, the less putty you need to use, the easier the shaping and the blending will be.

Building up the Nose The first step in building up the nose—the easiest feature to change three-dimensionally—should be to make a profile sketch of the shape you want, bearing in mind that no matter what the shape or size of the addition, it must appear to be an integral, living part of the face. This means that whatever additions you make to the nose must give the impression of being supported by bone and cartilage and must be so carefully blended into the natural skin that it is impossible to tell where the real nose leaves off and the false one begins.

Once you have a clear plan firmly in mind and know exactly what you intend to do, applying and shaping the nose putty is not difficult, but it does require patience. This is the procedure:

1. Keep your sketch in front of you and use two mirrors to give you a profile view of the nose as you work.
2. Make sure the skin is free from all grease and makeup before applying the putty. Cleansing the skin with absorbent cotton and rubbing alcohol, witch hazel, or skin toner, though not necessary, may be helpful.
3. Coat your fingers lightly with K-Y Lubricating Jelly (*not* petroleum jelly) to keep the putty from sticking to them. If you have no lubricating jelly, you can substitute wave set. (In case you have neither lubricating jelly nor wave set, vanishing cream or a very light coating of cleansing cream can be used.) Then separate a small piece of putty from the mass and knead it with your fingers until it is very pliable. If the putty should be too stiff and the heat of the hand does not soften it sufficiently, immerse it in hot water for a few minutes or place it near a radiator or some other heat source. Although it is possible to soften putty by the addition of a small amount of cleansing cream, the method is not recommended. There is a tendency to add too much cream, resulting in the putty's becoming too soft and mushy and quite unmanageable.
4. Stick the softened ball of putty on the part of the nose that is to be built up the most (Figure 13–2A), pressing it into the skin for good adhesion. If it does not seem to be securely attached, remove it, then paint the nose with spirit gum and let it dry before reapplying the putty. Or you can use both spirit gum and cotton under the putty, as described in the section on *Derma Wax*.

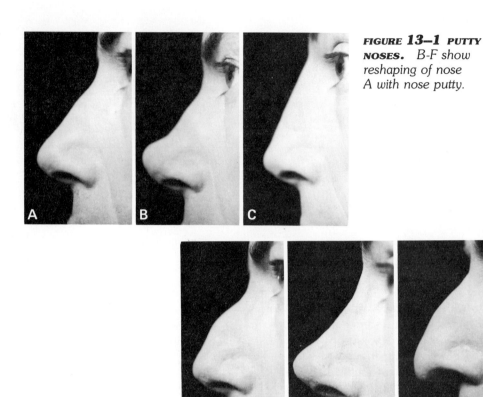

FIGURE 13–1 *PUTTY NOSES.* *B-F show reshaping of nose A with nose putty.*

5. Carefully blend the edges of the putty into the skin, shaping the nose as you work (Figure 13–2B). Use more lubricating jelly on your fingers if the putty sticks to them. Always confine the putty to as small an area as possible, being especially careful to keep it off areas *surrounding* the nose. If, in blending the edges, you tend to keep pulling the putty outward until it has spread well away from the area you want built up, blend in the opposite direction—*toward* the center of the nose.

6. When the blending is finished, you can make final adjustments in the shape. Using your sketch as a guide and two mirrors to check the nose from all angles, cover your fingers with more lubricating jelly and keep pressing, prodding, and massaging the putty until you have precisely the shape you want, always keeping in mind the image of flesh and skin over bone and cartilage. A final light massaging with lubricating jelly will help to eliminate unintentional cracks and bumps and give a completely smooth surface.

7. When the surface of the putty is smooth, the edges perfectly blended, and the lubricating jelly dried, stipple the putty with your black stipple sponge to give skin texture (see Figure 13–8K). Then, if the putty is lighter or less red than the skin, stipple it with rouge—dry rouge (applied with a damp sponge) or creme rouge (applied with either a stipple sponge or a flat red-rubber sponge). If creme rouge is used, powder it well, then brush off the excess powder.

A method of giving three-dimensional texture to putty by using a latex negative of a grapefruit, orange, or lemon rind is explained in Chapter 14. The method uses the same principle followed in creating texture on plastic eyebrow covers, illustrated in Figure 12–31C and D.

8. Powder the nose, pressing gently with the puff. Remove excess powder with a powder brush.

9. Stipple the foundation color (preferably creme or grease) over the entire nose (see Figure 13–8I), using a natural sponge for cake makeup and a flat red-rubber sponge for creme or grease. If this does not adequately cover the putty area, powder, then stipple on more of the foundation color. If you are using dry cake makeup, it will probably dry lighter than the same makeup applied directly to the skin. For that reason, it is not the best choice of makeup to use over nose putty. However, the problem can sometimes be corrected by coating the light area with more lubricating jelly. The water-soluble jelly

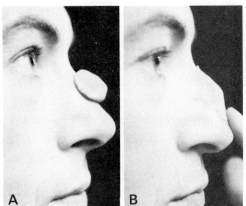

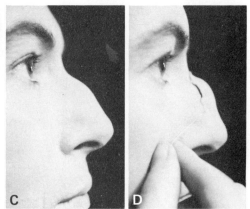

FIGURE 13–2 *MODELING A PUTTY NOSE. A. Ball of putty on nose. B. Putty being shaped and blended with fingers. C. Finished nose, made up and powdered. D. Removing the putty with a thread.*

will mix with the makeup and dry with a slight waxy sheen. Powdering will counteract this. If the color matching is still not satisfactory, coat the problem area with rubber-mask grease, making sure to blend the edges of the grease thoroughly into the skin, then powder. If the color of the rubber-mask grease you are using does not match the foundation color you plan to use for the makeup, you can either use the rubber-mask grease for the entire makeup or cover it, after it has been powdered, with the foundation color you are using on the rest of the face.

10. For most characters, you will want to add rouge to the nares and other parts of the nose to give it a more natural appearance. This can be done after the foundation coat has been applied or when the various colors of stipple or other finishing touches are being added. If it is done afterward, moist rouge can be stippled on, or dry rouge can be brushed on.

For illustrations of the use of nose putty, see Figures 13–1 and 13–7. Figures 13–3, 13–4, and 13–5 illustrate a variety of noses.

Removing the Putty A thread can be used to remove the putty. Starting at either the base or the bridge of the nose, run the thread along the nose under the putty (Figure 13–2D), pulling the thread tight with both hands. This does *not* preserve the putty nose intact for future use—it is simply a more efficient way of removing

the putty than pulling it off with the fingers. Any bits of putty remaining on the nose after the bulk of it has been detached with the thread can be removed by massaging with makeup remover until the putty is soft enough to be wiped off with tissues. Always do this gently in order to avoid irritation.

Building up the Chin Nose putty can also be used on other bony or cartilaginous areas, such as the chin. It is seldom practical, however, to apply it to parts of the face in which there is a great deal of movement of the muscles, for bubbles will very likely appear in the surface of the putty and ruin the effect.

When using putty on the chin, it is advisable first to cover the area with spirit gum. Let the gum become almost dry or tap it with one finger until it becomes very tacky (as shown on the nose in Figure 13–8B), then stick a ball of putty onto the tip of the chin and carefully work it outward in all directions until you have the desired shape. If at all possible, confine the building up to the bony area of the chin, keeping it off the softer parts, where muscular movement is very likely to result in wrinkling and bubbling. Blend the putty carefully into the skin so that there will be no visible edges when the makeup is finished. Massaging gently with lubricating jelly will help to smooth out any irregularities. Then follow the same steps suggested for building up the nose.

In applying beards or goatees to a putty chin, it is best to apply sealer to the putty before applying the spirit gum. Then proceed as usual.

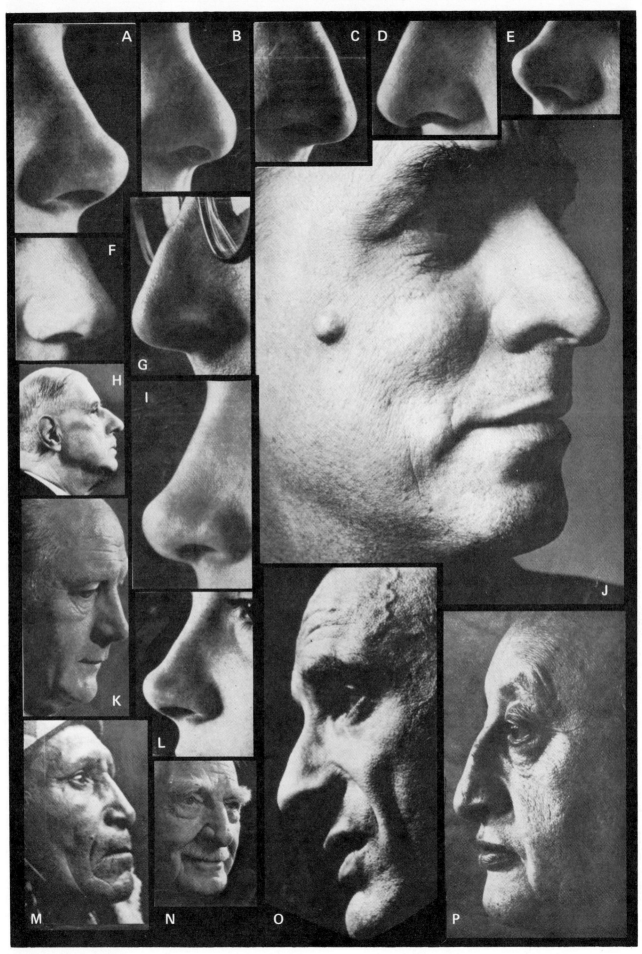

FIGURE 13—3 NOSES.

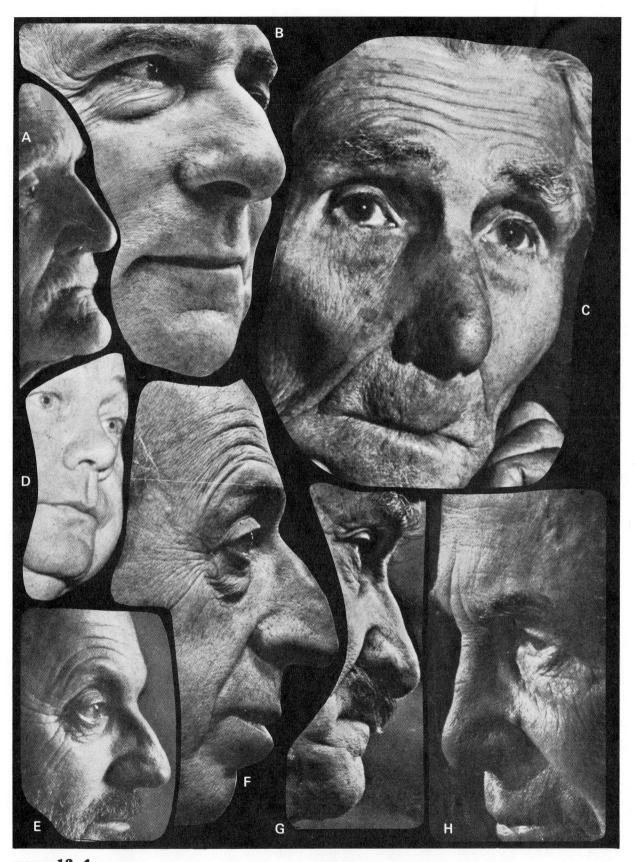

FIGURE 13–4 NOSES.

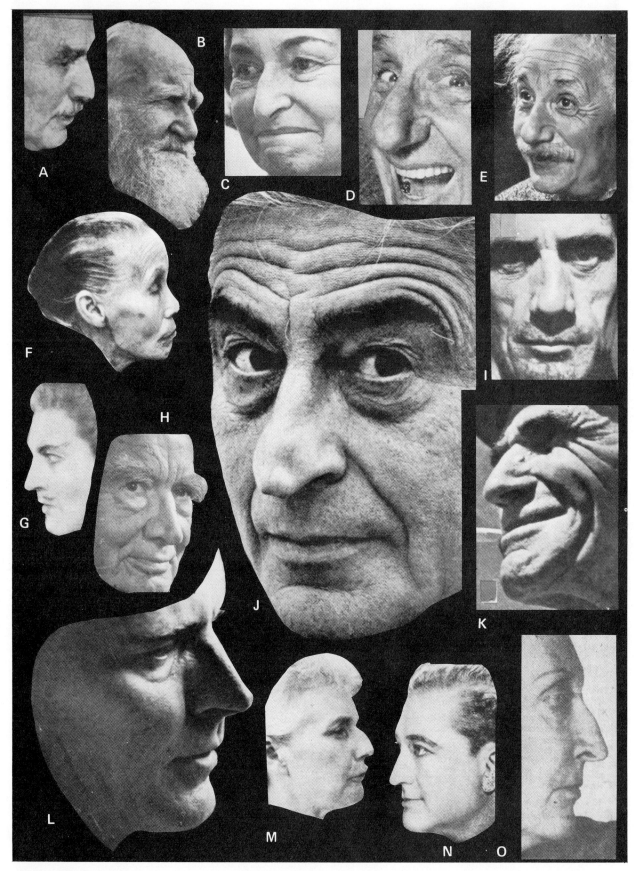

FIGURE **13–5** *NOSES.*

FIGURE 13–6 ELIZABETH I. *Eyebrows and hair around the face blocked out with derma wax. Nose built up with derma wax. Makeup by student Lee Austin on himself. (For a photograph of the makeup in progress, see Figure 16–3.)*

FIGURE 13–7 JOHANNES FUGGER. *Based on a portrait by Dürer. Eyebrows and sideburns blocked out with derma wax. Nose reshaped with nose putty. Makeup by student Lee Austin on himself. (For other makeups by Mr. Austin, see Figures H–21, H–22, and H–30.)*

DERMA WAX

Derma wax (see Appendix A) is softer than nose putty. It can be shaped and blended more easily, but it is also more easily damaged when touched than is nose putty and can loosen and fall off unless it is very firmly attached to the skin. Like nose putty, it should be confined to bony parts of the face. (See Figures 13–6 and 13–7.) For close work you may wish to blend the edges of the wax into the skin with alcohol and a soft brush.

Before using derma wax, apply a coat of spirit gum to the area of the skin to be covered in order to keep the wax from loosening. Let the spirit gum dry, then follow the same procedure as for applying nose putty.

Cotton under Derma Wax For still greater security, cotton fibers can be added to the undercoat of spirit gum before applying the derma wax, as follows:

1. Coat the nose with spirit gum. (Figure 13–8A.)
2. Tap the spirit gum repeatedly with your finger until it becomes very tacky. (Figure 13–8B.)
3. Place a layer of absorbent cotton over a slightly smaller area than that to be covered with derma wax (Figure 13–8C), then press the cotton firmly into the spirit gum.
4. When the spirit gum is dry, pull off all the loose cotton. (Figure 13–8D.)
5. Press a small amount of derma wax onto the cotton, and push it around firmly with one finger to make

sure the cotton fibers are embedded in the wax. (Figure 13–8F.)
6. Press a ball of derma wax into the center of the wax which has just been applied (Figure 13–8G), and mold it with the fingers into the precise shape you want. (Figure 13–8H.) Be sure that the edges are well blended. Using lubricating jelly on the fingers makes the blending easier.

Makeup can be applied directly over the derma wax (Figure 13–8I), or the wax can be coated first with sealer (see Appendix A). If cake makeup is to be used, apply it directly to the wax with no coating of sealer.

The makeup for the nose is completed in the usual way (Figure 13–8J through L).

Derma Wax over Nose Putty Derma wax can also be used over nose putty to provide a smooth surface and an imperceptible blend into the skin—not that this cannot be done with putty, but doing it with wax may be easier and in some cases can save time.

Latex over Derma Wax For greater protection than sealer will give to the surface of the derma-wax construction, latex can be used. This is the procedure:

1. Coat the wax construction with latex. This can be done with the fingers.
2. When the latex is dry, powder it.
3. Use a rubber-mask grease foundation over the latex.

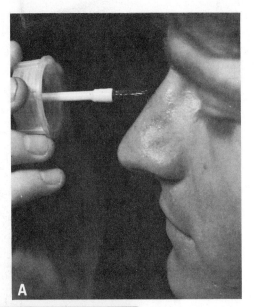

FIGURE 13—8 BUILDING UP THE NOSE WITH DERMA WAX OVER COTTON. (Tom Lindberg.) A. Applying spirit gum to the nose. B. Tapping the spirit gum to make it tacky. C. Applying the cotton. D. Pulling excess cotton off the nose after the spirit gum is dry. E. Cotton foundation for the derma wax. F. First application of derma wax. A small amount of wax is pressed into the cotton, then blended into the skin. G. Second application of derma wax. A ball of derma wax is pressed onto the nose at what is to be the most prominent part. H. Blending the derma wax with lubricating jelly. I. Applying creme makeup foundation with a red-rubber sponge. J. Powdering the nose. K. Pressing the wax with a stipple sponge to add skin texture. The entire nose was then stippled with creme rouge and a dark and light creme makeup for additional texture effect. L. Completed nose. M. Removing the derma wax with tissue.

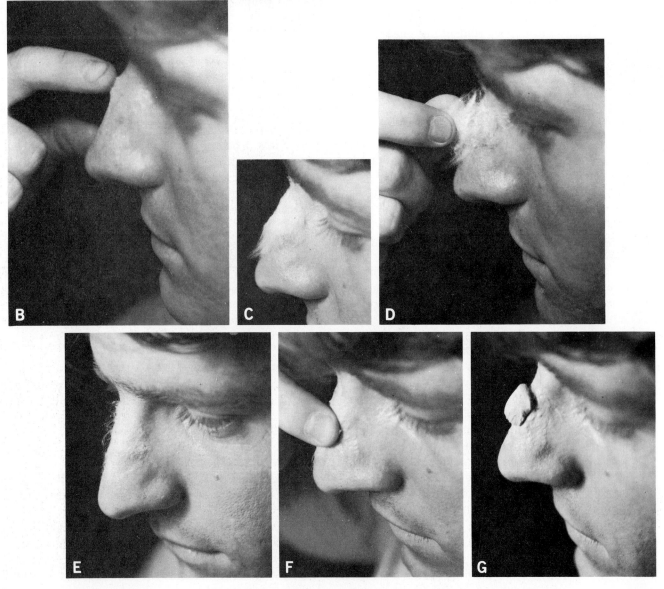

FIG. 13–8 Cont.

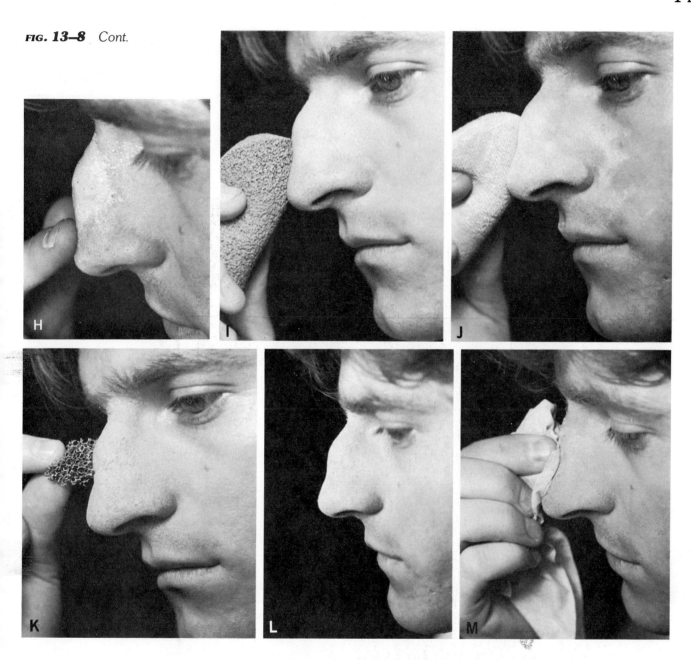

4. If the wax needs texture or wrinkles, they can be added at this point by pressing the wax with the latex negative of a grapefruit skin or with the tip of a brush handle to give a skin-texture effect or with an orangewood stick or a modeling tool to form wrinkles. In doing this, be careful not to puncture or tear the latex skin which protects the wax.
5. Complete the makeup.

Derma Wax Used on the Hands For the severed hand in Figure 13–9, derma wax was used to create the severed effect. For aging the hand in Figure 13–10 (and the witch's hand in Figure 18–23) it was used to build up the knuckles. Unless the makeup is to be used for photographs, tableaux, or very short scenes

in which the hands are not touched or used very much, there should be an undercoat of spirit gum and cotton, and the wax should be covered with latex.

For the hand in Figure 13–10, all of the joints were built up with a firm wax. Several coats of latex were then applied over the entire hand—not merely to protect the wax but to give the effect of wrinkled skin (see the section on *Latex*). The latex was allowed to dry with the fingers flexed, and additional coats were used over the joints. The fingernails were also coated with latex and made up, along with the rest of the hand, using creme makeup instead of the usual rubber-mask grease. The deepening of the wrinkles with brown shadow, which gives a slightly stylized effect, would not normally be done.

FIGURE *13—9* SEVERED HAND. *A section of the hand below the wrist was built up with derma wax to give the illusion of being cut off.*

FIGURE *13—10* AGING THE HAND WITH DERMA WAX AND LATEX. *Makeup by student Mark Frawley. A. Derma wax being applied to the knuckles. B. Derma wax being powdered. C. Clear wax being applied to the fingers. D. Wrinkles being deepened with shadow after several coats of latex have been applied. E. Fingernails being painted with creme makeup before being coated with clear latex. F. Completed hand.*

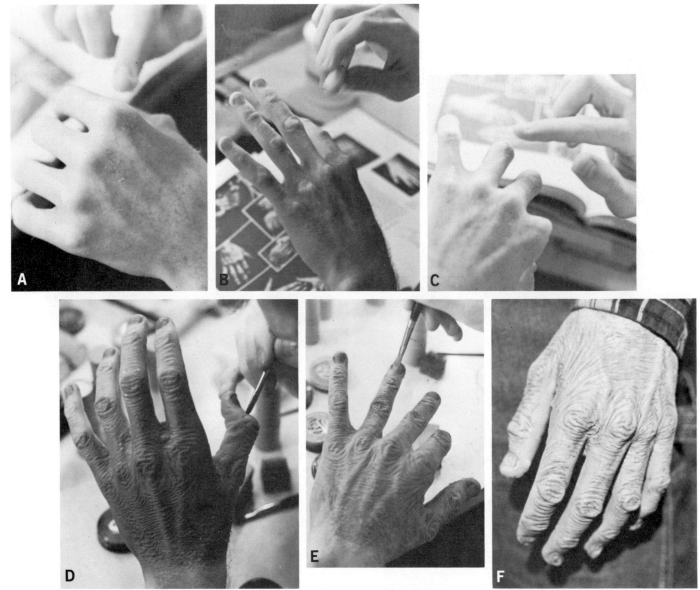

Removing Derma Wax If the derma wax has been applied directly to the skin without any sort of adhesive, most of it can simply be removed with the fingers and the remainder wiped off with makeup remover and tissues.

If spirit gum has been used under the wax, an all-purpose makeup remover (which removes spirit gum along with the rest of the makeup) may work better. If it doesn't, use some spirit-gum remover.

If you have used both spirit gum and cotton under the wax, you might do well, after peeling off as much of the construction as you can with your fingers, to remove the remainder with spirit-gum remover before using your regular makeup remover. If latex has been used over the derma wax, that can be peeled off first and the wax removed as usual.

PUTTY-WAX

A half-and-half mixture of nose putty and derma wax combines to some extent the advantages of each—the greater adhesives of the nose putty and the ease of blending of the derma wax. The mixture can be made up an ounce or so at a time by melting the two together in a double boiler. The mixture can then be poured into a container, cooled, and used as needed. If you are mixing only a small amount, it's simpler to remove half the contents of a metal container of derma wax, add a piece of nose putty to the remaining half, and place the container in a shallow pan of simmering water. When the wax and the putty are both melted, they can be stirred thoroughly, then cooled.

Putty-wax is applied in the same way as nose putty. If it doesn't adhere properly, use spirit gum or spirit gum and cotton under it. (See sections on *Nose putty* and *Derma wax*.)

Putty-wax has been used for the makeups in Figures 10–2 and 12–27.

Removing Putty-Wax Putty-wax can be removed in the same way as derma wax. If spirit gum or spirit gum and cotton have been used under it, see the instructions for removal in the sections on *Nose putty* and *Derma wax*.

GELATINE

Powdered gelatine mixed with hot water provides an efficient means of creating such three-dimensional effects as moles, warts, wounds, scars, and welts, that do not require great precision in modeling. The mixture makes a very thick liquid that solidifies as it cools. That means that you must work rapidly, for once the gelatine has congealed on the skin, it cannot be reshaped—unless, of course, you add more warm gelatine. If that doesn't give you the effect you want, you had better peel it all off and begin again. The congealed gelatine can be made up along with the rest of the face. This is the procedure:

1. Using soap and water or alcohol, cleanse the area of the skin on which the gelatine is to be used, since gelatine will not stick to a greasy or oily surface. Dry the skin thoroughly.
2. Put one envelope (one tablespoon) of gelatine into a small container. (If that makes more gelatine than you need, measure the powdered gelatine by the scant teaspoonful and add an equal number of teaspoonfuls of hot water.) If the container has a lid or can be covered, that will help keep the gelatine warm longer. Setting the container into a pan of hot water will also help. Then add one tablespoonful of very hot tap water and immediately begin stirring the mixture with some sort of rod or stick. An orangewood stick or a modeling tool works very well. Keep stirring until the mixture is very thick and syrupy.

   If you want to color the gelatine, one method is to add a little liquid food coloring of the appropriate color to the hot water, then check to make sure you've used the right amount of color before adding the water to the gelatine. Or you can add a bit of powdered rouge (see *Rouge, dry* in Appendix A) to the powdered gelatine either before or after adding the hot water. If you don't have powdered rouge, simply scrape the surface of a cake of dry rouge to obtain the powder. If you want a color other than red, use a cake of dry eyeshadow or any appropriate shade of cake makeup. For a mottled effect—say, in a mole—you might add to the powdered gelatine such ingredients as sesame seeds, chia seeds, grated nutmeg, or alfalfa seeds (see Figure 13–29). Or, for an unusual, nonrealistic effect, you might even add bits of glitter to the powdered gelatine.
3. The warm gelatine should be applied to the skin immediately with any suitable applicator, such as a modeling tool. Apply only as much as you think you will need. Agitating the gelatine with your applicator will speed the drying and cause the gelatine to become quite sticky and increasingly rubbery before solidifying. During the relatively short time this takes, you should maneuver the gelatine into the form you want. If more gelatine is required, you can add it at any point you like, either before or after the previous application has solidified. Practice will give you a feeling of how the gelatine should be handled.

   Gelatine can be applied to either smooth or hairy skin. Hairs on the skin, rather than creating a problem, as they do with latex, can be advantageous as they will help hold the gelatine in place. And even though

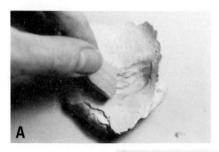

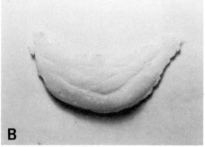

FIGURE *13–11* *MAKING A MOLDED EYE POUCH WITH* *GELATINE.* *A. Gelatine eye pouch being removed from the plaster mold. B. Molded gelatine eye pouch.*

they are embedded in the gelatine, they do not impede its removal.

4. Powder the solidified gelatine, pressing, not stroking, with the powder puff. Then remove excess powder with a powder brush. (If there are edges of the gelatine coming loose from the skin, they can be glued down with spirit gum, which can then be powdered after it has dried. If you are using latex to wrinkle the skin, the gelatine construction should be applied to the skin first, then covered with latex along with the rest of the skin.)

5. The makeup foundation can be applied over all, part, or none of the gelatine. On a wound, for example, the foundation might cover the swollen area but not the open part of the wound. A mole might very well not be covered with foundation, whereas a wart probably would be. Whether a foundation color is applied or not, you may wish to apply special coating to the gelatine construction, as on burns, for example, or fresh wounds (see *Burns* and *Wounds* in the latter part of the chapter under *Special Constructions*). This would be done with creme makeup, greasepaint, cake makeup, lipstick, eyebrow pencil, or dry rouge.

6. Powder the makeup unless powdering would be inappropriate—as, for example, when there is fresh blood in a wound or when you have colored the gelatine with dry rouge. Remove excess powder with a powder brush.

It is also possible to make the gelatine pieces on any smooth, flat surface, then powder them, peel them off the surface, and attach them to the skin with spirit gum. This will give better adhesion, of course. It is also useful when the pieces have to be applied during the performance. They can be made just before the performance, then attached quickly when they are needed.

When you prefer to exercise more precise control over the gelatine, you can pour it into a plaster mold of the three-dimensional addition you wish to make, then let the gelatine cool, lift it out of the mold, and apply it to the skin with spirit gum. (Instructions for making the molds are given in Chapter 14.) This might be done for *eye pouches*, for example, when you are pressed for time and need to make them quickly just before a performance. (For molding a gelatine eye pouch, see Figure 13–11.) There are, however, disadvantages in using gelatine pouches. They are heavier than latex pouches, and they can, of course, be used only once.

Whether made directly on the skin or molded, gelatine constructions should never be used onstage unless you have rehearsed with them under full dress-rehearsal conditions; heat can melt the gelatine and excessive perspiration can loosen it.

LATEX

Liquid latex (see Appendix A) can be used for casting prosthetic pieces (see Chapter 14); for painting on a flat, smooth surface (glass, for example) in order to create pieces, such as welts, that can be transferred to the skin after the latex has dried; and for applying directly to the skin to create three-dimensional wrinkles and skin texture. When using latex on the skin, use only the type that is intended for that purpose. If any latex feels as if it is burning the skin, *don't use it!* Try another brand or another technique that does not involve applying latex directly to the skin.

One method of using latex for aging is to apply clear latex (which is white when in liquid form but dries clear) over an age makeup. (See Figure 13–12.) If you use creme makeup or greasepaint, use as little as possible and set it with translucent powder. If you use cake makeup, which is water-soluble and tends to mix with latex, you will need to be very careful not to smear the makeup. Then, working on one area of the face at a time, pull the skin tight with the fingers and, using either a red-rubber or a foam latex sponge, stipple the latex over the completed makeup. If you don't happen to have a suitable sponge available, you can apply the latex with your fingers. When each area is dry, dust it with powder, then release the skin, which should form wrinkles. If you want deeper wrinkles, apply additional coats of latex in the same way. When the entire face has been covered, the makeup can be touched up with rubber-mask grease, greasepaint, creme makeup, or makeup pencils (provided you have suitable colors).

FIGURE 13–12 *CLEAR LATEX OVER AGE MAKEUP.* Makeup by student Barbara Murray. (For other makeups by Miss Murray, see Figures 12–62, 13–20, 18–9, and 18–10.)

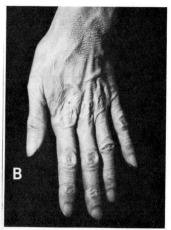

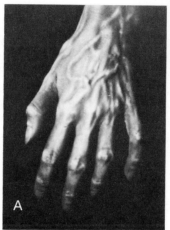

FIGURE 13–13 *HAND AGED WITH LATEX OVER MAKEUP.* Makeup by student Catherine Smith. A. Hand aged with cake makeup. B. Clear latex applied over the makeup.

If you prefer, you can apply the latex first, then add any makeup that seems necessary. For this method, you may or may not wish to tint the latex with a few drops of red, yellow, and blue food coloring (use mostly yellow, some red, and a tiny bit of blue) in order to provide a foundation color. In coloring liquid latex, remember that it turns much darker when it dries. Because latex can be irritating to some skins, it is advisable to coat the skin very lightly first with oil or grease. Any excess can be wiped off gently with a tissue. Powder before applying the latex.

In applying latex to the faces of women and girls or boys of pre-shaving age, using oil or grease may help to keep facial fuzz from becoming embedded in the latex, which could cause considerable discomfort and irritation on removal. Unfortunately, if there is much movement of the facial muscles, the latex may separate from the skin. The likelihood that this will happen is increased by the use of oil or grease, but there is always a chance that it may happen anyway—particularly around the mouth. If it does, loosen the edges of the latex and secure it to the skin with a good spirit gum, which should always be allowed to become tacky before the latex is pressed into it. If, for any reason, you suspect that areas of the latex may loosen before or during the performance, you can loosen them immediately and stick them down with spirit gum.

Latex can also be used to age the hands. But if the hands are hairy, make absolutely certain that the hairs are protected from becoming embedded in the latex, for that would almost certainly result in a good many of them being removed with the latex after the performance. To protect the hairs, coat hairy parts of the hand with spirit gum first, making sure that all of the hairs are embedded in the spirit gum, which should then be allowed to dry before the latex is applied. If there is only a little fuzz or a few short hairs, greasing the back of the hand lightly may provide sufficient protection.

Before applying the latex, stretch the skin tightly by making a fist. Then the latex can be applied, allowed to dry, and powdered. When the hand is relaxed, wrinkles will form. In Figure 13–13 the hand was aged first with cake makeup, then wrinkled with clear latex. For deeper wrinkles, use several coats of latex, making sure that each coat is dry before applying the next. Drying time can be shortened by using a hair dryer.

PLASTIC FILM

Liquid plastic film can be used in the same way as clear latex. *But make sure you use the plastic film intended for application directly on the skin* (see *Plastic film* in

Appendix A). The liquid dries very quickly—a considerable advantage.

Old Age Stipple   Dick Smith has created a remarkably effective latex stipple for aging the skin. This is the formula: (1) Place 90 grams of Schram Foam Latex Base in an 8-ounce paper cup. (2) In another paper cup mix together 10 grams of talc U.S.P., 6 grams of pulverized cake makeup of whatever shade you want for the makeup, and 1 teaspoon of plain Knox gelatine. (3) Stir 3 tablespoons of hot water into the powders, one at a time, until they are dissolved. (4) Stir the solution slowly into the latex, then pour the mixture into glass jars. (5) Place the open jars into hot water for 10 minutes, and stir occasionally. (6) Cap the jars and keep them refrigerated until needed. (7) To prepare the mixture for use, heat a jar of the mixture in hot water until the contents becomes liquefied. (8) To use the latex mixture, stipple it over the stretched skin, and keep the skin stretched until it is dry and has been powdered.

LATEX AND TISSUE

This technique involves the use of liquid latex and cleansing tissue (Figure 13–14) or a good quality of soft paper toweling. The toweling will, of course, give much deeper wrinkles than the tissues. It is usually best to cover the whole face with tissue (or toweling) in order to avoid unnatural contrasts in texture between the tissue-covered wrinkles and the relatively smooth skin. This is the procedure:

1. Be sure the skin is clean and dry. Then use a nonirritating liquid latex to paint the area to be wrinkled. *Avoid getting latex into the hair, eyebrows, eyelashes, or beard.* If the eyebrows are to be covered, block them out first by one of the methods suggested in Chapter 12 so that there are no free hairs. Then they can be safely covered with latex. If there is fuzz on the face, either try a small area first or else lightly oil or grease the skin, then powder it, before applying the latex. You may wish to use the oil or grease anyway to protect the skin, but remember that this can contribute to loosening of the latex during the performance.
2. Tear (do not cut) a single thickness of tissue to the approximate size and shape of the area to be covered, pull the skin tight with one hand, and with the other apply the tissue to the wet latex. For the area around the mouth, a broad smile will probably stretch the skin sufficiently. For best results, work on only a small area at a time.
3. Paint another layer of latex over the tissue and let it dry or force-dry it with a hair dryer.

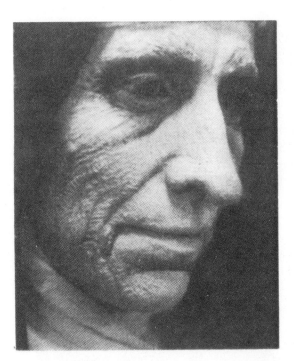

FIGURE 13–14   MAKEUP WITH LATEX AND TISSUE.

4. Release the skin and powder the latex. Wrinkles will form.
5. When all of the latex work is finished, cover it with rubber-mask grease (or greasepaint if rubber-mask grease is not available). If you have used a fairly dark latex, apply a lighter foundation color, catching only the tops of the wrinkles, leaving the darker latex showing through in the creases or tiny depressions. That will emphasize the texture as well as the wrinkles that have formed.
6. Complete the makeup as usual with highlights, shadows, and powder. In order to take advantage of the texture, keep the shading subtle. Touch-ups can be done with makeup pencils if you wish.

The latex can be peeled off quite easily after the performance.

If you want to build up parts of the face when using this technique, it can be done with either derma wax, putty-wax, or nose putty. It is best to keep the addition small, and care should be taken to blend it smoothly into the skin. The following method can be used:

1. Apply small amounts of putty or wax directly to the skin for jowls, nasolabial folds, etc. Avoid building up the mouth area if possible, and be sure to blend the wax or putty smoothly. Use spirit gum first if you prefer. If you use putty or wax on the nose and tissue on the rest of the face, be sure to give the nose some texture by pressing the surface of the putty or the wax with a grapefruit rind or by

stippling with a black plastic stipple sponge or a stiff-bristled brush to create tiny holes in the surface.

2. Apply latex over the entire area to be covered, doing a section at a time, stretching the skin as you go.
3. Apply tissue immediately to the wet latex, then brush another coat of latex over the tissue. Force-dry with a hair dryer before releasing the stretched skin.
4. Powder, then complete your makeup with a rubber-mask grease foundation. Stippling with various colors of paint is usually helpful.

In removing the makeup, peel off the latex. Most of the wax or putty will probably come off with it. Then use any good makeup remover. If you have used spirit gum first and it does not come off with your makeup remover, use spirit-gum remover or alcohol.

In using this technique, it's a good idea to experiment with small areas first, keeping the constructions small and simple.

Latex should never be used for a performance unless it has first been tried for at least one full rehearsal, preferably more. It sometimes works loose from the skin, especially if the actor perspires very much or if there is considerable movement of the muscles. The best solution to the problem is probably to use a method not requiring the direct application of latex to the skin. In the following method, which is generally to be preferred to the one just described, spirit gum is used as an adhesive.

SPIRIT GUM, TISSUE, AND LATEX

1. Coat the stretched skin with a good spirit gum, first letting the gum become tacky (or inducing tackiness by tapping the gum rapidly with the finger as described earlier and illustrated in Figure 13–8B).
2. Stretch the skin and apply single thicknesses of tissue that have been torn, not cut. Avoid straight edges. If you want to push the tissue into deeper wrinkles than those that will form naturally, do so at this point. Let the spirit gum dry or force-dry it with a hair dryer.
3. Stretch the skin again and apply a coat of latex. Let the latex dry or force-dry it with a hair dryer before releasing the skin.
4. Powder the latex.
5. Complete your makeup, using a rubber-mask grease foundation. Greasepaint or creme makeup can be used if rubber-mask grease is not available. Stipple as usual.

The makeup can be removed by brushing spirit-gum remover along the edge, then pulling the layers of tissue and latex up gradually, brushing with remover as you go in order to loosen the spirit gum.

LATEX, COTTON, AND SPIRIT GUM

In Figures 13–15 and 13–16 latex, cotton, and spirit gum have been used for two very different makeups—one requiring a skin texture appropriate for a frail old lady and the other, the abnormal, leathery skin of the young Elephant Man, whose eyes alone reveal his youthfulness. This is the technique:

1. Paint the skin with spirit gum, working on one section of the face at a time. The forehead is a good place to start. (See Figure 13–16A.) The eyes or the mouth can be done last. If you cover the eyebrows, flatten them out first with Kryolan's Eyebrow Plastic, Special Plastic, or derma wax so that they will not get stuck in the latex.
2. Tap the spirit gum with your finger until it is tacky, then lay on absorbent cotton (Figure 13–16A through E) and let the gum dry. Be sure the fibers follow in the direction you want the wrinkles to go—that is, vertically over the mouth, almost vertically down the cheeks, and horizontally on the forehead.
3. Pull off most of the cotton (Figure 13–16F). The less you leave on, the less pronounced the three-dimensional effect will be.
4. Cover the cotton with latex, using your finger rather than a brush. This step should be done with the skin tightly stretched. *Avoid getting latex into the hair, eyebrows, eyelashes, or beard!* Only one section

FIGURE 13–15 MAKEUP WITH LATEX, COTTON, AND SPIRIT GUM. *Rubber-mask grease foundation with cake makeup highlights and shadows. Makeup by student Sally Palmquist.*

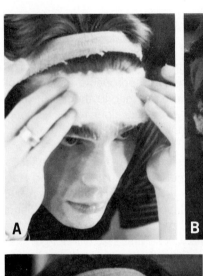

A

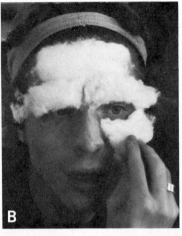

B

FIGURE 13–16 *SKIN TEXTURE WITH LATEX, COTTON, AND SPIRIT GUM.* *Makeup for* The Elephant Man *by student Milton Blankenship. A. Applying thick layer of cotton over spirit gum after the gum has become tacky. B. Applying cotton to the cheekbones. C. Applying cotton to the upper lip. D. Applying cotton to the jaw line, chin, and lower lip. E. Thick layer of cotton completed. F. Pulling off excess cotton. G. Applying latex to the chin area. H. Chin after latex has been dried. I. Stretching skin on cheek and jaw area as latex is being dried. J. Wrinkles on cheek and jaw after latex is dry. K. Drying latex on upper lip. L. Stretching skin over cheekbone as latex is being dried. M. Rubber-mask grease applied over the dried latex.*

C

D

E

F

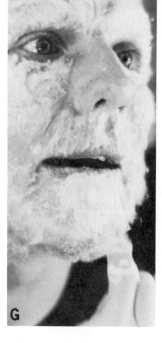

G

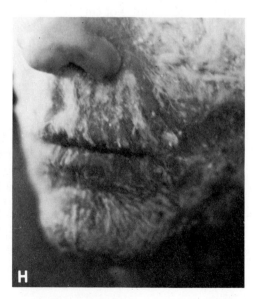

H

FIG. **13–16** *Cont.*

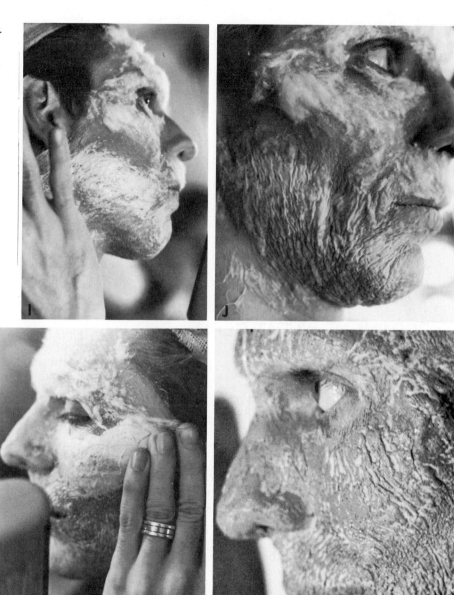

of the face should be done at a time. The mouth can be stretched with a broad smile, which must be held until the latex is dry. The skin of the cheeks can be pulled taut with the fingers (Figure 13–16L). A hair dryer can be used to speed the drying. When the latex is dry, release the skin, and it will fall naturally into wrinkles (Figure 13–16M).

5. If the eyebrows are covered, crepe-hair eyebrows can be attached with latex.

6. Give the latex a coat of rubber-mask grease (or greasepaint if rubber-mask grease is not available). With a velour puff, press a generous amount of powder into the grease, then remove the excess with a powder brush.

7. Finish the makeup with highlights and shadows of grease or creme makeup, then powder.

Most of the makeup can be peeled off, but because of the undercoat of spirit gum, it will peel less easily than latex usually does. The remainder of the gum can be cleaned from the skin with spirit gum remover or alcohol. In pulling the latex off and in dissolving the spirit gum, be extremely careful around the eyes and the eyebrows. To avoid pulling hairs out of the eyebrows, pull very slowly and brush a little alcohol or spirit gum remover into them as you go.

This technique can also be effective on the hands (see Figure 13–17).

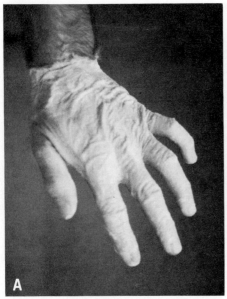

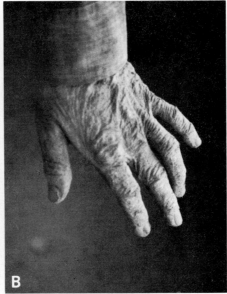

A

B

FIGURE **13–17** *HAND AGED WITH LATEX, COTTON, AND SPIRIT GUM.* Makeup by student Larry Lane. A. Cotton attached to the hand with spirit gum, then coated with latex. B. Foundation, 3 colors of stipple, and brown spots applied over the latex.

CORNMEAL, WHEAT GERM, OR BRAN WITH LATEX AND SPIRIT GUM

In order to give the skin a rough texture, with or without wrinkling, cornmeal (Figure 13–18), wheat germ, or miller's bran (Figure 13–19) can be used with the latex. This is the procedure:

1. Apply spirit gum to the skin and allow it to become tacky or induce tackiness by tapping the gum rapidly with one finger (as described earlier and illustrated in Figure 13–18B).
2. When the gum is sufficiently tacky, cover it with cornmeal, wheat germ, or bran (see Figure 13–19A).

FIGURE **13–18** *HAND AGED WITH LATEX AND CORNMEAL.* Makeup by student Howard Klein.

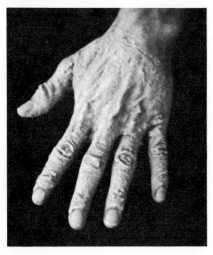

This can be done with the hands. Do *not* try to apply it with a tissue; the tissue will tend to stick to the spirit gum and tear, leaving small pieces that may be difficult to remove. If you want the skin to look wrinkled as well as rough, stretch it before applying the cornmeal, wheat germ, or bran.

3. Apply latex (Figure 13–19B) with the skin stretched or not stretched, as you prefer, and let it dry or force-dry it with a hair dryer. It is also possible, when using cornmeal, to mix it with the latex before applying it to the skin. (See Figure 13–21C.)
4. Complete the makeup, using a rubber-mask-grease foundation (Figure 13–19C).

Bran and latex, appropriately made up, can also be used to simulate wounds, growths, or diseased conditions of the skin.

TISSUE AND HONEY

For quick changes in which an age makeup is needed for the first scene and must be quickly removed for a subsequent scene, honey (or Karo syrup) can be used as an adhesive. The procedure is much the same as for latex and tissue.

1. Using the fingers or a stiff-bristled brush (a glue or paste brush will do), apply the honey to the skin. (As with other methods, this should be done one area at a time.)
2. Lay on a single thickness of peach-colored tissue, torn to the approximate size and shape of the area you are working on. If you prefer, tear the tissue after it is on.

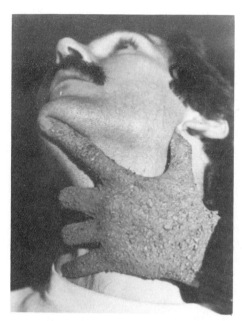

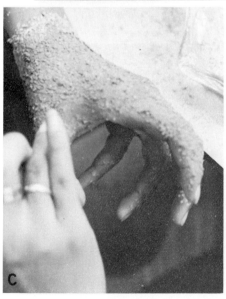

FIGURE 13–19 SKIN TEXTURED WITH LATEX AND MILLER'S BRAN. *Makeup by student Karyn Alston. A. Bran being applied to tacky spirit gum. B. Bran being covered with clear latex. C. Makeup being applied over latex. D. Hand after powdering.*

3. Follow the same procedure for other areas. If you are covering most of the face, you should also cover the neck.

4. If the honey has not soaked through all of the tissue, it is usually desirable to add a coat of honey on top of the tissue. If you do that, let it dry or force-dry it with a hair dryer, then press powder into it to eliminate any stickiness. Remove excess powder with a soft brush.

5. Cover both the tissue and all exposed skin with creme makeup or greasepaint. If, however, the peach-colored tissue blends with the skin tone and gives a suitable color, you may not need a foundation—a great convenience for quick changes. It is also possible to use the honey and colored tissue over a cake makeup. This is often done when the tissue is to be used on only part of the face (under the eyes, for example) or when there is a quick change involved.

6. With brush and fingers, add grease or creme shadows and highlights or, better yet, use fairly heavy cake shadows under the tissue and stipple on cake highlights over it. If this is done, the honey, with no foundation color, should be used over the tissue. The highlights and shadows may or may not be necessary, depending on the amount of projection required. For arena theater, particularly, the tissue alone, with or without foundation, may be quite sufficient.

7. Powder the makeup with translucent powder, and touch up if necessary.

Although this type of makeup is fairly stable for short periods, it will be loosened by excessive perspiration, which dissolves the honey. The makeup can easily be removed with a makeup remover or by peeling off the tissue, then cleansing the face with soap and water.

TISSUE AND SPIRIT GUM

Another method of achieving wrinkled skin texture involves using facial or bathroom tissue with spirit gum. (See Figure 13–20.) It is particularly effective in aging the hands (Figure 13–21B). This is the procedure:

1. Double the hand into a tight fist, then paint the back of the hand, from knuckles to wrist, with spirit gum.
2. Place tissue torn (not cut) to approximately the right size over the spirit gum, which can be fairly wet. (For deeper wrinkles in the final makeup, the tissue can be pushed into wrinkles at this point. If this is not going to be done, the spirit gum can be tacky instead of wet.) Then add a coating of spirit gum over the tissue.
3. Let the spirit gum dry or force-dry it with a hair dryer.
4. Powder the spirit gum and remove excess powder with a powder brush.
5. Apply spirit gum to the fingers.
6. Apply tissue to the fingers. (The fingers should be flexed when the tissue is applied so that when they are straightened out, the tissue will wrinkle at the joints.)

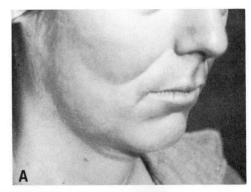

FIGURE 13–20 TISSUE AND SPIRIT GUM OVER AGE MAKEUP. *Makeup by student Barbara Murray. A. Highlights and shadows applied with creme makeup. B. Tissue and spirit gum applied over the makeup.*

7. Apply the foundation paint. If you are using cake makeup, stipple or press the makeup on with your sponge rather than stroking it on. If the cake makeup turns light or chalky, cover it with lubricating jelly and let the jelly dry.
8. Using a narrow brush, model the bones and veins with highlights and shadows. Or, if you prefer, you can do the highlighting and shadowing before the tissue is applied rather than after, in which case both shadows and highlights should be stronger than

FIGURE 13–21 HAND AGED WITH DIFFERENT TECHNIQUES. *A. Cake makeup. B. Tissue and spirit gum over cake makeup. C. Latex and cornmeal.*

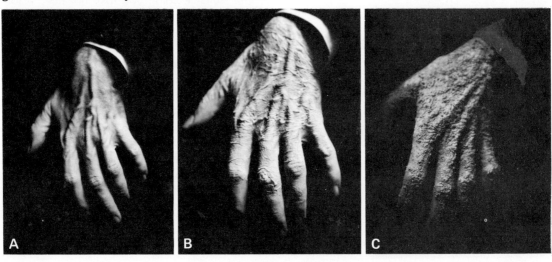

usual. When the shadows and highlights are completed, they should be powdered—unless, of course, they have been applied with cake makeup.

9. The hand can be stippled in various ways—by stippling two or three colors over the base, by eliminating the base color and stippling heavily over the tissue and spirit gum, or by stippling less heavily over the tissue and spirit gum, letting some of the natural color of the hand show through. Painting on the brown spots often seen on aged hands can also be helpful. This can be done instead of or in combination with stippling.

Be sure to carry the makeup far enough up the arm to be covered by the sleeve of the costume.

SPECIAL CONSTRUCTIONS

The constructions in the following list can all be made by direct methods. Some of them might also be done with the molded latex technique discussed in the next chapter.

Black Eye A black eye involving only swelling and bruising can be simulated with paint. It may involve only the orbital area or the checkbone as well. In either case, it changes color as it ages. There is more red at first, but then the inflammation subsides, leaving a deep purple color (giving the "black" effect), medium or dark gray, and the greenish yellow color typical of bruises which are no longer inflamed. See the photographs of the real black eye in Figure H–9 in the color section.

To create the effect of the drooping eyelid in Figure H–5A, close the eyes half-way, then make a tissue-paper pattern of the eyelid, using a soft eyebrow pencil. When the pattern of the eyelid has been marked on the tissue paper, cut the paper along the pencil line, and place the resulting paper pattern on the eyelid to test for accuracy. After making any necessary corrections, use the pattern to cut a matching shape on Johnson & Johnson Dermacil adhesive tape. Then attach the Dermacil piece to the eyelid, and make it up along with the rest of the eye. It will keep the eyelid half-closed even when the other eye is wide open.

The various stages of a black eye can be simulated by mixtures of red, purple, black, white, and greenish or lemon yellow. The purple can be deepened with black, and if the mixture is not red enough, red can be added. Or it can be stippled with black and red. Black and white can be mixed for the gray. For the yellowish tinge, lemon yellow can be mixed with just a little light gray (white with a touch of black) or stippled with light gray. The white can be used for highlights for light-skinned characters and stippled down later to give it the approximate

value. For dark-skinned characters, colors will be deeper and more grayed. All of the color can be applied with a brush or with a small black stipple sponge.

If the cheekbone is to be involved, you can highlight it just below the corner of the eye. The area immediately below the eye (including the lower lid) and the superciliary bone above the outer corner of the eye can also be highlighted. For light-skinned characters, white can be used for these highlights and stippled down later. For dark-skinned characters, it would be better to use a color a few shades lighter than the base. Gray shadow can then be stippled below all of the highlights and in the eye socket. Purple and black stipple can be added when appropriate. The shape of the darkened area will usually be a somewhat irregular oval. All edges of both highlights and shadows should be kept soft.

The red should be stippled on last. For a fresh black eye, it can cover the entire area but should be applied more heavily around the highlights and more lightly on them.

The swelling of the lid accompanying a black eye can be more effectively simulated with paint if the actor can keep the bruised eye partially closed. Since some people can do that more easily with one eye than the other, it would be best—unless there is an overriding reason for not doing so—to let that be the bruised eye.

Blindness The actor can usually suggest blindness by keeping the eyes nearly closed (see the photograph of Helen Keller, Figure 13–22K). For blindness involving disfigurement of the orbital area, you might cast a blind eye and make a molded latex piece from it (see Chapter 14 for casting methods); or if you have a plaster cast of the actor's head but don't have time to cast the blind eye, you could model a blind eye on the cast in clay, then paint latex over the clay. Although that would not have the texture or the detail of a cast piece, it would give you a molded piece that would fit the actor.

Whatever kind of piece you use, it should, of course, be appropriately painted or made up. For an open, staring eye, for example, or even a partially opened one, you might paint the eye on with either makeup or acrylic paint. You might even glue on false eyelashes. To enable the actor to see through the eye, a hole could be cut into the piece and gauze glued to the back, then painted to conceal it.

Bruises Even when accompanied by swelling, a bruise can usually be simulated with paint. (See Figure H–18 in the color section.) For Caucasians, red, gray, purple, greenish yellow, and light cream or ivory can be used. The fresher the bruise, the more red; the older it is, the more yellow. For darker-skinned characters, the colors should be adjusted to the color of the skin. The color being used can be either dabbed on the bruised area

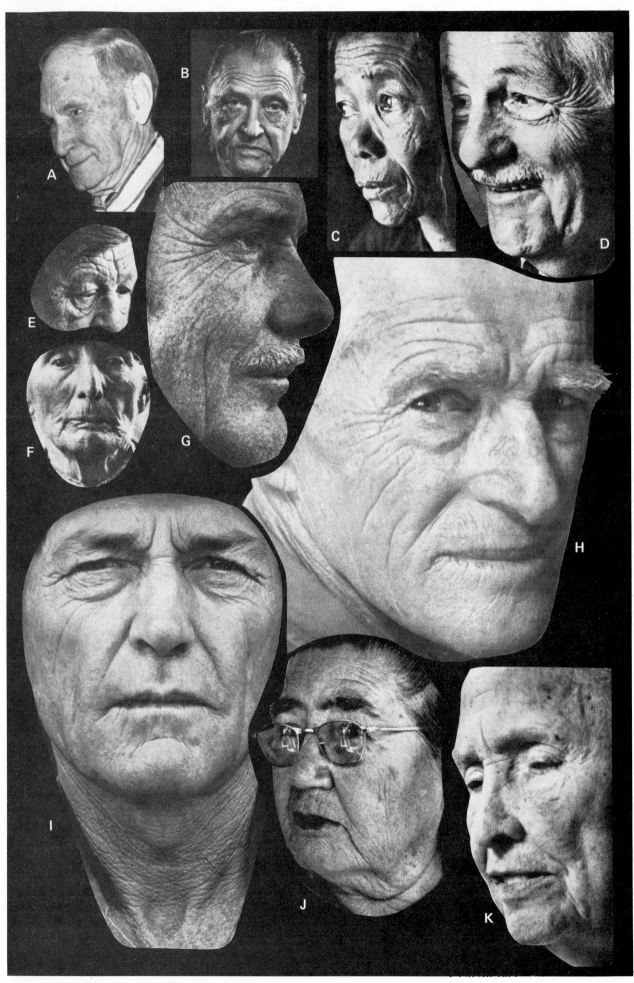

FIGURE **13–22** SKIN TEXTURE AND WRINKLES.

FIGURE **13–23** *SKIN TEXTURE AND WRINKLES.*

FIGURE **13—24** SKIN TEXTURE AND WRINKLES.

and then blended together with a brush, or stippled on. In either case, make sure that all edges are soft. If the bruised area is to be *very* swollen, you may want to build it up first with derma wax. (See *Welts*.)

Burns Minor burns can be simulated by stippling the skin with red makeup applied with a red-rubber sponge. For deeper burns, coat the skin with latex, which can be pulled loose and allowed to hang if you want it to. A single layer of cleansing tissue placed over the latex and then covered with another layer of latex will give more body to the hanging skin. Cotton can be used with the latex for burnt flesh. Makeup can be applied over the latex. For close work you might drop candle wax onto the latex to give the effect of blisters. (For a hand burned by scalding water, see Figure H–14.)

Cuts Superficial cuts can be painted on, with or without the use of artificial blood. Deeper cuts usually require building up the area with wax or putty, then cutting into it with a dull instrument, such as a palette knife (Figure H–19B). Plastic sealer can be painted over the construction at this point if you wish.

The inside of the cut can be painted red with greasepaint (Figure H–19B). For a cut that is still bleeding, a few drops or even a stream of artifical blood can be added to the cut with an eye dropper and allowed to run out onto the skin.

In some areas, such as the neck, where building up with putty or wax may not be practicable, latex can be painted directly onto the skin and allowed to dry thoroughly. The skin can then be pushed together into a crease in the middle of the strip of latex. The latex will stick to itself, forming a deep crease (Figure H–17A) that can be made to look like a cut with the addition of red makeup. Blood may or may not be running from the cut. In Figure H–17B bleeding has stopped, and most of the blood has been wiped off.

For a horizontal cut in the throat, be sure to use a natural crease in the skin if there is one. Pinching of the skin is not recommended but is sometimes done.

Ears If you are making up such characters as sprites, leprechauns, and devils, it may be necessary to make pointed ears. Although latex pieces should be used for close work, the following simple, direct construction can be used in an emergency:

1. Cut a paper pattern the exact size and shape of the tip to be added.
2. Cut a small square of muslin and trace the ear pattern onto it. Cut out around this about ¼ inch beyond the edge on all sides. You will need four of these pieces.
3. Stitch two of the pieces of muslin together on the penciled line, leaving the bottom open.
4. Turn this double piece inside out, insert a bent pipe cleaner, and shape it to the pointed tip, cutting it off a fraction of an inch above the bottom of the ear construction. Two pipe cleaners can be used for a thicker piece.
5. Stitch along the inner side of the pipe cleaner to hold it in place. Then trim the bottom of the piece to fit the real ear.
6. Attach the muslin or gauze to the ear with spirit gum, making sure you let the gum become tacky before attaching the piece. Both front and back of the upper curve of the ear should be painted with gum so that the two layers of muslin can encase the ear. The muslin can be coated with latex or with plastic sealer if you like.
7. When the gum is thoroughly dry, cover the pieces with rubber-mask grease or with greasepaint along with the rest of the ear. Touching the tip and the lobe with rouge will give a more lifelike quality. The tip can be removed with spirit-gum remover or alcohol and used a number of times.

Small additions can be made with putty (Figure 13–25). The putty should be covered with plastic sealer so as not to get stuck in the hair. Since it may not always hold its shape in hot weather on a hot stage, and since it must be made up fresh for every performance, it is less satisfactory than a latex piece.

Eyelid, Oriental (For real Oriental eyelids see Figures 12–16I, 12–18D,E, 12–23, 12–24, and 13–24A.) If the eye is so deepset as to make it difficult or impossible to create the effect of an Oriental eye with paint, and if

FIGURE 13–25 PHANTOM OF THE OPERA. *Ear modeled with putty-wax. Stylized silent-screen makeup by student Richard Brunner.*

a latex eyelid (Chapter 14) is not practicable, a satisfactory effect can usually be achieved with adhesive tape. This is one method:

1. Tear or cut slightly over 2 inches of tape from a roll at least 1 inch wide. This tape is represented by the broken line (A) in Figure 13–26.
2. Mark and cut as shown by the heavy lines (13–26B). This forms the eye opening and rounds off the upper edges so that the tape will be easier to conceal. (It is best to make a paper pattern first, then mark the tape.)
3. Cover the area indicated by C with makeup on the *back* of the tape. This gives a nonsticky area over the actor's own eyelid.
4. Attach the tape (usually slightly on the diagonal) so

FIGURE 13–26 DIAGRAM OF ORIENTAL EYELID MADE WITH ADHESIVE TAPE.

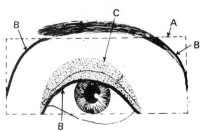

FIGURE **13–27** *ORIENTAL EYELID MADE WITH ADHE-SIVE TAPE.* *Edges are stippled with latex and the tape darkened with rubber-mask grease. Makeup is completed with eyebrow pencil and creme makeup. Notice how the flat tape is slightly rounded with shadowing.*

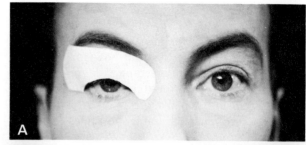

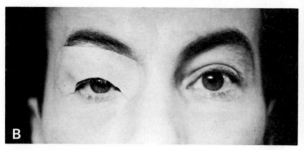

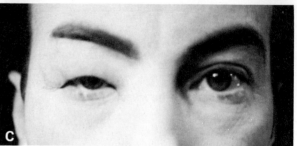

that the top falls just below the natural brow and covers the downward sweep of the outer end (Figure 13–27A). In order to prevent the eyebrow's appearing to be cut off too abruptly, lift a few hairs from under the tape and let them fall on the outside. Stipple the edges of the tape with latex cream adhesive to help conceal them.

5. When the latex is dry, cover the tape and the skin with foundation color (Figure 13–27B), and finish the makeup. If you are using cake makeup, cover the tape and a little of the skin around it with grease or creme makeup first; powder; then apply the cake makeup. In order to counteract the flatness of the tape, shadow the lower edge and highlight the center to give a puffy effect (Figure 13–27C).

The cutting of the tape can be greatly simplified by cutting 4 inches instead of 2, folding it double, sticky sides together, marking and cutting either side, then separating the two pieces. This will ensure that both eyes are exactly alike. If you place a piece of waxed paper between the two sticky sides, you will have no trouble getting them apart. Be sure the tape is not uncomfortable, that it does not interfere with the normal action of the eyelid, and that the actor can see without difficulty.

It is also possible to make Oriental eyelids with liquid plastic, using the technique described in the following section for making sagging eyelids. The main point of difference, aside from the change in shape, is that when the tab at the bottom (corresponding to A′ in Figure 13–28A) is folded up to create the almond-shaped opening for the lid, it will have to be clipped in several places in order to give a smooth curve.

A simpler tape construction can be used with equal effectiveness on certain eyes. This consists of a crescent-shaped piece of adhesive tape, the outer edge of which is attached to the side of the nose and under the inner end of the eyebrow. The inner edge of the crescent (which should be very nearly a half moon) hangs free. The purpose of the piece is to conceal the deep depressions (plane A, Figure 12–14) that are normal to the Caucasian eye.

Eyelid, Sagging A sagging eyelid (Figure 13–28) can be constructed in much the same way as an Oriental eyelid, except that the tape should slant down from the inner end of the eyebrow to the outer corner of the eye. The upper edge of the tape can correspond exactly to the bottom of the natural brow; or the tape can be used to block out part of the brow, and a new brow can be glued onto the tape or attached to the skin above the tape. The projection (A′) is folded under, along the dotted line, before the tape is attached to the skin. This gives the appearance of a fold of flesh.

Plastic film (see Appendix A) can be used instead of the tape in constructing the eyelid and is much to be preferred since it has greater flexibility, is less bulky, and has thinner edges. The piece shown in Figure 13–28C can be cut from a sheet of plastic film or formed by painting liquid plastic (see Appendix A) onto glass to conform to a pattern of the piece placed under the glass (Figure 13–28B).

The advantage of this method is that edges can be kept very thin, whereas the center portion can be given more firmness with additional coats of plastic. Since many coats of plastic may be needed to give the desired thickness, dropping the liquid plastic onto the area to be built up instead of brushing it on will speed up the process.

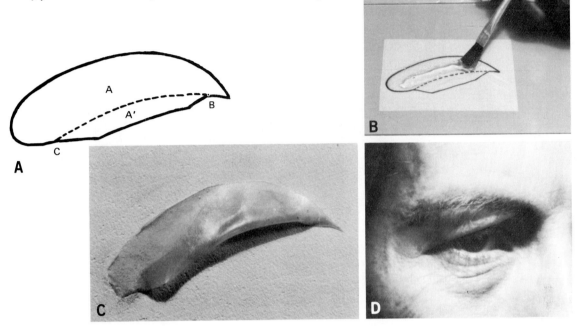

FIGURE 13–28 *SAGGING EYELID.* *A. Pattern for the sagging eyelid shown in C. and used for the makeup in D. (Reproduced here in the exact size used.) B. Painting plastic eyelid on glass. Pattern is placed under the glass. C. Plastic eyelid folded and ready for use. D. Plastic eyelid attached but not made up.*

When the plastic piece is dry, it should be powdered, then removed from the glass (see discussion under *Scars* and *Welts.*) The tab (A′) should be folded under and glued down or secured with translucent plastic tape (see *Adhesive tape* in Appendix A). The piece can then be applied with spirit gum. Before pressing it down into place, make sure that it is exactly where you want it. If you want to experiment first with various placements, coat the edges of the plastic with stubble adhesive (see Appendix A). The piece will then adhere temporarily to the skin. This experimentation should be done before any makeup is applied to the area.

In experimenting with the placement, try it with various expressions, such as a frown or raised eyebrows.

If any reshaping of the piece is necessary as a result of this experimentation, it can be done before the spirit gum is applied. Should this trimming result in any thickened edges, they can be thinned by placing the piece on the glass and brushing the edges with acetone until they are thinned down.

Makeup can then be applied as usual. As with any prosthetic piece, never use this eyelid for a performance unless it has first been worn for at least one entire rehearsal—preferably more.

Clear latex can be used in essentially the same way and builds up more quickly, though it may take longer to dry.

If you plan to use the eyelids for a number of performances, making molded latex eyelids (see Chapter 14) is much more efficient.

Fingernails Long fingernails can be cut out of used photographic film or sheets of acetate and glued onto the natural nails with spirit gum. They can be colored with nail polish or paint. Ready-made false fingernails, if they are long enough, provide a simpler solution to the problem.

Moles (Figures 13–29 and H–11.) These raised and sometimes hairy spots on the skin can be created with such materials or combinations of materials as derma wax, gelatine, cotton and spirit gum, gelatine and alfalfa or chia seeds, latex, and wheat germ. They can be formed directly on the skin before any makeup is applied or they can be made on any convenient smooth surface and attached with spirit gum after they have solidified. They can be appropriately colored when the rest of the makeup is applied. If a mole is to be hairy, the hairs can be embedded in the material as the mole is being made. If the mole is to be small and smooth, a few drops of latex can be transferred to any flat glass or other smooth, nonabsorbent surface with an orangewood stick, a small glass rod, or a brush handle and then allowed to dry. The latex must be thick enough so that it will not spread out when it touches the surface. And it must dry completely before it can be used.

FIGURE 13–29 **MAKING A MOLE WITH GELATINE AND ALFALFA SEEDS.** *A. Ingredients for the mole: gelatine, alfalfa seeds, and hot water. B. Mixing the ingredients. C. Forming the mole on the skin, using an orangewood stick. D. The finished mole. (Enlarged.) E, F. Gelatine moles, natural size.*

Since gelatine has a rather natural, flesh-like appearance, it is likely to require less makeup than other materials and may sometimes require none at all. When color is needed, powdered rouge or scrapings from cake rouge, cake eyeshadow, or cake makeup foundation can be added to the powdered gelatine before the hot water is added, or the gelatine mole can be touched up with cake eyeshadow, creme shading colors, or light, medium, or dark brown eyebrow pencils.

Moles can also be made by mixing liquid latex with alfalfa or chia seeds (and with scrapings from the top of an appropriate shade of brownish cake makeup if you want the mole to be colored), then pouring or spooning enough for one mole onto glass (or other smooth surface) and letting it dry. When it is dry, the top of the mole should be powdered, but the bottom must not be. If you want to attach the mole directly to the skin before applying any makeup, brush a spot of clear latex onto the skin and let it dry. Then carefully lift the mole off the glass with tweezers and press it onto the spot of dried latex on the skin.

Perspiration The effect of perspiration can be created by applying glycerine over the finished makeup. The glycerine should be applied with the fingers rather than with any sort of applicator, in order to avoid damaging the makeup.

Pimples Although pimples can be created three-dimensionally with latex, derma wax, sesame seeds, etc.,

they can also be painted on with tiny highlights, shadows, and creme rouge.

If there are to be a lot of them, and the whole area that they cover is to be reddened, the reddening can be done first by stippling, to whatever degree is appropriate, with a somewhat muted creme rouge. In order to determine the appropriate shade, observe the color of real pimples. The pimples, varying in size and irregularly placed, can then be modeled with highlights and shadows, using a very small brush. If, after the makeup is powdered, the pimples need toning down, that can be done with additional stippling, either with the creme rouge or with the foundation color, whichever is more appropriate.

For a single pimple or a few fairly large pimples, begin with a round, reddish spot a bit larger than the raised portion of the pimple in order to create the effect of an inflamed area around the pimple. To create the raised portion of the pimple, place a small, round highlight in the center of the reddish spot. Then, with a tiny brush, shadow around the bottom of the highlight as if you were modeling a sphere. The edges of all three colors in the pimple must be soft. Unless you are using cake makeup, the pimple or the pimpled area should, of course, be powdered.

Scabs Scabs can be made directly on the skin with derma wax, spirit gum and cotton, or gelatine. When gelatine or spirit gum and cotton are used, the scab can be made on any smooth surface (glass, marble, formica) and, when it has dried, attached to the skin with spirit gum. Or it can be made directly on the skin. It can be appropriately colored (see Figure H–10) either before or after it has been applied. Scabs can also be cast in latex and attached with spirit gum. (See Chapter 14.)

When gelatine is used to make the scab, the gelatine can be colored by adding various shades of dry rouge and cake makeup (especially browns and deep reds) before it is applied to the skin. Additional coloring can be added, if necessary, after the gelatine has solidified. When derma wax is used, spirit gum and cotton should be applied to the skin first—unless the skin is hairy, in which case the cotton may not be necessary. Or spirit gum and cotton can be used without the derma wax. In either case, coloring is added after construction of the scab has been completed.

Scabs can also be made by first painting the area of the scab with latex, then immediately placing a pinch or two of Red Zinger tea on the wet latex and letting the latex dry. Use a soft brush to remove any of the tea which is not anchored in the latex. For a thick scab, use more latex so that more of the tea will adhere to it. Or if you find, when the latex has dried, that the scab is too flat, simply paint on another coat of latex and add more tea. If the scab isn't exactly the color you want, touch it up with creme makeup colors and powder it.

With all of these direct methods, any hairs on the skin will become embedded in the artificial scab, as they do with real scabs, and will help to hold it in place.

Scars The traditional method of creating scars of the type illustrated in Figures 13–30F,I,J, and 13–31 is to paint the area to be scarred with nonflexible collodion before any makeup is applied. As the collodion dries, it will wrinkle and draw the skin. If the scar is not deep enough, successive coats can be applied. Each coat should be allowed to dry completely before another is added. The makeup is then applied as usual.

A better method is to use cake makeup as a foundation and apply the collodion over it. Makeup may or may not be needed over the collodion, depending on the effect you want. For additional protection to the skin, apply cleansing cream, moisture cream, or any good skin cream to the skin first, then wipe off the excess before applying the cake makeup. *Avoid using collodion close to the eye.*

As for color, recent scars will, of course, have more red in them than will old scars, which may have less color than the normal skin. For a 12-week-old surgical scar, see Figure H–13 in the color section. (Figure 13–32 shows the same scar in black and white.)

Collodion scars can be peeled off or removed with acetone. Because dermatologists consider this prolonged creasing of the skin undesirable, this method of making scars cannot be recommended. In addition, collodion may irritate the skin, though applying the collodion over the makeup rather than directly to the skin should cause less irritation. However, if there is any irritation at all, this method should not be used. Latex scars, which can be attached with spirit gum, can be used instead. Or you can use one of the methods described below.

One simple but effective method is to use cleansing tissue or absorbent cotton with latex and spirit gum. The spirit gum is applied first, then a very thin piece of cotton or tissue, then latex. The scarred area can be roughened as much as you like by pulling up bits of cotton or by wrinkling the tissue. Derma wax and other materials can also be used. (See Figure 13–33C and D.) Special coloring for the scar may or may not be necessary.

If latex has not been used in making the scar (or sometimes even if it has), it's a good idea to coat the scar with sealer after the makeup has been completed. That will not only protect the scar but also give it a slight natural sheen.

Another method is to pour or brush latex onto glass and, with a palette knife or an orangewood stick, swirl it and shape it into the size and kind of scar you want. Then allow it to dry, or force-dry it with a hair dryer, peel it off the glass, and apply it to the skin with spirit gum. When you complete the makeup, color the scar appropriately. This is a variation of the molded latex scars or welts described in Chapter 14. It is a particularly good technique for arena staging. For greater projection, combine the latex with cotton or tissue.

Similar techniques can be used to make scars with plastic sealer or liquid plastic film. The plastic is poured or smeared onto glass, then swirled with an orangewood stick to make bumps or ridges (Figure 13–34). This will give a semitransparent scar that can be applied to the skin with spirit gum. The scar can be colored and given more body by adding tinted face powder as the plastic is being swirled with the orangewood stick. For stronger coloring, powdered rouge can be used. If you don't have powdered rouge, simply scrape the top of a cake of dry rouge to produce a powder. Figure 13–34B shows scars with and without powder and rouge.

When the plastic scars are pulled off the glass, both sides should be powdered, as with latex pieces. When the scars are applied to the skin with spirit gum, the edges of the plastic can be dissolved and blended into the skin by brushing them with acetone. The makeup can then be applied. The plastic scar can be left without makeup or can be partially or completely made up with appropriate colors. As with latex, materials such as cotton or string can be used in the plastic scar. Figure 13–34C shows a plastic piece on the face before the edges have been blended.

Gelatine can also be used for making scars. The surgical scar shown in Figure H–18, for example, could be easily and quickly duplicated directly on the skin with

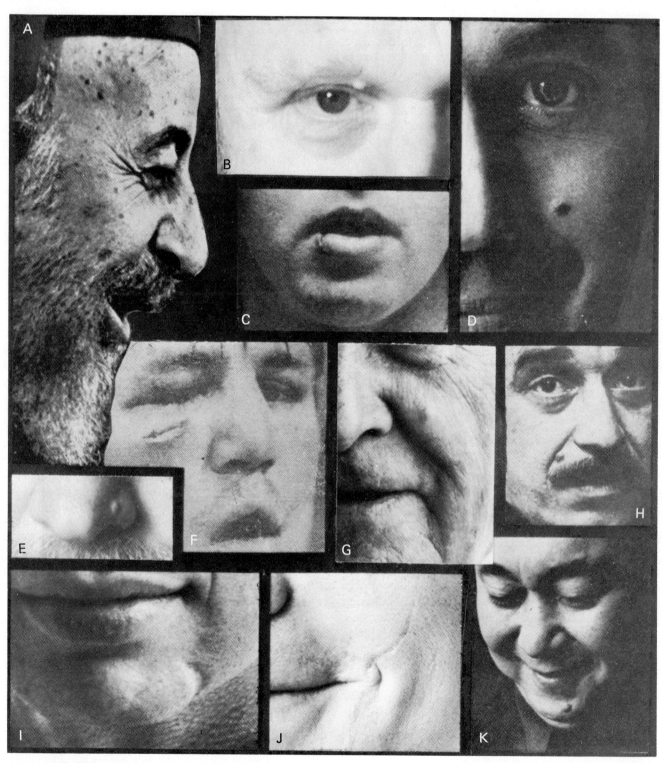

FIGURE **13–30** SCARS, CUTS, MOLES, AND WARTS.

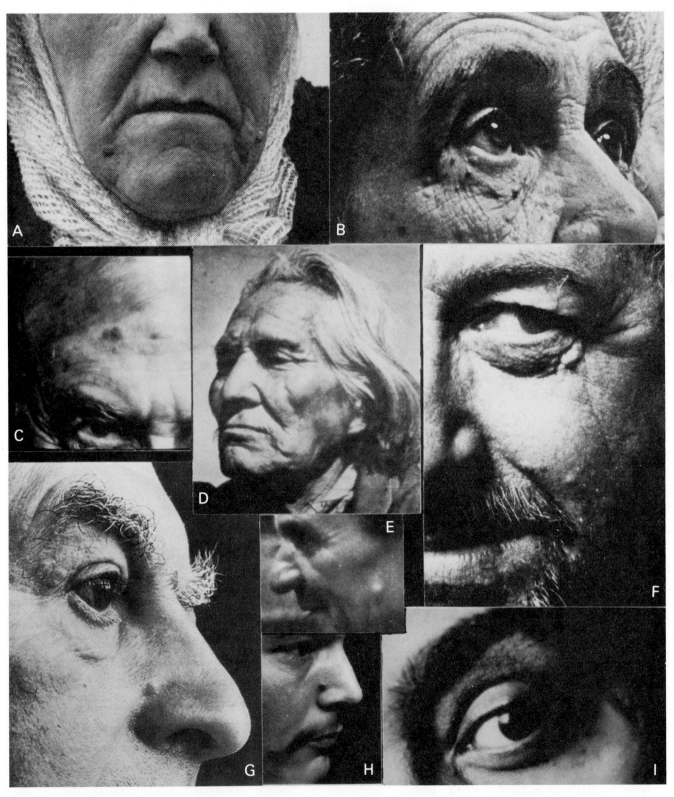

FIGURE 13–31 *SCARS, CUTS, MOLES, AND WARTS.*

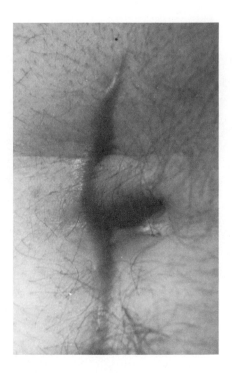

FIGURE *13–32* SURGICAL SCAR RE-SULTING FROM REPAIRING A KNIFE WOUND.

FIGURE *13–33 SCARS AND WELTS.*   A. Welt with cut. Derma wax with blood-red creme rouge in cut. Makeup by student Paul Lynch. B. Scar tissue. Derma wax covered with cake makeup. Makeup by student Joseph Rojas. C. Scar tissue. Left eye partially covered with adhesive tape and left side of face covered with layers of latex. Makeup by Bill Smith. D. Scar tissue. Latex, tissue, and derma wax. Makeup by student Jeanne Zavala.

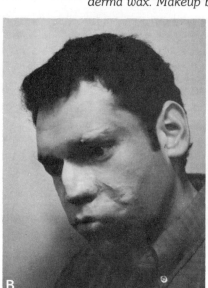

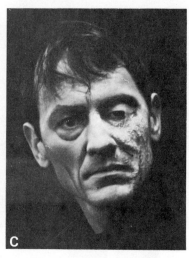

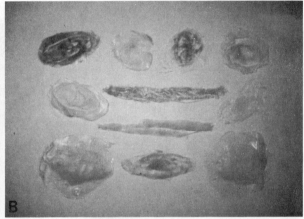

*FIGURE **13–34** PLASTIC SCARS, WELTS, AND GROWTHS.* *A. Making the pieces with liquid plastic. B. Finished pieces, some with color added. C. One of the pieces attached to the skin with spirit gum. Makeup has not yet been applied.*

gelatine. Or it could be made on glass or formica first, then attached with spirit gum.

Another method of making a raised scar is illustrated in Figure 13–35. Although it involves a number of steps, it is really quite simple and requires only following the illustrations and the captions. Having done that, you may wish to experiment with your own variations. The technique was devised for the 1986 Broadway revival of Eugene O'Neill's *The Iceman Cometh.*

Warts (See Figures 13–3J and 13–30D,G,H, and K.) Warts can be made with nose putty, derma wax, gelatine, molded latex, silicone, polyurethane, or latex foam. Nose putty, derma wax, and gelatine warts can be built up directly on the skin, whereas molded latex or foam warts must, of course, be molded first, then attached with spirit gum. Makeup can be applied to the wart with a small, flat shading brush. It can then be powdered along with the rest of the makeup.

Nonmolded latex warts, however, can be constructed directly on the skin by the following method:

1. Dip an orangewood stick, a glass rod, or the handle of a plastic rat-tail comb into a bottle of latex, then remove it and let it dry.
2. Starting at the top of the latex coating, which should not be powdered, remove the latex from the stick, rod, or comb handle by rolling it down from top to bottom, using the thumb and the forefinger.
3. When the latex is all off, squeeze it together into a

lump. If you want to reshape it further—to make it flatter on the bottom, for example—you can cut it with scissors.
4. Dab a spot of spirit gum (no smaller than the bottom of the wart) onto the skin (which must be free of makeup or grease) at the spot where the wart is to be placed, then tap the gum lightly with one finger until it becomes very tacky.
5. Press the bottom of the wart firmly into the spirit gum.
6. When the spirit gum is dry and the wart is securely attached to the skin, you can smooth out the surface of the wart with derma wax, blending it carefully into the skin, using a small, flat shading brush.
7. Powder the wart carefully and brush off excess powder with a powder brush. The wart is now ready to be made up.

The advantage of making a wart by this method is that if properly attached, it is unlikely to fall off or to be knocked out of shape if accidentally touched.

Welts Welts, like warts, can be made with nose putty, derma wax (Figure 13–33A), gelatine, molded latex, silicone, polyurethane, or latex foam. As with warts, welts of nose putty and gelatine can be built up directly on the skin, whereas molded latex or foam welts must be molded first, then attached with spirit gum. The method chosen may depend on the length of the welt and where it is to be used. A welt across the cheek, for example,

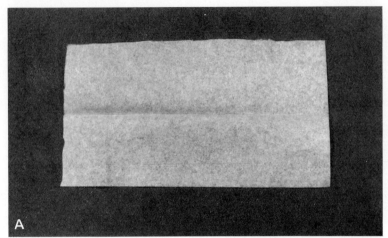

A

FIGURE **13–35** MAKING A SCAR. *A. Sheet of cleansing tissue. B. Spirit gum being applied along crease in tissue. C. Spirit gum powdered and tissue folded along crease. D. Tissue opened out. E. Tissue turned upside-down and spirit gum on tissue powdered. F. Crease in tissue pressed together. G. Tissue being torn around spirit-gummed area. H. All excess tissue removed. I. Ridge in tissue being flattened with scissors. J. Latex being applied to tissue. K. Tissue being folded, with latex inside. L. Excess tissue torn away. M. Sealer being applied to scar. N. Finished scar, powdered. O. Scar creased with orangewood stick, then attached to skin with spirit gum or latex.*

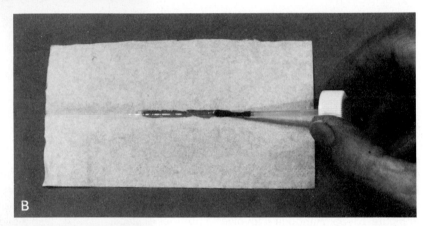

B

C

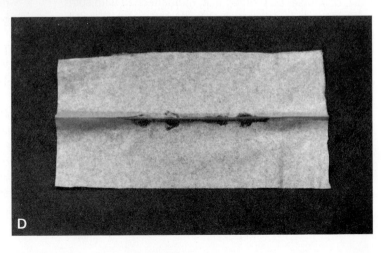

D

FIG. 13–35 *Cont.*

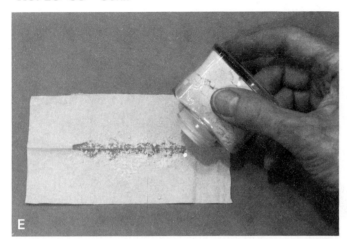

E

F

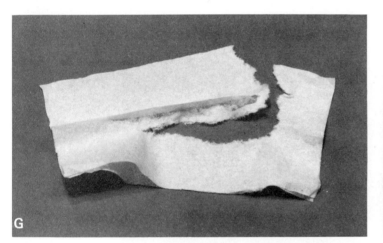

G

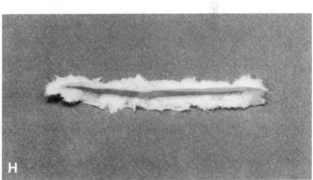

H

I

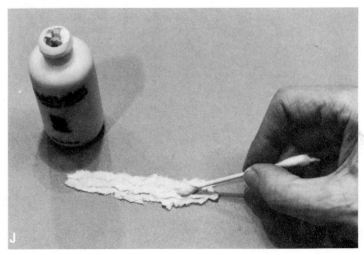

J

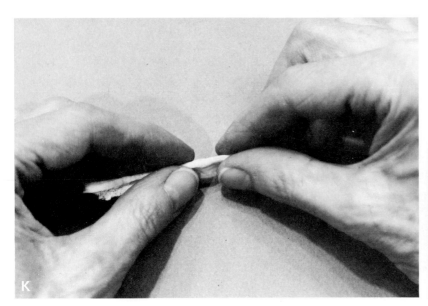

FIG. 13–35   Cont.

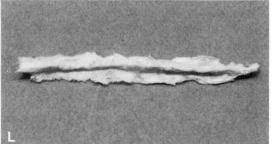

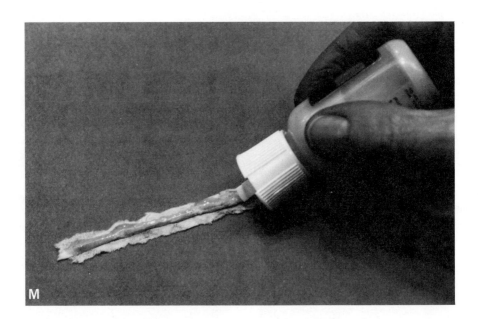

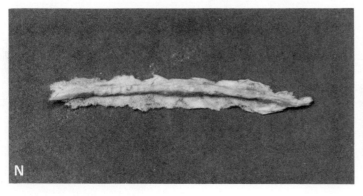

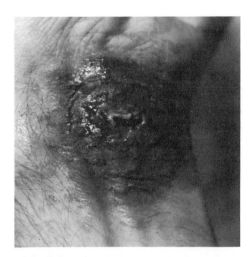

*FIGURE **13–36** PUNCTURE WOUND IN WRIST.* *Created with Red Zinger tea leaves and latex. (For a color photo of the wound, see Figure H–16.)*

most often found on the top of the head, the forehead, or the back of the neck. They can be made in the same way as warts; but because of their size, they should usually be made of foam latex or by the direct latex-and-wax method described for warts. They can also be made with gelatine (preferably molded), in which case they have to be made immediately before the performance and cannot be reused.

Wounds, Open Various materials, such as derma wax, putty wax, cotton, and latex, can be used to create open wounds. And various non-makeup items can be combined with those materials to produce interesting effects. In the wound illustrated in Figure H–18, for example, Red Zinger tea leaves were used in combination with latex.

The first step was to apply spirit gum to the area. The spirit gum was then tapped with one finger to make it tacky. The tea leaves were pressed into the spirit gum, and the entire area of the wound was painted with latex. When the latex was dry, it was made up to match the rest of the skin, and the central area was colored with two shades of creme rouge. The latex at the center of the wound was then cut open with scissors. (This was done with extreme care in order to avoid creating a *real* wound!) The opening was filled with stage blood, which was allowed to flow out, then smeared over the wound and onto the skin surrounding it.

could probably be made by whichever method was more convenient. But a long welt or a welt that is to be used under clothing and then revealed during the course of the play might better be made up in advance and attached with spirit gum.

Wens Similar to a wart in appearance but larger and more rounded; wens are usually flesh-colored and are

Problems

1. Model a nose with derma wax, then add skin texture, foundation, rouge, and stipple.
2. Model a nose meticulously, using derma wax (preferably flesh-colored). Then, instead of making up the nose with a foundation color, as you normally would, stipple it with what you consider to be the best possible colors to match your own nose in order to make the new nose look completely convincing to anyone standing and talking to you. (Yes, it *can* be done.) It would be advisable, of course, to avoid exaggerated shapes and to make only a small addition to your own nose. For this experiment, do not use sealer over the derma wax, but do powder it. If the powder is obvious, even after being dusted off with a powder brush, pat it lightly with a damp sponge. The best test of the makeup is, of course, deliberately to talk to someone who is unaware that the nose is not entirely your own in order to find out if it is noticed.
3. Model a nose with derma wax and cotton. Then add skin texture, foundation, rouge, and stipple.
4. Model a nose with nose putty, then add skin texture, foundation, rouge, and stipple.
5. Experiment with the various methods for creating the effect of wrinkled skin, and do a complete makeup using one of the methods.
6. Do a few special constructions, such as welts, warts, moles, scars, or burns.
7. Using whatever materials you wish to, create your own technique for making scars, wounds, or unslightly growths.
8. Design and execute a makeup using one or more three-dimensional makeup techniques.

14

Prosthetic Makeup

The most effective method of creating most three-dimensional additions to the face, neck, and hands is to use molded prosthetic pieces. For the stage, however, this type of makeup is not always practical since actors normally do their own makeup, and the creation of molded prostheses may require the services of a professional makeup artist.

However, the actor who wants to experiment with casting prosthetic pieces himself can certainly do so and will no doubt find it both interesting and useful. But whether the actor learns to make his own prosthetic pieces or has them made for him, the advantages of using this type of makeup are obvious—it can provide three-dimensional additions to the face impossible to achieve with nose putty and derma wax or other direct constructions (Figure 14–1, for example); the pieces can be modeled and remodeled on a plaster head until they are perfect and can then be reproduced indefinitely; and, unlike direct additions to the face, they can (for the stage, at least) be used several times.

CASTING FOR PROSTHESIS

The first step in prosthesis is to reproduce the actor's own face, or some part of it, in plaster. In order to do this, a negative mold must be made. The best way to make this negative mold is with a flexible *moulage* (see Appendix A), as illustrated in Figure 14–2.

Preparing the Subject If the entire face is being cast, it is best to have the subject sitting up straight or reclining only slightly in order to prevent the distortion of the jaw and neck area that can result when he is

FIGURE **14–1** *IONESCO'S THREE-FACED GIRL. Makeup by Richard Brunner. A. Molded latex piece for the second face. B. Latex piece attached and made up.*

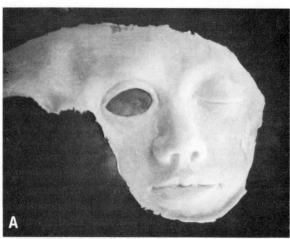

172

lying down. A barber's or a dentist's chair is ideal. A plastic makeup cape (Figure 14–2A) or a painter's fairly lightweight plastic drop cloth can be used to protect the clothing. It may or may not be taped to the skin at the neckline. The solidified moulage can be removed from the plastic later.

A better arrangement, suggested by makeup artist Paul Batson, is to use a lightweight but rigid "drip board" with a smooth, nonporous surface, 12 to 14 inches wide and at least 18 inches long, extending forward horizontally from the subject's collarbone. One end can be anchored to the subject with masking tape and the other end held up by the subject, with his elbows resting on the arms of the chair. If possible, one end of the board should have a semicircle cut out to fit around the subject's neck. The use of such a board makes it possible to retrieve and re-use globs of moulage or alginate which have dropped from the face much more efficiently than when they have dropped onto a plastic makeup cape.

If the top of the head or the entire head is to be cast, a plastic or a latex cap (see Figure 14–3) can be used to protect the hair and provide a smooth surface. If only the face is being cast, a cap can be used but is not always necessary. In any case, it's a good idea to mark the hairline on the cap. If this is done with an indelible pencil, it will later be visible on the cast.

The face requires no special preparation (except for removing mascara when alginate is used to make the mold, since alginate tends to stick to mascara), but psychologically the subject usually does require special preparation. It is essential that it be made clear to him that there is no danger. If for any reason the moulage interferes with his breathing, he need only expel his breath forcefully, open his mouth and break the mold, or remove the moulage from his nose or his mouth with his hands. Most subjects, once they have confidence in the operator, find the process pleasant and relaxing.

It is important that the facial muscles not be moved while the mold is being made. A smile or the raise of an eyebrow can ruin the mold. It's a good idea, especially with nervous subjects, to let them watch a mold being made on someone else first and also to explain to them as you go along exactly what you're doing. It is usually best to work in a private room which is relatively quiet with no extraneous noise or conversation and where the subject does not feel that he is being watched by a number of people. If others are watching (and this should be permitted only if the subject is willing), it is essential that they understand from the start that they must be quiet! Any remarks or noises that disturb the subject or tend to make him smile must not be permitted since they may very well result in a ruined cast and the work having to be done all over again.

It is also desirable for the person or persons doing the casting to avoid casual conversation with others unre-lated to the work being done. Knowing that he has the operator's undivided attention helps to give the subject confidence. Although it is not absolutely necessary, giving the subject a pencil and paper as a means of communication can add to his sense of security. If this is done, it would be best for someone other than the operator to be responsible for reading what the subject has written since the operator, particularly when he is using alginate rather than a reusable moulage, has to work very rapidly. The subject can also be given appropriate hand signals to enable the operator to ask him questions and get "yes" or "no" responses without the subject's having to answer by writing.

If, in spite of all the reassurances you can give him, the subject still seems apprehensive, you might suggest, making it clear that there is nothing unusual about it, that he let someone hold his hand. This can be very comforting to some subjects and therefore helpful to the operator as well. In any case, *never leave the subject alone until the mask has been removed*—he will feel more secure knowing you are there.

Negative Moulage Mold As has already been indicated, there are two types of moulage, one of which is reusable; the other, not. Both are used in the same way, but the preparation is different. To prepare reusable moulage for use, follow the directions that come with it. With Kryolan's Formalose, the material is added to boiling water, then allowed to cool to 42°C before being applied to the area being cast.

The second type of moulage is an alginate that is mixed with cold water for a minute or less (according to directions) and used immediately since it has a faster setting time than the reusable moulage—usually from 3 minutes (at 75°F or 24°C) to 5 minutes (at 65°F or 18°C). You should either mix small amounts at a time or else work very fast. It is helpful for two people to work together, one applying the moulage while the other mixes a fresh batch. The fast mixing is a considerable advantage, whereas the fast setting may or may not be, depending on how rapidly you can work. With reusable moulage, be sure to mix enough for the entire job before you begin. Slightly flexible plastic mixing bowls are recommended. Rubber kitchen spatulas are good for mixing. In using alginate, you should have available a bowl of water of the desired temperature for additional mixings.

In using either kind of moulage, brush it quickly over the face or the facial area being cast (Figure 14–2B), making sure there is a sufficiently thick layer (¼ to ⅓-inch—more over the ears if they are being cast, and perhaps over the nose). Avoid too thick a layer (and thus too much weight) on the softer areas of the face, which may sag and distort the final cast; but make very sure there are no areas that are too thin. In building up the moulage, remember that wet moulage will not adhere

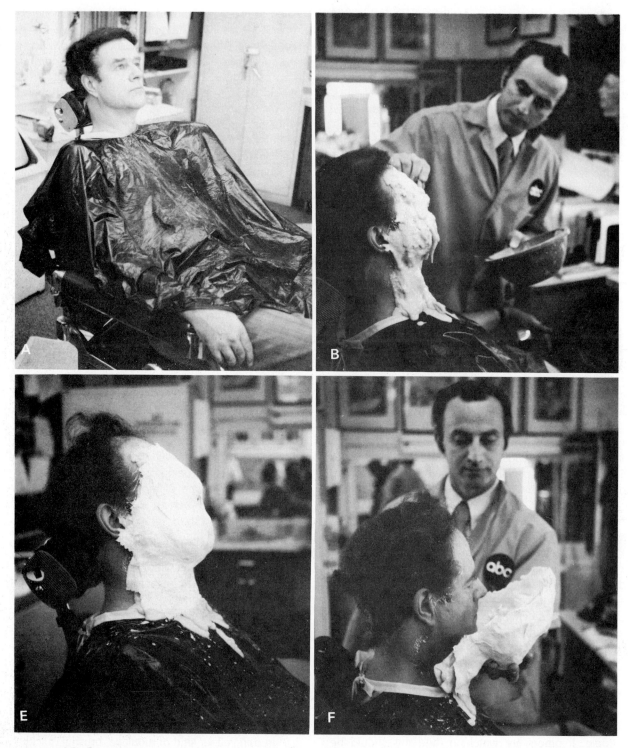

FIGURE 14–2 CASTING A FACE WITH MOULAGE. *A. Subject in barber's chair with protective plastic cape. If any of the head beyond the hairline were being cast, the hair would be covered with a plastic cap. B. Moulage (alginate) being applied with a brush. C. Partially completed moulage. D. Strips of plaster bandage being laid over solidified moulage. E. Completed negative mold on face. F. Removing negative mold from face. G. Brushing first layer of plaster or dental stone into negative mold. H. Negative mold being removed from completed positive impression in stone or plaster. Casting by Bert Roth, S.M.A.*

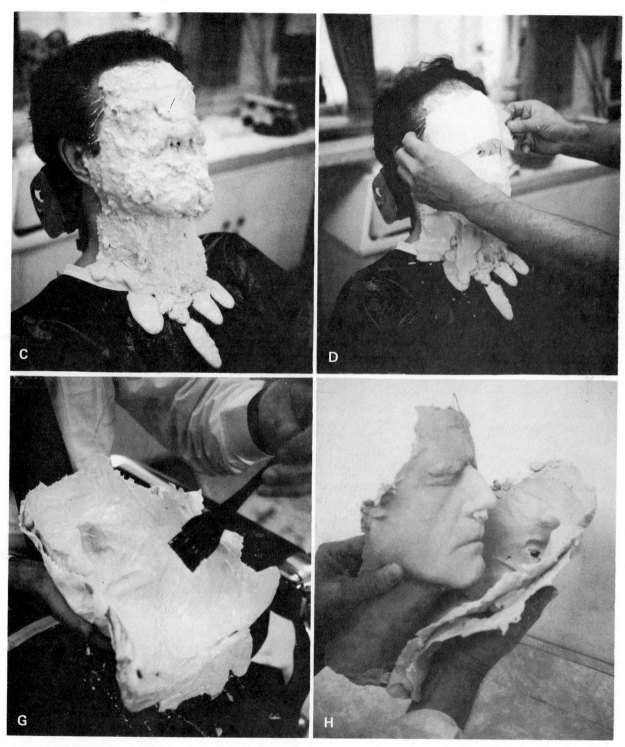

FIG. 14–2. *Cont.*

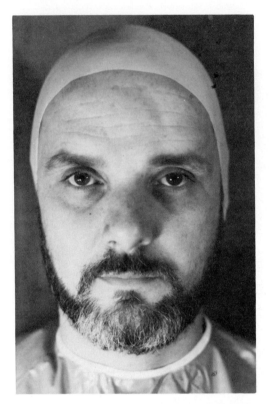

FIGURE *14–3* *LATEX CAP BEING WORN IN PREPARATION FOR MAKING A NEGATIVE MOULAGE MOLD.*

to moulage that has already solidified. This is an additional reason for working rapidly.

When the nose is being cast, you can either work very carefully around the nostrils with the fingers or a small brush, making sure that both nostrils are clear *at all times,* or you can ask the subject to take a deep breath and hold it, brush moulage quickly over the nose, then ask him to expel air forcefully through the nose. This will remove moulage from the nostrils. The first method is preferable. It will give a nervous subject a greater feeling of security if you cover the nose and leave proper holes for breathing before covering the mouth. Otherwise, leave the nose until last, when the subject is likely to feel more relaxed about the whole procedure. Then you can work around the nostrils very carefully and fill in the holes after the mold has been removed. You should explain to the subject that if moulage should cover the holes accidentally, he need only expel his breath forcefully to remove it. However, do your best to see that this doesn't happen.

It is also possible to insert straws or rolls of paper into the nostrils before beginning the casting. Derma wax around the straw will hold it in the nostril and make it impossible for the moulage to seep in. It is generally considered preferable, however, not to use straws since they may distort the shape of the nostrils. Also, it is possible

for a careless swipe of the moulage brush to dislodge them.

The eyes should be kept closed. Cotton can be stuffed into the ear opening. In casting the ears, be careful of undercuts that might interfere with the proper removal of the mold and might make the moulage much thicker there than on the rest of the face.

When the moulage has solidified (usually from 15 to 30 minutes is necessary for the reusable type unless you force-dry it with a hair dryer or cold cloths), it must be strengthened so that it will hold its shape when removed. The best way is to lay moistened strips of fast-drying plaster bandage (see Appendix A) over the moulage (Figures 14–2D and 14–4). Surgical gauze bandage dipped in wet plaster can be used instead. Four layers of bandage laid on in different directions and overlapping should be sufficient. When the plaster hardens, it will provide a rigid form to hold the shape of the moulage. (See Figure 14–2F and G.) Work around the nostrils carefully, crushing the bandage together as you go over the tip and between the nostrils. This will add greater strength. Do not use plaster bandage over the ears. Removal of the mask will be easier there if the thick layer of moulage is not completely rigid.

In removing the moulage, ask the subject to lean forward slightly and move his facial muscles in order to loosen the mold. Then it can be removed easily. (See Figure 14–2F.) It is best to loosen it first near the ear to let in the air. Remove it carefully and slowly, running your fingers around the edges between the skin and the

FIGURE *14–4* *CASTING PART OF THE FACE. Eyes being cast in preparation for making Oriental eyelids. Moulage has been covered with plaster bandage.*

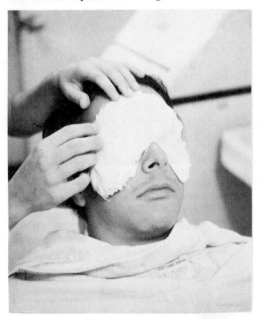

moulage. The moulage does not stick to skin or hair—one of its greatest advantages over plaster. If long hair should become embedded in the moulage, however, this can require extra care in removal.

When the negative mold is finished, the positive plaster cast should be made immediately in order to prevent the possibility of shrinkage of the moulage as it loses its moisture.

Positive Plaster Cast In preparing the plaster, first measure two or three cups of water into a bowl (preferably a plastic one), then slowly sift in plaster of Paris or dental stone (see Appendix A) until it reaches a level just barely below the surface of the water. Let the mixture stand without stirring until it begins to thicken. When it approaches a suitable consistency for pouring, it can be stirred very gently. It will then begin to harden quickly. After the plaster has been stirred, the bowl should be hit a few times on the bottom with the palm of the hand in order to force air bubbles to the surface.

Although plaster can be poured when it is thin and watery or as thick as mayonnaise, an in-between consistency (say, that of heavy cream) usually works best. If it is too thin, it will be hard to manage and will take longer to harden; if it is too thick, it may not conform to the shape of the mold. It should be pointed out, however, that thin plaster results in a harder, more durable cast than does thick plaster.

The wet plaster or dental stone should first be painted carefully over the inside surface of the negative mold, coating it completely. (See Figure 14–2G.) Then the rest of the stone or plaster can be either spooned or slowly and gently poured into the mold. In order to avoid having too heavy and cumbersome a cast, brush the plaster away from the center and up along the sides of the mold, leaving a shell of plaster rather than a solid block. If the plaster is too thin to do this, let it sit until it begins to thicken. In filling the mold, be sure it is adequately supported so that the shape will not be distorted. Be very careful to protect the nose, which is especially vulnerable to damage. Having someone hold the mold in his lap with his hands cupped around it for support works very well; or, if you prefer, you can set it into a box of crumpled-up cloth towels.

If you plan to hang the cast on a wall for storage, form a loop from a length of wire (part of a coat hanger will do) and embed the ends in the plaster before it hardens, leaving the loop outside and near the top of the cast. (See Figure 14–5.) This can prove to be a great convenience.

When the plaster is thoroughly hardened in the mold, the moulage can be peeled or broken off. Reusable moulage can be stored for future use. The moulage mixed from powder (alginate) can usually be removed from the plaster cast in one piece (Figure 14–2H) and some-

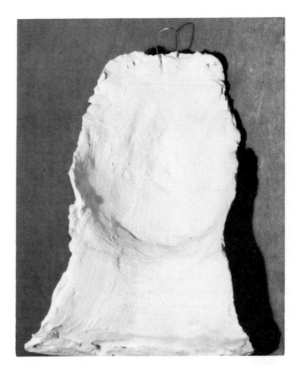

FIGURE 14–5 HANGER FOR PLASTER CAST. *Rear view of cast in Figure 14–2H. Hanger is embedded while the plaster is still wet.*

times be used to make a second cast of the same head. But this second casting should be done immediately, before the mold begins to shrink. If the mold is set aside and allowed to shrink, it can sometimes then be used to cast a shrunken head—a miniature version of the original. If for any reason you should want to do that, make sure the edges are not allowed to curl up, since that will give a deformed head. After the castings are done, the moulage is discarded.

The plaster cast should be allowed to dry thoroughly before being used. That may take several days. Then give the cast one or two coats of white shellac. You now have a reproduction of the actor's face (Figure 14–2H), on which you can model in clay the features you want to reproduce in latex.

Clay Models The modeling of individual features (Figures 14–6 and 14–7) is done with artists' modeling clay, which requires no special technique. You will do it largely with your fingers, though a clay modeling tool (Figure 1–4C) may be helpful for details. Be sure the clay is perfectly smooth, completely blended at the edges, and modeled in exactly the form you want the latex piece to take. You can simulate skin texture by dotting the clay with tiny depressions to represent pores. Remember that the slightest mark on the clay will be reproduced on the finished piece.

A useful trick for making skin texture quickly is to

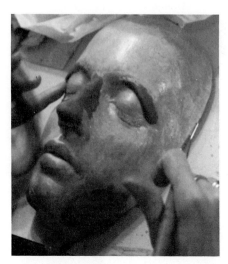

FIGURE *14—6* MODELING NOSE AND SAGGING EYELIDS IN CLAY ON A PLASTER CAST. *By student Catherine Smith.*

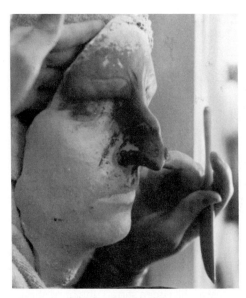

FIGURE *14—7* MODELING ONE-EYED WITCH'S NOSE ON A PLASTER CAST OF THE STUDENT'S FACE. *The right superciliary arch has been built up to distort the face. The left eye will be obliterated with clay. Makeup being created by student Barbara Murray.*

make a latex negative of a grapefruit, orange, or lemon skin, as mentioned in Chapter 13. This is done by painting liquid latex onto a section of the outside of the fruit— preferably one with skin which is not too smooth. Three to five coats will probably be necessary. When the latex is thoroughly dry, remove it from the fruit, powder it, and you will have a textured piece that can be pressed into the clay, transferring the texture. All clay models— except those for eyelids—should be textured so as to blend with natural skin texture.

Negative Plaster Mold The next step is to make a negative mold of the clay feature just as you made a negative mold of the actor's face. This casting from the clay, however, must be done with plaster or dental stone rather than moulage.

First, with some extra clay, build up a sort of fence or dike around the modeled feature to prevent the plaster from spilling over the cast. You can make the dike entirely of clay (Figure 14—8A), or you can make a low foundation of clay (Figure 14—9A) and set a cardboard tube (Figure 14—9B), a can, or a plastic container with both ends open, into the clay. The cardboard cylinder shown in Figure 14—9B was made from a container of cat food. The metal top of the container was, of course, removed when the contents were used. The bottom was then cut off in order to get rid of the metal rim, after which the edge was appropriately shaped to fit into the clay foundation.

When the cylinder is anchored securely in the clay and the clay pressed against it to prevent leakage, as has been done in Figure 14—9B, grease all exposed parts of the plaster cast and the clay sculpture that will be touched by the plaster when it is poured. This can be

done with mineral oil, cleansing cream, or preferably, with castor oil. In using a clay foundation with some sort of cylinder pressed into it, it is easier to grease the cast and the sculptured clay *before* pressing the cylinder into the clay foundation.

When the cast and the sculptured clay have been greased and the dike is firmly in place, make up your plaster or dental stone just as before and pour it over the new feature, giving plenty of thickness so that the mold will not break when you remove it.

When the plaster is hard, pull off the clay dike (Figure 14—8C). If you are using a cylinder in a clay foundation rather than a dike entirely of clay, you may wish to remove accessible portions of the clay foundation first, though this is not always necessary. Then maneuver the mold around until it can be easily slipped off. Now you have a negative mold (Figure 14—8D) from which you can make any number of prosthetic pieces. If, by chance, air bubbles have left little holes anywhere in the mold, fill them up with plaster.

Making a Negative Plaster Mold Directly on the Face If you do not have a plaster cast of the actor's face, it is possible to make a negative plaster mold of a character-feature directly on the face. For example, instead of modeling a clay nose on a plaster cast of the actor's face, the character-nose can be modeled with derma wax directly on his own nose exactly as it would be for a performance. The wax nose and the actor's entire face can then be covered with Vaseline.

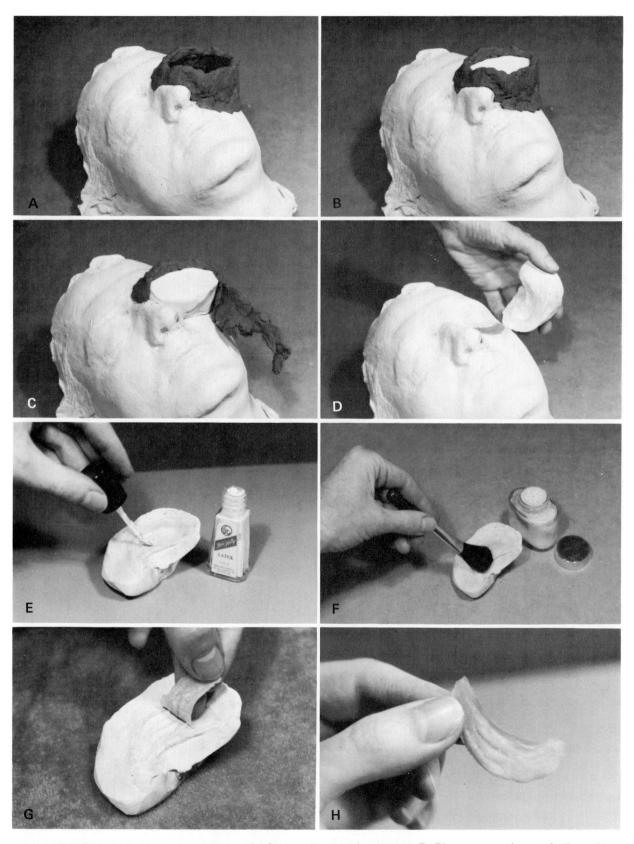

FIGURE 14—8 *CASTING AN EYE POUCH.*   A. Clay wall around eye area. B. Plaster poured in and allowed to harden. C. Clay wall partially removed. D. Negative plaster mold of pouch removed. E. Negative mold painted with latex. F. Dried latex being brushed with powder. G. Latex pouch being removed from mold. H. Latex pouch trimmed and ready for use.

FIGURE 14–9 *CASTING A LATEX NOSE.* *A. Plaster cast with nose modeled in clay, surrounded by a clay foundation for the cylinder to be used as a dike. B. Cardboard cylinder (a moist cat-food container with both ends removed) pressed into the clay. C. Pouring plaster into the cylinder. D. Removing the plastic mold. E. Latex nose being removed from the negative mold. F. Attached latex nose being made up for Kristoffer Tabori for his Dauphin in St. Joan. For the completed makeup, see Figure 14–10.*

As an added precaution, the eyelashes, the eyebrows, and any other facial hair should be heavily coverd with Vaseline, and the ears should be stuffed with cotton. A latex or a plastic cap can be worn over the hair.

Casting plaster can then be prepared (it should be thicker than usual so that it will hold its shape without clay dikes to contain it) and spooned over the actor's built-up nose. The actor can breathe through his mouth and thus avoid the usual straws in the nostrils. When the plaster is hard, it can be removed and used for casting latex noses in the usual way. Other character-features, such as the chin, can also be cast directly on the face. However, casting the eyes by this method is not recommended.

Positive Latex Cast There are two techniques for making latex prosthetic pieces from the plaster molds. One is a *painting* method; the other is a *slush* method.

For either method liquid latex is used (see Appendix A). The latex can usually be purchased in either flesh or natural white, which is almost transparent when it dries. It can also be tinted with food coloring or with special dyes. It is not necessary for the latex piece to match the base color, but if it is too different from the skin coloring, it may be more difficult to cover. The solidified latex will always be darker than the liquid latex.

The main requirement for a positive latex piece is to make the central parts of the piece thick enough to hold their shape and the edges thin enough to blend into the skin without an obvious line. In the brush technique (Figure 14–8E) a layer of latex is painted into the negative plaster mold, which requires no surface preparation. The type of brush used is a matter of choice. A soft bristle lets the latex flow on more easily, but it is also very difficult to clean; and unless extreme care is taken, it will probably not last very long. A stiff bristle is easier to clean but doesn't give as smooth a coat of latex. A flat, medium-stiff bristle is perhaps the most generally practical. Inexpensive brushes should be used. Brushes in use should be kept in soapy water and washed out thoroughly with soap the moment you have finished with them. Once the latex has solidified, it can seldom be removed from the brush.

Before painting in the first coat, it would be well to estimate about where you want the edge of the piece to be and to mark that with a pencil on the plaster. Then you can be sure to keep the latex thin along that line. Subsequent coats are painted in after the preceding coat is completely dry. Each subsequent coat can begin a little farther from the edge in order to provide a gradual thinning. The number of coats needed depends on the thickness of the coats. You will probably need a minimum of five, depending on the thickness of the latex and the requirements of the particular piece.

With the slush method, some of the latex is poured into the mold and gently sloshed around to build up layers of the latex. This is done by holding the plaster mold in the hand and moving or rocking it so that the latex runs first up to and just beyond the proposed edge, as marked with a pencil. Subsequent movements should keep the latex nearer and nearer to the center and farther and farther from the edge. If you have a problem in making the latex go exactly where you want it to, you can maneuver it with a clean modeling tool or an orangewood stick. When you think you have built up enough thickness, drain off the excess latex or take it up with cleansing tissues or absorbent cotton. Absorbing it instead of pouring it avoids a build-up of latex at the point at which it is poured. You can avoid the whole problem by pouring in a little at a time. It is better to have too little than too much since more can always be added.

Before removing the latex piece, be sure it is completely dry. In deep molds, such as noses, this may sometimes take several hours. Forcing hot air into the mold with a hair dryer can speed up the drying considerably. Then dust the surface of the latex with face powder to prevent its sticking to itself. (See Figure 14–8F.) Once it has been dusted, it will never stick again, even if you wash the powder off immediately. Then loosen the latex at a spot along the edge and carefully lift it away from the plaster (Figure 14–8G.) As you do so, dust more powder inside to keep that surface of the latex from sticking. Sometimes the piece comes away easily, sometimes it has to be pulled, but it will come. If you do have to pull hard, however, be sure not to pull it by the tissue-thin edge, which is likely to tear. Also, avoid pulling so hard that you stretch the piece permanently out of shape. As soon as you are able to loosen a little more of the piece, grasp it farther down to pull out the remainder. Tweezers can be helpful.

After you have removed the piece, try it on the actor who is to wear it or on the cast of his face. Check all blending edges to make sure they are very thin and lie flat against the skin. If the first piece you make from the mold is imperfect, make note of the problems. If they can be corrected by adjustments in the application of the liquid latex, make another piece, correcting the errors. If the problem is with the mold, see if there are any minor corrections that can be made. If not, make another mold—or as many more as necessary. When you have one you're satisfied with, label it with the date and the name of the actor, the character, and the play. If you then make duplicate molds, as you might want to do in order to make several pieces at once, number each one in the order in which it was made. There may be slight differences in the molds, and the identifying number could be useful. The plaster mold can be used indefinitely as long as the actual casting surface remains in good condition.

PROSTHETIC PIECES

Noses There are three basic criteria for a useful, workable latex nose—it must be rigid enough to hold its shape without wrinkling or sagging, the blending edges should be tissue thin, and the blend should, if possible, take place on a solid, rather than a flexible, foundation (on the actor's nose, that is, rather than on his cheeks or his nasolabial folds).

The first two of these criteria depend on the distribution of latex in the plaster cast and have already been discussed. The third requires careful placement of the clay used in building up the nose of the plaster cast. The actual modeling of the clay corresponds closely to the modeling of a putty nose—the accurate following of natural nose structure, the careful blending of edges, the limiting of the clay addition to as small an area as possible, and the final addition of skin texture.

The principal difference between modeling a clay nose and a putty one is that putty may, if necessary, cover the sides of the nose completely, but clay should not do so. It should, if possible, stop far enough short of the outer boundaries of the sides of the nose to allow for a blending edge of latex beyond the section that is being built up. (See Figure 14–9A. For the makeup using this nose in the final scene of *St. Joan*, see Figure 14–10.)

The latex piece need not cover the entire nose. On the contrary, the smaller the area it covers, the easier it will probably be to work with. A tilted tip or a small hump, for example, does not require modeling a complete nose. If the piece you make involves the nostrils (Figure 14–9A), they can be cut out of the piece after it has been cast in order to permit normal breathing.

Because the final latex piece can be no better than

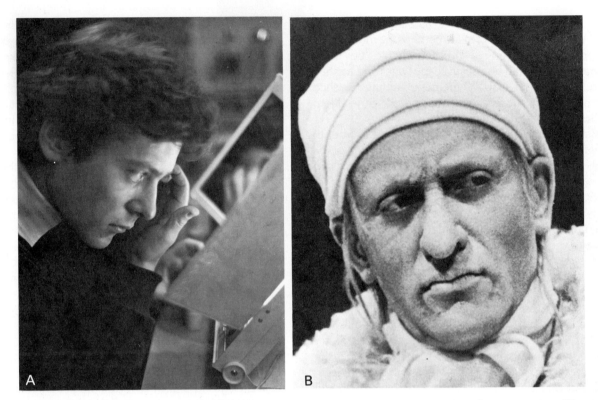

FIGURE 14–10 *A. ACTOR KRISTOFFER TABORI IN B. THE FINAL SCENE OF SHAW'S ST. JOAN.* The nose is shown being cast in Figure 14–9.

the clay nose from which it was cast, considerable care should be taken in the modeling. Once the model is perfected and cast, achieving an effective latex nose is largely a matter of careful manipulation of the liquid latex in the cast.

Eyelids Sagging eyelids are very helpful in aging youthful eyes. Figure 14–6 shows a pair being modeled in clay on a plaster head. In modeling the lids, work from photographs of older people, using more than one, if you like, and combining the most useful and adaptable features of each. The latex eyelids can stop just below the natural brow, which must then be aged; or they can cover the brow, making it possible to attach aged brows to the latex piece with crepe hair and latex or to ventilate eyebrows into the latex piece (see Chapter 15). Remember that only the edges that are to be attached to the skin should be thin. The edge that falls diagonally across the eye area hangs free and should be appropriately thick.

Latex eyelids are particularly useful in Oriental make-ups. In modeling them, be sure to give the clay sufficient thickness over the center of the eyeball so that the movement of the real eyelid will not be impeded. Before modeling Oriental lids, study the Oriental eyes in your morgue, as well as those in Figures 12–16I, 12–18D, 12–23, and 12–24.

Eye Pouches These are invaluable aids to aging and are one of the simplest pieces you can make (Figure 14–8). Again, you should work from photographs of real people (see Figures 12–16 through 12–19). Some pouches will be fairly smooth and definitely pouch-like. Others will be somewhat flat and a mass of fine wrinkles. There are countless variations. If there is a definite line of demarcation to the pouch you wish to make, then it will not be necessary to leave a thin edge on the bottom of the piece, though there should be one at the top. As usual, remember to give it skin texture.

If molded eye pouches are needed in a hurry, they can be made in a few minutes by using gelatine instead of latex—provided, of course, you have the molds. As mentioned in Chapter 13, however, there are disadvantages to gelatine pouches—they are heavier (and therefore less comfortable) than latex pouches, they can be used only once, and there is a possibility that they might be loosened by excessive perspiration.

In making gelatine additions in plaster molds, there is usually no need to apply a separator, such as castor oil, Vaseline, or mineral oil, to the mold, though you may prefer to do so. The gelatine should, of course, be poured into the mold before it congeals. Be sure to keep the gelatine at the level of the smooth area surrounding the negative mold so that the gelatine positive will lie flat against the skin. If, when the gelatine has congealed in the mold but has not yet been removed, the surface of the gelatine is rough, smooth it out by stroking it with cotton dipped in hot tap water. This will melt the surface of the gelatine and remove any excessive roughness that might prevent its fitting tightly against the skin.

Ears Rubber cauliflower ears can be slipped over the actor's real ears very simply. Rubber tips can be used for such characters as Puck or the leprechaun in *Finian's Rainbow*. Also, small ears can be enlarged—as they must be, for example, in a makeup for Abraham Lincoln.

The technique in making ears, partial or complete, is to make a shell that will fit over the natural ear. This requires a *split mold*. After you have modeled the clay ear on the plaster cast of the actor's natural ear and built your clay fence, place the cast so that the ear is horizontal. Then pour plaster up to the middle of the rim of the ear. It's a good idea to let the surface of the plaster be somewhat uneven. If the plaster is fairly thick, this will happen automatically, giving a bumpy or undulating surface. When the plaster is dry, grease the surface and pour in more plaster, covering the ear. When this plaster is dry, remove the clay fence, as ususal, then very carefully pry the two sections of plaster apart and remove both from the clay ear.

You can then fit the sections back together. If the surface is uneven, this will be no problem, for there will be only one way they will fit. This will give you a deep mold with a crevice into which you can pour the latex and slosh it around to cover all the surfaces of the negative mold. Any excess can be poured back out. It is better to build the ear up with several coats rather than trying to do the whole thing at once. Be sure to keep the latex thin at the edges, which will be glued to the natural ear, and thick around the rim so that the ears will hold their shape.

When you are sure the latex is dry (it's a good idea to force-dry it with a hair dryer), powder the inside, then carefully pry the mold apart, powdering as you do so.

The ear should then be trimmed around the edges. After the latex ear has been slipped over the natural ear and glued down, it should be made up to match the face.

In painting the mold with latex, you may not be quite sure how far out to bring the latex. After you have made and trimmed your first ear, however, you will be able to see where the boundaries should be. Then you can mark these boundaries on the plaster cast with a pencil to serve as guidelines for all future ears made from that mold. This will make it possible to keep the latex thin at all edges that are to be glued down.

Chin Receding chins can be built up or straight ones made to protrude; round chins can be made more square or square chins rounded. Goatees can be pasted on latex chins as well as on real ones and will not need to be remade for each performance. Frequently a chin can be combined in the same piece with a scrawny or a fat neck. If the chin addition is to be very large, a foamed latex piece (see the latter part of this chapter) would be preferable.

Wrinkled Forehead A wrinkled forehead can be modeled in clay on a plaster cast of the actor's head and a negative plaster mold made from the clay positive. Latex positives can then be made from the negative plaster mold. Ready-made latex forehead pieces are available. (See Figure 14–11.)

Neck It is possible to age the neck effectively from the front with paint, but the profile is difficult to change. A latex piece will, however, produce an old neck from any angle. (See Figure 14–12.) You can have prominent muscles and sagging flesh or transverse rolls of fat, or sagging jowls. For this type of construction, however, *Foamed* latex should be used. (See the latter part of this chapter and Figure 14–32.)

*FIGURE **14–11** MOLDED LATEX FORE-HEAD PIECE. (Available from Woochie In-dustries.)*

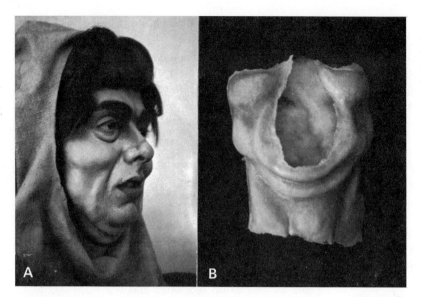

Scabs Scabs can be modeled in clay or derma wax on any smooth surface (such as glass or formica) and a negative plaster mold made from the positive. Latex positives can then be made from the negative mold. The scab or scabs can be powdered and attached to the skin with spirit gum, then appropriately colored (see the photograph of real scabs in Figure H–10 in the color section) and powdered again. For direct methods of making scabs, see Chapter 13.

Scars and Wounds These can be modeled with derma wax or modeling clay on a smooth surface, such as glass or formica, and a negative plaster mold made from the positives. From this, any number of latex positives can be made in the usual way. These can be appropriately colored after they have been attached to the skin and the rest of the makeup has been completed. Because scar tissue is smoother and somewhat shinier than the normal skin, a molded latex scar, which is not normally shiny, should be given a coat of liquid latex to provide a natural shine. If the scar is to be colored, the latex should not be applied until after that has been done—unless, of course, dry rouge is to be used for the coloring. For a photograph of a real scar, see Figure H–13 in the color section. For ready-made Vacu-form positives of scars and wounds, see *Scars and Wounds* in Appendix A.

Welts, Warts, and Moles These are extremely simple to make and can be pasted on quickly, like any other latex piece. They can be cast on any smooth surface without having a cast of a face or even a feature to work on. They can also be made without casting, as described in Chapter 13. (For a real mole, see Figure H–11 in the color section.)

Bald Caps One of the best methods of creating the effect of a bald head is to cover the hair with a latex or a plastic cap. The cap can be worn plain, or hair can be added (see Chapter 16).

In making a latex cap, the latex should be slushed or painted (a combination of the two is usually preferable) into a negative plaster head mold, which can be made from a suitably shaped wig block or millinery form. If the surface of the form is smooth, it may be possible to cast the plaster directly from the form after the usual greasing. If there is doubt about the surface, however, a thin layer of modeling clay can be used over it. Some reshaping can be done with the clay if that seems desirable. The normal hairline should be marked on the form with a pencil or a crayon that will then transfer to the plaster in order to simplify painting in the latex later. The usual clay dikes are built up, and the plaster poured over the form.

Obviously, since the top of the form is larger than the bottom, it cannot be removed from the plaster cast. There are two possible solutions to this. One is to cut the plaster cast in two with a thread while it is still soft. The two halves are allowed to dry and are then removed and put back together again. The join can be smoothed out and touched up with additional plaster.

A better method, if you have the right kind of form, is to slice the form into sections vertically. If you cut it twice each way, you will have nine sections, including a center one that will be in contact with the cast for only a few square inches on the top. A balsa-wood form is best for this purpose, since it is easily cut. Once the pieces have been cut, they are put back together and tied firmly at the base. The form is then covered with clay for a smooth surface. When the plaster is dry, the center section is removed from the bottom, releasing the other pieces so that they can be pulled out.

In making the cap in the negative mold, it is probably

easiest to pour in a quantity of latex and slosh it around, gradually building up the thickness of the latex. In order to have the thin front edge of the cap correctly shaped, that area should be painted in with a brush, using only one or two coats at the very edge. The back of the cap should be left long so that it will cover all of the neck hair and can be tucked into the collar. It this back tab is not needed, it can be cut off later.

Purchasing ready-made bald caps (either latex or plastic) will, of course, save a great deal of time. The ready-made cap illustrated in Figure 14–13 is made of extra-thin latex, with an unusually long nape, which can

FIGURE 14–13 APPLYING A LATEX CAP. *(Cap available from Woochie Industries. Photo courtesy of Paul Batson.) A. Subject assisting in putting on the cap. (Subject's hair has been plastered down with hair-setting gel.) B. Front of cap being smoothed out and distance from eyebrows adjusted. C. Applying spirit gum under front edge of cap. D. Pressing down front edge of cap firmly with dampened chamois or cloth. E. Attaching lower end of cap to skin with adhesive tape. F. Making marks to indicate front edge of ear and point at which ear joins head. G. Cutting cap to second mark. This should be done with great care! H. Applying spirit gum to under side of edge of cap, which will then be pressed firmly into place. I. Applying the rubber-mask greasepaint with sponge. J. Front edge of cap being stippled with Duo surgical adhesive for better blending. After stipple has dried and been powdered, cap is made up with rubber-mask greasepaint.*

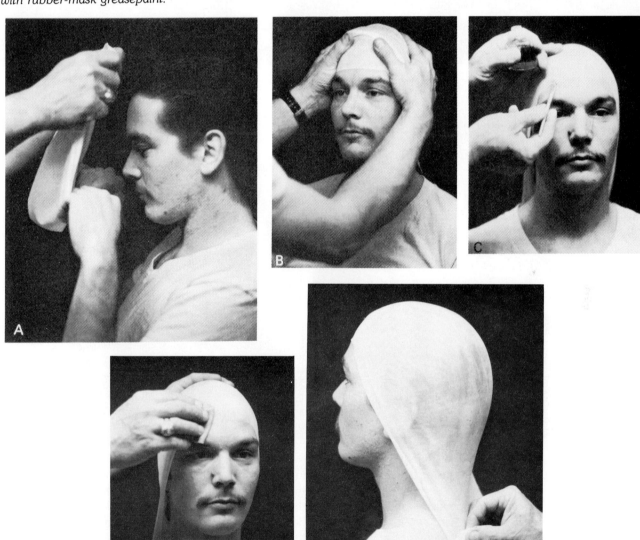

FIG. 14–13. *Cont.*

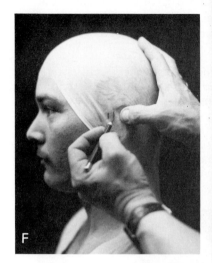

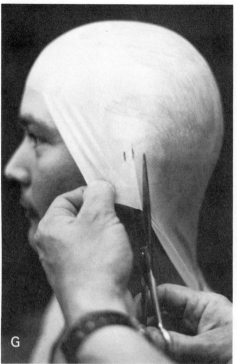

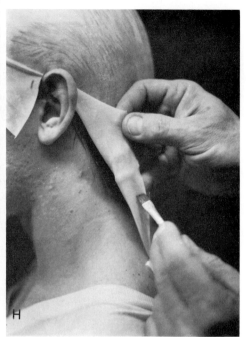

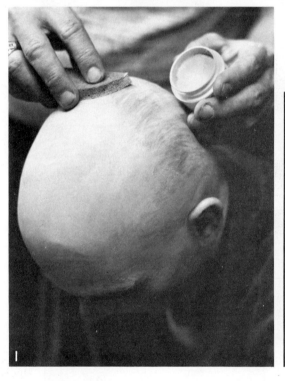

be shortened if you wish. Complete instructions for applying the cap come with it.

    (See also *Plastic caps* in Appendix A and *Soaping out the Hair* in Chapter 16.)

Hands Wrinkled and veined hands can be made up in the form of gloves, invaluable for quick changes. The gloves can be made by making up the hands with wax to build up knuckles, bones, and veins, then casting them, one at a time, by laying the hand, well oiled, palm down

in wet plaster and pushing down until the plaster covers the lower half of the hand, including the fingers. Let the plaster set until it has solidified. Before casting the back of the hand, make sure there are no free hairs that might become embedded in the plaster. If you can't flatten the hairs sufficiently with wax and petroleum jelly or cold cream, cut them off. If the subject objects to this, make plaster casts of the hands with moulage, then make a negative plaster mold from the positive plaster cast.

Whether you are casting directly from the hand or from a positive plaster cast of it, when the bottom half of the negative mold has solidified, remove the hand from the mold and grease the exposed area of the hardened plaster, return the hand to its original position, then pour fresh plaster over the hand. When the plaster has hardened, gently separate the two halves of the mold by moving the hand. When the two halves of the mold are thoroughly dry, they can be put back together and secured with masking tape. The mold is then ready for the latex, which can be poured in, sloshed around, then poured out. This can be repeated four or five times, each coat being allowed to dry thoroughly or force-dried with a hair dryer before the next one is added. For each drying period, place the mold with the fingers up so that latex will not accumulate in the finger tips. Extra coats may be added just to the back of the hand in order to stiffen knuckles, bones, and veins. These coats should dry with the mold flat and the palm up. Be patient and make sure that the latex is completely dry before separating the cast. Otherwise, the glove can be ruined.

Latex pieces to be pasted on the back of the hands are, of course, much simpler to make since only the back of the hand needs to be cast. (For hands aged this way using foamed latex, see Figure 17–6I.)

It is also possible to buy thin, snug, rubber surgical gloves and to attach the pieces to the gloves instead of to the hands.

Full Mask Although a full latex mask is normally made with foamed latex—and usually in sections, as illustrated in Figures 14–16 through 14–37—it is possible to use the slush-mold process. In general, the procedure is the same as for smaller pieces, though certain problems may be encountered, depending on the form of the particular mask and the way it is to be used. A mask of a human face is illustrated in Figure 14–14 and a non-human mask in Figure H–20.

APPLICATION OF PROSTHETIC PIECES

Attaching the Piece Latex pieces should be attached to the skin, which must be free of grease, before any makeup has been applied. This can be done with either liquid latex or spirit gum. The latex, however, may become loosened during the performance, and it has the added disadvantage of building up on the piece itself, thickening the edge, unless all traces of it are carefully removed after each use. Latex should not usually be used when the actor perspires freely or when there is facial activity that might tend to loosen it. Spirit gum is a safer choice.

FIGURE 14–14 LATEX FACE MASK. A full mask made by painting a number of coats of latex into a negative plaster mold made from a face cast built up with modeling clay. By Bert Roth, S.M.A.

These are the steps to be followed in attaching a latex piece (a nose, for example) with spirit gum.

1. Place the piece exactly where it is supposed to go, and check the fit. (Figure 14–15A.)
2. If the piece needs trimming, do it very carefully, keeping the blending edges thin and irregular. (Figure 14–15B.) Irregular edges are easier to conceal than straight ones. If you are applying a nose and the nostrils have not yet been cut out, that should also be done. Then try the piece on again and do any further trimming that may be necessary.
3. At this point it is usually a good idea to place the piece on the face exactly where you want it, then powder over and around it with face powder a few shades lighter or darker than the natural skin. When you remove the piece, there will be a clear outline of it on the face to guide you when you actually attach it.
4. Remove the piece from the face and brush spirit gum along all inside edges that are to be attached to the skin. (Figure 14–15C.)
5. Place the piece very carefully on the skin exactly where it is supposed to go. (Figure 14–15D.) Adjusting the position of the piece after the spirit-gummed edges are in contact with the skin can result in unsightly corrugations, which are difficult to conceal.
6. Press the edges down firmly with the fingers or with

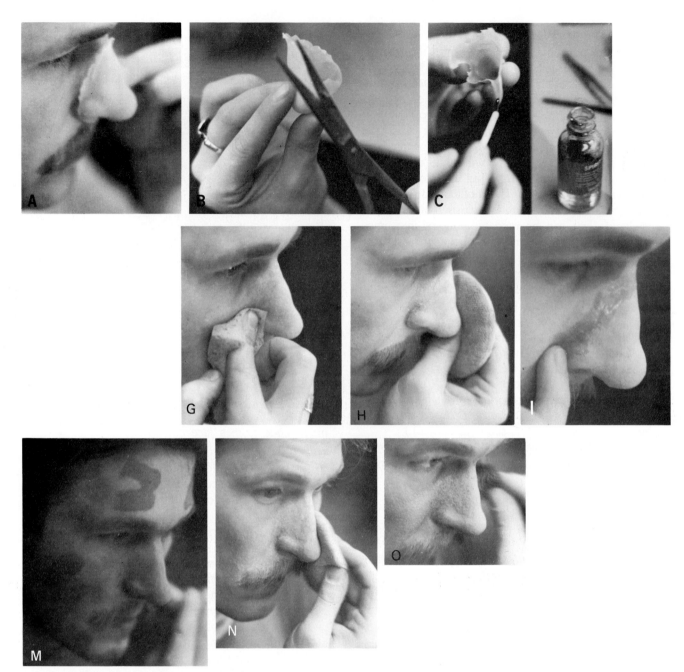

FIGURE 14—15 **APPLICATION OF A LATEX NOSE.** *Actor Tom Tammi applying a ready-made latex nose, using special precautions to deal with problem edges. A. Fitting the nose. Edges and nostrils have not yet been trimmed. B. Trimming the nostrils. C. Applying the spirit gum to the inside edges of the nose. D. Applying the spirit-gummed nose. Edges are being pressed down firmly with the fingers. This could also be done with a cloth or with a chamois. E. Pressing down edges around the nostrils with an orangewood stick. (Note: The next few steps—photographs F, G, and H—are intended to be followed only when there is a potential problem in concealing the edges—due, more often than not, either to their excessive thickness or to their tendency to corrugate.) F. Applying spirit gum over the blending edge. The spirit gum is then tapped with the finger until it becomes almost dry, after which it is set by pressing it with a damp sponge. G., H. Powder is then pressed into the spirit gum. I. Applying sealer over the spirit gum. The sealer is allowed to dry, then powdered. J. Applying latex over the sealer. The latex is allowed to dry, then powdered. K. Applying rubber-mask grease to the nose with a red-rubber sponge. L. Blending the rubber-mask grease into the area surrounding the nose. M. Applying creme stick makeup. This is then blended into the rubber-mask grease. (Or the rubber-mask grease could be used over the entire face.) N. Powdering the creme stick. O. Stippling the nose. After the nose has been powdered, three colors are applied with a black stipple sponge. Each color is powdered after it has been applied. P. Loosening the nose with spirit-gum remover.*

188

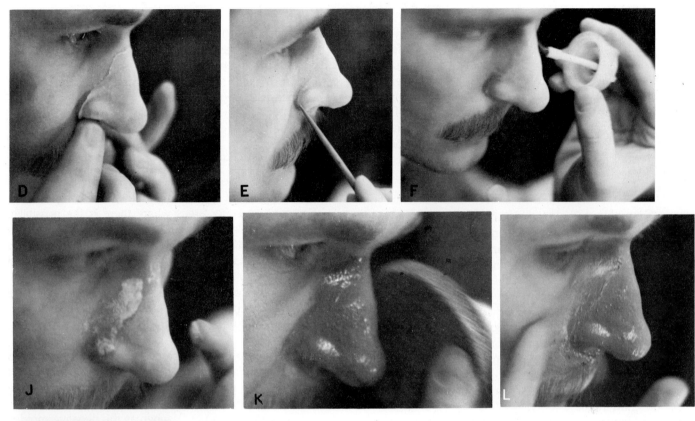

a lintless cloth or a chamois. Be very careful to press straight down and not at an angle in order to avoid creating wrinkles. An orangewood stick can be used to supplement the fingers in areas that are less easily accessible. (Figure 14–15E.)

Concealing the Edges Stippling the edges of the piece with latex cream adhesive (see Appendix A) will help to conceal them. The adhesive should, of course, be allowed to dry before the makeup is applied. If the edges are thicker than they should be or if they have a tendency to corrugate, the following procedure (or variations of it) may solve the problem:

1. Apply the piece as usual, using a very adhesive spirit gum. (Figure 14–15A through E.)

2. Paint all edges of the piece with matte spirit gum, overlapping onto the skin (Figure 14–15F), then tap the spirit gum with the finger until it is almost dry. Press it firmly with a wet cloth or a damp sponge (Figure 14–15G) to set it.
3. Press face powder firmly onto the spirit gum with a puff (Figure 14–15H), then remove excess powder with a powder brush.
4. (Optional) Apply a coat of sealer over the powdered spirit gum (Figure 14–15I) and allow to dry. Powder the sealer.
5. Apply liquid latex along the edge of the piece (Figure 14–15J), allowing it to overlap onto the skin. Allow to dry or force-dry with a hair dryer, then powder.
6. Apply rubber-mask grease as usual.

Applying the Makeup Rubber-mask grease, rather than the usual foundation paints, should be used over latex pieces and should be stippled on with a red-rubber sponge (Figure 14–15K). When you use rubber-mask greasepaint only for the latex piece and not for the rest of the makeup, be sure to stipple it over the edges of the piece and onto the skin immediately surrounding the piece. Then blend the edges of the rubber-mask grease into the skin with the fingers (Figure 14–15L) or with a brush in order to keep the edges from showing through the makeup used for the rest of the face. The rubber-mask grease can then be powdered by pressing in as much powder as the grease will absorb and brushing the excess off lightly with a powder brush. The rubber-mask grease needs more frequent powdering than regular greasepaint to keep it from developing a shine. This application of rubber-mask grease, including powdering, can be repeated one or more times if it seems necessary to do so in order to conceal the edges.

If a fairly large area of the face is covered by a latex piece or if there are a number of pieces used, you would probably do better to apply the rubber-mask grease over the entire face rather than just on the pieces.

Stippling To help conceal the edges of latex pieces, the rubber-mask grease foundation should be stippled with other colors. (See Chapter 11 for suggestions on stippling.) The stippling can be done with creme makeup or greasepaint instead of rubber-mask grease if you prefer. The following procedure or variations of it can be used:

1. Using a black stipple sponge (Figure 14–15O), stipple the piece with a color three or four shades darker than the base, concentrating on the edges of the piece and the adjacent areas of skin. Then powder.
2. Repeat step 1 using a color three or four shades lighter than the base. Powder.
3. Using a black stipple sponge, add some creme rouge if red is appropriate in that particular area of the face. (On the nose it usually is.) Powder again. If you wish to add additional red, that can be done very easily by brushing on a dry rouge of the appropriate shade.
4. Check to make sure that the edges of the latex piece are not apparent. If they are, do some detailed stippling along the edges, using a small pointed brush. Where the edge is revealed by shadows, use a light stipple to counteract the shadows; and where it is revealed by highlights, use a dark stipple. Check the effect in your mirror as you go along, continuing to stipple until the results are satisfactory.

Removing a Latex Piece If the piece has been attached with latex adhesive, it can be removed merely by pulling it off. The adhesive can usually be either pulled or rolled off the piece with the fingers. This should be done immediately upon removal of the piece if possible. The latex can be removed from the skin in the same way.

If the piece has been attached with spirit gum and if you expect to use the piece again, avoid pulling it off. Remove it instead by carefully loosening the edges with spirit-gum remover. This can be done by dipping a fairly firm-bristled flat brush into the remover, inserting the bristles between the edges of the latex piece and the skin, then running the bristles along under all of the edges. (Figure 14–15P.) The remover will dissolve the spirit gum as you go. The piece can then be lifted off easily. Pulling the piece off before the spirit gum is dissolved can stretch the edges, resulting in corrugations. After the piece has been removed, any spirit-gum residue should be cleaned off with more remover. This can be done with a wad of cotton. Makeup can be removed from the piece with alcohol or spirit-gum remover.

FOAMED LATEX

Although the hollow, shell-like latex pieces work well on bony parts of the face, their hollowness may become apparent on softer areas where there is the possibility of considerable movement. This problem can be overcome through the use of foamed latex, with which it is possible to make three-dimensional, spongy jowls and sagging necks that look and move like natural flesh.

The procedure for making foamed latex pieces is considerably more complicated than the slush-mold process previously described.

Closed Molds For foamed pieces it is necessary to use two molds—a positive and a negative—instead of the one open mold used with liquid latex. The positive mold duplicates the actor's own feature to be built up (as, for example, a nose), whereas the negative mold is taken of the same feature after it has been built up with clay and corresponds to the single mold used for painted-in latex pieces. When the two molds are fitted together, the space between will correspond precisely to the clay addition that has been built up on the plaster cast. This space is then filled with foamed latex by first pouring the latex into the negative mold, then fitting the positive mold into the negative mold, thus automatically squeezing out the excess latex, leaving the space between the two molds filled with latex foam. The foam in the closed mold is then cured (baked in an oven), after which the mold is separated and the foam—a spongy, three-dimensional piece—removed. The casting is done with gypsum or uncolored dental stone (see Appendix A), which is harder, less porous, and more durable than plaster. This is the procedure for making the closed mold:

1. Make a negative mold of the actor's face or of a single feature in the usual way. This mold can be of plaster. Then make two ½-inch balls of clay and cut them in half. That will give you four half spheres. Three of these (or all four, if you prefer) should be placed on the negative plaster mold, surrounding the face or feature. These will serve as keys or guides later in fitting the two molds together. Instead of using the semispherical clay pieces, you may, if you have a router bit available, drill into the positive stone cast (step 2) three depressions similar to those that would have been formed by the clay balls.
2. Build up high clay dikes around the mold, grease

the mold, and pour in the stone mixture (which is handled like plaster) to make a positive cast. When the stone has hardened, pull away the clay dikes, and separate the positive stone cast from the plaster negative.

3. Now proceed as for any latex piece, modeling the character face or feature in clay on the stone positive, including skin texture as usual. (See Figures 14–18 and 14–19.)

4. Build up a high clay dike on the positive cast; grease the cast and modeled clay features, then pour in stone to make a negative mold. This negative will be of the character face or feature.

5. When the stone has hardened, remove the dikes and separate the casts. Remove all clay and grease from the positive cast, and clean both casts thoroughly. Now you have two tight-fitting casts with semispherical keys to ensure an exact fit. The air space between the positive and the negative feature will be filled with foamed latex to form the prosthetic piece. Make sure the molds are thoroughly dry before using them with the foam. Drying can be done in the oven if you wish.

Foaming the Latex The companies that make latex for foaming have their own formulas for combining the various ingredients (either three or four, depending on the brand) in order to produce the foam. Whenever you use any foam latex for the first time, carefully follow the directions that come with it. Any experimentation should wait until after you have observed the results produced by following the maker's instructions. When you do begin experimenting with variations in the procedure, be sure to keep a precise record of all such variations, including all materials used and exact amounts of each, temperatures (both room and oven), beating times, and volume of foam. Date each entry and comment on the results. If the results are not entirely satisfactory, you might include any suggestions which occur to you for changes to be made in the next experiment. With each new experiment, only one variation should be made from the previous one.

Difficulties that can arise in the foamed latex process may be traced to such diverse sources as the type of beater used (improper foaming), too short a curing time or too low a temperature (foam too soft), excessive baking time or temperature (hard foam with an unpleasant odor), and too much moisture in the mold (latex skin becoming detached from the foam on or after removal from the mold.

Since formulas vary from brand to brand and since you will be following the instructions for your particular brand, the information given here is intended primarily for those who are not acquainted with the process but would like to have some idea of what is involved. Specific

amounts of the various ingredients will not be included. This is the general procedure:

1. Before beginning the mixing, grease the mold lightly with castor oil (preferably mixed with zinc stearate) or with rubber-mask grease. If you use the latter, the sponge will take on the color of the grease.

2. Weigh and mix with a spatula exact amounts of the curing agent and the foaming agent.

3. Weigh and add the exact amount of latex base specified, mixing carefully with the spatula.

4. Add the appropriate amount of colorant (latex dye or food coloring), and mix that in with the spatula.

5. In an electric mixer, whip the compound at high speed to approximately $3\frac{1}{2}$ or 4 (occasionally even to 5) volumes. This should take only a minute or so. The bowl in which you whip should be marked in advance for the desired numbers of volumes. The $3\frac{1}{2}$ volumes should give a firm sponge. For a softer sponge, increase the volumes.

6. Reduce the beater speed for a few minutes in order to refine the foam.

7. With the beater still running, add the gelling agent, carefully weighed, and beat for another minute.

8. Reduce the speed for a half a minute.

9. Reduce the speed still further for another half minute.

10. Pour or spoon the foamed latex into your negative mold.

11. Press the positive mold firmly into the negative, and give the foam time to set.

12. Place the mold in a preheated oven. The curing time will depend on the type of mold and the thickness. It will usually be a minimum of 3 hours.

13. When it is finished curing, the foamed piece can be removed immediately, if you wish, by separating the two halves of the cast and carefully lifting it out (Figure 14–24). The mold, however, should be allowed to cool slowly in the oven. Trim any ragged edges of the piece, but not too closely or too evenly—they should be very thin and somewhat irregular.

Application The foamed latex pieces can be attached with spirit gum, and Duo adhesive or stipple latex can be used to blend the edges. For areas in which there is a great deal of muscular activity, be sure the adhesive you use is reliable. Rubber-mask grease should be applied to the pieces with a sponge (Figure 17–6L). You may then want to adjust the color generally or locally (as with rouge, for example) by stippling on additional color with a coarse sponge. This helps to add texture and relieve the flatness of the rubber-mask grease foundation. Then press a generous amount of powder into the makeup to set it and remove all shine. To suggest even greater texture and color variation (as for broken blood vessels), use a coarse sponge or a brush to stipple additional colors over the powdered makeup—red-brown, grayed purple, dull brick red, rose, gray, lavender, creamy yellow, or whatever colors seen appropriate. This stippling should then be lightly powdered. If you wish the makeup to have a slight natural sheen (as you might for a bald head, for example), simply apply a light coating of K-Y Lubricating Jelly and allow it to dry or force-dry it with a hair dryer. Before working with foamed latex, study the series of photographs of the TV makeup for Hal Holbrook's Mark Twain in Figure 17–6 and of the movie makeup for Dustin Hoffman in *Little Big Man*, Figures 14–16 to 14–37.

MAKING AND APPLYING A FOAMED LATEX MASK. *The photographs on the following pages illustrate the creation of the makeup for Dustin Hoffman as the 120-year-old man in the film* Little Big Man. *MAKEUP BY DICK SMITH, S.M.A.*

FIGURE 14–16 *MAKING A PLASTER CAST OF DUSTIN HOFFMAN'S HEAD AND SHOULDERS.*

FIGURE 14–17 *PLASTER MODEL OF DUSTIN HOFFMAN'S HEAD.* *Clay models of every part of the latex mask were later sculpted over copies of this head or sections of it.*

MAKEUP BY DICK SMITH, S.M.A.

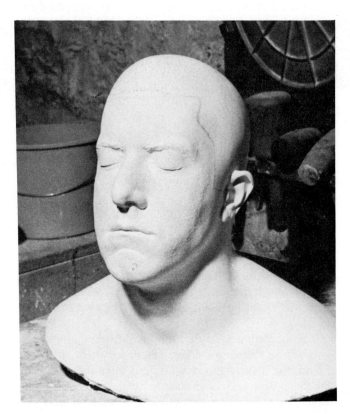

FIGURE **14–18** MAKEUP ARTIST DICK SMITH MAKING CLAY MODEL FOR FRONT HALF OF THE LATEX MASK.

MAKEUP BY DICK SMITH, S.M.A.

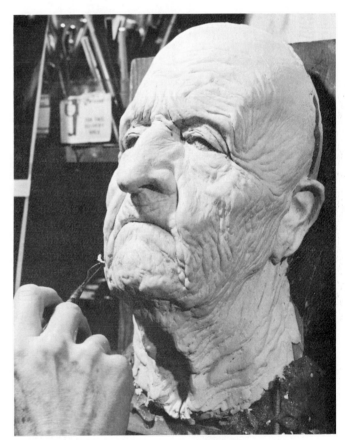

FIGURE **14–20** MODELING BACK OF HEAD ON A PLASTER SECTION OF DUSTIN'S HEAD.

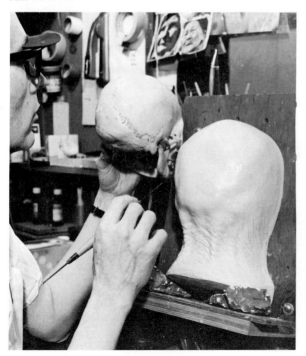

FIGURE **14–19** ROUGH MODEL. Will later be broken down into 8 parts—brow, nose, upper lip, eyelids, bags, lower lip and chin, and sides of face and neck.

FIGURE **14—21** *MAKING MOLDS OF CLAY MODELS OF BAGS, CHIN, AND NOSE.*

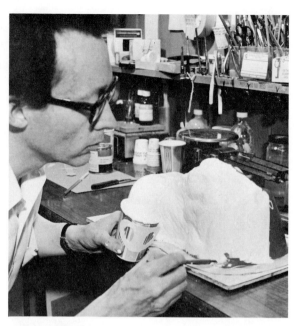

FIGURE **14—22** *MAKING SPECIAL EPOXY MOLD OF CLAY MODEL OF THE LARGEST PART OF THE MASK—SIDES OF FACE AND NECK.*

FIGURE **14—23** *FINISHING OUTER SURFACE OF THE MOLD OF THE SIDES OF THE FACE AND NECK SECTION. This exterior part of the mold is made of hard plaster.*

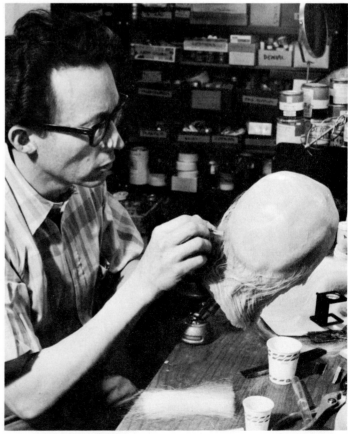

FIGURE **14–24** REMOVING LATEX.   *After mold has been baked to cure latex and positive cast of Dustin's face has been lifted out, the latex mask section is then carefully removed. (Pouring latex into the mold is illustrated in Figure 8–6.)*

MAKEUP BY DICK SMITH, S.M.A.

FIGURE **14–25** WHITE HAIR BEING IMPLANTED BIT BY BIT IN BACK SECTION OF LATEX MASK.

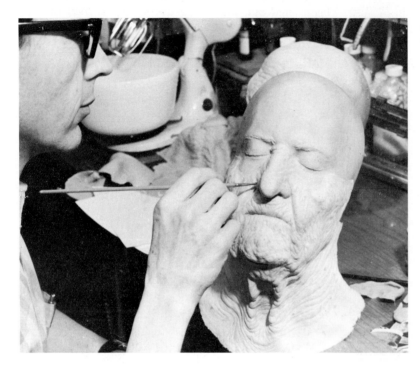

FIGURE *14–26. PAINTING "LIVER SPOTS" ON PART OF THE LATEX MASK.*

FIGURE *14–27 FINISHED MASK SEC-TIONS.*

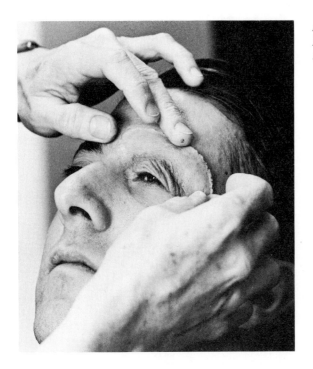

FIGURE 14–28 ATTACHING FOAM LATEX EYELID. *Piece is made thin enough and with enough folds sculpted into it so that it blinks naturally.*

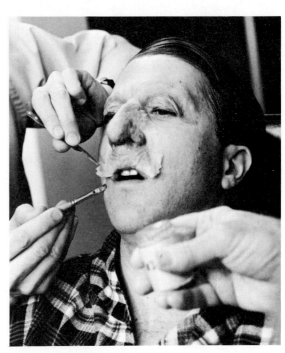

FIGURE 14–30 CHIN AND LOWER LIP BEING AT-TACHED. *All of the pieces were pre-colored to save time, leaving only minor coloring to do after they were glued on.*

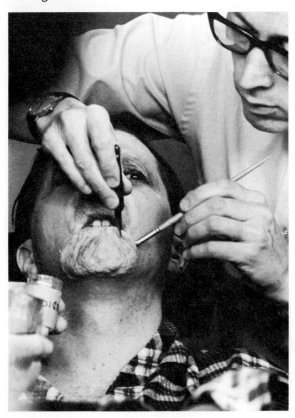

FIGURE 14–29 NOSE AND LIP PIECE. *Slomon's Medico Adhesive used near mouth for better adhesion.*

MAKEUP BY DICK SMITH, S.M.A.

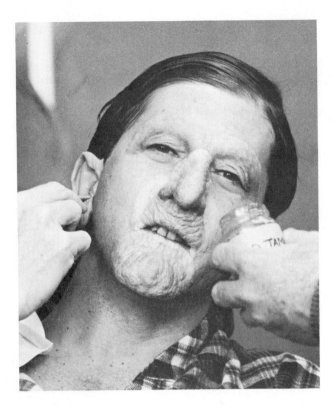

FIGURE **14–31** **ATTACHING THE EARS.** *Made of slush-molded lates. All others made of foam latex.*

MAKEUP BY DICK SMITH, S.M.A.

FIGURE **14–32** ATTACHING LARGE LATEX PIECE FOR CHEEKS AND NECK.

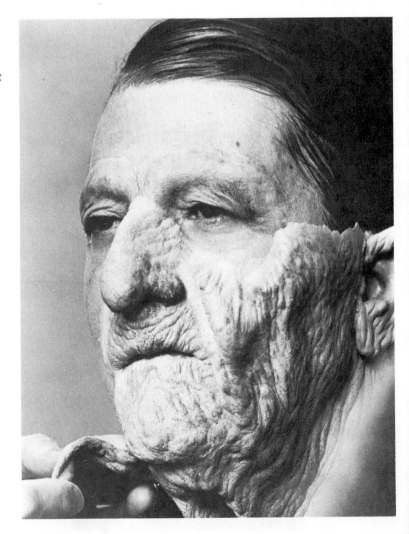

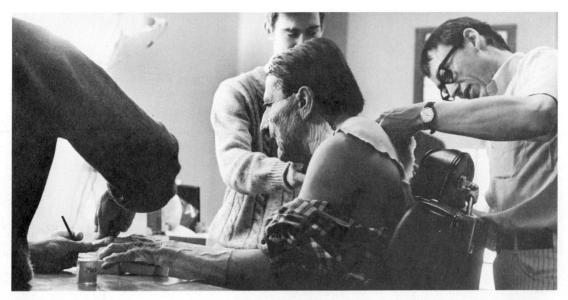

FIGURE *14—33* APPLYING SHOULDER HUMP AND HANDS.

FIGURE *14—34* HANDS WITH LATEX GLOVES AND FINGER-NAILS.

FIGURE *14—35* HEADPIECE BEING PUT ON. *Piece was constructed of 2 overlapping sections of foam latex, which were glued together before being put on.*

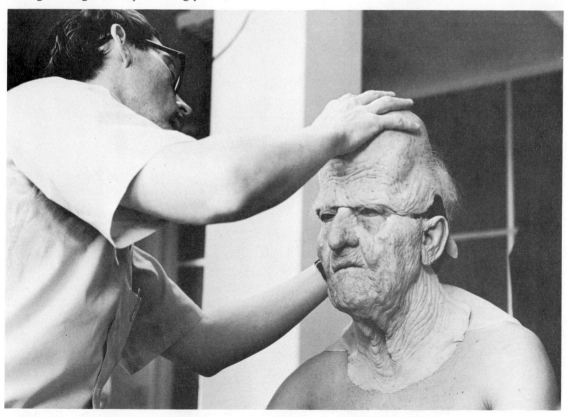

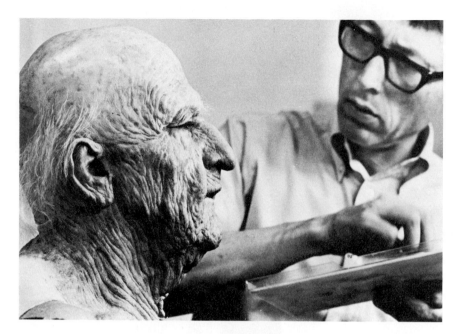

FIGURE **14–36** *FINAL TOUCH-UP OF LATEX MASK.*

MAKEUP BY DICK SMITH, S.M.A.

FIGURE **14–37** *DUSTIN HOFFMAN AS THE* **120**-YEAR-OLD *MAN IN* **LITTLE BIG MAN.** *(Photographs in Figures 14–25, 14–26, 14–27, 14–28, 14–29, 14–31, 14–32, and 14–33 by Mel Traxel, Cinema Center Films. All others by Dick Smith.)*

COLD-FOAM PROCESS

Polyurethane Foam A quick and relatively simple method for making foamed pieces in a closed mold, this process involves the use of a polyurethane foam with a latex skin. Instructions which come with the foam you're using should be carefully followed. In general, however, this is the procedure:

1. Cover surfaces of both the positive and the negative mold with a release agent, such as castor oil or rubber-mask grease (Figure 14–38A). Wipe off any excess

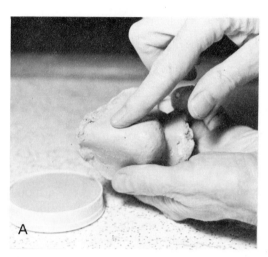

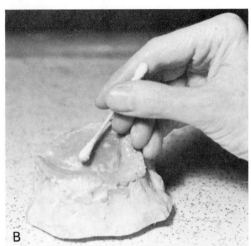

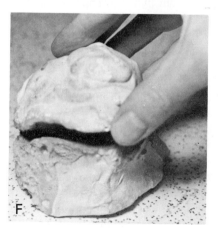

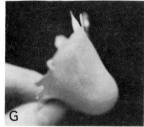

FIGURE *14–38* MAKING A NOSE WITH POLY-URE-THANE FOAM. *A. Coating the surface of the positive mold with rubber-mask grease. B. Coating the surface of the negative mold with latex. C. Adding the catalyst to the foaming compound. D. Stirring the catalyst and the foaming compound. E. Pouring the foam into the negative mold. F. Pressing the positive mold into the negative mold. G. The finished nose after it has been removed from the negative mold.*

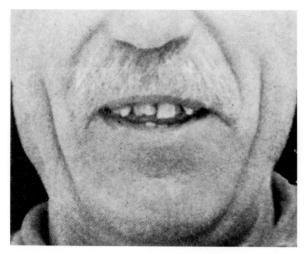

FIGURE *14–39* *TEETH OF AN ELDERLY MAN.*

FIGURE *14–40* *ACRYLIC POWDER AND LIQUID FOR MAKING FALSE TEETH.*

before proceeding. (Using rubber-mask grease adds color to the latex skin.)

2. Coat the inside of the negative mold with latex (Figure 14–38B), keeping it thin at the edges, then let it dry.

3. Add the catalyst to the foaming compound (Figure 14–38C) and stir well (Figure 14–38D), making sure the two are thoroughly mixed. Continue to stir until the moment the mixture begins to foam. *Do not lean over the mixture at this point to observe the foaming since the foaming process releases toxic fumes.*

4. Pour the mixture immediately into the negative mold (Figure 14–38E).

5. Press the positive mold tightly into the negative mold (Figure 14–38F), and let stand for the time specified in the instructions.

6. Carefully separate the two molds and remove the piece. If the latex skin separates from the foam, reattach it with spirit gum.

Silicone Foam This is a soft foam that does not require a latex skin. The brand you are using may already be flesh colored. If you want to deepen the color, add colorants before adding the catalyst. The foam is simple to mix and can be removed from the mold in from 7 to 10 minutes. It is fully cured in 24 hours. The manufacturer's directions should be followed.

TEETH

For enlarged or crooked teeth or fangs, acrylic caps can be made to fit over the natural teeth. The following materials—most of which are available from dental supply houses—will be required:

Disposable mouth trays—upper, lower, or both. (Be

sure to get the right size for the actor's mouth. Or get several sizes and keep the extras for possible future use. The mouth trays, though called "disposable," can be cleaned and reused.)
Dental impression cream
Dental stone
Mixing bowl for dental stone
Rubber form for making a base for the cast of the actor's teeth
Shellac
Modeling clay (preferably a light color)
Separating agent, such as Vaseline
Liquid Latex
Powdered acrylic and acrylic mixing liquid (Figure 14–40)
Coloring materials for teeth
Palette knife, stirring rod, modeling tool, spoon, utility brush

This is the procedure for making the teeth:

1. Fill a disposable mouth tray (upper or lower) with dental impression cream (which is supposed to dry in 3 minutes), and immediately place it in the actor's mouth (Figure 14–41A). After 3 minutes, in order to test for dryness, feel the overflow that has been forced through the holes in the tray. If it feels dry, wait another 30 seconds to make sure that *all* of the cream is dry before removing the tray.

2. Remove the tray from the mouth, mix the dental stone in a small bowl, and immediately brush it into the negative mold of the teeth before the impression cream starts to shrink. (The purpose of brushing rather than pouring the stone is to make sure that all crevices are filled and that there are no air holes.)

3. When the dental stone has hardened, separate it from the negative impression, which can then be

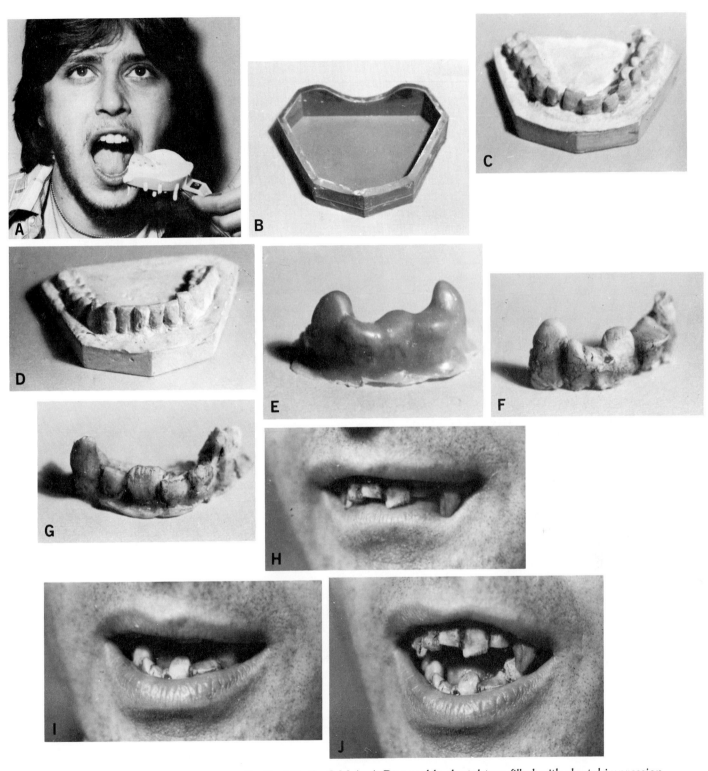

FIGURE 14—41 MAKING FALSE TEETH. *By Bert Roth, S.M.A. A Disposable dental tray filled with dental impression cream being placed in the mouth to make a negative mold of the upper teeth. (The casts of the teeth shown in the following illustrations were not made from this model.) B. Rubber mold for making a stone or plaster base for the positive cast of the teeth. C. Positive cast of the upper teeth set into a plaster base. D. Positive cast of the lower teeth. E. Negative latex mold for the false teeth. F. Acrylic caps for the upper front teeth. These made in the latex mold, then colored. G. Acrylic caps for the lower front teeth. H. Upper false teeth being worn. I. Lower false teeth being worn. J. Uppers and lowers being worn together.*

discarded. The disposable tray can be either discarded or washed and kept for future use.

4. Fill the rubber form (Figure 14–41B) with dental stone, and immediately set the positive cast of the teeth into it. Then let it dry until it has hardened.

5. Remove the rubber form from the stone cast.

6. When the teeth are thoroughly dry, coat them with shellac.

7. Using modeling clay, carefully model the false teeth on the cast of the actor's own teeth.

8. Paint the clay teeth and any exposed surfaces of the stone cast of the natural teeth with liquid latex. (It is not necessary to paint all of the teeth with latex—only those which have been built up with the clay.) Use at least 12 coats of latex, and let it dry.

9. When the latex is thoroughly dry, remove it from the cast. (Figure 14–41E shows a latex mold after it has been removed.)

10. Remove the clay from the stone cast of the teeth, wipe the teeth clean, then coat them with a separating agent.

11. Put acrylic powder into a mixing cup, and add the acrylic mixing liquid drop by drop, stirring until the mixture makes a paste. Then put the paste into the negative latex mold of the false teeth.

12. Push the positive stone cast of the natural teeth into the negative latex mold containing the acrylic paste. Let the acrylic dry. (It dries fairly fast.)

13. Remove the latex negative mold from the teeth, and separate the acrylic teeth from the stone cast of the natural teeth. When the actor is available, try on the acrylic teeth for fit.

14. Color the acrylic teeth appropriately, using any coloring medium (either paint or makeup) that will not rub off in the mouth or that for any other reason should not be used in the mouth. (It's a good idea to slip the acrylic teeth back onto the stone cast of the natural teeth when you do this.

The false teeth can be kept on the stone cast of the natural teeth and covered with the latex negative mold, or they can be wrapped in cotton or tissue paper and kept in a plastic box.

Figures 14–41H through J show a set of acrylic teeth being worn—uppers (H), lowers (I), and both together (J).

Problems

1. Cast a life mask.

2. Model a simple prosthesis (such as a nose or a pair of eye pouches) in clay on the plaster cast. Then make an open mold from the clay model and a latex prosthesis in the open mold.

3. Design and execute a makeup using the latex prosthesis you have made.

4. Make a simple prosthesis, using a closed mold and one of the cold-foam processes.

5. Design and execute a makeup using the foam piece you have made.

6. If you wish to do so, experiment with more complicated open-mold and/or closed-mold prostheses.

7. If you are interested in working in foam latex and have the necessary equipment available, experiment in making prosthetic pieces, using that method. Keep a careful record of procedures and results, specifying precise amounts used, volumes, temperatures, and timing.

8. Design a makeup requiring dental prosthesis, then make the teeth, and execute the makeup.

15

Beards and Mustaches

The first step in constructing a beard or a mustache is to make a rough sketch of what you have in mind. Presumably you will have done this when designing the makeup. Illustrations in this book and in your morgue should be helpful. The style you choose will, of course, depend on the period of the play and on the personality of the character. Period beard styles are illustrated in Appendix G.

You can make or buy beards or mustaches of real or synthetic hair ventilated on a lace foundation. This type of beard is the quickest to apply, the most comfortable to wear, and the most convincing. It is also the most expensive, but it will last for many performances. If you will be using a beard or a mustache for only a few performances and if your budget is limited, you will probably want to use crepe hair. In any case, you should become proficient in the technique of applying it. This applies primarily to men, of course, and to women who plan to make up men—or to make up *as* men. And women do sometimes use crepe hair for eyebrows in character makeups.

CREPE HAIR

Wool crepe is relatively inexpensive and, if skillfully manipulated, very effective. It can be used for beards, goatees, mustaches, sideburns, eyebrows, and occasionally to add to the natural hair. It is not usually satisfactory, however, for movie or television closeups.

Various shades of hair are available, and for realistic beards or mustaches, several shades should be mixed. This can be done by straightening braids of both shades, then combing them together. This will give a far more realistic effect than would a flat color. It is especially important for realistic makeups that pure black or pure white crepe hair never be used without being mixed with at least one other color. Black usually needs some gray or brown or red; and white, some blond or light gray.

PREPARATION OF CREPE HAIR

Crepe hair comes in braids of very kinky, woolly strands, which for straight- or wavy-haired actors should normally be straightened before the hair is applied. This is done by cutting the string that holds the braids together and wetting the amount of hair to be used. The portion of the hair that has been dampened can then be straightened by stretching it between the legs or arms of a chair, two clothes hooks, or any other solid objects not too far apart. Both ends of the stretched hair are tied with string to whatever moorings are being used and left to dry.

The damp hair can be straightened much more quickly, however, with an electric iron, but be careful to avoid scorching the hair. Pressing under a damp cloth or using a steam iron (Figure 15–1) is preferable.

After the hair is dry, it should be carefully combed with a wide-toothed comb, then cut into lengths as needed. A great deal of the hair will probably be combed out of the braid. This extra hair should be removed from the comb, gathered in bunches, and recombed as often as is necessary to make it useable for eyebrows, small mustaches, and the shorter lengths of hair needed in making beards. In combing, always begin near the end of the braid and work back, combing gently. Otherwise, you may tear the braid apart.

In case slightly wavy hair is desired, the crepe hair should be stretched less tightly while drying. Sometimes it need only be moistened and allowed to dry without stretching. It is also possible to use straightened hair and curl it with an electric curling iron after it has been properly trimmed. Crepe hair can also be curled by wrapping the straightened hair diagonally around a curling stick (a broom handle will do) and allowing it to dry or force-drying it with an electric dryer. Spraying the hair on the stick with hair spray or coating it with wave set will give it more body.

Occasionally it is possible to use unstraightened hair if a very thin, fluffy kind of beard is needed. To prepare

FIGURE **15—1** *STRAIGHTENING CREPE HAIR WITH A STEAM IRON.*

the hair, pull out the braid as far as it will go without cutting the string, grasp the braid with one hand, the loose end of the hair with the other, and pull in sharp jerks until a section of the hair is detached from the braid. The hair can then be spread out and fluffed up with the fingers. One method of fluffing is to pull the hair at both ends. Half of the hair will go with the left hand, half with the right. The two strands can then be put back together and the process repeated until there are no dark spots where the hair is thick and heavy. The curl is thus shuffled around so that it is no longer recognizable as a definite wave. If the hair is then too fluffy, it can be rolled briskly between the palms of the hands. This is nearly always done for mustaches when straightened hair is not used. The pulling and fluffing technique is particularly useful when skin should show through the beard in spots, as it sometimes does on the chin. It can also be used in an emergency if there is no straightened hair and no iron available to straighten it.

MIXING COLORS

Because combing wool crepe, even with a wide-toothed comb, tends to waste a good deal of hair, mixing can be accomplished more economically by first cutting the various shades of hair into whatever lengths you are going to need, always allowing extra length for the trimming. You can then proceed in one of two ways—either take strands of hair of each color and gradually put them together until the portions of the various colors you want

mixed are assembled into one pile, or put together all of the hair you want mixed and keep pulling the strands apart and putting them back together until they are sufficiently mixed. The principle, though not the technique, is the same as for shuffling cards.

The first method will probably give you a more even mixture. For some beards you will want to choose colors that are not too strongly contrasting in hue or value; for others you will want stronger contrasts. You might even, for example, use such strongly contrasting colors as black, white, and red.

If you wanted to give more subtlety to the color variation in a beard, you might work with three colors (which can be referred to as *a*, *b*, and *c*), mixing *a* and *b* to produce one mixture, *a* and *c* to produce another, and *b* and *c* to produce a third. Added to your original three colors, that would give you six different shades, which might vary only in value—variations of gray, for example—or in both value and hue—perhaps some red or brown mixed with the gray.

APPLICATION OF CREPE HAIR

The hair is commonly applied with spirit gum over the completed makeup. If creme makeup or greasepaint is applied in a very thin coat and well powdered, the gum should stick. How well it sticks will depend largely on how much the actor perspires and on the quality of the spirit gum used.

You will already have determined the shape of beard

you want. In applying the hair, always be aware of the natural line of hair growth, as shown in the diagram in Figure 15–2. The numbers indicate the most practical order of application. The procedure is as follows:

1. Paint the area to be covered by hair with spirit gum, and allow the gum to become quite tacky. Lightly tapping the gum repeatedly with the tip of a finger will speed up the process. It's a good idea to have some powder handy to dust on the fingers or on the scissors whenever they get sticky. During the application, the scissors can occasionally be cleaned with acetone and the fingers with alcohol or spirit-gum remover.

2. Separate a dozen or so hairs from one of your darkest piles, and, holding them firmly between the thumb and the forefinger of one hand, cut the ends on the bias (Figure 15–3). The hairs should be longer than required for the finished beard or mustache—they can be trimmed later. The darker hair should usually be used underneath; the lighter, on top. In observing bearded men, however, notice that in gray or partially gray beards, certain sections of the top layer are often lighter than others. Those areas normally match on both sides of the face.

3. When you have made sure that the gum is sufficiently tacky, apply the hair first to the underside of the chin (Figure 15–4A). Usually the application should be in three layers. Push the ends of the first layer into the gum under the chin, about ½ or ¾ of an inch back from the tip (#1 in Figure 15–2). Press with the scissors, a towel, or a damp chamois for a few seconds (Figure 15–4B), then add a second and a third layer (#2 and #3 in Figure 15–2), the latter starting from the lowest point on the neck where the hair grows naturally. The hair along the edge of this line should be very thinly spread. If you are making a full beard, the hair should be carried up to the highest point at which the beard grows on the underside of the jaw.

4. Next, apply hair to the front of the chin. The hair can first be attached in a roughly semicircular pattern, following the line of the tip of the chin (#4 in Figure 15–2). Then add thinner layers of hair (#5 and #6), following the line of the beard as outlined by the spirit gum. For full beards the hair should be built up gradually, starting at the chin and proceeding to the sideburns (Figure 15–2, #7–12; and Figure 15–4C). As the hair is usually not so heavy on the sides of the face, a few applications will be sufficient. Each application of hair should be pressed and allowed to dry slightly before another is made. Remember that ordinarily the thin layer of hair at the edge of the beard will be somewhat lighter in color than the hair underneath.

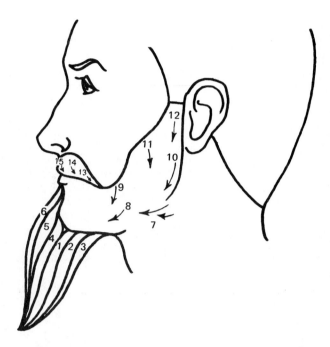

FIGURE **15–2** *DIAGRAM FOR APPLYING CREPE HAIR BEARD.* *Layers of hair are applied in the order indicated by the numbers.*

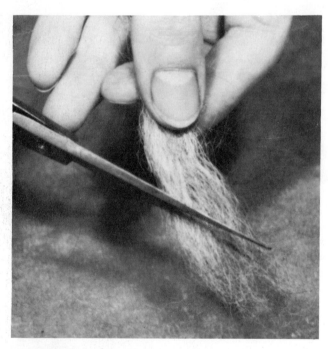

FIGURE **15–3** *CUTTING CREPE HAIR.* *Hair being cut on the bias before being applied to the face.*

5. When you have completed the application and have allowed the spirit gum time to dry, gently pull all of the hair in the beard in order to remove any stray hairs that are not firmly anchored. A beard that will

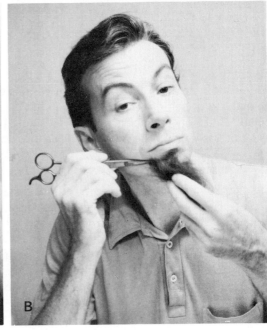

FIGURE 15–4 *CONSTRUCTING A BEARD WITH CREPE HAIR AND SPIRIT GUM.* Straightened hair is built up gradually in layers, using two or more shades of hair. All loose hairs are pulled out before the final trimming. Notice how the thinner hair on the cheek blends into the skin.

208

C   D

not resist this gentle pulling is not secure enough to wear on stage.

6. Holding your barber's shears vertically or nearly vertically, trim and shape the beard according to the style required, using a hand mirror when you need a profile view. If the beard is to be straggly, little or no trimming may be required; but a neat beard requires careful shaping.

7. Usually you will want to spray the beard with lacquer so that it will hold its shape. An unkempt beard may not need spraying; but, on the other hand, you may wish to use the spray to maintain the disorder.

Mustaches should not be stuck on in two pieces (except for distance work in which accurate detail is not necessary) but built up in the same manner as beards, starting at either end and working toward the center, letting the hair fall in the natural direction of growth (Figure 15–2, #13–15). One end of each hair should always be free. The ends of the mustache may be waxed to make them hold their shape. Better yet, the whole mustache can be sprayed with diluted spirit gum (see *Atomizer*, Appendix A) or hair lacquer.

In extending the sideburns, either separately or as part of a beard, it is sometimes possible, if the actor's hair is long and his sideburns are fairly full, to undercut the natural sideburns so that at least a quarter inch of real hair can be made to overlap the false hair, thus avoiding an obvious join. If, however, the natural sideburns are closely cropped, it will probably be more practical to continue the front edge of the false sideburns upward slightly in front of the real ones as far as necessary in order to make a smooth blend into the natural hair.

Removal In removing the crepe hair, brush on spirit-gum remover along the top edge of the beard or the mustache, then pull the hair off gently, continuing to

brush on the remover as you go. When all of the hair has been removed, clean the area where it was attached—first with the spirit-gum remover, then with your usual makeup remover.

Latex Base If you need the hair construction for more than one performance, you can make it up on a latex base rather than attaching it directly to the skin with spirit gum (Figure 15–5). Before painting latex on the face, it's a good idea to protect the skin with a light coating of cleansing cream or oil. Then powder the oiled skin and brush off the excess powder. If you should feel a burning sensation on your skin when you apply the latex, try another brand. If no other brand is immediately available or if you find all brands irritating, use spirit gum.

If you prefer to make the beard on a plastic face rather than on a real one, see Figure 15–6.

Following is the procedure for making a mustache. Essentially the same procedure would be used for beards and sideburns.

1. Paint the entire mustache area with liquid latex. If the character is to be aged, carry the latex application partially over the upper lip until the lip is as thin as you want it to be. When the first application is dry, add successive applications—usually two or three—until the latex seems thick enough to form a firm base.
2. When your crepe hair is ready to attach, paint on a final coat of latex and immediately push the ends of the hair into it. The ends will be firmly anchored when the latex dries. Because latex dries quickly, you should do only one small area at a time.
3. Pull out all loose hairs, and trim the mustache.

The mustache may now seem to be anchored solidly enough to leave it on for the first performance, but if

FIGURE 15–5 CREPE HAIR BEARD AND MUSTACHE. *Beard constructed on latex, using four colors of crepe hair—light gray, medium gray, light gray-brown, and blond. Mustache made of real hair ventilated on lace (see Figure 15–9B). Makeup by Bill Smith. (For another makeup by Mr. Smith, see Figure 13–33C.)*

there is much movement around the mouth or excessive perspiration, the latex may loosen and pull away from the skin. It is safer, therefore, to remove it as soon as the latex is dry and reattach it with spirit gum. This can be done simply by lifting one edge of the latex with a fingenail, tweezers, or an orangewood stick and pulling the mustache off. The back of the latex should be powdered immediately to prevent its sticking to itself. Rough edges should be trimmed before putting the mustache back on. In trimming the latex, be sure to leave as thin a blending edge as possible.

In reattaching the mustache, apply the spirit gum to the back of the latex, but only around the edges—unless there is to be so much movement that you would feel more secure with a greater area of adhesion. Let the gum become slightly tacky before attaching the piece to the skin. After the piece is in place, press with a towel for a few moments, just as in applying the hair directly with spirit gum. To conceal the edge of the piece, add a row of hair to the skin along the top edge of the mustache. This added row of hair will usually be the lightest hair you have prepared for use in making the mustache.

FIGURE 15–6 MUSTACHE ON A PLASTIC HEAD. *(The head is available from Bob Kelly.)*

On light-skinned actors, light hairs blend into the skin more readily than do dark ones.

Removal In removing the mustache, apply alcohol or spirit-gum remover around the edges of the latex to loosen it. Do not try to pull it off without first loosening the gum, as this may stretch or tear the latex. When the mustache has been removed, clean all the gum from the back of the latex with remover. It is possible to reattach the mustache with latex, but since the problem of security still remains, this is not advised.

In making both a beard and a mustache with latex base, make them separately or cut them apart after they are made in order not to restrict movement of the jaw.

BEARD STUBBLE

For an unshaven effect (see Figure 15–7), crepe hair is cut into tiny pieces and attached to the beard area with beard-stubble adhesive. There are several variations in the method. This is the simplest:

1. Wash the face with soap and water or clean it with alcohol or astringent to remove all grease. If the skin under the stubble is to be made up, use transparent liquid makeup.

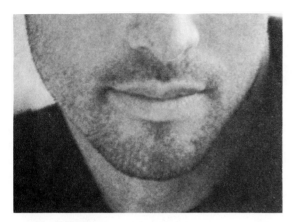

FIGURE 15—7 BEARD STUBBLE.

2. Choose the color of hair you want, then cut up tiny bits of it onto a piece of paper, your makeup table top, or any smooth surface.
3. Cover the beard area with a beard-stubble adhesive (see *Adhesives*, Appendix A). Uncolored mustache wax can also be used for the same purpose.
4. Push a dry rouge brush into the pile of hair bits (quite a few will stick to the brush), and, with the brush, transfer the bits to the face. The hair bits will spread out fairly evenly and will not pile up in clumps. (It would be best not to use your regular rouge brush for this but to have an extra one available for this purpose.) If you do not have a clean rouge brush available, you can transfer the hair bits to the face with a clean foam-rubber sponge. However, you may then need a clean brush (almost any kind of makeup brush will do) to remove clumps.

It is also possible to use matte spirit gum instead of the stubble adhesive, and it may be advisable to do so if there is likely to be any sort of activity that might dislodge the stubble from the wax adhesive. The spirit gum can be applied over whatever makeup you are using for the character. Regular spirit gum is not advisable because of the shine. When the gum is almost dry, the stubble can be attached by touching a fairly large clump of it to the gummed area repeatedly until the entire area is covered. Or you can spread the stubble over a towel, then apply it by pressing the towel against the gummed area of the face. In either case, loose hairs can be brushed off and final touching up can be done with the fingers or with tweezers. The spirit gum can be used over any makeup, though grease or creme makeup must, of course, be thoroughly powdered. The stubble adhesive works better on clean skin.

Removal Beard stubble applied with a wax adhesive can be removed with any makeup remover. When applied with spirit gum, it can be removed with spirit-gum remover or alcohol.

BEARD SHADOW

If, instead of a beard, only a beard shadow is required, simply stipple the beard area (over the finished makeup) with an appropriate color. (See Figure 15–8.) With medium or dark brown hair, charcoal brown is usually effective, but a lighter color would, of course, be used for lighter hair. For black hair, a dark gray makeup or gray mixed with black might be used; and for gray hair, a lighter gray. Experiment with colors to determine the right one. Unless you are stippling with cake makeup the stipple should always be powdered.

In stippling with creme makeup (or greasepaint), spread the color onto the back of the hand, then press the stipple sponge into the color on the hand rather than pressing it directly onto the cake. That gives you better control over the amount of color on the sponge. Then, touching the sponge very lightly to the face, do all of the stippling with great care in order to avoid mistakes,

FIGURE 15—8 BEARD SHADOW. Applied with Beard Stipple and a black stipple sponge. (Actor Kristoffer Tabori.)

which can be very time-consuming to correct. If you do make a mistake, try correcting it, if only a very small area is involved, by first blotting the mistake carefully with a tissue, then powdering it with a cotton ball or a cotton swab and, using a small brush, covering the spot with the foundation color. Powder again, then restipple. Depending on the size of the spot, it may be best to do the restippling with a small pointed brush rather than with your stipple sponge. Colors labeled "Beard Stipple" (usually a charcoal brown) are available.

EYEBROWS

Crepe hair can be used to supplement the natural brows, or it can be used to make completely new ones, as suggested in Chapter 12. In adding to the natural brows, it is possible to attach the crepe hair to the skin over the brow and comb it down into the brow or to stick tufts of crepe hair into the brow. The method used will depend on the form and the thickness of the natural brow and of the brow to be constructed.

Sometimes it is necessary to block out the eyebrows completely (see Chapter 12 for details) and build new ones. Ideally, this should be done by ventilating real hair onto net (see following section), but it can be done with crepe hair and spirit gum or latex. In using latex, be very careful not to get it into the real eyebrows, for it may be impossible to remove the latex without removing the hairs as well. Once the hairs have been completely matted down with spirit gum, wax, or sealer, however, it is usually safe to apply latex over them.

Removal Crepe hair eyebrows applied with spirit gum can be removed with spirit-gum remover. *When using spirit-gum remover on the eyebrows, always protect the eyes by bending over so as to cause the liquid to flow away from the eyes instead of toward them.* When applied with latex over blocked-out eyebrows, the crepe hair can simply be peeled off.

VENTILATED PIECES

The most convincing and convenient beards and mustaches are made of real or synthetic hairs individually knotted onto a net foundation. This knotting process is usually known as *ventilating*, though it is sometimes referred to as *working* or *knotting* the hair. Even in close-ups the hair appears to be actually growing out of the skin. The piece is easily attached and removed and, with proper care, will last for some time.

Materials Foundations may be of silk net, treated silk lace (plastic coated), nylon net, hairlace, cotton net,

silk gauze, or a combination of gauze and net. The gauze is a somewhat stiff, thin, tough, closely woven fabric. The better nets are also thin, fairly stiff, and somewhat transparent, so that when they are glued to the skin they become invisible from a short distance. For many years hairlace was considered the finest type of net available, but it has now been largely replaced with silk or nylon net (Figure 15–9A and B). Beards and mustaches are sometimes constructed with silk gauze for the body of the piece and edged with lace for the blend into the skin. The mustache in Figure 15–9D and E was ventilated onto silk gauze.

Both human and synthetic hair are used, but when greater stiffness is desired, yak hair may be substituted. It is less expensive, it can be dyed any color, and it does not mat or snarl as readily as human hair does.

The finest human hair is available in a variety of natural colors. Human hair that has been dyed is less desirable since the color may fade in time. Coarser human hair can be obtained at more reasonable prices. Hair comes in various lengths, tightly bound with string at the cut end, and may be either straight or curled. Hair is purchased by weight, the price depending on quality and color. Grays are usually the most expensive.

Various types of synthetic hair are available in a number of colors and at prices considerably lower than for human hair. Some types have a high sheen, giving a rather artificial look; others have less sheen, some of them being virtually indistinguishable in appearance from real hair. Real and synthetic hair are sometimes mixed. For sources of all types of hair, see Appendix A.

CONSTRUCTION OF VENTILATED PIECES

The first step in constructing a beard or a mustache is to draw the outline of the proposed piece on the face with an eyebrow pencil. This, of course, will indicate only the area of the skin from which the hair would normally grow—not the shape or styling of the beard or the mustache. In other words, a long handlebar mustache may grow from the same basic area as a short-clipped mustache. The only difference is that the hair itself is longer. The diagram in Figure 15–10 will serve as a general guide for outlining the area of growth. For individual variations in beard growth, see Figures 15–11, 15–12, Appendix G, and illustrations in your own morgue.

After the area is marked on the skin, lay a piece of thin, white translucent paper over the marked area and trace the outline onto the paper. Then cut out along the traced lines. This will give you an accurate paper pattern. For mustaches this is a very simple process, but

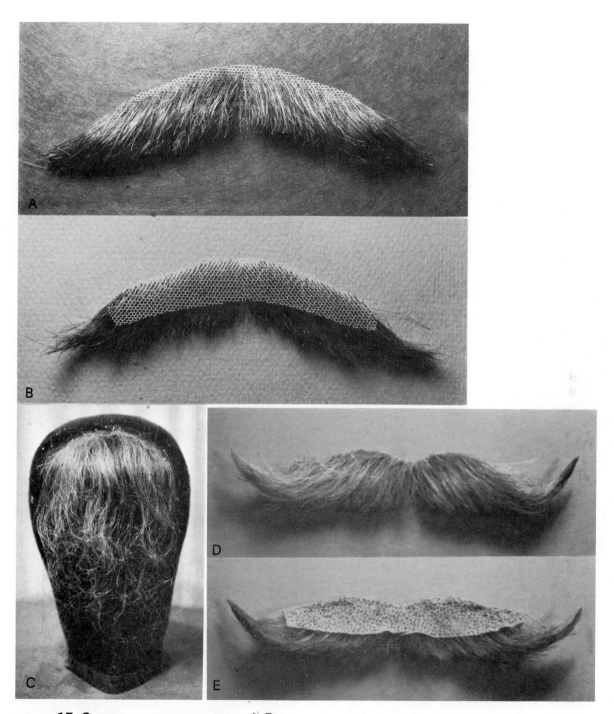

FIGURE 15—9 **VENTILATED MUSTACHES.** *A, B. Front and back of mustache ventilated on lace. C. Mustache (on wig block) ventilated on lace, shown before trimming. D, E. Front and back of mustache ventilated on gauze.*

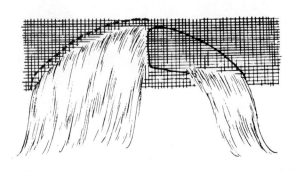

FIGURE 15—10 **VENTILATING A MUSTACHE ONTO NET OR GAUZE.** *The solid line represents the outline of the mustache, which should be drawn on paper underneath the net or, if gauze is used, on the gauze itself. The dotted line represents where the gauze or net will be trimmed.*

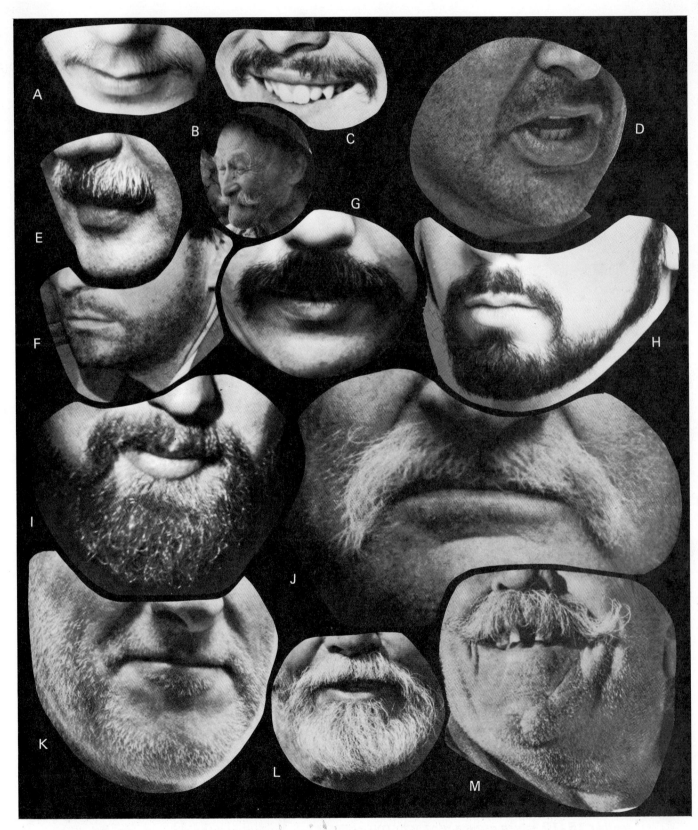

FIGURE **15—11** *MUSTACHES AND BEARDS.*

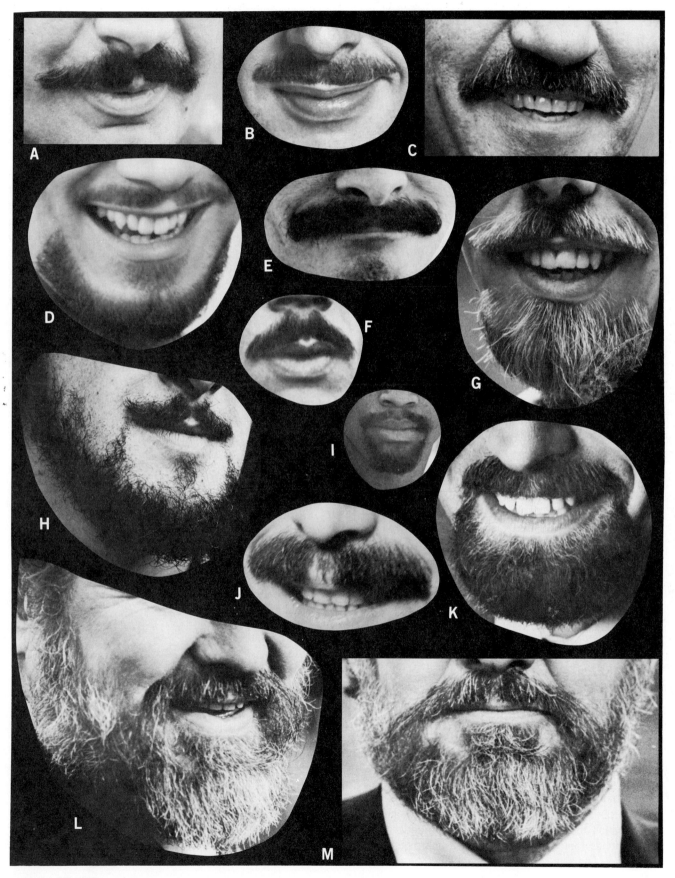

FIGURE 15–12 MUSTACHES AND BEARDS.

FIGURE *15–13* *BEARD BLOCK WITH VENTILATED BEARD.* (*Beard by Kryolan.*)

the needle is inserted. Needle sizes are designated by number, starting with 00—the larger the number, the larger the needle. For the body of a beard, a #1 or a #2 needle can be used, but for the edges a #00 is needed so that the knots will not be obvious. Larger needles should be used only where the knots are to be covered by subsequent layers of hair. For mustaches it is best not to use a needle drawing more than two or three hairs. For the top few rows a needle drawing only one hair should be used.

Figure 15–15 illustrates the ventilating technique. *Always keep in mind, in ventilating, that your hands must be pulling against each other from the moment the needle catches the hairs until the hairs are knotted.* Releasing the tension of the hairs before the knot is tied will probably result in their slipping off the needle. Releasing it before the ends of the hair are completely free of the knot may result in a loose knot, which will then have to be tightened by pulling it with the fingers. This is the procedure for ventilating:

1. (See Figure 15–15A.) Remove a very small bit of hair from the hank, and double it about a third of the way from the root end. If you are right-handed,

FIGURE *15–14* *VENTILATING A MUSTACHE ON A WIG FORM.* (*Student Gigi Coker.*)

for beards there is an obvious complication, since the hair grows both over and under the jawbone. The solution is to take a few tucks in the paper along the jaw line and crease it (making the folds under the jaw line) so that it fits the chin and the jaw snugly. Be sure to keep the upper edge—where the beard growth starts—absolutely smooth, with no tucks or wrinkles. Then cut with the tucks in it. After the paper pattern has been cut, open it out, lay it on the net, and cut the net flat.

The third step is to pin or tape (with masking tape) the pattern to a wig block (Figure 15–9C), a beard block (Figure 15–13), or a plaster cast of the actor's face, and lay a piece of lace over it. The lace should be about a half inch longer and wider than the pattern. It will be trimmed later. In Figure 15–10 the solid line represents the pattern of a mustache showing through the lace. Both the pattern and the lace should be pinned down with T-pins (see Appendix A), if you are using a canvas-covered or a styrofoam block (Figure 15–14), or with masking tape, thumb tacks, or a staple gun, on a woven block. When pins or tacks are used, be sure the lace is secured firmly, with the head of the pin or the tack resting tightly against it so that it is not pulled out of shape in the knotting process.

The ventilating needle is shown in Figure 15–15 and Appendix A. It consists of a handle about 3 inches long into which the needle is inserted. The needle is about 1½ inches long and curved with a sharp fishhook at the end. The size of this hook regulates the number of hairs that will automatically be drawn from the hank when

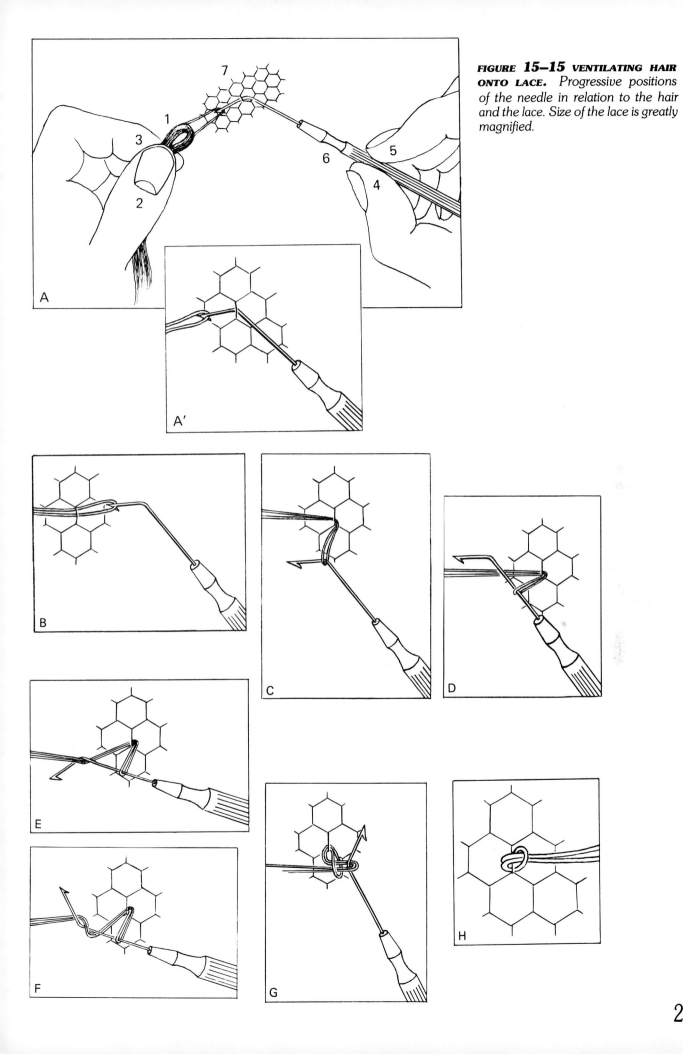

FIGURE **15—15** *VENTILATING HAIR ONTO LACE.* Progressive positions of the needle in relation to the hair and the lace. Size of the lace is greatly magnified.

217

grasp this loop (1) between the thumb (2) and the forefinger (3) of your left hand. With the thumb (4) and the forefinger (5) of your right hand, hold the needle (6) and slip it under one strand of the net (7). Then either thrust the hook of the needle into the hair or cast the hair over the hook of the needle (or do both simultaneously), and immediately withdraw the hook from the hair by moving the needle to the right. One or more hairs (the number depending on the size of the needle) should now be caught in the hook, as illustrated in Figure 15–15A.

2. Withdraw the needle from the lace, taking care to keep the hook from catching in the gauze. That can be done by rolling the needle slightly with the thumb and the forefinger in a counterclockwise direction and, at the same time, pushing the needle gently upward against the strand of the lace under which the hook must pass, enabling the smooth side of the needle to pass freely under the strand of the lace without the hook's becoming caught in the net. This may take a little practice, but it will soon become automatic. Then withdraw the hook far enough to clear the lace comfortably (Figure 15–15B); but be careful not to draw it too far, or you may pull out the short end of the hair. Until the knot is made, you must have a double hair to work with.

3. Then move the needle toward the left hand (Figure 15–15C,D), letting it cross over the hairs, then pressing it down slightly against the hairs, as illustrated in Figure 15–15E.

4. Now give the needle a half-turn clockwise (Figure 15–15F), then continue the clockwise turn until the hook is pointing slightly away from you, and draw the needle back through the loop (Figure 15–15G). Continue to draw it to the right until the entire length of the hair is through (Figure 15–15H). Pull the knot tight. The hairs will then lie in one direction, moving away from the left hand. Always move the right hand in the direction you wish the hairs to lie. Along the visible edges of your mustache you will probably place a hair in each tiny hole of the lace; but when you are using a larger needle, you will space the knots in order to give you the thickness of hair that you want.

Because single knots may sometimes loosen, causing hairs to be combed out of the piece, a double-knotting process can be used for added security. In step 4 above, after the needle has been drawn back through the loop (Figure 15–15G), but before the ends have been drawn through, the needle is once again hooked around the stems of the hair, as in Figure 15–15E, F. Then the needle is drawn back through the second loop that has been formed, the ends are drawn through, and the hair is pulled tight as usual.

Although this knotting procedure may sound com-plex, it is quite easy to learn. Once you have mastered the needle technique, you will make the necessary movements automatically and will be able to work quite rapidly.

In making a mustache, always begin at the outer corners and work along the bottom and upward (Figure 15–10). The top hair should always be the last to be knotted in. When the hair is in, trim the net about a quarter inch beyond the hair, as shown by the dotted line in Figure 15–10. The lace immediately under the nose may have to be trimmed closer than that, but avoid trimming it too close since the edges will eventually ravel and will have to be cut down still further.

You may want to do some preliminary trimming of the mustache before trying it on, for when you finish the ventilating, the hair will probably be as long as that in Figure 15–9C. When you are learning to trim and style beards and mustaches, carefully study photographs before you do any trimming at all. If you can find a photograph of exactly the style you want, so much the better. Cut the hair carefully with a good pair of barber's shears, a little at a time. Be sure to try on the mustache before doing the final trimming.

In constructing a beard, place the pattern on a form (such as a beard block or a plaster cast of the head) so that the original tucks can be taken. Then attach the edges of the pattern to the block with masking tape. Identical tucks can be taken in the net. These can be folded down as you attach the edges of the net to the block with masking tape, just as you did the pattern. You can secure the tucks simply by ventilating through the three thicknesses of net so that you are actually tying the tucks in with strands of hair.

If you want to make the body of the beard foundation with gauze, simply lay the gauze over the beard pattern as you would the net, but trim it down $3/8$ to $1/2$ inch below the upper outline of the beard. The gauze should not show when the beard is finished. Then lay on a strip of net along the edge, overlapping the gauze about $1/2$ inch and, of course, overlapping the edge of the pattern also. Along this edge, the hair can be ventilated through both net and gauze, tying them together.

For both beards and mustaches you should nearly always use more than one shade of hair. Facial hair is often darker underneath, lighter on top and along the edges. (See Figure 15–16.) The lighter hair along the edge, being nearer the color of the skin, is extremely helpful in making a subtle, realistic blend. With gray hair, the differences in color are especially marked. There may sometimes be dark brown or even black hairs underneath and white ones above. This can be reproduced very subtly in ventilating, since the hairs are put in individually. A few red or auburn hairs will give a gray beard added life. Observe real beards—gray ones are rarely, if ever, the same color throughout. There may be a salt-and-

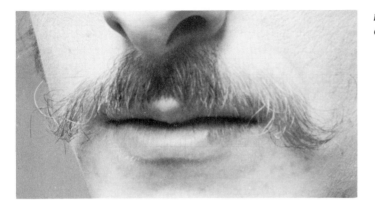

FIGURE 15–16 REAL MUSTACHE. *Note variation in color.*

pepper effect, with dark and light hair mixed, or the gray may be in streaks or areas, more or less matching on both sides of the face.

APPLICATION OF VENTILATED PIECES

A full beard can be applied in one piece or, if desired, cut into sections—usually three for actors or five for singers—each section being applied separately. In dividing the beard into sections, cut the lace very carefully, avoiding, if possible, cutting any of the hair. (Figure 15–18 shows a beard cut into three sections, plus a mustache.)

Following are the three basic steps for applying a beard, whether in one, three, or five sections:

1. Place the piece on your face to determine the correct position. If you have a beard or a mustache with a partial gauze foundation, you can secure it to the skin with double-faced toupee tape. If you are using a mustache with no gauze, set it on the face, then observe very carefully where it goes so that you can estimate where to place the spirit gum.
2. Brush a thin coat of matte spirit gum onto the clean skin, covering the entire area beneath the lace. For beards, you will normally place the gum only under the edges of the lace, though it is possible and sometimes desirable to cover the entire area if there is to be strong muscular activity, as in singing, or if for any reason you feel the need of the additional security. *Never use latex on hairlace!*
3. Let the spirit gum become slightly tacky. Then press the lace into the gum with a slightly dampened, clean, white, lintless towel, a piece of silk or nylon, or a damp chamois, being careful to press the lace straight down without letting it slide on the skin. This sliding could stretch it, causing unsightly corrugations or ripples, which might become permanent. Use a clean

section of the cloth or chamois each time you press. Keep pressing until the lace is dry. Then, with a toothbrush, a dye brush, or an eyebrow brush, lift any hairs that may have inadvertently been stuck down by the gum.

DRESSING VENTILATED PIECES

When the beard or the mustache is securely attached, it can be combed with a wide-toothed comb. But remember, in combing any hairpiece, always to hold the comb at an angle so that there is no possibility that the teeth will dig into the net foundation and tear it. This means holding it at the reverse angle from the one usually used in combing your own hair. Also, when the hair is fairly long, always begin combing at the ends and work toward the roots. Human hair in hairpieces of any kind becomes matted and tangled much more easily than the same hair would while growing on the head. This is because half of the hair is going against the natural direction of growth. In other words, the hair is knotted somewhere between the roots and the end, both of which are extended outward. A human hair is not quite the simple, smooth filament it appears to be—there are little scalelike projections, all going in the same direction. You can usually feel the difference by running a hair quickly between your thumb and forefinger in the direction of growth and then against the direction of growth. When hairs are not all going in the same direction, these tiny scales catch onto each other and cause matting. Therefore, special care is needed in combing any kind of hairpiece made from human hair.

If the hair does not naturally fall just as you would like it to, comb it with water, set it (pushing it into waves or making pin curls—on the ends of beards or mustaches—for example), and let it dry before recombing it. When the hair is dry, spray it with hair oil or hair spray, or apply a gel or cream dressing, then comb the hair and do whatever trimming and shaping may be

FIGURE 15—17 CAVALIER. *Mustache and goatee ventilated with synthetic hair on nylon net and dressed with Kryolan Eyebrow Plastic and hair spray. (Makeup, including mustache and goatee, by student Douglas Parker.)*

needed. If you want the hair to look dry or unhealthy or dirty, you can use colored powder or cake makeup to dull it.

The hair can also be curled with a curling iron if you prefer. Heat should be used with great care, however, on synthetic hair. Water waving is to be preferred. In order to maintain the wave in synthetic hair, it may be necessary to spray it with hair lacquer.

The ends of a mustache can be shaped with mustache wax, derma wax, or hair spray. The mustache and the goatee in Figure 15–17 were dressed with Kryolan Eyebrow Plastic and hair spray.

REMOVING AND CLEANING VENTILATED PIECES

To remove the beard or the mustache, dip a stiff brush into spirit-gum remover or alcohol, and press the bristles into the lace edge. *Do not scrub and do not pull up the lace by force.* Any good lace or net is very delicate and requires considerable care in handling to avoid stretching or tearing it. Keep flooding it with the remover

until the gum is softened and the lace comes up by itself. Then dip the lace edge (or the entire piece if there is spirit gum on all of it) into a dish of acetone to remove all traces of spirit gum and makeup. The lace must be kept absolutely clean if it is to remain invisible on the skin. It may be desirable, even when the gum has been used only on the edge, to soak the whole piece in acetone from time to time.

Beards and mustaches should be carefully stored so that they will be kept clean and the lace will not be damaged. It is best to stuff beards with cotton or tissue paper and to keep each one in a box large enough so that it will not press the beard or the mustache out of shape.

MEASURING FOR BEARDS

If you want to order a beard by mail, it would be well to include the measurements listed below. Letters refer to those in Figure 16–26, in which the heavy dotted lines represent beard measurements, and the light broken line, the beard line.

A. From sideburn to sideburn under chin
B. From lip to end of beard line under chin
C. Width across the front (average measurement, 3 inches)
D. Corner of lip to back of jawbone

If you are ordering a ready-made beard, not all of these measurements may be necessary, especially if you are renting it. But better too many than not enough.

ADAPTING BEARDS

One great advantage of ventilated pieces is that they can be restyled, often merely by combing, for a variety of characters. It is possible, for greater flexibility, to make a full beard in three pieces—one center and two side sections—with, of course, a separate mustache (see Figure 15–18). Then the pieces can be used singly or in any combination, as shown in Figure 15–19, in which all six makeups are done with a single wig and the four pieces shown in Figure 15–18. This is only a sampling of the variety that could be obtained by combining pieces and recombing.

It is most useful for an actor or any theater group to build up a stock of ventilated beards and mustaches. The best way to do that is to make whatever is required for each character you do instead of using crepe hair. Then the pieces can be saved and used in the future. This takes more time initially but pays off in the end, giving you a stock of realistic beards and mustaches to choose from.

FIGURE 15–18 ***FULL BEARD IN SEC-***
TIONS. *Sideburns, mustache, and
beard made of real hair ventilated on
nylon net. These pieces can be recombed, straightened, or curled and
used in various combinations, as illustrated in Figure 15–19.*

FIGURE 15–19 *A VERSATILE BEARD.* *Late nineteenth-century beard styles made by combining the four
ventilated hair pieces shown in Figure 15–18. The same hairlace wig was recombed and used throughout.*

Problems

1. With crepe hair, duplicate one or two beards and mustaches from photographs.
2. Design and execute, using suitable crepe-hair applications, makeups for two different characters.
3. Using real or synthetic hair, ventilate a mustache or a beard based on a drawing, a print, or a photograph.
4. Do another complete makeup for a specific character from a play, using your ventilated beard or mustache. Do a makeup worksheet first.

Hair and Wigs

The hair is always an important element in any makeup and is invaluable as a means of suggesting period, personality, and age. Failure to make the hair suit the character can ruin an otherwise skillful makeup.

NATURAL HAIR

Restyling More often than not the actor's own hair can be appropriately styled for the character being played. The same head of hair can be parted on the side, in the middle, or not at all. It can be combed straight back or straight forward. It can be well combed or mussed, straight or waved, close to the head or fluffed out.

For both men and women it is possible to wave the hair, if it is naturally straight, by setting it with pin curls or rollers or by curling it with a curling iron. If the hair is to look well groomed, it can be sprayed with hair oil or a commercial hair spray, or a hair dressing can be applied with the fingers and combed through the hair. A lacquer spray for keeping the hair in place is sometimes desirable, depending on how manageable the natural hair is and how well it stays combed.

For characters whose hair would be expected to look dull and lifeless, face powder the color of the hair can be dusted on, or a little cake makeup or liquid body makeup of the desired shade can be applied with a sponge to dull the hair. If the hair is to look stiff and matted, it can be heavily sprayed with a liquid hair set and shaped with the fingers rather than with a comb or a brush.

Cutting There are times when cutting the hair (Figure 16–1) is the simplest method of achieving the correct hair style for a character. If the actor is willing to have his hair cut, he can be sent to a barber or a hair stylist with sketches of the desired style. If he is not willing, a wig may be used instead. (See the section on *Wigs and Hairpieces* in this chapter.)

FIGURE **16–1** KRISTOFFER TA-BORI AS THE DAUPHIN IN ST. JOHN. *Natural hair cut in fif-teenth-century style. (Photo by George de Vincent.)*

Occasionally the style required may be so disfiguring that the actor may well object to having his hair cut for esthetic or other reasons. Possible solutions to the problem are to modify the hair style, to have a wig made for the actor to wear when he is not onstage, or to cast an actor who is willing to have his hair cut.

Coloring and Graying The hair can be colored or grayed with a temporary spray that can be washed out (see *Hair coloring*, Appendix A). Temporary sprays are available in gold, silver, black, and a variety of colors. The silver can be used when a silvery-gray effect is appropriate. The entire head can be sprayed, or the hair can be streaked with gray or with color, then carefully combed.

More than one color can be used when it seems appropriate to do so. For example, blond hair can be changed to brown streaked with gray merely by spraying first with the brown, then, when the brown is thoroughly dry, with silver. Black hair can be made blond, but it is usually recommended that the hair first be sprayed with red and then with blond, since the blond spray might not cover adequately.

One must be extremely careful in using such a spray to keep it off the face and to avoid patchiness. The best way to protect the skin is to cut a piece of paper to match the hairline and hold it over the forehead as the front of the hair is being sprayed. This cutout can be kept in the makeup kit for future use. The gray should usually be combed in after spraying.

If the silvery effect is inappropriate (as, for example, for a Bowery bum), liquid or stick hair whitener (see Appendix A), white or pale yellowish creme stick, makeup crayons, cake makeup, liquid body makeup, or colored spray can be used. Luminescent dry cake eyeshadow in white or silver is especialy useful for quick changes. Any hair whitener—no matter how it is applied—needs to be combed into the hair. If the whitener does not look natural on the hair—white on dark hair, for example, tends to look slightly bluish or chalky—the effect can be softened by the addition of yellow food coloring to the whitener before it is applied. A little silver spray applied in streaks and thoroughly combed into the whitened hair is also helpful. If the whitener you use looks too dull or too flat, a little hair oil can be sprayed on or combed in. Or you may prefer to experiment with various brands of hair whitener in order to determine which one will come closest to giving you the effect that you want. (For photographs of naturally gray hair and sideburns, see Figure 16–2.) White powder or cornstarch should be used only in an emergency and preferably not at all. It is seldom convincing, and any unusual activity on the part of the actor can send up a cloud of white dust.

For coloring the hair without using sprays, various techniques can be used. Cake makeup can be applied with a sponge or a brush, then combed in. Dry cake eyeshadow, matte or luminescent, can be brushed on for streaking or touching up. Luminescent copper eyeshadow (or a mixture of copper and brass or gold) can be used to give the effect of auburn hair.

For men whose hair is thin at the crown, cake makeup of the correct color can be used to darken the scalp. Should there be an emergency, makeup pencils, greasepaint, or creme makeup can be used for the same purpose, but they should usually be powdered to eliminate the shine.

Natural beards can be grayed or colored in the same way as natural hair.

FIGURE 16–2 GRAYING HAIR. *Naturally graying hair and sideburns.*

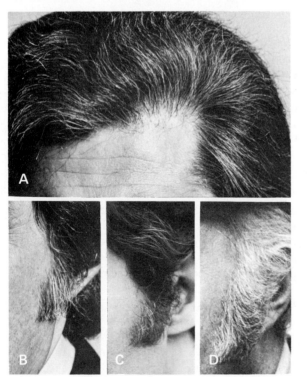

BLOCKING OUT THE HAIRLINE

When the hairline needs to be changed slightly—receding at the temples, for example, the sideburns shortened or removed, or the hairline raised—it can usually be done by blocking out sections of hair with Kryolan's Eyebrow Plastic or, as in Figure 16–3, with derma wax. How effectively it can be done will depend largely on the thickness, texture, and growth pattern of the actor's hair.

If the hair seems to lend itself to being blocked out, mat it down as flat as you can by stroking it firmly and repeatedly with the stick of Eyebrow Plastic, following the direction in which the hair is to be combed for the character. It works best, of course, if you are doing a little bit of the hairline or if the hair is fairly fine or not too thick.

When the hair is as flat and smooth as you can make it, press powder firmly into it with a velour puff. After removing the excess powder with a powder brush, give the blocked-out area a coat of plastic sealer. When that is dry, powder again, and apply your foundation makeup to the face and the blocked-out hair area. If the color of the hair shows through, it would be best to cover the blocked-out area with rubber-mask greasepaint.

This can be used for the entire makeup, or it can be blended into the foundation color, which should be either creme (*not* cake) makeup or greasepaint. Then complete the makeup as usual.

It is also possible to block out hair with spirit gum. The hair can be saturated with the spirit gum, combed carefully to eliminate clumps of hair, then, after the gum has become quite sticky, pressed down very firmly with a damp chamois or a cloth. Powder is then pressed into the gum and the excess removed with a powder brush. (If at this point it is evident that the blocked-out hair is not going to give a smooth surface, it can be smoothed out by going over it with a stick of Kryolan's Eyebrow Plastic.) Sealer is then applied and the foundation color applied over it.

A third method for blocking out the hair is illustrated in Figure 16–4. This is the procedure:

1. (Figure 16–4A.) Soap out the appropriate area of hair, using the method described under *Soaping out the Hair* (the following section in this chapter).
2. (Figure 16–4B.) Press powder into the dried soap.
3. (Figure 16–4C.) Coat the soaped-out area with spirit gum.
4. (Figure 16–4D.) Force-dry the spirit gum with a hair dryer.

FIGURE 16–3 BLOCKING OUT HAIR WITH DERMA WAX. *Makeup by Lee Austin. Hairline and eyebrows blocked out with derma wax for a makeup of Elizabeth I. Nose is also modeled with derma wax. For the final makeup with wig, see Figure 13–6.*

FIGURE 16–4 BLOCKING OUT THE HAIRLINE WITH SOAP, SPIRIT GUM, AND KRYOLAN'S EYEBROW PLASTIC. *Makeup by student Gigi Coker. A. Soaping out the hairline. B. Pressing powder onto the dried soap. C. Coating the soaped-out area with spirit gum. D. Force-drying the spirit gum with a hair dryer. E. Pressing powder onto the spirit gum after it is thoroughly dry. F. Waxing the flattened area with Eyebrow Plastic, which is then powdered. G. Applying sealer over the Eyebrow Plastic with the fingers. H. Rubber-mask greasepaint has been applied and is being powdered.*

FIG. **16—4.** *Cont.*

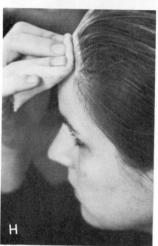

5. (Figure 16–4E.) Press powder into the spirit gum after it is thoroughly dry.
6. (Figure 16–4F.) Wax the flattened area with Kryolan's Eyebrow Plastic. Then powder.
7. (Figure 16–4G.) Using the fingers (or a brush, if you prefer), apply sealer over the Eyebrow Plastic, and let it dry. Then powder.
8. Stipple rubber-mask greasepaint heavily over the powdered sealer, using a red-rubber sponge. If the rubber-mask greasepaint is not to be used for the entire makeup but only for this area, blend it into the skin, then press it firmly with powder (Figure 16–4H), and proceed with the makeup, applying your foundation color over the rubber-mask greasepaint as well as the rest of the face. If the rubber-mask greasepaint is to be used as the foundation color over the entire face, obviously no additional foundation color need be applied.

For a more natural effect when you are creating a receding hairline or one higher than your own, soften the new hairline by shading it lightly with a color similar to the hair color. This should be done before the final powdering of the makeup. Matted hairs can be separated with a comb. If a wig is to be worn, it is not necessary, of course, to create a natural-looking hairline at the edge of the blocked-out area (see Figure 16–3).

Sometimes it may be necessary to block out sideburns entirely, as for an early fifteenth-century hair style. That is best accomplished by shaving the hair off, as was done for the makeup of the Dauphin in Figure 16–1. However, practical considerations—such as playing in repertory or filming for TV during the day and playing in the theater at night—may make that undesirable. In that case, blocking out the sideburns temporarily can solve the problem.

SOAPING OUT THE HAIR

Hair can also be blocked out with soap to create the effect of a shaved head (Figures 16–5 and 16–6), a bald pate (Figures 16–7, 16–8, and 16–9), or a receding hairline (Figure C–1). It is difficult for one to block out one's own hair to create a bald pate, but it can be done. (See

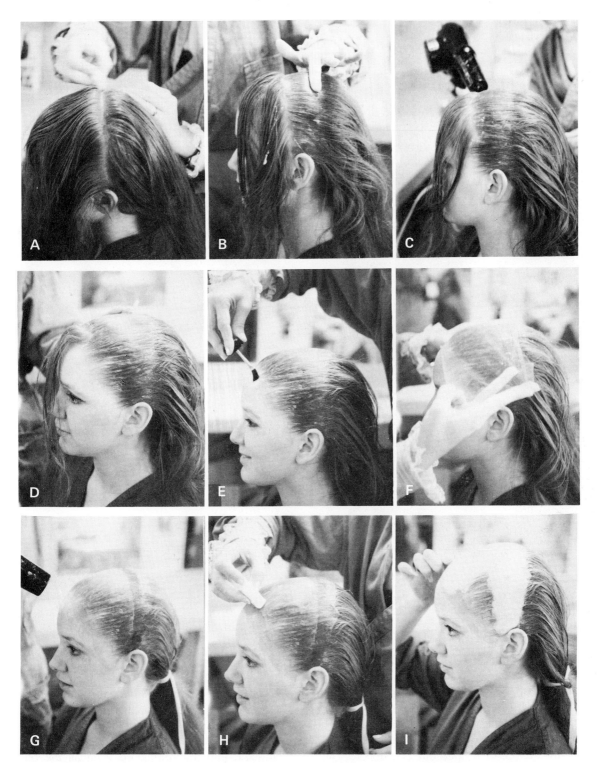

FIGURE **16–5** SOAPING OUT THE HAIR. *Hair is parted horizontally (A) at the highest point desired for the bald area, soaped down thoroughly in small sections (A–D), each section being dried with a hair dryer. Edges of the area are painted with spirit gum (E), and a piece of nylon stocking, cut approximately to size, is stretched over the soaped area (F) and pressed into the spirit gum. Any excess material around the edges is then trimmed. The spirit gum is dried (G) and the nylon covered with soap (H), which is dried, then covered with a creme or grease base (I). Powder is pressed into the makeup with a puff and the excess removed with a powder brush (J). The whole area, including the forehead and eyebrows, is brushed with sealer (K), then another coat of creme stick (L) and powder. M and N show two fifteenth-century makeups based on paintings by Jean Fouquet and Petrus Christus, illustrating the high shaved forehead fashionable at the time. Student makeup by Susan Thomas, assisted by Donna Kidder based on a technique devised by Professor Herbert C. Camburn. For other illustrations of the same technique, see Figures 16–6 and 16–7.*

227

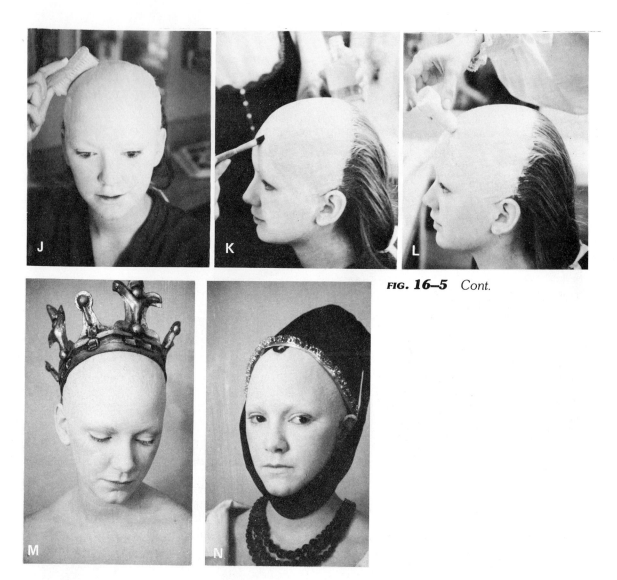

FIG. 16–5   Cont.

Figure 16–9.) If the blocking out is for a performance, the actor should have it done by one or two assistants. (See Figures 16–5 and 16–6.) In a makeup class the most practical arrangement is for two students who are blocking out their hair to work on each other. (See Figure 16–8.)

The procedure, which usually requires from one to three hours or more, depending on one's skill and on the size of the area to be soaped out, is as follows:

1. Part the hair at the line where you wish the bald pate to begin (Figure 16–5). For long hair, simply let the front hair hang forward over the face (Figure 16–5A). For shorter hair, pull all the top hair together, securing it with clips or pins (Figure 16–7A).
2. Soak cubes of a mild, nonirritating soap in water until the soap is fairly soft. (If there is no time for this presoaking, the wet soap can be used immediately.) Then soap down a few hairs at a time (Figure 16–5A and B), confining the soap to the area that is to be bald

and drying the soaped area with a hair dryer (16–5C) as you go. An assistant to handle the dryer as you work can be very helpful.

3. When the hair is completely flattened and dried, paint spirit gum along the forehead and the temples, just in front of the hairline (Figure 16–5E), then stretch a piece of nylon stocking over the area (Figures 16–5F and 16–8B). After pressing the front edge of the nylon into the spirit gum, glue all the other edges down with spirit gum along the borders of the soaped-out area, overlapping slightly on the forehead. Trim off the excess around the edges, and press out any wrinkles with the fingers or a flat modeling tool. It can be helpful in cutting the nylon if the stocking is first placed over the head and the outline of the area to be covered is drawn on the nylon with a felt-tipped pen or a grease pencil, as shown in Figure H19B. (The nylon is suggested because of its availability and the ease with which it can be stretched to conform to the shape of the head. For a partially bald head

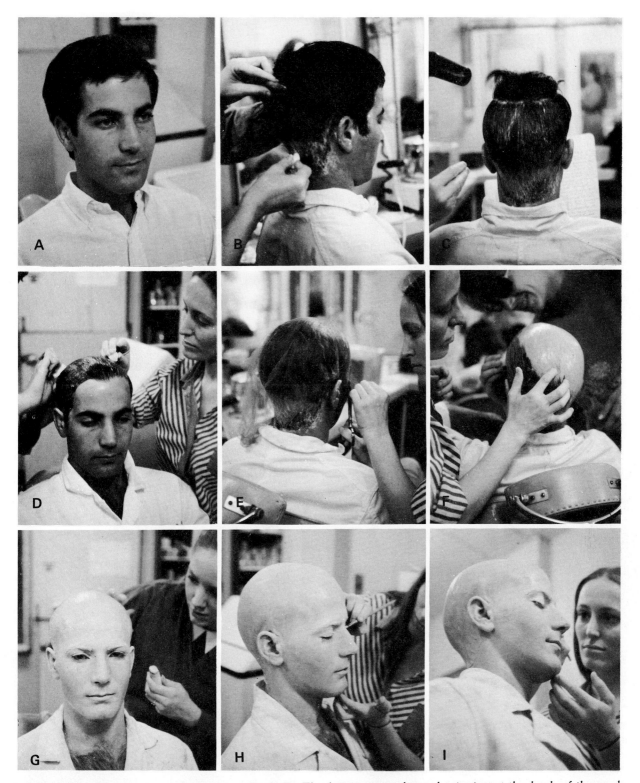

FIGURE 16—6 MAKING A BALD HEAD. *B, C, D. The hair is soaped out, beginning at the back of the neck and continuing upward and toward the front hairline. F, G. The entire soaped-out area is covered with a nylon stocking, which is then coated with soap, painted with creme stick. H and I show the makeup being completed. Makeup executed by students Donna Meyer and Susan Thomas.*

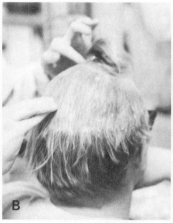
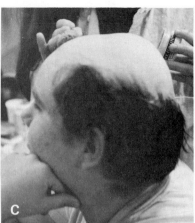

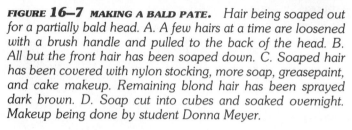

FIGURE 16—7 MAKING A BALD PATE. *Hair being soaped out for a partially bald head. A. A few hairs at a time are loosened with a brush handle and pulled to the back of the head. B. All but the front hair has been soaped down. C. Soaped hair has been covered with nylon stocking, more soap, greasepaint, and cake makeup. Remaining blond hair has been sprayed dark brown. D. Soap cut into cubes and soaked overnight. Makeup being done by student Donna Meyer.*

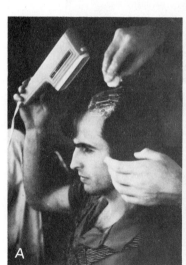
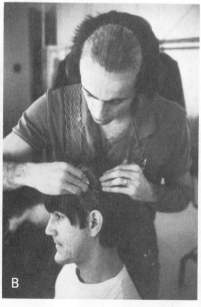

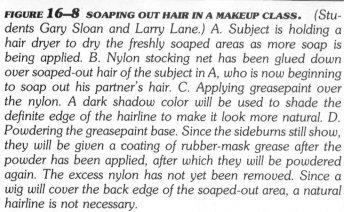
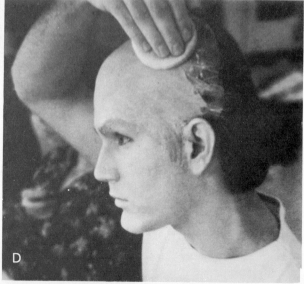

FIGURE 16—8 SOAPING OUT HAIR IN A MAKEUP CLASS. *(Students Gary Sloan and Larry Lane.) A. Subject is holding a hair dryer to dry the freshly soaped areas as more soap is being applied. B. Nylon stocking net has been glued down over soaped-out hair of the subject in A, who is now beginning to soap out his partner's hair. C. Applying greasepaint over the nylon. A dark shadow color will be used to shade the definite edge of the hairline to make it look more natural. D. Powdering the greasepaint base. Since the sideburns still show, they will be given a coating of rubber-mask grease after the powder has been applied, after which they will be powdered again. The excess nylon has not yet been removed. Since a wig will cover the back edge of the soaped-out area, a natural hairline is not necessary.*

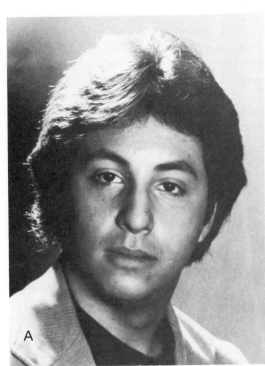

FIGURE *16–9* LIKENESS FROM A NINETEENTH-CENTURY PORTRAIT. *A. Natural hair is soaped out to create a bald pate (B). (This was done by the student himself without the help of an assistant.) Creme makeup, stippled. Improvised costume. Makeup by Harry Friedman.*

you might use the front section of a plastic cap, or make a piece of the required size and shape by painting liquid plastic film on a suitable head form. The advantage would be in the ease of blending the front edge. Another possibility would be to cover the soaped-out hair with derma wax, but this would not have the durabiliy of the nylon or the plastic.)

4. Soap the nylon (Figure 16–5H), and let it dry or force-dry it with the hair dryer.
5. Cover the bald pate and the forehead with rubber-mask grease to match your base (Figure 16–5I). If you are using a greasepaint base, finish the makeup, then powder. If you are using cake, be sure the rubber-mask grease is blended down over the forehead in order to avoid a line of demarcation where the grease stops; then powder the rubber-mask grease thoroughly (Figure 16–8D), brush off the excess powder (Figure 16–5J), and carefully sponge on the cake. If you are using creme makeup, it would be advisable to stipple it over the powdered rubber-mask grease when you do the rest of the face. If coverage of the bald pate is not complete, add more creme makeup and powder.
6. If the hairline is too definite, soften it by sponging lightly over the foundation color at the hairline with a shade of cake makeup to match the hair (Figure 16–7C) or, if the hair is very dark, a shade or so

lighter. Spots or skin discolorations can be sponged or brushed on if you like, and the pate can be highlighted or rouged to keep it from looking too even in color. If you are using cake makeup and want a slight sheen, cover it with K-Y Lubricating Jelly, and let it dry. The natural hair can be grayed or colored if you wish (see Figure 16–7C).

If the work is properly done and the bald head is treated with care, it will hold up satisfactorily. But it is easily damaged. If hats are going to be worn, they should be put on and taken off with care and no more often than necessary. It would also be helpful to paint a coat of plastic sealer over the entire soaped-out area after the makeup is finished. To cut down on the shine, you might add a coat of lubricating jelly. Even with this additional protection, any violent action involving the head could easily cause damage to the bald pate.

WIGS AND HAIRPIECES

If it is not possible to change the actor's own hair to achieve the effect needed for the character, a wig or a hairpiece is necessary. *Wigs* (Figure 16–10) cover the entire hair area, whereas *hairpieces* are used to supple-

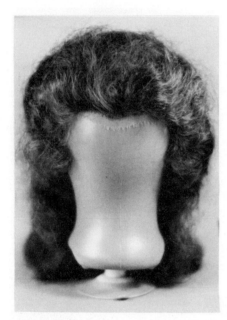

FIGURE ***16-10*** *HAND-VENTILATED WIG WITH REAL HAIR AND LACE FRONT.*

FIGURE ***16-11*** *SWITCH.   Constructed from weft (see Figure 16-15C).*

ment the natural hair. Hairpieces can be divided into two kinds—*toupees* (Figure 16-12D), which supply a front hairline and cover part or all of the top of the head, blending into the natural hair at the back and on the sides, and *falls* (Figure 16-23), which are attached to the natural hair (usually near the crown) in order to lengthen it in back. The natural hair is then combed over the edge of the fall and into the false hair. (See Figure 16-24.) The fall is extremely useful for period styles, especially for men with short hair. *Switches* (Figure 16-11) are used to extend the natural hair by making them into buns, braids, and chignons—as, for example, in Figures G-8A,C,I,K,L,N and G-19B and C.

Wigs can be classified by the type of construction,

type of hair, and length of hair. Naturally, in choosing a particular wig, the color will also be an important factor.

The construction of a wig involves both the type of foundation material to be used and the method by which the hair is to be added. Both of these depend to some extent on the direction in which the hair is to lie.

Foundations (Figure 16-14A) may be of cotton or imitation-silk net, elastic net, nylon net, hairlace, silk gauze, or a combination of these.

Probably the simplest form of wig is that made of net, edged and strengthened with webbing and usually made to hug the head by means of short lengths of steel spring or whalebone sewn into the foundation. These are curved slightly in order to press the edges of the foundation against the skin and are used at critical spots at which the foundation might tend to pull away from the head—normally at the front center, in front of the ears, and behind the ears at the very bottom of the foundation. There should be an elastic across the back of the neck to make the wig fit snugly. Stretch wigs (Figure 16-28) are constructed of a nylon net that will stretch to fit any head size. They also have a complete or a partial elastic band.

This type of wig makes no provision for a part and does not provide a realistic hairline in front, but it is quite suitable for wigs in which the hair is to be combed forward or which are meant to look like wigs rather than the natural hair—as, for example, the wigs worn in the eighteenth century (see Appendix G 13-16). This type of foundation could have a silk-gauze insert to make a parting possible. When the hair is to be separated in any way to expose the scalp, silk gauze must be used unless (as is the case with toupees) there is actually a bare scalp underneath the wig, in which case silk or nylon net can be used. For close inspection a *drawn parting* is necessary. This is a painstaking and delicate technique by which the hair is knotted into gauze, then the hairs are drawn individually through another piece of gauze so that no knots will be visible and the hair will seem to be growing directly out of the scalp. (See Figure 16-12A.) The effect is very realistic but is not necessary for stage work. It is used primarily for wigs for street wear.

If the hair is to be combed away from the face, revealing a natural-looking hairline, the best solution is to put a section of nylon net or hairlace in the front of the wig (Figure 16-13). The rest of the wig may be of silk gauze, caul netting, or a combination of the two. The nylon net should extend for at least half an inch beyond the hair so that it can be glued to the skin with spirit gum. Eventually this net edge will ravel and will need to be trimmed closer. As with ventilated beards, the wider it is originally, the longer the wig will last, but the more difficult it will be to conceal the net.

If the hairline of the wig is to be farther back than the actor's own hairline, a *blender* will be necessary to

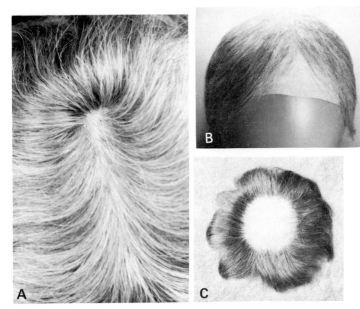
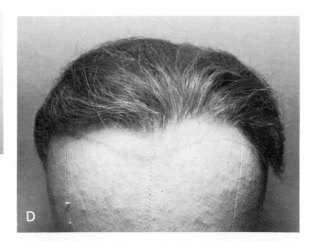

FIGURE *16–12 PARTS, PATES, AND HAIRLINES.* *A. Drawn parting. B. Blender wig. C. Monk's tonsure. D. Toupee with lace front. E. Ventilated hairline.*

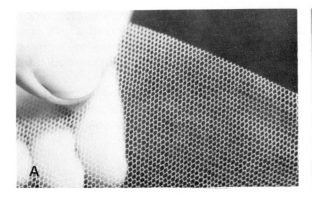
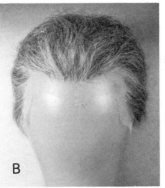
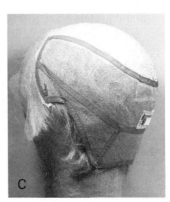

FIGURE *16–13 NYLON NET AND A LACE-FRONT WIG.* *A. Nylon net. B. Man's wig with lace front made of nylon net. C. Wig in B. turned inside-out to show construction.*

cover the natural hair in front (see Figures 16–12B and 17–5). The blender extends down onto the forehead, where its edge should be concealed with makeup. Suggestions for doing this are given under *Wearing the Wig.* Further information about blenders can be found under Constructing the Wig.

For makeups using wigs or hairpieces, see Figures 17–5, 17–6, and 17–8.

PERIOD HAIR STYLES

For period plays the hair styles should, of course, be correct for the period. If the natural hair can't be restyled to fit the period, false hair will need to be added.

The drawings in Appendix G illustrate representative hair styles for men and women from the early Egyptian to the present. These drawings by no means include all of the variations in style of any given period but merely show a few representative hair styles, most of them taken from paintings, sculptures, or photographs of the period. All of the drawings are of styles that were worn during the period indicated but were not necessarily at the height of fashion. They are intended to provide a handy makeup guide rather than a detailed historical study. For such a study see my book *Fashions in Hair*.

In referring to the drawings it is well to note the general style and basic silhouette of the period and to adapt the characteristics of that style to the individual character. In any period it will be found that social class is reflected in the hair style as well as in the dress. When you see an elaborate hair style illustrated for past centuries (Figures G–1E, G–3H, G–12T, G–13B, G–15K,N,O,P, and G–16A,C,D, for example) you may be sure it was worn by a person of high social standing. Obviously, such styles would be out of place on peasants or servants. The simpler styles that require little time or care in dressing are naturally more appropriate for those people who have less interest in fashion and less time and money to indulge in it. That does not mean, of course, that all simple styles are to be used for peasant classes only. Simple styles, as well as elaborate ones, may at times be fashionable.

Social standing and adherence to fashion do not always go together. An emperor's wife may be a very simple person with simple tastes, and this will be reflected in her hair style. But chances are that her hair, though not fashionably styled, will be carefully dressed. The personality must always be considered, especially since, in our present society, one can no longer assume that women who work at ordinary jobs on a relatively low social level do not have the time or the money to spend on their hair.

Age is also a factor. Sometimes older people will tend to dress their hair in a style that they have worn for many years and that may once have been fashionable.

This is more true in the past than in the present, and of course it may or may not apply to older women who are fashion-conscious. However, even if older women do follow the fashion of the moment, they do not always adopt the extremes of that fashion, which are designed primarily for younger women. As with the rest of the makeup, you should exercise your own judgment in choosing a hairstyle that will help to reveal the character.

CONSTRUCTING THE WIG

When the wig has been designed, you can either buy or make a foundation, and then attach the hair to the foundation. For a full wig you would do well to buy a net wig cap if it can be adapted to the type of wig you need. Such a cap is shown in Figure 16–14A. There are many types and qualities of net foundations, ranging from relatively inexpensive cotton ones, quite adequate for some types of wigs, to high quality, carefully constructed ones that fit better, look better, and are more comfortable. There are also elastic foundations for stretch wigs.

Most wigs, even those constructed on fairly simple foundations, have stays that hold the wig rather snugly to the head and an elastic at the nape of the neck to pull the wig tight. If the hair is to be combed back, revealing a natural-looking front hairline, a simple wig cap cannot be used, at least in its original form. Individually fitted wigs with a natural hairline are expensive and require a much better quality foundation cap, as illustrated in the wig in process of construction, Figure 16–15B.

Most foundations are available in white, gray, black, brown, and sometimes various shades of blond or auburn. Choose the color nearest that of the hair you plan to use.

FIGURE 16–14 CONSTRUCTING A WIG. A. Wig foundation. B. Detail of construction. C. Adjustable wig-block holder. (Bob Kelly Wig Creations.)

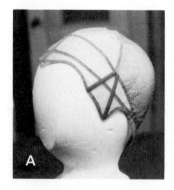
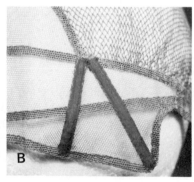
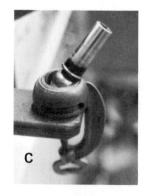

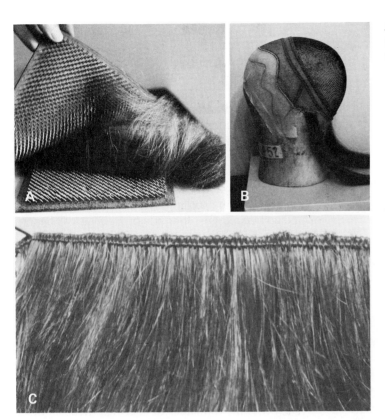

FIGURE 16–15 WIG CONSTRUCTION. A. Drawing mats with hair. B. Wig foundation in first stages of ventilating. (Bob Kelly Wig Creations.) C. Weft.

VENTILATING

The technique of ventilating a wig is the same as that for mustaches and beards (see Chapter 15). As with beards and mustaches, always begin with the hair that is to be underneath and finish with that which is to be on top—in other words, begin at the nape of the neck and work upward toward the crown, as shown in Figure 16–15B. The wig block can be held in the lap, or it can be placed on a wig stand or a wig holder with a tilt top and adjusted to a comfortable angle (See Figure 16–14C.)

As with beards, the hair can be mixed to a suitable basic color, but additional colors can be added as you ventilate—occasional hairs of another color to add interest, streaks of a different color, or a gradual lightening of the hair from the back to the front of the wig. For the latter effect you might want to mix two or more shades of hair and blend them as you ventilate. This blending of shades and making the wig lighter in front than in back is particularly effective with gray hair.

If the hair is to be combed back, simply work forward, toward the front hairline, always pulling the hair toward the back of the wig. Brushing or combing it occasionally as you work will keep stray hairs from getting in your way. The amount of hair you use will depend entirely on how thick you want the hair to be. Ordinarily, it is desirable to keep the wig as light in weight as possible

within the limits set by the effect you are trying to achieve. The hair can be knotted into the binding tapes as well as through the net.

When you approach the front hairline, use a smaller needle, and space your hair closer and very evenly. It is, in fact, usually a good idea to stop a half inch to an inch from the front edge, turn the wig block around, and work the hair from the opposite direction, beginning at the edge and letting the hair hang down as if over the face. When you reach the previous stopping place and all the hair is in, you can comb the front section back. It will then tend to stand up away from the forehead and make the hairline somewhat less obvious. Be sure that in ventilating along the front edge you catch the needle under the edge sufficiently so that when the wig is finished, none of the binding tape will show. If necessary, you can turn the wig inside out later and add a few hairs at the hairline.

If the hair is to be combed away from the crown in all directions, as it is in styles B, C, E, and a majority of the others in Figure G–7, you will proceed from the outer edges of the cap upward in an ever-narrowing circle so that the final hairs are knotted in at the crown. Always ventilate the hair in the direction in which it is to lie, except when you deliberately reverse direction in order to make the hair stand up rather than lie flat. That should be kept in mind as you work.

WEAVING

A simple wig, such as the one just described, can be made much more quickly and easily by sewing on rows of weft, particularly across the back, and ventilating only the front section. In fact, the entire wig can be made in this way provided the hair is to be combed back, but a much better hairline can be achieved by ventilating the front of the wig. The weft (which is made of lengths of hair woven on two, three, or four strings) is sewn to the wig cap, starting at the back and moving forward over the top of the head. The lengths of weft are usually about an inch apart but may be more or less than that. The closer they are, the heavier the hair will be. If they are too far apart, the foundation may show through. A wig made of weft is heavier to wear and much less versatile since the style of the wig can be changed very little, whereas a ventilated wig is light to wear and can be recombed in many ways.

Figure 16–16 illustrates the technique for making weft. A table or a bench with an overlapping edge is necessary. Two weaving sticks are clamped to it, as shown in Figure 16–16A. You can buy weaving sticks and clamps, or you can rig up your own. The essential elements are the three strings tied as shown. For fine weft, silk is used; but any heavy, strong thread, fishline, or very light cord will do. The strings should be as strong as possible without being bulky.

If you are sufficiently serious about wigmaking to be weaving hair, you should have a pair of drawing

FIGURE 16–16 WEAVING HAIR. A. Weaving sticks attached to table top. B. Threading the hair.

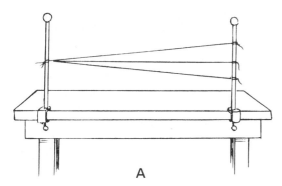

A

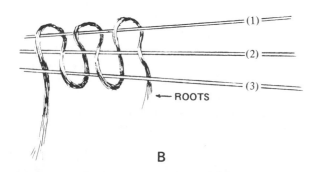

B

brushes or mats. The brushes have short, stiff bristles. The mats, which are preferable for knotting and weaving, are made of two rectangles of tough leather into which are inserted short wires, all bent down parallel to the mat in the same direction (Figure 16–15A). Hair that is to be woven is placed on one of the mats with the ends of the bent wires pointing toward the points (not the roots) of the hair. The root ends protrude slightly over the mat. The other mat is laid on top of the first one, wire side downward. The roots should be on the side of the mats facing the weaver and extending just enough so that they can be easily grasped. The amount of hair extending beyond the other side of the mats will depend entirely on the length of hair being used and is immaterial.

The purpose of the mats is to make it possible to draw from the hank as many hairs as you wish without disturbing the remainder of the hair. Ideally, drawing mats should be used in knotting as well as weaving.

This is the procedure for weaving:

1. Draw a strand of hair from the braid (the more hairs you use, the heavier the weft will be), and hold it in your left hand with the root ends protruding upward.
2. Then, holding the strand of hair behind the strings, reach with the forefinger of your right hand between strings 2 and 3 (Figure 16–16B), and pull the hair through and up over the top of 1.
3. Reach between 1 and 2; grasp the hair; pull it forward (toward you, that is) between 1 and 2.
4. Reach between 1 and 2 and grasp the hair from behind. Pull it away from you under 3, then forward between 1 and 2, and back over the top of 1.
5. Reach between 1 and 2 and grasp the hair. Pull it forward between 1 and 2.
6. Reach between 1 and 2 and pull the hair under 3, away from you, and up and out toward you between 1 and 2, then over the top.
7. Reach between 1 and 2, and pull the hair forward.
8. From behind, reach forward between 2 and 3, and pull the hair back.
9. Now, holding both ends of the hair, pull it close together and tight so that it seems to be hanging from a little knot. The root ends of the hair should be short—not much more than an inch hanging down. The other end will, of course, be long.

Keep repeating this process, each time pushing the hair to the left and making sure it is as tight as you can make it. You can press the knots with a pinching iron (illustrated in Figure 16–18D) if you have one. When you have the necessary length, cut the strings and tie both ends securely. Then the weft is ready to sew onto the wig foundation. There are a number of methods of weaving (see the eighteenth-century engraving, Figure 16–17E,A,F,B,C, and D), but this is one of the most

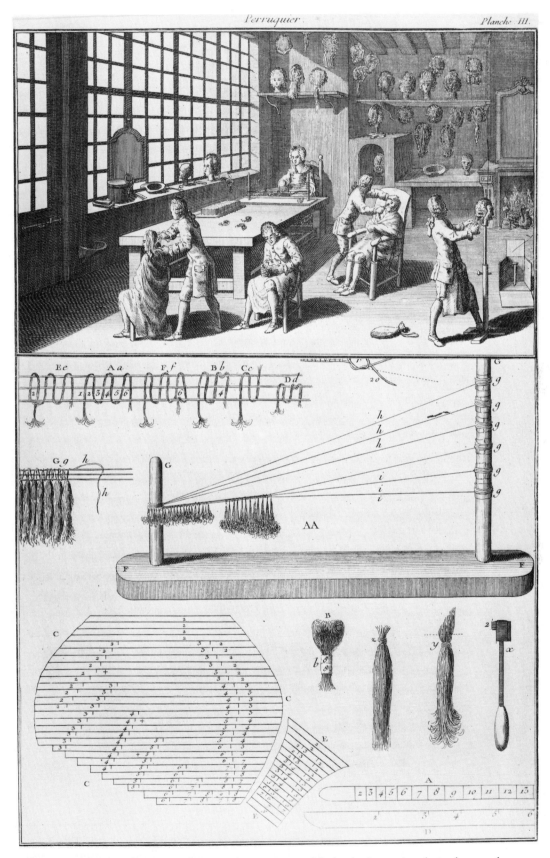

FIGURE 16–17 EIGHTEENTH-CENTURY WIG SHOP. *Method of weaving hair shown above.*
Diagram lower left is a white paper marked to indicate arrangement of hair on the wig.
Garsault's Art du Perruquier.

FIGURE 16–18 *EIGHTEENTH-CENTURY WIGMAKER'S TOOLS.* *K, Q. Hackles. F. Powder. G. Powder bag. H. Powder puff. I. Powder cone. C. Curl paper. g. Razors. a. Barber's basin. M, N, O. Machine for binding pigtails. Garsault's Art du Perruquier.*

FIGURE 16–19 HACKLE. *Hair being drawn through hackle, which is attached to table top with clamps.*

common ones for making weft to be used in wigs. The technique is not nearly so complicated as it appears, and a little practice will make it possible to weave very quickly.

MIXING HAIR

You will usually do well to mix two or more colors of hair to achieve a natural look. This requires the use of a hackle (or card), which is a wooden block with numerous sharp, steel spikes projecting from it. The spikes may be either vertical or slightly angled. The design of the hackle has changed very little since the eighteenth century (see Figure 16–18K). In using the hackle, you will need to secure it to a bench or a table with clamps (see Figure 16–19).

Straight hair is more easily mixed than curly. In mixing, grasp in one hand the root ends of the two hanks of hair to be mixed. Then slap the hair down onto the hackle and pull it through (Figure 16–19), mixing the two hanks with both hands as you pull. Keep repeating this process until the two colors are thoroughly blended. If you wish to add a third color, follow the same procedure. If you are not sure how much of a second color you wish to add to the first, blend in a little at a time. The purpose of the hackle in this blending process is simply to keep the hair from tangling. Hair that is already tangled can be drawn through the hackle for untangling.

CRIMPING HAIR

If you have straight hair (real or synthetic) and want it crimped, it can be done very easily and quickly with an electric crimping iron (see Figure 16–20). If you want

crimped hair in a wig (or a beard) you plan to make, the wig or the beard should be constructed with straight hair, which can then be crimped.

REMODELING THE WIG CAP

It is always best, of course, to buy a wig foundation suitable for the wig you're making, but if that is impractical, you may be able to remodel one that you already have. If you want a natural hairline, for example, the simple,

FIGURE 16–20 ELECTRIC CRIMPING IRON. *A. Crimping iron in normal (open) position. B. Hot crimping iron being squeezed together to crimp hair. C. Crimped hair.*

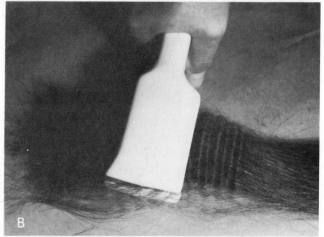

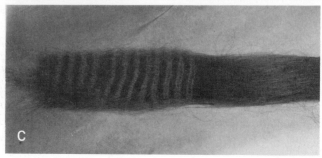

ready-made wig cap can still be used by cutting off the front portion and replacing it with hairlace or nylon net. (On the foundation in 16–14A you might remove everything up to the second tape.) As with beards and mustaches, a paper pattern of the desired hairline should be made first, then pinned to the wig block under the lace. Remember that the lace should extend at least ½ inch beyond the hairline, preferably more. It can be trimmed later, if you wish. The smallest ventilating needle, which pulls out just one hair at a time, should be used for the last few rows along the front edge in order to create a natural-looking hairline. If you use more than one hair at a time, the knots are likely to show. As before, you may ventilate either forward or backward, depending on whether you wish the hair to stand up slightly or to lie flat.

It may sometimes be necessary to remove more of the foundation than just the front section. If you need to go farther back, you may have to resew one of the tapes so that the cap will hold its shape. When the hair is all in, trim the lace or net at the front, no closer than ½ inch from the hairline.

If you need a part in the wig, insert a section of silk gauze about an inch wide and of whatever length is necessary, at the spot where you want the part. Then ventilate toward the part from each side, using a 1-hair needle on the gauze section. Tapes should be sewn on around the edges of the section of gauze to give firmness. The gauze parting will, in most cases, be a continuation of a front section of lace at the hairline. If the wig is to be used over a bald head, nylon lace can be used instead of gauze so that the skin will show through.

BLENDERS

These are constructed of a tightly woven, thin fabric that can be covered with greasepaint to match the foundtion color on the skin. Several different fabrics are used. A high-grade shirting is satisfactory, or silk gauze (see Appendix A) can be used. Whatever your fabric, the selvage and not a raw edge must cross the forehead and be used for the blend. (See Figure 16–12B.)

It is simplest to start with a ready-made wig foundation, and remove the front and as much of the top as necessary, the exact amount depending on how far back the new hairline is to go. The blender, which is attached to the side pieces of the wig foundation, must fit very tightly across the forehead. Be particularly careful at the temples to prevent wrinkling. That, of course, would ruin the entire effect. The hair is ventilated into the gauze or shirting in the usual way, using a 1-hair needle for the first few rows or, if the hair is to be thin on top, for a

number of rows. A good blender wig must be very carefully fitted to be successful, and the snug fit across the forehead is essential (see Figure 17–5).

A more satisfactory blend can be achieved by using a head band or a cap (see *Bald Wigs* below) of plastic or latex under a lace-front wig (see Figure 17–6J,K, and O). The plastic or latex will cover any natural hair that is to be concealed, and the false hairline can recede as much as you like. The lace can be glued to the plastic (or latex), which has a much thinner edge than the fabric blender and is thus easier to blend.

BALD WIGS

The most satisfactory method of constructing a bald wig is to make or buy a snug plastic (Figure 16–21) or latex (Figure 14–13) cap (see Chapter 14) and attach the necessary hair (real, synthetic, or crepe) with latex or spirit gum. But it would be advisable to ventilate the top few rows of sparse hair into the cap for a more realistic effect. (See the photographs of balding heads in Figure 16–22.) Or all of the hair can be ventilated instead of being glued on. However, gluing ventilated pieces to the cap is quicker and easier than ventilating all of the hair into the cap and is preferable to gluing hairs directly to the cap.

TOUPEES AND SIDEBURNS

A toupee is usually constructed of a silk-gauze piece, bound with tape somewhat larger than the bald spot it is intended to cover. Toupees with the hairline showing should have a lace front and, if there is to be a part, a lace insert. Toupees made without the lace front but with the hair combed back usually look exactly like toupees. They are less expensive to have made and far simpler to put on and take off, and they last much longer; but they seldom fool anybody. A good toupee requires a lace front unless the hair is to be combed in such a way that the hairline is concealed.

Making a convincing toupee for street wear is a job requiring both skill and experience and should usually be left to professional wigmakers. But a satisfactory hairpiece for stage wear can be made by an actor or a makeup artist who has reasonable proficiency in ventilating.

In Figure 17–2A, for example, we see an actor who is to be made up as Woodrow Wilson. Obviously his top hair is too sparse to be recombed in any way that would prove adequate. Therefore, a small hairpiece was made on nylon net (Figure 17–2B). Since the hair was combed forward and only a fraction of an inch of the

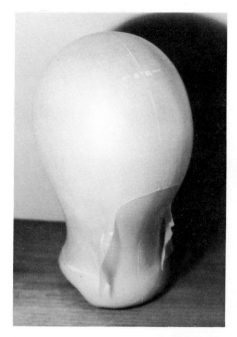

FIGURE **16–21** PLASTIC CAP. *Shown on the plastic head form on which it was made. Cap can be trimmed to fit when used.*

FIGURE **16–21a** FITTING NYLON STOCKING OVER A PLASTIC HEAD FORM.

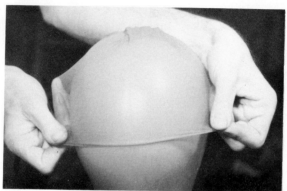

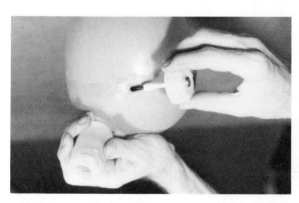

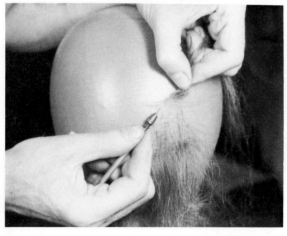

FIGURE **16–21b** COATING STOCKING WITH LIQUID PLASTIC.

FIGURE **16–21c** VENTILATING HAIR INTO THE NYLON AND PLASTIC.

lace showed, great skill in wigmaking was not required. Sometimes a pointed tuft of hair—a sort of widow's peak—is needed to change the actor's hairline. That can easily be made on lace in a few minutes. The technique is the same as for beards and mustaches. First, draw the new hairline on the skin with eyebrow pencil, trace and cut a paper pattern and place the hairlace or nylon net over it on the wig block, leaving the usual ½ inch or more for pasting down. Then, carefully selecting hair to match the color of the actor's own, work the hair with a small needle.

It is often necessary to conceal sharply cut sideburns, and that can easily be done with two small hairpieces with hair long enough to brush back over or behind the actor's ears and into his own hair. If his hair is long enough, these hairpieces will sometimes suffice. If not, he may need to combine the hairpieces with a fall pinned under his own hair in back. In Figures G-9T and G-11A we can see hair styles that might require this treatment.

Again, a pattern is made and the net placed over it on the block. The new side hair may follow the actor's natural hairline, or it may extend farther onto the face.

As is always the case in making a natural-looking hairline with dark hair, it is helpful to make the last row of a lighter shade of hair, partly to soften the line and partly to avoid having a row of dark knots, which spoil the naturalness of the effect.

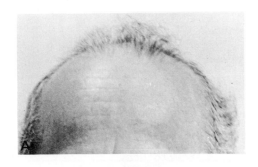

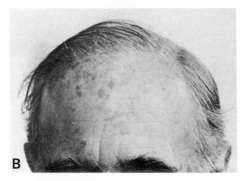

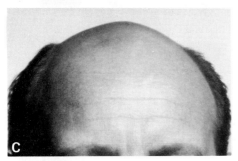

FIGURE 16–22 BALDING HEADS.

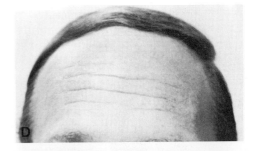

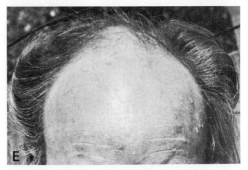

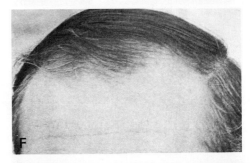

FALLS

Falls, as indicated earlier, are hairpieces used to lengthen the back hair while using the natural hair in front. This avoids the problem of creating a natural front hairline or of concealing the blender or the lace.

The fall can take various forms, depending on the use to which it is to be put. For a cascade of curls for women, it can be constructed of weft in a sort of basket weave—that is, the rows of weft are laid out diagonally, about 1 inch apart, sewed together where they cross, and stiffened with fine wire to give more body to the foundation. Usually, small loops are formed across the top of the piece for pinning to the natural hair, or small combs (see Figure 16–23) can be sewn into the piece for attaching it. The fall is then attached and the front and top hair combed back over the join and blended with the false hair, as in Figure 16–24. If the fall takes

the form of a mass of curls, it can simply be pinned on top of the natural hair. (See Figure G–19M.)

The fall may also take the form of a Juliet cap, with the front band across the top of the head from ear to ear (Figure 16–27, #3) and the bottom band around the nape of the neck. It is then constructed like the top and back of a wig. This is particularly useful for men or for women with short hair. In constructing such a piece, remember that the front of the fall must lie flat and not be too heavy.

FIGURE 16–23 FALL, WITH HAIR SEWN ON STIFF GAUZE. *A small comb has been sewn to the top edge of the gauze for attaching the fall to the natural hair.*

FIGURE 16–24 PHILIP IV. *Based on Velásquez' portrait. Cake makeup with putty nose. Eyebrows partially blocked out with spirit gum and putty wax. Crepe hair mustache. Natural front hair with fall. Makeup by student Larry Liles.*

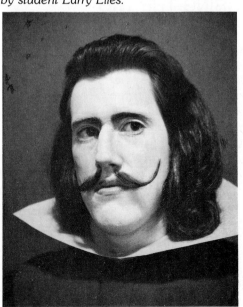

An even smoother, flatter edge can be achieved by using a net front instead of the tape. A heavier, sturdier net can be used than would be suitable for blending at the forehead. In either case it will be necessary to pin the fall securely to the hair and then comb the natural front hair over and into it to make a perfect blend.

If the actor has very short hair and there is not time for the side hair to grow over the ears, it is possible either to add separate side pieces on lace (see preceding section on sideburns) or to make such pieces part of the fall itself. If this is done, the side pieces, when glued to the skin, serve as additional support to hold the fall in place.

The hair in a fall can be of any length and can be dressed and redressed in any style. Since it is to be blended with the actor's own hair, it should be made from real hair or a convincing synthetic. It can be constructed entirely of weft, entirely ventilated, or a combination of the two.

Falls can also be attached to a wig, providing a practical means of increasing the flexibility of the wigs you have in stock and also of dealing with emergencies when you find unexpectedly that you don't have the type of wig you need.

BRAIDS

Braids can be easily made from switches by first separating the hair into three approximately equal sections, then braiding them (Figure 16–25) as follows:

1. Cross section B over section C.
2. Cross section C over section A.
3. Cross section A over section B.

FIGURE 16–25 MAKING A BRAID FROM A SWITCH.

Keep repeating steps 1, 2, and 3 until the braid is complete, then tie the ends together. (If you prefer to begin by crossing B over A and proceeding with A over C and C over B, it will work just as well.) The smaller you want the braid to be, of course, the less hair there should be in the switch. If you want quite small braids, you may be able to use braids of crepe hair, in which case both ends of the braid should be tied off. Crepe hair braids could be used around the topknot of the wig in Figure 7–2.

DRESSING THE WIG

Whether you have made your own wig or rented or bought a good one, its effectiveness will depend to a great extent on how skillfully it is dressed. If a rented wig doesn't look the way you want it to, you may be able to change the styling. Cheap mohair wigs on buckram cannot be changed and are usually a waste of money, but any human-hair wig or good (not necessarily expensive) synthetic one can be redressed, at least within the limits imposed by its particular construction. Although a rented wig must not be cut or damaged, there is usually no reason for its not being redressed.

The first step in dressing any wig is to pin or tack it to your wig block and brush and comb it out thoroughly. Bear in mind previous instructions for holding the comb in working with wigs or beards. If a very simple style is required and you are pressed for time, you can curl the ends with an electric curling iron.

You can do a more thorough job, however, by combing the hair with water until it is quite wet, then putting it up in pin curls (Figure 16–26B) or on rollers, (Figure 16–26A). Pin curls are made by forming a flat coil from a strand of hair and pinning it down flat to the head with a hairpin or a bobby pin. All pin curls in one row are usually coiled in the same direction though they may be coiled in opposite directions on either side of a part. The direction of the coil can be reversed in alternate rows. If you want the entire head of hair to be wavy, you will put it all up in flat pin curls, starting at the front hairline and moving back and down. Often there will be some natural wave in the hair. This can be encouraged with a damp comb, and the hair may need no further curling except at the ends.

When the pin curls are thoroughly dry (the drying can be forced with a hair dryer), comb them out. A little hair dressing may be necessary to provide a natural, healthy sheen. (In an emergency, liquefying cleansing cream can be rubbed on the palms of the hands and then transferred to the hair.) Then arrange the hair in waves, curls, or puffs, combing it section by section as you go, and securing it with hairpins when necessary. Be sure the hairpins are inserted carefully so that they do not show. A rat-tail comb is often helpful in making rolls or curls. A hair-lacquer spray may be used to set the hair after it has been dressed.

If the wig belongs to you and the hair needs any additional trimming, that can be done with barbers' shears and a comb and also with thinning shears if any thinning is required. However, if the wig is rented or borrowed, the hair obviously must not be trimmed or thinned—unless, of course, you have permission, preferably in writing.

For graying or adding temporary color to a wig, see the suggestions for coloring and graying natural hair at the beginning of this chapter. However, if the wig is not your own, you should not color or gray it without permission.

WEARING THE WIG

Wigs must be handled carefully if they are to keep their shape and fit snugly. In putting on any full wig, grasp the lower back edge of the wig foundation with both hands, slide it up over the forehead until the hairline approaches within an inch or two of where you want it to be, then pull the wig down snugly over the head. Then, with both hands resting on the wig, move it back still further until the hairline is in the correct position. If the actor's own hair is long, it should be pulled up toward the top of the head first and pinned flat. A wide band around the head is frequently helpful in making sure that no stray hairs escape. (Figure 17–5C shows a wig being put on.)

To remove the wig, grasp the back edge with both hands, and pull up and forward. *Never remove the wig by pulling on the hair.*

If the wig or the toupee has a hairlace front, the procedure is the same as for applying beards on lace

FIGURE 16–26 DRESSING THE WIG. A. Wig in rollers. B. Wig in pin curls.

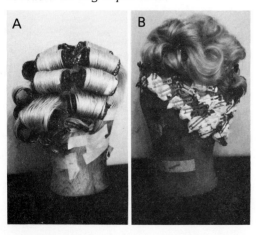

(see Chapter 15). Always attach the lace edge to the skin with spirit gum before makeup is applied. In removing any hairpiece with a lace edge, always dissolve the spirit gum with spirit-gum remover until the lace comes away from the skin naturally. Never *pull* the lace off the skin because it may cause the lace to stretch or tear.

If the wig has a blender, it should be put on in the same way, making sure that the blender covers the natural hairline and that it fits snugly against the skin. It should be attached with spirit gum. You may then wish to stipple the edge of the blender with latex cream adhesive at the line where the blender meets the skin. That can be done by dotting the edge in such a way that the adhesive overlaps both blender and skin, thus helping to break the line across the forehead. The stippling must be done when the skin is clean and dry and before any makeup has been applied. If the blender is too thick at the edge to be concealed by the adhesive, Kryolan's Eyebrow Plastic can be used instead. Then the Eyebrow Plastic can be coated with sealer, and the makeup can be applied when the sealer is dry.

If the blender is well made in the first place and the edge is kept clean, it should be thin enough to be concealed with adhesive and paint or, if you prefer, with paint alone. The secret of concealing the line is, first to match the color of the blender perfectly to the color on the skin, bearing in mind that a given color of paint will not necessarily look the same on the fabric of the blender as it does on the skin. Second, it is essential to make up the blender as if it were the real forehead, with the usual shadows and highlights and wrinkles. Ordinarily it should become lighter as it approaches the hairline, at least if the hairline is a receding one. Third, the area in which the blender joins the skin should be so broken up with color that the line is lost. Shadows at the temples and highlights on the superciliary arch make a good start. A stippling technique (see Chapter 11) is almost essential. Grease or cream makeup should be used rather than cake when a blender is to be concealed (see Figure 17–5D). Using a plastic strap or cap, as suggested earlier, will simplify the problem of concealment.

When you remove the wig, it is not necessary to clean the entire blender each time, but you should clean the edge carefully and thoroughly with acetone. Any accumulation of adhesive and makeup will render a good blend impossible.

Toupees may or may not have a lace front. If they do, the lace is attached with spirit gum; if they do not, the front is attached with toupee tape (Appendix A). The back can be attached to the scalp with tape or to the hair in back of the crown with a French clip, which can be sewn onto the underside of the toupee.

In putting on a toupee with a lace front, place the toupee in position, then attach the lace front to the skin with spirit gum, being extremely careful to avoid corruga-tions in the lace. After pressing the gum dry, grasp the back edge of the toupee and gently but firmly pull it back so that it hugs the head, then press down, thus sticking the toupee tape to the skin. If a French clip is being used instead of toupee tape, it can be attached to a strand of hair about an inch wide. Since the clip makes a slight bump under the toupee (not noticeable except to the touch) and since the clip pulling on the hair may be slightly uncomfortable, the tape is usually preferred.

In removing the toupee, always soak the lace with spirit-gum remover until it loosens, then clean it thoroughly with acetone after it is removed. Toupees without lace fronts are easier to put on and take off and require less care, but they rarely look as convincing—unless, of course, they are dressed to conceal the hairline.

When a wig is properly dressed before being worn, if should require little or no rearranging after it is on. For subsequent wearings, however, it may require some recombing. Check the wig carefully before each performance for styling and condition of the hair, and do whatever redressing is necessary.

CARE OF THE WIG

Good wigs are expensive and should be given painstaking care. Any elaborately dressed wig or any wig with a lace front should be kept on a wig block between performaces. At other times it can be stuffed with tissue paper and stored in an individual box.

To be effective, wigs must be kept clean. That can best be done by dipping them into wig cleaner. The cleaner will not materially affect the wave in the hair.

It is also possible to clean wigs by dipping them up and down in a detergent solution, then rinsing, but that removes all temporary wave and may result in a good bit of tangling no matter how carefully the dipping is done. *Never under any circumstances shampoo a human-hair wig!* Any rubbing of the hair in water can result in hopeless matting and tangling and a ruined wig.

RENTING OR BUYING WIGS

The usual means of obtaining wigs (other than making them) is to rent them if the play is to have only a few performances and to buy them if it is expected to have a longer run. Whether renting or buying, you should obtain a wig that looks good, even though it may be inexpensive. Wigs made of mohair, for example, are relatively cheap, but they seldom look good enough to be used in realistic plays. Hand-ventilated, lace-front wigs, on the other hand, look very good indeed but are quite expensive to buy. Since lace fronts are fragile and easily damaged, the wigs are not usually available for rent.

The solution to the problem may often be to buy a synthetic-hair stretch wig. There are many to be had quite reasonably. A particularly good one, intended primarily for street wear for both men and women, has the front and top hair ventilated by machine into flexible plastic. The sides and the back of the wig are constructed of weft sewn to flexible net. One great advantage of these wigs over usual stretch wigs is the absence of ventilating knots. Therefore, the top hair can be parted—either before or after the wig has been dressed—wherever you want it parted, and the part will look completely natural. But since the front edge of the plastic top does not produce a natural-looking hairline, the wigs should always be dressed so that the front hairline is concealed (See Figure 16–28.) The advantage of these machine-ventilated wigs over hand-ventilated ones is, of course, the price. The major disadvantage is that eventually the plastic will stiffen and tear apart, ruining the wig.

In either renting or buying, it is important, if ordering by mail, to send adequate measurements and to allow plenty of time for the wig to be dressed and sent through the mail. In some cases the wig will not be in stock and will have to be made up specially, in which case as much as three or four weeks' additional time may be required.

When possible, it is preferable to buy a wig, unless it is a very special style that you are unlikely to use again. Buying the wig usually costs more for the particular play but saves money in the end—provided the wig is used for a sufficient number of subsequent productions.

MEASURING FOR WIGS

If you are ordering a wig or a toupee, it is important to supply the wigmaker with accurate measurements. The numbers below refer to Figure 16–27, in which the heavy broken lines represent wig measurements. The first five measurements are the most important. The others are not always used.

1. Around the head (over the ears) from the front hairline to the nape of the neck and back. (Average measurement, 22 inches.)
2. From the front hairline to the nape of the neck over the top of the head. (Average measurement, 14 inches.)
3. From ear to ear over the top of the head. This is sometimes taken over the crown instead. (Average measurement, 12 inches.)
4. Temple to temple around the back of the head. (Average measurement, 16 inches.)
5. Ear to ear across the forehead at the hairline.

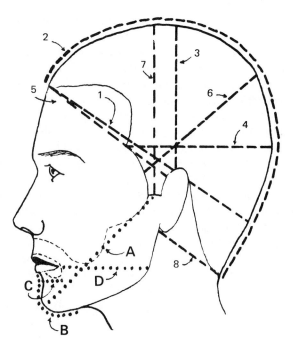

FIGURE 16–27 DIAGRAM FOR WIG AND BEARD MEASUREMENTS. *The heavy broken line represents wig measurements and the heavy dotted line, measurements for a beard.*

6. Sideburn to sideburn over the crown. (Infrequently used.)
7. Bottom of sideburn to bottom of sideburn over the top. (Infrequently used.)
8. Bottom of ear to bottom of ear around the back of the neck. (Infrequently used.)

If there is to be a part, be sure to indicate how many inches from the center and on which side. If the wig or the toupee is being made to order, it is also important to include an exact outline of the hair at the temples.

ADAPTING WIGS

Fortunately, it is not necessary to have a different wig for every different hair style. Any reasonably good wig can be redressed in various styles within the limitations set by its basic construction. The front hairline, the part or lack of one, and the length are crucial features. The color can be changed with sprays, though it would be better to avoid that if possible. If the hair is too short, a fall or a switch can sometimes be added to give the necessary length.

Length and color aside, we can classify wigs generally into the following groups:

1. Hair combed forward, concealing the hairline, as in

Figure G–7B,C,D,E,F. This is more often than not a male style.

2. Hair combed back, no parting, as in Figure G–14A,B,G. This ordinarily requires either a lace front or a blender except, for example, in the eighteenth-century styles that in many cases (though not all) represent wigs rather than real hair. Style A in Figure G–14 is certainly a wig, but N is the natural hair.
3. Center part, as in Figure G–6K,M,N,Q.
4. Side part, as in Figure G–17F,G,J,P.
5. Blender front, necessitated by a receding hairline or a hairline farther back than that of the actor who is to use the wig. Styles shown in Figures G–2K and G–11A, for example, would very likely require blenders or plastic bands or caps. The hair may be combed as in 1, 2, 3, or 4 above; but since blender wigs are not usually interchangeable with other types, they are listed separately.
6. Special styles, such as those with a horizontal part (Figure G–1Q), double part (Figure G–5A), or tonsure (Figures G–5P and 16–12C).

On the basis of this breakdown of types of wigs, it will be clear that many of the styles shown in the plates can, with a little ingenuity and the use of supplementary falls and switches, be achieved with a relatively small number of wigs. It is obvious, for example, that Figures G–2B,E, G–5E,I,M, and G–9A,D could be approximated with nothing more than a simple redressing of a single wig of type 1. Among the wigs with partings there are, perhaps, even more possibilities.

It must not be assumed, however, that *every* center-part style or *every* forward-combed style, for example, can be made from one specific center-part or forward-combed wig with just the addition of hair. There are other elements that must be considered, such as, for example, the thickness of the hair. Although sparse hair can be fluffed up somewhat and heavy hair can be sleeked down, the possibilities are not unlimited. But they are much greater than one would suspect at first glance.

Learning to design hair styles and dress and care for wigs is an important part of the makeup process. If you also know how to construct wigs, so much the better. In the professional theater, actors are not usually expected to design or to dress their own wigs, but they are sometimes expected to take care of them between performances. Professional makeup artists should have a thorough knowledge of wigs, but they do not have to make them and do not usually have to dress them. In the nonprofessional theater, however, both actors and makeup artists may sometimes have to do both. A thorough knowledge of how to deal with hair, real or false, will not only contribute greatly to the effectiveness of the makeup, but it can also help trim the makeup budget.

FIGURE 16–28 THE SAME SYNTHETIC-HAIR STRETCH WIG DRESSED IN 3 DIFFERENT STYLES. A, B, and C. Wig styled by brushing and combing.

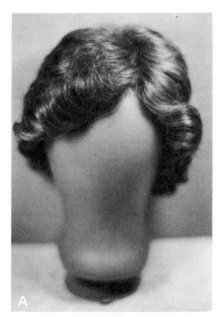 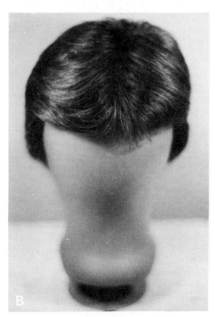 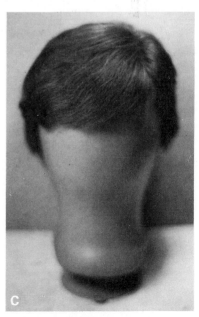

Problems

1. If you have the necessary equipment and material available, ventilate a mustache, a beard, or eyebrows.
2. Do a makeup for a middle-aged or elderly character from a play, using a wig, facial hair, or both.

17

Creating a Likeness

For most makeups there is considerable latitude in choice of details—the height of the forehead, the line of the eyebrows, the shape of the nose. But in recreating real people whose faces are well known, the objective should be, of course, to achieve as accurate a likeness as possible.

The first step is to compare the face of the character with that of the actor who is to portray him, noting points of difference and of similarity. The comparison should include shape of the face; shape, length, and color of the hair and the beard; color of the skin; and precise conformation of individual features, including height and width of the forehead; length, breadth, and shape of the nose; distance from nose to mouth and from mouth to tip of the chin; width of the mouth; thickness and shape of the lips; line of the jaw; prominence of the cheekbones; line and thickness of the eyebrows; size, shape, prominence, and slant (if any) of the eyes; distance between the eyes; and the line, in profile, of the forehead, nose, mouth, chin, and neck. The points of similarity can be emphasized and the differences minimized. If the actor's nose is too small, it can be enlarged and reshaped with putty. If it is too large, it can be shadowed to make it seem less large, and attention can be drawn to other features. Wigs, beards, and spectacles can be enormously helpful.

An excellent way of training yourself to observe details and to reproduce them is to copy portraits. Photographs, with their myriad of details, may prove less useful to the beginner than works of art (paintings, drawings, engravings) with their simplifications. In using these artists' representations, however, you should keep in mind that your objective, except when you are deliberately working with stylization, is to achieve a realistic, believable makeup. It should be your purpose to recreate in three dimensions the artist's subject, not to reproduce his technique. Whereas the artist is permitted to show brush marks and to use a cross-hatching of lines to represent

FIGURE 17–1 CREATING A LIKENESS IN A MAKEUP WORKSHOP. *Note the careful arrangement of the portrait and the close-up mirror for easy comparison between the portrait and the likeness. (Makeup by student Clista Towne-Strother. For other makeups by the same student, see Figures 12–51B and 12–75.)*

249

FIGURE 17–2 ACTOR WILSON BROOKS AS WOOD-ROW WILSON.

shadows, the makeup artist, in doing a realistic makeup, is permitted no such license. You may also have to make certain compromises in minor features that cannot reasonably be duplicated on the actor's face. But a good likeness can usually be achieved in spite of inevitable minor variations from the original.

WOODROW WILSON

In creating the makeup for Woodrow Wilson shown in Figure 17–2, it was immediately obvious that the actor (Mr. Wilson Brooks, Figure 17–2A) had a bone structure lending itself easily to the makeup. Since President Wilson's face was wider, Mr. Brooks' hair was puffed out a little at the sides to increase the apparent width of the head, and a small ventilated hairpiece on nylon net was used to match Wilson's hair style. Observe carefully the following relatively minor but extremely important changes in individual features:

1. Wilson's eyes have a heavy-lidded effect caused by sagging flesh that actually conceals the upper lid completely when the eye is open. For this makeup a latex piece was used over the eye. The piece was made by the method described in Chapter 14. Since Wilson's eyebrows were straighter than Mr. Brooks', the latex was allowed to cover part of the inner end of each brow.

   The shape of the eyebrows is always important and should be copied as accurately as possible. In this case the inner ends were raised slightly, the brows darkened, and the point just beyond the center of each brow was exaggerated. Shadows under the eye were deepened with cake makeup.

2. The nostrils were highlighted, though it does not show in the photograph, and the nose was narrowed slightly by shadowing.

3. The shape of both upper and lower lips was altered slightly, and the lower lip was highlighted. Shadows at the corners of the mouth were deepened. Observe also the highlights and shadows just below the mouth.

4. A slight cleft in the chin was painted in with highlights and shadows.

5. Forehead wrinkles were accentuated with highlights and shadows. The superciliary arch was highlighted.

6. The cheekbones were brought out with highlights and shadows, and the nasolabial folds were deepened. Although the line of Mr. Brooks' folds is not quite the same as Wilson's, the difference has little effect on the likeness. An actor's own wrinkles, particularly the nasolabial folds, can be deepened or flattened out, shortened or lengthened; but if they are at all pronounced, the natural line should be followed. Otherwise, a smile will reveal that the real fold does not coincide with the painted one, and the credibility of the makeup will be destroyed.

7. The ears were made to stick out slightly with nose putty.

8. The final touch was added with a pair of pince-nez.

   It was observed frequently during the making up that very slight changes—reshaping the lips or the eyebrows, a shadow here, a highlight there—made considerable difference in the likeness. Because it is impossible to have *every* detail perfect, it is important to make the most of what the actor's face will permit.

MARK TWAIN

Actor Hal Holbrook (Figure 17–3), in his brilliant recreation of Mark Twain, is as meticulous in his makeup as in his acting. No detail is too small or too unimportant to be given careful attention each time the makeup is applied. And for every performance he devotes more than three hours to perfecting these details. That his makeup takes so long is perhaps less significant than that he is willing to spend that amount of time doing it.

In discussing his problems of recreating Mark Twain physically, Mr. Holbrook says: "The jaw formation is similar, and so is the cheekbone. My eyes have the *possibility*. His eyes had an eagle sort of look, but you can create that with makeup. And, of course, his nose was very distinctive—long and somewhat like a banana. Mine's too sharp. The nose alone takes an hour. I have a smooth face, and if I don't break it up, the texture is wrong. Also, I have to shrink three and one-half inches. Part of this is done by actual body shrinkage—relaxation all the way down as though I were suspended on a string from the top of the head. Part of it is illusion—the way the suit is made and the height of the furniture on stage. The coat is a little bit longer than it should be. There's

a downward slope to the padded shoulders. There's a belly, too—not much of one, but it pulls me down. The lectern, the table, and the chair are built up a little higher."

Materials The makeup is done with a combination of creme stick, grease-stick liners, pencils, and powder. Three shades of creme stick are used—FS-5-c/d for the base, OF-2-b for highlights, and S/FS-10-e for shadows. Three grease sticks are also used—a deep brown, a maroon, and a rose. All three are used for shadows and accents and the red for additional pink color in the cheeks, on the forehead, eyelids, and ears, for example. There are also brown and maroon pencils for deep shadows.

Application Except for the base and the first general application of creme-stick shadows to the cheeks and eye sockets and sides of the nose, all of the makeup is done with brushes, most of them flat sables in various widths. The smaller wrinkles are done with 1/8-inch and 3/16-inch brushes and some of the larger areas with a 3/8-inch brush. The makeup is taken directly from the stick. The color is sometimes taken up from the two sticks and mixed on the brush; but more frequently, the various shades are applied separately, one after the other. Mr. Holbrook uses three shadow colors—the S/FS-10-e, the maroon, and the dark brown—and he sometimes adds a bit of rose to give the shadow more life.

All shadows and highlights, as can be observed in Figure 17–5A, are exaggerated since they are to be powdered down. If cake were being used instead of grease,

FIGURE **17–3** *ACTOR HAL HOLBROOK AS HIMSELF.* Chicago Tribune, *photo by John Austad.*

FIGURE **17–4** *HAL HOLBROOK AS MARK TWAIN.* Chicago Tribune, *photo by John Austad.*

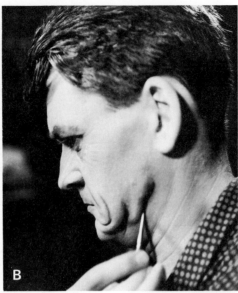

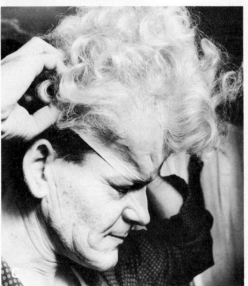

this initial heightening would not be necessary. However, once one has determined what effect the powder will have, one way is as effective as the other. For the detailed brushwork used on this makeup (the whole makeup is approached almost as if it were a painting), the creme-stick and grease method is probably easier. As always, choice of materials is a personal matter.

One of the greatest problems in making up youth for age is to eliminate expanses of smooth skin. It is at this point that otherwise technically competent makeups often fail. The problem has been solved in this case by covering the smooth expanses with wrinkles, puffiness, hollows, and sagging flesh. You will notice in the accompanying photographs, especially Figure 17–5D, that the

entire face and the neck (except for the forehead, which is concealed by the wig blender, and the upper lip, which will be concealed by a mustache) are almost completely covered with shadows and highlights. Very little of the original base color shows through.

After the makeup has reached approximately the stage shown in Figure 17–5B, the cheek area in front of the ears is stippled (using a small brush) with dots of maroon, rose, and the creme-stick base. This is then softened somewhat with a clean ⅜-inch brush. When further toned down with powder, the effect, even in the dressing room, is remarkably convincing. (See Figure 17–4.)

After the stage shown in Figure 17–5B has been

reached and that much of the makeup powdered, the lower part of the forehead, across the bottom of the sideburns to the ears, is covered with spirit gum, and the wig is put on in the usual way (Figure 17–5C). Ordinarily it is safer to put the wig on first, then apply the spirit gum underneath the blender, though with a very tight wig this may be difficult. Practice makes it possible, however, to apply the spirit gum in the right place and to put the wig on exactly right the first time so as to avoid the difficulties with the gum. The blender in this case extends down to the eyebrows.

The next problem, and a crucial one, is to adjust the blender perfectly so that there are no wrinkles, no air bubbles, nothing to destroy the illusion. This must be done quickly, before the spirit gum becomes too tacky. Again, it takes practice to know exactly how to adjust the blender and what sort of minor imperfections are likely to cause trouble later. Once the blender is perfectly adjusted, it is pressed hard with a towel all along the edge in order to stick it tight to the skin and to make it as smooth as possible. The blender is always cleaned with acetone after the performance in order to make sure the edge will be as thin as possible.

In concealing the edge of the blender, the creme stick base is applied to the blender somewhat irregularly with a ⅜-inch brush. Then the shadow is applied with a brush to the temples, crossing the edge of the blender. A little light red is worked spottily into either side of the frontal area, keeping away from the hairline. Wrinkles are then drawn on the blender with maroon and the shadow color and highlighted with OF-2-b. Then the temples are stippled with maroon and rose and the shadow color. This is a very important step, since it further helps to hide the blender line by breaking up the color in the area. (See Figure 17–5D.)

The eyebrows are made shaggy by sticking several tufts of gray hair with spirit gum into the natural brows. The mustache (ventilated on gauze) is attached with spirit gum, the hair is combed, and the makeup is completed. (See Figure 17–4).

The preceding paragraphs about Mr. Holbrook's makeup were written for the third edition of *Stage Makeup*. It is interesting to note that by the time *Mark Twain Tonight* appeared on Broadway in 1966, Mr. Holbrook had made several changes in his makeup—notably, from a blender wig to one with a lace front (putting on the wig was far easier and the effect from the audience was essentially the same) and in the use of sponges for stippling (as described in Chapter 11) instead of brushes. The effect was equally good though not quite the same. Whereas the sponge method took away the youthful smoothness of the skin, which then looked convincingly

aged, the brush technique, giving equal age, suggested discolorations of the skin typical of old age. For Mr. Holbrook's television special in 1967 a three-dimensional makeup had to be created for Mark Twain using foamed latex (see Figure 17–6). Since then, Mr. Holbrook has made further changes in his makeup for the stage—a latex nose, false eyebrows, and a plastic cap underneath the wig to conceal his own hairline.

There are several lessons to be learned from Mr. Holbrook's makeup:

1. An effective makeup should be carefully planned and rehearsed. Any but the simplest sort of makeup may well require a certain amount of experimentation, sometimes a great deal. Even experienced makeup artists do careful research and planning on any makeup involving historical characters.
2. The makeup should be an integral part of the characterization. Mr. Holbrook over a period of years studied photographs and even an old film of Mark Twain, read everything he could find by or about him, and talked with people who had known or seen him. His makeup developed along with his performance and was the result of considerable planning and experimentation.
3. It is essential, in making up, to adapt the makeup to the actor's face. Mr. Holbrook does not duplicate a portrait of Mark Twain on his own face. As he makes up, he continually twists and turns and grimaces in order to make sure that every shadow or wrinkle he applies follows the natural conformations of his own face so that there is not the slightest chance that a passing movement or expression will reveal a painted wrinkle different from a real one.
4. One of the secrets of aging the youthful face is to concentrate on eradicating *all* signs of youth, including a smooth, youthful skin. This Mr. Holbrook has done. The numerous wrinkles in the Mark Twain makeup are less important individually than for their effect in breaking up smooth areas of skin with light and shade and color. Unwrinkled areas are textured with stippling. Mr. Holbrook has taken a positive approach to every area of the face and has made sure that nothing remains to betray the actor beneath the makeup.

Because the remarkable recreation of Twain's likeness is essential to the effectiveness of the performance, Mr. Holbrook feels that he must cut no corners and that even if the audience were unaware of any imperfections, *he* would know, and in his own mind the performance would suffer. This is an example of the dedicated artist to whom no amount of effort is too great if it will in any way contribute to his performance.

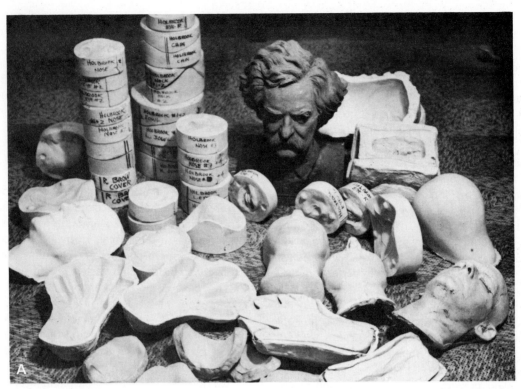

FIGURE 17-6 *TELEVISION MAKEUP FOR HAL HOL-BROOK'S MARK TWAIN. The series of photographs on the following pages show the step-by-step creation of Dick Smith's makeup for the CBS-TV special of Mark Twain Tonight. Although Mr. Holbrook does his own makeup for the stage (see Figures 17–3, 17–4, and 17–5), three-dimensional constructions were required for television. Mr. Smith spent eight to ten weeks preparing for the makeup. This involved making more than 50 casts (A) and a number of experimental tests. Three complete makeups were created before the final one was chosen. With the help of an assistant, Mr. Smith was able to cut the 5-hour application time to 4½ hours and removal time to 1 hour. The method of making casts and foam-latex pieces like those on the following pages is described in Chapter 14.*

The makeup involved both expected and unexpected problems. In order to prevent the smearing of makeup when Mr. Holbrook put his hands into the pockets of his white suits, Mr. Smith painted the backs of the hands (after the foam-latex pieces had been attached) with a mixture of latex and acrylic paint. Then at the dress rehearsal it was discovered that the edges of the large latex appliances were working loose around the mouth because of muscular activity—a common problem with any prosthetic application in that area. The use of Slomon's Medico Adhesive in troublesome spots successfully prevented any loosening of edges during the performance.

Although the three-dimensional television makeup shown here would obviously not be practical for regular use in the theater, some of the techniques might very profitably be incorporated into makeups for the stage.

The first step was to flatten Mr. Holbrook's front hair with spirit gum. B. After the gum was brushed on, it was pressed down with a wet towel. Stipple-latex was then applied to the eyelids, dried with a hair dryer, and powdered to prevent sticking. C. Foam-latex eye pouches were attached with stipple-latex and adjusted with tweezers. D. Eyebrows were flattened with spirit gum and covered with foam-latex pieces. E. The foam-latex nose was attached with spirit gum and stipple-latex. F. The large foam-latex appliance (neck, jowls, nasolabial folds) was set in place and attached with spirit gum on the lower parts and stipple-latex on the top edges. The edges were blended with Scar Plastic Blending Liquid. G. Piece completely attached. H. Duo adhesive was then applied as a sealer. I. Meanwhile, foam-latex pieces were being attached to the backs of the hands by an assistant.

J. A plastic forehead piece was needed to give the effect of seeing the scalp through the thin and fluffy front hair of the wig. K. After it was attached with gum, the edge of the plastic piece was dissolved with acetone to blend it imperceptibly into the natural skin. L. A light rubber-mask greasepaint base was applied over the entire face, then stippled with other colors, using a coarse sponge (M) and in some cases a brush. N. Eyebrows were attached over the latex covers. O. The wig was then put on, the front lace glued down with matte plastic, and the hair brushed. P. After the mustache (ventilated on a net foundation) was attached, the entire makeup was touched up wherever necessary. Q shows the final result.

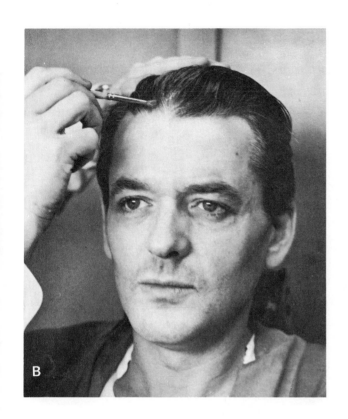

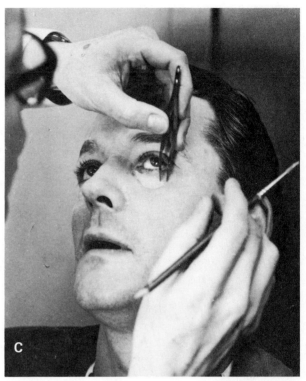

MAKEUP BY DICK SMITH, S.M.A.

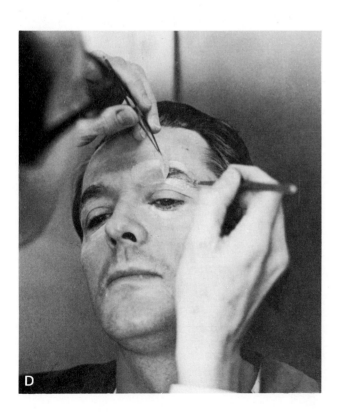

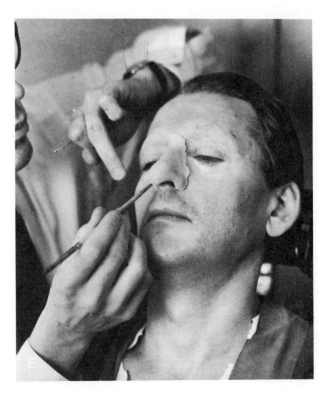

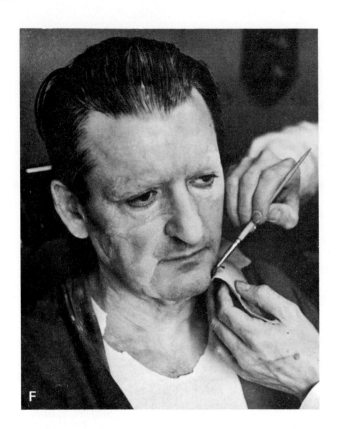

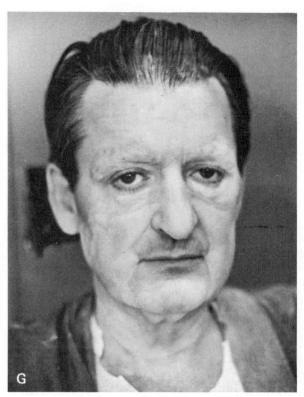

MAKEUP BY DICK SMITH, S.M.A.

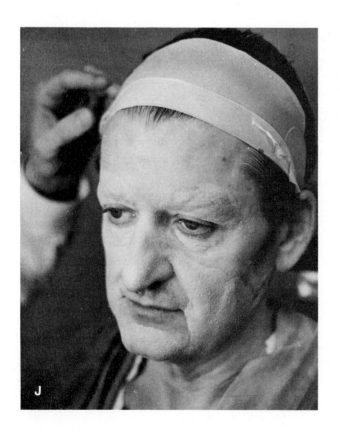

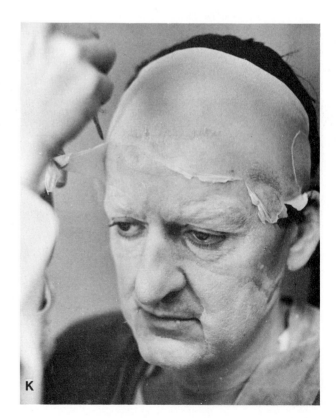

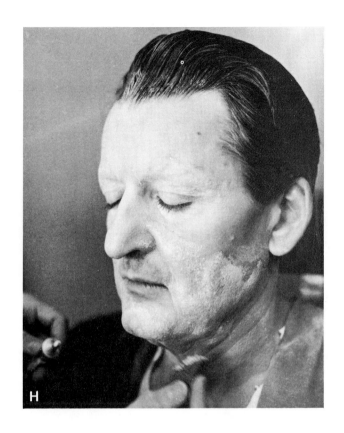

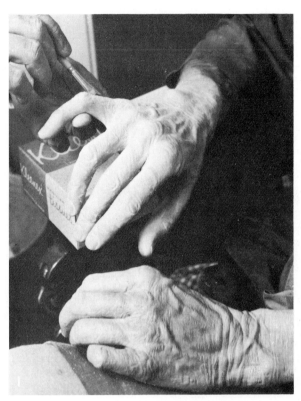

MAKEUP BY DICK SMITH, S.M.A.

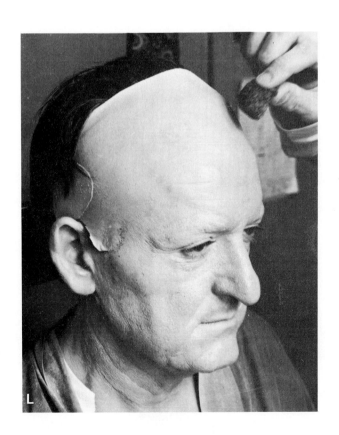

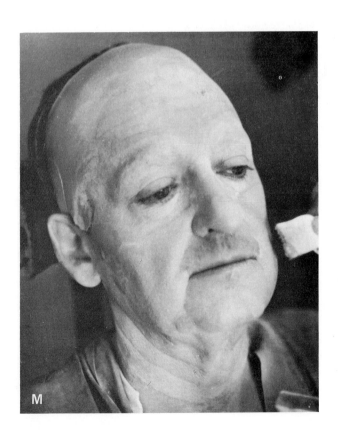

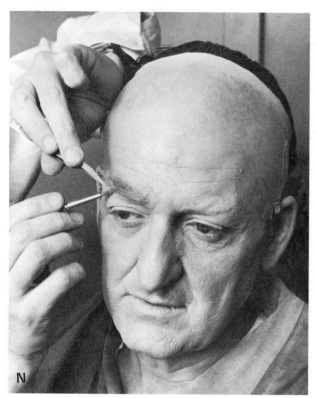

N

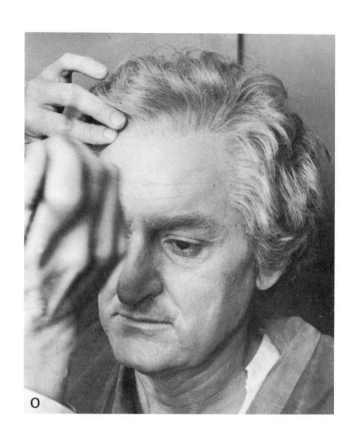

O

MAKEUP BY DICK SMITH, S.M.A.

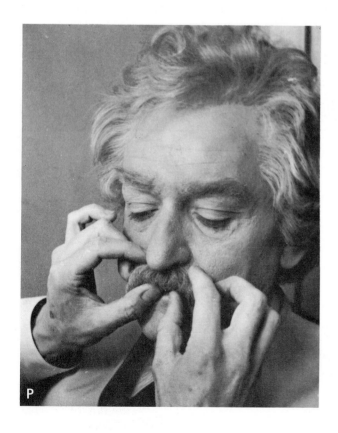

P

Q

Peter Falk   Falk as Stalin, Acts I & II   Act III

FIGURE 17–7 PENCIL SKETCHES OF PETER FALK AS HIMSELF AND AS JOSEF STALIN.

STALIN AND TROTSKY

In designing the makeups for historical characters, such as Stalin and Trotsky in Paddy Chayefsky's *The Passion of Josef D.*, it is helpful, as suggested in Chapter 7, to work from photographs of the actor. In doing character drawings from these photographs, one should be careful to do only what can actually be done with makeup in the given situation. If, for example, the makeup has to be done quickly (as in the change from the young Stalin to the older one, shown in Figure 17–7), changes should be kept simple. Although it is not necessary, there is some advantage in doing a sketch of the actor as well as of the character. Having both sketches for comparison, as in Figures 17–7 and 17–9, adds considerably to the effectiveness of the presentation in discussing the makeup with the director and the actor and in reassuring them that the transformation is feasible.

In using this method, be sure, as suggested in Chapter 7, that the photograph is a reasonably recent one, and use both front view and profile. If all your preliminary work is based on a firm jaw and a smooth skin, an unexpectedly wrinkled face with sagging muscles can be disastrous. Furthermore, a face that appears, from the front, reasonably easy to make into the likeness of a historical personage can present problems in profile.

Peter Falk as Stalin The major elements in the change to the young Stalin were the mustache and the eyebrows. Adding the mustache (real hair ventilated on lace) was a simple matter; changing the eyebrows was not quite so simple. Whereas Mr. Falk's eyebrows were heavy and slanting down, Stalin's had to be thin and slanting up. Thus, the actor's natural eyebrows had to be completely blocked out. This was done with spirit gum and fabric. (See Chapter 12.) After the foundation, highlights, and shadows had been applied, the beard area was darkened somewhat with gray, then stippled

with dark brown for an unshaven effect. Finally, the mustache was attached with spirit gum, and Mr. Falk's own hair was arranged to suit the character.

For the more mature Stalin, the wig was put on (Figure 17–8C) and the lace front attached with spirit gum. Then the youthful makeup was covered with a cake foundation and appropriate highlights and shadows added.

Alvin Epstein as Trotsky Alvin Epstein presented an additional problem in that he was expected not only to look like Trotsky but to achieve the likeness in a quick change. He was playing three characters, each one totally unlike any of the others; but only Trotsky needed to be a recognizable historical personage.

In addition to adding a wig, a goatee, and a mustache (Figure 17–9), Mr. Epstein reshaped and darkened his own blond eyebrows. The pale, translucent skin that Mr. Epstein wanted for Trotsky was achieved with white cake makeup lightly applied, then partially removed with liquid cleanser, letting the natural skin color show through and leaving a very slight shine. The bone structure was then accentuated with highlights and shadows and the eyes with black and light red. A touch of red was added immediately under the eyebrows.

THE MAD HATTER

Likenesses can also be based on illustrations of fictional characters. Once it is determined, by examining the face in the mirror at the same angle and with the same expression as that in the illustration, that a likeness is possible, the procedure is essentially the same as when working with a drawing of a real person. For the Mad Hatter, the eyebrows, eyelids, and nose were the features requiring the most obvious changes. Figure 17–10 shows the step-by-step procedure.

FIGURE 17—8 *PETER FALK TO STALIN.*   A. Blocking out natural eyebrows. B. Human-hair eyebrows, ventilated on net, being attached with spirit gum. C. Wig being adjusted, front lace not yet trimmed. D. Makeup completed, wig being combed. Photos by Werner J. Kuhn.

Alvin Epstein

Epstein as Trotsky

FIGURE 17—9 *PENCIL SKETCHES OF ALVIN EPSTEIN AS HIMSELF AND AS TROTSKY.*

FIGURE 17—10 *THE MAD HATTER FROM ALICE IN WONDERLAND.* Based on the Tenniel illustration.

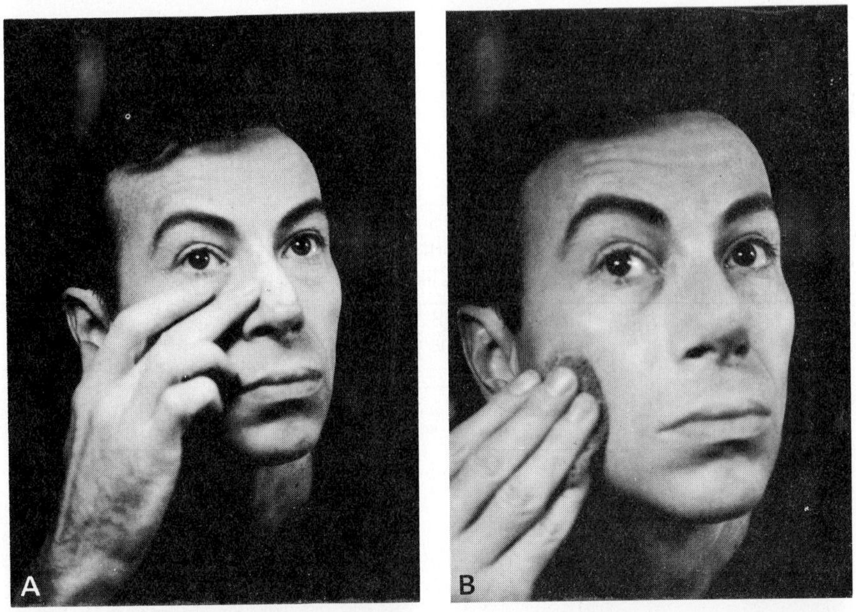

FIGURE **17–11** *MAKEUP FOR THE MAD HATTER.* A. Nose being built up with putty-wax. B. Cake makeup foundation being applied. C, D, E. Face being modeled with highlights and shadows. F. Eyebrows being made up. G. Hairlace being pressed into spirit gum. H. Finished makeup.

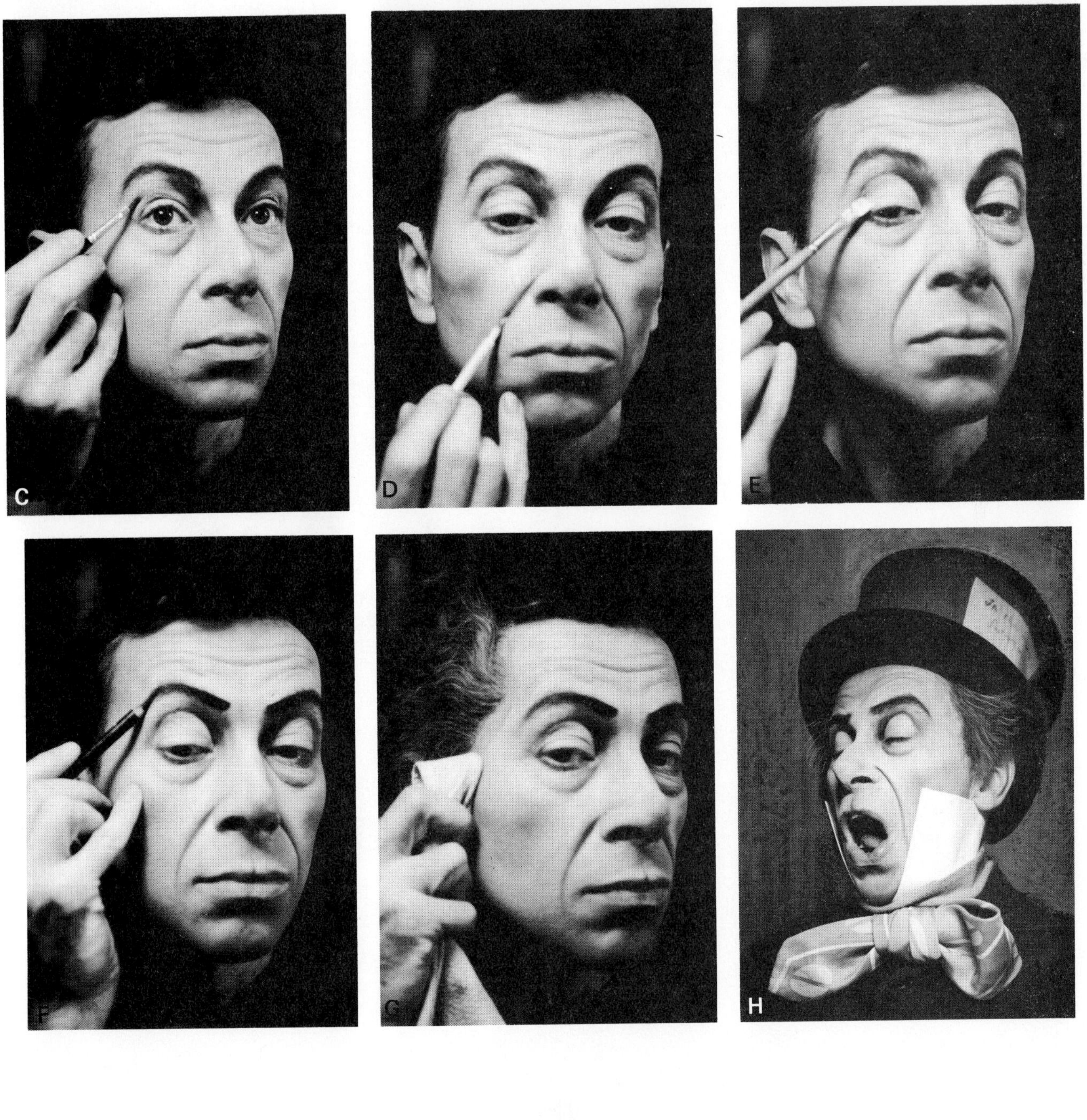

Problems

1. Make yourself up as a historical character from a play.
2. Create a likeness from a portrait—not necessarily of a historical figure and preferably a painting rather than a photograph. Make sure before you begin that a recognizable likeness is possible.

18

Nonrealistic Makeup

Nonrealistic makeup comprises makeups not only for realistic and nonrealistic characters made up in one of various nonrealistic styles (Figures 18–1B, 18–2, 18–3, 18–4, and 18–5), but also for nonrealistic, that is, fanciful or nonhuman characters—such as trolls, demons, and apes—made up in a realistic style (Figure 18–8).

NONREALISTIC STYLES

The nonrealistic styles can range from theatrical realism or *theatricalism* (Figures 18–1B and 18–2, for example) to nonrealism (Figures 18–3B, 18–4, and 18–5). When this nonrealism results from imposing a particular style on the design of the makeup, it is referred to as *stylization*.

Stylization In designing a stylized makeup, you might begin by thinking in terms of using line, color, and form to heighten, exaggerate, simplify, clarify, satirize, symbolize, or perhaps amuse. Instead of consulting photographs for inspiration, you might consult paintings (Figure 18–4), drawings (Figure 18–7), prints, caricatures, masks (Figures 18–5 and H–20), mosaics (Figures 18–6 and H–29), toys (Figure 18–20), sculpture, or stained glass. Then, from your various ideas, you could select for your designs those that seemed best suited to the character, the play, and the style of production.

For a stylized production of a French farce using black-and-white sets and costumes, for example, black-and-white makeups are an obvious, but potentially amus-

FIGURE 18–1 ALAN SUES AS PROFESSOR MORIARTY IN THE ADVENTURES OF SHERLOCK HOLMES. An example of theatricalism. A. Alan Sues as himself. B. Alan Sues as Professor Moriarty. (Photograph by Martha Swope.)

FIGURE 18—2 THE RED QUEEN FROM THROUGH THE LOOKING GLASS. *Natural eyebrows soaped out. Putty wax nose. An example of theatricalism. Student makeup by Rebecca Colodner.*

A

B

FIGURE 18—3 MEPHISTOPHELES. *Makeup in two different styles. A. Theatricalism. B. Stylization.*

FIGURE 18—4 MAKEUP IN THE STYLE OF PAINTER KARL SCHMIDT-ROTTLUFF.

FIGURE 18—5 MAKEUP COPIED FROM AN ORIENTAL MASK. *By student Elaine Herman. (For other makeups by the same student, see Figure 6–1.)*

FIGURE 18—6 *THIRTEENTH-CENTURY MO-SAIC HEAD.* San Marco, Venice.

FIGURE 18—7 *THE DUCHESS FROM ALICE IN WONDERLAND.* With Alice, Cook, Baby, and Cheshire Cat. Illustration by Sir John Tenniel.

ing, choice. For a Medieval morality play, you might design makeups to look like mosaics (Figures 18–6 and H–29, for example) or stained glass. For the production of a play by Brecht, you could relate the makeups to the work of German artists of the period.

Relating the Makeup to the Audience In addition to relating to the style of the production, to the play, and to the character, a nonrealistic makeup should also relate to the audience. Although audiences are usually quite willing to go along with innovations in style, there are certain areas of resistance the actor or the makeup artist should be aware of. Our ideas about some nonrealistic characters may be rather unspecific and are thus open to fresh interpretation. But our ideas about other nonrealistic characters—such as those in *Alice in Wonderland* and *Through the Looking Glass*, for example, are not so flexible. Sir John Tenniel created visual images of the characters in *Alice* (Figure 18–7, for example) that have become the definitive representations of those characters, and most audiences will tend to relate to them more readily onstage if they look rather like the ones with which they're familiar.

NONREALISTIC AND NONHUMAN CHARACTERS

Makeups for nonrealistic and nonhuman characters may or may not be nonrealistic in style. Sometimes—as when an actor is playing a flower, for example—there is no choice since an actor simply cannot be made up realistically as a flower. Or as a cat. But he can be made up quite realistically as an ape (Figure 18–8).

The following suggestions may provide some ideas for dealing with a variety of nonrealistic characters. When referring to these suggestions, bear in mind that the descriptions are based largely on literature, art, and folklore; and though they may sometimes be stated dogmatically, they represent only a convenient point of departure. You may wish to vary them to suit your purpose.

Angels First determine the style of the production and the sort of angel required. If an ethereal angel is called for, you may wish to work with pale lavenders, blues, or whatever color seems appropriate. The features will probably be idealized human ones. But if you were doing *The Green Pastures*, the angels could achieve the comic effect required only with a realistic makeup.

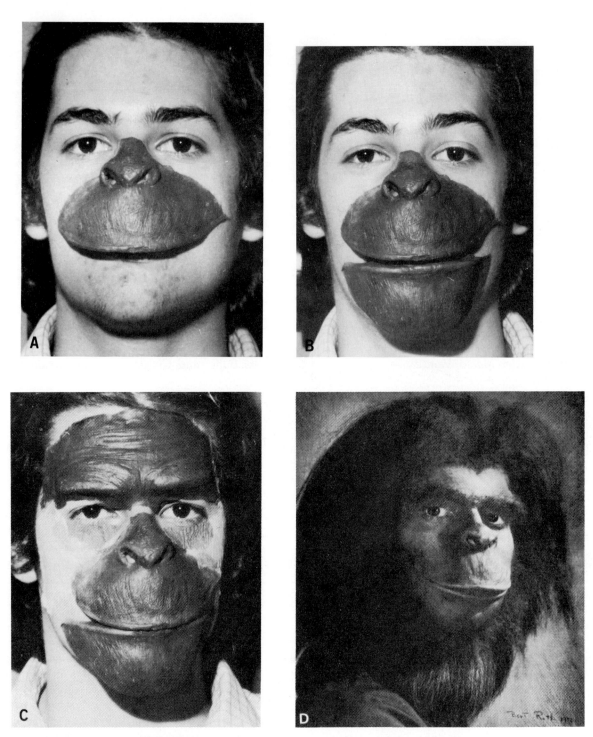

FIGURE 18—8 APE. *Foamed latex mask, made in 3 pieces. Makeup by Bert Roth, S.M.A.*

Animals When animals are played by humans (Figure 18–9), the style of the makeup may be either realistic or nonrealistic. Papier mâché heads or masks (Figure 18–12) or latex constructions (Figure 18–8) can be used and sometimes should be; but if the style of the production permits, you may prefer merely to suggest animal features on a human face. That can be done in a completely nonrealistic or a modified realistic style with paint (Figures 18–10 and 18–11), or the paint can be combined with three-dimensional makeup. Crepe hair can also be used. Split lips can be drawn on (Figure H–27), foreheads can be lowered, real or painted whiskers can be added, and paws can be made from gloves.

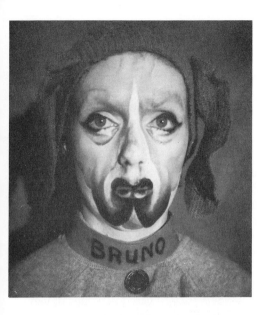

FIGURE **18–9** BRUNO. *Stylized makeup for children's play. Improvised headdress. Makeup by student Barbara Murray. (For other makeups by the same student, see Figures 12–62, 13–12, 13–20, 18–10, and 18–23.)*

FIGURE **18–10** STYLIZED RABBIT. *Makeup by Barbara Murray. A. Blocking out eyebrows with Kryolan Eyebrow Plastic. B. Eyes being made up. C. Areas of color being painted on. D. Completed makeup with improvised headdress. Teeth are painted on over the lips.*

FIGURE 18–11 TIGER. *Makeup by student Kathy Ross.*

Birds Bird faces can be built up with three-dimensional additions, such as large beaks (Figure 18–13) or completely stylized with painted details. Sometimes the two may be combined. Birds with small beaks and large eyes (owls, for example) are, of course, easier to do with paint than are large-beaked birds. The beak of the parrot in Figure 18–13 was molded with latex and painted a brilliant red-orange. Brightly colored feathers were attached with spirit gum. A complete mask would, of course, have been more practical if the makeup had to be repeated. For smaller-beaked birds being done with makeup rather than masks, putty might be used instead of latex. Color can be as realistic or as fanciful as the birds themselves.

Clowns *Circus* clowns wear stylized makeups of various types, each individually designed. Traditionally, they always design their own makeups and never copy the makeup of another clown. *Shakespearean* clowns are not really clowns at all in the contemporary meaning of the word and require a makeup—either *realistic* or *theatrical*—appropriate for the individual character.

The first step in designing a makeup for a circus clown is to decide what sort of clown you want—sad, happy, elegant, shy, brash, suspicious, ineffectual. Then design an exaggerated, stylized makeup to fit the conception. For a sad clown, for example, the eyebrows and the corners of the mouth will probably slant downward. A happy clown will, of course, have the corners of the mouth turned up. If your clown is to be a tramp (see Figure 18–14), he will presumably have painted-on beard stubble. Sketching your design on paper first is likely to save time and result in a better makeup.

Clown white (see Appendix A) is usually used as a foundation. All exposed areas of flesh should be evenly

FIGURE 18–12 BIRD AND ANIMAL MASKS. *By Bill Smith. A. Sketches. B. Masks.*

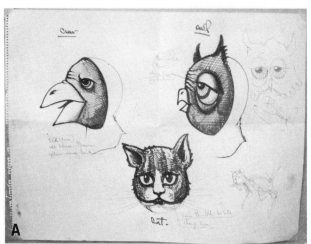

FIGURE *18–13* PARROT. *Coral-colored beak made of molded latex. Gold, yellow, green, red, and purple feathers attached to the face with latex. Makeup by student Gordon Hayes.*

FIGURE *18–14* TRAMP-CLOWN MAKEUP. *By student Jan Vidra.*

colored. Then with pencils, brushes, and shading colors, you can duplicate your design. Bulbous clown noses can be molded with latex or purchased ready-made. Red-rubber balls are sometimes used. The hair should be treated in a style harmonious with the rest of the makeup. A skull cap or a wig is usually worn.

Death Death is usually pictured as having a skull for a head (see Figure 18–15). The facial bones can be highlighted with white or ivory and shadowed with gray, charcoal-brown, or both. If the head is not going to be covered, a white skull cap or a plastic or a latex cap should be worn. The cap, which should cover the ears, can be painted the same color as the face and the edges blended carefully into the foundation. The eyebrows should always be blocked out (see Chapter 12).

If the makeup is to be luminous, the white paint can be dusted with fluorescent or phosphorescent powder (see Appendix A) before any shading is done. Or fluorescent or phosphorescent paint can be brushed over the completed makeup in the appropriate places. With fluorescent makeup, an ultraviolet ray must be used on a dark stage to cause luminosity.

If Death is to appear part of the time disguised as a human, a normal though pale, makeup can be used instead of white and the fluorescent paint or pigment applied only to the bones of the skull. Under normal stage lights the makeup will look normal, but under the ultraviolet ray the skull will appear. If the hands are to be visible, they should, of course, be made up in harmony with the makeup on the face. It is also possible to present Death in other ways—as a coldly beautiful woman, perhaps, or as a black-hooded figure with no face at all. Or as a clown.

FIGURE *18–15* DEATH. *Cake makeup. Makeup by student Dennis Drew.*

FIGURE **18–16** DEVIL AS JESTER. *From an old print.*

FIGURE **18–17** SIXTEENTH-CENTURY DEVIL'S HEAD.

FIGURE **18–18** DEMON. *English door knocker.*

FIGURE **18–19** CARVED WOODEN MASKS, LIGHTED FROM ABOVE AND BELOW.

Devils and Demons (Figures 18–16, 18–17, 18–18, 18–19) The conventional devil (Figure 18–16) usually has a long face with sharp, pointed features, prominent cheekbones, long, hooked nose, well-defined lips, dark, upward-slanting eyebrows, close together, and deepset eyes. He may also have a mustache and a small, pointed beard. Conceptions of demons are usually less conventional and more imaginative.

Dolls China or porcelain dolls can be made up with a creamy white, ivory, or pale pink foundation. The rouge, usually pink, should be applied in a round spot in the center of each cheek, and the spot should be blended somewhat at the edges. The lips should be small with a pronounced cupid's bow. The natural eyelashes can be darkened with mascara or false ones added. The eyes should be made to look as round as possible. An inexpen-

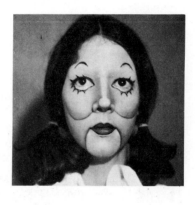

FIGURE **18–20** RAG DOLL. *Eyebrows blocked out with spirit gum and fabric. Black, white, and red cake makeup. Red yarn wig. Makeup by student Jeanne Zavala. (For another makeup by the same student, see Figure 13–33D.)*

FIGURE **18–21** MARIONETTE. *Eyebrows blocked out. Cake makeup with black eyebrow pencil. Makeup by student Sarah Barker.*

sive wig with shiny, synthetic hair is usually preferable to an expensive one. Other types of dolls will, of course, require other kinds of makeup.

Elves   Elves are usually pictured as very small with pointed or butterfly-shaped ears, large mouths, small turned-up noses or long pointed ones, and round or slanted eyes. The hair may be short or long. Older elves usually have beards. Red cheeks are appropriate for good-natured elves of any age.

Fairies   Fairies tend to be diminutive and graceful—unless they have turned bad, in which case they will appear more evil and witch-like. Wicked fairies (Carabosse in *The Sleeping Beauty*, for example) are more like wicked witches and are sometimes played by men, giving them stronger, less feminine features. Emphasis in the makeup should, of course, be on wickedness—dark, slanting eyebrows, close together, evil, piercing eyes, etc. (See *Witches.*) Good witches may tend to look more like fairies.

The skin color for good fairies is usually light and delicate—shell pink, lavender, orchid, pale blue or green, gold, or silver are possibilities. Red shades, being more human, should be avoided. Metallic flakes or sequins are sometimes used. The flakes usually adhere to greasepaint. If they don't, you might try rubber-mask grease, or you might use stubble paste (see Appendix A) as an adhesive. Sequins can be attached with a latex adhesive or spirit gum.

The features should be delicate and well formed. The ears may or may not be pointed. A delicate lip coloring should be used but no cheek rouge. The eyebrows and sometimes the eyes may be slanted. The hair of female fairies is usually long and golden.

Flowers   These obviously cannot be given a realistic treatment. They are usually created by surrounding the face with oversize, artificial petals, but there can be a variety of approaches to the face itself. One possibility is illustrated in Figure H–21, in which the entire face is covered with real petals.

Ghosts   Ghosts are usually thought of as being pale and rather indistinct. Highlighting is, of course, essential in achieving an appropriate ghostly effect. As for the makeup, pale, bloodless colors—such as white or lighter, grayed tints of blue, lavender, greenish yellow, or yellowish green—might be used. The bone structure can be highlighted with white or pale tints of the base color and shadowed with gray, especially in the eye sockets, which should be the most deeply shadowed areas of the face. Hair on the head and on the face can be white or gray.

The ghost of a specific character should usually resemble the character—except, of course, in color. The makeup in Figure H–8D, though not intended as the makeup of a ghost, might, with less warmth in the coloring, be so used.

A gray nylon stocking worn over the face (with or without makeup underneath) will increase the effect of ghostliness.

Gnome   Gnomes are commonly thought of as living underground. They are always mischievous and nearly always unfriendly. They may be very ugly, even deformed. A long nose, prominent cheekbones, jutting brow and receding forehead, pointed chin, receding chin, fat cheeks, sunken cheeks, large ears, very bushy eyebrows, no eyebrows, pop eyes, small and beady eyes, and bulg-

FIGURE 18–22 SMALL PERSON WITH FLOWERED HAT. *Cake makeup, eyebrow pencil, lip rouge, ventilated mustache. Surrealistic makeup by student Christine Donish.*

ing forehead are possible characteristics. Older gnomes may have long and flowing beards. The skin may be very wrinkled and either very pale or very sallow.

Goblins Goblins are believed to be evil and mischievous. Rough and swarthy skin, slanted slits for eyes, enormous mouths, flat or long and carrot-shaped noses, extremely large ears, and pointed teeth are possibilities to be considered in the makeup.

Grotesques Grotesques are creatures (human or nonhuman) that are in some way distorted or bizarre. (See Figure 18–22.) The Weird Sisters in *Macbeth* are sometimes made up as Grotesques.

Monsters This category covers a variety of creatures, from mechanical men to werewolves. If the monster is to be animalistic, the hair should grow low on the forehead and perhaps cover a good deal of the face. The nose usually needs to be widened and flattened. False teeth made to look like fangs will make the monster more terrifying. But if the creature is to appear in a children's play, it should be conceived with some discretion. Gory details, such as blood streaming from an open wound and eyes torn out of their sockets, might well be saved, if they are to be used at all, for adult horror plays. Foreheads can be raised and heads squared off, eyes rearranged, teeth made large and protruding, and so on. Skin-texture techniques—tissue with latex, tissue and spirit gum, latex and bran or cornmeal—can be used to good effect.

Ogres An ogre is usually conceived to be a hideous monster who feeds on human beings. Prosthetic applications will undoubtedly be needed. You might consult the suggestions for making up a gnome and then exaggerate them.

Pan Pan is the mythological Greek god of forests, flocks, and pastures. His head and body are those of an elderly man, and his lower parts are those of a goat. He is usually depicted with horns.

Pierrot Pierrot and Pierrette are often made up with a white foundation covering all exposed flesh. Ivory or very pale pink can be used if preferred. The lips should be small and quite red with a pronounced cupid's bow. The natural brows should be blocked out and high arched ones painted on with black eyebrow pencil. The eyes should be well defined, and the rouge should be two round spots. For a more completely stylized makeup, rouge, lips, and eyebrows might all be in the shape of diamonds or other simple geometric figures. The design of the costume should harmonize.

Statuary All exposed flesh should be made up, the color depending on the color of the material of which the statue is supposedly made. Grays, grayed blues, grayed greens, and grayed violets are useful for shadowing. Avoid warm tones unless the statue is of a color that would require warm shadows. Whether or not the makeup should be powdered will depend on the material of which the statue is supposedly made. If the finish would naturally be shiny, a creme or a grease foundation without powder can be used. A dull finish requires a water-soluble or a powdered creme or grease foundation.

Gold, silver, or bronze statues can be made with metallic body makeup. The effect is excellent, but the technique should be used with care (see discussion in Appendix A under *Metallic Makeup*).

Toys Makeup for toys other than dolls—as, for example, tin or wooden soldiers or marionettes (see Figure 18–21)—can best be copied from the actual toys. Their unreality should be stressed in order to counteract the obvious lifelike qualities of the actor.

Trolls Trolls live underground or in caves and are usually thought of as being stupid, ugly, and hateful. They have been described as having large, flabby noses, enormous ears, rotten teeth, and disgusting skin. For the skin, the face might be covered with latex over mounds of derma wax. For a rougher texture, miller's bran could be added. (For wonderful illustrations of trolls, goblins, brownies, elves, and other faerie creatures, *see Faeries*, a book by Brian Froud and Alan Lee.)

Vampires A vampire is a preternatural being that spends its days in a coffin and comes out only at night to drink blood. Since it never sees the light of day, it invariably has a pale, bloodless complexion—with the exception of the lips, which are sometimes abnormally red. Dark hair is conventional, with dark eyebrows slanting upward. The face should usually be thin and rather emaciated.

Witches Traditional witches (see Figure 18–23), usually have sharp, hooked noses, prominent cheekbones, sunken cheeks, thin lips, small sunken eyes, prominent pointed chins, numerous wrinkles, straggly hair, clawlike hands, warts and hair on the face, and seldom more than one or two good teeth. The complexion may be light or dark, sallow or swarthy, gray or puce. It might even be yellow, red, blue, green, or violet.

Witches can, however, be good or bad, young or old, ugly or beautiful. And the makeup can be realistic or stylized. Whereas a wicked old witch might have a face the texture and color of a dried apple, a good young witch might have a face of alabaster with hair of metallic gold. A bad (but sophisticated) young witch, on the other hand, could have a face with a glint of steel, slashed with jet black eyebrows over heavily lashed, slanted eyes. And then there are those witches who look exactly like everybody else and not like witches at all.

FIGURE 18–23 WITCH FROM SNOW WHITE AND THE SEVEN DWARFS. *Derma wax on chin, nose, and knuckles. Makeup by student Nancie Underwood.*

FIGURE 18–24 3 WITCHES, A DEVIL, AND A DEMON.

Problems

1. Make sketches for makeups based on visual images suggested to you by three of the following adjectives: Gross. Mean. Fantastic. Disoriented. Confused. Odd. Square. Melting. Broken. Discordant. Eroded. Slimy. Strange. Startled.
2. Design a realistic and a nonrealistic makeup for the same character.
3. Design two makeups for nonrealistic characters from plays, and execute one of the makeups. Following are some suggestions for possible characters:
   Oberon, Titania, Puck, Peaseblossom (*A Midsummer Night's Dream*); Mephistopheles; one of the Witches (*Macbeth*); Ko-ko, Pooh-Bah, Katisha, the Mikado (*The Mikado*); The Green Thing (*The Gods of the Mountain*); Red Queen, White Queen (*Through the Looking Glass*); King of Hearts, Queen of Hearts (*Alice in Wonderland*); He (*He Who Gets Slapped*); Ariel, Caliban (*The Tempest*); Elvira (*Blithe Spirit*); Pagliacci; Ghost (*Hamlet*); Trolls (*Peer Gynt*); Insects (*The Insect Comedy*); one of the Orcs (*Lord of the Rings*).

19

Quick-Change Makeups

Makeups that progress from one stage to another during the course of the play (Figure 19–1) and makeups that must be changed quickly from one character to another present a special problem since both involve a limitation on the time available for doing the makeup. This usually requires not only speeding up the application of the makeup, but also devising more efficient methods and procedures for accomplishing that end. It may also require special techniques not normally used.

ORGANIZING THE QUICK CHANGE

Organization is extremely important in most quick changes, and for a really fast change it can be crucial. The organization of any quick-change makeup falls into three basic categories—simplifying the makeup, selecting the materials, and formulating a detailed plan for actually making the change.

Simplifying the Makeup The makeup itself and the process of changing into it can nearly always be simplified if that should be necessary in order to save time. One way is to stipple the foundation color over the first makeup with a sponge instead of stroking it on, thus adding texture along with the color. Highlights and shadows can be applied either before or after the stippling, and they can be sponged on, brushed on, or, for the major highlights, applied with crayons or blemish-cover sticks and blended with the fingers. Or they can be stippled directly over the first makeup, thus eliminating the application of a foundation color, as was done for the makeup in Figure 19–1B. However, if the first makeup is very light, you might do well to apply a fairly dark foundation color before beginning your stippling for the second makeup. Since this will cut down considerably on the amount of shadowing required (see Chapter 12), it will probably save time in the long run.

If your makeup would normally include time-consuming details, such as forehead wrinkles and tiny wrinkles around the eyes, all carefully modeled, those might be eliminated. Or you might substitute less time-consuming techniques for the ones you usually use. Instead of applying forehead wrinkles in the usual way, each with a carefully modeled highlight and shadow, you might, for example, simply stipple the forehead heavily with a dark foundation color, then wrinkle the forehead as deeply as you can and stipple lightly with your highlight color. For wrinkles around the eyes, you can smile broadly before stippling the highlight over the wrinkle area. In aging the mouth, purse the lips tightly before highlighting. This should, however, be considered only an emergency measure to be used when time is limited.

If you are not using a stipple sponge for applying the highlights, you can use either a makeup crayon or a light blemish-cover stick since either is more efficient than a brush in making quick changes.

Selecting the Materials Time can be saved by selecting those materials that can be applied with the greatest efficiency. That means, for example, choosing crayons, blemish-cover sticks, lipsticks, eyeshadow sticks, hair-whitening sticks, and makeup pencils instead of makeup which is transferred from the container to the skin or the hair with brushes, sponges, or the fingers. If possible, avoid using spillable liquids for quick changes. If you need to use spirit gum, of course, you have no choice. You can, however, make sure that the bottle is securely anchored to the dressing table with masking tape or, better yet, placed in one of the Woochie spirit-gum bottle holders, designed to prevent nasty accidents. The holders are illustrated in Appendix A. You should also choose a brand of spirit gum (such as Kryolan's) that has strong adhesive qualities and dries fairly fast. The Kryolan plastic bottle, incidentally, has several advantages—a good-sized brush, a large, unbreakable plastic

FIGURE 19–1 *KING CHARLES VII IN YOUTH AND AGE.* *A. Kristoffer Tabori (with Kitty Winn) as the Dauphin in Shaw's* St. Joan. *(Construction of the latex nose is illustrated in Figure 14–8.) B. The King in the Epilogue. This makeup was done on top of the makeup in A. Highlights (Bob Kelly creme stick S-21) were stippled on and, when small areas or hard edges were involved, applied with sharpened makeup crayons (Bob Kelly CR-21). Medium shadows were added with a sharpened crayon (Bob Kelly CR SL-16) and deepened with creme shading color (Bob Kelly SL-17). Dry rouge (Bob Kelly DRC-1) was brushed around the eye and into the wrinkles. The makeup was then powdered. Photos by George de Vincent. (Note: Mr. Tabori's makeup for the Old King in Figure 14–10 was done for a later production of the play with a different cast.)*

cap that can be unscrewed more easily than most, and a conveniently wide mouth, which is easy to get the brush into when you're in a hurry.

Efficiency can also be increased by choosing the right brushes. In selecting flat shading brushes, for example, choose the widest brush suitable for the use to which it's going to be put. (You should always do that anyway, but it's especially important when time is limited.) In order to avoid having to clean the brushes during a change or, worse yet, inadvertently using a dirty brush and having your highlights streaked with shadow color, make sure there will be two brushes or two sets of brushes, one for highlights and one for shadows. (If you do have to clean any brushes during a change, have an open bottle of brush cleaner taped to the table, within easy reach.) It's a good idea, by the way, to keep the highlight and the shadow brushes separated on the dressing table by putting them in separate containers, such as drinking glasses or coffee mugs. They are more easily accessible when standing up than when lying flat. They also take up less space, and they won't roll off onto the floor.

If the change is being made at a table in the wings, a mirror and a light will, of course, be needed. Obviously,

the mirror must be securely anchored so that it won't be inadvertently knocked over in the rush of making the change. The makeup box shown in Figure 19–2 provides a very practical solution to the problem. The makeup needed for the change can be put into the compartments in the box, which can then be set up on the table in the wings. The various makeup items can be left in the box or removed and arranged on the table—whichever is more convenient. If spirit gum is being used, the bottle should be set into one of the Woochie spirit-gum-bottle holders illustrated in Appendix A. After the change has been made, the makeup box can be returned to the dressing room by the assistant stage manager.

If beards or mustaches are required for quick changes, obviously they should be made in advance. Ideally, they should be ventilated into a net foundation. But if that isn't possible, they can be constructed of crepe or synthetic hair on a latex foundation, which can be removed and reattached with spirit gum. For greater strength and durability, a lightweight fabric or netting can be built into the foundation by pressing it into the latex, then applying additional coats of latex over it.

If the style or the color of the hair is to be changed,

FIGURE **19–2** *MAKEUP BOX.*

the change can usually be accomplished most efficiently with a wig, which should, of course, be dressed and placed on a wig stand within easy reach. The back of the wig should be facing the actor so that he can grasp it easily by the bottom corners of the foundation, using both hands, and slip it on over his own hair in a matter of seconds.

The use of makeup crayons, can speed up the quick change considerably.

Planning and Rehearsing the Change The actual step-by-step procedure for making a quick change should always be carefully planned and rehearsed as often as necessary. The planning is normally done by the actor, though if he is working with a makeup artist, they can do it together. It should include not only making a detailed outline of the change, noting each step in order, but also listing all materials to be used and making a notation (or a diagram) to indicate where on the makeup table each item is to be placed. That will depend largely on whether you are right- or left-handed, the order in which each item is to be used, and, if you are methodical, your customary placement of the various items on your makeup table. It is important, for maximum efficiency, that you know where each item is and not have to search for it.

When the change is being rehearsed, it should be timed. If it's too long, additional simplifications and short-cuts may be necessary. Rehearsing the change will, of course, reduce the time somewhat. A quick change should always be rehearsed until you *know* you can make it, preferably with time to spare.

ONSTAGE CHANGES

Occasionally, quick changes take place onstage, and more often than not, the change consists of removing a disguise. If the disguise is intended to fool the audience as well as the other characters and to astonish them with its removal, it is obviously essential that the makeup be convincing and that it be removed as quickly as possible. Wigs, beards, mustaches, and false eyebrows can provide dramatic changes in the appearance and can be removed rather quickly. Latex pieces can also be used, though removing them may leave the face rather messy. If you are onstage very long after the removal and have no way to clean up your face, this could prove distracting to the audience.

The time available for putting the makeup on can be a determining factor in the decision as to what kind of makeup to use and how much. If it has to be a quick change—that is, if the character has already appeared as himself and in the next act (or even in the same act) has to reappear in the disguise—the possibilities are limited, and one is more likely to rely on wigs, beards, and mustaches than on latex pieces. How much additional makeup, highlighting, shadowing, rouging, etc., is done will depend not only on the time available for putting it on but on how effectively it can be removed onstage.

A good disguise, of course, does not have to be complicated. By choosing the elements of the disguise carefully and applying them skillfully, you can achieve a makeup that is both simple and effective.

DOUBLE MAKEUPS

An alternative technique for making a quick change when only two makeups are involved is to do one makeup on top of the other and to make the change by removing the top makeup (the one the audience will see first), revealing the one underneath.

Lubricating-Jelly Separation The under-makeup can be done very much as it would be if there were no quick change involved. It must, however, be done with creme makeup, greasepaint, or rubber-mask grease. Water-soluble makeup (cake makeup, liquid makeup, or Kryolan's Vitacolor) cannot be used. The makeup, including highlights, shadows, rouge, and stippling (if used) is powdered as usual. Three-dimensional additions to this first makeup (including false eyebrows, beard, and mustache) should not be used unless they are also appropriate for the makeup that is to cover it or can be added to the under-makeup in the time available after the top makeup has been removed. With false eyebrows, beards, and mustaches, that may be possible. With other three-dimensional additions (such as putty

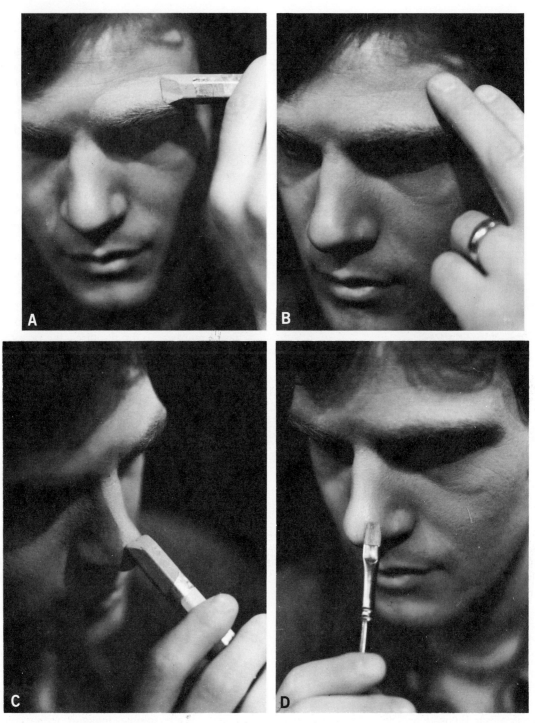

FIGURE *19—3* HIGHLIGHTING WITH MAKEUP CRAYONS. *(Actor Eugene Bicknell.) A. Highlighting the superciliary bone. B. Blending the highlight with the fingers. C. Highlighting the nose. D. Blending the highlight.*

or latex noses), it usually is not. The natural eyebrows can, however, be covered in the under-makeup (if they are inappropriate for either makeup), and eyebrows can be painted on with water-soluble makeup in the top makeup. Either three-dimensional or painted eyebrows can then be added to the first makeup after the second makeup has been removed.

In any case, when the under-makeup has been powdered, it is coated with lubricating jelly (see Appendix A). When the jelly is dry, the top makeup is carefully applied over the one which has just been completed.

For this top makeup, a water-soluble makeup works particularly well. It is possible, though not desirable, to use a cream or grease makeup; but if you do, an extra-heavy coating of lubricating jelly may be needed to facilitate removal. The makeup, water-soluble or not, should be applied with a sponge by pressing the sponge firmly against the skin with a stippling motion instead of stroking it across the face, since that might smear the makeup underneath. If one coat is insufficient to conceal dark areas of the under makeup, additional coats can be added. Highlights, shadows, and rouge can be applied very gently with a brush, and stippling can be done with a stipple-sponge as usual. Even when you are using water-soluble makeup, creme rouge can be used on the lips and then carefully wiped off as the first step in making the quick change. It is best not to coat the lips with lubricating jelly to facilitate removal, since the removal might occur gradually and unintentionally during the performance.

If painted (rather than three-dimensional) eyebrows are to be used, it's best to apply them with a brush. An eyebrow pencil *can* be used; but if it is, make sure to stroke it on very gently so that the point of the pencil does not penetrate the coating of lubricating jelly. If the natural eyebrows are used and require makeup, they can be darkened with a brush or a pencil.

In making the change, the top makeup, including the water-soluble jelly, is removed with water. It is, of course, essential to have either a sink or a large basin of clean, tepid water to lean over as this is being done.

When the top makeup has been removed, the face should be blotted very gently with tissues to dry it. The under-makeup can then be retouched, if necessary, re-powdered, and any details, such as false eyebrows or a mustache, added.

The 1–2–1 Variation If there is a change from one makeup to another, and then a change back to the first makeup, the procedure will be much the same as for a single quick change except that the actor will appear in the first makeup to be applied before covering it with the second. For the reappearance in the first makeup, the second makeup will be removed, revealing the first one. Other variations can be devised, depending on the demands of a particular play or a particular production.

20

Sex Reversals

Men and women may reverse sexes in theatrical productions because the script requires it (Rosalind, Portia), because it has become an established convention (Kabuki Theater), because the particular production requires it (see Figure 20–1), because the performer chooses to do it (female impersonators), or because the director has arbitrarily decided to have a particular character played by the performer of the opposite sex (Lady Bracknell played by a man).

MEN AS WOMEN

A successful male-to-female makeup change requires, first of all, careful casting. An actor with a strong chin and a rugged jaw line cannot—no matter how handsome he is—be transformed into a convincingly pretty girl. Beard shadows can be concealed, eyebrows can be thinned, and lips can be painted on, but little can be done about a bone structure that is too aggressively masculine—except, of course, to create a strong-faced woman. Given an actor with a less aggressively masculine bone structure, however, a convincingly female face is not difficult to achieve. The basic approach is to follow the general principles of female corrective or character makeup, noting a few special problems.

Eyebrows If the eyebrows are too wide, as they usually are, they can be narrowed and reshaped by blocking out part of them and leaving whatever part you want to keep for the new eyebrows, or by completely blocking them out and painting on new ones, as was done for the makeup in Figure 20–1D. For instructions in blocking out eyebrows, see Chapter 12.

Beard Shadow An actor playing a female part should shave immediately before applying his makeup. Then, if any trace of beard shadow remains, it can be counteracted with an application of creme makeup or greasepaint a few shades lighter than the foundation to be used. This beard cover should be well powdered and the excess powder dusted off before the foundation is applied. A creme, cake, or greasepaint foundation can be used over the beard cover, but it should be sponged or patted on, not stroked on, in order to avoid smearing the beard cover.

Lips Techniques for changing the shape of the lips are described in Chapters 10 and 12.

Hair If the actor's hair is not long enough, or if for some other reason (a receding hairline, for example) it cannot be suitably dressed for the female character, a wig can be worn.

WOMEN AS MEN

When women are made up as men, the changes required may involve facial structure, coloring, hair, and the possible addition of beards and mustaches.

Facial Structure Since curves tend to make a face look more feminine, and angles more masculine, making curved lines more angular and exaggerating whatever angular features the woman already has will help to give a more masculine look.

The angle of the jaw can be modeled with highlights and shadows to give it a less rounded and more muscular look; and the chin, if it is softly rounded, can be similarly "corrected" to appear more angular. The nose, if it is small and feminine, can be built up with nose putty to make it look more masculine. However, using corrective makeup for lengthening or broadening or both may give

FIGURE *20–1* SIX CHARACTERS FROM THE BALL SCENE IN PATRIOT FOR ME. *A. Peter Colley as Salome. B. Bryan Young as the Tsarina. C. Warren Burton as a Lady of Fashion. D. Tom Tammi as a Medieval Lady. E. Carl Jessop as Marie Antoinette. F. Luis Cepero as a Shepherdess.*

Preliminary designs were based on the costume sketches of Freddy Wittop, following consultation with the actors and the director. Final makeups were the result of work with the actors and observations of the effects during dress rehearsals. Throughout the run of the play off Broadway, the actors did their own makeups, following the final approved designs.

FIGURE 20–2 MAKING UP AS MADAME TUSSAUD. *Makeup by student Joe Allen Brown. A. Applying the foundation with creme stick. The eyebrows have been blocked out with Kryolan's Eyebrow Plastic, and the nose has been built up with nose putty. Since the face was cleanshaven, no special makeup was required to cover it. B, C, D, and E. Modeling the face with highlights and shadow. F. Giving the neck a final touch-up.*

FIGURE 20–3 THE QUEEN OF HEARTS FROM ALICE IN WONDERLAND. *(For other makeups on and by the same actor, see Figure 12–80.)*

FIGURE 20–4 **PENCIL DRAWINGS FOR MALE CHARACTER MAKEUPS ON A FEMALE FACE.** *A. Corrective makeup from Figure 10–1A. B, C. Male makeups that could be done on the same face by cutting and restyling or covering the hair, changing the shape of the nose, modeling with highlights and shadows, and adding a mustache and, in B, a small beard.*

the nose a sufficiently masculine look—at least from the front—without using nose putty. It will, of course, have no effect on the profile.

A softly rounded forehead can be made to look more masculine by highlighting the frontal bone to give it greater prominence and by shadowing the inner corners of the eye socket just below the frontal bone. Lightly shadowing the infratemporal area may also be helpful in squaring off a rounded forehead. Emphasizing the cheekbones by modeling them with highlights and shadows can also be useful in creating a more angular face.

Coloring The foundation color should, of course, be darker than is usually used for women. If a beard is not going to be worn, a slight beard shadow will give a more masculine look. (See Chapter 15.) If you use color in the cheeks, apply it as you would for men. It is usually better not to use color on the lips.

Eyeshadow and eyelash makeup should also be avoided. The eyebrows should not be darkened excessively, but they nearly always need to be made fuller. A slight angle in the brow will give a more masculine look than a soft curve. Experiment with various eyebrow shapes before deciding which one is most effective. Eyebrows can sometimes be reshaped convincingly by filling them out with an eyebrow pencil applied very carefully with a sketching technique, using short, light strokes to give the effect of natural hair. If this doesn't prove satisfactory, crepe hair eyebrows or, preferably, real-hair eyebrows ventilated on lace can be used.

Beards and Mustaches When appropriate, beards and mustaches can, of course, be very helpful in achieving a masculine look. They can be constructed of crepe hair; but real or synthetic hair, ventilated on lace, is preferable. (For instructions in making beards and mustaches, see Chapter 15.)

Hair The hair style should, of course, be one that is appropriate for men—or for the particular man being portrayed. A wig may or may not be required. For short hair with sideburns, a hand-made lace-front wig may be necessary. If the hair can be longer and need not have close-cropped sideburns, a good ready-made men's stretch wig with synthetic hair may be satisfactory. If the actress's hair is too long to be concealed under a wig, it may have to be cut—either in a style appropriate for the character or merely short enough to be concealed under a wig appropriate for the character.

PLANNING THE MAKEUP

In planning a sex-reversal makeup, it's a good idea to make pencil drawings of the character on tracing paper, over a photograph of the actor or actress in order to make sure, first of all, that an effective makeup can be done, and secondly, what actually needs to be done. This will save a great deal of time in experimenting on the face with various makeup possibilities. (See Figure 20–4.)

Makeup Materials

The following pages contain an alphabetical listing of materials from various makeup companies. The materials can be obtained directly from the companies, from makeup supply houses, or occasionally from your local drugstore. Addresses of the makeup companies and various distributors of their makeup are listed in Appendix B.

Absorbent Cotton   Used for stuffing in the cheeks to enlarge them and for building up the face, neck, or hands in combination with spirit gum or latex.

Accent Colors   Colors used to "accent" the face, such as rouge, lipstick, and eye makeup, or to decorate it— as in clown, Kabuki, or other stylized makeups. Bright reds, oranges, yellows, blues, greens, purples, and all metallic colors are in this category. These are available from the various makeup companies in creme makeup, cake makeup, and greasepaint and are listed, in their brochures, under various headings—*Lining Colors, Creative Colors, Rouge, Lipstick, Eyeshadow, Pressed Shadow,* and so forth.

Acetone   A clear liquid solvent for plastic film, sealer, collodion, and spirit gum. Since it evaporates very rapidly, it should be kept tightly sealed. Obtainable at drugstores or much more reasonably by the gallon from beauty supply houses, which usually label it "nail polish remover." Avoid breathing the fumes, and keep it away from the eyes.

Adhesives   Spirit gum is the adhesive most frequently used in makeup. (See *Spirit Gum.*) Johnson & Johnson's Duo Surgical Adhesive is used for stippling to help conceal edges of prosthetic pieces and wig blenders. Kryolan's *Stoppelpaste* is a wax adhesive for beard stubble (see *Stubble Paste*). Dicor Adhesives 209 (paste) and 210 (liquid) are used largely in prosthesis. Appliance adhesives are available from Joe Blasco.

Spirit gum can be obtained from any makeup supply house, Duo Adhesive from drugstores, *Stoppelpaste* from the various Kryolan distributors and Alcone, and Dicor and Medico from the sources listed in Appendix B.

Adhesive Tape   Occasionally used to draw the skin in order to change the shape of the eyes or the mouth or to construct false Oriental or sagging eyelids. A clear plastic tape called *Dermacil* is available in drugstores in ½-inch and 1-inch widths.

Kryolan has a clear plastic tape in ½-inch and 2-inch widths as well as an unusually effective double-faced adhesive tape, which comes in large and small rolls and is made with a very thin layer of strong adhesive on a brown paper tape. When the tape has been pressed into place, the brown paper is peeled off, leaving the adhesive. In using the tape, *tear* off the length you want— don't cut it. Tearing the tape makes it much easier to separate the tape from the brown paper. The same type of tape is also available from Bob Kelly and other wigmakers in precut, short strips packaged in small plastic boxes for the convenience of toupee wearers who want to carry a small supply of tape with them.

All Kryolan tapes are available from Alcone and from the various Kryolan distributors. Both cloth and plastic toupee tape can be obtained from wigmakers, and both can be used to attach mustaches and beards for quick changes, as well as to secure toupees.

Age Stipple   Liquid latex for wrinkling the skin. It can be applied (using a stippling technique) with a red-rubber sponge or with any soft synthetic sponge. It should *not* be applied with a black stipple sponge. It should be allowed to dry with the skin stretched, then powdered. Available from Ben Nye.

Alcohol   Rubbing alcohol can be used to remove spirit gum. Obtainable at drugstores.

Alfalfa Seeds   Can be used with gelatine or latex for such three-dimensional constructions as moles or scabs. (See Chapter 13.) Obtainable at natural-food stores.

Alginate   A nonreusable impression powder for making molds. Available from dental supply houses and from Alcone. (See also *Moulage.*)

Aquacolor Wet Makeup   A Kryolan moist cake makeup. Available in three sizes and many shades. There is also a water-soluble, nonmetallic makeup in gold, silver, copper, and bronze, called *Aquacolor-Interferenz.* Both have excellent coverage. (See also *Cake Makeup.*)

Artificial Snow   A remarkably effective instant artificial snow, which is sprayed from an aerosal can, is available from Joe Blasco. Although artificial snow is more likely to be used on props or costumes, it can also be used on beards or hair, from which it can be removed by shaking it off, brushing it off, or combing it out.

Ash Powder   Simulates ash for makeup or costume aging. Available from Ben Nye.

Atomizers   Useful for spraying brilliantine on the hair, diluted spirit gum on crepe hair to help it hold its shape, and alcohol on the face and on rubber pieces to remove spirit gum.

Bandoline   A thick, hair-setting liquid.

Base Colors   See *Foundation Colors.*

Beard Block   (See Figure 15–13.) A shaped wooden block used in ventilating beards. Available from wigmakers' supply houses. A plastic beard block mounted on an aluminum pipe is available from Bob Kelly. (See Figure 15–6.) A plaster cast of the actor's head can be substituted if no beard block is available or if a more nearly perfect fit is required. The hairlace can be taped to the plaster with masking tape. If you want to attach the plaster head to a wig-block holder, embed a 1-inch pipe into the plaster while it is still wet—the pipe will fit over a standard holder. For temporary use, a pipe might be taped to the back of the cast.

Beards   Instructions for making beards can be found in Chapter 15. Excellent ready-made ventilated beards and mustaches are available from Kryolan. (See Figure A–1, A–2.) Ready-made beards can also be purchased

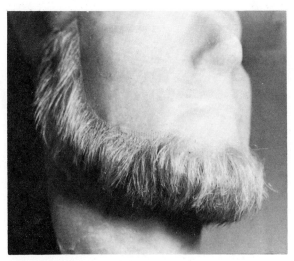

FIGURE *A–1* READY-MADE BEARD.   *Available from Kryolan.*

FIGURE *A–2* READY-MADE GOATEE.   *Available from Kryolan.*

from some wigmakers and costumers. Made-to-order beards are available from Bob Kelly.

Beard Stubble Adhesive   An adhesive wax in stick form used to attach beard stubble for an unshaven effect. It is made by Kryolan and is available from their distributors. Bob Kelly has a somewhat similar product called *Beard Stubble Adhesive Stick.*

Black Wax   Used for blocking out teeth. It is softened in the hand, then applied to the teeth to be blocked out after they have been dried with a tissue. It can also be used to block out parts of teeth to make them appear broken or uneven. It can be removed with a dry tissue. Black tooth enamel (see *Tooth Enamel*) serves the same purpose. Using black eyebrow pencil as a substitute for black wax is discussed in Chapter 12. Black wax is available from Mehron and Bob Kelly and also from Paramount and most other makeup distributors.

Blemish-Cover Sticks These are small makeup sticks in lipstick cases used to cover skin blemishes or minimize wrinkles. They usually come in a limited number of shades, ranging from light to medium flesh tones. The lighter shades can also be used for highlighting. They are particularly useful for quick changes (see Chapter 19). Bob Kelly's is called *Blot-out,* and Kryolan's is called *Erase.*

Blending Powder See *Face Powder.*

Blood, Artificial Stage blood can be classified into two categories, according to the use to which it is to be put—external (used outside the body) or internal (flowing from the mouth). External blood should never be used internally. For internal blood, gelatine capsules, obtainable from your local pharmacist in various sizes, can be filled with blood formulated specifically for internal use, held in the mouth, then crushed at the appropriate time to release the blood. (For certain external uses, capsules of blood can be held in the hand and crushed.) In deciding which brand of blood to use, you should consider the ease with which the blood can be removed from costumes and from the skin. Some brands of blood can be wiped off the skin easily without leaving a stain, whereas others leave a temporary stain, which can be removed with soap and water. Consider also the thickness of the blood and how believable it looks as it runs on the skin. The color, of course, should also be believable. Artificial blood is obtainable from the makeup companies and their distributors. Ben Nye's and Mehron's are both called *Stage Blood.* Joe Blasco's and Bob Kelly's are called *Artificial Blood.* Kryolan has several types—blood for external use, blood for internal use, blood for bloodshot eyes, washable blood, thick blood, packets of blood (external and internal), capsules of powdered blood (internal), and plastic blood in tubes (called *Fixblut*) for a dried blood effect. The *Fixblut* dries quickly, does not rub off, and is removed with acetone. Kryolan also has what they call *Magic Blood,* consisting of two reacting chemicals, both liquid, one of which is applied to the skin and allowed to dry. Then, at whatever point the other liquid touches it, the two chemicals combine and turn dark red. This might be used, for example, by applying one liquid to the skin and the other to a dull knife blade, then drawing the blade lightly across the skin to create the effect of a cut. Magic Blood should, however, be used cautiously. *It is not a toy, it should not be played with, and it should not be used by children. It should never be used near the eyes or any mucous membranes. It should be applied only on normal, healthy skin, and it should be removed thoroughly after use.*

For blood coming from the mouth, Batson's *Blood* (mint flavored and formulated specifically for use in the mouth) is excellent in both color and consistency. Red toothpaste can also be used. Mixing it with adhesive powder for false teeth will produce an effect of dried blood.

Blot-out Bob Kelly's blemish-cover stick. (See *Blemish-Cover Sticks.*)

Body Makeup Available as an opaque liquid, a transparent liquid, or a powder. Opaque liquid body makeup is a greaseless foundation comparable to cake makeup except that it is in liquid form. It can be obtained from the various makeup companies and their distributors in a variety of shades. It is applied with a sponge and is removable with soap and water or makeup remover.

Hanz-N-Neck, a body makeup by Joe Blasco, does not rub off on costumes and is designed especially for use on the hands and the neck.

Kryolan has a special makeup called *Liquid Brightness*—a nonmetallic makeup that can be mixed with other liquid body makeups to make the skin glisten. Kryolan also has a transparent liquid called *Exotenteint,* and Bob Kelly has one called *Body Makeup Tint.* Transparent liquid makeup is intended only for coloring the skin and does not cover blemishes or provide a foundation for other makeup, though other types of makeup can be used over it. The color can be varied by adding food coloring. It is also possible to make a transparent liquid body makeup by simply adding food coloring to water.

Kryolan's *Body Makeup Powder* is applied with a damp sponge and dries rather quickly. Rubbing it slightly after it is dry will produce a natural-looking sheen. It is available in 33 shades. (See also *Texas Dirt* and *Metallic Makeup.*)

Bran Can be used with latex for creating rough skin texture (see Chapter 13). Miller's bran—not processed cereals—should be used. It is obtainable at natural-food stores.

Brilliantine Can be used to give a sheen to the hair. After the brilliantine has been sprayed on, the hair should be combed or brushed. Sprays and commercial hair dressings are more frequently used.

Brush Cleaner A liquid for cleaning brushes. Available from Ben Nye and his distributors in three sizes. The 2-ounce size is convenient to have on the makeup table for cleaning brushes as you work. If you want to economize, you can buy a larger bottle and refill the small bottle from it or simply use it to fill a suitable container of

FIGURE A–3 BEN NYE'S BRUSH CLEANER.

your own. Large-size bottles (16-ounce) are available from both Ben Nye and Joe Blasco.

Brushes, Chinese or Japanese (See Figure A–4F.) Watercolor brushes with a fine, sharp point, useful in accenting wrinkles. Obtainable at art supply stores and in some Oriental shops.

Brushes, Dye (See Figure A–4H.) Available in various forms. Some are shaped like toothbrushes and can be used for applying spirit-gum remover to hairlace in removing wigs, toupees, beards, and mustaches. Available from Bob Kelly.

Brushes, Eyebrow (See Figure A–4I.) Used for brushing the eyebrows. Available from Joe Blasco, Mehron, Kryolan, and Bob Kelly. Eyebrow brushes combined with tiny eyebrow combs (Figure A–4J) are also available.

Brushes, Eyeliner High-quality, sable eyeliner brushes are available from Joe Blasco and from Kryolan. The handle of the Blasco brush is shorter and rounded at the end—a worthwhile safety factor when working around the eyes.

Brushes, Eyeshadow (Figure A–4K.) Small, soft brushes used to apply pressed eyeshadow. They are also useful for applying dry rouge in small areas, such as wrinkles.

Brushes, Lip (See Figure A–4E.) Narrow flat brushes used for applying lip rouge. Mehron and Kryolan have excellent short-handled sable ones. Joe Blasco has a retractable lip brush in a metal case.

Brushes, Mascara Small, stiff-bristled brushes for applying mascara.

Brushes, Moulage Used for applying moulage in casting. Available from Paramount. Other kinds of brushes can, however, be used for the same purpose.

Brushes, Powder and Rouge (See Figure A–4M and L.) Available from Ben Nye, Mehron, Kryolan, and Bob Kelly. The quality of powder and rouge brushes can be judged to a very large extent by the softness of the bristles.

Brushes, Shading (See Figure A–4A,B,N, and O.) Several flat—preferably sable—brushes of various widths are practically indispensable in doing character makeups. The bristles should be fine, tapered, and very springy. Kryolan has excellent ones in a good range of widths (see Figure 12–2). Their extremely useful extra-wide, short-bristled sable brush (Figure A–4A) is particularly noteworthy. Kryolan brushes are available from their distributors. Joe Blasco also has excellent sable brushes in several widths and with both long and short handles. Two of the brushes (one long-handled and one short-handled) have wedge-cut bristles. These are especially useful for modeling nasolabial folds, for highlighting and shadowing around the eyes, and for modeling forehead wrinkles. Sable brushes can also be obtained from art supply stores. The often inconveniently long handles can be cut down if you wish. Good quality flat synthetic brushes are available from Ben Nye in six widths and from Bob Kelly in two. Ben Nye has round red-sable brushes in four sizes, and Bob Kelly has synthetic ones in two sizes.

Brushes, Utility (See Figure A–4G.) Can be used to apply sealer, spirit gum, or collodion. They are available from Bob Kelly or at artists' supply stores.

Burnt Cork Used for minstrel makeup only. Available from some makeup supply houses.

Cake Makeup A greaseless, water-soluble foundation that is applied with a dampened sponge. There are two types—dry and moist. Kryolan makes a moist type called *Aquacolor.* (See *Aquacolor Wet Makeup.*) Blending highlights and shadows is somewhat easier with moist cake makeup than with dry. The moist type is also better for stippling. Dry cake makeup is available from Mehron, Kryolan, Grimas, and Kelly. In judging costs, be sure to check comparative net weights.

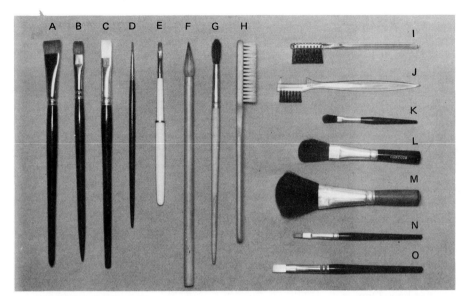

*FIGURE **A—4** BRUSHES.* A-B. *Long-handled flat sable brushes (Kryolan). C. Long-handled flat synthetic brush (Ben Nye). D. Long-handled pointed sable brush (Kryolan). E. Sable lip brush in white plastic holder (Kryolan). F. Pointed Chinese water-color brush. G. Camel's hair utility brush (Bob Kelly). H. Brush for cleaning hairlace. I. Eyebrow brush. J. Eyebrow brush-and-comb (Kryolan). K. Soft brush for applying dry eyeshadow. L. Contour or rouge brush. M. Powder brush (Mehron). N. Short-handled flat sable brush. O. Short-handled flat synthetic brush (Bob Kelly).*

Camouflage Creme See *Dermacolor* and *Cosmediflo.*

Castor Oil Can be mixed with ground-up cake makeup to make a rather sticky rubber-mask greasepaint. Because castor oil does not rot rubber, it is safe to use on latex.

Chamois Can be used to press down the net in attaching hairlace wigs, beards, and mustaches with spirit gum. Can also be used in applying crepe hair. Available at most art supply, paint, or hardware stores.

Chiffon Used for covering the eyebrows when blocking them out (see Chapter 12).

Chromaflo A Joe Blasco liquid facial and body makeup. It is applied with a damp sea sponge and is water-resistant.

Clay See *Modeling Clay.*

Cleansing Cream See *Makeup Removers.*

Cleansing Tissues Indispensable for removing makeup. They can also be used for creating three-dimensional skin texture (see Chapter 13).

Clown White An opaque white paint used primarily for clowns. Available from Ben Nye, Mehron, and Bob Kelly.

Cold-Foam Systems Two types are available from Kryolan—the Hagen Foam System (#8010), for a rigid foam with a latex skin, and the 2-Part Cold Foam System (#8040), for a soft foam appropriate for facial and body appliances requiring flexibility.

Collodion A clear, viscous solution of cellulose nitrates in alcohol and ether. There are two types of collodion—

*FIGURE **A—5** GRIMAS CAKE MAKEUP.*

flexible and nonflexible. The nonflexible type is used directly on the skin for making scars or pock marks (see Chapter 13). It can be diluted with acetone. It is available from Kryolan, Mehron, and Bob Kelly. Mehron also has nonflexible collodion. Collodion can be peeled off the skin or removed with acetone.

Combs   A wide-toothed comb is used for combing out crepe hair and wigs. The kit should also contain a comb to be used for hair with temporary coloring in it, one to be used with clean hair, and a rat-tail comb. Eyebrow combs and brushes combined (Figure A–4J) are available from Kryolan.

Cornmeal   Can be used with latex for creating three-dimensional skin texture (see Chapter 13).

Cornstarch   Formerly used for graying the hair. One of the hair whiteners (see *Hair Whiteners*) should be used instead. For quick-change makeups or when the gray must be removed during the play, it may be necessary to use white face powder, which, though not satisfactory, is preferable to cornstarch.

Cosmediflo   A highly pigmented liquid makeup for covering skin discolorations. Available from Joe Blasco in 10 colors, but can be made up, on special order, in any of the Joe Blasco professional foundation colors.

Cotton Swabs   Cotton-tipped sticks (such as Q-Tips), used for removing small areas of makeup when correcting mistakes or making minor adjustments and sometimes for blending or for applying dry rouge to small areas. They can also be used in applying latex to open molds and for removing excess latex from them.

Crayons   A creme makeup in crayon form. It has the advantage of giving a somewhat more matte finish than does most creme makeup. It can be applied directly with the crayon or transferred from the crayon to the face with either the fingers or a brush, as with regular creme makeup. The crayons are very convenient for modeling the face with highlights and shadows, especially when it must be done quickly. (See Figures 9–3 and 19–3.) (See also *Creme Makeup*.)

Creme Makeup   A velvety, nongreasy makeup foundation applied with the fingers or (for highlights and shadows) with a brush. There are those who prefer to use a foam sponge for applying it as a foundation. (For applying creme makeup, see Chapter 9.)

Crepe Hair   Used for making beards and mustaches and occasionally eyebrows. There are two types—crepe-wool and human crepe hair. Crepe wool comes in tightly

FIGURE A–6 *CREME MAKEUP.*
Bob Kelly's Cremestick.

woven braids and is usually purchased by the yard. It is available from most of the makeup companies and their distributors in such colors as blond, auburn, light brown, medium brown, dark brown, light gray, and medium gray. Human crepe hair is available from Kryolan and its distributors.

Datex   A de-ammoniated appliance adhesive. Available from Joe Blasco.

Dep   A thick, hair-setting liquid. Available from beauty supply houses.

Dermaceal   A highly pigmented, waterproof makeup by Joe Blasco for covering skin discolorations, scars, birthmarks, burns, etc. It is available in 10 colors but can be made up to order in any color in the Joe Blasco line. It can be worn on the street as well as on the stage. It should be applied with one's finger rather than with a brush.

Dermacolor   A very effective camouflage creme by Kryolan. It is designed primarily for street wear for both men and women to cover skin discolorations, such as birthmarks or uneven pigmentation. It can also be used for the stage to cover temporary or permanent skin discolorations difficult to cover with most stage makeup. It can be used as a foundation color over the entire face or applied only to the discolored areas, then covered with stage makeup for the overall foundation. It has been used successfully by actors who are allergic to other kinds of makeup, and it has the additional advantage of being waterproof. It can also be used as a foundation color by black actors with very dark skins when they want to achieve a much lighter skin tone. If you are uncertain about what shade you should have, there are two very

FIGURE ***A—7*** *CREME MAKEUP.* A. *Ben Nye's Creme Foundation.* B. *Joe Blasco's Creme Base and Shading Color.*

handy mini-palettes, each containing 16 of the available colors. If no one color is exactly right, you can experiment with mixing the colors in the palette and order the ones you require. Palette D/1 is designed primarily for street wear and D/2, for theatrical use.

Dermatex A Joe Blasco foundation makeup for use on prosthetic appliances. Available in 40 colors. It does not need to be powdered, and it will not rub off on costumes.

Derma Wax A soft wax for building up areas of the face. It is easier to apply and to remove than nose putty but is less adhesive. It can also be mixed with nose putty as explained in Chapter 13. It is available from the various makeup companies and their distributors. Ben Nye's Nose and Scar Wax is a mixture of derma wax and putty. (See *Putty-Wax.*) Kryolan has a special wax for street wear (called Dermacolor Skin Plastic) for concealing scars. The wax is then covered with Dermacolor makeup.

Drawing Mats (See Figure 16–15A.) Used in wig-making for drawing hair.

Duo Adhesive A Johnson & Johnson creme latex adhesive. Obtainable in drugstores. Will eventually deteriorate in the tube.

Dye Brushes See *Brushes, Dye.*

Equipoise A pre-base lotion for dry skin, available from Joe Blasco.

Erase Kryolan's blemish-cover stick. (See *Blemish-Cover Sticks.*)

Eyebrow Brushes See *Brushes, Eyebrow.*

Eyebrow Pencils Wooden pencils with soft grease lead used for darkening the eyebrows. (See *Makeup Pencils.*)

Eyebrow-Pencil Sharpeners Because ordinary pencil sharpeners are not really satisfactory for eyebrow pencils, special eyebrow-pencil sharpeners should be used. Particularly well-designed ones are available from Kryolan. Other eyebrow-pencil sharpeners can be obtained at most cosmetics counters. For giving pencils a flat cut, a single-edged razor blade or a sharp mat knife can be used.

Eyebrow Plastic (Figure A–8) A firm wax in stick form for blocking out eyebrows. For further information and additional illustrations, see *Eyebrow Plastic* in the index. Available from Kryolan distributors, Grimas, and Paramount.

Eyelashes, False Used for straight or corrective eye makeup. They should usually be trimmed before using. Sometimes each lash can be cut in half to make a pair (see Chapter 10). Lashes with a feathered look are available and tend to look more natural. False eyelashes can be obtained from Kryolan, Paramount, or any cosmetics counter. They are applied with special eyelash adhesive or with Duo Adhesive.

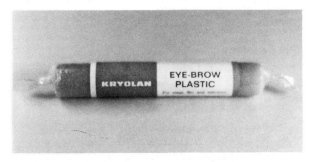

FIGURE ***A—8*** *KRYOLAN'S EYE-BROW PLASTIC.*

Eyeliner Brush   A narrow brush suitable for lining the eyes. Very good sable eyeliner brushes are available from the various makeup companies and their distributors.

Eyeliners   Water-soluble cake eyeliners are available in several colors. Liquid eyeliners are also available.

Eyeshadow   Available in creme and brush-on cakes and sometimes sticks. Kryolan's creme eyeshadows are also available in a palette containing 16 shades. Brush-on cake eyeshadows (available from Ben Nye and Joe Blasco) can be applied with either a dry or a wet brush.

Face Powder   Used over creme or grease makeup. It comes in a variety of tints and shades, most of which are unnecessary. A translucent face powder, the purpose of which is to cause less distortion in makeup colors than the regular powders, is available from the various makeup companies and their distributors. Most translucent powders, unfortunately, have some darkening effect when used over white or very light colors. Mehron's *Colorset*, however, has relatively little and is, therefore, recommended for any makeup in which there are light highlights. A similar product (*Transparentpowder*) is available from Grimas.

Tinted powders are available from Kryolan and from Ben Nye.

If you want to add a satiny sheen to your makeup, Kryolan also has an effective nonmetallic powder (*Satinpuder*), available in four colors—pearl, gold, yellowish, and silver. Before using *Satinpuder* over a makeup, experiment with it over a patch of the foundation color on your hand or your arm in order to determine what the effect will be. You might, in fact, experiment with trying whatever *Satinpuder* colors you have over a variety of makeup colors for possible future use in nonrealistic makeups.

FIGURE A–9 EYESHADOW. *Joe Blasco's brush-on cake eyeshadow.*

False Eyelashes   See *Eyelashes, False.*

Fixative A   A very useful liquid plastic sealer made by Mehron. (See *Sealer.*)

Foam-Latex System (McLaughlin's)   A foam-latex system developed by makeup artist Tom McLaughlin that produces a soft, low-shrinkage foam. There are four components—the latex, a curing agent, a foaming agent, and a gelling agent. It can be cast in plaster, silicone, fiberglass, or metal molds. The first three components are blended at high speed for 1 minute, then at slow speed for 2 minutes. The gelling agent is then added, and the mixture is blended at slow speed for an additional minute before being poured into the mold, which is then put into a 200°F oven for 2 hours. Available from Alcone Company, Inc.

Formalose   A reusable moulage that can be liquefied by adding it to boiling water. See *Negative Moulage Mold* in Chapter 14. Available from Kryolan.

Foundation Colors   Colors used to provide an appropriate skin color for the character and to serve as a foundation for *contour* and *accent* colors. Foundation colors are available in creme makeup, cake makeup, and greasepaint in a wide range of flesh colors. Foundation colors are also known as *base* colors.

Gauze, Surgical   Can be dipped in plaster and used over negative moulage molds. Available in drugstores and surgical supply houses.

Gauze, Wigmakers'   A thin, tough foundation material for wigs and beards. It is usually available in various qualities and grades. Can be obtained from wigmakers' supply houses and from Kryolan. The Kryolan gauze is available in both silk and polyester, both of excellent quality. The silk is considerably stiffer than the polyester.

Gelatine   Can be used for certain types of quick three-dimensional work (see Chapter 13). Available in grocery stores, boxed in envelopes, each containing 1 tablespoon of powdered gelatine.

Glatzan L.   See *Plastic Film, Liquid.*

Glitter   Available from Kryolan in a variety of colors, including gold and silver and in three forms—powder, tiny bits, and stars. The glitter can be easily attached by coating the skin with Glitter Gel, then transferring the glitter to the gel-coated area with a soft brush.

Glitter Gel A transparent gel for attaching glitter directly to the skin or over makeup. It can be applied with the fingers and removed with water.

Glycerine Can be brushed or sponged onto the body to make it shine or used as a base for metallic powders. The powders can be either patted on over the glycerine or mixed with it before it is applied. Mehron has a *Mixing Liquid* that can be used with metallic powders as well as with other dry pigments. Glycerine can be obtained at drugstores, and the *Mixing Liquid* is available from Mehron and their distributors. (See also *Metallic Makeup.*)

Greaseless Makeup See *Cake Makeup* and *Body Makeup.*

Greasepaint The traditional foundation paint used to give the basic skin coloring. It is made in a variety of colors and in both a soft and a hard consistency. Mehron's soft, lanolin-enriched foundation paint comes in the same type of container as their cake makeup. Kryolan's soft greasepaint comes in convenient plastic cases in three sizes. Kryolan also has greasepaint sticks in two sizes. (See also *Shading Colors* and *Creme Makeup.*)

Greasepaint (including rubber-mask greasepaint) deteriorates with age. If any makeup smells rancid, throw it out.

Hackle (See Figure 16–18.) An instrument combining the functions of a comb and a brush, constructed of metal spikes in a wooden block, used for combing or untangling skeins of hair. Available from Paramount.

Hair, Crepe See *Crepe Hair.*

Hair, Human Used for fine wigs, toupees, falls, and other hairpieces, and for ventilated beards and mustaches. Waved hair comes in a loose corkscrew curl that forms a natural wave in the wig. Unlike crepe hair, real hair should not normally be straightened before use. It is usually available in lengths from 10 to 24 inches, in a variety of colors, and is sold by the pound (or the ounce). The price per pound varies with the length and the color. Available from DeMeo Brothers. Human crepe hair is available from Kryolan.

Hair, Synthetic See discussion in Chapter 15. Synthetic hair with a high sheen is suitable only for certain stylized wigs and beards. Synthetic hair of a better quality can be used as a substitute for human hair or blended with human hair. Available from Kryolan or from Paramount in a number of shades, which can easily be mixed. Synthetic hair is sold by the ounce and is considerably cheaper than human hair.

FIGURE A–10 BEN NYE'S SILVER GREY HAIR COLOR.

Hair, Yak Sometimes used for wigs but more often for beards and mustaches. It is also less expensive than human hair.

Hair Coloring Temporary color sprays are available from Kryolan and Paramount and at drugstores and cosmetics counters. Kryolan has a number of opaque shades that can be used for covering dark hair with light colors.

Hair Dryer Can be used to speed the drying time of latex and other rather slow-drying liquids and, of course, for drying hair. Make sure the one you use does not contain asbestos. Available at drugstores, appliance shops, department stores, etc.

Hairlace A net foundation used in making wigs, toupees, beards, and mustaches (see Chapters 15 and 16). Available from Kryolan in three grades. Number 2430 is their finest flesh-colored nylon lace, excellent for street wear or for films but finer than necessary for the stage. Number 2431 is only slightly less fine. Number 2433 is a more durable lace, practical for stage wear. Numbers 2432 and 2434 are strong and slightly stiff nylon netting, which can be used by students for practice in ventilating as a substitute for the rather fragile hairlace.

Hair Spray A spray used for keeping the hair in place. (See also *Hair Coloring.*) Colorless hair sprays are available in drugstores, at cosmetics counters, and from Kryolan.

Hair Whiteners Ben Nye has an excellent liquid whitener, called Silver Grey Hair Color, that produces a very natural effect. Bob Kelly and Kryolan have sticks, and Mehron has a white liquid. All are available from the makeup companies and their distributors.

Hand-Lac A clear liquid that can be applied over makeup on the hands. It dries quickly, forming a protective film that helps keep the makeup from rubbing off on costumes. It can be applied with a brush or with the fingers of the other hand. Available from Kryolan distributors.

Hanz-N-Nek A Joe Blasco liquid makeup for hands and neck. It does not rub off on costumes but is easily removed with soap and water. Available in 20 colors.

Highlight Colors Contour colors used for highlighting in corrective and character makeups. The values in standardized numbers usually range from 1 to 3½ for light and medium highlights, the hues from FS to OF, and the values from a to d.

Honey Can be used as an adhesive with cleansing tissue for wrinkling the skin (see Chapter 13).

Ink, Simulated A viscous liquid used to simulate ink which has to be spilled. It is available in dark blue or black and can be thinned with water. It is nonstaining and is easily removable with soap and water. Available from Joe Blasco.

Knotting Needles *See Ventilating Needles.*

K-Y Lubricating Jelly Can be used in blending nose putty and derma wax. Can also be used as a protective film over a grease or creme makeup, then removed for a quick change (see Chapter 19). Available in drugstores in large and small tubes.

Latex, Liquid Used for building up flexible prosthetic pieces (see Chapter 14), attaching crepe hair (Chapter 15), or creating wrinkles and texture for age (Chapter 13). Latex is normally an off-white but can be colored by the addition of small amounts of concentrated vegetable dye, food coloring, or even makeup powders to arrive at whatever flesh tone is required. White latex dries clear; colored latex normally dries darker. If your bottle of latex has a brush in the cap, always return the cap to the bottle as quickly as possible so as not to expose the brush to the air any longer than necessary. Once latex dries on the brush, the brush is ruined. Liquid latex is available from the various makeup companies. Kryolan's latex (Gummimilch) is available in clear (four sizes) and flesh-colored (three sizes); Ben Nye's flesh-colored Liquid Latex, in three sizes; Mehron's white (clear) Latex, in two sizes; and Bob Kelly's, in two sizes. Joe Blasco's colored latex is called *Datex* and is available in a 1-oz. bottle, convenient for small makeup kits.

Because some latices cause a burning sensation when applied to the skin, for use directly on the skin, always use a latex that does not! The ones mentioned here are intended for use on the skin and do not normally create a burning sensation when applied. However, as sensitivity to a particular latex can vary with individuals, any latex you plan to use should be tried on your skin well in advance of the time you intend to use it.

Latex Caps (See Figures 14–13 and A–11.) For creating a bald-head effect. (See also *Plastic Caps.*) Available from Kryolan distributors and from Woochie Industries. The Woochie caps are thinner than the Kryolan caps and are designed to be used only once. When removed with sufficient care, however, they can usually be reused.

Latex Pieces Ready-made latex pieces (noses, chins, pouches, Oriental eyelids, wrinkled foreheads, scars, warts, burns, etc.) are available from Kryolan, Bob Kelly, and Paramount. If you are ordering from Bob Kelly, make sure you get pieces with thin edges. He also has thick-edged pieces intended for Halloween, masquerades, etc. With some pieces, getting a perfect fit may not be possible. Ready-made chins and noses, for example, are usually designed to fit "average" features. Even so, they may not always fit such features perfectly since there are many possible variations in the shape of features of approximately the same size. Other pieces, such as eye pouches, are more easily adaptable.

Lip Rouge or Lip Color Creme makeup for coloring the lips. It is usually applied with a lip brush.

FIGURE A–11 *LATEX CAP ON HEAD. By Kryolan.*

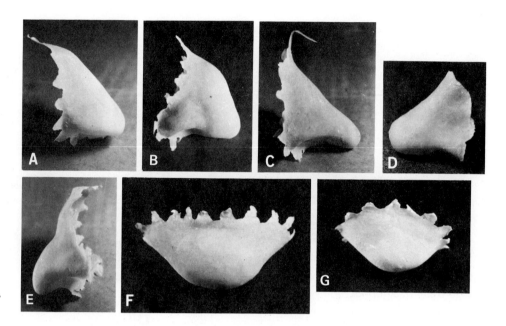

FIGURE A–12 KRYOLAN LA-
TEX NOSES AND CHINS.

Lipsticks   These can be used in the individual makeup kit but for sanitary reasons have no place in group kits. Available from Ben Nye, Bob Kelly, and Kryolan in a variety of colors. Ben Nye's #7 lipstick is an excellent natural color which can be used for both men and women.

Liquid Brightness   A Kryolan product. See *Metallic Makeup.*

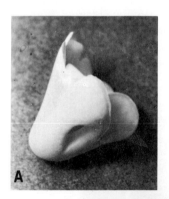

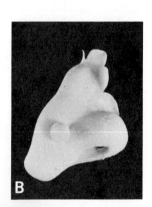

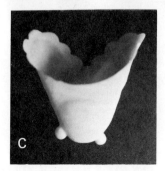

FIGURE A–13 LATEX NOSES (A,B) AND WITCH'S CHIN (C) BY PAUL BATSON.   *Available from Paramount.*

Liquid Makeup   Any makeup in liquid form. It is usually referred to as *Body Makeup* except when it is intended only for the face. See *Body Makeup.*

Liquid Plastic   See *Plastic Film, Liquid.*

Liquitex   A pressure-sensitive appliance adhesive. Available from Joe Blasco.

Luminous Paints   For a makeup which must glow in the dark, either fluorescent or phosphorescent paints and pigments can be used. The fluorescent ones must be excited by an ultraviolet light; the phosphorescent ones require no ultraviolet light but are less brilliant. A number of shades of both kinds of paints and pigments are available from Kryolan distributors and from Paramount.

Makeup, Non-Allergenic   Makeup which is advertised as being non-allergenic may be successful with some individuals and not with others. Kryolan's Dermacolor (see *Dermacolor*), a high-quality camouflage makeup, has also been used very successfully by individuals with allergy problems when non-allergenic makeups have failed.

Makeup Cape   Used for protecting the clothing. Paramount has a translucent white plastic cape, and Kryolan has a plastic bib for covering just the shoulders and the chest.

Makeup Kits   (See Figures 8–1, A–14.) Available from the various makeup companies in creme makeup (Ben

FIGURE A-14 MAKEUP KITS. *A. Ben Nye creme makeup kit. B. Contents of Bob Kelly makeup kit.*

Nye, Joe Blasco), creme makeup or cake makeup (Bob Kelly), cake makeup or greasepaint (Mehron), and moist cake makeup or greasepaint (Kryolan). Ben Nye also has miniature color kits ("SFX Color Kits")—small, round, plastic containers, each divided into four sections, containing makeup colors designed for a specific purpose. The kits (or palettes, Figure A–15) include "Burns and Blisters," "Age Stipple," "Bruises," and "Severe Exposure."

Makeup Palettes   Kryolan has convenient makeup palettes (Figure A–15) in color selections for stage, black-and-white TV, color TV, color film, and darkskinned actors—also one with only eyeshadows and rouges. Colors can be mixed in the cover of the box, as can the colors in a palette box by Grimas. Kryolan palettes are available from Alcone. Kryolan also has a palette of 16 rouge or eyeshadow colors in a thin plastic case (Figure A–16B). Larger quantities of makeup paints in plastic boxes can be obtained from Kryolan and from Bob Kelly. You can also buy empty palette boxes and fill them with colors of your own choice, as suggested in Chapter 8. An exceptionally useful palette box (Figure 8–3) is made by Grumbacher and can be obtained from artists' supply stores. If it is not available locally, your dealer can probably order it from the Grumbacher catalog.

Makeup Pencils   Wooden pencils with soft grease lead. When used for darkening the eyebrows, they are usually called *eyebrow pencils.* They are available in a variety of colors in addition to the usual brown and black. Pencils to be used for shading can be sharpened flat with a razor blade, rather like an artist's shading pencil. (See Figure 12–11 and the discussion in Chapter 12 in the section on eye pouches.)

Before using any *red* pencil in a makeup, test it on

the skin to see if it leaves a red stain when removed. If it does, try another shade, or use another type of red makeup.

Makeup Removers   Available in a cream or a liquid. Both Mehron and Kryolan have excellent makeup removers—Mehron's Liquefying Cream and their Makeup Remover and Kryolan's Makeup Remover. Kryolan has a special remover for Dermacolor. Ben Nye and Bob Kelly have liquid makeup removers that remove spirit gum along with the makeup. Ben Nye's is called *Quick and Clean.* The removers can be obtained from the makeup companies and their distributors. Various brands of cleansing cream, cold cream, and baby oil can be obtained in drugstores. (See also *Spirit-Gum Remover.*)

FIGURE A-15 BEN NYE'S RAINBOW WHEEL—A 6-COLOR MAKEUP PALETTE.   *The colors are red, orange, yellow, blue, green, and black.*

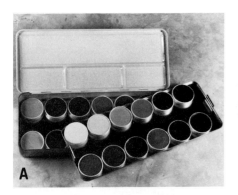

FIGURE A–16 MAKEUP PALETTES. A. Kryolan palette box. Metal palette box with 2 removable trays, each containing 12 colors. Brushes can be kept between the rows of colors. Also available in a 12-color and a 6-color box in various combinations of colors. B. Mehron's Makeup Palette.

Mascara Used primarily for coloring the eyelashes, sometimes the eyebrows, and occasionally the hair. It is made in brown, black, white, and various colors, such as blue, green, blond, and henna. Ben Nye and Bob Kelly have creme mascara with a roll-on wand; Bob Kelly also has liquid mascara. Cake mascara can be obtained from Kryolan and Mehron. Kryolan's is available in black, gray, blue, brown, and white in a case with mirror in a plastic box containing two colors. Having a combination of black or brown with white can be very convenient, since the white is useful for aging. Mascara is available from the makeup companies and their distributors and from any cosmetics counter.

Matte Adhesive A nonshiny spirit gum, available from Kryolan and from Joe Blasco.

Metallic Makeup Greasepaints are available in gold and silver from Kryolan; makeup pencils, from Bob Kelly and Ben Nye; and shading colors or eyeshadow, from Mehron and Kryolan. Kryolan's metallic makeup is called *Interferenz* and is available in a mini-palette of 16 shades, as well as individually.

Kryolan also has an effective water-soluble, nonmetallic gold and silver makeup called *Aquacolor Interferenz*, which can be applied with the fingers or with a damp sponge or a brush. Normal application gives a solid metal-

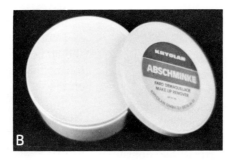

FIGURE A–17 MAKEUP REMOVERS. A. Mehron's Liquefying Cream. B. Kryolan's Makeup Remover. C. Ben Nye Makeup Remover.

lic effect, but a light application over other makeup gives a slight metallic sheen. Available from Kryolan distributors. Kryolan also has a nonmetallic liquid makeup, called *Glanzliquid* or *Liquid Brightness,* in gold, silver, and copper. It can be applied with a brush, a sponge, or the fingers, directly on the skin or over other makeup. It can also be mixed with other liquid makeup before it is applied. Either technique will give variations on the basic colors (red-gold, green-gold, silver-blue, etc.). Any unevenness can be smoothed out after the makeup is dry by stroking lightly with tissues or cotton.

Joe Blasco has a very effective Metallic Liquid Body Makeup, available in light gold, dark gold, copper, purple, green, brown, red, and blue.

Although gold and silver powders can be used on the hair for graying or adding brilliance, they are difficult to remove and ruinous to any grease or creme makeup upon which they happen to fall. Silver and gold sprays are preferable. The powders can be mixed with Mehron's *Mixing Liquid* and applied to the body for special effects. The powders are usually available in silver (aluminum), gold, copper, red, blue, and green. Mehron has gold and silver. Flakes or sequins are also available. These can be used for certain scintillating, sparking effects in stylized makeups. Kryolan has glitter (they call it *Glimmer*) in various colors and in various forms, including creme and spray.

No metallic paint should remain on the entire body longer than necessary and should not be used at all unless the actor is in good health. It is considered safe for very short periods, but if it is left too long on the entire body or a large portion of its area, the effects could be extremely dangerous. As a precaution, at least a few square inches of skin—even if the actor is completely nude—should be free of the makeup to allow that much of the skin to "breathe." Should the actor wearing the metallic makeup show any sign of faintness—no matter what you *think* the cause may be—the makeup should be removed immediately!

Mineral Oil   Can be sprayed on the face to simulate perspiration.

Mirror   A double-faced mirror (one side magnifying) is very useful in the makeup kit. Whenever possible, of course, makeup should be done before a large, well-lighted mirror, but the small mirror is essential in getting back and profile views. Portable lighted makeup mirrors are very useful—especially those that allow for adjusting the color of the light and have triple mirrors—two adjustable side panels and a center panel with a plain mirror on one side and a magnifying mirror on the other.

Mixing Liquid   A clear liquid for mixing with metallic powders and dry makeup pigments. Available from Mehron and its distributors.

Modeling Clay   Oil-base modeling clay, which does not dry out, is used in modeling heads when studying facial structure and also in modeling features for prosthesis. Obtainable at art supply stores, usually in 1-pound or 5-pound blocks in various colors.

Modeling Tools   Artists' modeling tools are used in clay modeling and sometimes in modeling nose putty or derma wax. Available from art supply stores in various styles.

Modeling Wax   See *Derma Wax.*

Moist Cake Makeup   See *Cake Makeup.*

Moulage   A gelatinous material used in making plaster or stone casts for prosthesis (see Chapter 14). A reusable type, called Formalose, is available from Kryolan. An alginate that is much faster but is not reusable is available from dental supply houses.

Mousseline de Soie   A gauzelike silk or rayon cloth often used in making facial lifts. Obtainable at dry-goods counters.

Movie Mud   A Joe Blasco makeup for simulating mud or dirt.

Mustaches   Excellent ready-made mustaches, ventilated on net (see Figure A–18), are available from Kryolan distributors. Instructions for making beards and mustaches are given in Chapter 15.

Mustache Wax   Available from Kryolan and from Bob Kelly.

Needles, Knotting or **Ventilating**   See *Ventilating Needles.*

Netting   Used as a foundation for wigs, toupees, beards, and mustaches. Available in silk, nylon, plastic, and cotton. The more expensive nettings (or hairlace) should be used for good wigs, toupees, and beards. Cotton netting can be used for practice work. All nettings and laces are available from Kryolan distributors.

Nose Putty   Used for building up the nose and other bony parts of the face. Available from Kryolan distributors in two degrees of stiffness, the softer of which is called *Plastici.* Kryolan and Grimas have a very pliable Soft Putty. Ben Nye's Nose and Scar Wax is a blend of putty and wax.

Old Skin Plast   A Kryolan product. (See *Plastic Film, Liquid.*)

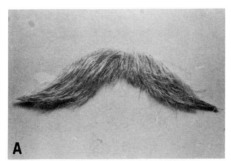

FIGURE *A–18* *READY-MADE MUSTACHES AND SIDEWHISKERS.* By Kryolan. A. Mustache. B. Mustache with sidewhiskers.

Old Stipple   A Kryolan liquid latex which can be used for wrinkling the skin. (See *Age Stipple.*)

Paint, simulated   A thick, liquid, nonstaining, easily removable makeup used to simulate high gloss paint which has to be spilled. Available on special order from Joe Blasco.

Pan-Cake   Factor's trade name for cake makeup.

Pan-Stik   Factor's trade name for creme stick.

Pencils   See *Makeup Pencils.*

Perspiration   Glycerine can be used to achieve the effect of perspiration by patting—not rubbing—it on the skin with the fingertips. Glycerine can be purchased at any pharmacy.

Phosphorescent Paints   See *Luminous Paints.*

Plaster Bandage   Rolls of gauze impregnated with plaster for use in making molds with alginate or reusable moulage. Can be obtained from art stores, medical supply houses, and some drugstores. Surgical gauze dipped into plaster can be substituted.

Plaster of Paris   Used in making both positive casts and negative molds in rubber prosthesis (see Chapter 14). Can be obtained at paint stores.

FIGURE *A–19* NOSE PUTTY.

Plastic, Liquid   See *Plastic Film, Liquid.*

Plastic Caps   Used for a bald-head effect. Available from Kryolan distributors. (See also *Plastic Film, Liquid* and *Plastic Head Forms.*) If the makeup you are using does not adhere to the cap, use Kryolan's Fixier Spray or Glatzan L (matte finish) to coat the cap before applying the makeup. If a cap has lost its flexibility, warm it with a hair dryer.

Plastic Film, Liquid   Kryolan has a liquid plastic called Glatzan L, which can be used to make bald caps and can also be painted on glass to make a plastic film in any shape or size. The film can be used for making eyebrow covers (see Chapter 12) as well as scars and sagging eyelids (see Chapter 13). It should be used in a well-ventilated room. Glatzan L matt can be used over Glatzan L to provide a matte finish. A Glatzan hardener is also available for making a stiffer plastic film. The Glatzan liquid *must not be used on the skin.* Glatzan that has become too thick can be thinned with acetone.

Kryolan's Old Skin Plast is a clear liquid that can be applied to the skin to wrinkle it. The liquid is brushed on over stretched skin (lightly coated with skin cream or creme makeup). It dries in a matter of seconds and can then be powdered. When the skin is released, wrinkles form. For deeper wrinkles, repeat the process. For still deeper wrinkles, apply torn pieces of cleansing tissue (white or colored) to the first layer of Old Skin Plast, then brush on another layer over the tissue. The liquid plastic is available in a matte finish, which makes powdering unnecessary. It can also be used as a sealer over derma wax, Eyebrow Plastic, etc. It can be removed with Kryolan's OSP Remover or with Kryolan's Mild Spirit Gum Remover. Mehron's Fixative A (see *Sealer*) can be used in the same way as Old Skin Plast.

Plastic Head Forms   For use in making plastic caps. Available from Kryolan distributors.

Plastici   A soft nose putty made by Kryolan. (See *Nose Putty.*)

Powder Puffs   Velour powder puffs are available from Ben Nye, Mehron, Bob Kelly, and any cosmetics counter. Large (5-inch diameter) velour puffs are available from Joe Blasco.

Pressed Eyeshadow   Dry cake eyeshadow. (See *Eyeshadow.*)

Prosthetic Adhesive.   A special adhesive for use with prosthetic appliances. Available from Alcone.

Putty   See *Nose Putty.*

Putty-Wax   A soft putty made by melting nose putty and derma wax together (see Chapter 13). Ben Nye's Nose and Scar Wax is a ready-made mixture of derma wax and nose putty.

Q-Tips   See *Cotton Swabs.*

Rouge, Creme   For coloring cheeks, lips, and areas of the face or hands that are to be reddened. Also used for stippling. Available from the various makeup companies.

Rouge, Dry   A cake (or sometimes powdered) rouge that can be applied with a puff or a soft brush, or with a damp sponge, over an otherwise completed makeup. Cake rouges in various shades are available from Kryolan, Bob Kelly, and Ben Nye. Mehron has powdered French rouge in bottles.

Brush-on (or blush-on) rouge—a somewhat powdery cake, sometimes called a "blusher," is applied dry with a soft brush. It is available in softer, more subtle colors than most dry rouges. Ben Nye and Bob Kelly both have brush-on rouges.

Rubber   See *Latex, Liquid.*

Rubber-Mask Greasepaint   A special castor-oil base greasepaint for use on latex. Available from Mehron, Bob Kelly, and Kryolan. Kryolan's is available in palette boxes (6 or 12 colors) as well as in individual containers. See also *Dermatex.*

Satinpuder or **Satin Powder**   Kryolan's nonmetallic powder which gives a satiny sheen to the makeup. It comes in four shades—pearl, gold, yellowish, and silver. Available from Kryolan distributors.

FIGURE *A–20* CREME ROUGE.

FIGURE **A—21** SATIN POWDER. *Available from Kyrolan.*

Scar Plastic See *Tuplast.*

Scars and Wounds Molded latex scars and wounds can be made quite easily by obtaining a Vacu-form mold of scars and wounds (available from Kryolan), making a negative plaster cast in the Vacu-form mold, then making latex positives from the negative plaster cast. (See Figure A–22.)

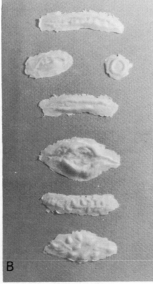

FIGURE **A—22** SCARS AND WOUNDS. *A. Negative plaster cast made in a Vacu-form mold. B. Latex positives made in the plaster cast. Available from Kyrolan.*

Scissors (See Figure A–23.) Necessary for trimming crepe hair and frequently useful for other purposes, such as trimming latex pieces. Barbers' shears are best for hair work.

Sealer A liquid plastic skin adhesive containing polyvinyl butyral, castor oil and isopropyl alcohol. It is used to provide a protective coating for various makeup constructions. It can also be used to wrinkle the skin (see *Plastic Film, Liquid*). It is an important item in any makeup kit. It is available from Mehron and their distributors in a convenient bottle with brush and is called *Fixative A.* It is also available from Kryolan and from Joe Blasco. Blasco's is available in two types—regular and matte.

Separating Agents Used in casting between the positive and the negative to make it possible to separate them easily. Kryolan has an excellent separating agent called Trens-Mittel. Vaseline, cleansing cream, or mineral oil can also be used.

Shading Colors The term is used in two ways—specifically to refer to contour colors used for shadowing and, in a more general sense, to include all contour and accent colors. Shading colors (in both the general and the specific meaning) are available from all of the makeup companies. Particularly useful colors for shadowing are Ben Nye's #40, Bob Kelly's #16, Kryolan's EC4, Blasco's Character Gray, and Mehron's RC11, RC12, and RC14.

Silk Gauze See *Gauze, Wigmakers'.*

Soap Used for blocking out the hair (see Chapter 16). Glycerine soaps or good quality, mild toilet soaps can be used.

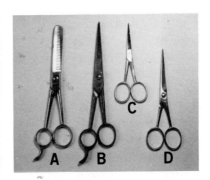

FIGURE **A—23** SCISSORS.
A. *Thinning shears.*
B. *Barber's shears.*
C. *Mustache scissors.*
D. *Small barber's shears.*

Spirit Gum   (Figures A–24, A–25.) A liquid gum adhesive used to attach crepe hair and other three-dimensional makeup to the skin. There is a difference in adhesiveness and in drying time among the various brands. Regular spirit gum is shiny when dry. For use with hairlace, a matte gum (dull surface when dry) is preferable. If the brush that comes in the bottle is too small, a larger brush can be used instead. In applying crepe hair, you should wipe the brush from time to time with an old cloth to remove the hair that sticks to it. And it's a good idea to tape the bottle to your makeup table to avoid the possibility of knocking it over. Or you may prefer to use the spirit-gum bottle holders described below. Spirit gum is available from the various makeup companies and their distributors. Kryolan's unusually adhesive spirit gum comes in regular, matte, quick-drying, and water-soluble. Their bottle and brush are the best available. In ordering Kryolan spirit gum, be sure to specify the plastic bottle with brush unless you prefer one of the larger, more economical sizes, in which case you can order any number of the small empty plastic bottles-with-brush and fill them yourself. Kryolan also has a thinner spirit gum for those who prefer it. It comes in a square glass bottle with a smaller brush. Ben Nye's Matte Adhesive Spirit Gum comes in a plastic bottle and is available in both 1-oz. and ½-oz. sizes.

Spirit-Gum Remover   Available from the various makeup companies. Kryolan has an Extra-Mild Spirit-Gum Remover (MME) that is particularly recommended for sensitive skins. Spirit gum can also be removed with alcohol or acetone.

FIGURE **A–24** KRYOLAN'S SPIRIT GUM.

FIGURE   **A–25** SPIRIT GUM.   By Kryolan.

Spirit-Gum Bottle Holders   (Figure A–26.) Heavy holders for spirit-gum bottles to prevent the bottles' tipping over. The holders are made in 5 sizes (as shown) for 1-ounce bottles from the various makeup companies. Useful whenever there is an open spirit-gum bottle on a dressing table and especially when there are quick changes requiring the use of spirit gum. Can prevent very messy accidents! Available from Woochie Industries. In ordering the holders, be sure to specify which brand of spirit gum you plan to use.

Sponges   Natural-silk sponges are used primarily for applying cake or liquid makeup. Red-rubber sponges are used for creating skin-texture effects with stippling and for applying rubber-mask grease. Foam sponges are sometimes used for applying creme makeup or for stippling with latex. Black stipple sponges are, of course, used for stippling. Natural-silk sponges are available from

FIGURE A—26 *SPIRIT GUM BOTTLE HOLDERS.* *Designed to fit the bottles of all major brands of spirit gum. (Available from Woochie Industries.)*

Mehron; black stipple sponges from Ben Nye or Bob Kelly; red-rubber sponges from Bob Kelly; and various types of foam sponges from Kryolan, Bob Kelly, and Ben Nye. Handy wedge-cut sponges, as well as the usual square-cut ones, are available from Joe Blasco.

Stick Makeup Various kinds of makeup are made in stick form—lipsticks, blemish-cover sticks, creme sticks, crayons, beard-stubble adhesive, eyebrow cover, hair white, etc. But the term is used, more often than not, to apply specifically to greasepaint foundation and shading colors in stick form, though it can logically refer to creme sticks as well. Stick makeup (greasepaint, that is) is available from Kryolan, Leichner, and Stein.

Stone, Dental Comes in powder form to be mixed with water and is used for making casts in the same way as plaster. The resulting cast is harder than plaster and must be used when the cast is to be subjected to considerable pressure. Available from dental supply houses.

Stoppelpaste or **Stubble Paste** Kryolan's Beard Stubble Adhesive. (See *Beard Stubble Adhesive.*)

Stumps Paper stumps are small, pointed, pencil-like rolls of paper sometimes used for shadowing and high-lighting. Brushes should be used instead, but stumps are useful for blending when drawing with charcoal and chalk.

They can be obtained from any artists' supply store. Chamois stumps are more expensive but last much longer.

Tape, Adhesive See *Adhesive Tape.*

Tears Apply glycerine with an eyedropper just below the corner of the eye. Glycerine can be purchased at any pharmacy.

Temple Stick A hair-graying stick made by Kryolan. Available in three colors from Kryolan distributors.

Texas Dirt An effective body makeup that comes in powder form and is applied with a damp sponge. It can be removed with soap and water. It is available from Mehron in Gold, Silver, and Plain and from Bob Kelly in one color only. Mehron's Plain dries with a dull finish; their Gold is about the same color but has a gold sheen; and their Silver has a silver sheen. (See also *Body Makeup.*)

Thread Common cotton or silk thread or dental floss is useful in removing nose putty. When the thread is passed between the skin and the putty, most of the putty will come off easily.

Tooth Enamel Available from Kryolan distributors in six colors—black, brown, white, red, ivory, and nicotine. The nicotine is particularly effective in aging the teeth. The black can be used for blocking out teeth, shortening them, or making them appear broken. The enamel is applied to dry teeth with a brush that comes in the bottle. The enamel can be removed by wiping the teeth firmly with cleansing tissues. Any specks of color remaining can be removed by brushing the teeth.

Toupee Tape See *Adhesive Tape.*

T-pins T-shaped pins for securing wigs to wig blocks. They come in various sizes and can be obtained from any wig-supply company. Kryolan has a very convenient magnetic container for T-pins.

Tuffy Head A life-size rubber head (face and neck only) that can be used for making beards with a latex base rather than making them directly on the face. If the beard is to be sprayed, it should be done with the beard on the Tuffy head rather than on the face. The Tuffy head is available from Kryolan distributors.

FIGURE A–27 *MAGNETIC CONTAINER WITH T-PINS.* Container available from Kryolan.

Tuplast   A thick, liquid plastic that can be used on the skin to build up three-dimensional scars. It can also be used in open molds to make three-dimensional molded pieces. (Eye pouches, for example, can be made in much the same way as in using gelatine. See Figure 13–11. Edges can be dissolved with acetone for blending.) Available from Kryolan distributors.

Tweezers   Handy for removing stray hairs in dressing crepe-hair beards or mustaches or in attaching small latex pieces.

Velvet Stick   Stein's trade name for creme stick.

Ventilating Needles   Used for knotting hair into net or gauze for wigs or beards (see Chapters 15 and 16). Available from Kryolan or any wigmakers' supply company. They should be ordered by number, the smallest usually being 00. The needle holder is ordered separately. For three different styles of needle holder, see Figure A–28.

Vitacolor Greasepaint   A soft greasepaint intended for sensitive skins.

Vitacolor Wet Makeup   A water-soluble paint in tube form by Kryolan. When used as a foundation, it should be patted on—preferably with a slightly damp or dry synthetic sponge. However, red-rubber, foam latex, and even natural sponges can be used. The natural sponge would be used damp, of course, and the others dry. It should not be stroked on. It can be applied either lightly or heavily. Although the paint can be transferred directly from the tube to the sponge, it's usually best to squeeze out some paint onto the back of your hand, then take it up from there with the sponge. (If you don't have the exact color you want, it can be mixed on the back of your hand.) When the foundation coat has dried, it can be rubbed gently with a tissue or a soft cloth, if you wish, to give a more transparent, natural look. However, you may prefer the opaque effect.

Vitacolor highlights and shadows can be used over either a cake makeup foundation or a Vitacolor Wet Makeup foundation. They should be applied with a dry brush. Vitacolor is easier to blend than dry cake makeup but has the same advantage of not having to be powdered.

It can also be used for stippling. Spread the paint fairly generously on the back of the hand, smoothing it out with the fingers, then press the stipple sponge into the paint and apply as usual. Since, like Aquacolor, it is a moist makeup, it has an advantage over dry cake makeup when used for stippling. Vitacolor can be removed with any makeup remover or with soap and water. Available in all of the Kryolan shades.

Water-Soluble Makeup   See *Cake Makeup, Body Makeup,* and *Vitacolor Wet Makeup.*

Wax, Black   See *Black Wax.*

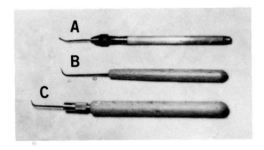

FIGURE A–28 *VENTILATING NEEDLES.* A. Metal handle with adjustable clamp for needle. B. Wooden handle with needle. C. Wooden handle with adjustable metal clamp for needle. (Available from Kryolan.)

Wax, Derma *See Derma Wax.*

Weaving Frames For weaving hair. (See Chapter 16.) Available from wigmakers' supply houses.

Wheat Germ Can be used with latex for special texture effects. Available from natural-food stores and grocery stores. (See also *Bran.*)

Wig Blocks (See Chapter 16.) Available from Kryolan or any wigmakers' supply house.

Wig Hangers Kryolan has a lightweight, easily stored wig hanger made of cloth-covered wire. It is available in two styles—N for hanging from a hook and K for hanging over a rod (Figure A–29). Available from Kryolan distributors.

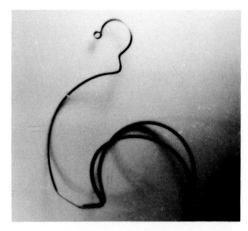

FIGURE ***A–29*** ***WIG HANGER.*** *Available from Kryolan. Made of strong, cotton-covered wire. The one shown (Kryolan #2400) has a loop at the top for hanging on a hook.*

B

Sources of Makeup Materials

ALCONE COMPANY, INC., Paramount Theatrical Supplies, 5–49 49th Avenue, Long Island City, New York 11101.
Mail-order source of makeup of all brands, as well as hair supplies. Write for catalog.

AMERICAN RAINBOW THEATRICAL SERVICES, 149 So. Edwards, Kalamazoo, Michigan 49007
Nationwide mail-order service for makeup supplies. Catalog available.

BLASCO, JOE, MAKEUP CENTER, 1708 Hillhurst Avenue, Los Angeles, California 90027

CALIFORNIA THEATRICAL SUPPLY, 256 Sutter Street, San Francisco, California 94102.
West Coast distributors of Kryolan makeup.

DOW CHEMICAL COMPANY, 55 W. Sheffield, Englewood, New Jersey 07631.
Dow Corning Prosthetic Foam—a quick-setting silicone foam.

FACTOR, MAX, MAKEUP STUDIOS, 1655 North McCadden Place, Hollywood, California 90028.

FERO CORPORATION, Cleveland, Ohio.
Colorants for silicone foam.

FIBRE PRODUCTS (DIVISION OF IKELHEIMER ERNST INC.), 601 West 26th Street, New York City 10001.
A variety of sample cases, some of them suitable for makeup kits.

JAARI HAIR PROCESSING CORPORATION, 168 Fifth Avenue, New York City 10010.
Hair in bulk and wigmakers' supplies, including ventilating needles and hairlace.

KELLY, BOB, 151 West 46th Street, New York City 10036. Phone: 212 245-2237.
Complete line of stage makeup. Also makes wigs, beards, and mustaches. If you are in New York, you can purchase makeup or rent wigs at the address above.

KRYOLAN CORPORATION, 132 Ninth Street, San Francisco, CA 94103–2603. Phone: 415 863-9684.
Complete line of theatrical makeup, available through Paramount and various theatrical distributors in the United States.

MAKEUP CENTER LTD., 150 West 55th Street, New York City 10019. Phone: 212 997-9494.
A convenient source of makeup in New York.

MEHRON MARKETING, INC., 45E, Route 303, Valley Cottage, N.Y. 10989. Phone: 212 997-1011.
Complete line of stage makeup. Write for brochure. All Mehron products are also available from Paramount and other distributors.

NYE, BEN, INC., 11571 Santa Monica Blvd., Los Angeles, California 90025. Phone: 213 447-0443.
Complete line of makeup for stage, screen, and TV. Write for brochure.

PARAMOUNT THEATRICAL SUPPLIES (ALCONE COMPANY), 5–49 49th Ave., Long Island City, New York. Phone: 718 361-8373.
A convenient mail-order source of makeup for all brands, as well as hair supplies. Fast air-mail service when needed. Write for catalog. They will do their best to supply most of the makeup and hair items listed in this book.

PLASTODENT, INC., 2882 Middletown Rd., New York City.
Dental supplies.

ROSCO LABORATORIES INC.,   36 Bush Avenue, Port Chester, New York. Phone: 914 937-1300.
They have a polyurethane foam which they call Haussmann Foam. For prosthetics, the most useful grade is their A-10 flexible foam, used with their standard B-55 catalyst.

SLOMON'S LABORATORIES,   43–28 Van Dam Street, Long Island City, New York 10001.
Source of Medico Adhesive.

M. STEIN COSMETIC COMPANY,   430 Broome Street, New York City 10013.
Complete line of stage makeup. Mail orders only.

WOOCHIE INDUSTRIES,   5011 College Avenue, San Diego, California 92115.
Batson's Burn, Scar, and Wound Effect, latex noses, spirit-gum-bottle holders, etc.

SOURCES OUTSIDE THE UNITED STATES

CAFFERATA & CO., LTD.,   Newark-on-Trent, Nottingham, England.
Casting plaster.

DUNLOP SEMTEX, LTD.,   Industrial Products Division, Chester Road Factory, Erdington, Birmingham 24, England.

FOX, CHARLES H., LTD.,   25 Shelton Street, Upper St. Martin's Lane, London, W.C. 2, England.

GRIMAS, NIJVERHEIDSWEG 35A,   2102 LK Heemstede, Harlem, Holland.

KRYOLAN, GMBH,   1 Berlin 51, Papierstrasse 10, Federal Republic of Germany.

MALABAR, LTD.,   14 McCaul Street, Toronto, 2B, Canada.
Distributors of Kryolan makeup.

RUBBER LATEX, LTD.,   Harling Road, Wythenshawe, Manchester, 17, England.
Latex adhesives and latex foam (Easifoam #117H).

SIEGI'S MAKEUP CENTRE,   Commissiouer, Van Kruis St., 409 State Bldg., Johannesburg, Tvl.
Distributors of Kryolan makeup.

A Makeup Workshop

To the student:

You will probably be able to complete the first 8 or 9 assignments in about forty hours, preferably divided into five 8-hour sessions or, if that is not possible, into ten 4-hour sessions. In order to do this, it is absolutely essential that you study the text in advance of each session, *including the first one.* There will be no lectures and no demonstrations. Since this is a workshop course, you will spend your time actually making up. By following the assignments given, you will be able to progress at your own speed. When one assignment has been approved, you will be free to proceed to the next. But keep in mind that it is more important to master fundamentals than to complete a specific number of assignments. (The remainder of the assignments are intended to be used for an advanced workshop.)

ASSIGNMENTS:

1. PREPARATION. Study Chapters 1 through 12 before the first class.
2. CORRECTIVE MAKEUP. Chapter 10, problems 2, 4, 5, 9, 10.
3. MODELING WITH PAINT. Chapter 12, problem 3. Repeat this makeup until you are satisfied with the results.
4. MODELING WITH PAINT. Chapter 12, problems 7, 9, 12.
5. MODELING WITH PAINT. Chapter 12, problem 14.
6. THREE-DIMENSIONAL MAKEUP. Chapter 13, problems 2, 4, 5.
7. BEARDS AND MUSTACHES. Chapter 15, problem 2 (1 character).
8. CREATING A LIKENESS. Chapter 17, problem 2. Before you begin the makeup, be sure that you will be able to do the appropriate hair style with either your own hair or a wig and that any necessary headdresses, hats, and partial costumes are available so that the likeness can be as effective as possible. For this assignment, a painting is preferable to a photograph.
9. NONREALISTIC MAKEUP. Chapter 18, problem 4.
10. VENTILATING BEARDS AND MUSTACHES. Chapter 15, problem 4.
11. EXPERIMENTAL MAKEUP. Do a complete makeup, using an original technique or a material not usually used in makeup.
12. PROSTHETIC MAKEUP. Chapter 14. Model, cast, and complete at least one successful latex piece.
13. MAKEUP WITH PROSTHETIC PIECE. Do a complete makeup for a specific character, using the prosthetic piece you have made.

FIGURES C–1 AND C–2 MAKEUPS BY STUDENT DOUG MASSEY FOR ASSIGNMENTS #8 AND #9. *In Figure C–1* the front hair has been soaped out and Mr. Massey's natural blonde hair has been darkened with brown spray. In Figure C–2 the nose was elongated and the growth on the cheek constructed with nose putty. The natural eyebrows were blocked out and new ones created with crepe hair.

A Basic Makeup Kit

The materials listed below are those which are more or less essential for learning basic makeup techniques. They can be supplemented by additional materials as needed. The relatively few colors have been carefully selected to make it possible to mix practically any color required. The colors have been designated by the standardized color numbers, which can be used, by referring to Appendix J, to determine the appropriate color numbers in the various brands of makeup.

Foundation Colors (Creme Makeup or Greasepaint) for Light-skinned Actors:

A highlight color, such as FS-1-c, SF-1½-b, or CO-2-b

A light flesh color, such as S-4-b, S-5-b, SF-4-a, SF-4-b

A fairly deep tan color, such as FS-13-e, FS-12-e, or SF-12-f

A sallow color, such as FS-8-e/f, 0-8-g/h, SF-8-h, or PR-10-g

Foundation Colors (Creme Makeup) for Dark-skinned Actors:

A light color, such as F/SF-5-c/d, F-6-d/e, SF-7-e, F-7-e

A medium color, such as F/SF-10-d/e, F-8½-d, FS-10-d/e, FS-10-e, or FS-10-f

A medium dark color, such as F-13-f, SF-11-e, SF-11-f, or FS/SF-12-g

A dark color, such as OF-17-e, F-19-f, FS-19-e, FS-16-g, or SF-17-f

Contour and Accent Colors for Light-skinned Actors:

White
Yellow
Blue
Red
Brown
Dark gray

Highlight: OF-1-b, OF-1-c, F-1-a, F-2-e, FS-1-d, FS-3-a

Medium shadow: PR-12-g, S-13-f, S-14-d/e, SF-12-h, SF-12-i, FS-13-d, FS-13-g, SF-10-e, SF-10-e/f, SF-11-f, RP-12-g

Deep shadow: P/RP-15-d, SR-17-g, S/FS-18-e, S-18-e, FS-16-g, SF-17-h

Contour and Accent Colors for Dark-skinned Actors:

White
Yellow
Blue
Red
Brown
Black
A deep shadow color, appropriate for the actor's skin color

Creme Rouge:

RS-10-d, RS-8-c, or SR/RS-9-a/b

Dry Rouge:

R-9-a, PR-8-a/b, or FS-9-b

Face Powder:

Translucent

Additional Items:

Powder puff
Powder brush

Rouge brush
1 flat shading brush, narrow width
1 or 2 flat shading brushes, medium width
1 flat shading brush, wide
1 eyeliner brush
Makeup pencils: brown, black
Nose putty
Derma wax
Kryolan Eyebrow Plastic
Crepe hair: gray and color to match your own hair
Spirit gum
Spirit-gum remover
Latex

Scissors
Comb
Eyebrow-pencil sharpener
Stipple sponges
Absorbent cotton
Makeup remover
Tissues
Hand mirror

NOTE: *As an alternative to buying all of the foundation and shading colors separately, you might prefer to get one of the makeup palettes mentioned in Appendix A. The palette could then be supplemented with any additional colors you might need.*

Racial Characteristics

The purpose of the following information is to provide a guide in making up characters of races other than your own. Nowadays, however, there is such an intermingling of the races and of ethnic groups that it is frequently impossible to pinpoint specific features and skin colors as being truly characteristic. The following suggestions, therefore, should be taken only as generalizations.

Alpine Includes Swiss, Russian, Czech, Balkan, and northern French peoples. Faces tend to be broad and short with straight noses, either medium or narrow in width. Brown, wavy hair is typical. Skin color is largely in the F, OF, and SF groups, light to medium in value, with high to medium intensity.

Arabian (Figure E–1L.) The face is usually narrow with a medium or narrow, straight or convex nose. Hair is black or brown and likely to be wavy. Skin colors tend to range from fairly light to medium dark in the middle intensities of the F, OF, and FO groups.

Armenoid Includes Turkish, Syrian, Persian, Russian, and Greek. Faces tend toward the long and narrow, with long, convex noses. Dark, wavy hair is typical. Skin color ranges from light to medium, mostly in the OF and FO groups and in the middle intensities.

Celtic Includes the English, Scottish, Irish, and Welsh. The pure type has a long face with a straight, narrow nose, but there is much variation. Light to medium brown hair, as well as reddish, is typical. Complexions tend to be light. The S through F groups can all be used. Rosy cheeks are common.

Chinese (Figures 12–23 and E–1H, K.) Faces tend to be broad, with short, broad, somewhat flat noses, concave or straight. Eyes have the epi-canthic fold and are often oblique. Hair is straight and black. The O, O/CO, and OC groups are particularly suitable for the skin color, which ranges from light to medium with medium to low intensity.

Czech See *Alpine.*

Danish See *Nordic.*

Dutch See *Nordic.*

East Baltic This includes Balkan, Finnish, and some Russian and German. Faces tend to be broad. In the pure type, the nose is concave and of medium width. Hair is likely to be ash blond or brown. Complexions range from light to medium, mostly in the warm groups—S through F—with fairly high intensity.

East Indian See *Indian, East.*

Egyptian The ancient Egyptians' faces ranged from narrow to broad. Noses were usually broad and straight or sometimes convex. The hair was usually brown. Complexions ranged from medium to dark, largely in the O and OF groups, with low intensity.

English See *Celtic* and *Nordic.*

Eskimo (Figure E–1B.) Faces tend to be broad with concave noses of medium width. Eyes may be almond-shaped. The hair is black and straight. Complexions range from medium light to medium dark, mostly in the low intensities of the O group.

Finnish See *East Baltic.*

French For northern French, see *Alpine*; for southern, see *Mediterranean.*

German For north German, see *Nordic*; for south German, see *East Baltic.*

313

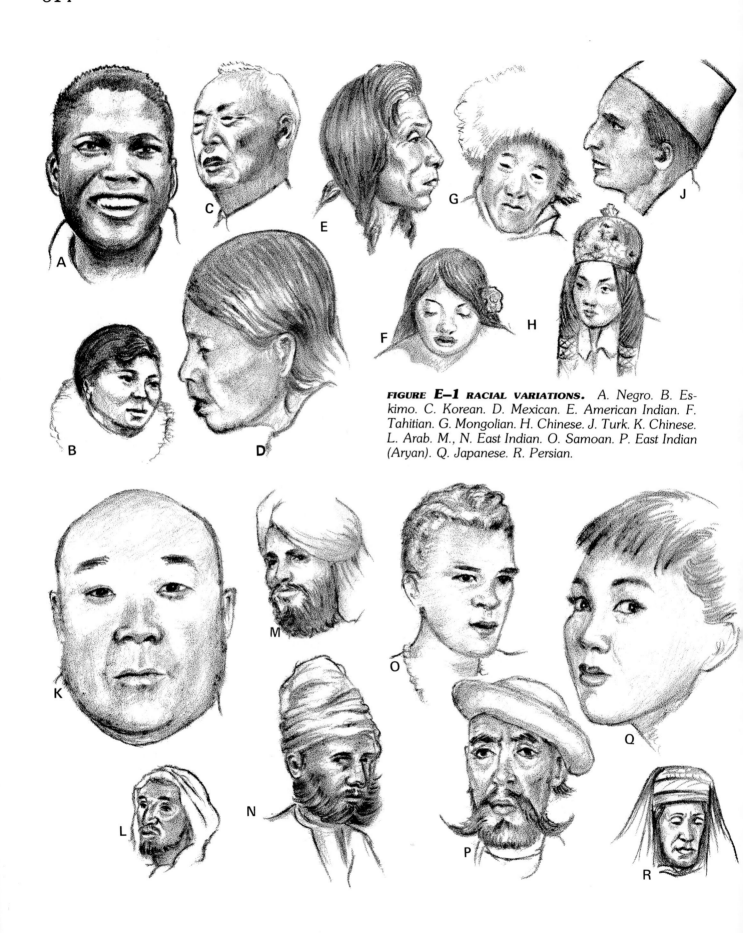

FIGURE E–1 RACIAL VARIATIONS. A. Negro. B. Eskimo. C. Korean. D. Mexican. E. American Indian. F. Tahitian. G. Mongolian. H. Chinese. J. Turk. K. Chinese. L. Arab. M., N. East Indian. O. Samoan. P. East Indian (Aryan). Q. Japanese. R. Persian.

Greek See *Armenoid*. The ancient Greeks were evidently lighter than the present-day ones and are typified by the classic Greek nose.

Hawaiian See *Polynesian*.

Indian, American (Figure E–1E.) Faces are broad in the middle with prominent cheekbones and straight or convex noses of medium width. Hair is black and straight. The skin is usually medium dark. Low intensities of the F and SF groups can be used. Avoid making Indians brick red!

Indian, East (Figure E–1M, N.) The Dravidian faces are of medium width with a broad, convex nose and curly black hair. The skin is dark (low intensities of the O group). Aryans have narrower faces, wavy dark hair, and lighter complexions.

Irish See *Celtic*.

Italian See *Mediterranean*.

Japanese (Figure E–1Q.) Some faces are long, some broad, with convex, straight, or concave noses, narrow, medium, or broad. Eyes have the epicanthic fold and tend to be almond-shaped. Hair is black and usually straight. Skin colors vary from light to medium. Grayed colors in the CO and OC groups are perhaps the most generally useful. You may have to mix colors to get what you want.

Mediterranean This includes French, Spanish, Portuguese, and Italian. Faces vary but tend more toward the narrow than the wide, with noses medium or wide and straight or convex. Among southern Italians, convex noses seem to predominate. The hair ranges from ash blond or light brown to black. The usual complexion is medium light to medium olive (F or OF, with *e* or *f* intensity). Southern Italians tend to be darker than northern.

Mexican (Indian) (Figure E–1D.) Faces tend toward broadness, though this is variable. Noses may be concave, convex, or straight. Hair is black and either straight or wavy. Complexions also vary from medium light to dark. The *f* and *g* intensities in the OF group are good possibilities.

Mongolian (Figure E–1G.) Complexion is similar to Chinese.

Negro (Figure E–1A.) There is great variation through intermingling of the races, but the more nearly pure Negro characteristics tend toward flat, broad, concave noses, wooly black hair, and very dark skins, which may appear close to black but

are actually a low value and low intensity of brown. The mixture of races has resulted in skin coloring ranging from medium light to very dark—low in intensity, mostly in the OF and FO groups.

Nordic This includes Scandinavian, North German, Dutch, and some English and Scottish. Faces tend to be long and narrow, with broad or convex noses (medium or narrow), and wavy gold or ash blond hair. Complexions are light, sometimes pale, sometimes pink. Light colors of *a*, *b*, and *c* intensity in the F, SF, FS, and RS groups can be used.

Norwegian See *Nordic*.

Persian (Figure E–1R.) See *Armenoid*.

Polynesian (Figure E–1F.) This includes Samoan (Figure E–1O), Tahitian, and Hawaiian. Faces tend to be long and narrow, with broad or medium noses. Hair may be wavy or straight, black or brown. Skin color varies from medium light to medium dark, in grayed tones of the SF through OF hues.

Portuguese See *Mediterranean*.

Roman See *Mediterranean*.

Russian See *Alpine*, *Armenoid*, and *East Baltic*.

Samoan (Figure E–1O.) See *Polynesian*.

Scandinavian See *Nordic*.

Scottish See *Celtic* and *Nordic*.

Siamese The typical face is broad, with a concave nose of medium width and almond-shaped eyes. Hair is straight and black. The skin color ranges from medium light to medium, in low intensities of the O, O/CO, and CO groups.

Swedish See *Nordic*.

Swiss See *Alpine*.

Syrian See *Armenoid*.

Tahitian See *Polynesian*.

Tibetan Faces tend to broad, with almond eyes and medium-wide, concave noses. Hair is straight and black. The skin colors range from light to medium, in low intensities of the O through CO groups.

Turkish (Figure E–1J.) See *Armenoid*.

Welsh See *Celtic*.

Yugoslav See *Alpine* and *East Baltic*.

Fashions in Makeup

One of the determining factors in any realistic makeup for the stage is the historical period to which the character belongs. This applies not only to the hair style but, in many cases, to the facial makeup as well. The kohl-lined eyes of the ancient Egyptians, the whitened faces of eighteenth-century ladies, the fashionably pale lips of the early 1960s—all must be taken into consideration in creating makeups for those periods.

The brief notes in this chapter are intended to give an overall view of the subject and to serve as a reference in doing period plays. Although hair styles are mentioned from time to time along with the makeup, more extensive information can be found in the 40 plates of hair-style drawings in Appendix G.

ANCIENT PEOPLES

Among the Egyptians, both men and women used makeup. The eyelids were frequently colored with green malachite and the eyes heavily lined and the eyebrows darkened with black kohl (powdered antimony sulfide). Carmine was used on the lips; for coloring the cheeks, red clay was mixed with saffron. Veins, especially on the bosom, were sometimes accented with blue. White lead was occasionally used for whitening the skin. Both men and women shaved their heads and wore wigs. The hair was usually dark brown, though at the height of Egyptian civilization it was sometimes dyed red, blue, or even green. Beards were often false and tied on with a ribbon or a strap; no attempt was made to make them look natural. Sometimes they were even made of gold or other metal.

The Assyrians and the Persians also dyed their hair and their beards, the Assyrians preferring black, the Persians, henna color. The eyes were lined with kohl, though not so heavily as those of the Egyptians. The brows,

however, were often made very heavy and close together. Both natural hair and wigs were worn, and the hair was curled with tongs. On special occasions it was sometimes decorated with gold dust and intertwined with gold threads.

Upper-class Greek women sometimes painted their cheeks and lips rose or earthy red, whitened their faces, darkened their eyebrows, shadowed their eyelids, and, upon occasion, dyed their hair or wore wigs. Red hair was popular, and blue, it is reported, was not unknown.

Fashionable Roman women and some men whitened their faces, rouged their cheeks and lips, darkened their eyebrows, and sometimes dyed their hair blond or red. During the period of the extremely elaborate and rapidly changing hair styles for women, wigs were frequently worn. Men sometimes wore wigs or painted on hair to cover their baldness. Both sexes wore beauty patches made of leather.

THE MIDDLE AGES

Upper-class Medieval women liked a pale complexion and in the late Middle Ages frequently used white lead to achieve it. Cheek and lip rouge were often used. In the thirteenth century, rouge was in general use among women; often rose or pink was worn by the upper classes and a cheaper brownish red by the lower. Fifteenth-century French women sometimes painted their cheeks and their lips with a crimson rouge. Throughout the Middle Ages, rouge seems usually to have been applied in a round spot with some attempt at blending.

Various colors of eyeshadow were used to some extent in the Middle Ages, and the upper lid was sometimes lined with black. Eyebrows were natural until the late Middle Ages and early Renaissance, when women of fashion (and in England, at least, even lower-class women)

FIGURE **F–1** *SIXTEENTH-CENTURY LADY.* *Makeup based on a contemporary portrait. Front hair soaped out and brows blocked out with spirit gum and derma wax. Latex nose. Makeup by student Carol Doscher.*

plucked their brows to a fine, arched line (Figure F–1). Sometimes, it seems, the eyebrows were shaved off completely. The hairline was also plucked so that little or no hair would show below the headdresses. The plucking was even done in public.

Both black and blond hair were fashionable, but red was not and would not be until Elizabeth I made it so.

THE SIXTEENTH CENTURY

The Renaissance brought a marked increase in the use of cosmetics but not, unfortunately, much improvement in the knowledge of how to make them safe for the skin. Frequently, irritating and poisonous artists' pigments were used to paint the face as if it were a living canvas. The skin was whitened and the cheeks and lips rouged. In *Love's Labours Lost* Byron says:

Your mistresses dare never come in rain.
For fear their colours should be washed away.

Spanish wool and Spanish papers (wool or small leaves of paper containing powdered pigment) were popular for rouge (and sometimes for the white as well) and continued to be used for several centuries.

By the end of the sixteenth century the artificially high forehead for women was no longer in fashion. Women had stopped plucking their eyebrows to a thin line, and some of them had begun to spot their faces with black patches.

Although some men painted their faces, this was not looked upon with favor by either sex. Nonetheless, Henri III is said to have gone about the streets of Paris "made up like an old coquette," his face plastered with white and red, his hair covered with perfumed violet powder.

Wigs were sometimes worn (both Elizabeth I and Mary Queen of Scots had large numbers of them); false hair was used; and beards, as well as hair and wigs, were sometimes dyed. Elizabeth favored red hair and thus made it a popular color. White or tinted powder was sometimes used on the hair. Venetian women in particular sat for days in the sun bleaching their hair and, according to contemporary reports, occasionally suffered severe reactions from overexposure to the sun. Blond wigs were sometimes worn instead.

Elizabeth's teeth, like so many people's of the time were yellow, spotted, and rotting away.

THE SEVENTEENTH CENTURY

Cosmetics were more widely used in the seventeenth century. Spanish papers in red and white were still in use. Samuel Pepys in his diary referred to his cousin, Mrs. Pierce, as being "still very pretty, but paints red on her face, which makes me hate her." On the other hand, the Earl of Chesterfield wrote to his well-painted Miss Livingston: "Your complexion is none of those faint whites that represents a Venus in the green sickness, but such as Apollo favours and visits most."

It is important to remember in doing Restoration plays that country girls still relied on their natural coloring but that ladies who wore makeup made no attempt to conceal the fact. Faces were usually whitened with powder or washes. Dark complexions were considered common.

Rouge worn by the upper classes was usually rose colored, whereas that used by lower-class women was an ochre red, often applied excessively.

Eyebrows were occasionally darkened, and a creme eyeshadow in blue, brown, or gray was sometimes worn by upper-class women. It was usually concentrated on the upper lid near the eye but might occasionally, in a burst of enthusiasm, be allowed to creep up toward the eyebrow.

Rouge, pink or flesh powder, and sometimes a touch of lip rouge were worn by men of fashion in the last decade of the century. Patches were worn by some fashionable men—whether or not they wore makeup—and in profusion by fashionable ladies. Some, according to Beaumont and Fletcher, were "cut like stars, some in half moons, some in lozenges." There were other shapes as well. Their placement was not without significance— a patch close to the eye was called *la passionée*, one beside the mouth, *la baiseuse*, on the cheek, *la gallante*, and so on. Ladies were seldom content with one patch. According to John Bulwer, writing in 1650 in his *Anthro-*

pometamorphosis, "Our ladies have lately entertained a vaine custom of spotting their faces out of an affectation of a mole, to set off their beauty, such as Venus had; and it is well if one black patch will serve to make their faces remarkable, for some fill their visages full of them, varied into all manner of shapes and figures." Bulwer includes an illustration of a "visage full of them." Eight years later, in *Wit Restored,* there appeared a few lines on the subject:

> Their faces are besmear'd and pierc'd
>   With severall sorts of patches.
> As if some cats their skins had flead
>   With scarres, half moons, and notches.

The patches were usually made of black taffeta or Spanish leather (usually red) or sometimes of gummed paper. It was also suggested in *Wit Restored* that patches might be of some practical use in covering blemishes. It is reported, in fact, that the Duchess of Newcastle wore "many black patches because of pimples around her mouth." Plumpers, made of balls of wax, were sometimes carried in the mouth by aging ladies to fill out their sunken cheeks.

The fashion of wigs for men was begun by Louis XIII; black wigs were popularized by Charles II. At the end of the century, light powder (mostly gray, beige, and tan, but not white) was used on the hair. Hair styles even developed political significance for a time—whereas the Cavaliers wore their hair long, the Puritans cut theirs short and were called Roundheads. Beards and mustaches were carefully groomed with special combs and brushes and kept in shape with perfumed wax.

Teeth were still poorly cared for, and they often looked it.

THE EIGHTEENTH CENTURY

Face painting and patching continued to flourish in the eighteenth century. In Wycherly's *Love in a Wood,* published in 1735, Dapperwit, who is trying to arouse Miss Lucy, says to Ranger, "Pish, give her but leave to gape, rub her Eyes, and put on her Day-Pinner, the long Patch under the left Eye, awaken the Roses on her Cheeks with some Spanish Wool. . . . Doors fly off the Hinges, and she into my Arms."

As for patches, a prominent marquise is reported to have appeared at a party wearing sixteen of them, one in the shape of a tree on which were perched two love birds. Sometimes the patches had political significance—Whigs patching on the right side and Tories on the left. Ladies who had not made up their minds patched on both sides.

Face painting became more garish in the second half of the eighteenth century. The ladies "enamelled" their faces with white lead and applied bright rouge heavily and with little subtlety. Horace Walpole, in writing of the coronation of George III, mentions that "lord Bolingbroke put on rouge upon his wife and the duchess of Bedford in the Painted Chamber; the Duchess of Queensbury told me of the latter, that she looked like an orange-peach, half red, half yellow."

In *The Life of Lady Sarah Lennox* we read that a contemporary of Lady Caroline Mackenzie remarked that she wore "such quantities of white that she was terrible" and that the Duchess of Grafton "having left red and white quite off is one of the coarsest brown women I ever saw." A guest at a party in 1764 was described as wearing on her face "rather too much yellow mixed with the red; she . . . would look very agreeable if she added blanc to the rouge instead of gamboge."

The white paints, according to *The Art of Beauty* (written anonymously and published in 1825),

> affect the eyes which swell and inflame and are rendered painful and watery. They change the texture of the skin, on which they produce pimples and cause rheums; attack the teeth, make them ache, destroy the enamel, and loosen them. . . . To the inconveniences we have just enumerated, we add this, of turning the skin black when it is exposed to the contact of sulphureous or phosphoric exhalations. Accordingly, those females who make use of them ought carefully to avoid going too near substances in a state of putrefaction, the vapours of sulphur . . . and the exhalation of bruised garlic.

FIGURE F-2 LADY WITH PATCHES. *English woodcut, c.1680.*

The warnings about the white lead paints were hardly exaggerated. Walpole wrote in 1766 that the youthful and attractive Lady Fortrose was "at the point of death, killed like Lady Coventry and others, by white lead, of which nothing could break her." At least they did not lose their lives through ignorance of the dangerous nature of their paints.

Despite the seemingly excessive makeup used by English ladies, they still lagged behind the French. Walpole reported that French princesses wore "their red of a deeper dye than other women, though all use it extravagantly." Lady Sarah Lennox found the Princesse de Condé to be the only lady in Parisian society who did not "wear rouge, for all the rest daub themselves so horribly that it's shocking."

Casanova was of the opinion that the rouge, though excessive, had its attractions and that the charm of the ladies' painted faces lay in the carelessness with which the rouge was applied, without the slightest attempt at naturalness.

The rouge was sometimes applied in a triangular pattern, sometimes more rounded. About 1786 hairdresser William Barker described French fashions in makeup:

> From a little below the eye there is sometimes drawn a red streak to the lower temple and another streak in a semicircular form to the other line. If the eyebrows are not naturally dark, they make them so. . . . Sometimes the French ladies . . . put on rouge of the highest color in the form of a perfect circle, without shading it off at all.

But Mr. Barker added that Marie-Antoinette had introduced a more natural application of rouge. A red pomade was used on the lips as well. One recipe for lip pomade suggested that the lady might add some gold leaf if she wished.

But it was not only the women who used cosmetics. In 1754 a correspondent wrote to *Connoisseur*:

> I am ashamed to tell you that we are indebted to Spanish Wool for many of our masculine ruddy complexions. A pretty fellow lacquers his pale face with as many varnishes as a fine lady. . . . I fear it will be found, upon examination, that most of our pretty fellows who lay on carmine are painting a rotten post.

Wigs were almost universally worn by men, much less frequently by women. Powdered hair was in fashion until near the end of the century. White powder was introduced in 1703; but tinted powder—gray, pink, blue, lavender, blond, brown—continued to be worn. Facial hair was never fashionable and rarely worn except, in some instances, by soldiers. Military hair styles were strictly regulated.

The wigs and high headdresses and powdered hair passed, however, and with them the garish makeup. At the end of the century a more-or-less natural makeup was in vogue.

THE NINETEENTH CENTURY

In the early years of the nineteenth century, fashionable cheeks were rouged. A portrait by Sir Thomas Lawrence, painted about 1803, shows the rose-colored rouge applied in a round pattern. The lips were also rose. But excessive rouging was not always looked upon with favor. The Countess of Granville wrote disapprovingly to her sister of ladies whose makeup she considered ill-bred: "Mrs. Ervington, dressed and rouged like an altar-piece but still beautiful . . . Miss Rodney, a very pretty girl, but with rather too much rouge and naivete . . . Lady Elizabeth Stuart by dint of rouge and an auburn wig looks only not pretty but nothing worse." A Mrs. Bagot she described as being "rouged to the eyes."

The *Art of Beauty*, published in 1825, noted that it was "not the present fashion to make so much use of red as was done some years ago; at least, it is applied with more art and taste. With very few exceptions, ladies have absolutely renounced that glaring, fiery red with which our antiquated dames formerly masked their faces."

In Victorian England there was a reaction against any form of paint on the face, though creams and lotions and a little powder were acceptable. Makeup was used nonetheless, but so subtly (by "nice" women, that is) that it was often undetectable. A woman who would not dare buy rouge in a public shop was often not above rubbing her cheeks with a bit of red silk dipped in wine or trying some other homemade artifice.

As the Victorian influence became more pervasive, the use of cosmetics became more furtive, particularly in the United States. Despite the example of George Washington, who was perfumed and powdered along with other men of his class, sentiment against any use of cosmetics by men was becoming exceedingly strong—so much so, in fact, that the revelation that Martin Van Buren used such cosmetic aids as Corinthian Oil of Cream, Double Extract of Queen Victoria, and Concentrated Persian Essence helped to end his political career. But in other countries, essential items for the gentleman's toilet included hair oil, dye for the hair and beard, perfumed chalk for sallow complexions, and a little rouge, which was to be used with great care so as to avoid detection.

The use of cosmetics was revived to some extent in the 1860s, and it was reported that rouge was "extensively employed by ladies to brighten the complexion" and to give "the seeming bloom of health to the pallid

FIGURE F–3 *LATE NINETEENTH-CENTURY LADY.* *Natural look. (After a drawing by Friedrich von Kaulbach.)*

or sallow cheek." Eyebrows were dark, full, moderately thick, and attractively curved. The Empress Eugénie is believed to have introduced the use of mascara, and Charles Meyer, a German teenager trained in wigmaking, introduced Leichner's theatrical makeup—the first greasepaint to be made in America.

By the end of the century the shops were well supplied with fascinating and irresistible cosmetics. Not only did women not resist them, but they were known brazenly to repair their makeup in public. In 1895 the editor of the *London Journal of Fashion* wrote:

> Rouge, discreetly put on, of course, forms a part of every toilet as worn by fashionable women, and some among these are beginning to use their toilet-powders somewhat too heavily. Even those who do not use rouge aim at producing a startling effect of contrast by making the lips vividly red and the face very pale, with copiously laid on powder or enamel—which when badly put on is of very bad effect, and, in point of fact, greatly ages a woman. Still, the entirely unaided face is becoming more and more rare, almost everybody uses other makeup effects, if not rouge, and an almost scarlet lip-salve.

It should be particularly noted, in planning your own makeup for a Victorian woman, that well-bred young girls never used makeup, though they did pinch their cheeks occasionally. Married women might resort to a delicate rouge, very subtly applied so as to look like natural color, but they did not rouge their lips. They might, however, employ various methods of bringing the blood to the surface, such as biting; and they might soften the lips with cream. Lipstick was used mainly by actresses on stage and by courtesans. Victorian eyebrows were natural (Figure F–3).

Early in the century, wigs for women were fashionable. Black and blond were both popular colors. By the 1820s black was favored. *The Art of Beauty* included a recipe for "Grecian Water for Darkening the Hair," which, the reader was warned, was not only dangerous to the skin, but might eventually turn the hair purple. In the second half of the century the preference was for brown or black hair, and dyes were freely used by both men and women—the men for their beards as well as their hair.

In 1878 Mrs. Haweis wrote that red hair was all the rage; and in 1895 the *Journal of Fashion* announced that "the coming season will be one of complexions out of boxes . . . and the new colour for the hair a yellow so deep as to verge on red. It is not pretty, it is not becoming, and it is somewhat fast-looking because manifestly unreal."

THE TWENTIETH CENTURY

At the turn of the century, many women were using henna to turn their hair fashionably auburn. The purpose of makeup was still to enhance the natural beauty rather than to look frankly painted. Some women, including Queen Alexandra, tended to defeat their purpose by applying their makeup quite heavily, though the colors used were delicate. The English and the Americans lagged behind the French in the frank and open application of paint. In the second decade the use of eyeshadow, eyebrow pencil, mascara, and lipstick became widespread.

In the early twenties, beauty experts in England and America were still advising natural-looking makeup, but it was a losing battle. In the mid-twenties, geranium or raspberry lips and a pale complexion were fashionable, and eyebrows were being plucked into a thin, hard line. In 1927 it was reported, with marked disapproval, that some women actually used eyeshadow. They were also lining their eyes with black and painting their lips cerise. By the end of the decade, heavily painted, bee-stung lips, plucked eyebrows, and short hair were the mark of the emancipated woman.

It was in the late twenties that sun-tanned faces became popular, and dark powders were made available for those who did not tan well or had no time to lie in the sun. Orange rouge and lipstick were in fashion, and the lips were overpainted with an exaggerated cupid's bow. Beauty experts recommended that eyeshadow be applied close to the lashes, then blended out to elongate the eye. Brown was recommended for day use, blue for night. Rouge and lipstick also came in day and evening colors—light for day, dark for evening.

Early in the thirties, orange lipstick went out and

raspberry came in. Even schoolgirls used makeup. Their older sisters bleached their hair platinum, and their mothers or even their grandmothers rinsed away their gray. Hollywood set the styles. For the first time in history women made their mouths larger—Joan Crawford style. The beestung lips were gone. Fingernails and toenails were painted various shades of red, gold, silver, green, blue, violet, and even, for a time, black. Polish had been used for some years previously, but it was either colorless or natural pink.

In the forties and fifties, extremes of artificial makeup subsided somewhat, though lips were still heavily painted. Rouge became less and less used and eventually was omitted entirely by fashionable women. Makeup bases in both water-soluble cake and cream form were available in a variety of shades, ranging from a pale pink to a deep tan, and were usually applied too heavily. Eye makeup was still more or less natural. Eyebrows were no longer plucked to a thin line, colored eyeshadow was used mostly for evening wear, and mascara and false eyelashes were intended to look natural.

In the early half of the sixties, however, the natural look was out. Makeup became as extreme as the hair styles, with a shift of emphasis from the mouth to the eyes. Lips were not only pale (either unpainted or made up with a pale lipstick), they were, for awhile, even painted white. This fashion, like most others, began in Paris. Eye makeup became heavier and heavier, with colored eyeshadow generously applied for daytime wear and the eyes heavily lined with black in a modified Egyptian style. False eyelashes became thick and full, and sometimes several pairs were worn at once. It was a time for restless dissatisfaction and experimentation. White and various pale, often metallic, tints of eyeshadow were tried. Eyebrows were even whitened to try to focus attention on the eye itself, and extremely pale makeup bases were worn. The objective seemed to be great dark eyes staring out of a colorless blob. Hair was tinted, rinsed, dyed, teased, ironed, and wound on enormous rollers, which, during the daytime, were sometimes worn in public. Sometimes the hair was just left to hang (possibly a beatnik influence), framing a pale face with great black furry-lashed eyes.

The 1970s began with a flurry of artificiality—red eyelashes, green hair, colored polkadots around the eyes, doll-like makeup on the cheeks, heavy black eyelashes painted on the skin, eyebrows blocked out with makeup. No innovation seemed too bizarre. But reaction set in, and a greater naturalness in makeup took over. In 1972, however, severely plucked eyebrows were once again in fashion—sometimes no more than the thin line of the twenties. But rouge was natural, and lip color varied with the season. By 1974 the variations included stronger colors—both very bright and very dark—than had been worn for a number of years.

In 1975 the tawny look was fashionable, with cheek coloring tending to be muted and lips either muted or bright and clear. Eyes were shadowed with such colors as Evergreen, Parsley, Walnut, Plum, or Heather and highlighted with tints like pink, lavender, or pale yellow. Eyebrows were light or medium.

In the latter part of 1976 there was a shift among some makeup artists toward pink and rose and plum. Among some women who continued to wear the brown tones, coral lips were popular, but others preferred the deeper, tawnier shades. Lips were outlined with makeup pencils, filled in with brushes, then covered with colored gloss. Eyeshadow colors were often tinged with silver, copper, or gold.

Makeup in 1977 was darker and stronger, with rich, dark reds ranging from brownish to plum. Eyes were shadowed with earth tones—browns, grays, muted greens—and lip coloring might be brownish, deep and rich, or bright and clear. Makeup for evening frequently glimmered with gold or silver.

The emphasis in 1978 was definitely away from the browns and corals and more toward burgundy, magenta, fuchsia, and bluish pinks. The fashionable look was less natural and more sophisticated, with bolder, brighter makeup—deeper eyeshadow colors, bright rouge instead of soft blushers, with even more gloss on the lips. Eye lining was less smudged but still softened with no hard lines. For evening, lighter foundations were worn with smoky, shadowed eyes, bright rouge, and bright, glossy lips.

Continuing the trend, makeup in 1979 was supposed to look like makeup, and a woman with Sunset Rose cheeks, Spirited Rhubarb lips, and Honest Amber eyelids (highlighted with Pearlfrost Pink) might merely be on her way to the supermarket.

The new decade began quietly, on the one hand, with natural-looking eyebrows, soft, opalescent colors, and no hard lines around the eyes. But on the other hand, there were startlingly pale-faced punk rockers with charcoal-smudged eye sockets and bleached blond or dyed black hair shellacked into fierce points and sprayed in streaks or spots with brilliant purple, green, or orange. For summer the tawny look was in fashion—grey-brown or olive green on the eyes and a brownish red on the mouth. This look continued into the fall, when colors were sometimes muted, sometimes exploding into a dazzling array of magentas, mauves, and fuchsias vying with coppery reds and oranges and eyes accented with blue, violet, or green mascara. The eyebrows, however, were still natural-looking.

In 1982 makeup tended to match the natural skin color, with no hard lines and, for awhile, no strong, contrasting colors. In the fall, however, colors deepened, with tones of red, purple, and bronze. Cheek and lip coloring was subtle, but eye coloring was not. Two or three colors, including metallics, might be used on the eyes, along with heavy, slightly smudgy black lines surrounding them. Eyebrows were pale.

Emphasis on the eyes continued into 1983, with charcoal and black still surrounding the eye, but with less color. Eyebrows ranged from pale to very dark. Lip and cheek coloring remained generally subtle, often pale. In mid-year, however, the "assymetrical look" was in vogue. Various colors were applied casually to the eyelids, but not the same colors on both eyelids—nor, in fact, was the same foundation color used on both sides of the face. The effect was, predictably, bizarre. In more conservative makeup, emphasis on the eyes continued for awhile but by the winter had become more natural-looking.

The natural look continued into 1984, with softer, paler tones intended to enhance one's appearance rather than to attract attention. When strong color was used, it was likely to be on a single feature—usually the eyes or the lips.

In the spring of 1985 eyebrows were usually unplucked but darkened a bit if they were light, the eyes accented with deep colors (black, gray, purple, blue, bronze), often with more than one color. Lips might be pink, purplish, bright red, or red-orange. Foundation colors were usually natural-looking, tending toward the warm tones, and the general intent seemed to be to look healthy rather than bizarre. However, the purples, which were fairly popular, tended to defeat this.

In 1986 popular colors, according to *Vogue*, were orange, metallic, and lavender, used separately or in various combinations—a bronze foundation, for example, with lavender on the eyelids, cheeks, and lips, or a pale foundation with bronze on the eyelids, cheeks, and lips. All-bronze makeups were also worn, with variations of brown and bronzy red around the eyes, as well as on the cheeks and lips. In the autumn, colors were warmer and more intense, and there was a greater variety of colors and fewer rules about their application. Metallic eyeshadows were available in gold, silver, and copper; and blushers, in bronzed pink, soft apricot, or coral. The objective for the final makeup was, it was said, to create a "natural" look.

In 1987 glittery, bronzy colors were out, and the new matte makeup featured a variety of tints as well as texture. Although the rose tints were popular, especially among the more conservative, yellow lips, pink eyeshadow, and brightly colored mascara could be seen on the more adventurous. Eyebrows were not only darkened but were sometimes brushed upward to make them fuller and slightly shaggy, with dark eyeshadows surrounding the eye. With this strong emphasis on eye makeup, cheek and lip makeup was fairly natural. But for the young and less conservative, the hair was sometimes boldly streaked with bright colors. And by the end of 1987 women were once again using compacts and powdering their faces in public.

Fashions in Hair

The following pages illustrate men's and women's fashions in hair from ancient times to the present day.

Sumerian

Egyptian

Egyptian

Egyptian

Sumerian

Egyptian

Hittite

Egyptian

Egyptian

Egyptian

Egyptian

Egyptian

Assyrian

Assyrian

Assyrian

Etruscan

Etruscan

Etruscan

Etruscan

Persian

FIGURE G—1 ANCIENT PEOPLES, MEN.

A Greek
B Greek
C Greek
D Greek
E Greek
F Greek
G Greek
H Greek
I Roman
J Roman
K Roman
L Roman
M Roman
N Roman
O Roman
P Roman
Q Roman
R Roman
S Egyptian
T Roman
U Roman
V Roman
W Roman
X Roman

FIGURE **G—2** *ANCIENT PEOPLES, MEN.*

A Egyptian
B Sumerian
C Semitic Akkadian
D Egyptian
E Egyptian
F Egyptian
G Egyptian
H Egyptian
I Egyptian
J Egyptian
K Etruscan
L Greek
M Greek
N Greek
O Greek
P Greek
Q Greek
R Greek
S Etruscan

FIGURE G–3 ANCIENT PEOPLES, WOMEN.

Greek

B

Egyptian

Greek

C

D

Roman

E Roman

F

Roman

G

Roman

H

Roman

I

Roman

J

Roman

K

Roman

L

Roman

M

Roman

N

Roman

O

Roman

P

Roman

Q

Roman

R

Roman

S

Roman

T

Roman

FIGURE G–4 ANCIENT PEOPLES, WOMEN.

A
6th century

B
Byzantine

C
c.547

D
c.750

E
c.879

F
10th century

G
c.1130

H
c.1150

I
13th century

J
c.1150

K
c.1160

L
c.1235

M
c.1245

N
13th century

O
13th century

P
14th century

Q
14th century

R
14th century

S
14th century

T
c.1376

U
c.1390

V
1390

W
c.1409

FIGURE G—5 MEDIEVAL MEN.

A c.400

B Byzantine

C Byzantine

D 1083

E 1180

F c.12th century

G

H 13th century

I 13th century

J 12th or 13th century

K c.1340

L 14th century

M 14th century

N c.1310

O 14th century

P After 1320

Q 1364

R 14th century

S c.1360

FIGURE G—6 MEDIEVAL WOMEN.

A Early, French

B 1412

C Early, English

D 1416

E Early, French

F German

G c.1440

H 1448

I 1445

J Mid-century

K Mid-century

L 1480

M 1476

N 1491

O 1488

P Late, Italian

Q Late, Italian

R 1486

S Late, Italian

T c.1490

U Late, Italian

V c.1495

W Late, Italian

FIGURE G—7 FIFTEENTH-CENTURY MEN.

A

c.1400

B

1st half

C

Mid-century

D

1st half

E

c.1440

F

1447

G

c.1470

H

Last quarter

I

1488

J

Last quarter

K

Last quarter

L

Last quarter

M

Last quarter

N

Last quarter

O

Last quarter

P

1495

Q

Last quarter

R

1492

S

Last quarter

T

c.1500

FIGURE **G—8** FIFTEENTH-CENTURY WOMEN.

Early years

1510

2nd. quarter

1520

E
1520

F
GERMAN

G
1529

H
1530

I
1530

J
1535

K
1540's

L
2nd. quarter

M
N
Mid - century

O
3rd. quarter

P
3rd. quarter

Q
3rd. quarter

R
c. 1575

S
Last quarter

T
Mid - century

U
1594

V
1596

W
1599

FIGURE G—9 SIXTEENTH-CENTURY MEN.

A c. 1512

B c. 1515

C c.1515

D Before 1520

E 1520

F 1st. quarter

G c. 1550

H c. 1550

I c. 1550

J c. 1550

K c. 1560

L c. 1560

M First half

N c. 1575

O Last quarter

P 1560's

Q Last quarter

R Last quarter

S Last quarter

T c. 1595

U c. 1597

FIGURE **G–10** SIXTEENTH-CENTURY WOMEN.

A Before 1616

B 1614

C 1614

D 1628

E Early 1600's

F c. 1630

G c. 1630

H c. 1630

I c. 1630

J c. 1630

K c. 1630

L c. 1640

M 1632

N 1635

O c. 1635

P 1645

Q 1645

R 1649

S c. 1650

T c. 1650

U c. 1680

V 1688

FIGURE G–11 SEVENTEENTH-CENTURY MEN.

FIGURE **G–12** SEVENTEENTH-CENTURY WOMEN.

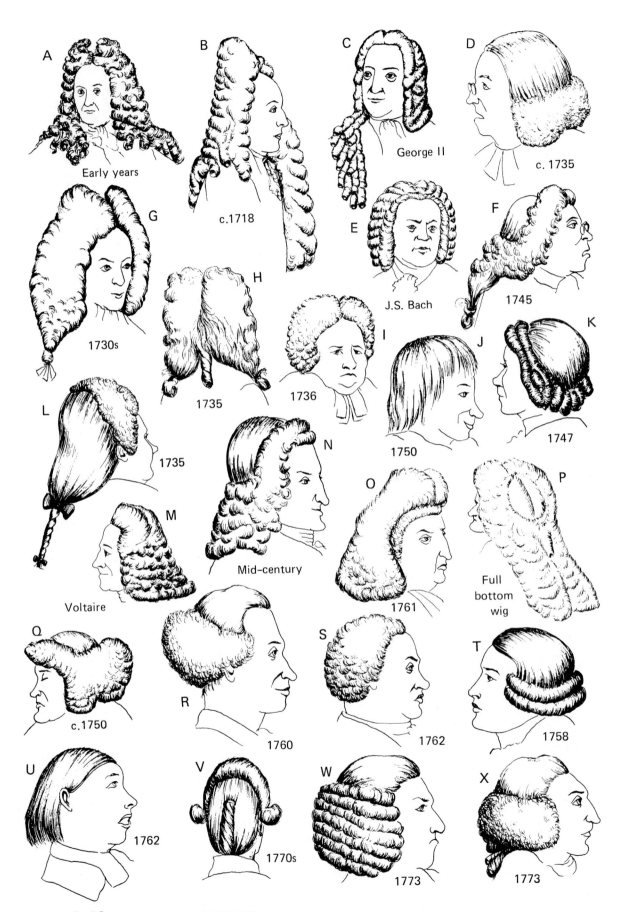

A Early years

B c.1718

C George II

D c.1735

G 1730s

E J.S. Bach

F 1745

H 1735

1736

I 1750

J

K 1747

L 1735

M Voltaire

N Mid-century

O 1761

P Full bottom wig

Q c.1750

R 1760

S 1762

T 1758

U 1762

V 1770s

W 1773

X 1773

FIGURE G—13 EIGHTEENTH-CENTURY MEN.

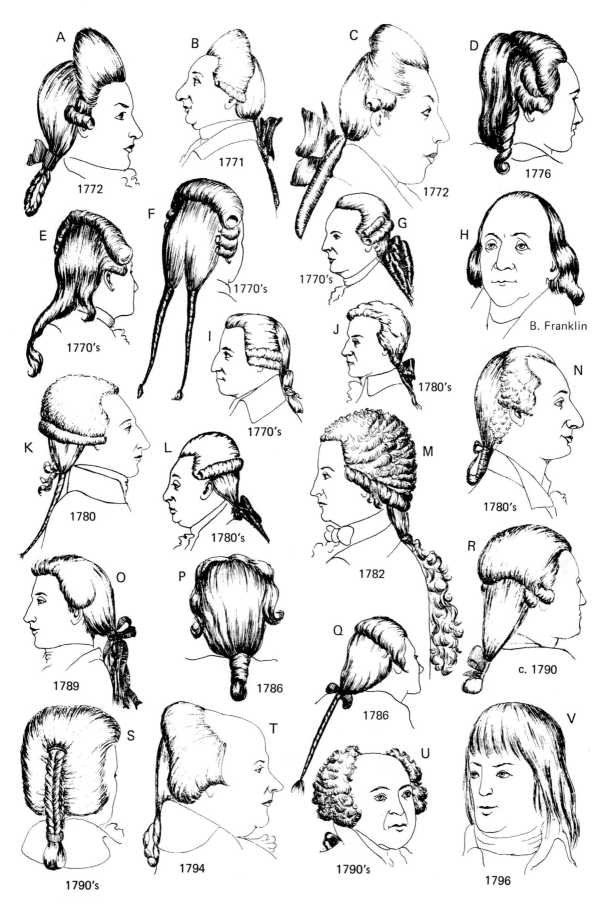

A 1772
B 1771
C 1772
D 1776
E 1770's
F 1770's
G 1770's
H B. Franklin
I 1770's
J 1780's
K 1780
L 1780's
M 1782
N 1780's
O 1789
P 1786
Q 1786
R c. 1790
S 1790's
T 1794
U 1790's
V 1796

FIGURE **G–14** EIGHTEENTH-CENTURY MEN.

A c. 1700
B c. 1702
C 1732
D c. 1730
E c. 1735
F c. 1750
G 1750's
H 1760's
I 1764
J c. 1770
K c. 1770
L 1774
M 1773
N 1774
O c. 1776
P c. 1776
Q 1776
R 1778

FIGURE G—15 EIGHTEEN-CENTURY WOMEN.

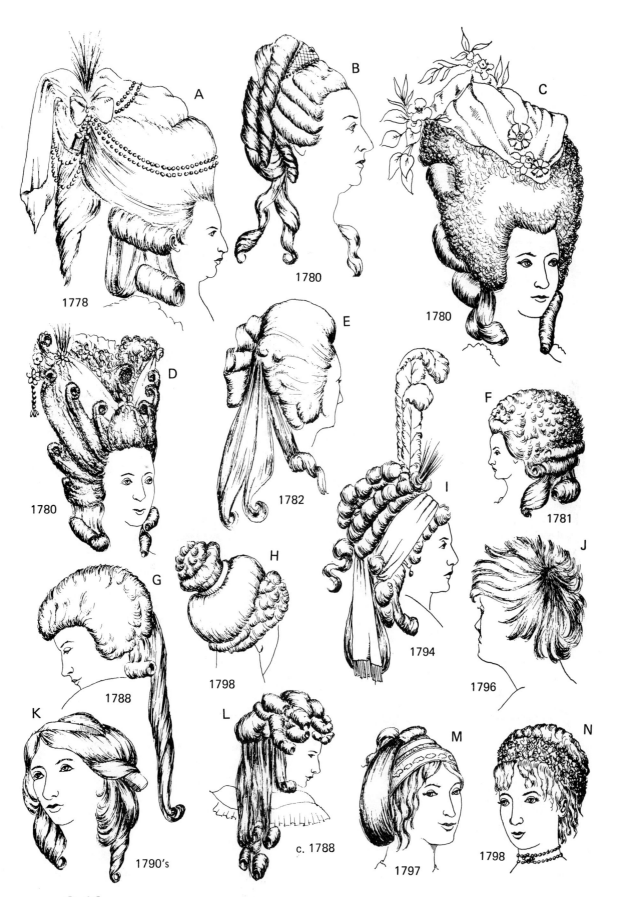

A 1778
B 1780
C 1780
D 1780
E 1782
F 1781
G 1788
H 1798
I 1794
J 1796
K 1790's
L c. 1788
M 1797
N 1798

FIGURE G—16 EIGHTEENTH-CENTURY WOMEN.

A Early years

B Early years

C George IV

D 1820

E Disraeli

F Chopin

G Mid-century

H Napoleon III

I Mid-century

J 3rd. quarter

K c. 1850

L c. 1860

M 2nd. half

N 2nd. half

O 3rd. quarter

P 2nd. half

Q 2nd. half

R 2nd. half

S 1880's

T 1880's

U 1880's

V 1880's

W 1880's

X 1880's

FIGURE G-17 NINETEENTH-CENTURY MEN.

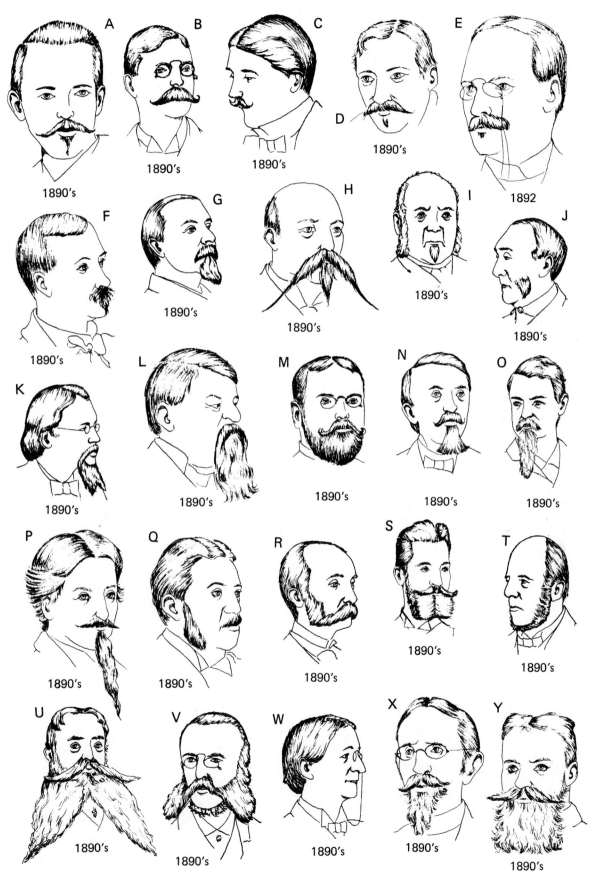

FIGURE G—18 NINETEENTH-CENTURY MEN.

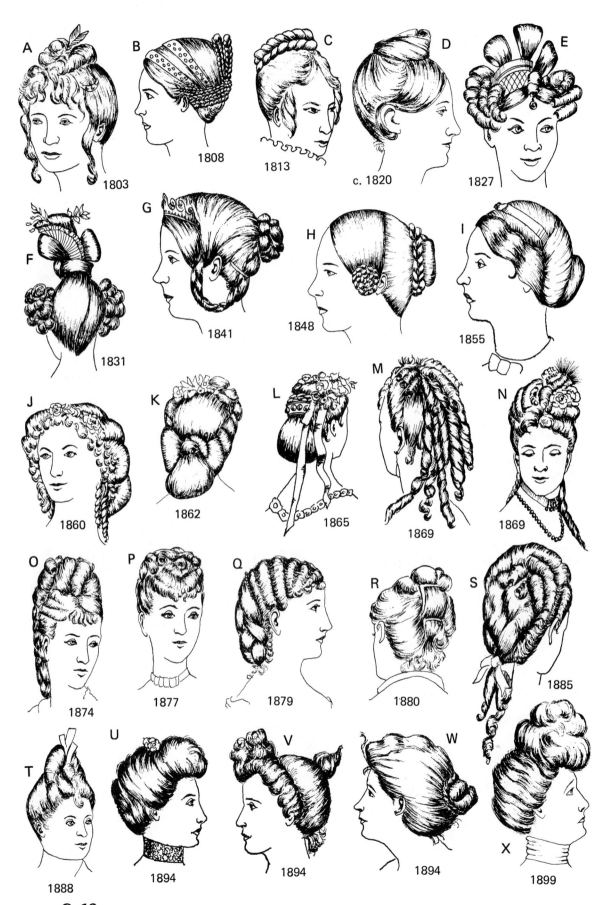

FIGURE G—19 NINETEENTH-CENTURY WOMEN.

A
1905

B
Early years

C
Early years

D
Early years

E
Early years

F
Early years

G
c.1922

H
1926

I
1929

J
1930's

K
1937

L
1940

M
1953

N
1956

O
1958

P
1959

Q
1961

R
1961

S
1961

T
1962

U
1962

V
1963

W
1965

X
1966

Y
1966

FIGURE G–20 TWENTIETH-CENTURY MEN.

FIGURE G–21 TWENTIETH-CENTURY WOMEN.

FIGURE G–22 TWENTIETH-CENTURY MEN.

A 1967
B 1967
C 1968
D 1969
E 1969
F 1969
G 1969
H 1970
I 1970
J 1970
K 1970
L 1970
M 1970
N 1970
O 1971
P 1971
Q 1972
R 1972
S 1973
T 1973
U 1973
V 1973
W 1973
X 1973
Y 1973

FIGURE G–23 TWENTIETH-CENTURY WOMEN.

A 1973

B 1974

C 1974

D 1974

E 1975

F 1975

G 1975

H 1975

I 1975

J 1975

K 1975

L 1976

M 1976

N 1976

O 1976

P 1976

Q 1976

FIGURE **G—24** *TWENTIETH-CENTURY MEN.*

FIGURE G—25 TWENTIETH-CENTURY WOMEN.

A 1976

B 1976

C 1976

D 1976

E 1976

F 1976

G 1977

H 1977

1978

J 1978

K 1978

L 1978

M 1978

N 1980

O 1980

P 1979

Q 1979

R 1980

S 1980

FIGURE G–26 *TWENTIETH-CENTURY MEN.*

FIGURE G–27 TWENTIETH-CENTURY WOMEN.

A
1981

B
1981

C
1981

D
1981

E
1981

F
1982

G
1982

H
1982

I
1982

J
1982

K
1983

L
1983

M
1983

N
1983

O
1983

P
1984

Q
1984

R
1984

S
1984

T
1984

FIGURE G—28 TWENTIETH-CENTURY MEN.

FIGURE G–29 TWENTIETH-CENTURY WOMEN.

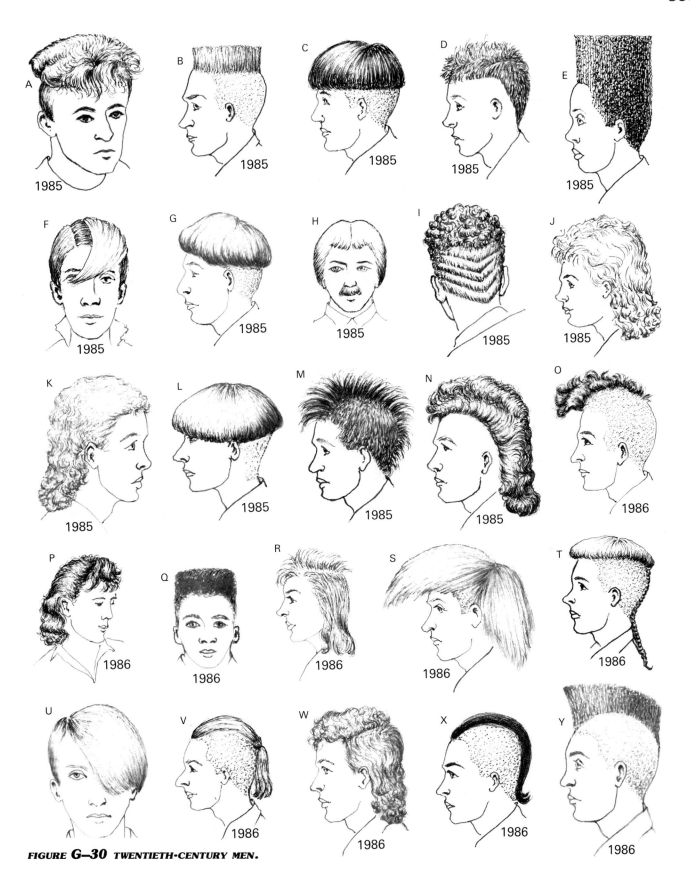

A 1985 B 1985 C 1985 D 1985 E 1985

F 1985 G 1985 H 1985 I 1985 J 1985

K 1985 L 1985 M 1985 N 1985 O 1986

P 1986 Q 1986 R 1986 S 1986 T 1986

U V 1986 W 1986 X 1986 Y 1986

FIGURE G–30 TWENTIETH-CENTURY MEN.

A 1985

B 1985

C 1985

D 1985

E 1985

F 1985

G 1985

H 1985

I 1985

J 1985

K 1985

L 1985

M 1985

N 1985

O 1985

P 1985

Q 1985

R 1985

S 1985

FIGURE G—31 TWENTIETH-CENTURY WOMEN.

A 1985 B 1985 C 1985 D 1985

E 1985 F 1985 G 1986 H 1986 I 1986

J 1986 K 1986 L 1986 M 1986 N 1986

O 1986 P 1986 Q 1986 R 1986 S 1986

FIGURE **G–32** TWENTIETH-CENTURY WOMEN.

FIGURE G–33 *TWENTIETH-CENTURY WOMEN.*

FIGURE **G-34** *TWENTIETH-CENTURY MEN.*

A 1987

B 1987

C 1988

D 1988

E 1988

F 1988

G 1988

H 1988

I 1988

J 1988

K 1988

L 1988

M 1988

N 1988

O 1988

P 1988

Q 1988

R 1988

S 1988

T 1988

U 1988

V 1988

W 1988

FIGURE G–35 TWENTIETH-CENTURY WOMEN.

A 1987
B 1987
C 1987
D 1987
E 1987
F 1987
G 1987
H 1987
I 1987
J 1987
K 1987
L 1987
M 1987
N 1987
O 1987
P 1987
Q 1987
R 1987
S 1987
T 1987

FIGURE **G—36** TWENTIETH-CENTURY WOMEN.

A 1988
B 1988
C 1988
D 1988
E 1988
F 1988
G 1988
H 1988
I 1988
J 1988
K 1988
L 1988
M 1988
N 1988
O 1988
P 1988
Q 1988
R 1988
S 1988
T 1988
U 1988
V 1988
W 1988
X 1988

*FIGURE **G–37** TWENTIETH-CENTURY WOMEN.*

FIGURE G—38 TWENTIETH-CENTURY WOMEN.

FIGURE G–39 TWENTIETH-CENTURY WOMEN.

A 1989
B 1989
C 1989
D 1989
E 1989
F 1989
G 1989
H 1989
I 1989
J 1989
K 1989
L 1989
M 1989
N 1989
O 1989
P 1989
Q 1989
R 1989
S 1989
T 1989
U 1989
V 1989
W 1989
X 1989

FIGURE G—40 *TWENTIETH-CENTURY WOMEN.*

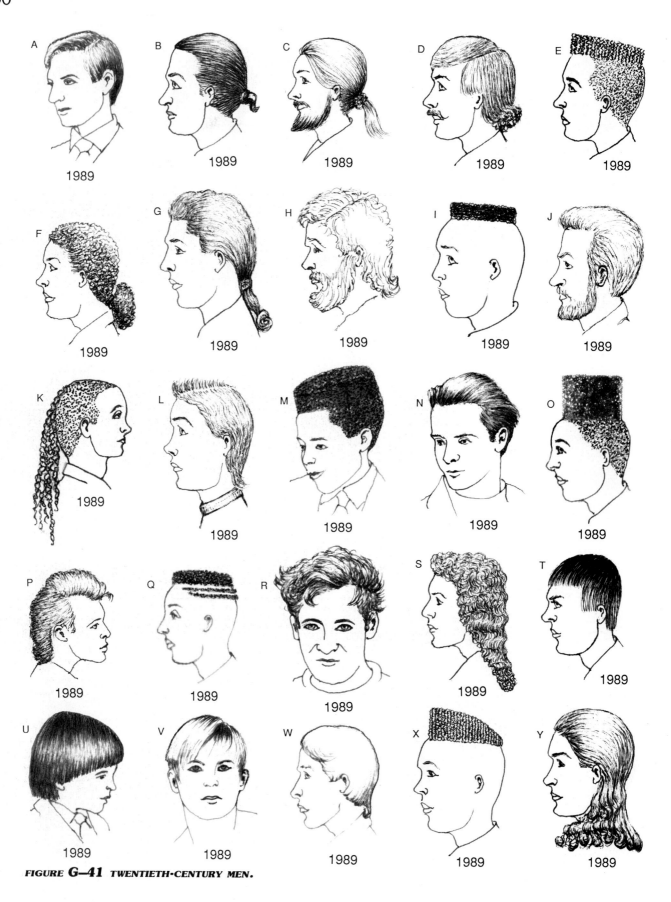

A 1989

B 1989

C 1989

D 1989

E 1989

F 1989

G 1989

H 1989

I 1989

J 1989

K 1989

L 1989

M 1989

N 1989

O 1989

P 1989

Q 1989

R 1989

S 1989

T 1989

U 1989

V 1989

W 1989

X 1989

Y 1989

FIGURE **G—41** *TWENTIETH-CENTURY MEN.*

Makeups In Color

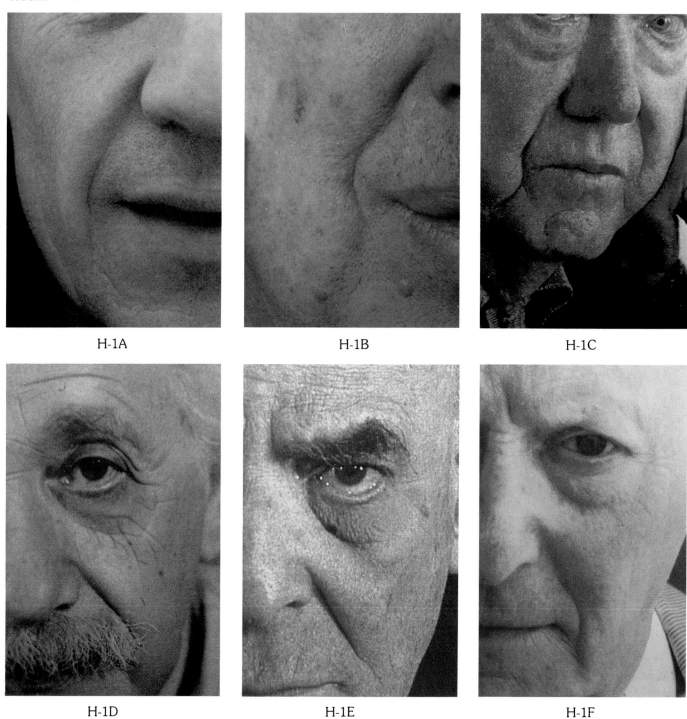

H-1A   H-1B   H-1C

H-1D   H-1E   H-1F

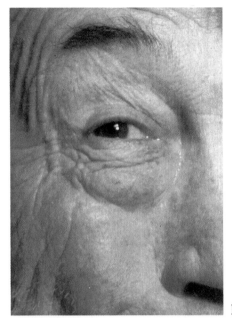

H-2A

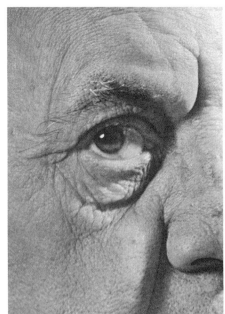

H-2B

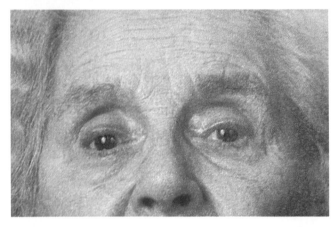

H-2C

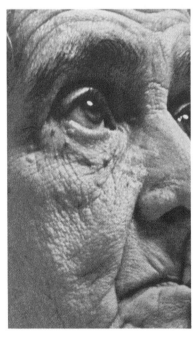

H-2D

H-2E

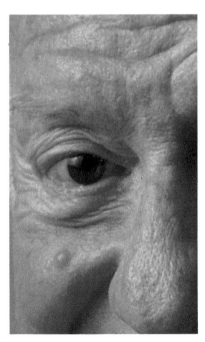

H-2F

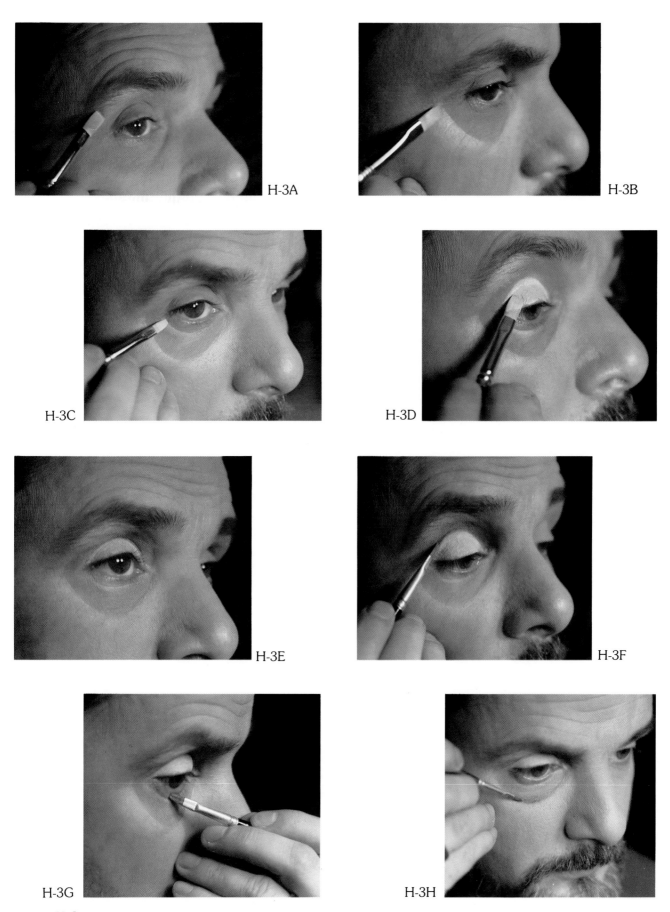

FIGURE H-3. BRUSH TECHNIQUE FOR APPLYING HIGHLIGHTS AND SHADOWS. (Subject: New York stage manager John Handy.)

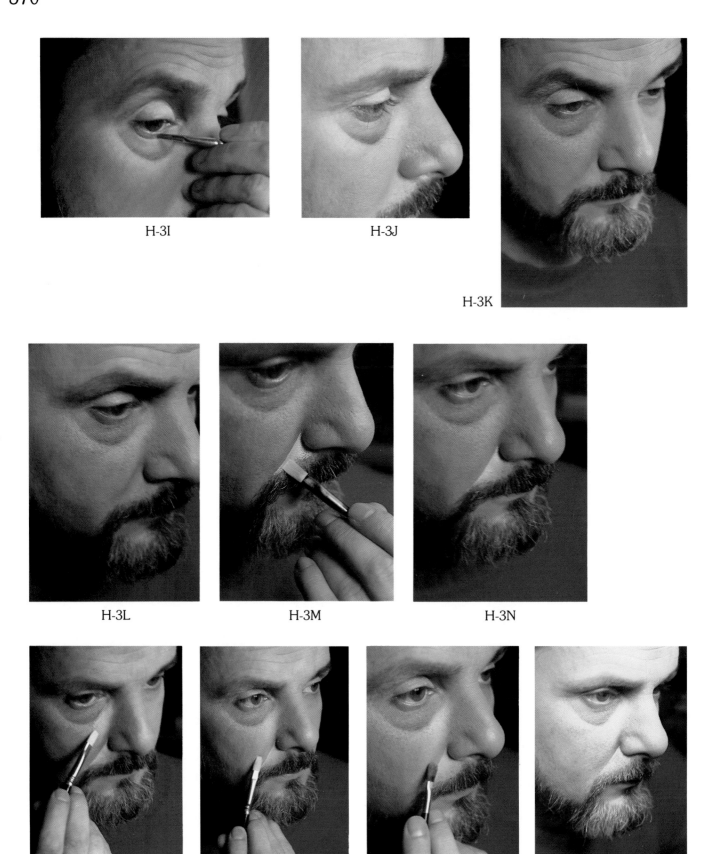

H-3I

H-3J

H-3K

H-3L

H-3M

H-3N

H-3O

H-3P

H-3Q

H-3R

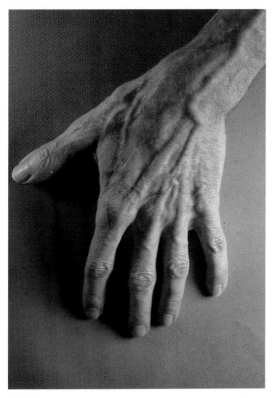

H-4A

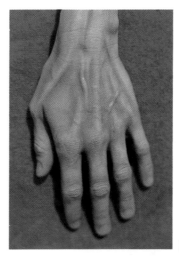

H-4B

H-4C

FIGURE *H-4A. HAND (REAL).*

FIGURE *H-4B. AGED HAND.* Makeup by student Gigi Coker.

FIGURE *H-4C. HAND BEING AGED WITH MAKEUP.* (Student Joe Allen Brown.)

FIGURE *H-4D. AGED HAND.* Highlighted, shadowed, and stippled for texture and color. Makeup by student Milton Blankenship.

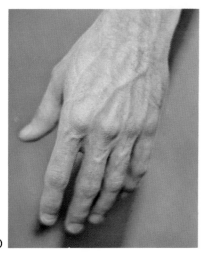

H-4D

FIGURE *H-5. COLOR AND TEXTURE IN THE FACE.*

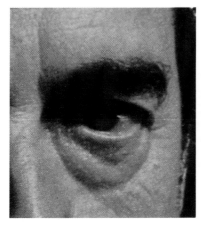

H-5A

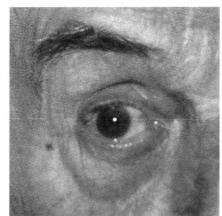

H-5B

H-5C

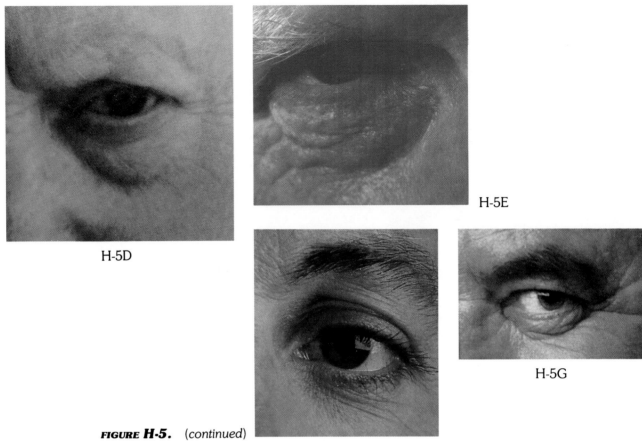

H-5E

H-5D

H-5G

*FIGURE **H-5.*** (continued)

H-5F

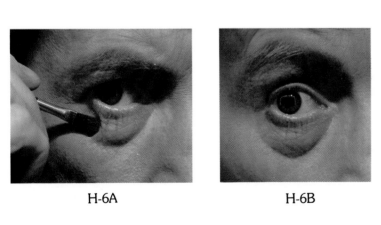

H-6A

H-6B

*FIGURE **H-6.** AGING THE FACE WITH HIGHLIGHTS AND SHADOWS.*

H-6C

FIGURE *H-7.* MODEL FOR FIGURE *H-8,* SHOWN WITHOUT MAKEUP.

FIGURE *H-8.* MAKEUP WITH LATEX AND TISSUE.

(From Kryolan's series of makeup color slides.)
A-B. Latex and tissue being applied. Head has been covered with a plastic cap.
C. Shadowing begun.
D. Makeup completed with wig, beard, and additional shadowing.
E. Removing the makeup.

H-7

H-8A

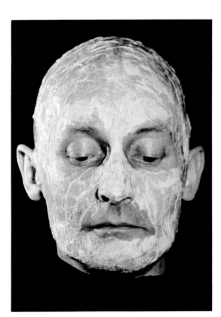

H-8B

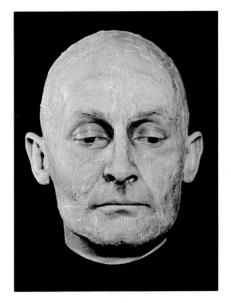

H-8C

H-8D

H-8E

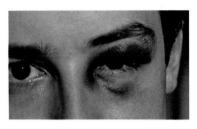

H-9A   H-9B

FIGURE H-9. BLACK EYE. *Photographs of a real black eye in its fifth day. Note that the red inflammation has disappeared.*

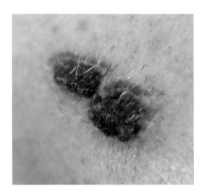

FIGURE H-10. SCABS (REAL).

FIGURE H-11. MOLE (REAL).

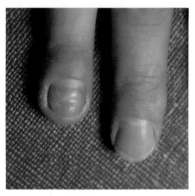

FIGURE H-12. BRUISED AND SWOLLEN FINGER.

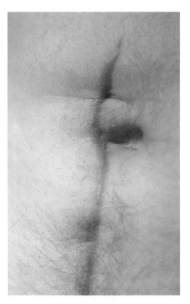

FIGURE H-13. SCAR FROM ABDOMINAL SURGERY. *(About 12 weeks.)*

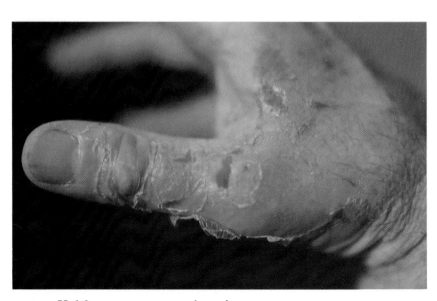

FIGURE H-14. SCALDED HAND (REAL).

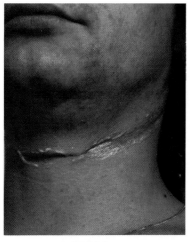

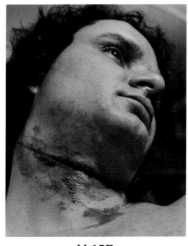

H-15A

H-15B

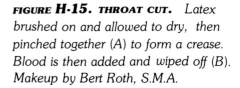

FIGURE **H-15.** THROAT CUT. *Latex brushed on and allowed to dry, then pinched together (A) to form a crease. Blood is then added and wiped off (B). Makeup by Bert Roth, S.M.A.*

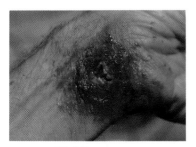

FIGURE **H-16.** PUNCTURE WOUND *IN WRIST.* *(See Chapter 13.)*

H-17A

H-17B

FIGURE **H-17.** MAKING A DEEP CUT. *Forehead area built up with derma wax, then cut with a palette knife. Grays, purples, and reds (A) are mixed to create a bruise. Creme rouge is then painted into the cut (B).*

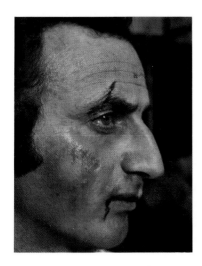

FIGURE **H-18.** SCAR AND BRUISE. *Collodian scar, artificial blood running from the mouth, and cheek painted to appear bruised and swollen. Makeup by Bert Roth, S.M.A.*

H-19A

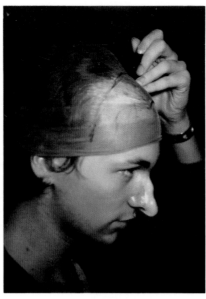

H-19B

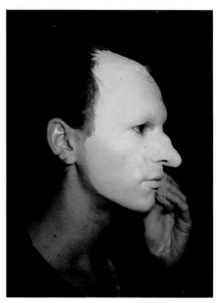

H-19C

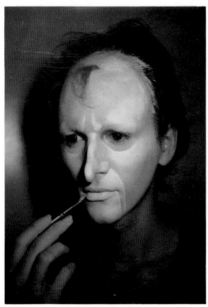

H-19D

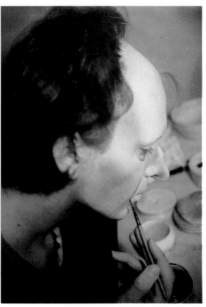

H-19E

H-19F

FIGURE H-19. MAKING UP AS FESTE IN TWELFTH NIGHT.
A. Soaping out front hair. Nose built up with putty.
B. Making outline of bald area with nylon stocking, which will cover soaped-out hair.
C. Applying the foundation with a sponge. Eyebrows have been blocked out.
D-E. Modeling the face with highlights and shadows.
F. Completed makeup, with painted eyebrows, rouge, and full lower lip. Makeup by student Lee Austin. (For other makeups by Mr. Austin, see Figures 13–7 and 13–8.)

FIGURE *H-20*. STYLIZED MAKEUP COPIED FROM AN ORIENTAL MASK. *Makeup by student Lee Austin.*

FIGURE *H-21*. FLOWER GIRL. *Petals from fresh flowers attached to the face with spirit gum. Makeup by student Barbara Murray.*

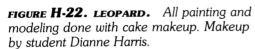

FIGURE *H-22*. LEOPARD. *All painting and modeling done with cake makeup. Makeup by student Dianne Harris.*

FIGURE *H-23*. BOTTOM THE WEAVER AS A JACKASS. *Latex mask with articulated lower jaw. Makeup by Paul Batson.*

FIGURE *H-24.* SIXTEENTH-CENTURY LADY.   *Based on a portrait by Leonardo da Vinci. Makeup by student Gaye Bowan.*

FIGURE *H-25.* FIFTEENTH-CENTURY LADY.   *Makeup by student Camille Carrell.*

FIGURE *H-27.* STYLIZED RABBIT MAKEUP.   *By student Barbara Murray.*

FIGURE *H-26.* CLOWN MAKEUP.   *By student Barbara Murray.*

H-28A

H-28B

H-28C

H-28D

FIGURE *H-28. NON-REALISTIC MAKEUP IN PROGRESS.* By student Lee Austin.

FIGURE **H-29.** STYLIZED MAKEUP BASED ON A MOSAIC OF THE EMPEROR JUSTINIAN. *Makeup by student Sheila Hargett.*

380

FIGURE *H-30.* MAKEUPS BY MARGARET SPICER.

FIGURE *H-31.* MAKEUPS FOR BETTY (TOP) (ACT I) AND GERRY (BOTTOM) (ACT II) IN CLOUD NINE. Theatre Department production at the California State University in Long Beach. Both characters were played by Steven Wickoff. Makeups were by instructor Robert Maverick.

FIGURE *H-32.* LIZARD MAN. Latex slush mold and bald cap. Makeup by Robert Maverick.

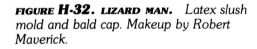

Makeup Color Charts

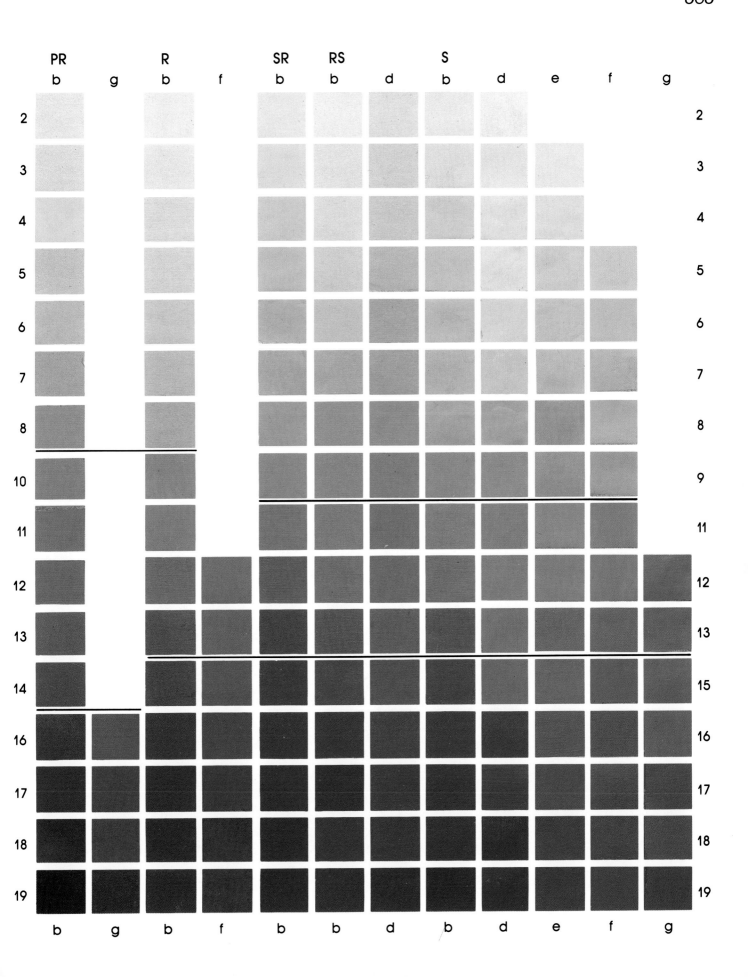

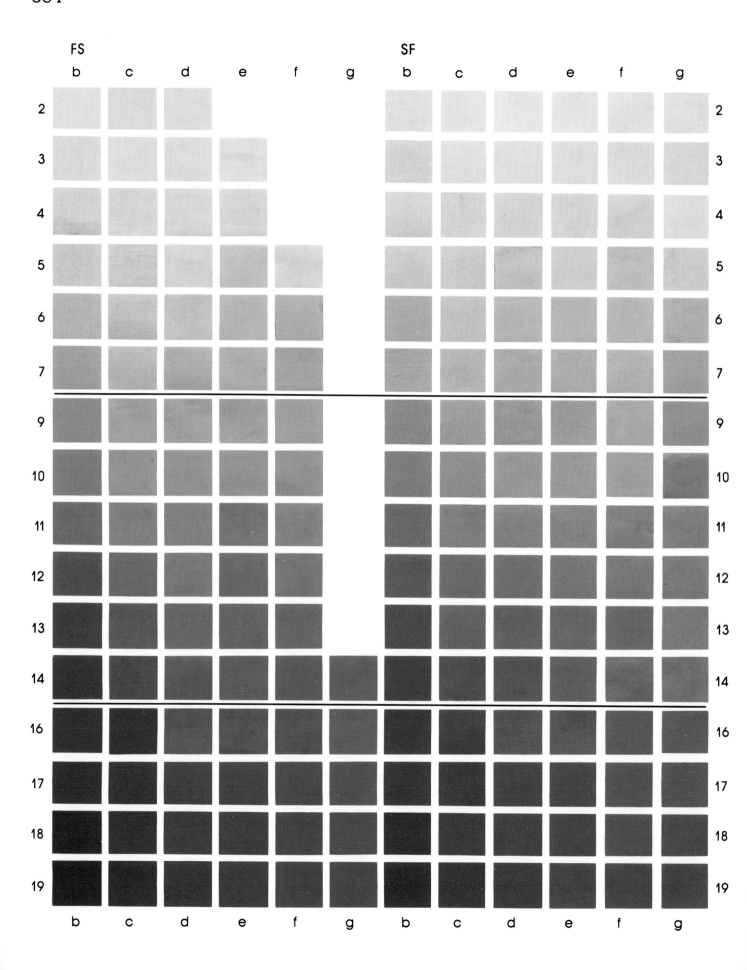

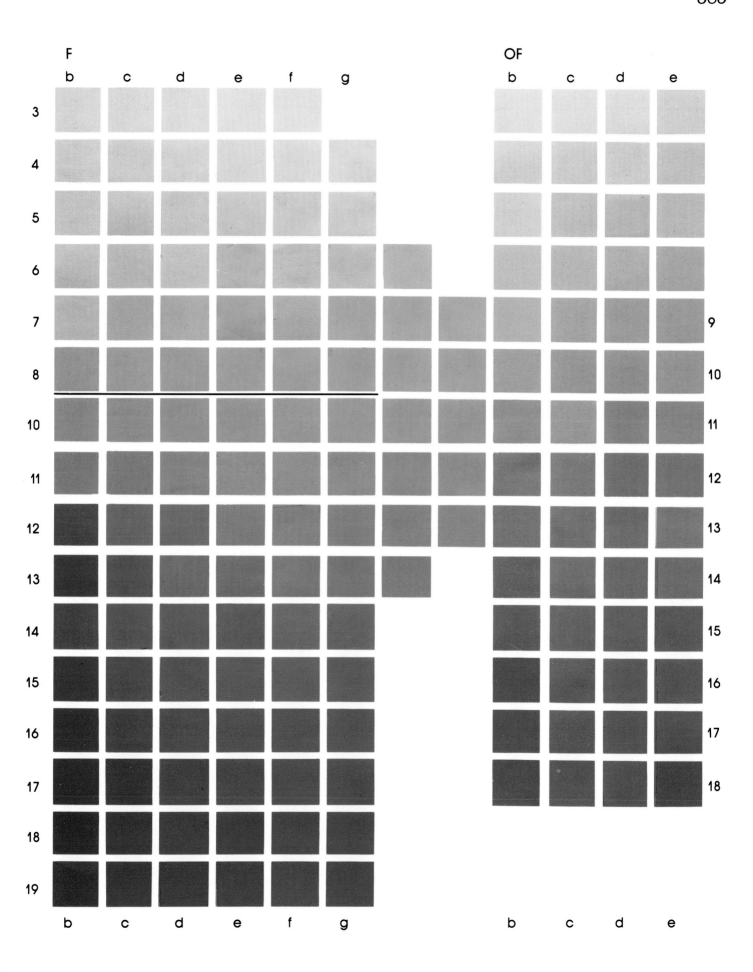

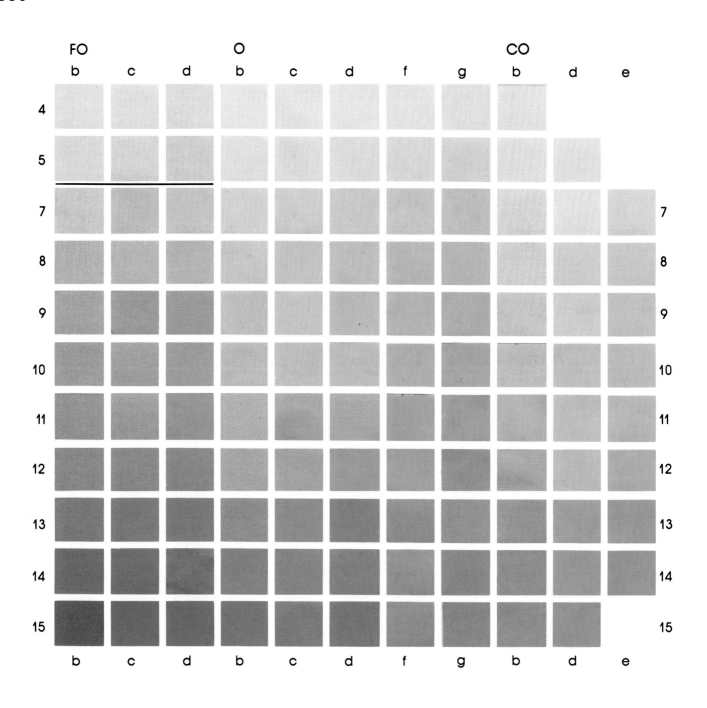

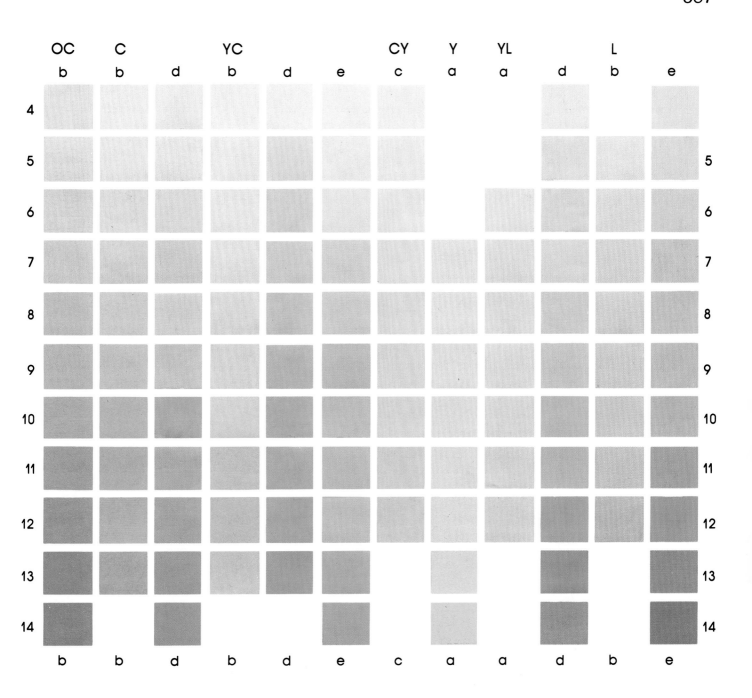

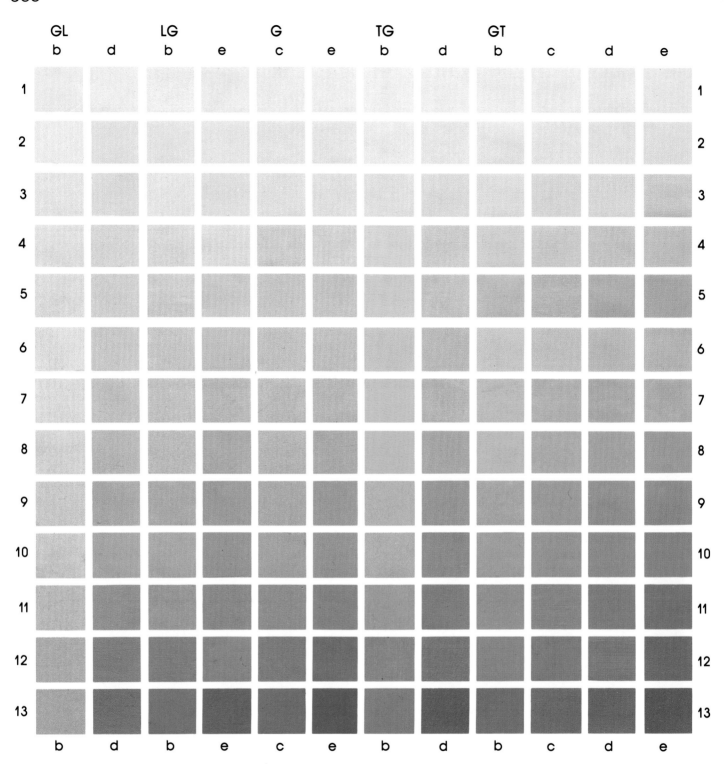

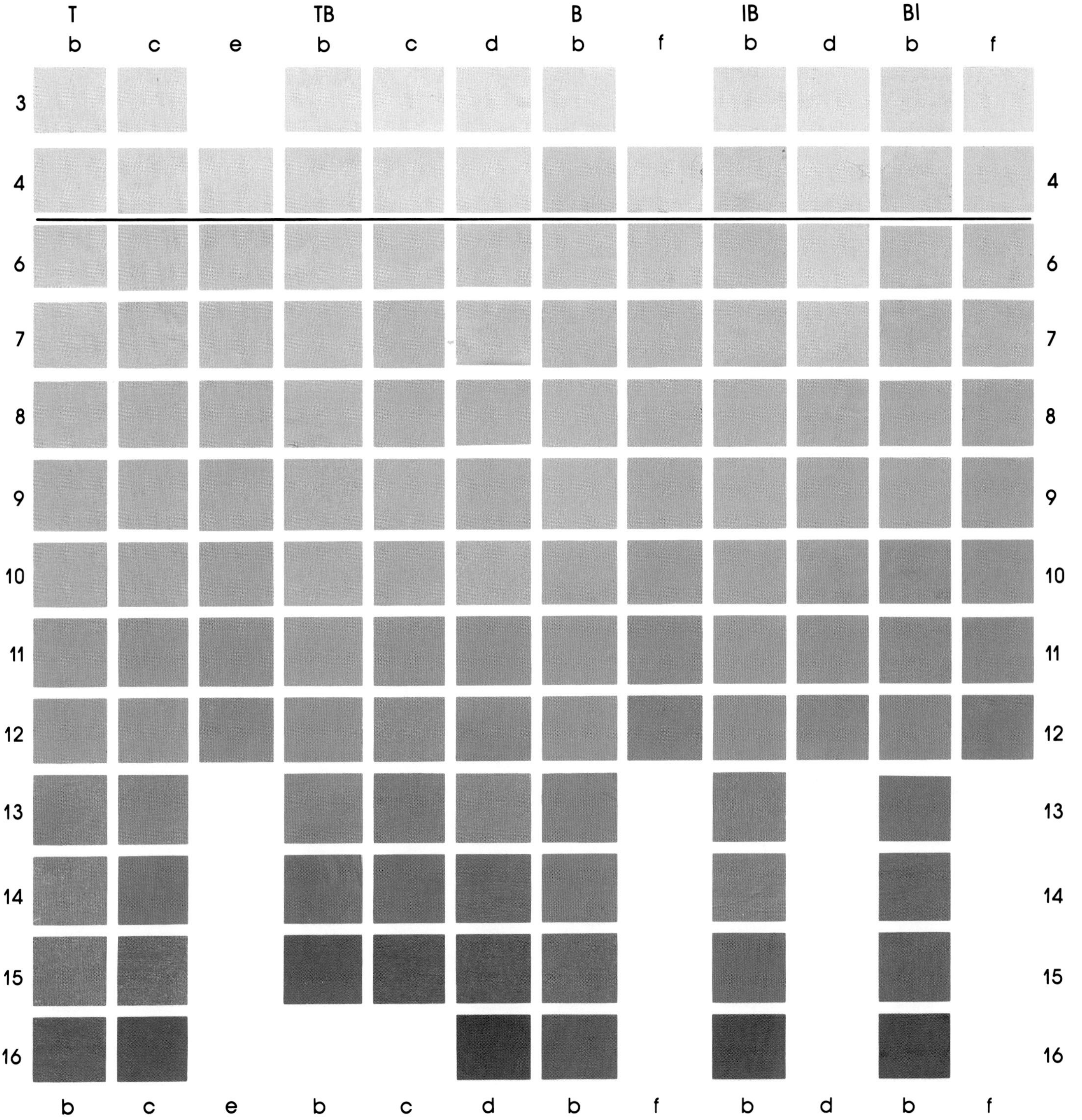
T
TB
B
IB
BI
b c e b c d b f b d b f
3
4
6
7
8
9
10
11
12
13
14
15
16
b c e b c d b f b d b f

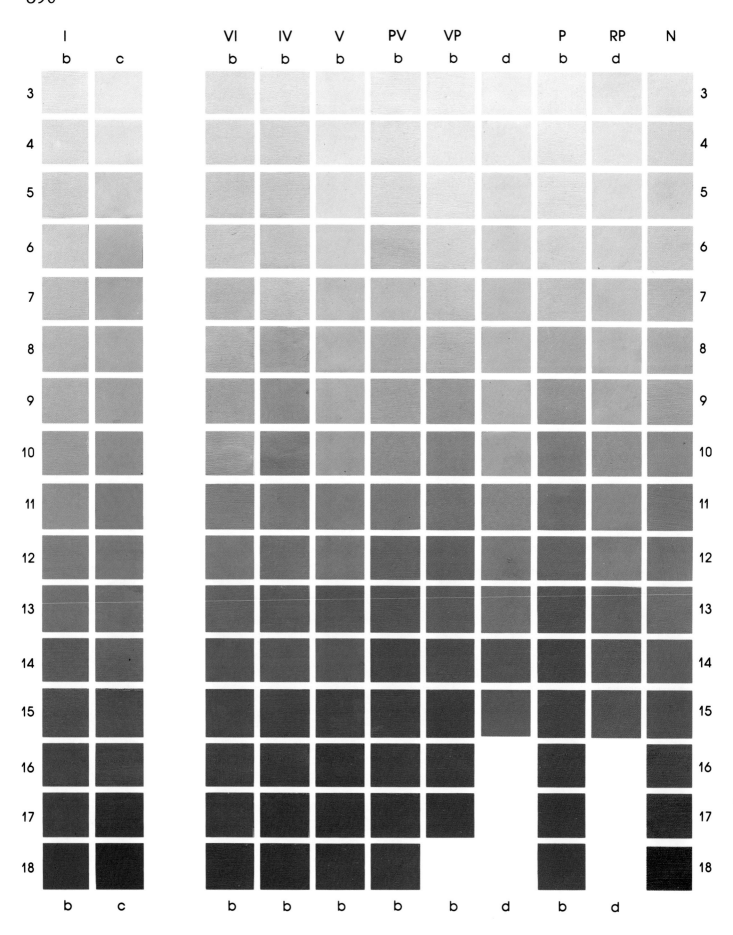

Makeup-color Tables

On the following pages colors are listed by both the standardized numbers and the numbers under which they are sold by the various makeup companies.

When you want to find out what makeup paints correspond to a particular standardized number, consult Table 1, which lists the colors currently available, along with the makeup companies that make them and the numbers they use to designate them.

If you should want to know what color a certain brand number actually represents, consult Table 2, which lists makeup by the brand name, along with the standardized numbers.

If you want to find the number of the paint in one brand of makeup that is equivalent to a certain number in another brand, refer first to the listing by company (Table 2) to find the standardized number, which will enable you to refer to Table 1, where you will find equivalent paints listed.

In Tables 1 and 2 the abbreviations used are:

bcs blemish-cover stick
br brush-on rouge
c cake makeup
cf creme foundation
cr creme rouge

dr dry rouge (pressed cake or powder)
es eyeshadow
ess eyeshadow stick
f foundation colors
h highlight colors
l lipstick
lr lip rouge
mc moist cake makeup
p makeup pencils
ps pressed shadow
rmg rubber-mask greasepaint
s shading colors
R Red
S Scarlet
F Flame
O Orange
C Chrome
Y Yellow
L Lime
G Green
T Turquoise
B Blue
I Indigo
V Violet
P Purple

TABLE 1   THE STANDARDIZED COLOR NUMBERS AND THEIR EQUIVALENT COLOR NUMBERS USED BY THE VARIOUS MAKEUP COMPANIES

RP/PR

RP/PR-11-a
  STEIN: *dr* 18
RP/PR-11-d
  STEIN: *dr* 20

PR

PR-2-a
  MEHRON: *f* 2
PR-5-a
  KELLY: *dr* Female
PR-6-a
  KELLY: *cr* SR-2
  MEHRON: *cr* 11
PR-7-a
  BLASCO: *dr* Rose
PR-8-a/b
  KELLY: *dr* SRC-4
PR-9-a
  MEHRON: *cr* 10
PR-9-a/b
  KELLY: *cr* SR-4
PR-9-d
  NYE: *l* 7
PR-10-a
  STEIN: *dr* 14
PR-10-a/b
  KELLY: *cr* SR-5
PR-10-g
  KRYOLAN: EC2
PR-12-a
  NYE: *dr* Raspberry
  STEIN: *cr* 5
PR-12-g
  KELLY: *s* SL-16
PR-13-a
  STEIN: *cr* 7; *dr* 16
PR-13-h
  KELLY: *cf* 32-E
PR-14-b
  KRYOLAN: Carmin 3
PR-16-a
  STEIN: *s* 21
PR-16-g
  NYE: *ps* Burgundy
PR-17-a
  KRYOLAN: Carmin 4
PR-17-b
  KRYOLAN: Altrot
PR-18-a
  KRYOLAN: 086
  MEHRON: *lr* CR
PR-18-b
  STEIN: *s* 13

PR-19-c
  BLASCO: *s* Maroon
  MEHRON: *lr* Maroon

R/PR

R/PR-7-b
  KELLY: *dr* Male
R/PR-13-a
  STEIN: *cr* 3
R/PR-14-b
  KRYOLAN: 083
R/PR-15-a
  MEHRON: *lr* Cherry
R/PR-16-a
  MEHRON: *lr* Dark
R/PR-16-a/b
  KRYOLAN: 082

R

R-1-a
  KELLY (MIRAGE):
    Pink
R-3-f
  KRYOLAN: 072
R-4-d
  NYE: *ps* Sterling Pink
R-8-a
  KELLY: *cr* SR-9
  MEHRON: *cr*10
R-9-a
  KELLY: *dr* DRC-1
R-9-a/b
  NYE: *cf* Misty Pink
R-10-a
  KELLY: *cr* SR-3
  KRYOLAN: R6
R-10-b
  BLASCO: *dr* Mauve
R-10-h
  MEHRON: *s* RC12
R-11-a
  NYE: *dr* Red
R-12-a
  NYE: *dr* Flame Red
R-12-a/b
  KELLY: *l* LP-3
R-12-c
  KELLY: *l* Zebra
  NYE: *dr* Brick Red
R-12-f
  STEIN: *cf* 50
R-13-a
  KELLY: *l* LP-1
R-13-b

NYE: *l* 5
R-14-a
  MEHRON: *lr* Cherry
R-16-a
  BLASCO: *s* Blood
    Color
R-16-b
  KELLY: *s* Sl-18
  STEIN: *s* 12
R-16-b/c
  NYE: *l* 9

R/SR

R/SR-10-a
  NYE: *cr* CR-4

SR

SR-2-a
  KRYOLAN: Naturell
  MEHRON: *f* 1
SR-2-b
  KRYOLAN: G14
  KELLY: *cf* S-2
SR-3-a
  KRYOLAN: 03
SR-3-a/b
  BLASCO: *cf* Stage
    Base 1
SR-4-a
  BLASCO: *cf* Fair Pink
SR-6-a/b
  BLASCO: *cf* Stage
    Base 2
  KELLY: *cr* SR-1
SR-7-b
  KELLY: *dr* Bronze
SR-8-a
  KELLY: *cr* SR-10
  KRYOLAN: 031
SR-9-a
  KRYOLAN: R5
SR-10-a
  BLASCO: *dr* Coral
SR-10-d
  KELLY: *l* Cinnamon
SR-11-a
  KRYOLAN: 078
SR-12-a
  KELLY: *l* LP-4
  STEIN: *cr* 6
SR-13-a
  STEIN: *s* 14
SR-14-a
  KRYOLAN: 081

MEHRON: *lr* Medium
  STEIN: *cr* 4
SR-14-e
  BLASCO: *cf* Death
    Purple
SR-14-g
  MEHRON: *s* RC-14
SR-16-b
  NYE: *s* Maroon
SR-17-b
  STEIN: *cf* 9

SR/RS

SR/RS-8-b
  KELLY: *l* LP-5
SR/RS-8-b/c
  MEHRON: *f* LM D
SR/RS-10-a
  NYE: *dr* Coral Red
SR/RS-10-b
  NYE: *cr* Dusty Rose
SR/RS-10-c
  KRYOLAN: 012
SR/RS-11-a/b
  STEIN: *cr* 8
SR/RS-12-a
  BLASCO: Red
  KRYOLAN: Carmin 2
  NYE: *s* Fire Red

RS

RS-2-b
  NYE: *cf* P-2
RS-5-b
  MEHRON: *f* 5
RS-6-d/e
  KELLY: *cf* Coppertone
RS-6½-a/b
  KRYOLAN: B
RS-8-a
  KRYOLAN: R3
RS-8-a/b
  KRYOLAN: *dr* TC1
  NYE: *l* Coral
RS-8-b
  BLASCO: *cf* Stage
    Base #3
RS-10-a
  KELLY: (MIRAGE)
    Pink Strawberry
  NYE: *cr* Coral
  STEIN: *dr* 3
RS-10-a/b
  KELLY: (MIRAGE)

TABLE 1 (CONTINUED)

Bronze
KRYOLAN: *dr*
Mandarin
RS-10-b
BLASCO: *cr* Coral
Rose
RS-10-c
KRYOLAN: *dr* R20
RS-10-d
KELLY: *cr* SR-Bronze
RS-11-b
MEHRON: *cr* 20
RS-11-b/c
MEHRON: *f* 10b
RS-12-a
KELLY: *l* LP-9
KRYOLAN: 079
MEHRON: *lr* L
RS-12-b
KELLY: *l* LP-2
KRYOLAN:
Schattierrot
RS-12-e
NYE: *ps* Burgundy
RS-13-a
KRYOLAN: Carmin 1
STEIN: *cf* 48; *s* 18; *cr* 1
RS-13-a/b
NYE: *cr* Dk.
Technicolor
RS-13-c
KELLY: *cf* CVA-Red
RS-13-e
MEHRON: *c* Red
Brown
RS-14-a
KELLY: *cf* Red
KRYOLAN: Jugendrot
NYE: *cr* Red; *l* 14
RS-14-c/d
NYE: *l* 12
RS-15-a
KRYOLAN: 080
MEHRON: *f* Red
RS-15-a/b
NYE: *s* Blood Red
RS-15-d/e
MEHRON: *s* RC11
RS-17-d
KRYOLAN: 046

S/RS

S/RS-1½-a/b
STEIN: *f* 1½

S

S-½-a
MEHRON: *c* 1B

S-1-a
MEHRON: *c* 2b
S-2-a/b
MEHRON: *f* B
S-2-g
STEIN: *ess* 1
S-2½-b
KRYOLAN: 2
S-3-a/b
MEHRON: *f* 3B; *c* 5B,
24A
S-3-c
KRYOLAN: 101 (B)
S-3-c/d
KRYOLAN: G15
S-3-e
KRYOLAN: G104
S-4-a
STEIN: *f* 2
S-4-b
KELLY: *cf* S-4
S-4-d
KRYOLAN (B): F11
S-5-a
KRYOLAN: 449
S-5-a/b
MEHRON: *f* 7B
S-5-b
MEHRON: *f* 7
S-5-d
KELLY: *cf* S-3
S-5-g
STEIN: *f* 13
S-6-b
KRYOLAN: 3½ (B)
S-6-e
KRYOLAN: 160
S-6-f
MEHRON: *f* 11B
S-7-a
KRYOLAN: R9
S-7-c
KELLY: *cf* S-6
S-8-a/b
KRYOLAN: *dr* G113
S-8-b
KELLY: *l* LP-6
S-8-c/d
MEHRON: *f* 9
S-8-d
KELLY: *cr* SR-6
S-8-e
MEHRON: *c* 43
S-8-h
MEHRON: *c* 11B
S-9-a
KELLY: *cr* SR-8
S-9-d/e
KELLY: *l* Coffee

S-9-h
KRYOLAN: EC5
S-10-b/c
MEHRON: *f* 12
S-11-a
KELLY: *l* LP-8
S-11-e
KRYOLAN: 431
S-11-g
KRYOLAN: 4½
S-11-h
MEHRON: *c* 37
S-12-a
KELLY: *l* LP-Orange
NYE: *cr* Red
S-12-c
KELLY: *cf* S-15
S-12-d
KRYOLAN: 075
S-13-d
NYE: *dr* Chestnut
STEIN: *f* 9
S-13-f
NYE: *s* 40
S-13-g
MEHRON: *c* 38
S-14-a
KRYOLAN: 416
S-14-b
KRYOLAN: Hellrot
S-14-d
MEHRON: *s* RC10
S-16-b
BLASCO: *cf* Stage
Base 4
S-16-d/e
STEIN: *cf* 41A
S-17-d
KRYOLAN: 30
S-18-b/c
MEHRON: *lr* Sp. 5
S-18-e
KRYOLAN: 050
S-19-b
STEIN: *s* 22

S/FS

S/FS-3-e
KRYOLAN: K1
S/FS-4-c
KRYOLAN: F10 (B)
S/FS-6-d/e
STEIN: *cf* Natural B
S/FS-7-d/e
MEHRON: *c* 41
S/FS-9-b/c
STEIN: *f* 7F
S/FS-9-d/e
MEHRON: *c* 42

S/FS-10-e
KELLY: *cf* S-10
S/FS-10-e/f
KELLY: *cf* BK-1
S/FS-11-d
STEIN: *f* 10
S/FS-12-e/f
KELLY: *cf* BK-7
S/FS-12-f
KELLY: *cf* BK-2
S/FS-12-g
KELLY: RMG-5
S/FS-14-c/d
STEIN: *cf* 37
S/FS-15-b/c
STEIN: *cf* 41

FS

FS-1-a
BLASCO: *h* Pink
Highlight 1
MEHRON: *f* A
FS-1-b
STEIN: *f* 4
FS-1-c
KELLY: *cf* S-21; *mc*
Ivory
FS-2-a
KRYOLAN: 576
FS-2-b
MEHRON: *c* 21
STEIN: *cf* Natural A
FS-2-e
KRYOLAN: F7
FS-3-a
NYE: *h* Extra Lite
FS-3-c
KRYOLAN: FF21
FS-3-g
BLASCO: *cf* Death
Gray
FS-3½-c
KRYOLAN: G41
FS-4-b
MEHRON: *c* 3B
FS-4-c
BLASCO: *h* Pink
Highlight 2
MEHRON: *c* 40
FS-4-e
KRYOLAN: F5
FS-4-j
KRYOLAN: FF1
FS-4½-c
KRYOLAN: FA
FS-5-a
STEIN: *f* 3
FS-5-b
MEHRON: *c* 25A

TABLE 1 (CONTINUED)

FS-5-c/d
  KRYOLAN: 6
  STEIN: *cf* Natural Blush
FS-5-d/e
  STEIN: *cf* Tan Blush
FS-5-e
  BLASCO: *cf* Stage
    Base 6
FS-6-b
  KELLY: *mc* Rose
FS-6-b/c
  MEHRON: *c* 26A
FS-7-b/c
  MEHRON: *c* 27A
FS-7-c
  BLASCO: *cf* AD1
FS-8-a
  MEHRON: 7½ B
FS-8-b
  MEHRON: *c* 9B
FS-8-b/c
  BLASCO: *cr* Pastel
    Rose
  MEHRON: *c* 28A
FS-8-d/e
  KRYOLAN: F13
FS-8-e
  KRYOLAN: F12 (B)
FS-8-e/f
  KELLY: *cf* S-8
FS-9-b
  MEHRON: *c* 12B
  NYE: *dr* Coral
FS-9-b/c
  KELLY: *l* LP-7
  MEHRON: *f* 6
FS-9-c
  MEHRON: *c* 29A
  STEIN: *cf* 45
FS-9-e
  KRYOLAN: F6
FS-9-f
  KRYOLAN: EC8
FS-9½-c
  MEHRON: *c* 30A
FS-10-b
  BLASCO: *dr* Peach
FS-10-b/c
  MEHRON: *c* 10B
FS-10-c
  MEHRON: *c* 31A
  STEIN: *cf* 7
FS-10-c/d
  BLASCO: *cr* Nat.
    Cheek Color Regular
FS-10-d
  KELLY (MIRAGE):
    Warm Red

FS-10-d/e
  KELLY: *cf* Bronzetone
  KRYOLAN: 035
FS-10-e
  KELLY: RMG 3
FS-10-f
  KELLY: *cf* SC-50
FS-11-c
  KRYOLAN: 9
  LEICHNER: *f* 8
  MEHRON: *rmg* LM 11
FS-11-d
  KRYOLAN: 4
FS-11-d/e
  KELLY: *cf* S-14
FS-11-e
  STEIN: *cf* 38
FS-11-e/f
  KELLY: *cf* BK-6
FS-12-a
  KRYOLAN: Zinnober
  NYE: *cr* Blush Coral
FS-12-b
  STEIN: *dr* 12
FS-12-d
  KELLY: *cf* S-22
FS-12-d/e
  MEHRON: *c* 31
FS-12-f
  KELLY: *cf* S-23
  KRYOLAN: G5
FS-13-b
  STEIN: *cf* 42
FS-13-e
  KELLY: *cf* S-7
  KRYOLAN: F14
FS-13-g
  BLASCO: *s* Character
    Gray
FS-16-e
  KELLY: RMG 4
FS-16-g
  NYE: *s* 44
FS-17-e
  KELLY: *cf* S-18
FS-18-b/c
  KRYOLAN: *dr*
    Schattierbraun
FS-18½-b
  MEHRON: *s* 8½
FS-19-e
  KRYOLAN: 047
FS-19-f/g
  KRYOLAN: 103

FS/SF

FS/SF-12-g
  KRYOLAN: 039
FS/SF-13-a/b

KELLY (MIRAGE):
  Grape

SF

SF-1½-b
  KRYOLAN: 01
SF-2½-b
  MEHRON: *f* 22
SF-3-a
  KRYOLAN: 02
  STEIN: *f* 21
SF-3-a/b
  KELLY: *bcs* Light
  MEHRON: *f* C
  STEIN: *f* 2½
SF-3-b
  KRYOLAN: FF2
  STEIN: *cf* Cream Blush
SF-3-b/c
  KELLY: *cf* Olive
  KRYOLAN: FF3
SF-3-c
  STEIN: *cf* Cream B
SF-3½-b
  STEIN: *cf* 44
SF-4-a
  KRYOLAN: 2½
SF-4-a/b
  MEHRON: *f* D
SF-4½-a/b
  KRYOLAN: 104
SF-4½-b
  KRYOLAN: P3
SF-5-b
  KRYOLAN: FB
  MEHRON: *rmg* LM5
  NYE: *f* P-3
SF-6-a/b
  MEHRON: *f* F
SF-6-b
  KELLY: *br* Amber
SF-6-c
  KELLY: *cf* Natural Tan
SF-6-d
  BLASCO: *cf* Blushtone
    1
SF-6-f
  KRYOLAN: FF4
SF-7-d
  BLASCO: *cf* Blushtone
    2
  KRYOLAN: 3
SF-7-e
  STEIN: *cf* Tan A
SF-7-e/f
  BLASCO: Natural
    Shading 1
SF-7-f/g
  KELLY: *cf* Deep Olive;

RMG 2
SF-8-b
  BLASCO: *cr* AD-2
SF-8-b/c
  MEHRON: *f* 28A
SF-8-d
  MEHRON: *f* 40
SF-8-e
  BLASCO: Natural
    Shading 2
  KRYOLAN: FF14
SF-8-e/f
  KELLY: *br* Tawny
SF-8-h
  KRYOLAN: EC6
SF-9-a/b
  STEIN: *f* 8
SF-9-b/c
  KELLY: *cr* SR-7
SF-9-c
  BLASCO: *cr* CTV
  STEIN: *cf* 2
SF-9-c/d
  KRYOLAN: FE
SF-9-d
  BLASCO: *f* DW #3
SF-9-e
  MEHRON: *cr* 9
SF-9-f
  BLASCO: *s* 1
SF-9-g
  NYE: *ps* ES-10
SF-9½-e
  KRYOLAN: EC1
SF-10-b
  BLASCO: *cr* Coral
    Orange
  NYE: *s* Sunburn Stipple
SF-10-c/d
  KELLY: *cf* Golden Tan
  KRYOLAN: *dr* 665G
SF-10-e
  BLASCO: *cf* Rugged
    Tan 2
  STEIN: *cf* Tan B
SF-10-f
  BLASCO: *s* Shading 2
  MEHRON: *s* 9
SF-10-g
  KELLY: *s* KS-1
SF-10-h
  KRYOLAN: EC7
SF-10½-c
  MEHRON: *f* 8B
SF-11-d
  BLASCO: *cf* Rugged
    Tan 1
SF-11-e
  KRYOLAN: F31

TABLE 1 (CONTINUED)

SF-11-f
  KELLY: cf BK-5
SF-12-a
  NYE: dr Dark
    Technicolor
SF-12-a/b
  BLASCO: cf Stage
    Base #5
SF-12-d/e
  STEIN: cf 39
SF-12-e
  KELLY: cf S-17
SF-12½-b
  BLASCO: mr Light
    Burnt Orange
SF-13-c
  NYE: s Sunburn Stipple
SF-13-c/d
  STEIN: cf 35
SF-13-d
  BLASCO: mr Dark
    Burnt Orange
SF-13-e
  KRYOLAN: 8
  MEHRON: f 37
SF-13-f
  STEIN: ess 2
SF-14-d
  STEIN: cf 36
SF-16-a/b
  STEIN: cr 9
SF-17-f
  KRYOLAN: 453
SF-18-c
  KRYOLAN: 113
SF-18-d
  MEHRON: rmg LME
SF-19-d
  STEIN: ess 7
SF-20-d
  BLASCO: cf Dark Skin
    Shading 4

F/SF

F/SF-6-d
  KELLY: bcs Dark
F/SF-8-d
  BLASCO: cf
    Summertan
  KELLY (MIRAGE):
    Blender Tone
F/SF-10-b
  BLASCO: cr Rose
    Orange
F/SF-10-c
  STEIN: f 14
F/SF-10-d
  KELLY (MIRAGE):
    Terra cotta

F/SF-10½-g
  KRYOLAN: EC4
F/SF-16-a
  KELLY (MIRAGE):
    Darkest Tone
F/SF-16-d
  BLASCO: cf Ruddy
    Dark Skin Base 6
F/SF-17-e
  BLASCO: cf Ruddy
    Dark Skin Base 7
F/SF-19-f
  BLASCO: cf Ruddy
    Dark Skin Base 8

F

F-1-a
  KRYOLAN: 406
F-1-f
  BLASCO: cf TV White
F-2-b
  BLASCO: cf Stage
    Base 8
F-2-c
  BLASCO: cf Ruddy
    Ultra Fair 1
F-2-e
  KELLY (MIRAGE):
    Ivory
F-2½-f
  KRYOLAN: 513
F-3-b
  STEIN: cf Cream A
F-3-c
  BLASCO: cf Fair
  KELLY (MIRAGE):
    Rose Glow
F-3½-c
  BLASCO: h Orange
    Highlight 1
F-3-d
  KRYOLAN: FS4
F-4-b
  KELLY: cf Fairest
F-4-e
  KELLY: mc Natural
F-4½-b
  BLASCO: cf Cream
F-4½-b/c
  BLASCO: cf Peachtone
    1
F-4½-c
  KELLY: cf Lady Fair
  KRYOLAN: F2
F-5-b
  KRYOLAN: F2(B)
F-5-c
  BLASCO: h Orange

Highlight 2
  KRYOLAN: F4(B)
F-5-d
  KRYOLAN: 034
F-5½-b
  KRYOLAN: 033
  MEHRON: f E
  NYE: cf L-1
F-5½-b/c
  BLASCO: cf
    Peachtone 2
F-5½-c
  KELLY: cf Light
    Brunette
  KRYOLAN: P2
F-5½-d
  KRYOLAN: F4
F-6-a/b
  KRYOLAN: FS8
F-6-b
  KELLY: bcs Medium
  MEHRON: f 2½
  NYE: cf L-2
F-6-c
  KELLY: cf Medium
    Brunette
  KRYOLAN: FF13
F-6-d
  KELLY: cf Tantone
  KRYOLAN: F3
  STEIN: cf Tan Blush 2
F-6-d/e
  KELLY: cf Medium
    Olive
F-6½-b
  NYE: cf L-3
F-6½-c
  KRYOLAN: FF5
F-6½-c/d
  KRYOLAN: FF
F-7-a/b
  STEIN: f 3½
F-7-b
  MEHRON: c 6½B; f G
  NYE: cf L-5
F-7-b/c
  BLASCO: cf
    Peachtone 3
  NYE: cf L-5
F-7-d
  KELLY: cf Dark
    Brunette
  KRYOLAN: F17
F-7-d/e
  KRYOLAN: F16
F-7-e
  KRYOLAN: 438
F-7½-b

MEHRON: f 8B
F-7½-e
  KELLY: cf BK-3
F-8-b
  MEHRON: rmg LM-8
F-8-b/c
  STEIN: f 7
F-8-c/d
  KELLY: br Cocoa
  KRYOLAN: 017
  STEIN: cf Tan Blush 3
F-8-d
  BLASCO: cf
    Blushtone 3
F-8½-d
  KELLY: cf BK-4
F-9-a/b
  BLASCO: cf EF 3
F-9-b/c
  BLASCO: cf
    Peachtone 4
F-9-c/d
  BLASCO: cf
    Blushtone 4
F-9-d
  NYE: cf M-1
F-10-a
  KRYOLAN: 032
F-10-a/b
  BLASCO: cf EF 4
F-10-b
  BLASCO: cf EF 9
F-10-d
  MEHRON: f 28
  NYE: cf M-2
F-10-i
  KRYOLAN: F9
F-11-b
  BLASCO: mr Brick
F-11-c/d
  BLASCO: cf DW #4
F-11-d
  BLASCO: cf California
    Tan
  KELLY (MIRAGE):
    Dark Average
  NYE: cf M-3
  MEHRON: f 29A
F-11-g
  KRYOLAN: 425
F-12-c
  BLASCO: cf EF 8
F-12-c/d
  BLASCO: cf Men's
    Cheekcolor
F-12-d
  BLASCO: s Natural
    Shading 3

TABLE 1   (CONTINUED)

NYE: *cf* M-5
F-12-d/e
　MEHRON: *f* 30
F-12-f
　KRYOLAN: G1
F-12-f/g
　MEHRON: *c* 4C
F-12½-f/g
　MEHRON: *c* 5C
F-13-d
　KELLY: *mc* Bronze
F-13-g
　MEHRON: *f* 6C
F-13-h
　MEHRON: *f* 7C
F-14-d
　KRYOLAN: 13
F-14-f
　NYE: *ps* Bronzed Sable
F-14-g
　MEHRON: *c* 14B
F-15-f
　KRYOLAN: EC3
　NYE: *s* 43
F-15-h
　MEHRON: *f* 8C
F-16-e
　KELLY: *cf* S-2
F-16½-e
　KELLY: *cf* S-11
F-17-c
　KELLY: *cf* S-16
　KRYOLAN: 470
F-17-d
　NYE: *cf* P-8
F-17-e
　BLASCO: *s* Dark
　　Brown
F-17-h
　MEHRON: *f* 9C
F-17-i
　MEHRON: *c* 17B
F-18-b
　KRYOLAN: 08
　STEIN: *s* 1
F-18-d
　BLASCO: *s* Dark Skin
　　Shading 3
F-18½-b
　BLASCO: *cf* Stage
　　Base 10
F-19-f
　KELLY: *cf* SC-54
F-19-h
　MEHRON: *f* 10C
F-20-f
　STEIN: *f* 16

F/OF

F/OF-5-b
　KRYOLAN: FS9
F/OF-5-d
　BLASCO: *cf* Medium
　　Olive
F/OF-5½-c/d
　KRYOLAN: F3
F/OF-8-b
　MEHRON: *f* H
F/OF-8-f
　KRYOLAN: F10
F/OF-10-c/d
　BLASCO: *cf* Dark
　　Bronzetone
F/OF-11-b
　BLASCO: *cf* EF10
F/OF-11-b/c
　BLASCO: *cf* EF6
F/OF-14-c/d
　BLASCO:*s* Shading 4

OF

OF-1-b
　MEHRON: *h* 17
OF-1-c
　KELLY: *s* HL-1
OF-2½-b
　KRYOLAN: P1
OF-3-c
　BLASCO: *cf* Sp. Olive
　　Beige
OF-3½-b
　KELLY: *s* HL-2
OF-4-c
　MEHRON: *h* 18
OF-4½-b
　KELLY: RMG #1
OF-4½-c
　BLASCO: *cf* Ruddy
　　Ultra Fair 2
OF-5-a/b
　NYE: *h* Lite
　STEIN: *f* 5½
OF-5-b
　BLASCO: *cf* DW #1
　KELLY: *cf* Medium Fair
　KRYOLAN: FP
　NYE: *cf* TW-20
OF-5-c
　BLASCO: *cf* Olive
　KELLY (MIRAGE): *f*
　　Lady Fair
　MEHRON: *f* 23
OF-5-d
　BLASCO: *cf* Alabaster

OF-6-a/b
　NYE: *h* Medium
OF-6-b
　KRYOLAN: 016
　NYE: *cf* TW-22
OF-6-c
　BLASCO: *cf* Ruddy
　　Ultra Fair 3
　KRYOLAN: FC
　MEHRON: *f* 24A
OF-6-c/d
　STEIN: *f* 24
OF-6-d
　KRYOLAN: FD
OF-6-e
　KRYOLAN: F8
OF-7-b
　BLASCO: *cf* Stage
　　Base #9
　NYE: *h* Deep
OF-7-c
　KRYOLAN: P4
　MEHRON: *f* 25A
OF-7-c/d
　BLASCO: *cf* Teentone
OF-7-d
　KRYOLAN: FL
OF-7-e
　KRYOLAN: P5
OF-8-a
　KRYOLAN: 030
OF-8-b
　KRYOLAN: 108
　NYE: *h* Dark
OF-8-b/c
　NYE: TW-24
OF-8-c
　BLASCO: *cf* Ruddy
　　Beige 2
　MEHRON: *f* 26A
OF-8-c/d
　BLASCO: *cf* SR
　NYE: *cf* P-5
OF-8½-a/b
　STEIN: *f* 6
OF-9-b/c
　NYE: *cf* TW 25
OF-9-c
　BLASCO: *cf*
　　Bronzetone
　KRYOLAN: FN
　MEHRON: *f* 27A
　NYE: *cf* Y-1
OF-9-c/d
　BLASCO: *cf* CTV 7W
　KELLY (MIRAGE):
　　Light Dark

OF-9-d
　BLASCO: *cf* Hal
　　Linden
OF-9-d/e
　KELLY (MIRAGE): *f*
　　Bronze Glow
OF-9½-c
　BLASCO: *cf* Ruddy
　　Dark Skin Base 1
OF-10-b
　BLASCO: *cf* EF 5
OF-10-b/c
　BLASCO: *cf*
　　Coppertone
　NYE: *cf* TW-26
OF-10-c/d
　BLASCO: *cf* Ruddy
　　Beige 4
　NYE: *cf* Y-3
OF-10-d
　BLASCO: *cf* Olive
　　Tan 2
OF-10-e
　KRYOLAN: 014
OF-10½-c
　BLASCO: *cf* Ruddy
　　Dark Skin Base 2
OF-10½-c/d
　BLASCO: *cf* Hawaiian
　　Tan
OF-11-a/b
　BLASCO: *cf* EF 1
OF-11-b
　BLASCO: *cf* EF 11
OF-11-b/c
　KRYOLAN: 118
OF-11-c
　BLASCO: *cf* Tantone
　NYE: *cf* TW 27
OF-11-c/d
　BLASCO: *cf* Malibu
　　Tan
　NYE: *cf* TW-28
OF-11½-c
　BLASCO: *cf* Ruddy
　　Dark Skin Base 3
OF-11-d
　BLASCO: *s* Character
　　Cold
　KRYOLAN: 115
　NYE: *cf* Y-5
OF-12-a
　MEHRON: *cr* 15
OF-12-a/b
　BLASCO: *cf* EF2
OF-12-b
　BLASCO: *cf* EF7

OF-12-c/d
  NYE: *cf* TW-29
OF-12-e
  KRYOLAN: 09
OF-12½-c
  BLASCO: *cf* Ruddy
    Dark Skin Base 4
OF-13-a
  NYE: *s* CL-7
  KRYOLAN: Mandarin
OF-13-d
  BLASCO: *s* Shading 3
OF-13½-c
  BLASCO: *s* Natural
    Shading 4
OF-13½-c/d
  BLASCO: *cf* Ruddy
    Dark Skin Base 5
OF-14-b
  NYE: *s* Dark Sunburn
OF-14-c/d
  BLASCO: *s* Character
    Warm
  NYE: *s* Cinnamon
OF-15-a/b
  BLASCO: *cf* EF 14
OF-15-d
  BLASCO: *s* Medium
    Brown
OF-16-a/b
  BLASCO: *cf* EF 15
OF-16-c
  MEHRON: *s* 8
OF-16-e
  STEIN: *s* 6
OF-16-g
  NYE: *ps* Dark Brown
OF-17-c/d
  KELLY (MIRAGE):
    Medium Dark
OF-18-d
  STEIN: *cf* 32
OF-20-c
  STEIN: *s* 7

OF/FO

OF/FO-7-c
  KRYOLAN: 021
OF/FO-7-c/d
  BLASCO: *cf* Natural
    Beige 2
OF/FO-8-c/d
  BLASCO: *cf* Deep
    Olive
OF/FO-8½-b
  NYE: *s* FS-1
OF/FO-9-c

NYE: *cf* T-1
OF/FO-9½-b
  BLASCO: *cf* DW #2
OF/FO-9½-c
  BLASCO: *cf* Palm
    Springs Tan
OF/FO-9½-c/d
  BLASCO: *cf* Olive Tan
    1
OF/FO-10-c
  BLASCO: *cf* Dark SR
  NYE: *f* T-2
OF/FO-11-a/b
  BLASCO: *cf* EF 12
OF/FO-11-b/c
  BLASCO: *h* Dark Skin
    Highlight
OF/FO-11-c
  BLASCO: *cf* Dark Skin
    Shading 1
OF/FO-11½-e
  KELLY (MIRAGE):
    Dark Skin #4
OF/FO-13-b
  BLASCO: *cf* EF 13
OF/FO-15-c/d
  BLASCO: *cf* Dark Skin
    Shading 2

FO

FO-2-b
  KRYOLAN: 01s
  STEIN: *f* 22
FO-2-c
  BLASCO: *cf* Fair Olive
FO-3-b
  KRYOLAN: O
FO-4-c
  BLASCO: *cf* Olive
    Beige 2
FO-4½-b
  KRYOLAN: 05
FO-5-b
  KRYOLAN: G3
FO-6-c/d
  KRYOLAN: 06
FO-8-a
  KRYOLAN: 508
FO-8-b/c
  KRYOLAN: G2
FO-8-c
  BLASCO: *cf* Olive
    Beige 4
  KRYOLAN: 010
FO-8-c/d
  BLASCO: *cf* Light
    Oriental

FO-9-a/b
  NYE: FS-3
FO-9-b
  KRYOLAN: 111
FO-9-b/c
  MEHRON: *f* K
FO-9-c
  KRYOLAN: G4
FO-9-c/d
  BLASCO: *cf* Dark
    Oriental
FO-9½-c
  NYE: FS-2
FO-10-a
  MEHRON: *f* Orange
FO-10-b
  NYE: *cf* P-7
FO-10-b/c
  MEHRON: *f* L
FO-10-c
  BLASCO: *cf* Suntone
FO-10-d
  BLASCO: *cf* Natural
    Beige 4
FO-11-a
  BLASCO: Orange
  MEHRON: *cr* 15
FO-11-b/c
  MEHRON: *f* M
FO-13-b
  BLASCO: *h* Dark Skin
    Highlight 2
FO-13-d
  KRYOLAN: 468
FO-14-d
  BLASCO: *s* Light
    Brown
FO-16-b
  STEIN: *s* 2
FO-15-b/c
  KRYOLAN:
    Schattierbraun
FO-16-c
  STEIN: *es* 1
FO-17-d
  KRYOLAN: 7
FO-18-d
  STEIN: *cs* 52
FO-20-d
  MEHRON: *f* 17
FO-20-i
  KELLY: *des* SESC-7

O

O-4-a/b
  MEHRON: *c* 16B
O-4-b

KRYOLAN: 015
O-4-d
  STEIN: *f* 23
O-5-d
  MEHRON: *c* 6B
O-6-f/g
  KRYOLAN: F11
O-7-b
  MEHRON: *f* 16
O-8-b
  KRYOLAN: G24
O-8-c
  KRYOLAN: 109
O-8-g
  KRYOLAN: F12
O-10-c
  STEIN: *cf* 39½
O-10-f
  KRYOLAN: F15
O-11-b
  KRYOLAN: C
O-12-a
  MEHRON: *cr* 15
O-12-f
  STEIN: *cf* 40
O12-g
  KRYOLAN: 040
O-15-e
  KELLY: *s* SL-7
O-16-c
  KELLY: *s* SL-8
O-16-d
  KRYOLAN: 579
O-16-h
  KRYOLAN: 28a
O-18-d
  KELLY: *cf* S-19
O-18-e
  KELLY: *cf* S-20
O-19-c
  STEIN: *cf* 51
O-19-d
  MEHRON: *f* 15
O-19-f
  KRYOLAN: 101
O-20-c
  MEHRON: *f* 14B
O-20-g
  KRYOLAN: 102
O-20-h
  KRYOLAN: 11
  STEIN: *f* 11

O/CO

O/CO-4-d
  KRYOLAN: F18
O/CO-6-c

KRYOLAN: 04
O/CO-7-b
  KRYOLAN: 07
O/CO-8-a
  KRYOLAN: 106
O/CO-10-b/c
  KRYOLAN: 466
O/CO-15-d
  KRYOLAN: 045
O/CO-18-f
  KRYOLAN: 043

CO

CO-1-b
  MEHRON: f 4B
CO-2½-b
  KRYOLAN: F1
CO-4-b
  KRYOLAN: 5
CO-4½-b
  MEHRON: rmg LM O
CO-5-b
  KELLY: s SL-19
  KRYOLAN: K
CO-10-c
  KRYOLAN: 022a
CO-13-b
  KRYOLAN: 107
CO-17-c
  KRYOLAN: 421
CO-18-g
  KRYOLAN: 462
CO-19-c
  MEHRON: rmg LM N

OC/CO

OC/CO-16-c
  KRYOLAN: 024

OC

OC-2-b
  KRYOLAN: G16
OC-3-a
  NYE: cf P-4
OC-3-b
  STEIN: f 5
OC-4-b
  KRYOLAN: 04a
  MEHRON: f 4½
OC-5-b
  NYE: h MY1
OC-6-a
  KRYOLAN: 303
OC-6½-c
  NYE: MY2
OC-7-b
  STEIN: cf 40½

OC-8-b
  KELLY: s SL-15
OC-12-b
  KRYOLAN: 022
OC-13-c
  KRYOLAN: 507
OC-14-g
  BLASCO: s Green-
    Gray 3
OC-15-e
  KRYOLAN: 041
OC-16-g
  BLASCO: s Green-
    Gray 4

C/OC

C/OC-10-b
  BLASCO: s Gold-Olive

C

C-2-a/b
  MEHRON: c 4B
C-3-a/b
  MEHRON: c 4½B
C-5-b
  KELLY: s SL-14
C-8-b
  BLASCO: s Gold-
    Yellow
  KELLY: cf S-9
  STEIN: f 12
C-8-j
  BLASCO: s Green-
    Gray 1
C-9-a/b
  NYE: s Goldenrod
C-9-b
  KRYOLAN: 8a
C-9-i
  BLASCO: s Green-
    Gray 2
C-11-b
  BLASCO: s Yellow-
    Gold

YC

YC-1-a
  NYE: ps ES-1
YC-2-b
  KRYOLAN: 521
YC-4-a
  KRYOLAN: 436
YC-4-d
  KRYOLAN: 522
YC-13-c
  KRYOLAN: 10
YC-14-b/c

KRYOLAN: 308
YC-14-f
  KRYOLAN: 503
YC-15-h
  KRYOLAN: 459

CY

CY-6-b
  BLASCO: cf Death
    Straw
CY-10-a
  MEHRON: s 16
CY-10-b
  KRYOLAN: 305
CY-11½-d
  KRYOLAN: 8b
CY-12-d
  KRYOLAN: 452
CY-17-f
  KRYOLAN: 16

Y

Y-1-a
  KRYOLAN: G10
Y-2-b
  KRYOLAN: G9
Y-4-d
  KRYOLAN: G7
Y-6-a
  KRYOLAN: G92
Y-9-a
  NYE: s Yellow
Y-10-a
  MEHRON: f 4½;
    c 4½ B; s 11
Y-11-a
  STEIN: s 16
Y-11-d
  KRYOLAN: 477
Y-12-a
  KRYOLAN: 509
  KELLY: cf Yellow
Y-13-c
  KRYOLAN: 607
Y-13-d
  KRYOLAN: 504
Y-14-e
  KRYOLAN: 606

LY

LY-1-c
  KRYOLAN: 00
LY-5-a
  BLASCO: s Yellow
LY-10-a
  MEHRON: s 16

LY-15-d
  KRYOLAN: 304

YL

YL-1-a
  KRYOLAN: 523
YL-2-b
  KRYOLAN: Grün 11
YL-8-e
  KRYOLAN: G103
YL-11-a
  KRYOLAN: 534

L

L-6-f
  BLASCO: cf Death
    Green
L-9-c
  KRYOLAN: Grün 1
L-9-d
  BLASCO: s Light
    Yellow-Green
L-13-c
  BLASCO: s Medium
    Yellow-Green
L-14-d
  KRYOLAN: 502

GL

GL-3-a
  KRYOLAN: 092
GL-5-b
  KRYOLAN: Grün 9
GL-6-d
  KELLY: des SESC-6
GL-8-c
  KELLY: des SESC-8
GL-11-d
  KELLY: s SL-5
GL-12½-d
  STEIN: s 19, es 16
GL-13-c
  BLASCO: s Dark
    Yellow-Green
GL-13-f
  STEIN: es 17
GL-13-g
  KRYOLAN: 454
GL-14-g
  STEIN: cf 46

LG

LG-5-a/b
  KRYOLAN: 511
LG-12-b
  KRYOLAN: 512

LG-13-c
  BLASCO: *s* Green

G

G-9-b
  KELLY: *cf* Green
G-10-f
  NYE: *ps* Forest Moss
G-12-c
  NYE: *s* Green
G-13-c
  MEHRON: *s* 5

TG

TG-1-c
  KRYOLAN: FF7
TG-4-d
  BLASCO: *s* Icy Green

GT

GT-6-a
  KELLY: *des* SESC-4
  STEIN: *es* 6
GT-7-c
  KELLY: *s* SL-20
GT-9-b/c
  STEIN: *ess* 11
GT-11-a
  KRYOLAN: Grün 21
GT-11-b
  KRYOLAN: Grün 20
GT-13-c
  MEHRON: *s* 4
GT-14-a/b
  KRYOLAN: 096

T/GT

T/GT-11-a
  KRYOLAN: Grün 30
T/GT-13-d
  NYE: *s* Forest Green
T/GT-16-a
  KRYOLAN: 095

T

T-2-a
  KRYOLAN: 097
T-8-c
  BLASCO: *s* Turquoise
T-10-e
  STEIN: *es* 3
T-13-b
  KRYOLAN: Grün 31
  MEHRON: *f, c* Green
T-14-b

KRYOLAN: 094
T-17-c
  KELLY: *s* SL-6

BT

BT-6-e
  KRYOLAN: G81
BT-8-c
  STEIN: *ess* 6
BT-9-b
  MEHRON: *s* 2½

TB

TB-8-b
  KRYOLAN: 090
TB-9-b
  KELLY: *cf* Blue
TB-11-d/e
  KRYOLAN: 193
TB-14-c
  KRYOLAN: 093
TB-15-b
  STEIN: *s* 20

B

B-1-a
  MEHRON: *f* 19
B-9-b
  KRYOLAN: 549
  MEHRON: *f* Blue
B-10-e
  NYE: *s* Peacock

IB

IB-6-d
  STEIN: *ess* 5
IB-7-d
  KELLY: *des* SESC-3
IB-14-a
  MEHRON: *s* 2

BI

BI-½-a/b
  MEHRON: *c* 19B
BI-4-a
  KRYOLAN: G82
BI-4-d
  KELLY: *des* SESC-2
  KRYOLAN: G83
BI-6-a
  KRYOLAN: 587
BI-6-c
  KRYOLAN: Blau 1
BI-8-b
  STEIN: *s* 11

I/BI

I/BI-8-g
  STEIN: *es* 11

I

I-6-f
  BLASCO: *cf* Death
    Blue-Gray
I-7-a
  BLASCO: *s* Icy Blue
  MEHRON: *s* 3
I-7-a/b
  KELLY: *s* SL-1
I-8-a
  BLASCO: *s* Sky Blue
  KELLY (MIRAGE):
    Clear Blue
  NYE: *s* Sky Blue: *ps*
    Blue
I-9-a
  KELLY: *des* SESC-1
I-9-a/b
  STEIN: *es* 19
I-10-a
  KRYOLAN: Blau 3
I-10-b
  KRYOLAN: 091
I-11-a
  STEIN: *s* 8
I-11-b
  STEIN: *ess* 3
I-12-a
  MEHRON: *s* 1
I-13-a
  KRYOLAN: 510
  NYE: *s* Blue
I-14-d
  MEHRON: *f* Blue
I-19-a/b
  STEIN: *es* 19

I/VI

I/VI-4-a
  KRYOLAN: G56
  NYE: *ps* Blue Mist
I/VI-9-c
  NYE: *s* Blue-Gray
I/VI-10-a
  STEIN: *s* 9
I/VI-10-d
  BLASCO: *s* Blue-Gray
I/VI-11-a
  KRYOLAN: Blau 5
  STEIN: *cf* 47
I/VI-12-a
  BLASCO: *s* Blue

KELLY: *s* SL-2

VI

VI-1-c
  MEHRON: *c* 20B
VI-4-h
  KRYOLAN: 173
VI-6-a/b
  KRYOLAN: 483
VI-10-a
  STEIN: *es* 2
VI-15-a
  STEIN: *es* 20; *s* 10
VI-16-a
  KELLY: *s* SL-3

IV/VI

IV/VI-3½-a/b
  KRYOLAN: 087
IV/VI-8-b
  STEIN: *cf* 49

IV

IV-1-a/b
  KRYOLAN: 481
IV-10-a/b
  MEHRON: *s* 6

V

V-3-a/b
  KRYOLAN: 482
V-8-b
  NYE: *s* Misty Violet; *ps*
    Violet
V-11-a
  KELLY: *cf* Purple
V-13-e
  BLASCO: *s* Gray-
    Violet

PV

PV-7-b
  STEIN: *ess* 8
PV-10-b
  KELLY: *s* SL-4
PV-15-b
  KRYOLAN: 098
PV-16-a
  KRYOLAN: 545

VP

VP-5-b
  MEHRON: *f* 20B
VP-11½-b
  STEIN: *s* 23; *es* 4
VP-12-c

KRYOLAN: Lila
NYE: *s* Purple
P/VP-13-d
   BLASCO: *s* Blue-Violet

P

P-3-b
   BLASCO: *cf* Stage
     Base #7
P-6-b
   KRYOLAN: G108
P-13-c
   BLASCO: *s* Purple
P-15-a
   KELLY: *s* SL-21

P/RP

P/RP-15-d
   KELLY: *s* SL-17

RP

RP-8-a/b
   BLASCO: *s* Pink-Purple
RP-9-a
   NYE: *ps* Misty Lilac
RP-10-b
   BLASCO: *s* Lavender-
     Purple
RP-12-e
   BLASCO: *s* Gray-Rose
RP-12-g
   KELLY (MIRAGE):
     Cool Grey
RP-14-a
   MEHRON: *lr* Plum
RP-16-a
   STEIN: *s* 2; *es* 5

N

N-1

KELLY: *cf* Frankenstein
   Grey
N-2
   KRYOLAN :073
N-3½
   KRYOLAN: 074
N-4
   KRYOLAN: 32b
   STEIN: *cf* 34
N-5
   KRYOLAN: 089
N-6
   KELLY: *s* SL-10
N-7
   NYE: *s* Gray
   STEIN: *es* 18
N-8
   BLASCO: *s* Gray
   KELLY: *s* KS-2
   MEHRON: *f* 18
   STEIN: *s* 3

N-10
   KRYOLAN: 32a
N-11
   MEHRON: *s* 7
N-12
   KELLY: *s* SL-11
N-13
   KELLY: *mc* Grey
   KRYOLAN: 517
   STEIN: *es* 8; *s* 4
N-14
   KRYOLAN: 501
N-15
   KRYOLAN: 32c
   MEHRON: *c* 18B
   NYE: *s* Steel Gray
     ps Charcoal
   STEIN: *s* 5
N-16
   KRYOLAN: 088
N-18
   BLASCO: *s* Charcoal

TABLE 2 COLOR NUMBERS OF THE VARIOUS MAKEUP COMPANIES AND THEIR EQUIVALENT STANDARDIZED NUMBERS

BYE NYE CREME FOUNDATIONS:

P-1: White
P-2: RS-2-b
P-3: SF-5-b
P-4: OC-3-a
P-5: OF-8-c/d
P-6: F-7-b
P-7: FO-10-b
P-8: F-17-d
P-9: Black
L-1: F-5½-b
L-2: F-6-b
L-3: F-6½-b
L-5: F-7-b/c
T-1: OF/FO-9-c
T-2: OF/FO-10-c
M-1: F-9-d
M-2: F-10-d
M-3: F-11-d
M-5: F-12-d
Y-1: OF-9-c
Y-3: OF-10-c/d
Y-5: OF-11-d
TW-20: OF-6-b
TW-22: OF-7-b
TW-24: OF-8-b/c
TW-25: OF-9-b/c
TW-26: OF-10-c
TW-27: OF-11-c
TW-28: OF-11-c/d
TW-29: OF-12-c/d

BEN NYE CREME LINING COLORS:

Cl-1: White
CL-2: T/GT-13-d
CL-3: G-12-c
CL-5: Y-9-a
CL-6: C-9-a/b
CL-7: OF-13-a
CL-9: SF-10-b
CL-10: OF-14-b
CL-11: OF-14-c/d
CL-13: SR/RS-12-a
CL-14: RS-15-a/b
CL-15: SR-16-b
CL-17: V-8-b
CL-18: VP-12-c
CL-19: I-13-a
CL-21: B-10-e
CL-22: I-8-a
CL-23: I/VI-9-c
CL-25: N-15

BEN NYE CREME CHEEK ROUGE:

CR-1: S-12-a
CR-2: SR/RS-10b
CR-4: R/SR-10-a
CR-5: RS-13-a/b
CR-7: RS-10-a
CR-8: RS-12-a

BEN NYE DRY CHEEK ROUGE:

DR-1: R-12-a
DR-2: FS-9-b
DR-3: PR-12-a
DR-5: R-12-c
DR-6: R-9-a/b
DR-7: SR/RS-10-a
DR-9: SF-12-a
DR-10: S-13-d

BEN NYE LIPSTICKS:

3: RS-8-a/b
5: R-13-b
7: PR-9-d
9: R-16-b/c
12: RS-14-c/d
14: RS-14-a

BEN NYE CREME HIGHLIGHTS:

CH-1: FS-3-a
CH-2: OF-5-a/b
CH-3: OF-6-a/b
CH-4: OF-7-b
CH-5: OF-8-b

BEN NYE CREME SHADOWS:

CS-1: S-13-f
CS-2: OF-14-c/d
CS-3: F-15-f
CS-4: FS-16-g

BEN NYE MELLOW YELLOW:

MY-1: OC-5-b
MY-2: OC-6½-c

BEN NYE FIVE O' SHARP:

FS-1: OF/FO-8½-b
FS-2: FO-9½-c
FS-3: FO-9-a/b

BEN NYE PRESSED EYESHADOW:

ES-1: YC-1-a
ES-2: RP-9-a
ES-3: V-8-b
ES-7: G-10-f
ES-9: OF-16-g
ES-10: SF-9-g
ES-11: I/VI-4-a
ES-13: N-15
ES-14: F-14-f
ES-15: RS-12-e

JOE BLASCO OLIVE BASES:

TV White: F-1-f
Fair Olive: FO-2-c
Special Olive Beige: OF-3-c
Alabaster: OF-5-d
Olive: OF-5-c
Medium Olive: F/OF-5-d
Deep Olive: OF/FO-8-c/d
Suntone: F0-10-c
Olive Tan 1: OF/FO-9½-c/d
Olive Tan 2: OF-10-d
Olive Tan 3: OF-11½-c/d
Hawaiian Tan: OF-10½-c/d
Olive Beige 2: FO-4-c
Olive Beige 4: FO-8-c
Light Oriental: FO-8-c/d
Dark Oriental: FO-9-c/d
CTV 7W: OF-9-c/d

JOE BLASCO RUDDY BASES:

Fair: F-3-c
Fair Pink: SR-4-a
Cream: F-4½-b
Ruddy Ultra Fair 1: F-2-c
Ruddy Ultra Fair 2: OF-4½-c
Ruddy Ultra Fair 3: OF-6-c
Peachtone 1: F-4½-b/c
Peachtone 2: F-5½-b/c
Peachtone 3: F-7-b/c
Peachtone 4: F-9-b/c

Blushtone 1: SF-6-d
Blushtone 2: SF-7-d
Blushtone 3: F-8-d
Blushtone 4: F-9-c/d
Ruddy Beige 2: OF-8-c
Ruddy Beige 4: OF-10-c/d

JOE BLASCO STAGE BASES:

Stage Base #1: SR-3-a/b
Stage Base #2: SR-6-a/b
Stage Base #3: RS-8-b
Stage Base #4: S-16-b
Stage Base #5: SF-12-a/b
Stage Base #6: FS-5-e
Stage Base #7: P-3-b
Stage Base #8: F-2-b
Stage Base #9: OF-7-b
Stage Base #10: F-18½-b
DW#1: OF-5-b
DW#2: OF/FO-9½-b
DW#3: SF-9-d
DW#4: F-11-c/d
EF 1: OF-11-a/b
EF 2: OF-12-a/b
EF 3: F-9-a/b
EF 4: F-10-a/b
EF 5: OF-10-b
EF 6: F/OF-11-b/c
EF 7: OF-12-b
EF 8: F-12-c
EF 9: F-10-b
EF 10: F/OF-11-b
EF 11: OF-11-b
EF-12: OF/FO-11-a/b
EF 13: OF/FO-13-b
EF 14: OF-15-a/b
EF 15: OF-16-a/b

JOE BLASCO RUDDY TAN BASES:

Bronzetone: OF-9-c
Dark Bronzetone: F/OF-10-c/d
Tantone: OF-11-c
Coppertone: OF-10-b/c
Palm Springs Tan: OF-FO-9½-c
Summertan: F/SF-8-d
California Tan: F-11-d
Malibu Tan: OF-11-c/d
Rugged Tan 1: SF-11-d
Rugged Tan 2: SF-10-e

TABLE 2   (CONTINUED)

JOE BLASCO NATURAL BEIGE BASES:

Natural Beige 2: OF/FO-7-c/d
Natural Beige 4: FO-10-d
Teentone: OF-7-c/d
SR: OF-8-c/d
Dark SR: OF/FO-10-c

JOE BLASCO DARK SKIN BASES:

Ruddy Dark Skin Base 1: OF-9½-c
Ruddy Dark Skin Base 2: OF-10½-c
Ruddy Dark Skin Base 3: OF-11½-c
Ruddy Dark Skin Base 4: OF-12½-c
Ruddy Dark Skin Base 5: OF-13½-c/d
Ruddy Dark Skin Base 6: F/SF-16-d
Ruddy Dark Skin Base 7: F/SF-17-e
Ruddy Dark Skin Base 8: F/SF-19-f

JOE BLASCO AUXILIARY BASES:

Hal Linden: OF-9-d
White Base: White
Clown White: White
Black Base: Black

JOE BLASCO SHADING COLORS:

Shading 1: SF-9-f
Shading 2: SF-10-f
Shading 3: OF-13-d
Shading 4: F/OF-14-c/d
Character Cold: OF-11-d
Character Warm: OF-14-c/d
Character Gray: FS-13-g
Natural Shading 1: SF-7-e/f
Natural Shading 2: SF-8-e
Natural Shading 3: F-12-d
Natural Shading 4: OF-13½-c

Dark Skin Shading 1: OF/FO-11-c
Dark Skin Shading 2: OF/FO-15-c/d
Dark Skin Shading 3: F-18-d
Dark Skin Shading 4: SF-20-d

JOE BLASCO HIGHLIGHTING COLORS:

Pink Highlight 1: FS-1-a
Pink Highlight 2: FS-4-c
Orange Highlight 1: F-3½-c
Orange Highlight 2: F-5-c
Dark Skin Highlight 1: OF/FO-11-b/c
Dark Skin Highlight 2: FO-13-b

JOE BLASCO CHEEK COLORS:

AD 1: FS-7-c
AD 2: SF-8-b
CTV: SF-9-c
Men's Cheekcolor: F-12-c/d
Natural Cheekcolor Regular: FS-10-c/d
Coral Rose: RS-10-b
Pastel Rose: FS-8-b/c
Rose Orange: F/SF-10-b
Coral Orange: SF-19-b
Light Burnt Orange: SF-12½-b
Dark Burnt Orange: SF-13-b
Brick: F-11-b

JOE BLASCO DRY CHEEK COLORS:

Rose: PR-7-a
Mauve: R-10-b
Coral: SR-10-a
Peach: FS-10-b

JOE BLASCO DEATH COLORS:

Death Straw: CY-6-b
Death Blue-Gray: I-6-f
Death Green: L-6-f
Death Purple: SR-14-e
Death Gray: FS-3-g

JOE BLASCO CREATIVE COLORS:

Blood Color: R-16-a
Red: SR/RS-12-a
Orange: FO-11-a
Gold-Yellow: C-8-b
Yellow-Gold: C-11-b
Yellow: LY-5-a
Gold-Olive: C/OC-10-b
Light Yellow-Green: L-9-d
Medium Yellow-Green: L-13-c
Dark Yellow-Green: GL-13-c
Green: LG-13-c
Icy Green: TG-4-d
Turquoise: T-8-c
Gray: N-8
Green-Gray 1: C-8-i
Green-Gray 2: C-9-i
Green-Gray 3: OC-14-g
Green-Gray 4: OC-16-g
Icy Blue: I-7-a
Sky Blue: I-8-a
Blue: I/VI-12-a
Blue-Gray: I/VI-10-d
Blue-Violet: P/VP-13-d
Gray-Violet: V-13-e
Pink-Purple: RP-8-a/b
Lavender-Purple: RP-10-b
Purple: P-13-c
Maroon: PR-18-c
Gray-Rose: RP-12-e
Light Brown: FO-14-d
Medium Brown: OF-15-d
Dark Brown: F-17-e
Charcoal: N-18

JOE BLASCO DERMATEX:

1: FO-1-a
2: OF-5-c/d
3: FO-7-c
4: OF-7-c
5: OF/FO-9½-c
6: OF/FO-10-c/d
7: O-10-d
8: OF-6-d
9: OF-5-b
10: OF/FO-7-b
11: F-6-b
13: OF-9-c
14: OF-8-c
15: FS-9-b
16: FS/SF-13-a/b

17: F-9-d/e
18: P-3-b
19: OF/FO-10-b
20: OF-10-b/c
21: OF-11-b/c
23: FO-11-b
24: OF/FO-10-b
25: OF/FO-12-b
26: OF/FO-15-c/d
27: White
28: Black
29: F-15-f
30: FO-13-d
31: OF-11-c
32: OF-12-a
33: YC-7-a
34: N-8
35: Y-8-e
36: S-12-a
37: Y-9-a
38: LG-13-c
39: I/VI-12-a
40: OF-16-d

JOE BLASCO DERMACEAL:

1: FO-3-c
2: OF-7-c/d
3: FO-10-c
4: OF-10-c/d
5: OF-7-c
6: F-7-c
7: OF-8-b
8: OF-11-c
9: OF/FO-12-c
10: OF-12-d

BOB KELLY CREME STICK:

S-1: White
S-2: SR-2-b
S-3: S-5-d
S-4: S-4-b
S-5: S-9-d
S-6: S-7-c
S-7: FS-13-e
S-8: FS-8-e/f
S-9: C-8-b
S-10: S/FS-10-e
S-11: F-16½-e
S-12: F-16-e
S-14: FS-11-d/e
S-15: S-12-c
S-16: F-17-c
S-17: SF-12-e
S-18: FS-17-e

TABLE 2 (CONTINUED)

S-19: O-18-d
S-20: O-18-e
S-21: FS-1-c
S-22: FS-12-d
S-23: FS-12-f
BK-1: S/FS-10-e/f
BK-2: S/FS-12-f
BK-3: F-7½-e
BK-4: F-8½-d
BK-5: SF-11-f
BK-6: FS-11-e/f
BK-7: S/FS-12-e/f
32-E: PR-13-h
CVA-Red: RS-13-c
Frankenstein Grey: N-1
SC-50: FS-10-f
SC-54: F-19-f
Fairest: F-4-b
Medium Fair: OF-5-b
Lady Fair: F-4½-c
Olive: SF-3-b/c
Medium Olive: F-6-d/e
Deep Olive: SF-7-f/g
Light Brunette: F-5½-c
Medium Brunette: F-6-c
Dark Brunette: F-7-d
Tantone: F-6-d
Natural Tan: SF-6-c
Golden Tan: SF-10-c/d
Coppertone: RS-6-d/e
Bronzetone: FS-10-d/e
Blue: TB-9-b
Green: G-9-b
Purple: V-11-a
Red: RS-14-a
Yellow: Y-12-a

BOB KELLY CAKE MAKEUP:

Since cake-makeup shades are supposed to match creme-stick shades, they are not listed separately.

BOB KELLY MOIST CAKE MAKEUP (RAIN BARREL):

Ivory: FS-1-c
Flesh Tone: SF-3½-c
Natural: F-4-e
Rose: FS-6-b
Tan: FS-9-d
Olive Rose: SF-3-c
Latin: FS-10-d/e
Sunburn: FS-19-b
Sportsman: RS-7½-d/e

Egyptian: FS-10-d
Bronze: F-13-d
American Indian: S/FS-11-e/f
Arabian: FS-12-e
Old Age: FS-8-e/f
Grey: N-13

BOB KELLY CREME SHADING COLORS (LINER/EYE SHADOW):

SL-1: 1-7-a/b
SL-2: I/VI-12-a
SL-3: VI-16-a
SL-4: PV-10-b
SL-5: GL-11-d
SL-6: T-17-c
SL-7: O-15-e
SL-8: O-16-c
SL-9: Black
SL-10: N-6
SL-11: N-12
SL-12: White
SL-14: C-5-b
SL-15: OC-8-b
SL-16: PR-12-g
SL-17: P/RP-15-d
SL-18: R-16-b
SL-19: CO-5-b
SL-20: GT-7-c
SL-21: P-15-a
HL-1: OF-1-c
HL-2: OF-3½-b
KS-1: SF-10-g
KS-2: N-8

BOB KELLY CREME ROUGE:

SR-1: SR-6-a/b
SR-2: PR-6-a
SR-3: R-10-a
SR-4: PR-9-a/b
SR-5: PR-10-a/b
SR-6: S-8-d
SR-7: SF-9-b/c
SR-8: S-9-a
SR-9: R-8-a
SR-10: SR-8-a
SR-Bronze: RS-10-d

BOB KELLY DRY ROUGE:

Female: PR-5-a
Male: R/PR-7-b
DRC-1: R-9-a

SRC-4: PR-8-a/b
Bronze: SR-7-b

BOB KELLY BRUSH-ON ROUGE:

Amber: SF-6-b
Tawny: SF-8-e/f
Cocoa: F-8-c/d

BOB KELLY LIPSTICK:

LP-1: R-13-a
LP-2: RS-12-b
LP-3: R-12-a/b
LP-4: SR-12-a
LP-5: SR/RS-8-b
LP-6: S-8-b
LP-7: FS-9-b/c
LP-8: S-11-a
LP-9: RS-12-a
Cinnamon: SR-10-d
Coffee: S-9-d/e
Orange: S-12-a
Zebra: R-12-c

BOB KELLY RUBBER-MASK GREASEPAINT:

RMG #1: OF-4½-b
RMG #2: SF-7-f/g
RMG #3: FS-10-e
RMG #4: FS-16-e
RMG #5: S/FS-12-g

BOB KELLY CAKE EYESHADOW:

SESC-1: I-9-a
SESC-2: BI-4-d (Silver)
SESC-3: IB-7-d (Silver)
SESC-4: GT-6-a
SESC-5: White
SESC-6: GL-6-d (Gold)
SESC-7: FO-20-i
SESC-8: GL-8-c

BOB KELLY BLEMISH-COVER STICK (BLOT-OUT):

Light: SF-3-a/b
Medium: F-6-b
Dark: F/SF-6-d

BOB KELLY MIRAGE:

Pink: R-1-a
Pink Strawberry: R-10-a
Bronze: R-10-a/b

Warm Red: FS-10-b
Grape: FS/SF-13-a/b
Blender Tone: F/SF-8-d
Terra Cotta: F/SF-10-d
Darkest Tone: F/SF-16-a
Ivory: F-2-e
Rose Glow: F-3-c
Dark Average: F-11-d
Lady Fair: OF-5-c
Light Dark: OF-9-c/d
Bronze Glow: OF-9-d/e
Medium Dark: OF-17-c/d
Dark Skin #4: OF/FO-11½-e
Clear Blue: I-8-a
Cool Grey: RP-12-g

MEHRON FOUNDATION COLORS:

1: SR-2-a
2: PR-2-a
2½: F-6-b
3: S-3-a/b
4: CO-1-b
4½: OC-4-b
5: RS-5-b
6: FS-9-b/c
6½: FS-8-b/c
7: S-5-b
8: SF-10½-c
9: S-8-c/d
10: RS-11-b/c
11: S-6-f
12: S-10-b/c
14: O-20-c
15: O-19-d
16: O-7-b
17: FO-20-d
18: N-8
19: B-1-a
20: VP-5-b
21: FS-2-b
22: SF-2½-b
23: OF-5-c
24: OF-6-c
25: OF-7-c
26: OF-8-c
27: OF-9-c
28: F-10-d
29: F-11-d/e
30: F-12-d/e
31: FS-12-d/e
37: SF-13-e

TABLE 2   (CONTINUED)

38: S-13-g
40: FS-4-c
41: S/FS-7-d/e
42: S/FS-9-d/e
43: S-8-e
RB: RS-13-e
24A: S-3-a/b
25A: FS-5-b
26A: FS-6-b/c
27a: FS-7-b/c
28A: FS-8-b/c
29A: FS-9-c
30A: FS-9½-c
31A: FS-10-c
1B: S-½-a
2B: S-1-a
3B: FS-4-b
4B: C-2-a/b
4½B: C-3-a/b
5B: S-3-a/b
6B: O-5-d
6½B: F-7-b
7B: S-5-a/b
7½B: FS-8-a
8B: F-7½-b
9B: FS-8-b
10B: FS-10-b/c
11B: S-8-h
12B: FS-9-b
14B: F-14-g
16B: O-4-a/b
17B: F-17-i
18B: N-15
19B: BI-½-a/b
20B: VI-1-c
A: FS-1-a
B: S-2-a/b
C: SF-3-a/b
D: SF-4-a/b
E: F-5½-b
F: SF-6-a/b
G: F-7-b
H: F/OF-8-b
K: FO-9-b/c
L: FO-10-b/c
M: FO-11-b/c
Red: RS-15-a
Blue: I-14-d
Green: T-13-b
Yellow: Y-10-a
Orange: FO-10-a
4C: F-12-f/g
5C: F-12½-f/g
6C: F-13-g
7C: F-13-h
8C: F-15-h
9C: F-17-h
10C: F-19-h

MEHRON RUBBER-MASK GREASEPAINT (MASK COVER):

LM 5: SF-5-b
LM 8: F-8-b
LM 11: FS-11-c
LM D: SR/RS-8-b/c
LM O: CO-4½-b
LM N: CO-19-c

MEHRON CREME ROUGE (BLUSHTONE):

9: SF-9-e
10: R-8-a
11: PR-6-a
15: O-12-a
20: RS-11-b

MEHRON LIP ROUGE:

Light: RS-12-a
Medium: SR-14-a
Dark: R/PR-16-a
Cherry: R/PR-15-a
Crimson: PR-18-a
Special #5: S-18-b/c
Maroon: PR-19-c
Plum: RP-14-a

MEHRON SHADING COLORS (SHADO-LINERS):

1: I-12-a
2: IB-14-a
2½: BT-9-b
3: I-7-a
4: GT-13-c
5: G-13-c
6: IV-10-a/b
7: N-11
8: OF-16-c
8½: FS-18½-b
9: SF-10-f
RC10: S-14-d
RC11: RS-15-d/e
RC12: R-10-h
RC14: SR-14-g
16: CY-10-a
17: OF-1-b
18: OF-4-c

STEIN GREASEPAINT:

1½: S/RS-1½-a/b
2: S-4-a
2½: SF-3-a/b

3: FS-5-a
3½: F-7-a/b
4: FS-1-b
5: OC-3-b
5½: OF-5-a/b
6: OF-8½-a/b
7: F-8-b/c
7F: S/FS-9-b/c
8: SF-9-a/b
9: S-13-d
10: S/FS-11-d
11: O-20-h
12: C-8-b
13: S-5-g
14: F/SF-10-c
16: F-20-f
21: SF-3-a
22: FO-2-b
23: O-4-d
24: OF-6-c/d

STEIN CREME MAKEUP (VELVET STICK):

Natural Blush: FS-5-c/d
Natural A: FS-2-b
Natural B: S/FS-6-d/e
Cream Blush: SF-3-b
Cream A: F-3-b
Cream B: SF-3-c
Tan Blush: FS-5-d/e
Tan Blush #2: F-6-d
Tan Blush #3: F-8-c/d
Tan A: SF-7-e
Tan B: SF-10-e
2: SF-9-c
7: FS-10-c
9: SR-17-b
32: OF-18-d
33: Black
34: N-4
35: SF-13-c/d
36: SF-14-d
37: S/FS-14-c/d
38: FS-11-e
39: SF-12-d/e
39½: O-10-c
40: O-12-f
41½: OC-7-b
41: S/FS-15-b/c
41A: S-16-d/e
42: FS-13-b
43: White
44: SF-3½-b
45: FS-9-c
46: GL-14-g
47: I/VI-11-a
48: RS-13-a

49: IV/VI-8-b
50: R-12-f
51: O-19-c
52: FO-18-d

STEIN CAKE MAKEUP:

Since cake-makeup shades are supposed to match creme-makeup shades, they are not listed separately.

STEIN SOFT SHADING (LINING) COLORS:

1: F-18-b
2: FO-16-b
3: N-8
4: N-13
5: N-15
6: OF-16-e
7: OF-20-c
8: I-11-a
9: I/VI-10-a
10: VI-15-a
11: BI-8-b
12: R-16-b
13: PR-18-b
14: SR-13-a
15: White
16: Y-11-a
17: Black
18: RS-13-a
19: GL-12½-d
20: TB-15-b
21: RP-16-a
22: S-19-b
23: VP-11½-b

STEIN CREME EYESHADOW:

1: FO-16-c
2: VI-10-a
3: T-10-e
4: VP-11½-b
5: RP-16-a
6: GT-6-a
8: N-13
11: I/BI-8-g
16: GL-12½-d
17: GL-13-f
18: N-7
19: I-19-a/b
20: VI-15-a

TABLE 2 (CONTINUED)

STEIN EYESHADOW STICK:

1: S-2-g
2: SF-13-f
3: I-11-b
5: IB-6-d
6: BT-8-c
7: SF-19-d
8: PV-7-b
11: GT-9-b/c

STEIN CREME ROUGE:

1: RS-13-a
3: R/PR-13-a
4: SR-14-a
5: PR-12-a
6: SR-12-a
7: PR-13-a
8: SR/RS-11-a/b
9: SF-16-a/b

STEIN LIPSTICK:

Since lipstick shades are supposed to match creme-rouge shades, they are not listed separately.

STEIN DRY ROUGE:

3: RS-10-a
12: FS-12-b
14: PR-10-a
16: PR-13-a
18: RP/PR-11-a
20: RP/PR-11-d

FACTOR GREASEPAINT:

1: SR-2-b
1A: S-4-b
1½: R-4-b
2: SR-2½-c
2A: SF-4-c
2½: S-5-c
3: S-10-c/d
4: OC-1-a/b
4A: F/SF-2-c
4½: FS-2-b
5: CO-6-b
5A: SF-4½-c
5½: F/SF-7-d
6: FS-10-h
6A: F/SF-8-d
7: F/SF-5-c
8: F-9-c

8A: F-16-d/e
9: SF-9½-b
10: S-11-c
11: O/CO-18-g
14: VP-1-d
16: OC-18-f
17: CO-18-h
18: SR-11-b

FACTOR PAN-CAKE:

Pan-Cakes and Pan-Stiks with the same numbers are approximately the same color.

Natural No. 1: F-3-b
Olive: F-4-d
Deep Olive: F-5-d
Tan No. 1: F/OF-6-e
Tan No. 2: F-9-d
Café Honey: OF-10-f
Cocoa Tan: OF-12-h
Chinese: CO-8-d
Dark Egyptian: O-15-h
Indian: SF-10-e/f
Negro No. 1: O-16-h
Negro No. 2: FO-15-g
Eddie Leonard: FS-19-g

The following shades have been discontinued but are included for the convenience of those who have them and wish to replace them with similar colors in other brands:

21: FS-2-b
22: FS-3-b
23: FS-4-b
24: F-5-c
25: F-6-c
26: F-7-c
27: F-8-d
28: F-9-d
29: F-10-d
30: F-11-d
31: F-12-d

FACTOR PAN-STIK:

1N: FS-3-a
3N: SF-3-a
5N: OF-5-b
6N: OF-6-b
7N: OF-7-b
8N: F-8-d
10N: F-10-b

2A: SF-7-c
4A: SF-2-a
7A: S/FS-11-c
Olive: F-4-d
Deep Olive: F-5-b
Natural Tan: SF-7-e
Golden Tan: SF-10-f
Light Egyptian: SF-14-f/g

KRYOLAN MAKEUP COLORS:

The same Kryolan color numbers are used for all of their paints.

01: SF-1½-b
01s: FO-2-b
02: SF-3-a
03: SR-3-a
04: O/CO-6-c
04a: OC-4-b
05: FO-4½-b
06: FO-6-c/d
07: O/CO-7-b
08: F-18-b
09: OF-12-e
010: FO-8-c
012: SR/RS-10-c
014: OF-10-e
015: O-4-b
016: OF-6-b
017: F-8-c/d
021: OF/FO-7-c
022: OC-12-b
022a: CO-10-c
024: OC/CO-16-c
030: OF-8-a
031: SR-8-a
032: F-10-a
033: F-5½-b
034: F-5-d
035: FS-10-d/e
039: FS/SF-12-g
040: O-12-g
041: OC-15-e
043: O/CO-18-f
045: O/CO-15-d
046: RS-17-d
047: FS-19-e
050: S-18-e
072: R-3-f
073: N-2
074: N-3½
075: S-12-d
078: SR-11-a
079: RS-12-a
080: RS-15-a

081: SR-14-a
082: R/PR-16-a/b
083: R/PR-14-b
086: PR-18-a
087: IV/VI-3½-a/b
088: N-16
089: N-5
090: TB-8-b
091: I-10-b
092: GL-3-a
093: TB-14-c
094: T-14-b
095: T/GT-16-a
096: GT-14-a/b
097: T-2-a
098: PV-15-b
101: 0-19-f
102: 0-20-g
103: FS-19-f/g
160: S-6-e
173: VI-4-h
193: TB-11-d/e
303: OC-6-a
304: LY-15-d
305: CY-10-b
308: YC-14-b/c
406: F-1-a
416: S-14-a
421: CO-17-c
425: F-11-g
431: S-11-e
436: YC-4-a
438: F-7-e
449: S-5-a
452: CY-12-d
453: SF-17-f
454: GL-13-g
459: YC-15-h
462: CO-18-g
466: O/CO-10-b/c
468: FO-13-d
470: F-17-c
477: Y-11-d
481: IV-1-a/b
482: V-3-a/b
483: VI-6-a/b
501: N-14
502: L-14-d
503: YC-14-f
504: Y-13-d
507: OC-13-c
508: FO-8-a
509: Y-12-a
510: I-13-a
511: LG-5-a/b
512: LG-12-b
513: F-2½-f
517: N-13

521: YC-2-b
522: YC-4-d
523: YL-1-a
534: YL-11-a
545: PV-16-a
549: B-9-b
576: FS-2-a
579: O-16-d
587: BI-6-a
606: Y-14-e
607: Y-13-c
F1: CO-2½-b
F2: F-4½-c
F3: F-6-d
F4: F-5½-d
F5: FS-4-e
F7: FS-2-e
F8: OF-6-e
F9: F-10-i
F10: F/OF-8-f
F11: O-6-f/g
F12: O-8-g
F15: O-10-f
F16: F-7-d/e
F17: F-7-d
F18: O/CO-4-d

KRYOLAN "B" SERIES:
00: LY-1-c
2: S-2½-b
2½: SF-4-a
3: SF-7-d
3½: S-6-b
4: FS-11-d
4½: S-11-g
5: CO-4-b
6: FS-5-c/d
7: FO-17-d
8: SF-13-e
8a: C-9-b

8b: CY-11½-d
9: FS-11-c
10: YC-13-c
11: O-20-h
12: Black
13: F-14-d
16: CY-17-f
28a: O-16-h
30: S-17-d
32a: N-10
32b: N-4
32c: N-15
101: S-3-c
104: SF-4½-a/b
106: O/CO-8-a
107: CO-13-b
108: OF-8-b
109: O-8-c
111: FO-9-b
113: SF-18-c
115: OF-11-d
118: OF-11-b/c
B: RS-6½-a/b
C: O-11-b
EC1: SF-9½-e
EC2: PR-10-g
EC3: F-15-f
EC4: F/SF-10½-g
EC5: S-9-h
EC6: SF-8-h
EC7: SF-10-h
EC8: FS-9-f
F2: F-5-b
F3: F/OF-5½-c/d
F4: F-5-c
F6: FS-9-e
F10: S/FS-4-c
F11: S-4-d
F12: FS-8-e
F13: FS-8-d/e

F14: FS-13-e
F31: SF-11-e
FA: FS-4½-c
FB: SF-5-b
FC: OF-6-c
FD: OF-6-d
FE: SF-9-c/d
FF: F-6½-c/d
FF1: FS-4-j
FF2: SF-3-b
FF3: SF-3-b/c
FF4: SF-6-f
FF5: F-6½-c
FF7: TG-1-c
FF13: F-6-c
FF14: SF-8-e
FF21: FS-3-c
FL: OF-7-d
FN: OF-9-c
FP: OF-5-b
FS4: F-3-d
FS8: F-6-a/b
FS9: F/OF-5-b
G1: F-12-f
G2: FO-8-b/c
G3: FO-5-b
G4: FO-9-c
G5: FS-12-f
G7: Y-4-d
G9: Y-2-b
G10: Y-1-a
G14: SR-2-b
G15: S-3-c/d
G16: OC-2-b
G24: O-8-b
G41: FS-3½-c
G56: I/VI-4-a
G81: BT-6-e
G82: GI-4-a
G83: BI-4-d

G92: Y-6-a
G103: YL-8-e
G104: S-3-e
G108: P-6-b
K: CO-5-b
K1: S/FS-3-e
O: FO-3-b
P1: OF-2½-b
P2: F-5½-c
P3: SF-4½-b
P4: OF-7-c
P5: OF-7-e
R3: RS-8-a
R5: SR-9-a
R6: R-10-a
R9: S-7-a
Naturell: SR-2-a
Mandarine: OF-13-a
Jugendrot: RS-14-a
Zinnober: FS-12-a
Carmin 1: RS-13-a
Carmin 2: SR/RS-12-a
Carmin 3: PR-14-b
Carmin 4: PR-17-a
Hellrot: S-14-b
Altrot: PR-17-b
Schattierrot: RS-12-b
Schattierbraun: FO-15-b/c
Blau 1: BI-6-c
Blau 3: I-10-a
Blau 5: I/VI-11-a
Lila: VP-12-c
Grün 1: L-9-c
Grün 9: GL-5-b
Grün 11: YL-2-b
Grün 20: GT-11-b
Grün 21: GT-11-a
Grün 30: T/GT-11-a
Grün 31: T-13-b

Index